NETWORKING
FOR BIG DATA

Chapman & Hall/CRC
Big Data Series

SERIES EDITOR
Sanjay Ranka

AIMS AND SCOPE

This series aims to present new research and applications in Big Data, along with the computational tools and techniques currently in development. The inclusion of concrete examples and applications is highly encouraged. The scope of the series includes, but is not limited to, titles in the areas of social networks, sensor networks, data-centric computing, astronomy, genomics, medical data analytics, large-scale e-commerce, and other relevant topics that may be proposed by potential contributors.

PUBLISHED TITLES

BIG DATA : ALGORITHMS, ANALYTICS, AND APPLICATIONS
Kuan-Ching Li, Hai Jiang, Laurence T. Yang, and Alfredo Cuzzocrea

NETWORKING FOR BIG DATA
Shui Yu, Xiaodong Lin, Jelena Mišić, and Xuemin (Sherman) Shen

Chapman & Hall/CRC
Big Data Series

NETWORKING FOR BIG DATA

EDITED BY

SHUI YU
DEAKIN UNIVERSITY
BURWOOD, AUSTRALIA

XIAODONG LIN
UNIVERSITY OF ONTARIO INSTITUTE OF TECHNOLOGY
OSHAWA, ONTARIO, CANADA

JELENA MIŠIĆ
RYERSON UNIVERSITY
TORONTO, ONTARIO, CANADA

XUEMIN (SHERMAN) SHEN
UNIVERSITY OF WATERLOO
WATERLOO, ONTARIO, CANADA

CRC Press
Taylor & Francis Group
Boca Raton   London   New York

CRC Press is an imprint of the
Taylor & Francis Group, an **informa** business

A CHAPMAN & HALL BOOK

Contents

Preface

WE HAVE WITNESSED THE dramatic increase of the use of information technology in every aspect of our lives. For example, Canada's healthcare providers have been moving to electronic record systems that store patients' personal health information in digital format. These provide healthcare professionals an easy, reliable, and safe way to share and access patients' health information, thereby providing a reliable and cost-effective way to improve efficiency and quality of healthcare. However, e-health applications, together with many others that serve our society, lead to the explosive growth of data. Therefore, the crucial question is how to turn the vast amount of data into insight, helping us to better understand what's really happening in our society. In other words, we have come to a point where we need to quickly identify the trends of societal changes through the analysis of the huge amounts of data generated in our daily lives so that proper recommendations can be made in order to react quickly before tragedy occurs. This brand new challenge is named Big Data.

Big Data is emerging as a very active research topic due to its pervasive applications in human society, such as governing, climate, finance, science, and so on. In 2012, the Obama administration announced the Big Data Research and Development Initiative, which aims to explore the potential of how Big Data could be used to address important problems facing the government. Although many research studies have been carried out over the past several years, most of them fall under data mining, machine learning, and data analysis. However, these amazing top-level killer applications would not be possible without the underlying support of network infrastructure due to their extremely large volume and computing complexity, especially when real-time or near-real-time applications are demanded.

To date, Big Data is still quite mysterious to various research communities, and particularly, the networking perspective for Big Data to the best of our knowledge is seldom tackled. Many problems wait to be solved, including optimal network topology for Big Data, parallel structures and algorithms for Big Data computing, information retrieval in Big Data, network security, and privacy issues in Big Data.

This book aims to fill the lacunae in Big Data research, and focuses on important networking issues in Big Data. Specifically, this book is divided into four major sections: Introduction to Big Data, Networking Theory and Design for Big Data, Networking Security for Big Data, and Platforms and Systems for Big Data Applications.

Section I gives a comprehensive introduction to Big Data and its networking issues. It consists of four chapters.

Chapter 1 deals with the challenges in networking for science Big Data movement across campuses, the limitations of legacy campus infrastructure, the technological and policy transformation requirements in building science DMZ infrastructures within campuses through two exemplar case studies, and open problems to personalize such science DMZ infrastructures for accelerated Big Data movement.

Chapter 2 introduces some representative literature addressing the Virtual Machine Placement Problem (VMPP) in the hope of providing a clear and comprehensive vision on different objectives and corresponding algorithms concerning this subject. VMPP is one of the key technologies for cloud-based Big Data analytics and recently has drawn much attention. It deals with the problem of assigning virtual machines to servers in order to achieve desired objectives, such as minimizing costs and maximizing performance.

Chapter 3 investigates the main challenges involved in the three Vs of Big Data—volume, velocity, and variety. It reviews the main characteristics of existing solutions for addressing each of the Vs (e.g., NoSQL, parallel RDBMS, stream data management systems, and complex event processing systems). Finally, it provides a classification of different functions offered by NewSQL systems and discusses their benefits and limitations for processing Big Data.

Chapter 4 deals with the concept of Big Data systems management, especially distributed systems management, and describes the huge problems of storing, processing, and managing Big Data that are faced by the current data systems. It then explains the types of current data management systems and what will accrue to these systems in cases of Big Data. It also describes the types of modern systems, such as Hadoop technology, that can be used to manage Big Data systems.

Section II covers networking theory and design for Big Data. It consists of five chapters.

Chapter 5 deals with an important open issue of efficiently moving Big Data, produced at different geographical locations over time, into a cloud for processing in an online manner. Two representative scenarios are examined and online algorithms are introduced to achieve the timely, cost-minimizing upload of Big Data into the cloud. The first scenario focuses on uploading dynamically generated, geodispersed data into a cloud for processing using a centralized MapReduce-like framework. The second scenario involves uploading deferral Big Data for processing by a (possibly distributed) MapReduce framework.

Chapter 6 describes some of the most widespread technologies used for Big Data. Emerging technologies for the parallel, distributed processing of Big Data are introduced in this chapter. At the storage level, distributed filesystems for the effective storage of large data volumes on hardware media are described. NoSQL databases, widely in use for persisting, manipulating, and retrieving Big Data, are explained. At the processing level, frameworks for massive, parallel processing capable of handling the volumes and complexities of Big Data are explicated. Analytic techniques extract useful patterns from Big Data and turn data into knowledge. At the analytic layer, the chapter describes the techniques for understanding the data, finding useful patterns, and making predictions on future data. Finally, the chapter gives some future directions where Big Data technologies will develop.

Chapter 7 focuses on network configuration and flow scheduling for Big Data applications. It highlights how the performance of Big Data applications is tightly coupled with the performance of the network in supporting large data transfers. Deploying high-performance networks in data centers is thus vital, but configuration and performance management as well as the usage of the network are of paramount importance. This chapter discusses problems of virtual machine placement and data center topology. In this context, different routing and flow scheduling algorithms are discussed in terms of their potential for using the network most efficiently. In particular, software-defined networking relying on centralized control and the ability to leverage global knowledge about the network state are propounded as a promising approach for efficient support of Big Data applications.

Chapter 8 presents a systematic set of techniques that optimize throughput and improve bandwidth for efficient Big Data transfer on the Internet, and then provides speedup solutions for two Big Data transfer applications: all-to-one gather and one-to-all broadcast.

Chapter 9 aims at tackling the trade-off problem between energy efficiency and service resiliency in the era of Big Data. It proposes three energy-aware survivable routing approaches to enforce the routing algorithm to find a trade-off solution between fault tolerance and energy efficiency requirements of data transmission. They are Energy-Aware Backup Protection 1 + 1 (EABP 1 + 1) and Energy-Aware Shared Backup Protection (EASBP) approaches. Extensive simulation results have confirmed that EASBP could be a promising approach to resolve the above trade-off problem. It consumes much less capacity by sacrificing a small increase of energy expenditure compared with the other two EABP approaches. It has proven that the EASBP is especially effective for the large volume of data flow in ever-escalating data environments.

Section III focuses on network and information security technologies for Big Data. It consists of four chapters.

Chapter 10 focuses on the impact of Big Data in the area of network intrusion detection, identifies major challenges and issues, presents promising solutions and research studies, and points out future trends for this area. The effort is to specify the background and stimulate more research in this topic.

Chapter 11 addresses the challenging issue of Big Data collected from network threat monitoring and presents MapReduce-based Machine Learning (MML) schemes (e.g., logistic regression and naive Bayes) with the goal of rapidly and accurately detecting and processing malicious traffic flows in a cloud environment.

Chapter 12 introduces anonymous communication techniques and discusses their usages and challenges in the Big Data context. This chapter covers not only traditional techniques such as relay and DC-network, but also PIR, a technique dedicated to data sharing. Their differences and complementarities are also analyzed.

Chapter 13 deals with flow-based anomaly detection in Big Datasets. Intrusion detection using a flow-based analysis of network traffic is very useful for high-speed networks as it is based on only packet headers and it processes less traffic compared with packet-based methods. Flow-based anomaly detection can detect only volume-based anomalies which cause changes in flow traffic volume, for example, denial of service (DoS) attacks, distributed DoS (DDoS) attacks, worms, scans, and botnets. Therefore, network administrators will have hierarchical anomaly detection in which flow-based systems are used at earlier stages of high-speed networks while packet-based systems may be used in small networks. This chapter also explains sampling methods used to reduce the size of flow-based datasets. Two important categories of sampling methods are packet sampling and flow sampling. These sampling methods and their impact on flow-based anomaly detection are considered in this chapter.

Section IV deals with platforms and systems for Big Data applications. It consists of four chapters.

Chapter 14 envisions and develops a unified Big Data platform for social TV analytics, mining valuable insights from social media contents. To address challenges in Big Data storage and network optimization, this platform is built on the cloud infrastructure with software-defined networking support. In particular, the system consists of three key components, a robust data crawler system, an SDN-enabled processing system, and a social media analysis system. A proof-of-concept demo over a private cloud has been built at the Nanyang Technological University (NTU). Feature verification and performance comparisons demonstrate the feasibility and effectiveness.

Chapter 15 discusses the use of cloud infrastructures for Big Data and highlights its benefits to overcome the identified issues and to provide new approaches for managing the huge volumes of heterogeneous data through presenting different research studies and several developed models. In addition, the chapter addresses the different requirements that should be fulfilled to efficiently manage and process the enormous amount of data. It also focuses on the security services and mechanisms required to ensure the protection of confidentiality, integrity, and availability of Big Data on the cloud. At the end, the chapter reports a set of unresolved issues and introduces the most interesting challenges for the management of Big Data over the cloud.

Chapter 16 proposes an innovative User Data Profile-aware Policy-Based Network Management (UDP-PBNM) framework to exploit and differentiate user data profiles to achieve better power efficiency and optimized resource management. The proposed UDP-PBNM framework enables more flexible and sustainable expansion of resource management when using data center networks to handle Big Data requirements. The simulation results have shown significant improvements on the performance of the infrastructure in terms of power efficiency and resource management while fulfilling the quality of service requirements and cost expectations of the framework users.

Chapter 17 reintroduces the fundamental concept of circuits in current all-IP networking. The chapter shows that it is not difficult to emulate circuits, especially in clouds where fast/efficient transfers of Big Data across data centers offer very high payoffs—analysis in the chapter shows that transfer time can be reduced by between half and one order of magnitude. With this performance advantage in mind, data centers can invest in implementing a flexible networking software which could switch between traditional all-IP networking (normal mode) and special periods of circuit emulation dedicated to rare Big Data transfers. Big Data migrations across data centers are major events and are worth the effort spent in building a schedule ahead of time. The chapter also proposes a generic model called the Tall Gate, which suits many useful cases found in practice today. The main feature of the model is that it implements the sensing function where many Big Data sources can "sense" the state of the uplink in a distributed manner. Performance analysis in this chapter is done on several practical models, including Network Virtualization, the traditional scheduling approach, and two P2P models representing distributed topologies of network sources and destinations.

We would like to thank all the authors who submitted their research work to this book. We would also like to acknowledge the contribution of many experts who have participated in the review process, and offered comments and suggestions to the authors to improve their work. Also, we would like to express our sincere appreciation to the editors at CRC Press for their support and assistance during the development of this book.

Editors

Shui Yu earned his PhD in computer science from Deakin University, Victoria, Australia, in 2004. He is currently a senior lecturer with the School of Information Technology, Deakin University, Victoria, Australia. His research interests include networking theory, network security, and mathematical modeling. He has published more than 150 peer-reviewed papers, including in top journals and top conferences such as IEEE TPDS, IEEE TIFS, IEEE TFS, IEEE TMC, and IEEE INFOCOM. Dr. Yu serves the editorial boards of *IEEE Transactions on Parallel and Distributed Systems, IEEE Communications Surveys and Tutorials, IEEE Access*, and a number of other journals. He has served on many international conferences as a member of organizing committees, such as TPC cochair for IEEE BigDataService 2015, IEEE ATNAC 2014 and 2015, publication chair for IEEE GC 2015, and publicity vice chair for IEEE GC 16. Dr. Yu served IEEE INFOCOM 2012–2015 as a TPC member. He is a senior member of IEEE, and a member of AAAS.

Xiaodong Lin earned his PhD in information engineering from Beijing University of Posts and Telecommunications, China, and his PhD (with Outstanding Achievement in Graduate Studies Award) in electrical and computer engineering from the University of Waterloo, Canada. He is currently an associate professor with the Faculty of Business and Information Technology, University of Ontario Institute of Technology (UOIT), Canada.

Dr. Lin's research interests include wireless communications and network security, computer forensics, software security, and applied cryptography. He has published more than 100 journal and conference publications and book chapters. He received a Canada Graduate Scholarships (CGS) Doctoral from the Natural Sciences and Engineering Research Council of Canada

(NSERC) and seven Best Paper Awards at international conferences, including the 18th International Conference on Computer Communications and Networks (ICCCN 2009), the Fifth International Conference on Body Area Networks (BodyNets 2010), and the IEEE International Conference on Communications (ICC 2007).

Dr. Lin serves as an associate editor for many international journals. He has served and currently is a guest editor for many special issues of IEEE, Elsevier, and Springer journals and as a symposium chair or track chair for IEEE conferences. He has also served on many program committees. He currently serves as vice chair for the Publications of Communications and Information Security Technical Committee (CISTC)—IEEE Communications Society (January 1, 2014–December 31, 2015). He is a senior member of the IEEE.

Jelena Mišić is professor of computer science at Ryerson University in Toronto, Ontario, Canada. She has published more than 100 papers in archival journals and more than 140 papers at international conferences in the areas of wireless networks, in particular, wireless personal area network and wireless sensor network protocols, performance evaluation, and security. She serves on editorial boards of *IEEE Network, IEEE Transactions on Vehicular Technology, Elsevier Computer Networks and Ad Hoc Networks*, and Wiley's *Security and Communication Networks*. She is a senior member of IEEE and Member of ACM.

Xuemin (Sherman) Shen (IEEE M'97-SM'02-F09) earned his BSc (1982) from Dalian Maritime University (China) and MSc (1987) and PhD (1990) in electrical engineering from Rutgers University, New Jersey (USA). He is a professor and university research chair, Department of Electrical and Computer Engineering, University of Waterloo, Canada. He was the associate chair for Graduate Studies from 2004 to 2008. Dr. Shen's research focuses on resource management in interconnected wireless/wired networks, wireless network security, social networks, smart grid, and vehicular ad hoc and sensor networks. He is a coauthor/editor of 15 books, and has published more than 800 papers and book chapters in wireless communications and networks, control, and filtering. Dr. Shen is an elected member of IEEE ComSoc Board of Governors, and the chair of Distinguished Lecturers Selection Committee. Dr. Shen served as the Technical Program Committee chair/cochair for IEEE Infocom'14 and IEEE VTC'10 Fall, the symposia chair for IEEE ICC'10, the tutorial chair for IEEE VTC'11 Spring and IEEE ICC'08, the Technical Program Committee chair for IEEE Globecom'07, the general cochair for ACM Mobihoc'15, Chinacom'07, and QShine'06, and the chair for IEEE Communications Society Technical Committee on Wireless Communications and P2P Communications and Networking. He has served as the editor-in-chief for *IEEE Network, Peer-to-Peer Networking and Applications,* and *IET Communications;* a founding area editor for *IEEE Transactions on Wireless Communications;* an associate editor for *IEEE Transactions on Vehicular Technology, Computer Networks, and ACM/Wireless Networks,* etc.; and as a guest editor for *IEEE JSAC, IEEE Wireless Communications, IEEE Communications Magazine,* and *ACM Mobile Networks and Applications,* etc. Dr. Shen received the Excellent Graduate Supervision Award in 2006, and the Outstanding Performance Award in 2004, 2007, and 2010 from the University of Waterloo, the Premier's Research Excellence Award (PREA) in 2003 from the Province of Ontario, Canada, and the Distinguished Performance Award in 2002 and 2007 from the Faculty of Engineering, University of Waterloo. Dr. Shen is a registered professional engineer of Ontario, Canada, an IEEE Fellow, an Engineering Institute of Canada Fellow, a Canadian Academy of Engineering Fellow, and a distinguished lecturer of the IEEE Vehicular Technology Society and the Communications Society.

Contributors

Michel Adiba
Laboratory of Informatics of Grenoble
and
University of Grenoble
Grenoble, France

Reaz Ahmed
D.R. Cheriton School of Computer Science
University of Waterloo
Waterloo, Ontario, Canada

Adnan Al-Anbuky
School of Engineering
Auckland University of Technology
Auckland, New Zealand

Fadi Alhaddadin
School of Computer and Mathematical
    Sciences
Auckland University of Technology
Auckland, New Zealand

Elmustafa Sayed Ali
Electrical and Electronics Engineering
    Department
Red Sea University
Port Sudan, Sudan

Mustafa Ally
Faculty of Business, Education, Law, and Arts
University of Southern Queensland
Toowoomba, Queensland, Australia

Erik Blasch
Information Directorate Air Force
    Research Laboratory
Rome, New York

Noureddine Boudriga
Communication Networks and Security
    Research Lab
University of Carthage
Tunis, Tunisia

Raouf Boutaba
D.R. Cheriton School of Computer
    Science
University of Waterloo
Waterloo, Ontario, Canada

Prasad Calyam
Department of Computer Science
University of Missouri—Columbia
Columbia, Missouri

Juan Carlos Castrejón
Laboratory of Informatics of Grenoble
and
University of Grenoble
Grenoble, France

Chen Chen
Department of Computer and Information
    Sciences
Towson University
Towson, Maryland

Minghua Chen
Department of Information Engineering
The Chinese University of Hong Kong
Hong Kong, China

Shihabur Rahman Chowdhury
D.R. Cheriton School of Computer Science
University of Waterloo
Waterloo, Ontario, Canada

Tat-Seng Chua
School of Computing
National University of Singapore
Singapore

Saptarshi Debroy
Department of Computer Science
University of Missouri—Columbia
Columbia, Missouri

Matthew Dickinson
Department of Computer Science
University of Missouri—Columbia
Columbia, Missouri

Yacine Djemaiel
Communication Networks and Security
    Research Lab
University of Carthage
Tunis, Tunisia

Lautaro Dolberg
Interdisciplinary Centre for Security,
    Reliability, and Trust
University of Luxembourg
Luxembourg, Luxembourg

Thomas Engel
Interdisciplinary Centre for Security,
    Reliability, and Trust
University of Luxembourg
Luxembourg, Luxembourg

Javier A. Espinosa-Oviedo
Laboratory of Informatics of Grenoble
and
Franco-Mexican Laboratory of Informatics
    and Automatic Control
Grenoble, France

Boutheina A. Fessi
Communication Networks and Security
    Research Lab
University of Carthage
Tunis, Tunisia

Jérôme François
Inria Nancy Grand Est
Villers-lès-Nancy, France

Linqiang Ge
Department of Computer and Information
    Sciences
Towson University
Towson, Maryland

Chuanxiong Guo
Microsoft Corporation
Redmond, Washington

Jairo A. Gutiérrez
School of Computer and Mathematical
    Sciences
Auckland University of Technology
Auckland, New Zealand

Jing He
College of Engineering and Science
Victoria University
Melbourne, Victoria, Australia

Han Hu
School of Computer Engineering
Nanyang Technological University
Singapore

Guangyan Huang
School of Information Technology
Deakin University
Melbourne, Victoria, Australia

Zahra Jadidi
School of Information and
 Communication Technology
Griffith University
Nathan, Queensland, Australia

Francis C. M. Lau
Department of Computer Science
The University of Hong Kong
Hong Kong, China

Lichun Li
School of Electrical and Electronic
 Engineering
Nanyang Technological University
Singapore

Wenjuan Li
Department of Computer Science
City University of Hong Kong
Kowloon Tong, Hong Kong

Xuelong Li
Chinese Academy of Sciences
Shaanxi, China

Zongpeng Li
Department of Computer Science
University of Calgary
Calgary, Alberta, Canada

William Liu
School of Computer and Mathematical
 Sciences
Auckland University of Technology
Auckland, New Zealand

Rongxing Lu
School of Electrical and Electronic
 Engineering
Nanyang Technological University
Singapore

Bing Luo
School of Computer and Mathematical
 Sciences
Auckland University of Technology
Auckland, New Zealand

Weizhi Meng
Infocomm Security Department
Institute for Infocomm Research
Singapore
and
Department of Computer Science
City University of Hong Kong
Kowloon Tong, Hong Kong

Vallipuram Muthukkumarasamy
School of Information and
 Communication Technology
Griffith University
Nathan, Queensland, Australia

Rashid A. Saeed
Electronics Engineering School
Sudan University of Science and
 Technology
Khartoum, Sudan

Kalvinder Singh
School of Information and
 Communication Technology
Griffith University
Nathan, Queensland, Australia

Elankayer Sithirasenan
School of Information and
 Communication Technology
Griffith University
Nathan, Queensland, Australia

Jeffrey Soar
Faculty of Business, Education, Law, and Arts
University of Southern Queensland
Toowoomba, Queensland, Australia

Shaojie Tang
Department of Computer and
    Information Science
Temple University
Philadelphia, Pennsylvania

Genoveva Vargas-Solar
Laboratory of Informatics of
    Grenoble
and
Franco-Mexican Laboratory of
    Informatics and Automatic
    Control
and
French Council of Scientific Research
Grenoble, France

Yang Wang
School of Computer Engineering and
    Science
Shanghai University
Shanghai, China

Yonggang Wen
School of Computer Engineering
Nanyang Technological University
Singapore

Peter Wlodarczak
Faculty of Business, Education, Law, and
    Arts
University of Southern Queensland
Toowoomba, Queensland, Australia

Chuan Wu
Department of Computer Science
The University of Hong Kong
Hong Kong, China

Jie Wu
Department of Computer and
    Information Science
Temple University
Philadelphia, Pennsylvania

Guobin Xu
Department of Computer and
    Information Sciences
Towson University
Towson, Maryland

Wei Yu
Department of Computer and
    Information Sciences
Towson University
Towson, Maryland

José-Luis Zechinelli-Martini
Fundación Universidad de las
    Américas, Puebla
Puebla, Mexico

Hanling Zhang
Department of Computer and
    Information Sciences
Towson University
Towson, Maryland

Linquan Zhang
Department of Computer Science
University of Calgary
Calgary, Alberta, Canada

Wu Zhang
School of Computer Engineering and
    Science
Shanghai University
Shanghai, China

Marat Zhanikeev
Department of Artificial Intelligence,
    Computer Science, and Systems
    Engineering
Kyushu Institute of Technology
Fukuoka Prefecture, Japan

Wanlei Zhou
School of Information Technology
Deakin University
Melbourne, Victoria, Australia

I

Introduction of Big Data

CHAPTER 1

Orchestrating Science DMZs for Big Data Acceleration

Challenges and Approaches

Saptarshi Debroy, Prasad Calyam, and Matthew Dickinson

CONTENTS

INTRODUCTION

What Is Science Big Data?

In recent years, most scientific research in both academia and industry has become increasingly data-driven. According to market estimates, spending related to supporting scientific data-intensive research is expected to increase to $5.8 billion by 2018 [1]. Particularly for data-intensive scientific fields such as bioscience, or particle physics within academic environments, data storage/processing facilities, expert collaborators and specialized computing resources do not always reside within campus boundaries. With the growing trend of large collaborative partnerships involving researchers, expensive scientific instruments and high performance computing centers, experiments and simulations produce petabytes of data, namely, Big Data, that is likely to be shared and analyzed by scientists in multi-disciplinary areas [2]. With the United States of America (USA) government initiating a multimillion dollar research agenda on Big Data topics including networking [3], funding agencies such as the *National Science Foundation, Department of Energy*, and *Defense Advanced Research Projects Agency* are encouraging and supporting cross-campus Big Data research collaborations globally.

Networking for Science Big Data Movement

To meet data movement and processing needs, there is a growing trend amongst researchers within Big Data fields to frequently access remote specialized resources and communicate with collaborators using high-speed overlay networks. These networks use shared underlying components, but allow end-to-end circuit provisioning with bandwidth reservations [4]. Furthermore, in cases where researchers have sporadic/bursty resource demands on short-to-medium timescales, they are looking to federate local resources with "on-demand" remote resources to form "hybrid clouds," versus just relying on expensive overprovisioning of local resources [5]. Figure 1.1 demonstrates one such example where science Big Data from a Genomics lab requires to be moved to remote locations depending on the data generation, analysis, or sharing requirements.

Thus, to support science Big Data movement to external sites, there is a need for simple, yet scalable end-to-end network architectures and implementations that enable applications to use the wide-area networks most efficiently; and possibly control intermediate network resources to meet quality of service (QoS) demands [6]. Moreover, it is imperative to get around the "frictions" in the enterprise edge-networks, that is, the bottlenecks introduced by traditional campus firewalls with complex rule-set processing and heavy manual intervention that degrade the flow performance of data-intensive applications [7]. Consequently, it is becoming evident that such researchers' use cases with large data movement demands need to be served by transforming system and network resource provisioning practices on campuses.

Demilitarized Zones for Science Big Data

The obvious approach to support the special data movement demands of researchers is to build parallel cyberinfrastructures to the enterprise network infrastructures. These parallel infrastructures could allow bypassing of campus firewalls and support "friction-free" data-intensive flow acceleration over wide-area network paths to remote sites at 1–10 Gbps speeds for seamless federation of local and remote resources [8,9]. This practice is popularly referred to as building science demilitarized zones (DMZs) [10] with network designs that can provide high-speed (1–100 Gbps) programmable networks with dedicated network infrastructures for research traffic flows and allow use of high-throughput data transfer

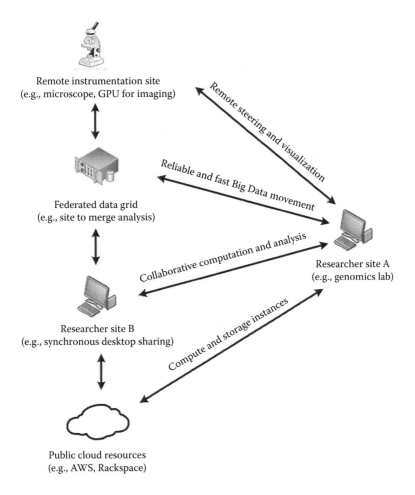

FIGURE 1.1   Example showing need for science Big Data generation and data movement.

protocols [11,12]. They do not necessarily use traditional TCP/IP protocols with congestion control on end-to-end reserved bandwidth paths, and have deep instrumentation and measurement to monitor performance of applications and infrastructure. The functionalities of Science DMZ as defined in Dart et al. [4] include

- A scalable, extensible network infrastructure free from packet loss that causes poor TCP performance

- Appropriate usage policies so that high-performance applications are not hampered by unnecessary constraints

- An effective "on-ramp" for local resources to access wide-area network services

- Mechanisms for testing and measuring, thereby ensuring consistent performance

Following the above definition, the realization of a Science DMZ involves transformation of legacy campus infrastructure with increased end-to-end high-speed connectivity (i.e., availability of 10/40/100 Gbps end-to-end paths) [13,14], and emerging computer/network virtualization management technologies [15,16] for "Big Data flow acceleration" over wide-area networks. The examples of virtualization management technologies include: (i) software-defined networking (SDN) [17–19] based on programmable OpenFlow switches [20], (ii) remote direct memory access (RDMA) over converged Ethernet (RoCE) implemented between zero-copy data transfer nodes [21,22], (iii) multidomain network performance monitoring using perfSONAR [23] active measurement points, and (iv) federated identity/access management (IAM) using Shibboleth-based entitlements [24].

Although Science DMZ infrastructures can be tuned to provide the desired flow acceleration and can be optimized for QoS factors relating to Big Data application "performance," the policy handling of research traffic can cause a major bottleneck at the campus edge-router. This can particularly impact the performance across applications, if multiple applications simultaneously access hybrid cloud resources and compete for the exclusive and limited Science DMZ resources. Experimental evidence in works such as Calyam et al. [9] shows considerable disparity between theoretical and achievable goodput of Big Data transfer between remote domains of a networked federation due to policy and other protocol issues. Therefore, there is a need to provide fine-grained dynamic control of Science DMZ network resources, that is, "personalization" leveraging awareness of research application flows, while also efficiently virtualizing the infrastructure for handling multiple diverse application traffic flows.

QoS-aware automated network convergence schemes have been proposed for purely cloud computing contexts [25], however there is a dearth of works that address the "personalization" of hybrid cloud computing architectures involving Science DMZs. More specifically, there is a need to explore the concepts related to application-driven overlay networking (ADON) with novel cloud services such as "Network-as-a-Service" to intelligently provision on-demand network resources for Big Data application performance acceleration using the Science DMZ approach. Early works such as our work on ADON-as-a-Service [26] seek to develop such cloud services by performing a direct binding of applications to infrastructure and providing fine-grained automated QoS control. The challenge is to solve the multitenancy network virtualization problems at campus-edge networks (e.g., through use of dynamic queue policy management), while making network programmability-related issues a nonfactor for data-intensive application users, who are typically not experts in networking.

Chapter Organization

This chapter seeks to introduce concepts related to Science DMZs used for acceleration of Science Big Data flows over wide-area networks. The chapter will first discuss the nature of science Big Data applications, and then identify the limitations of traditional campus networking infrastructures. Following this, we present the technologies and transformations needed for infrastructures to allow dynamic orchestration of programmable network resources, as well as for enabling performance visibility and policy configuration in Science DMZs. Next, we present two examples of actual Science DMZ implementation use cases with one incremental Science DMZ setup, and another dual-ended Science DMZ federation. Finally, we discuss the open problems and salient features for *personalization* of hybrid cloud computing architectures in an on-demand and federated manner. We remark that the contents of this chapter build upon the insights gathered through the theoretical and experimental research on application-driven network infrastructure personalization at the Virtualization, Multimedia and Networking (VIMAN) Lab in University of Missouri-Columbia (MU).

SCIENCE BIG DATA APPLICATION CHALLENGES

Nature of Science Big Data Applications

Humankind is generating data at an exponential rate; it is predicted that by 2020, over 40 zettabytes of data will be created, replicated, and consumed by humankind [27]. It is a common misconception to characterize any data generated at a large-scale as Big Data. Formally, the four essential attributes of Big Data are: *Volume,* that is, size of the generated data, *Variety,* that is, different forms of the data, *Velocity,* that is, the speed of data generation, and finally *Veracity,* that is, uncertainty of data. Another perspective of Big Data from a networking perspective is any aggregate "data-in-motion" that forces us to look beyond traditional infrastructure technologies (e.g., desktop computing storage, IP networking) and analysis methods (e.g., correlation analysis or multivariate analysis) that are state of the art at a given point in time. From an industry perspective, Big Data relates to the generation, analysis, and processing of user-related information to develop better and more profitable services in, for example, Facebook social networking, Google *Flu trends* prediction, and United Parcel Service (UPS) route delivery optimization.

Although the industry has taken the lead in defining and tackling the challenges of handling Big Data, there are many similar and a few different definitions and challenges in important scientific disciplines such as biological sciences, geological sciences, astrophysics, and particle mechanics that have been dealing with Big Data-related issues for a while. For example, genomics researchers use Big Data analysis techniques such as MapReduce and Hadoop [28] used in industry for web search. Their data transfer application flows involve several thousands of small files with periodic bursts rather than large single-file data sets. This leads to large amounts of small, random I/O traffic which makes it impossible for a typical campus access network to guarantee end-to-end expected performance. In the following, we discuss two exemplar cases of cutting-edge scientific research that is producing Big Data with unique characteristics at remote instrument sites with data movement scenarios that go much beyond simple file transfers:

1. *High Energy Physics*: High energy physics or particle mechanics is a scientific field which involves generation and processing of Big Data in its quest to find, for example, the "God Particle" that has been widely publicized in the popular press recently. Europe's Organization for Nuclear and Particle Research (CERN) houses a *Large Hadron Collider* (LHC) [29,30], the world's largest and highest-energy particle accelerator. The LHC experiments constitute about 150 million sensors delivering data at the rate of 40 million times per second. There are nearly 600 million collisions per second and after filtering and refraining from recording more than 99.999% of these

streams, there are 100 collisions of interest per second. As a result, only working with less than 0.001% of the sensor stream data, the data flow from just four major LHC experiments represents 25 petabytes annual rate before replication (as of 2012). This becomes nearly 200 petabytes after replication, which gets fed to university campuses and research labs across the world for access by researchers, educators, and students.

2. *Biological Sciences and Genomics*: Biological Sciences have been one of the highest generators of large data sets for several years, specifically due to the overloads of omics information, namely, genomes, transcriptomes, epigenomes, and other omics data from cells, tissues, and organisms. While the first human genome was a $3 billion dollar project requiring over a decade to complete in 2002, scientists are now able to sequence and analyze an entire genome in a few hours for less than a thousand dollars. A fully sequenced human genome is in the range of 100–1000 gigabyte of data, and a million customers' data can add up to an exabyte of data which needs to be widely accessed by university hospitals and clinical labs.

   In addition to the consumption, analysis, and sharing of such major instruments generated science Big Data at campus sites of universities and research labs, there are other cases that need on-demand or real-time data movement between a local site to advanced instrument sites or remote collaborator sites. Below, we discuss the nature of four other data-intensive science application workflows being studied at MU's VIMAN Lab from diverse scientific fields that highlight the campus user's perspective in both research and education.

3. *Neuroblastoma Data Cutter Application*: The Neuroblastoma application [9] workflow as shown in Figure 1.2a consists of a high-resolution microscopic instrument on a local campus site generating data-intensive images that need to be processed in real time to identify and diagnose Neuroblastoma (a type of cancer)-infected cells. The processing software and high-performance resources required for processing these images are highly specialized and typically available remotely at sites with large graphics processing unit (GPU) clusters. Hence, images (each on the order of several gigabytes) from the local campus need to be transferred in real time to the remote sites for high resolution analysis and interactive viewing of processed images. For use in medical settings, it is expected that such automated techniques for image processing should have response times on the order of 10–20 s for each user task in image exploration.

4. *Remote Interactive Volume Visualization Application (RIVVIR)*: As shown in Figure 1.2b, the RIVVIR application [31] at a local campus deals with real-time remote volume visualization of large 3D models (on the order of terabyte files) of small animal imaging generated by magnetic resonance imaging (MRI) scanners. This application needs to be accessed simultaneously by multiple researchers for remote steering and visualization, and thus it is impractical to download such data sets for analysis. Thus, remote users need to rely on thin-clients that access the RIVVIR application over network paths that have high end-to-end available bandwidth, and low packet loss or jitter for optimal user quality of experience (QoE).

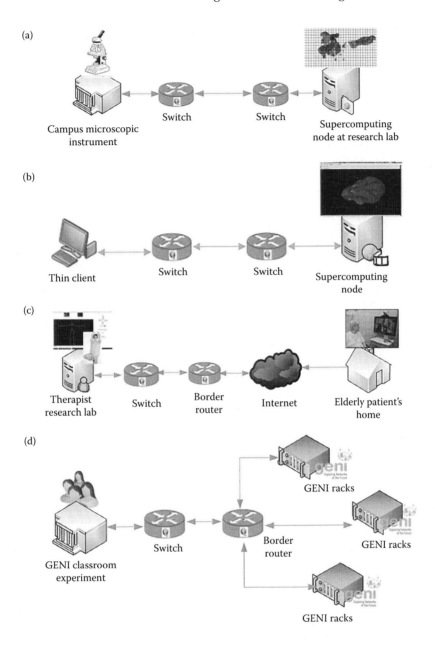

FIGURE 1.2 Science Big Data movement for different application use cases: (a) Neuroblastoma application, (b) RIVVIR application, (c) ElderCare-as-a-Service application, and (d) GENI classroom experiments application.

5. *ElderCare-as-a-Service Application*: As shown in Figure 1.2c, an ElderCare-as-a-Service application [32] consists of an interactive videoconferencing-based tele-health session between a therapist at a university hospital and a remotely residing elderly patient. One of the tele-health use cases for wellness purposes involves performing physiotherapy exercises through an interactive coaching interface that not only involves video but also 3D sensor data from Kinect devices at both ends. It has

been shown that regular Internet paths are unsuitable for delivery adequate user QoE, and hence this application is being only deployed on-demand for use in homes with 1 Gbps connections (e.g., at homes with Google Fiber in Kansas City, USA). During the physiotherapy session, the QoE for both users is a critical factor especially when transferring skeletal images and depth information from Kinect sensors that are large in volume and velocity (e.g., every session data is on the order of several tends of gigabytes), and for administration of proper exercise forms and their assessment of the elders' gait trends.

6. *Classroom Lab Experiments*: It is important to note that Big Data-related educational activities with concurrent student access also are significant in terms of campus needs that manifest in new sets of challenges. As shown in Figure 1.2d, we can consider an example of a class of 30 or more students conducting lab experiments at a university in a Cloud Computing course that requires access to large amount of resources across multiple data centers that host GENI Racks* [32]. As part of the lab exercises, several virtual machines need to be reserved and instantiated by students on remotely located GENI Racks. There can be sudden bursts of application traffic flows at the campus-edge router whose volume, variety, and velocity can be significantly high due to simultaneous services access for computing and analysis, especially the evening before the lab assignment submission deadline.

Traditional Campus Networking Issues

1. *Competing with Enterprise Needs:* The above described Big Data use cases constitute a diverse class of emerging applications that are stressing the traditional campus network environments that were originally designed to support enterprise traffic needs such as e-mail, web browsing, and video streaming for distance learning. When appropriate campus cyberinfrastructure resources for Big Data applications do not exist, cutting-edge research in important scientific fields is constrained. Either the researchers do not take on studies with real-time data movement needs, or they resort to simplistic methods to move research data by exchanging hard-drives via "snail mail" between local and remote sites. Obviously, such simplistic methods are unsustainable and have fundamental scalability issues [8], not to mention that they impede the progress of advanced research that is possible with better on-demand data movement cyberinfrastructure capabilities.

   On the other hand, using the "general purpose" enterprise network (i.e., Layer-3/IP network) for data-intensive science application flows is often a highly suboptimal alternative; and as described earlier in previous section, they may not at all serve the purpose of some synchronous Big Data applications due to sharing of network

---

* GENI Racks are future Internet infrastructure elements developed by academia in cooperation with industry partners such as HP, IBM, Dell, and Cisco; they include Application Program Interface (API) and hardware that enable discovery, reservation, and teardown of distributed federated resources with advanced technologies such as SDN with OpenFlow, compute virtualization, and Federated-IAM.

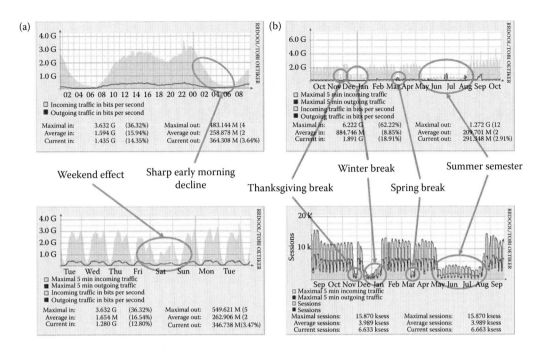

FIGURE 1.3   Campus access network usage trend at MU.

bandwidth with enterprise cross-traffic. Figure 1.3 illustrates the periodic nature of the enterprise traffic with total bandwidth utilization and the session count of wireless access points at MU throughout the year. In Figure 1.3a, we show the daily and weekly usage patterns with peak utilization during the day coinciding with most of the on-campus classes with a significant dip during the latter hours of the night, and underutilization in the early weekends especially during Friday nights and Saturdays. Figure 1.3b show seasonal characteristics with peak bandwidth utilization observed during the fall and spring semesters. Intermediate breaks and the summer semester shows overwhelmingly low usage due to fewer students on campus. For wireless access points' session counts shown in the bottom of Figure 1.3b, the frequent student movements around the campus lead to a large number of association and authentication processes to wireless access points, and bandwidth availability varies at different times in a day, week, or month time-scale. It is obvious that sharing such traditional campus networks with daily and seasonally fluctuating cross-traffic trends causes significant amount of "friction" for science Big Data movement and can easily lead to performance bottlenecks.

To aggravate the above bottleneck situation, traditional campus networks are optimized for enterprise "security" and partially sacrifice "performance" to effectively defend against cyber-attacks. The security optimization in traditional networks leads to campus firewall policies that block ports needed for various data-intensive collaboration tools (e.g., remote desktop access of a remote collaborator using remote desktop protocol (RDP) or virtual network computing (VNC) [33], GridFTP data movement utility [34]). Federal regulations such as HIPAA in the United States that deal with privacy issues of health-related data also increase the extent to which network access lists are tightly controlled and performance is compromised to favor higher security stances. The blocking of ports in traditional campus networks decreases the risk of malicious access of internal-network data/resources, however it severely limits the ability of researchers to influence campus security policies. Even if adhoc static firewall exceptions are applied, they are not scalable to meet special performance demands of multiple Big Data application-related researchers. This is because of the "friction" from hardware limitations of firewalls that arises when handling heavy network-traffic loads of researcher application flows under complex firewall rule-set constraints.

2. *Hardware Limitations:* In addition to the friction due to firewall hardware limitations, friction also manifests for data-intensive flows due to the use of traditional traffic engineering methods that have: (a) long provisioning cycles and distributed management when dealing with under or oversubscribed links, and (b) inability to perform granular classification of flows to enforce researcher-specific policies for bandwidth provisioning. Frequently, the bulk data being transferred externally by researchers is sent on hardware that was purchased a number of years ago, or has been repurposed for budgetary reasons. This results in situations where the computational complexity to handle researcher traffic due to newer application trends has increased, while the supporting network hardware capability has remained fairly static or even degraded. The overall result is that the workflows involving data processing and analysis pipelines are often "slow" from the perspective of researchers due to large data transfer queues, to the point that scaling of research investigations is limited by several weeks or even months for purely networking limitations between sites.

   In a shared campus environment, hosts generating differing network data-rates in their communications due to application characteristics or network interface card (NIC) capabilities of hosts can lead to resource misconfiguration issues in both the system and network levels and cause other kinds of performance issues [35]. For example, misconfigurations could occur due to internal buffers on switches becoming exhausted due to improper settings, or due to duplex mismatches and lower rate negotiation frequently experienced with new servers with 1 Gbps NICs communicating with old servers with 100 Mbps; the same is true when 10 Gbps NIC hosts communicate with 1 Gbps hosts. In a larger and complex campus environment with shared underlying infrastructures for enterprise and research traffic, it is not always possible to predict whether a particular pathway has end-to-end port configurations for high network speeds, or if there will be consistent end-to-end data-rates.

   It is interesting to note that performance mismatch issues for data transfer rates are not just network related, and could also occur in systems that contain a large array of solid-state drives (versus a system that has a handful of traditional spinning hard drives). Frequently, researchers are not fully aware of the capabilities (and limitations) of their hardware, and I/O speed limitations at storage systems could manifest as bottlenecks, even if end-to-end network bandwidth provisioning is performed as "expected" at high-speeds to meet researcher requirements.

TRANSFORMATION OF CAMPUS INFRASTRUCTURE FOR SCIENCE DMZs

An "On-Ramp" to Science DMZ Infrastructure

The inability of traditional campus infrastructures to cater to the real time or on-demand science Big Data application needs is the primary motivation behind creating a "parallel infrastructure" involving Science DMZs with increased high-speed end-to-end connectivity and advanced technologies described previously in Section "What Is Science Big Data?" They provide modernized infrastructure and research-friendly firewall policies with minimal or no firewalls in a Science DMZ deployment. In addition, they can be customized per application needs for on-ramp of data-intensive science flows to fast wide-area network backbones (e.g., Internet2 in the United States, GEANT in Europe, or APAN in Asia). The parallel infrastructure design thus features abilities such as dynamic identification and orchestration of Big Data application traffic to bypass the campus enterprise firewall and use devices that foster flow acceleration, when transit selection is made to leverage the Science DMZ networking infrastructure.

Figure 1.4 illustrates traffic flow "transit selection" within a campus access network with Science DMZ capabilities. We can see how intelligence at the campus border and department-level switches enables bypassing of research data flows from campus firewall-restricted paths onto research network paths. However, enterprise traffic such as web browsing or e-mails are routed through the same campus access network to the Internet through the firewall-policed paths. The research network paths typically involve extended virtual local area network (VLAN) overlays between local and remote sites, and services such as AWS Direct Connect are used for high-speed layer-2 connections to public clouds. With such overlay paths, Big Data applications can use local/remote and public cloud resources as if they all reside within the same internal network.

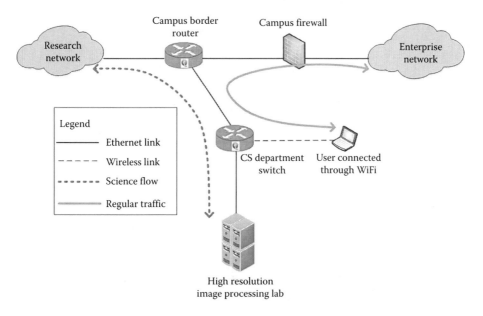

FIGURE 1.4   Transit selection of Science flows and regular traffic within campus.

Moreover, research traffic can be isolated from other cross-traffic through loss-free, dedicated "on-demand" bandwidth provisioning on a shared network underlay infrastructure. It is important to note that the "last-mile" problem of getting static or dynamic VLANs connected from the research lab facilities to the Science DMZ edge is one of the harder infrastructure setup issues. In case of Big Data application cases, having 100 Gigabit Ethernet (GE) and 40–100 Gbps network devices could be a key requirement. Given that network devices that support 40–100 Gbps speeds are expensive, building overlay networks requires significant investments from both the central campus and departmental units. Also, the backbone network providers at the regional (e.g., CENIC) and national-level (e.g., Internet2) need to create a wide footprint of their backbones to support multiple-extended VLAN overlays simultaneously between campuses.

Further, the end-to-end infrastructure should ideally feature SDN with OpenFlow switches at strategic traffic aggregation points within the campus and backbone networks. SDN provides centralized control on dynamic science workflows over a distributed network architecture, and thus allows proactive/reactive provisioning and traffic steering of flows in a unified, vendor independent manner [20]. It also enables fine-grained control of network traffic depending on the QoS requirements of the application workflows. In addition, OpenFlow-enabled switches help in dynamic modification of security policies for large flows between trusted sites when helping them dynamically bypass the campus firewall [18]. Figure 1.5 shows the infrastructural components of a Science DMZ network within a campus featuring SDN connectivity to different departments. Normal application traffic traverses paths with intermediate campus firewalls, and reaches remote collaborator sites or public cloud sites over enterprise IP network to access common web applications. However, data-intensive science application flows from research labs that are "accelerated" within Science DMZs bypass the firewall to the 10–100 GE backbones.

Handling Policy Specifications

Assuming the relevant infrastructure investments are in place, the next challenge relates to the Federated-IAM that requires specifying and handling fine-grained resource access policies in a multiinstitution collaboration setting (i.e., at both the local and remote researcher/ instrument campuses, and within the backbone networks) with minimal administrative overhead. Figure 1.6 illustrates a layered reference architecture for deploying Science DMZs on campuses that need to be securely accessed using policies that are implemented by the Federated-IAM framework. We assume a scenario where two researchers at remote campuses with different subject matter expertise collaborate on an image processing application that requires access to an instrument facility at one researcher's site, and an HPC facility at the other researcher's site.

In order to successfully realize the layered architecture functions in the context of multiinstitutional policy specification/handling, there are several questions that need to be addressed by the Federated-IAM implementation such as: (i) How can an researcher at the microscope facility be authenticated and authorized to reserve HPC resources at the collaborator researcher campus?; (ii) How can an OpenFlow controller at one campus be authorized to provision flows within a backbone network in an on-demand manner?; and

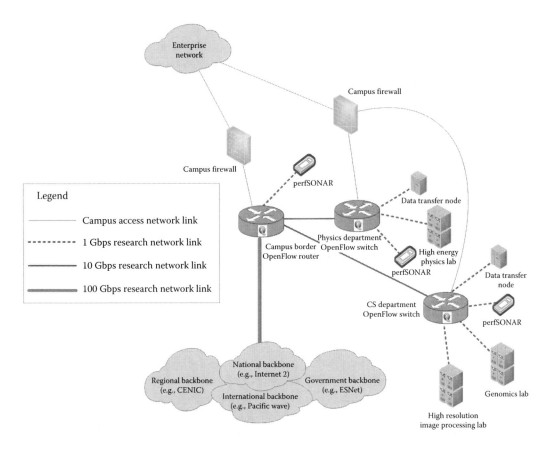

FIGURE 1.5 A generic Science DMZ physical infrastructure diagram.

even (iii) How do we restrict who can query the performance measurement data within the extended VLAN overlay network that supports many researchers over time?

Fortunately, standards-based identity management approaches based on Shibboleth entitlements [24] have evolved to accommodate permissions in above user-to-service authentication and authorization use cases. These approaches are being widely adopted in academia and industry enterprises. However, they require a central, as well as an independent "service provider" that hosts an "entitlement service" amongst all the campuses that

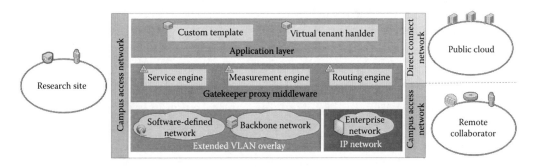

FIGURE 1.6 Campus Science DMZ logical schematic showing architecture layers.

federate their Science DMZ infrastructures. Having a registered service provider in the Campus Science DMZ federation leads to a scalable and extensible approach, as it eliminates the need to have each campus have bilateral agreements with every other campus. It also allows for centrally managing entitlements based on mutual protection of privacy policies between institutions to authorize access to different infrastructure components such as intercampus OpenFlow switches.

In order to securely maintain the policy directories of the federation, and to allow institutional policy management of the Science DMZ flows, a "gatekeeper-proxy middleware" as shown in Figure 1.6 is required. The gatekeeper-proxy is a critical component of the Science DMZ as it is responsible to integrate and orchestrate functionalities of a Science DMZ's: (a) OpenFlow controller through a "routing engine" [36], (b) performance visibility through a "measurement engine," and (c) "service engine" which allows the functioning of the user-facing web portals that allow a researcher request access to overlay network resources.

To effectively maintain the gatekeeper-proxy to serve diverse researcher's needs concurrently on the shared underlay infrastructure, the role of a "performance engineer" technician within a campus Science DMZ is vital. We envisage this role to act as the primary "keeper" and "helpdesk" of the Science DMZ equipment, and the success of this role is in the technician's ability to augment traditional system/network engineer roles on campuses. In fact, large corporations that typically support data-intensive applications for their users (e.g., disaster data recovery and real-time analytics in the financial sector, content delivery network management in the consumer sector) have well-defined roles and responsibilities for a performance engineer.

Given that researcher data flows in Science DMZs are unique and dynamic, specialized technician skill sets and toolkits are needed. The performance engineer needs to effectively function as a liaison to researchers' unique computing and networking needs while coordinating with multidomain entities at various levels (i.e., building-level, campus-level, backbone-level). He/she also has to cater to each researcher's expectations of high-availability and peak-performance to remote sites without disrupting core campus network traffic. For these purposes, the performance engineer can use "custom templates" that allow repeatable deployment of Big Data application flows, and use virtualization technologies that allow realization of a "virtual tenant handler" so that Big Data application flows are isolated from each other in terms of performance or security. Moreover, the tools of a performance engineer need to help serve the above onerous duties in conjunction with administering maintenance windows with advanced cyberinfrastructure technologies, and their change management processes.

Achieving Performance Visibility

To ensure smooth operation of the fine-grained orchestration of science Big Data flows, Science DMZs require end-to-end network performance monitoring frameworks that can discover and eliminate the "soft failures" in the network. Soft failures cause poor performance unlike "hard failures" such as fiber cuts that prevent data from flowing. Particularly, active measurements using tools such as Ping (for round trip delay), Traceroute (for network topology inference), OWAMP (for one-way delay), and BWCTL (for TCP/UDP through-put) are essential in identifying soft failures such as packet loss due to failing components, misconfigurations such as duplex mismatches that affect data rates, or routers forwarding packets using the management CPU rather than using a high-performance forwarding hardware. These soft failures often go undetected as the legacy campus network management and error-reporting systems are optimized for reporting hard failures, such as loss of a link or device.

Currently, perfSONAR [21] is the most widely deployed framework with over 1200 publicly registered measurement points worldwide for performing multidomain active measurements. It is being used to create "measurement federations" for collection and sharing of end-to-end performance measurements across multiple geographically separated Science DMZs forming a research consortium [37]. Collected measurements can be queried amongst federation members through interoperable web-service interfaces to mainly analyze network paths to ensure packet loss free paths and identify end-to-end bottlenecks. They can also help in diagnosing performance bottlenecks using anomaly detection [38], determining the optimal network path [39], or in network weather forecasting [40].

Science DMZ Implementation Use Cases

Below we discuss two ideologically dissimilar Science DMZ implementation use cases. First, we present a three-stage transformation of a campus science infrastructure for handling data-intensive application flows. Next, we shed light on a double-ended Science DMZ implementation that connects two geographically distant campus Science DMZs for Big Data collaboration between the two campuses.

1. *An Incremental Science DMZ Implementation*: In Figure 1.7, we show the stages of the University of California-Santa Cruz (UCSC) campus research network evolution to support data-intensive science applications [41]. Figure 1.7a shows the UCSC campus research network before Science DMZ implementation with a 10 Gbps campus distribution core catering the three main Big Data flow generators, for example, Santa Cruz Institute of Particle Physics (SCIPP), a 6-Rack HYADES cluster, and Center for Biomolecular Science & Engineering. A traditional (i.e., non-OpenFlow) Dell 6258 access switch was responsible to route research data to campus border router through core routers and ultimately to the regional Corporation for Education Network Initiatives in California (CENIC) backbone. However, buffer size limitations of intermediate switches created bottlenecks in both research and enterprise networks, particularly the dedicated 10GE links to research facilities could not support science data transfer rates beyond 1 Gbps. In 2013, UCSC implemented a quick-fix solution to the problem as shown in Figure 1.7b, which involved a Cisco 3560E OpenFlow switch connected with perfSONAR nodes and multicore delay-tolerant networking (DTN). The Science DMZ switch currently at this time of writing has direct links to all Big Data applications and is connected to the border router with 10 GE on both ends. In future, UCSC has plans to install dedicated Science DMZ switches connected through 10 GE links with individual data-intensive services, and a master switch

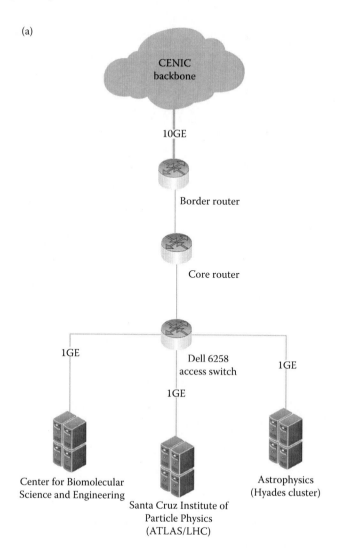

(a)

FIGURE 1.7 An exemplar incremental campus Science DMZ implementation: (a) past Science application flow path. *(Continued)*

connected to CENIC backbone through 100 GE link, as shown in Figure 1.7c. This three-stage transformation is a common trend in campus network evolution that has been seen in many other cases, and is increasing the footprint of software-defined network elements (OpenFlow-compatible) in support of Big Data applications across campus environments.

2. *A Double-Ended Science DMZ Transformation Example*: Figure 1.8 shows how both The Ohio State University (OSU) and MU campuses have transformed their Science DMZ infrastructures for intercampus research collaborations. They are both connected through an extended VLAN overlay that involves an Internet2 Advanced Layer 2 Service (AL2S) connection by way of local regional networks of OARnet in

(b)

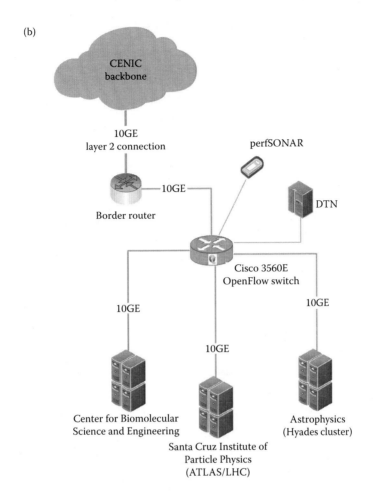

FIGURE 1.7 (*Continued*) An exemplar incremental campus Science DMZ implementation: (b) present Science DMZ architecture. (*Continued*)

Ohio, and GPN/MoreNet in Missouri, respectively. Each Science DMZ has a matching DTNs equipped with dual Intel E5-2660, 128 GB of memory, 300 GB PCI-Express solid-state drive, and dual Mellanox 10 Gbps network cards with RoCE support. Each Science DMZ has perfSONAR measurement points for continuous monitoring at 1–10 Gbps network speeds. A common Dell R610 node in the OSU Science DMZ is used to run an OpenFlow controller that controls both the OSU and MU Science DMZ OpenFlow switches. Two HP 3800s are used to attach to the various nodes in the Science DMZ, and a single NEC PF5820 aggregates the two connections at OSU. A NEC switch is connected to OSU's 100 Gbps Cisco Nexus router at 10 Gbps, and has the ability to scale to 40 Gbps as the Science DMZ grows to support future researchers and applications. At MU, the Science DMZ features OpenFlow switches include a Brocade VDX 8770 switch to attach various nodes in the Science DMZ, and a 100 Gbps Brocade MLXE router at 10 Gbps interface speeds, with the ability to scale up to 100 Gbps speeds. This double-ended Science DMZ deployment between

(c)

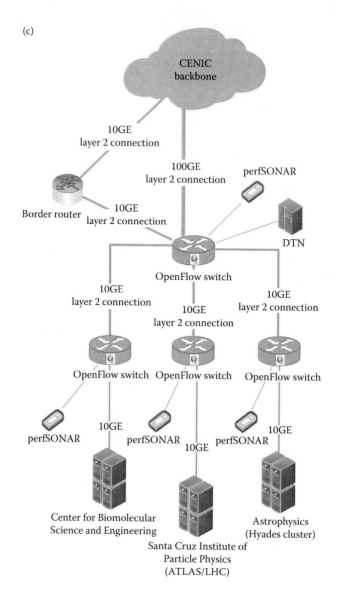

FIGURE 1.7 (*Continued*) An exemplar incremental campus Science DMZ implementation: (c) future Science DMZ upgrade plan.

OSU and MU has garnered support and fostered new collaborations between a number of researchers on the two campuses, and is being viewed as model infrastructure for "team science" projects.

NETWORK-AS-A-SERVICE WITHIN SCIENCE DMZs

If multiple applications accessing hybrid cloud resources compete for the exclusive and limited Science DMZ resources, the policy handling of research traffic can cause a major

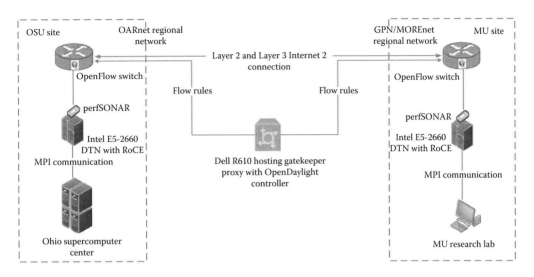

FIGURE 1.8   An exemplar double-ended campus Science DMZ implementation.

bottleneck at the campus edge router and impact the performance across applications. Thus, there is a need to provide dynamic QoS control of Science DMZ network resources versus setting a static rate limit affecting all applications. The dynamic control should have awareness of research application flows with urgent or other high-priority computing needs, while also efficiently virtualizing the infrastructure for handling multiple diverse application traffic flows [42]. The virtualization obviously should not affect the QoS of any of the provisioned applications, and also advanced services should be easy-to-use for data-intensive application users, who should not be worrying about configuring underlying infrastructure resources.

Consequently, there is a need to provide fine-grained dynamic control of Science DMZ network resources, that is, "personalization" leveraging awareness of research application flows, while also efficiently virtualizing the infrastructure for handling multiple diverse application traffic flows. More specifically, there is a need to explore the concepts related to ADON with novel cloud services such as "Network-as-a-Service" to intelligently provision on-demand network resources for Big Data application performance acceleration using the Science DMZ approach. The salient features of ADON are as follows:

- ADON intelligently provisions on-demand network resources by performing a direct binding of applications to infrastructure with fine-grained automated QoS control in a Science DMZ.

- In ADON, "network personalization" is performed using a concept of "custom templates" to catalog and handle unique profiles of application workflows.

- Using the custom templates and VTH concepts, ADON manages the hybrid cloud requirements of multiple applications in a scalable and extensible manner.

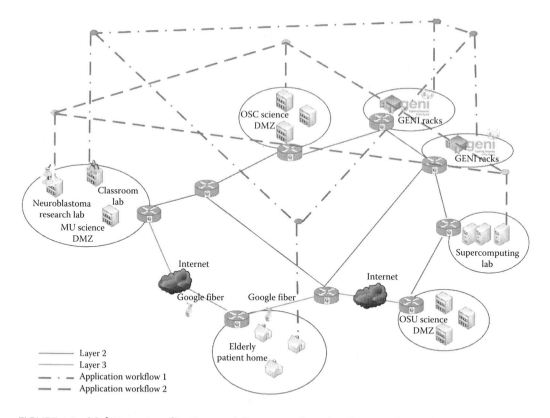

FIGURE 1.9   Multitenant application workflows on a shared wide-area physical infrastructure.

- ADON ensures predictable application performance delivery by scheduling transit selection (choosing between Internet or extended VLAN overlays) and traffic engineering (e.g., rate limit queue mapping based on application-driven requirements) at the campus-edge.

Figure 1.9 shows how, through the ADON, data-intensive applications can coexist on top of a shared wide-area physical infrastructure topology, with each application demanding local/remote network or compute resources with unique end-to-end QoS requirements. We can notice how multiple science Big Data applications such as Neuroblastoma, ECaaS, and Classroom Lab with different QoS requirements are orchestrated through overlay networking without compromising the overall end-to-end performance. Such an approach of application-driven orchestration of Science DMZs seeks to lay the foundation for solving even harder issues that may transform the way science Big Data research is carried out through collaborations across communities.

CONCLUDING REMARKS

What Have We Learned?

To summarize, the exponential growth of science Big Data traffic and ensuing accelerated movement requirements are revolutionizing the way campus networks are being designed and operated. The volume and velocity of science Big Data has necessitated a complete paradigm shift from legacy campus network architecture principles and policies, especially in terms of resource provisioning, QoS management, and coupling performance visibility and control. To meet the need to make cross-campus Big Data movement friction free, today's campus networks are making provisions for on-demand proprietary access of high-speed physical resources by Big Data applications through various network virtualization approaches. Such exclusive access in order to isolate Big Data traffic from enterprise traffic is an intellectual evolution from the traditional ways campus access networks were designed a decade ago where applications used to share resources using best-efforts networks.

Moreover, in legacy campus access networks, the service providers used to jointly manage QoS for campus-related business and research traffic. However, with adoption of Science DMZ infrastructures by research campuses to accelerate Big Data movement, the QoS initiative is shifting from being "service provider"—governed to "Big Data researcher and application"—steered. On-demand application-driven orchestration using intelligent resource allocation and network virtualization with application-imposed QoS guarantees has become the widely accepted future direction of campus access network design for effective Big Data handling.

Finally, making performance monitoring an integral part of science Big Data networking to better steer data-intensive science flows within-and-outside the campus network is providing robustness and fault-tolerance capabilities to the campus network in its goal to handle Big Data. Strategically located measurement instrumentation, and application-driven performance metrics have facilitated better visibility and control on Big Data transfer performance between campuses, and are enabling the identification and proactive avoidance of performance bottleneck scenarios and network soft-spots.

The Road Ahead and Open Problems

Transformation of legacy campus infrastructures with adoption of Science DMZs has facilitated "Big Data Highways" that use cutting-edge technologies, such as SDN, end-to-end performance monitoring, and network-virtualization. Typically, these efforts so far have been mostly incremental where network engineers and designers upgrade the campus access network with faster devices, gigabit fiber cables and intelligent flow control to cater specific data-intensive applications' needs. However, a truly "Research-defined Network" (RDN), built to control and troubleshoot all the networking aspects of data-intensive science applications, is still to be realized by network researchers and service providers. Such RDNs need to support the full life cycle of campus Big Data, from creation to computation and consumption.

Through RDNs, Big Data researchers will be able to dictate policies, security features, and QoS guarantees specific to their applications. Making data-intensive research a driving force behind campus Big Data network design will enable the network designers to better address open issues, such as: (a) assurance of satisfactory user QoE when simultaneously scheduling multiple science Big Data applications, (b) standardizing performance engineering techniques and protocols for easy use and wide-adoption, and (c) selectively replicating time sensitive or mission critical data across multiple platforms for reliability purposes and prudently selecting replication sites to avoid end-to-end performance bottlenecks.

Building such RDNs is a first step to federate different "Big Data highways" to create a "Big Data interstate system" where different campus Big Data network infrastructures seamlessly come together. Creating such federations should be aimed toward faster sharing of research data, enhancing cross-campus research collaboration, and quicker troubleshooting of network performance bottlenecks. Although early efforts led by Clemson University [37] are taking shape in creating such multicampus Science DMZ federations, there exist a number of open challenges in realizing such collaborations.

The open challenges can be summarized as follows: (a) coordination of federated resources with adherence to policies of multiple-domains, (b) enforcing federated and transparent access control mechanisms over local autonomy to facilitate broader sharing, (c) building secured middle grounds for performance visibility and network control across Science DMZ domains, and (d) creating social platforms or extending existing platforms for scientific collaborations, such as Science Gateway [43] or HUBzero [44] where Big Data researchers, network designers, and policymakers belonging to the same society can mingle, share data and expertise, collaborate, and create new policies and rules for the federation. Solving these open issues are fundamental in the future explorations that will lead to an *Internet for Big Data* in our society.

SUMMARY

To summarize, the key takeaways from this chapter are

- The unique characteristics and data movement requirements of science Big Data pose novel networking challenges.

- These challenges motivate the need for creation of Science DMZs that are parallel infrastructures to enterprise infrastructures to accelerate performance of science Big Data flows.

- Application-driven orchestration of science Big Data flows is essential within the Science DMZ to obtain expected performance and avoid performance bottlenecks.

REFERENCES

1. A. Robbins, Network modernization is key to leveraging big data, http://www.federaltimes.com/.
2. H. Yin, Y. Jiang, C. Lin, Y. Luo, Y. Liu, Big Data: Transforming the design philosophy of future internet, *IEEE Network Magazine*, 28(4), 14–19, 2014.
3. Obama administration unveils "Big Data" initiative: Announces $200 million in new R&D investments, *Office of Science and Technology Policy, The White House*, 2012.
4. E. Dart, L. Rotman, B. Tierney, M. Hester, J. Zurawski, The science DMZ: A network design pattern for data-intensive science, *Proceedings of IEEE/ACM Supercomputing*, 2013.
5. A. Das, C. Lumezanu, Y. Zhang, V. Singh, G. Jiang, C. Yu, Transparent and flexible network management for big data processing in the cloud, *Proceedings of USENIX HotCloud*, 2013.

6. X. Yi, F. Liu, J. Liu, H. Jin, Building a network highway for Big Data: Architecture and challenges, *IEEE Network Magazine*, 28(4), 5–13, 2014.

7. L. Borovick, R. L. Villars, The critical role of the network in Big Data applications, *Cisco White paper*, 2012.

8. L. Zhang, C. Wu, Z. Li, C. Guo, M. Chen, F. Lau, Moving Big Data to the cloud: An online cost-minimizing approach, *IEEE Journal on Selected Areas in Communications*, 31(12), 2710–2721, 2013.

9. P. Calyam, A. Berryman, E. Saule, H. Subramoni, P. Schopis, G. Springer, U. Catalyurek, D. K. Panda, Wide-area overlay networking to manage accelerated science DMZ flows, *Proceedings of IEEE ICNC*, 2014.

10. Science DMZ network design model, http://fasterdata.es.net/science-dmz.

11. H. Subramoni, P. Lai, R. Kettimuthu, D. K. Panda, High performance data transfer in grid environment using GridFTP over InfiniBand, *Proceedings of IEEE CCGrid*, 2010.

12. B. Tierney, E. Kissel, M. Swany, E. Pouyoul, Efficient data transfer protocols for Big Data, *Proceedings of IEEE e-Science*, 2012.

13. A. Rajendran, P. Mhashilkar, H. Kim, D. Dykstra, G. Garzoglio, I. Raicu, Optimizing large data transfers over 100 Gbps wide area networks, *Proceedings of IEEE/ACM CCGrid*, May 2013.

14. E. Kissel, M. Swany, B. Tierney, E. Pouyoul, Efficient wide area data transfer protocols for 100 Gbps networks and beyond, *Proceedings of NDM*, 2013.

15. H. Luo, H. Zhang, M. Zukerman, C. Qiao, An incrementally deployable network architecture to support both data-centric and host-centric services, *IEEE Network Magazine*, 28(4), 58–65, 2014.

16. Y. Ren, T. Li, D. Yu, S. Jin, T. Robertazzi, B. Tierney, E. Pouyoul, Protocols for wide-area data-intensive applications: Design and performance issues, *Proceedings of IEEE/ACM Supercomputing*, 2012.

17. Y. Cui, S. Xiao, C. Liao, I. Stojmenovic, M. Li, Data centers as software defined networks: Traffic redundancy elimination with wireless cards at routers, *IEEE Journal on Selected Areas in Communications*, 31(12), 2658–2672, 2013.

18. I. Monga, E. Pouyoul, C. Guok, Software-defined networking for big data science, *Proceedings of IEEE/ACM Supercomputing*, 2012.

19. M. V. Neves, C. A. De Rose, K. Katrinis, H. Franke, Pythia: Faster Big Data in motion through predictive software-defined network optimization at runtime, *Proceedings of IEEE IPDPS*, 2014.

20. N. McKeown, T. Anderson, H. Balakrishnan, G. Parulkar, L. Peterson, J. Rexford, S. Shenker, J. Turner, Enabling innovation in campus networks, *ACM SIGCOMM Computer Communication Review*, 38(2), 69–74, 2008.

21. P. Lai, H. Subramoni, S. Narravula, A. Mamidala, D. K. Panda, Designing efficient FTP mechanisms for high performance data-transfer over InfiniBand, *Proceedings of ICPP*, 2009.

22. E. Kissel, M. Swany, Evaluating high performance data transfer with RDMA-based protocols in wide-area networks, *Proceedings of IEEE HPCC*, 2012.

23. A. Hanemann, J. Boote, E. Boyd, J. Durand, L. Kudarimoti, R. Lapacz, M. Swany, S. Trocha, J. Zurawski, perfSONAR: A service oriented architecture for multi-domain network monitoring, *Proceedings of ICSOC*, 2005. (http://www.perfsonar.net).

24. R. Morgan, S. Cantor, S. Carmody, W. Hoehn, K. Kligenstein, Federated security: The Shibboleth approach, *EDUCAUSE Quarterly*, 27(4), 12–17, 2004.

25. W. Kim, P. Sharma, J. Lee, S. Banerjee, J. Tourrilhes, S. Lee, P. Yalagandula, Automated and scalable QoS control for network convergence, *Proceedings of INM/WREN*, 2010.

26. S. Seetharam, P. Calyam, T. Beyene, ADON: Application-driven overlay network-as-a-service for data-intensive science, *Proceedings of IEEE CloudNet*, 2014.

27. J. Gantz, D. Reinsel, The digital universe in 2020: Big data, bigger digital shadows, and biggest growth in the far east, *IDC: Analyze the Future*, 2012.

28. Hadoop Tutorial, http://hadoop.apache.org/docs/r1.2.1/mapred_tutorial.html.

29. C. Lefevre, LHC Guide, English version. A collection of facts and figures about the Large Hadron Collider (LHC) in the form of questions and answers, *CERN-Brochure-2008-001-Eng. LHC Guide*, 20, 2013.
30. G. Brumfiel, High-energy physics: Down the petabyte highway, *Nature, 469, 19*, 2011.
31. P. Calyam, A. Berryman, A. Lai, M. Honigford, VMLab: Infrastructure to support desktop virtualization experiments for research and education, *VMware Technical Journal*, 2012.
32. P. Calyam, S. Seetharam, R. Antequera, GENI laboratory exercises development for a cloud computing course, *Proceedings of GENI Research and Educational Experiment Workshop*, 2014.
33. P. Calyam, A. Kalash, N. Ludban, S. Gopalan, S. Samsi, K. Tomko, D. E. Hudak, A. Krishnamurthy, Experiences from cyberinfrastructure development for multi-user remote instrumentation, *Proceedings of IEEE e-Science*, 2008.
34. W. Allcock, GridFTP: Protocol extensions to FTP for the grid, *Global Grid Forum GFD-R-P.020*, 2003.
35. M. A. Sharkh, M. Jammal, A. Shami, A. Ouda, Resource allocation in a network-based cloud computing environment: Design challenges, *IEEE Communications Magazine*, 51, 2013.
36. W. Jia, L. Wang, A unified unicast and multicast routing and forwarding algorithm for software-defined datacenter networks, *IEEE Journal on Selected Areas in Communications*, 31, 2013.
37. J. B. Bottum, R. Marinshaw, H. Neeman, J. Pepin, J. B. von Oehsen, The Condo-of-Condos, *Proceedings of XSEDE*, 2013.
38. P. Calyam, J. Pu, W. Mandrawa, A. Krishnamurthy, OnTimeDetect: Dynamic network anomaly notification in perfSONAR deployments, *Proceedings of IEEE/ACM MASCOTS*, 2010.
39. S. Tao, K. Xu, A. Estepa, R. Guerin, J. Kurose, D. Towsley, Z. L. Zhang, Improving VoIP quality through path switching, *Proceedings of IEEE INFOCOM*, 2005.
40. B. Gaidioz, R. Wolski, B. Tourancheau, Synchronizing network probes to avoid measurement intrusiveness with the network weather service, *Proceedings of IEEE HPDC*, 2000.
41. L. Smarr, UC-wide cyberinfrastructure for data-intensive research, *Invited Talk @ UC IT Leadership Council in Oakland, California*, 2014.
42. R. Jain, S. Paul, Network virtualization and software defined networking for cloud computing: A survey, *IEEE Communications Magazine*, 51(11), 24–31, 2013.
43. N. Wilkins-Diehr, Science gateways: Common community interfaces to grid resources, *Concurrency and Computation: Practice and Experience*, 19(6), 743–749, 2007.
44. HUBzero platform for scientific collaboration, https://hubzero.org.

CHAPTER 2

A Survey of Virtual Machine Placement in Cloud Computing for Big Data

Yang Wang, Jie Wu, Shaojie Tang, and Wu Zhang

CONTENTS

INTRODUCTION

Cloud-based Big Data analytics is driving the rapid advancement of cloud computing services [1]. With the rapid growth in cloud computing, it provides reasonable cost and better performance for many Big Data systems. Big Data in clouds also adds more stress to CPU in servers, memory in storage, and bandwidth in network. As one of the key technologies for cloud computing, virtualization brings great benefits to modern data centers including cost savings, efficient resource management, and scalability. The virtual machine placement problem (VMPP) is important to data centers, and has attracted much attention in recent years. Virtual machine (VM) placement is the process of choosing the most suitable configuration between the mapping of VMs and servers. The desired configuration may be different, depending on the goals intended to be achieved.

VMPP algorithms typically have three generic goals. The first is to reduce server cost, which is usually represented by the number of servers used, or by the power consumption. According to Greenberg et al. [2], the cost of data centers can be roughly estimated to consist of server, infrastructure, power consumption, and network cost, which accounts for 45%, 25%, 15%, and 15%, respectively. Clearly, decreasing the server number by increasing the server utilization has a large positive impact on data centers. Other research works use server power consumption to represent the server cost, because once the scale of a data center is determined (i.e., the total number of servers is fixed), the major cost comes from power consumption. At the same time, server power consumption and server number are strongly related: the more servers that are turned on, the more power consumption incurred. Some CPU utilization-based power consumption models are introduced in Verma et al. [3], Kumar et al. [4], and Fan et al. [5]. Another factor that will impact server cost is server multidimension resource utilization. Whenever one type of resource in a server is exhausted, we cannot assign additional VMs to this server, even though there are plenty of other resources available on the server. Otherwise, it will be overloaded. To make full use of the server, we should try to balance the usage of each type of resource.

The second general goal is to reduce network cost. Networks are another important issue for data centers, especially when the scale of a data center expands and the servers communicate with one another more densely. The traditional approach to optimizing the network and improving the scalability of data centers is to introduce new network architectures. A new way to tackle the problem is to formulate a good VM placement strategy in a given architecture. For example, once the network architecture is given, we can optimize network traffic by placing the VMs with heavy traffic rates close to each other, and by choosing proper routing paths between VMs. In addition to considering network traffic between VMs, we should also consider the access latency between VMs and data servers. Data access latency is an important metric for data-intensive applications, which are very popular in cloud computing. Since it is infeasible to store the data locally in each computation server, a large number of computation servers need to remotely access the data servers connected to network attached storage (NAS) or storage area network (SAN) devices, and this process can lead to a large network cost.

The final goal is to improve user application performance. The application performance is generally weighed by a Service Level Agreement (SLA), which is a contract between the service provider and the user, and guarantees that the user will get the agreed target response time from the service provider. For VMPP, a key factor related to application performance is the live migration cost (i.e., migrate running VMs without shutting them down). When we dynamically migrate VMs between servers toward our desired configuration, the application performance will be adversely impacted. This is because on both the source and destination servers, some CPU, memory, and network bandwidths are needed by the migration process, and thus the running application will have fewer resource bandwidths and will take a longer time to finish. The migration cost is usually measured by performance loss during the migration duration, and should be minimized.

BACKGROUND

Virtualization can be defined as the technology of creating virtual resources on physical resources including, but not limited to, physical servers, storage devices, and computer networks, such that a single physical resource can be the host of multiple virtual resources on which the applications run. The concept of virtualization can be traced back to the 1960s, when it was implemented by IBM to divide a mainframe computer into multiple VMs, in order to run multiple different applications simultaneously. Nowadays, virtualization has become one of the core technologies of the emerging and rapidly expanding cloud computing. A virtualization technique called hypervisor is responsible for managing the VMs, and makes it possible that each VM appears to own part of its host's physical resources and that multiple VMs can run on a single host. The flexibility of VM creation and management enables data centers to operate more efficiently. The problem concerning the deployment or redeployment of VMs on physical machines is referred to as VMPP.

Most current data centers follow a three-tier architecture [6]. The lowest tier is the access tier, where each server connects to an access switch. Then, all the access switches connect to aggregation switches at the intermediate aggregation tier (refer to Figure 2.1 as an example). And finally, at the highest tier, the core tier, all the aggregation switches connect

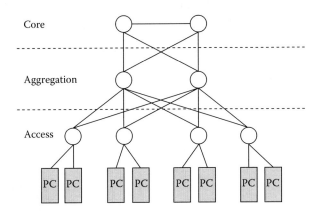

FIGURE 2.1   An example of three-tier architecture.

to core switches which also contain gateways for data transfer between the data center and the outside. Many three-tier architectures are proposed to improve the cost effectiveness and scalability of data centers, such as VL2 [7] and FatTree [8]. Furthermore, some new multilevel architectures are also proposed, such as BCube [9] and DCell [10]. (Refer to Popa et al. [11] for a comparison between recent data center network architectures.) While all the above works focus on introducing new architectures, many recent literatures [12–16] begin to consider improving networks in a given architecture, by choosing a desired VM placement strategy. We will review the main results of these research works in this chapter.

VMPP ALGORITHMS

Because of the significance of VM placement strategy to data centers, much research has been focusing on this problem. The purpose of this chapter is to introduce some representative literature, which may help us have a clearer and more comprehensive view of this problem. In this chapter, we mainly focus our attention on

- Minimizing server cost

- Minimizing network cost

- Jointly minimizing server cost and network cost

- Trade-off between cost and utility

Server Cost Minimization Algorithms

Server cost minimization is the most basic problem of VMPP, and has been studied extensively. The problem can be described as minimizing the used server number, while at the same time satisfying the resource demand of VMs such as CPU, memory, and network.

Basic Algorithm

1. The basic server number minimization VMPP can be treated as a static one-dimensional bin packing problem (BPP) [17]: the sets of VMs and servers are given and assumed to be static; the resource is simplified as one dimensional (e.g., CPU); the objective is to pack all VMs to servers, such that the used number of servers is minimized, and the capacity of each server is not less than the resource demand of the VMs packed on it. This VMPP can be solved by the first-fit bin packing algorithm [17], that is, assigning each VM, one after another, to the first server that has enough remaining resource capacity for the VM, until all the VMs are packed.

Multidimensional Resources

In practice, to run applications, VMs need multidimensional resources such as CPU, memory, and network resources. Mishra and Sahoo [18] proposed a method to deal with the server number minimization VMPP with respect to multidimensional resources, which is similar to the vector BPP. For simplicity, we demonstrate the main idea in two dimensions, as in Figure 2.2.

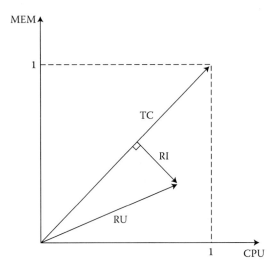

FIGURE 2.2 Depiction of resource vectors.

The horizontal axis represents the normalized CPU, and the vertical axis represents the normalized memory. Vector TC and RU denote the total capacity and the resource utilization of a server, respectively. Vector RI, which is the difference between vector RU and RU's projection on TC, can be used as a metric to measure the resource imbalance of a server. The smaller the vector RI is, the more balanced the server resource utilization is. By minimizing the imbalance of server resource utilization (i.e., the magnitude of vector RI), we can increase the multidimensional server resource utilization, and thus, reduce the needed server number. The main idea of this bin packing heuristic can be described as follows. First, assign the least imbalanced VM to the first server. Second, assign the next VM that meets the following two requirements to the current PM: (1) the resource demand of the VM is less than the remaining capacity of the current server; (2) after the VM has been assigned, the current server has the least value of RI. If the current server does not have enough remaining capacity to host any VM, then open a new server. Finally, repeat the above process, until all VMs are packed.

Dynamic Resource Demand
For dynamic VMPP, the future VM demand is unknown, and will change in a short time. So we need to recompute the placement configuration, and redeploy the VMs, preferably in a shorter time than is required of a significant change of resource demand. One way of solving dynamic server cost minimization VMPP is by first predicting the future VM demand and treating the demand as deterministic, and then solving the problem as static BPP. Bobroff et al. [19] provided a prediction technique, and has solved the VMPP using First Fit Decreasing (FFD) algorithm [20]. More prediction approaches can be found in Wood et al. [21].

But a recent study [13,22] has shown that data center network traffic patterns are highly volatile, and it is unreliable to treat the VM network demand as deterministic. Wang et al.

[23] proposed to treat the future network bandwidth usage as a random variable obeying Gaussian distribution, for online VMPP (an online problem refers to the situation in which new VMs may arrive, old VMs may leave, and the information cannot be known in advance). This VMPP is a stochastic bin packing problem (SBPP). The difference between BPP and SBPP is that when we reduce the latter to the former, the size of a VM demand will depend on the other VMs packed on the same server. To minimize the server number, we need to first consider which VMs should be packed together so that their sizes are reduced, and then solve the problem as BPP. Wang et al. [23] and Breitgand and Epstein [24] both proposed some methods on how to divide the VMs into different groups.

The advantage of treating server minimization VMPP as BPP is that we can find some efficient algorithms such as fit-first and FFD to solve the problem fast, while the disadvantage is that these algorithms do not guarantee an optimal solution.

Alternatives to Bin-Packing

Instead of treating the sever number minimization problem as a BPP, Hermenier et al. [25] treats the problem as a constraint satisfaction problem (CSP) [26], which can be generally defined as finding the solution for a set of objectives under some constraints. For this VMPP, server number is the objective to minimize, and the constraints can be expressed as: for every server, its resource capacity is not less than the total resource demand of the VMs on it. This CSP can be solved by dynamic programming [27]. The advantage of treating VMPP as CSP is that the solution is better than those of heuristics based on local optimization algorithms such as first-fit and FFD, and that the optimal solution can be found frequently. The disadvantage lies in the excessive time needed for problem solving. Hermenier et al. [25] proposed some methods to reduce the computation time as well.

Network Cost Minimization Algorithms

Compared with server cost minimization VMPP, network cost minimization VMPP is relatively new. The traditional method to handle network problems is with respect to improving the underlying network architecture. An early work that considers minimizing network cost with respect to VMPP is done in Meng et al. [13].

Minimizing Network Costs between VMs

For VMPP, traffic cost between two VMs i and j can be defined as $T_{ij}D_{ij}$ in which $T_{ij}d_mT_{ij}d_m$ denotes traffic rate from VMs i to j, and D_{ij} denotes the communication cost between the two hosts of VMs i and j. Traffic rate can be represented by the amount of data transferred in a unit time, and communication cost can be represented by the number of switches on the routing path.

In Meng et al. [13], each server is treated as consisting of several slots, and a slot represents a portion of server resources. For simplicity, the number of slots and VMs are assumed to be equal, and the mapping between slots and VMs should be one-to-one. The goal is to find a permutation function d_m $\pi:[1, \ldots, n] \to [1, \ldots, n]$ to minimize the total traffic cost $\sum_{i=1}^{n} \sum_{j=1}^{n} T_{ij}D_{\pi(i)\pi(j)}d_m$. The formulated problem is a quadratic assignment problem [28], and is known to be NP-hard. To solve the problem, one can exploit the proposition below:

Proposition:

Suppose. $0 \leq a_1 \leq a_2 \cdots \leq a_n d_m$ and the following inequalities hold for any permutation π on $[1, \ldots, n]$ [29]:

$$\sum_{i=1}^{n} a_i b_{n-1+i} \leq \sum_{i=1}^{n} a_i b_{\pi(i)} \leq \sum_{i=1}^{n} a_i b_i$$

According to the proposition above, to minimize the total traffic cost, we should assign the VM pairs with heavy traffic rates to slot pairs with low communication costs. The main idea of the algorithm can be divided into two steps. In step 1, the slots are partitioned into k clusters, such that slots with low communication costs are in one slot cluster, and VMs are also partitioned into k clusters, such that VMs with heavy mutual traffic rates are in one VM cluster. At the same time, the partition process must satisfy the requirement that each slot cluster has a corresponding VM cluster with the same size. After the partition, do a one-to-one mapping between slot clusters and VM clusters based on propositions introduced in Hardy et al. [29]. In step 2, within each mapped slot-VM cluster, repeat step 1 recursively until each slot and VM are mapped. The partition process is based on algorithms introduced in Gonzalez [30] and Saran and Vazirani [31].

A similar work to Meng et al. [13] is introduced in Shrivastava et al. [14]. Shrivastava et al. [14] aims to find a server for every overloaded VM to migrate in such a way that the total network traffic cost is minimized. Shrivastava et al. [14] proposed a greedy algorithm to migrate each VM based on its traffic rate. The total traffic rate of VM i can be represented by $\sum_{j \in O(i)} T_{ij}$ in which $O(i)$ denotes the set of VMs that have data transfer with VM i. The main idea of the algorithm is as follows: first, sort all the overloaded VMs in decreasing order with respect to their total traffic rate; second, beginning with the first overloaded VM, migrate each overloaded VM one after another to servers having enough remaining resource capacity, such that the VM being migrated will have minimum traffic cost after its migration. Shrivastava et al. [14] also introduced some techniques to improve performance and reduce computation costs of the algorithm.

Compared to Meng et al. [13], whose algorithms can achieve bounded approximation ratios, Shrivastava et al. [14] have considered more factors, by taking server resource capacity into account. However, in Shrivastava et al. [14], they did not give any theoretical guarantees on the performance bound of their greedy algorithm.

Minimizing Network Costs between VM and Data Stores
Both Meng et al. [13] and Shrivastava et al. [14] have only considered network costs derived from communication between VMs, while network costs can also be caused by access latency between VMs and data servers. Alicherry and Lakshman [15] proposed an approach to minimize the data access latency. In Alicherry and Lakshman [15], the locations of data servers are given, and the latency between computation servers and data servers, which is proportional to network bandwidth usage, is given. Each VM on computation servers can only be paired with one data server, and vice versa. The goal is to minimize the total latency

by choosing the proper VM for each data server. By making the number of VMs and data servers equal, Alicherry and Lakshman [15] have transformed this VMPP into a classic linear sum assignment problem [32]. The corresponding assignment problem can be represented and solved as a 0–1 linear program: the objective to minimize is $\sum_{i=1}^{n}\sum_{j=1}^{n} l_{ij} m_i x_{ij}$, in which n denotes the number of data servers and VMs, l_{ij} denotes the latency between data server i and VM_j, m_i denotes the amount of data needed to be processed on data server i, and x_{ij} denotes the mapping between data server i and VM_j; the constraint can be described as: for any $i, j = 1, \ldots, n$, $x_{i,j} \in \{0, 1\}$ for any $i = 1, \ldots, n$, $\sum_{j=1}^{n} x_{ij} = 1$; and for any $j = 1, \ldots, n$, $\sum_{i=1}^{n} x_{ij} = 1$. This problem can be solved by the Hungarian algorithm [32].

Server and Network Jointly Cost Minimization Algorithms

In Sections "Server Cost Minimization Algorithms" and "Network Cost Minimization Algorithms," we have seen VPMM algorithms that focus only on server cost or only on network cost. In this section, we will introduce some algorithms that jointly consider both costs.

VMPP Algorithms Using Markov Chains

As we have introduced, Meng et al. [13] and Shrivastava et al. [14] only focus on network cost minimization by finding a good VM placement strategy, while assuming that the routing path between two VMs is single. Jiang et al. [16] proposed an algorithm that takes both VMPP and multipath routing into account. Furthermore, its objective is to minimize weighted server costs and network costs. By using an approximation technique introduced in Jiang et al. [16], Chen et al. [33] have transformed the original minimization problem into a new problem whose optimal solution, which associates a probability $p_{s_i}^*(x)$ to each configuration, can be easily calculated. We can use the Markov chain as a time-sharing strategy among different configurations to approximately solve the original problem. The Markov chain can be built as below (refer to Figure 2.3 as an example): each state s_i represents a feasible configuration, and the stationary distribution is according to $p_{s_i}^*(x)$. We build a link between two states that can be transferred from one to the other by only migrating one VM. We also design the Markov chain as time-reversible, so we can get the proper transition rate $q_{s_i \to s_j}$, which only depends on the target state s_j, between two connected states s_i and s_j.

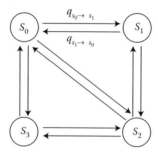

FIGURE 2.3   An example of time-reversible Markov chain.

For a static VMPP given a snapshot of network topology and a set of VMs, we can find the target configuration by the following steps: start from a feasible configuration s_0 and probabilistically transfer to another configuration s_i based on transition rate $q_{s_0 \to s_i}$; then compare the weighted total cost of the two configurations, choose the one with smaller cost, and repeat the transfer and comparison process for a given number of times.

Jiang et al. [16] proposed a greedy algorithm to reduce the feasible configuration numbers in order to save computation time. A similar online algorithm is also given by Jiang et al. [16], based on Markov chain approximation.

VMPP Algorithms Using Binary Search

Different from the above network cost-related papers, which assume that the traffic rate between VMs is given and which calculate the network cost based on it, Li et al. [12] argued that in practice, network traffic is difficult to know, and has defined the network cost function based on VM interserver communication patterns and sizes of communicating VM parts. The network cost between VMs on the same server is ignored. For a simplified central model example that only considers communication patterns, if n VMs of an application are divided into W parts and are placed on W servers, and one of the servers is the central node (e.g., project manager) so that all the other servers only communicate with it, then the network cost is $W - 1$. (Refer to Li et al. [12] for more cost functions that consider the sizes of VM parts and other communication patterns.)

In Li et al. [12], all servers are assumed to have the same capacity, while the applications can be homogeneous or heterogeneous, that is, the VM number for each application can be equal or different. The weighted relation between τ (the unit cost of opening a new server) and δ (the unit cost of adding a new communication link) is defined as $\tau = \mu\delta(\mu > 1)$. The objective is to find a strategy to divide into parts and pack all the VMs of each application, such that the total weighted cost is minimized. The solution process of this VMPP consists of two stages. In stage one, according to different cost functions and application characteristics (i.e., homogeneous or heterogeneous), several packing algorithms are proposed to minimize the network cost for a given number of servers. In stage two, the binary search algorithm [34] is employed to compute the optimal number of servers that minimizes the total weighted cost of a configuration, during which the network cost of a configuration, as one part of the total weighted cost, is calculated based on network cost minimization algorithms in stage one, and the server cost is calculated based on the number of servers turned on.

For the case of homogeneous applications with the central model-based network cost function as given above, the corresponding packing algorithm given by Li et al. [12] can provide the optimal solution; for the heterogeneous applications case, the corresponding packing algorithm can achieve a two-approximation ratio.

Minimizing Migration Cost

For dynamic VMPP, we should pay special attention to VM migration cost, because the migration process, which needs resources such as CPU, memory, and network bandwidths, will lead to the increase of both server cost and network cost. Large-scale migration

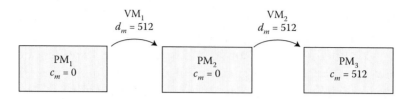

FIGURE 2.4 A sequence of migration.

processes may result in huge costs that offset the benefit of reduced server or network costs under certain optimized configurations.

Hermenier et al. [25] presented an approach to minimize the migration cost from one configuration to another. A migration is feasible only when the destination server has enough remaining resource capacity for the migrating VM. Migrations that are not immediately feasible are subject to one of two constraints: sequential constraint and cyclic constraint. For simplicity, we use memory as the resource to show the examples of these two constraints, as in Figures 2.3 and 2.4. For each VM, d_m denotes its memory demand; and for each physical machine (PM), c_m denotes its current remaining memory capacity.

In Figure 2.4, the goal includes two operations: (1) migrate VM_1 from PM_1 to PM_2; (2) migrate VM_2 from PM_2 to PM_3. But because of the memory constraint of PM_2 operation 1 can only be performed after operation 2 is finished.

In Figure 2.5, the goal is to exchange two VMs on two PMs as shown in Figure 2.5a, but the exchange cannot be done directly because both VMs are waiting for the other side to move first, while no VM can do so due to the memory constraints of the PMs. To solve this deadlock situation, another server PM_3 is needed to temporarily host one VM that needs to be migrated, as shown in Figure 2.5b. With the help of PM_3, we can complete the exchange process by first migrating VM_1 from PM_1 to PM_3, then migrating VM_2 from PM_2 to PM_1, and at last, migrating VM_1 from PM_3 to PM_2.

Considering the above sequential and cyclic migration, we can minimize and calculate the migration cost from one configuration to another with properly arranged migration steps, as introduced in Hermenier et al. [25]. The main idea is to migrate the VMs in the

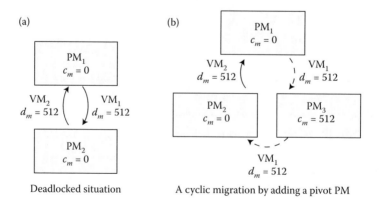

(a)

Deadlocked situation

(b)

A cyclic migration by adding a pivot PM

FIGURE 2.5 A cyclic migration.

minimum number of steps, and with the maximum simultaneous migrations in each step. We can then treat the minimum migration cost as the reconfiguration cost from one configuration to another.

The VMPP is divided into two CSPs in Hermenier et al. [25]. The objective of the first CSP is to minimize the server number and find a sample candidate configuration, as introduced in Section "Server Cost Minimization Algorithms" (notice that with the same minimized server number, there can be many different candidate configurations). The objective of the second CSP is to find the target configuration that minimizes the reconfiguration cost, subject to the constraints similar to the first CSP, and an additional constraint that the server number used in the target configuration that is given by the first CSP.

Trade-Off between Cost and Utility

In previous sections, we have discussed the VMPP algorithms for cost minimization. However, this is only one perspective based on the service providers, and we should take a broader view to consider the experience of users, as well. At the same time, we can bring in the concept of utility to better reflect the welfare of both service providers and users. For providers, the utility is mainly determined by two factors: the rent paid by users, which produces a positive utility, and the power consumption, which produces a negative utility. For users, the positive utility is derived from the efficient application performance of VMs, and the negative utility is derived from the rent and SLA violation. An optimal objective for VMPP should be the maximization of the social welfare, that is, the positive utility of both providers and users. For simplicity, we can ignore the different preferences for money between providers and users; thus, the influence of rent to social welfare is offset, and the total utility can be represented by the difference between positive utility of application performance and negative utility of power consumption.

Maximizing Total Utility

Cardosa et al. [35] proposed an algorithm to maximize total utility. A major difference between preciously introduced papers and Cardosa et al. [35] is that in the former scenarios, we treat the VM demand as a single value, and once a VM is placed on a server, it will be assigned this single value of resources. Meanwhile, Cardosa et al. [35] state that in practice, many virtualization technologies, such as VMware [36], Xen [37], allow administrators to set a minimum, and a maximum amount of resources required by a VM, as well as its share of the spare resources, and we should exploit this advantage. For example, if a VM is more important to us, we should assign more resources to it. In Cardosa et al. [35], an algorithm is proposed to maximize the objective, that is, the difference between performance utility and power consumption, while treating the VM demand as adjustable between a minimum and a maximum value. The performance utility of a VM is a user-defined function of its assigned resource amount, such that the more resources the VM is assigned, the more utility we get from the VM, as long as the assigned resource is no larger than the maximum demand of the VM. The power consumption of a server is incurred once it is turned on. So for every configuration plan, we can calculate the corresponding objective value. To maximize the objective,

Cardosa et al. [35] adopt a metric called NodeUtility to represent the achievable maximum utility of a given set of servers hosting VMs. Here, NodeUtility is defined as the maximum utility of the nodes we can get by only adjusting the resource amount assigned to VMs without other operations such as VM migrations. For example, suppose VM_1 and VM_2 are packed in server 1, and VM_1 is more utility-efficient than VM_2, that is, VM_1 can produce more utility than VM_2 with one unit of resource; then, we can compute the NodeUtility of server 1 as follows: we assign the resources to VM_1 and VM_2 based on their minimum demands, and if there are remaining resources on server 1, we preferentially assign the resources to VM_1, and then to VM_2, until the resources are used up or the maximum demands of VM_1 and VM_2 are reached. The utility we get from server 1 by performing the above operation is the NodeUtility of server 1. By using the NodeUtility, we can solve the VMPP as follows: pack each VM, one after another, on servers in such a way that the entailed increase of difference between NodeUtility and power consumption is maximized after each step of packing, and repeat the process until all the VMs are packed.

A more comprehensive algorithm to maximize total utility is proposed in Jung et al. [38]. The objectives include application performance, power consumption, and overheads caused by adaptation actions and the decision-making process. Here, an adaptation action can be one of the following: increasing/decreasing CPU amount assigned to a VM, adding/removing a VM, live-migrating a VM, and turning on/off a server. Based on some estimation models [38], each different objective is represented by a corresponding utility, so that they can be compared (the utility from adaptation actions and decision-making process can be measured based on their impact to application performance and power consumption). Jung et al. [38] treated this utility maximization VMPP as a graph search problem: a configuration is represented by a vertex, and the utility associated with each vertex can be calculated based on the estimating models; a link between two vertices represents just one adaption action between two configurations. The main idea of Jung et al. [38] is to find the shortest distance from the current vertex (configuration) to the target vertex, by using A^* graph search algorithm [39].

FUTURE RESEARCH DIRECTIONS

Although a large amount of research has been done on VMPP in recent years, there are still some unsolved problems that need further work. In this section, we present some open issues to be addressed in future.

Social-Oriented Algorithms

When devising VMPP algorithms, most current researchers put themselves in the shoes of cloud providers, and propose algorithms to help minimize cost consumptions. However, there is a trade-off between cost consumptions and application performance, as we mentioned before. Focusing only on cost minimization may affect user satisfaction which is also important for cloud computing to be widely accepted. So we should pay more attention to user utility when we try to design comprehensive VMPP algorithms, and carry a social-oriented view to balance cost consumption and user utility.

Data Uncertainty

In most of the literature we have introduced, the algorithms assume that all the parameters are known, while in reality, cloud data centers are highly volatile systems and it is hard to precisely know some parameters. For example, most literatures addressing network cost VMPP have assumed that the network traffic between VMs is known. But as Li et al. [12] claims, it is hard to know the network traffic because the system is greatly dynamic. Accordingly, algorithms working on real cloud systems should take into account and address estimation errors and unexpected events. Future algorithms need to be robust enough to cope with such situations.

Algorithm Evaluation

To evaluate the soundness of an algorithm, it is preferable if we can prove its properties through mathematical analysis. Or, if dealing with the general case is too tricky, we can at least analyze some simplified special cases and make the algorithm more understandable and reliable. However, some of the literature has not given any theoretical analysis about the properties of proposed algorithms. In the absence of analytical evaluation, the second evaluation method is by meaningful comparison of the simulation results based on different algorithms. Unfortunately, there is no generally accepted standard benchmark for VMPP, because the literature holds different assumptions and addresses distinct objectives. As a result, some literatures only compare with trivial algorithms or compare different versions of their own algorithms, and some make no comparison at all. The lack of meaningful comparison compromises the soundness of the algorithms. Given this situation, future research should also take into consideration the development of a rigorous evaluation system for VMPP.

CONCLUSION

With the prevalence of virtualization technology in data centers, addressing VMPP has been an important issue for data centers to improve efficiency and reduce costs. In this chapter, we have introduced various objectives of VMPP that may be concerned in different scenarios, especially under various stresses from Big Data applications on CPU, memory, and networks. Based mainly on two perspectives, server cost and network cost, we have introduced the representative literature, presenting and comparing their main ideas and algorithms. We have seen that because VMPPs are generally computationally complex problems, especially when multiobjectives are considered jointly, many approximate algorithms are proposed on this issue. The future trends include devising efficient and comprehensive algorithms that can be implemented for data centers to reduce expenditure, enhance efficiency, and improve scalability. At the same time, we should also consider the algorithms from the user's point of view, and address the problems of data uncertainty and algorithm evaluation.

REFERENCES

1. A. Divyakant, S. Das, and A. E. Abbadi, Big Data and cloud computing: Current state and future opportunities, in *ACM 14th International Conference on Extending Database Technology*, pp. 530–533, 2011.

2. A. Greenberg, J. Hamilton, D. A. Maltz, and P. Patel, The cost of a cloud: Research problems in data center networks, *SIGCOMM Computer Communication Review*, 39(1), 68–73, 2009.
3. A. Verma, P. Ahuja, and A. Neogi, pMapper: Power and migration cost aware application placement in virtualized systems, in *ACM 9th International Middleware Conference*, Leuven, Belgium, pp. 243–264, 2008.
4. S. Kumar, V. Talwar, V. Kumar, P. Ranganathan, and K. Schwan, Loosely coupled platform and virtualization management in data centers, in *Proceedings of the IEEE International Conference on Autonomic Computing*, Barcelona, Spain, pp. 127–136, 2009.
5. X. Fan, W. Weber, and L. Barroso, Power provisioning for a warehouse-sized computer, in *Proceeding of the 34th ACM International Symposium On Computer Architecture*, San Diego, California, USA, pp. 13–23, 2007.
6. Cisco Data Center Infrastructure 2.5 Design Guide, http://www.cisco.com/c/en/us/td/docs/solutions/Enterprise/Data_Center/DC_Infra2_5/DCI_SRND_2_5a_book.html.
7. A. Greenberg, J. Hamilton, N. Jain, S. Kandula, C. Kim, P. Lahiri, D. A. Maltz, P. Patel, and S. Sengupta, VL2: A scalable and flexible data center network, *SIGCOMM Computer Communication Review*, 39(4), 51–62, 2009.
8. C. E. Leiserson, Fat-trees: Universal networks for hardware efficient supercomputing, *IEEE Transactions on Computers*, 34(10), 892–901, 1985.
9. C. Guo, G. Lu, D. Li, H. Wu, X. Zhang, Y. Shi, C. Tian, Y. Zhang, and S. Lu, Bcube: A high performance, Server-centric Network Architecture for Modular Data Centers, *SIGCOMM Computer Communication Review*, 39(4), 63–74, 2009.
10. C. Guo, H. Wu, K. Tan, L. Shi, Y. Zhang, and S. Lu. Dcell, A Scalable and Fault-tolerant Network Structure for Data Centers, *SIGCOMM Computer Communication Review*, 38(4), 75–86, 2008.
11. L. Popa, S. Ratnasamy, G. Iannaccone, A. Krishnamurthy, and I. Stoica, A cost comparison of datacenter network architectures, in *Proceeding of the 6th International Conference, Co-NEXT*, (16), pp. 1–12, 2010.
12. X. Li, J. Wu, S. Tang, and S. Lu, Let's stay together: Towards traffic aware virtual machine placement in data centers, in *Proceedings of the IEEE INFOCOM*, pp. 1842–1850, 2014.
13. X. Meng, V. Pappas, and L. Zhang, Improving the scalability of data center networks with traffic-aware virtual machine placement, in *Proceedings of the IEEE INFOCOM*, pp. 1–9, 2010.
14. Y. Shrivastava, P. Zerfos, K. won Lee, H. Jamjoom, Y.-H. Liu, and S. Banerjee, Application-aware virtual machine migration in data centers, in *Proceedings of the IEEE INFOCOM Mini-Conference*, pp. 66–70, 2011.
15. M. Alicherry and T. V. Lakshman, Optimizing data access latencies in cloud systems by intelligent virtual machine placement, in *Proceedings of the IEEE INFOCOM*, pp. 671–679, 2013.
16. J. W. Jiang, T. Lan, S. Ha, M. Chen, and M. Chiang, Joint VM placement and routing for data center traffic engineering, in *Proceedings of the IEEE INFOCOM*, pp. 2876–2880, 2012.
17. http://en.wikipedia.org/wiki/Bin_packing_problem.
18. M. Mishra and A. Sahoo, On theory of VM placement: Anomalies in existing methodologies and their mitigation using a novel vector based approach, 2011 IEEE International Conference on Cloud Computing, pp. 275–282, 2011.
19. N. Bobroff, A. Kochut, and K. Beaty, Dynamic placement of virtual machines for managing SLA violations, in *Proceedings of the 10th IFIP/IEEE International Symposium on Integrated Network Management (IM)*, pp. 119–128, 2007.
20. Y. Ajiro and A. Tanaka, Improving packing algorithms for server consolidation, in *Proceedings of the International Conference for the Computer Measurement Group*, pp. 399–406, 2007.
21. T. Wood., L. Cherkasova, K. Ozonat, and P. Shenoy, Predicting Application Resource Requirements in Virtual Environments, HP Laboratories, Technical Report HPL-2008–122, http://www.hpl.hp.com/techreports/2008/HPL-2008-122.pdf, 2008.

22. T. A. Benson, A. Anand, A. Akella, and M. Zhang, Understanding data center traffic characteristics, In *ACM SIGCOMM WREN Workshop*, pp. 65–72, 2009.
23. M. Wang, X. Meng, and L. Zhang, Consolidating virtual machines with dynamic bandwidth demand in data centers, in *Proceedings of the IEEE INFOCOM*, pp. 71–75, 2011.
24. D. Breitgand and A. Epstein, Improving consolidation of virtual machines with risk-aware bandwidth oversubscription in compute clouds, in *Proceedings of the IEEE INFOCOM Mini-Conference*, pp. 2861–2865, 2012.
25. F. Hermenier, X. Lorca, J. M. Menaud, G. Muller, and J. Lawall, Entropy: A consolidation manager for clusters, in *VEE '09: Proceedings of the 2009 ACM SIGPLAN/SIGOPS International Conference on Virtual Execution Environments*, pp. 41–50, 2009.
26. http://en.wikipedia.org/wiki/Constraint_satisfaction_problem.
27. M. Trick, A dynamic programming approach for consistency and propagation for Knapsack constraints, in *Proceedings of the Third International Workshop on Integration of AI and OR Techniques in Constraint Programming for Combinatorial Optimization Problems*, pp. 113–124, 2001.
28. J. P. O. B.-N. P. H. Eliane Maria Loilola, N. M. M. de Abreu, and T. Querido, A survey for the quadratic assignment problem, *European Journal of Operational Research*, 176, 657–690, 2007.
29. G. G. Hardy, J. E. Littlewood, and G. Polya, *Inequalities*. London and New York: Cambridge University Press, 1952.
30. T. Gonzalez, Clustering to minimize the maximum intercluster distance, *Theoretical Computer Science*, 38, 293–306, 1985.
31. H. Saran and V. V. Vazirani, Finding k cuts within twice the optimal, *SIAM Journal on Computing*, 38(1), 101–108, 1995.
32. R. E. Burkard and E. Cela, Linear assignment problems and extensions. *Handbook of Combinatorial Optimization: Supplement Volume A*, Dordrecht, 1999.
33. M. Chen, S. C. Liew, Z. Shao, and C. Kai, Markov approximation for combinatorial network optimization, in *Proceedings of the IEEE INFOCOM*, pp. 1–9, 2010.
34. http://en.wikipedia.org/wiki/Binary_search_algorithm
35. M. Cardosa, M. Korupolu, and A. Singh, Shares and utilities based power consolidation in virtualized server environments, in *Proceedings of the 11th IFIP/IEEE International Conference on Symposium on Integrated Network Management*, pp. 327–334, 2009.
36. VMWare, http://www.vmware.com/
37. P. Barham, B. Dragovic, K. Fraser, S. Hand, T. Harris, A. Ho, R. Neugebauer, I. Pratt, and A. Warfield, Xen and the art of virtualization, in *Proceedings of Symposium on Operating Systems Principles*, pp. 52–65, 2003.
38. G. Jung, M. A. Hiltunen, K. R. Joshi, R. D. Schlichting, and C. Pu, Mistral: Dynamically managing power, performance, and adaptation cost in cloud infrastructures, in *Proceedings of the 2010 IEEE 30th International Conference on Distributed Computing Systems*, Genova, Italy, pp. 62–73, 2010.
39. S. J. Russell and P. Norvig, *Artificial Intelligence: A Modern Approach*. Prentice Hall, Jersey, 2003.

CHAPTER 3

Big Data Management Challenges, Approaches, Tools, and Their Limitations

Michel Adiba, Juan Carlos Castrejón, Javier A. Espinosa-Oviedo, Genoveva Vargas-Solar, and José-Luis Zechinelli-Martini

CONTENTS

INTRODUCTION

Big Data is the buzzword everyone talks about since it concerns every human activity generating large quantities of digital data (e.g., science, government, economy). However, it is still difficult to characterize the Big Data phenomenon since different points of view and disciplines attempt to address it. It is true that everyone sees behind the term a data deluge for processing and managing big volumes of bytes (peta 10^{15}, exa 10^{18}, zetta 10^{21}, yotta 10^{24}, etc.). But beyond this superficial vision, there is a consensus about the three Vs [1] characterizing Big Data: *volume*, *variety* (different types of representations: structured, not-structured, graphs, etc.), and *velocity* (streams of data produced continuously).

Big Data forces to view data mathematically (e.g., measures, values distribution) first and establish a context for it later. For instance, how can researchers use statistical tools and computer technologies to identify meaningful patterns of information? How shall significant data correlations be interpreted? What is the role of traditional forms of scientific theorizing and analytic models in assessing data? *What you really want to be doing is looking at the whole dataset in ways that tell you things and answers questions that you're not asking* [2,3]. All these questions call for well-adapted infrastructures that can efficiently organize data, evaluate and optimize queries, and execute algorithms that require important computing and memory resources. With the evolution toward the cloud, data management requirements have to be revisited [4,5]. In such setting, it is possible to exploit parallelism for processing data, and thereby increasing availability and storage reliability thanks to replication. Organizing Big Data in persistence supports (cache, main memory, or disk), dispatching processes, producing and delivering results implies having efficient and well-adapted data management infrastructures. These infrastructures are not completely available in existing systems. Therefore, it is important to revisit and provide systems architectures that cope with Big Data characteristics. The key challenge is to hide the complexity of accessing and managing Big Data and also to provide interfaces for tuning them according to application requirements.

By focusing on data management issues, the chapter examines the main challenges involved in the three Vs of Big Data and discusses systems architectures for proposing *Vs model aware data management solutions.* Accordingly, the remainder of the chapter is organized as follows. The section "The Big Data Vs" characterizes Big Data in terms of the Vs model. In particular, it insists on the aspects that lead to new challenges in data management and on the expected characteristics of processed Big Data. The section "Big Data-Processing Platforms" describes data-processing platforms including parallel approaches, NoSQL systems, and Big Data management systems (BDMS). The section "Big Data-Processing Platforms" introduces the life cycle of Big Data processing. It also describes the possible application markets underlining the expected requirements that will lead to push the limits of what can be expected when fine-grained data are observed. Finally, the section "Conclusions and Perspectives" concludes the chapter and discusses Big Data perspectives.

THE BIG DATA Vs

While some initial successes have already been achieved such as the Sloan Digital Sky Survey [6], genome databases, the Library of Congress, and so on, there remain many technical challenges that must be addressed to exploit the full potential of Big Data. For instance, the *sheer size* of the data is a major challenge and is the one that is most easily recognized. However, there are challenges not just in *volume*, but also in *variety* (heterogeneity of data types, representation, and semantic interpretation) and *Velocity* (rate at which data arrive and the time in which it must be processed) [7].

Variety

Data variety has been a recurrent issue since it has been possible to digitalize multimedia data and since the production of documents has become a day-by-day practice in organizations and in the domestic context. Continuous work has been carried out for modeling data and documents that are digitalized in different formats. Raw data representation has been standardized (PDF documents, JPEG, GIF for images, MP3 for audio, etc.) and then coupled with data models to facilitate manipulation and information retrieval operations.

In the 1980s the relational model (structured data model) was defined on a solid theoretical basis namely mathematical relations and first-order logic. The relational approach does an important distinction between the schema (intention) and the extension of the relation. This dichotomy schema-data is fundamental to the database approach. Relations enable the manipulation of structured data independently of their physical representation in a computer. Given that a relation is a set of tuples that only contains atomic values, several consequences have to be considered. First, a relation cannot contain repeated data; in a tuple an attribute cannot have as associated value a set, a table, or another relation; there cannot be an undefined or missing value in a tuple. These constraints led to extensions to the relational model, which is considered not expressive enough. The first approach was to relax the first normal form of relations and authorize attribute values to be of type relation. Generalizing the use of constructors of type Cartesian product and set, and then adding lists and tables led to the definition of the complex object model, which is more expressive. Attempts have been made to define object-oriented database management systems (DBMS) and these systems are characterized in Atkinson et al. [8].

The structured and semistructured models (HTML, XML, JSON) are today managed by existing DBMS and by search engines exploring the Web and local files on computers. Semistructured data are mostly electronic documents that emerged on the Web. We consider also that object-oriented databases influenced the JavaScript Object Notation (JSON) model today used as a data exchange model on the Web. JSON is a generic format for textual data derived from the Javascript object notation.[*]

Later, the NoSQL systems being vague, other data models have emerged and are being used for dealing with Big Data. The key-value[†] data model associates a key to a simple or complex value. Records are distributed across nodes within a server network using, for example, a hash function over the key. The key-value model being the simplest model is used for dealing with noncomplex data, such as those in logs, user sessions, shopping cart data, that have to be retrieved fast and where there is no manipulation of the value elements. In the document model, data are semistructured documents corresponding to nested structures that can be irregular (similar to markup languages like XML).[‡] In the column

---

[*] Several NoSQL systems such as CouchDB [42] proposed in 2005 and MongoDB in 2009 are based on JSON (see NoSQL section).

[†] Memcached, Redis, and Riak are examples of systems that use this model.

[‡] MongoDB and CouchDB are the most prominent examples of systems adopting this model.

TABLE 3.1   Data Models Proposed by NoSQL Systems

Type	Operation	Data Models	Description
Key	Read (key)	Key Value, Graph, Document, Column-Family, Relational	*Read* a single record based on *primary key*
	Insert (key, *value*)		*Insert* a single record based on *primary key*
	Update (key, value)		*Update* a single record based on *primary key*
	Delete (key)		*Delete* a single record based on *primary key*
Aggregation	Read (pattern)	Document, Column-Family, Relational	*Read* all entities that conform to the specified *pattern*
	Insert (value)		*Insert* a single record with the specified *pattern*
	Update (pattern, *value*)		*Update* all entities that conform to the specified *pattern*
	Delete (pattern)		*Delete* all entities that conform to the specified *pattern*
Connection	Read (relationship)	Graph, Relational	*Read* all entities that conform to the specified *relationship*
	Insert (relationship)		*Create* a *relationship* between entities
	Update (oldRel, newRel)		*Update* a *relationship* between entities
	Delete (relationship)		*Delete* a *relationship* between entities

model, data are grouped into columns in contrast to traditional relations stored in rows. Each element can have a different number of columns (non-fixed schema).* Document and column-family models are mainly used for event logging, blogging, and Web analytics (counters on columns). The manipulation of documents is executed on the content with few atomicity and isolation requirements and column families are manipulated with concurrency and high throughput. Graph models provide concepts such as nodes, edges, and navigation operations for representing objects and querying operations. Nodes and edges can have properties of the form <key, value>.† Graph data models are adapted for highly connected data used for when information is retrieved based on relationships. Every model has associated manipulation operations that are coupled to the data structure it relays on (see Table 3.1). The figure shows the way data can be looked up and retrieved: by key, aggregating data, and navigating along relationships. For every possibility, there are specific functions provided by the NoSQL system's APIs.

Semantic content representations also appeared in order to support the Semantic Web (ontology languages such as OWL and tagging models such as RDF) and lookup tools deployed on computers and other devices. For improving scalability, current research [9] is applying parallel models to the execution of reasoning engines where ontologies and linked data have millions of nodes and relationships.

This diversity is somehow the core of Big Data challenges (and of database integration in general), since it is no longer pertinent to expect to deal with standardized data formats, and to have generic models used for representing the content. Rather than data models, the tendency is to have data representations that can encourage rapid manipulation, storage, and retrieval of distributed heterogeneous, almost raw data. Key challenges are (i) to cope

---

* HBase, Cassandra, and Hypertable are examples of systems that adopt this data model.
† Neo4J is an example of system that uses this model.

database construction (data cleaning) with short "time to market" (despite the volume of data and its production rate) and (ii) to choose the right data model for a given dataset considering data characteristics, the type of manipulation and processing operations applied to data, and "nonfunctional properties" provided by the system. "Nonfunctional properties" of systems include the performance of lookup functions given the possibility of associating simple or complex indexing structures to data collections.

Volume

The first thing anyone thinks about Big Data is its size [10,11]. In the era of Internet, social networks, mobile devices, and sensors producing data continuously, the notion of size associated to data collections has evolved very quickly [7,12]. Today it is normal for a person to produce and manage terabytes of information in personal and mobile computing devices [13]. Managing large and rapidly increasing volumes of data has been a challenging issue for many decades [13–15]. In the past, this challenge was mitigated by processors getting faster, following Moore's law, to provide us with the resources needed to cope with increasing volumes of data. However, there is a fundamental shift underway now: data volume is scaling faster than computing resources and CPU speeds are not significantly evolving. Cloud computing now aggregates multiple disparate workloads with varying performance goals (e.g., interactive services demand that the data-processing engine returns an answer within a fixed response time cap) [5]. This level of resources sharing on expensive and large clusters requires new ways of determining how to (i) run and execute data-processing jobs to meet cost-effectively the goals of each workload and (ii) deal with system failures that occur more frequently on large clusters [12,11].

Velocity

The term *velocity* refers to the speed of data generation and the time for processing it. Big Data is the result of a fine-grained continuous reading of the environment, society, and organizations, and is a natural and social phenomenon. Observations are done under different conditions and with different devices and therefore Big Data are heterogeneous, raw continuously produced data (i.e., streams) that must be processed for extracting useful information. A stream is a sequence (a priori infinite) of couples (t_i, v_i), where t_i is a time stamp and v_i is a (simple or complex) value. There are two possible interpretations for a stream, either as a *data flow* or as an *event flow*. Two aspects must be considered: data and users mobility in a spatio-temporal context, and the existence of several data or event streams produced continuously that must be processed under real-time constraints more or less strict.

Several works have addressed stream processing and have proposed stream management systems (SMS) and complex event processing (CEP). Briefly, the difference between both approaches relies on the semantics associated with the data. For instance, an SMS computes the average of temperature during the day, while a CEP tests whether the temperature in a room is not higher than a threshold and if it then reacts in consequence [16].

There are two main reasons to consider stream processing. First, it is not possible to store the data in their entirety: in order to keep storage requirements practical some level of analysis must occur as the data streams in. The issue is not just the velocity of the incoming data: it is possible to stream fast-moving data into bulk storage for later batch processing, for example. The importance lies in the speed of the feedback loop, taking data from input to decision. The second reason to consider streaming is where the application mandates immediate response to the data. Thanks to the rise of mobile applications and online gaming, this is an increasingly common situation.

BIG DATA-PROCESSING PLATFORMS

Schematically, (relational) databases and Web data management have evolved in parallel. On one hand, there is the success of relational, parallel DBMS with SQL. On the other hand, specific distributed systems for managing Web data were developed using the MapReduce model (see NoSQL systems). The classical database approach seemed unsuitable to manage Web data because it required successive design phases (Extract, Transform, and Load [ETL]). These phases were considered too rigid with respect to (i) nonstructured data sources (e.g., documents); (ii) specific Web applications; and (iii) high availability and scalability for an increasing number of users. Furthermore, DBMS are expensive systems with few open source proposals such as MySQL-C. Big Data-processing platforms offer strategies with good performance despite the data volume and greedy processing algorithms. Today these strategies start to converge and exploit the best of both worlds. From an application point of view, the question is how they can be combined to exploit Big Data?

Three architectures have emerged to address Big Data analytics: NoSQL systems, MapReduce/Hadoop, and extended RDBMS. At the beginning, these architectures were implemented as completely separate systems. Today, the trend is to develop innovative hybrid combinations of the three architectures. For example, Cisco and Oracle have delivered the first-ever enterprise class NoSQL solution deployed on Cloudera for harnessing large volumes of real-time unstructured and semistructured Big Data [17,18].

NoSQL Systems

At the end of the 1990s with the development of the Web and companies such as Google, Yahoo!, Facebook, or Amazon, offering efficient data management solutions became crucial. Monolithic SQL databases built for OLTP and OLAP were rejected as being too expensive, too complex, and/or not fast enough. The "Not Only SQL" movement was born [19,20]. For instance, Google and Amazon developed their own answers (BigTable and Dynamo, respectively) to meet these needs, and then the Apache open-source community created corresponding clones such as HBase and Cassandra, two of todays most popular and scalable key-value stores. Several systems have emerged providing their own implementations of the different data models and specific manipulation functions. The site of NoSQL databases* provides a list of existing systems.

The main objectives of NoSQL systems are to increase scalability and extensibility, using the Classic Hardware. They also ensure reliability, fault tolerance, and good performance despite the increasing number of requests. The common characteristic of these systems is

---

* The site http://nosql-database.org/ gathers 150 systems with different models and functions.

that they enable data manipulation without having to define a schema, so data are mainly semistructured. Thereby, they avoid schema definition and database loading after data cleaning. The characteristics of these systems architecture are: horizontal extensibility for executing distributed simple operations on a multitude of servers, data partitioning and duplication on several servers (data sharding), low-level interfaces for accessing the systems, concurrent access model more flexible than ACID transactions, distributed indexing and in-memory storage, and easy data structure evolution [5]. They provide basic Create, Read, Update, and Delete (CRUD) functions adapted for efficiently manipulating data structures according to their underlying data model.

Parallel Data Processing with MapReduce

MapReduce is a programming model (MR [21]) for developing data processing by defining the functions Map and Reduce inspired by functional programming. It is possible to parallelize data processing by partitioning and duplicating data on N machines, assuming that data are managed by a distributed file system. The function Map implements an operation based on a divide and conquer strategy. The idea is to divide a dataset modeled as <key, value> tuples into smaller datasets that can be processed independently. Both key and value elements can be of atomic or complex data types. Reduce combines the result of the Map function and reduces them by applying aggregation or summation functions. Developers must write these functions but they can rely on a platform that provides tools for coordinating the jobs executing these functions in parallel.

MR execution platforms consist, in general, of a distributed file system for storing input and output data and a process manager that coordinates parallel job execution. The first proposal, namely, the Google File System (GFS) [22], appeared in 2003. The architecture consists of millions of interconnected shared-nothing machines for incrementing data availability and reducing response time; ensuring the reliability of the system duplicating both servers and data; exploiting the inherent parallelism of the architecture. This system processes URL, user data (most recent query results), and geographical information (location of the points of interest in a region, such as boutiques, hotels, satellite street images). The scale factor is high with millions of URL, different versions of pages, millions of users, millions of queries per second, and hundreds of TB of satellite images. GFS offers a familiar byte-stream-based file view of data randomly partitioned over hundreds or even thousands of nodes in a cluster [23]. GFS is coupled with the programming model MR, to enable programmers to process Big Data by writing two user-defined functions, Map and Reduce. Google builds distributed applications with MR functions that are then executed by Hadoop [24], an open source MR execution platform.

Concerning the architecture, the Hadoop nodes are of different types and all have HDFS (Highly Distributed File System open source version of GFS [24]) and MR layers. HDFS is based on a master–slave architecture consisting of a master, the *name node* (an instance per cluster), that manages metadata for the data in each node; the *backup node* of the name node; the *data node*, an instance deployed in every machine of the cluster, manages data storage on disk. Similarly, MR components are distributed and manage jobs: with the *name node* there is a *job tracker*, and with the *data node*, a *task tracker* executing the MR functions on local data. This architecture scales toward millions of nodes that can manage PB of data. Data blocks are large enough for avoiding overcharging data access from the disk. Data are stored in each block in three copies for ensuring fault tolerance, instead of using mirror disks (e.g., RAID). Data location is invisible to the upper layers and this opens room for optimizations like those implemented by RDBMS.

Several works have been devoted for implementing relational operators using MR [25,26]. For example, a selection corresponds to a filter for Map. Projection is also expressed by a simple Map function. For a join, Map [27,28] provides tuples with the join attribute as key and Reduce performs the join. Thus, a relational query can be implemented as a set of parallel MR jobs. This kind of approach is provided by Hive [29] or Pig [30] built on top of Hadoop that provide SQL-like languages for programming data processing and associated execution environments.

Big Data Management Systems

Parallel RDBMS use a "shared-nothing" architecture where data are spread over a cluster based on a partitioning strategy, usually hash based, but sometimes range or random partitioning. Queries are processed by using parallel, hash-based divide-and-conquer techniques [31]. Parallel architectures address two factors expecting to get a linear behavior: (1) linear speedup, using the double of resources so that the program runs twice as fast, for example, processing 10TB using 8 nodes instead of 4 and thereby dividing the execution time by two; (2) linear speedup, double the resources used for processing a database twice bigger in the same response time, for example, process 10TB on 4 nodes and 4 disks and then process 20TB using 8 nodes and 8 disks. In reality, linear speedup is a theoretical vision since other factors are to be considered: interconnection time between processors, load balancing among distributed servers.

In Stonebraker et al. [32], there is a comparison of RDBMS with the Hadoop platforms for specific data analytics tasks. RDBMS seem to achieve good performances under the condition of appropriate tuning as good as Hadoop solutions or even better in some cases. These systems are robust and stable, but expensive (no open source system available). In contrast, Hadoop platforms are accessible and require less tuning efforts but they lack transparency and require algorithmic design effort when implementing binary operations like joins. Application development is always ad hoc in Hadoop since there is no general one-size-fits-all like in RDBMS. Thus, Stonebraker et al. [32] believe that there is a need for designing a highly scalable platform for next-generation information storage, search, and analytics: a BDMS. This can be done by combining and extending ideas drawn from semistructured data management, parallel databases, and first-generation data-intensive computing platforms (notably Hadoop/HDFS). ASTERIX* aims to be able to access, ingest, store, index, query, analyze, and publish very large quantities of semistructured data. The design of the ASTERIX BDMS is well suited to handling use cases that range all the way from rigid, relation-like data collections—whose structures are well understood and largely invariant—to flexible and more complex data, where little is planned ahead of time and the data instances are highly variant and self-describing.

---

* http://asterix.ics.uci.edu

Discussion

Different comparisons have been made between RDBMS, NoSQL, and Hadoop platforms [33–35]. NoSQL systems seem to provide too simple indexing strategies in comparison to relational DBMS. They encourage the programming of queries using the MR model in contrast to the declarative and optimized approach of relational DBMS. In contrast, Hadoop can process data directly without defining a schema as for relational DBMS. Hadoop and NoSQL solutions do not provide general "one-fits-all" systems, and it requires a lot of expertise and programming effort for implementing solutions. In all cases, extensibility and fault tolerance are aspects addressed by all systems according to their characteristics. In response to the drawbacks of Hadoop and NoSQL systems, recently, Google Cloud Dataflow* has been proposed. The objective is to make data and analytics accessible to everyone [36] through a data-centric model. With Dataflow programmers can easily express data-processing pipeline, monitor its execution, and get actionable insights from data, without having to deploy clusters, tuning configuration parameters, and optimizing resource usage.

BIG DATA LIFE CYCLE AND APPLICATIONS

"Big Data is a paradigm shift in how we think about data assets, where do we collect them, how do we analyze them, and how do we monetize the insights from the analysis," says Kimball [37]. Therefore, it is important to analyze Big Data life cycle and underline the challenges in each of these phases. Only analytic results matter. In the case of Big Data the whole processing phases are challenging: what to keep and what to throw? In which conditions are data acquired and cleaned? What is volatile or persistent, for how long? Are results transient or should they be used in further analysis?

Data Acquisition

Data are collected from some data-generating source. Much data are of no interest, and they can be filtered and compressed by orders of magnitude [10–12,38]. One challenge is to define these filters in such a way that they do not discard useful information. Data acquisition calls for research in the information reduction science that can intelligently process raw data to a size that its users can handle while not missing the needle in the haystack. Furthermore, "on-line" analysis techniques are required to process streaming data on the fly, since it is not possible to store first and reduce afterwards.

Furthermore, it is necessary to automatically generate the right metadata to describe what data are recorded and measured. Another important issue is data provenance. Recording information about the data at its birth is not useful unless this information can be interpreted and carried along through the data analysis pipeline [39]. Thus, research is required for both generating suitable metadata and designing data systems that carry the provenance of data and its metadata through data analysis pipelines.

---

* See http://googlecloudplatform.blogspot.fr/2014/06/sneak-peek-google-cloud-dataflow-a-cloud-native-data-processing-service.html

Data Cleaning

Given the heterogeneity of data flood, it is not enough merely to record it and store it into a repository. This requires differences in data structure and semantics to be expressed in computer understandable forms, and then "robotically" tractable. There is a strong body of work in data integration that can provide some of the answers. However, considerable additional work is required to achieve automated error-free difference resolution. Usually, there are many different ways to store the same information, each of them having their advantages and drawbacks. We must enable other professionals, such as domain scientists, to create effective database designs, either through devising tools to assist them in the design process or through foregoing the design process completely and developing techniques so that databases can be used effectively in the absence of intelligent database design.

Data Analysis and Mining

Methods for querying and mining Big Data are fundamentally different from traditional statistical analysis on small samples. Big Data are often noisy, dynamic, heterogeneous, interrelated, and untrustworthy. Nevertheless, even noisy Big Data could be more valuable than tiny samples. Indeed, general statistics obtained from frequent patterns and correlation analysis usually overpower individual fluctuations and often disclose more reliable hidden patterns and knowledge.

Big Data are enabling the next generation of interactive data analysis with real-time answers. In the future, queries toward Big Data will be automatically generated for content creation on websites, to populate hot lists or recommendations, and to provide an ad hoc analysis of datasets to decide whether to keep or to discard them [40]. Scaling complex query-processing techniques to terabytes while enabling interactive response times is a major open research problem today.

Analytical pipelines can often involve multiple steps, with built-in assumptions. By studying how best to capture, store, and query provenance, it is possible to create an infrastructure to interpret analytical results and to repeat the analysis with different assumptions, parameters, or datasets. Frequently, it is data visualization that allows Big Data to unleash its true impact. Visualization can help to produce and comprehend insights from Big Data. Visual.ly, Tableau, Vizify, D3.js, R are simple and powerful tools for quickly discovering new things in increasingly large datasets.

Big Data Aware Applications

Today, organizations and researchers see tremendous potential value and insight to be gained by warehousing the emerging wealth of digital information [41]: (i) increase the effectiveness of their marketing and customer service efforts; (ii) sentiment analysis; (iii) track the progress of epidemics; (iv) studying tweets and social networks to understand how information of various kinds spreads and/or how it can be more effectively utilized for the public good. In a broad range of application areas, data are being collected at an unprecedented scale. Decisions that previously were based on guesswork, or on painstakingly constructed models of reality, can now be made based on the data itself.

The Sloan Digital Sky Survey [6] has become a central resource for astronomers worldwide. The field of astronomy was transformed. Back in the old days, taking pictures of the sky was a large part of an astronomer's job. Today these pictures are all in a database already and the astronomer's task is to find interesting objects and phenomena. In the biological sciences, there is now a well-established tradition of depositing scientific data into a public repository, and also of creating public databases for use by other scientists. In fact, there is an entire discipline of bioinformatics that is largely devoted to the analysis of such data. As technology advances, particularly with the advent of next-generation sequencing, the size and number of experimental datasets available is increasing exponentially.

In the context of education, imagine a world in which we have access to a huge database where every detailed measure of every student's academic performance is collected. These data could be used to design the most effective approaches to education, starting from reading, writing, and math, to advanced, college-level courses. We are far from having access to such data, but there are powerful trends in this direction. In particular, there is a strong trend for massive Web deployment of educational activities, and this will generate an increasingly large amount of detailed data about students' performance.

Companies are able to quantify aspects of human behavior that were not accessible before. Social networks, news stream, and smart grid, are a way of measuring "conversation," "interest," and "activity." Machine-learning algorithms and Big Data tools can identify whom to follow (e.g., in social networks) to understand how events and news stories resonate, and even to find dates [9].

CONCLUSIONS AND PERSPECTIVES

The Big Data wave has several impacts on existing approaches for managing data. First, data are deployed on distributed and parallel architectures. Second, Big Data affects the type and accuracy of the models that can be derived. Big Data implies collecting, cleaning, storing and analyzing information streams. Each processing phase calls for greedy algorithms, statistics, models that must scale and be performed efficiently. Scaling data management depends on the type of applications using data analytics results: critical tasks require on-line data processing while more analytic tasks may accept longer production time. Applying different algorithms produces results of different precision, accuracy, and so on (i.e., veracity).

These complex processes call for new efficient data management techniques that can scale and be adapted to the traditional data-processing chain: storage, memory management (caching), filtering, and cleaning. New storage technologies, for instance, do not have the same large spread in performance between the sequential and random I/O performance. This requires a rethinking of how to design storage systems and every aspect of data processing, including query-processing algorithms, query scheduling, database design, concurrency control methods, and recovery methods [31]. It is also important to keep track of the type of processes applied to data and the conditions in which they were performed, since the processes must be reproduced, for instance, for scientific applications. These techniques must be guided by hardware characteristics, for example, memory, storage, and computing resources and the way they are consumed. Particularly, in cloud architectures that are guided by "pay-as-you-go" business models.

Future BDMS should take into account the analytic requirements of the applications, the characteristics of data (production rate, formats, how critical they are, size, validity interval), the resources required, and the economic cost for providing useful analytic models that can better support decision-making, recommendation, knowledge discovery, and data science tasks.

REFERENCES

1. D. Laney, 3D Data Management: Controlling Data Volume, *Velocity & Variety*, Technical Report, META-Group, 2001.
2. B. Grinter, A big data confession, *Interactions*, vol. 20, no. 4, Jul. 2013, pp. 10–11.
3. A. Halevy, P. Norvig, and F. Pereira, The unreasonable effectiveness of data, *IEEE Intell. Syst.*, vol. 24, no. 2, Mar. 2009.
4. S. Chaudhuri, What next?: A half-dozen data management research goals for big data and the cloud, in *Proceedings of the 31st PODS Symposium on Principles of Database Systems (PODS'12)*, Scottsdale, Arizona, USA, 2012.
5. S. Mohammad, S. Breß, and E. Schallehn, Cloud data management: A short overview and comparison of current approaches, in *24th GI-Workshop on Foundations of Databases*, 2012.
6. A. S. Szalay, J. Gray, A. R. Thakar, P. Z. Kunszt, T. Malik, J. Raddick, C. Stoughton, and J. VandenBerg, The SDSS skyserver: Public access to the sloan digital sky server data, in *Proceedings of the International Conference on Management of Data (SIGMOD'02)*, Madison, Wisconsin, 2002.
7. A. K. Hota, and D. Madam Prabhu, No problem with Big Data. What do you mean by Big?, *Journal of Informatics*, 2012, pp. 30–32.
8. M. Atkinson, D. Dewitt, D. Maier, K. Dittrich, and S. Zdonik, The object-oriented database system manifesto, in *Object-Oriented Database System: The Story of O₂*, Morgan Kaufmann, 1992, pp. 1–17.
9. J. Langford, Parallel machine learning on big data, *XRDS Crossroads, ACM Mag. Students*, vol. 19, no. 1, Sep. 2012, pp. 60–62.
10. P. Lyman, H. R. Varian, J. Dunn, A. Strygin, and K. Swearingen, How much information?, *Counting-the-Numbers*, vol. 6, no. 2, 2000.
11. P. C. Zikopoulos, C. Eaton, D. DeRoos, T. Deutsch, and G. Lapis, *Understanding Big Data*. McGraw-Hill, USA, 2011.
12. DBTA, *Big Data Sourcebook*, Unisphere Media, 2013.
13. M. L. Kersten, S. Idreos, S. Manegold, and E. Liarou, The researcher's guide to the data deluge: Querying a scientific database in just a few seconds, *Proceedings of the VLDB Endowment*, vol. 4, no. 12, 2011, pp. 1474–1477.
14. L. Hoffmann, Looking back at big data, *Communications of the ACM*, vol. 56, no. 4, Apr. 2013, pp. 21–23.
15. A. Kleiner, M. Jordan, T. Ameet, and S. Purnamrita, The big data bootstrap, in *Proceedings of the 29th International Conference on Machine Learning*, Edinburgh, Scotland, 2012.
16. H. Andrade, B. Gedik, and D. Turaga, *Fundamentals of Stream Processing*. Cambridge University Press, New York, 2014.
17. Oracle Corporation, Oracle NoSQL Database Compared to MongoDB, White-Paper, 2011.
18. P. Zikopoulos, D. DeRoos, K. Parasuraman, T. Deutsch, J. Giles, and D. Corrigan, *Harness the Power of Big Data*. McGraw-Hill, New York, 2013.
19. R. Cattell, Scalable SQL and NoSQL data stores, *SIGMOD Record*, vol. 39, no. 4, May 2011, pp. 12–27.
20. P. J. Sadalage and M. Fowler, *NoSQL Distilled: A Brief Guide to the Emerging World of Polyglot*. Addison Wesley, Crawfordsville, Indiana, 2012.

21. J. Dean and S. Ghemawat, MapReduce: Simplified data processing on large clusters, *Communications of the ACM*, vol. 51, no. 1, Jan. 2008, pp. 107–113.

22. S. Ghemawat, H. Gobioff, and S.-T. Leung, The Google file system, in *Proceedings of the 19th ACM SOSP Symposium on Operating Systems Principles (SOSP'03)*, The Sagamore, Bolton Landing, New York, vol. 37, no. 5, 2003.

23. M. Cafarella, A. Halevy, W. Hsieh, S. Muthukrishnan, R. Bayardo, O. Benjelloun, V. Ganapathy, Y. Matias, R. Pike, and R. Srikant, Data management projects at Google, *SIGMOD Record*, vol. 37, no. 1, 2008, pp. 34–38.

24. D. Borthakur, HDFS Architecture Guide, Apache-Report, pp. 1–13, 2010.

25. J. Dittrich and J.-A. Quiané-Ruiz, Efficient big data processing in Hadoop MapReduce, *Proceedings of the VLDB Endowment*, vol. 5, no. 12, Aug. 2012, pp. 2014–2015.

26. F. Li, B. C. Ooi, M. T. Özsu, and S. Wu, Distributed data management using MapReduce, *ACM Computing Surveys*, vol. 46, no. 3, pp. 31–42, Feb. 2014.

27. A. Okcan and M. Riedewald, Processing theta-joins using MapReduce, in *Proceedings of the 2011 ACM SIGMOD International Conference on Management of Data (SIGMOD '11)*, Athens, Greece, 2011.

28. J. D. Ullman, Designing good MapReduce algorithms, *XRDS Crossroads, ACM Magazine Students*, vol. 19, no. 1, Sep. 2012, pp. 30–34.

29. A. Thusoo, J. Sen Sarma, N. Jain, Z. Shao, P. Chakka, N. Zhang, S. Antony, H. Liu, and R. Murthy, Hive—A petabyte scale data warehouse using Hadoop, in *Proceedings of the 26th ICDE Int. Conference on Data Engineering (ICDE'10)*, Long Beach, California, USA, 2010.

30. C. Olston, B. Reed, U. Srivastava, R. Kumar, and A. Tomkins, Pig latin: A not-so-foreign language for data processing, in *Proceedings of the International Conference on Management of data (SIGMOD'08)*, Vancouver, Canada, 2008.

31. V. R. Borkar, M. J. Carey, and C. Li, Big data platforms: What's next? *XRDS Crossroads, ACM Magazine Students*, vol. 19, no. 1, Sep. 2012, pp. 44–49.

32. M. Stonebraker, D. Abadi, and D. DeWitt, MapReduce and parallel DBMSs: Friends or foes? *Communications of the ACM*, Vol. 53, no. 1, 2010, pp. 64–71.

33. 451-Research, Mysql vs. nosql and newsql: 2011–2015, Report, 2012.

34. C. Mohan, History repeats itself: Sensible and NonsenSQL aspects of the NoSQL hoopla, in *Proceedings of the 16th EDBT International Conference on Extending Database Technology (EDBT'13)*, Genoa, Italy, 2013.

35. V. Borkar, M. J. Carey, and C. Li, Inside 'Big Data Management': Ogres, onions, or parfaits? in *Proceedings of the 15th Int. Conf. on Extending Database Technology (EDBT'12)*, Berlin, Germany, pp. 3–14, 2012.

36. K. Ren, Y. Kwon, M. Balazinska, and B. Howe, Hadoop's adolescence: An analysis of Hadoop usage in scientific workloads, *Proceedings of the VLDB Endowment*, vol. 6, no. 10, Aug. 2013, pp. 853–864.

37. Chris Forsyth, For big data analytics there's no such thing as too big, *Forsyth-Communications*, 2012.

38. Chris Sherman, What's the big deal about big data? *Online Search.*, vol. 38, no. 2, 2013.

39. P. Agrawal, O. Benjelloun, A. Das Sarma, C. Hayworth, S. Nabar, T. Sugihara, and J. Widom, Trio: A system for data, uncertainty, and lineage, in *Proceedings of the 32nd International Conference on Very Large Databases (VLDB'06)*, Seoul, Korea, 2006.

40. S. Idreos, I. Alagiannis, R. Johnson, and A. Ailamaki, Here are my data files. Here are my queries. Where are my results?, in *Proceedings of the 5th CIDR Biennial Conference on Innovative Data Systems Research (CIDR'11)*, Asilomar, California, pp. 10–21, 2011.

41. K. Michael and K. Miller, Big data: New opportunities and new challenges, *Computer (Long. Beach. Calif)*., vol. 46, no. 6, 2013, pp. 22–24.

42. NoSQL Database Technology, Report, 2014.

CHAPTER 4

Big Data Distributed Systems Management

Rashid A. Saeed and Elmustafa Sayed Ali

CONTENTS

B IG DATA DEALS WITH large scales of data characterized by three concepts: volume, variety, and velocity known as the 3Vs of Big Data. Volume is a term related to Big Data, and as known data can be organized in sizes by gigabytes or terabytes of data storage but Big Data means there are a lot of data amounting to more than terabytes such as petabytes or exabytes and it is one of the challenges of Big Data that it requires a scalable storage. Really, data volume will continue to grow every day, regardless of the organized sizes because of the natural tendency of companies to store all types of data such as financial data, medical data, environmental data, and so on. Many of these companies' datasets are within the terabytes range today, but soon they could reach petabytes or even

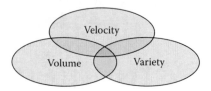

FIGURE 4.1   The 3 Vs of Big Data.

exabyte and more. Variety of Big Data is an aggregation of many types of data and maybe structured or unstructured including social media, multimedia, web server logs, and many other types of information forms. With the explosion of sensors, smart devices as well as social networking, data in an enterprise has become complex because it includes not only structured traditional relational data, but also semistructured and unstructured data and velocity becomes more reality in these types of data [1].

The velocity of data in terms of the frequency of its generation and delivery is also a characteristic of Big Data (Figure 4.1). A conventional understanding of velocity typically considers how quickly the data arrives and is stored, and how quickly it can be retrieved. In Big Data, velocity should also be applied to data in motion, which represents the speed at which the data is flowing. The various information streams and the increase in sensor network deployment have led to a constant flow of data at a pace that has made it impossible for traditional systems to handle.

Today data has deeply affected our lives than ever before. We can gather more information from the daily life of every human being and use data in many applications, such as to solve problems, improve well-being, and to generate economic prosperity. The collection, analysis, and storage of data has become increasingly more and also unbounded, and the growing number of sensor technologies embedded in devices of all kinds which deal with most Big Data drivers that use data such as science data, Internet data, finance data, mobile device data, sensor data, RFID data, GPS data, and streaming data require more processing power, and require high costs of computation and storage. Coupled with recent advances in machine learning and reasoning, as well as rapid rises in computing power and storage, we are transforming our ability to make sense of these increasingly large, heterogeneous, noisy, and incomplete datasets collected from a variety of sources [2].

BIG DATA CHALLENGES

Since Big Data deals with large volumes of data measured and collected from multiple resources as shown in Figure 4.2 in terabytes, petabytes, exabytes, zetabytes, and beyond, some of the challenges Big Data faces are such as storage and transport issues, management issues and processing issues.

The storage and transport challenge is due largely to social media. Moreover, data is being created by everyone and everything (devices) and also as heretofore, by professionals such as scientist, journalists, writers, and so on, and as known the current storage media technology limits are about 4 terabytes per disk. So, 1 exabyte would require 25,000 disks. Even if an exabyte of data could be processed on a single computer system, it would be unable to directly attach the requisite number of disks. Moreover, transferring an exabyte

FIGURE 4.2   Big Data resources.

may take several hours, if we assume that a sustained transfer could be maintained. So a design of hierarchical storage architecture is needed.

The most difficult problem in management issue is to address the Big Data. Current technologies of data management systems are not able to satisfy the needs of Big Data, and the increasing speed of storage capacity is much less than that of data; thus new technologies are required for information management, processing, and to rebuild a new framework for the Big Data. Other consideration is that previous computer algorithms are not able to effectively storage data that is directly acquired from the actual world, due to the heterogeneity of the Big Data. However, they perform well in processing homogeneous data. Therefore, how to reorganize data is one big problem in Big Data management. Virtual server technology can increase the problem, raising the prospect of overcommitted resources, especially if communication is poor between the application, server, and storage administrators [3].

Processing issue is one of the most important challenges of Big Data, while processing a query in Big Data; speed is a significant demand. Processing of large volumes of data required a very long processing time maybe in years to process and analyze these data, if we assume that a processor expends 100 instructions on one block at 5 GHz, we know that the time required for end-to-end processing would be 20 ns. To process 1K petabytes would require a total end-to-end processing time of approximately 635 years. Thus, effective processing of exabytes of data will require extensive parallel processing and new analytics algorithms in order to provide timely and actionable information. Therefore, a traditional model of data processing and management does not have the ability to handle the Big Data concept processing and management since the traditional model is not able to provide a process of multiple cloud resources to interact with multiple data clouds such as enterprise, social media, public data, and so on. A traditional data processing and management shown in Figure 4.3 can only handle the current types of data, and not able to deal with Big Data management since an operational data store (ODS) database responsible for collecting data from multiple sources for operational data that are used by enterprise systems and applications, and the ODS is able to store short-term data or data currently in use by operational systems or applications, and it requires an engine mechanism to operate,

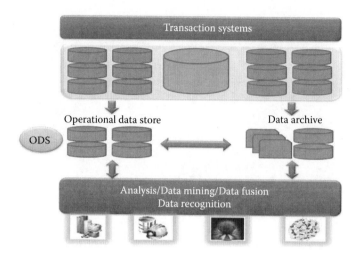

FIGURE 4.3   Traditional data management.

and allow to process a huge amount of data to deal with the concept of Big Data processing and management.

Computation and analysis of Big Data may take time because mostly it cannot traverse all the related data in the whole database in a short time. In this case, index will be an optimal choice. At present, indices in Big Data are only aiming at a simple type of data, while Big Data is becoming more complicated. The combination of appropriate index for Big Data and up to date preprocessing technology will be a desirable solution when we encountered this kind of problems. Application parallelization is natural computational paradigms for approaching Big Data problems. However, getting additional computational resources is not as simple as just upgrading to a bigger and more powerful machine on the fly. The traditional serial algorithm is inefficient for the Big Data. If there is enough data parallelism in the application, users can take advantage of the cloud's reduced cost model to use hundreds of computers for a short-term costs [4].

BIG DATA MANAGEMENT SYSTEMS

Many researchers have suggested that commercial database management systems (DBMSs) are not suitable for processing extremely large-scale data. The classic architecture database server will be in potential bottleneck when faced with peak workloads. To adapt various large data processing models, Kossmann et al. [5] presented four different architectures based on classic multitier database application architecture which includes partitioning, replication, distributed control, and caching architecture. It is clear that the alternative providers have different business models and target different kinds of applications; Google seems to be more interested in small applications with light workloads whereas Azure, a Microsoft cloud platform, is currently the most affordable service for medium to large services. Most of recent cloud service providers are utilizing hybrid architecture that is capable of satisfying their actual service requirements. In this section, we mainly discuss Big Data architecture from three key aspects: distributed file system, nonstructural, and semistructured data storage.

Distributed File System

Google file system (GFS) is a fraction of based distributed file system that supports fault tolerance by data partitioning and replication. As an underlying storage layer of Google's cloud computing platform, it is used to read input and store output of MapReduce. Similarly, Hadoop also has a distributed file system as its data storage layer called Hadoop Distributed File System (HDFS), which is an open source counterpart of GFS. GFS and HDFS are user level file systems that do not implement an IEEE programming interface (POSIX) semantics and heavily optimized for the case of large files measured in gigabytes. Amazon Simple Storage Service (S3) is an online public storage web service offered by Amazon heavily optimized for the case of large files also measured in gigabytes [6]. Amazon Simple Storage Service (S3) is an online public storage web service offered by Amazon Web Services. This file system is targeted at clusters hosted on the Amazon Elastic Compute Cloud server on demand infrastructure. S3 aims to provide scalability, high availability, and low latency at commodity costs. ES2 is a cloud data storage system [5], which is designed to support both functionalities within the same storage. The system provides efficient data loading from different sources, flexible data partitioning scheme, index and parallel sequential scan. In addition, there are general file systems that have not to be addressed such as the Moose File System (MFS) and Kosmos Distributed File system (KFS) [7].

Nonstructural and Semistructured Data Storage

With the success of Web 2.0, more and more IT companies have increasing needs to store and analyze the ever-growing data, such as search logs, crawled web content, and click streams, usually in the range of petabytes, collected from a variety of web services. However, web datasets are usually nonrelational or less structured and processing such semistructured datasets at scale poses another challenge. Moreover, simple distributed file systems mentioned above cannot satisfy service providers like Google, Yahoo!, Microsoft, and Amazon. All providers have their purpose to serve potential users and own their relevant state of the art Big Data management systems in cloud environments. Bigtable is a distributed storage system of Google for managing structured data that is designed to scale to a very large size such petabytes of data across thousands of commodity servers. Bigtable does not support a full relational data model. However, it provides clients with a simple data model that supports dynamic control over data layout and format. PNUTS [8] is a massive-scale hosted database system designed to support Yahoo!'s web applications. The main focus of the system is on data serving for web applications, rather than complex queries. Upon PNUTS, new applications can be built very easily and the overhead of creating and maintaining these applications is nothing much. The Dynamo [9] is a highly available and scalable distributed key/value-based data store built for supporting internal Amazon's applications. It provides a simple primary-key only interface to meet the requirements of these applications. However, it differs from the key value storage system. Facebook proposed the design of a new cluster-based data warehouse system, as in Lin [10], a hybrid data management system that combines the features of row-wise and column-wise database systems. They also describe a new column-wise file format for Hadoop called CFile, which provides better performance than other file formats in data analysis.

BIG DATA ANALYTICS

Analytics can be looked at as that fact which makes Big Data understandable. It encounters a number of technologies in different computer fields. Moreover, analytics usually feed Big Data revolution and at the same time create new sets of Big Data values. The big datasets could either be stored or retrieved for reuse completely or selectively regardless of the analytics concepts.

Data Mining

Data mining is an expression referring to computational process that can discover large dataset modes. It is a convergence of many academic research fields, computer science, applied mathematics, statistics, databases, machine learning, and artificial intelligence. Data mining like any new technology has an advanced research and development stage to develop new computer programs and algorithms; it also has later phases of commercialization and application of data. Data mining algorithms can be trained to find modes either by supervised learning or unsupervised learning. Supervised learning is used because the algorithm is seeded with manually curated examples of the pattern to be recognized. In unsupervised learning, the algorithm tries to find related parts of data without prior seeding. A recent success of unsupervised learning algorithms was a program that can search millions of images on the web [11].

The desired output of data mining can take several forms, each with its own specialized algorithms such as classification algorithms, which attempt to assign objects or events to known categories; regression algorithms, also called numerical prediction algorithms, try to predict numerical quantities; clustering algorithms make a group of objects or events into categories; association techniques try to find relationships between items in their dataset; and detection algorithms look for untypical examples within a dataset [12].

Data mining sometimes confused with machine learning makes use of machine learning, as well as other disciplines; while machine learning has applications in fields other than data mining, for example, robotics. There are limitations, both practical and theoretical, to what data mining can fulfill, as well as limits to how delicate it can be. It may cover patterns and relationships, but usually it cannot tell the user the value or significance of these patterns. For example, supervised learning based on the characteristics of known criminal persons might find similar persons, but they might or might not be criminals; and it would miss different classes of criminals who do not fit the profile [13].

Image and Speech Data Recognition

Image and speech recognition technologies have both the ability to extract information, and in some limited cases approaching human understanding, from images, videos, and recorded or broadcast speech. Extraction of the urban scene can be accomplished using a variety of data sources from photographs and videos to ground-based on remote sensing technique using lasers (LiDAR). In the government sector and city models, these approaches become more accurate for urban planning and visualization. They are equally important for a broad range of academic disciplines including history, archeology, geography, and computer graphics research. Digital city models are also central to popular consumer mapping and visualization applications such as Google Earth and Bing Maps, as well as GPS-enabled navigation systems. Scene extraction is an example of the accidental capture of personal information and can be used for data fusion that reveals personal information.

Modern systems nowadays are able to track any objects across an area covered by cameras and sensors detecting unusual activities in a large dedicated area by combining information from different sources, as well as many objects as in video surveillance in crowded environments in public areas, known as scene extraction techniques like the Google Street View technology which used to capture photos for use in Street view and may contain personal and sensitive information about any people who are unaware they are being observed and photographed. Social media data can be used as an input source for scene extraction techniques. When these data are posted, however, users are unlikely to know that their data would be used in these aggregated ways and that their social media information, although public, might appear synthesized in new forms [14]. Automated speech recognition has existed since 1950s approximately, but recent developments over the last 10 years have allowed for novel new capabilities like a spoken text such as news broadcasters reading part of a document can today be recognized with an accuracy of higher than 95% using state-of-the-art techniques. Spontaneous speech is much harder to recognize accurately. In recent years there has been a dramatic increase in the corpuses of spontaneous speech data available to researchers, which has allowed for improved accuracy [15]. Over the next few years speech recognition interfaces will be in many more places, for example, multiple companies are exploring speech recognition to control televisions, cars, find a show on TV, or to choose any object in Glass Corning's vision technology. Google has already implemented some of this basic functionality in its Google Glass product, and Microsoft's Xbox One system already integrates machine vision and multimicrophone audio input for controlling system functions [16].

Social Network Data Analysis

Social network analysis refers to information extraction from variable interconnecting units under the assumption that their relationships are important and that the units do not behave autonomously. Social networks often emerge in an online context and the most famous online social networks are Facebook, Twitter, and LinkedIn, which provide new access to social interaction by allowing users to connect directly with each other over the Internet to communicate and share their information. There are other types of social networks on platforms and mobiles such as whats App, Tango, and other chatting programs. Offline human social networks may also leave analyzable digital traces, such as in phone call metadata records that record which phones have exchanged calls or texts, and for how long. Analysis of social networks is increasingly enabled by the rising collection of digital data that links people together, especially when it is correlated to other data or metadata individually [17]. This type of analysis requires available and developed tools [18] motivated in part by the growing amount of social network content accessible through open application programming interfaces to online social media platforms, which have become an active area for researches [19].

Social network analysis complements analysis of conventional databases, and some of the techniques use clustering in association networks and the analysis can be more powerful because of the easy association of diverse kinds of information for making considerable data fusion possible. It lends itself to visualization of results, which aids in interpreting the results of the analysis and can be used to learn about people through their association with others who have some similarities to themselves [20]. A recent study by researchers at Facebook analyzed the relationship between geographic location of individual users and that of their friends. From this analysis, they were able to create an algorithm to predict the location of an individual user based on the locations of a small number of friends in their network, with higher accuracy than simply looking at the user's IP address [21].

Data Fusion and Integration

Data fusion is the process of merging of multiple heterogeneous datasets into one homogeneous representation to be better processed for data mining and management, and it is used in a number of technical domains such as sensor networks, video and image processing, robotics, intelligent systems, and elsewhere. Data integration is differentiated from data fusion in that integration, more broadly datasets, combines and retains the larger set of information while in data fusion, there is usually a reduction or replacement technique and it is facilitated by data interoperability, the ability for two systems to communicate and exchange data.

Data fusion and data integration is together a set of techniques for business intelligence that is used to integrate online storage for catalog of sales databases to create more completed pictures for the customers. Taking the example of this Williams Sonoma [22], an American consumer retail company has integrated customer databases with information on 60 million households. Variables including household income, housing values, and number of children needs are tracked. It is claimed that targeted emails based on this information yield 10–18 times the response rate of emails that are not targeted. This is a simple illustration of how more information can lead to better inferences. Such techniques that can help preserve privacy are emerging [23]. There is a great amount of interest today in multi-sensor data fusion. The biggest technical challenges being tackled today, generally through development of new and better algorithms, related to data precision and resolution: Outliers and spurious data, conflicting data, modality both heterogeneous, homogeneous data and dimensionality, data correlation, data alignment, association within data, centralized versus decentralized processing, operational timing, and the ability to handle dynamic versus static phenomena [24]. Privacy concerns may arise from sensor fidelity and precision as well as correlation of data from multiple sensors. A single sensor's output might not be sensitive, but the combination from two or more may raise privacy concerns [25].

MANAGEMENT OF BIG DATA DISTRIBUTED SYSTEMS

Over the last years many companies designed distributed data systems to overcome the challenges of large-scale data such as in Google Company as an example. Google designed, implemented, and deployed a distributed storage system for managing structured data called Bigtable. Bigtable is designed to reliably scale to petabytes of data and thousands of machines and it has achieved several goals namely wide applicability, scalability, high performance, and high availability [34,35]. Moreover, it is used by more than 60 Google

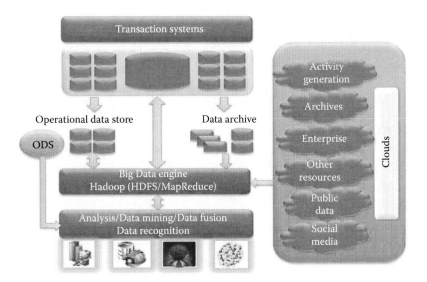

FIGURE 4.4   Next-generation Big Data management.

products and projects, including Google Analytics, Google Finance, Personalized Search, and Google Earth. The following section discusses some of the Big Data technologies that used a concept of distributed data systems management deal with the whole clouds available that required new technologies for Big Data processing and management such as Hadoop technology as shown in Figure 4.4.

Hadoop Technologies

Hadoop is a framework that provides open source libraries for distributed computing using MapReduce software and its own distributed file system, which is known as the HDFS. It is designed to scale out from a few computing nodes to thousands of machines, each offering local computation and storage. One of Hadoop's main value propositions is that it is designed to run on commodity hardware such as commodity servers or personal computers, and has high tolerance for hardware failure. In Hadoop, hardware failure is treated as a rule rather than an exception [32,36–38].

Hadoop Distributed File System (HDFS)

HDFS is a fault-tolerant storage system that can store huge amounts of information, scale up incrementally, and survive storage failure without losing data. Hadoop clusters are built with inexpensive computers. If one computer (sometimes called node) fails, the cluster can continue to operate without losing data or interrupting work by simply redistributing the work to the remaining machines in the cluster. HDFS manages storage on the cluster by breaking files into small blocks and storing duplicated copies of them across the pool of nodes. Compared with other redundancy techniques, including the strategies employed by Redundant Array of Independent Disks (RAID) machines, HDFS offers two key advantages. First, HDFS requires no special hardware as it can be built from a common hardware. Second, it enables an efficient technique of data processing in the form of MapReduce [33].

Hadoop MapReduce

Most enterprise database management systems are designed to make simple queries run quickly. Typically, the data is indexed so that only small portions of the data need to be examined in order to answer a query. This solution, however, does not work for data that cannot be indexed, namely in semistructured form (text files) or unstructured form (media files). To answer a query in this case, all the data has to be examined. Hadoop uses the MapReduce technique to carry out this exhaustive analysis quickly.

MapReduce is a data processing algorithm that uses a parallel programming implementation. That means MapReduce is a programming paradigm that involves distributing a task across multiple nodes running a "map" function. The map function takes the problem, splits it into subparts, and sends them to different machines so that all the subparts can run concurrently. The results from the parallel map functions are collected and distributed to a set of servers running "reduce" functions, which then takes the results from the subparts and recombines them to get a single answer [26]. Semistructured and unstructured datasets are the two fastest growing data types in the digital universe. Analysis of these two data types will not be possible with traditional database management systems. Hadoop HDFS and MapReduce enable the analysis of these two data types, giving organizations the opportunity to extract insights from bigger datasets within a reasonable amount of processing time. Hadoop Map Reducing parallel processing capability has increased the speed of extraction and transformation of data and also can be used as a data integration tool by reducing large amounts of data to its representative form which can then be stored in the data warehouse [39,40]. At the current stage of development, Hadoop is not meant to be a replacement for scaling up storage but it is designed more for batch processing rather than for interactive applications. It is also not optimized to work on small file sizes as the performance gains may not be considerable when compared with huge data processing [26].

NoSQL Database Management System (NoSQL DBMS)

NoSQL database management systems (DBMSs) are available as open source software and designed for use in high data volume applications in clustered environments. They often do not have fixed schema databases and are nonrelational, unlike the traditional SQL database management system also known as RDMS in many data warehouses today. As they do not adhere to a fixed schema database, NoSQL DBMS permit more flexible usage, allowing high-speed access to semistructured and unstructured data. However, SQL interfaces are also increasingly being used alongside the MapReduce programming paradigm. There are several types of NoSQL DBMS as the following:

1. Key value stores and key value pair (KVP) tables are used to provide persistence management for many of the other NoSQL technologies. The concept of two keys is that the table has two columns one is the key and the other is the value. The value could be a single value or a data block containing many values, the format of which is determined by program code. KVP tables may use indexing, hash tables, or sparse arrays

to provide rapid retrieval and insertion capability, depending on the need for fast lookup, fast insertion, or efficient storage. KVP tables are best applied to simple data structures and on the Hadoop MapReduce environment [26].

2. Document-oriented database is a database designed for storing, retrieving, and managing document-oriented or semistructured data such as Apache's Couch DB and Mongo DB. The central concept of a document-oriented database is the notion of a document where the contents within the document are encapsulated or encoded in some standard format such as JavaScript Object Notation (JSON), Binary JavaScript Object Notation (BSON), or XML.

3. Bigtable database is a distributed storage system based on the proprietary GFS for managing structured data that is designed to scale to very large size petabytes of data across thousands of commodity servers, and it is also known as Distributed Peer Data Store. This database is almost similar to relational database except that the data volume to be handled is very high and the schema does not dictate the same set of columns for all rows. Each cell has a time stamp and there can be multiple versions of a cell with different time stamps. To manage the huge tables, Bigtable splits tables at row boundaries and saves them as tablets and each tablet is around 200 MB; also each server saves about 100 tablets. This setup allows tablets from a single table to be spread among many machines. It also allows for load balancing and fault tolerance. An example of a Bigtable database is Cassandra DB [26].

4. Graph database is a graph database that contains nodes, edges, and properties to represent and store data. In a graph database, every entity contains a direct pointer to its adjacent element and no index lookups are required. A graph database is useful when large-scale multilevel relationship traversals are common and is best suited for processing complex many to many connections such as social networks. A graph may be captured by a table store that supports recursive joins such as Bigtable and Cassandra [27].

With the Big Data movement comes a series of use cases that conventional schematic DBMS is not meant to address. These cases typically include providing data processing and access environments for large-scale, compute-intensive analytics. The fact that NoSQL has been developed to handle data management problems well outside the realm of traditional databases spells new opportunities for the technology. NoSQL databases are designed to be able to scale out on commodity hardware (adopting the principle of the Hadoop framework) to manage the exploding data and transaction volumes. The result is that the cost per gigabyte or transactions per second for NoSQL can be many times less than the cost for RDBMS, allowing more data storage and processing at a lower price point. However, it is important to recognize that the NoSQL database can realistically focus on two of the three properties of consistency, availability, and partition tolerance (CAP Theorem). NoSQL databases need partition tolerance in order to scale properly, so it is very likely that they will have to sacrifice either availability or consistency [41].

Software as a Service (SaaS)–Based Business Analytics

Software as a Service (SaaS) is software owned, delivered, and managed remotely by one or more providers. A single set of common code is provided in an application that can be used by many customers at any one time. SaaS-based business analytics enable customers to quickly deploy one or more of the prime components of business analytics without significant IT involvement or the need to deploy and maintain an on forward solution [42,43]. The prime components and analytic applications support performance management with prepackaged functionality for specific solutions and the business analytics platforms provide the environment for development and integration, information delivery, and analysis; then the information management infrastructures provide the data architecture and data integration infrastructure [28]. Leveraging the benefits of cloud computing, SaaS-based business analytics offers a quick, low-cost, and easy-to-deploy business analytics solution. This is especially the case for enterprises that do not have the expertise to set up an in-house analytics platform nor the intention to invest in internal business analytics resources. SaaS-based business analytics may be useful for medium and small enterprises that have yet to invest in any form of on-premise business analytics solutions [29].

Master Data Management

Master data is the official, consistent set of identifiers and extended attributes, which describes the core entities of the enterprise, such as customers, prospects, locations, hierarchies, assets, and policies. Master data management (MDM) is a technology-enabled discipline in which businesses and IT departments work together to ensure the uniformity, accuracy, stewardship, and accountability of the enterprise's official, shared master data assets. MDM helps to reconcile different data silos to create a master data "single version of the truth," either through physically consolidating data into a single data store or federation of the best source of record data from multiple sources. It is an example of an information-sharing environment that represents a key part of an enterprise information management initiative [44]. MDM helps organizations to break down operational barriers. It can help to ensure that all master data is "clean" in a business analytical framework, which can then improve the ability of users to make decisions more effectively, leading to increased performance and agility, process integrity, and cost optimization [30].

Master data management (MDM) domains have a direct impact on the business, for example, MDM for customer data creates a centralized system of records for customer data such that all applications and business processes go to the system to determine whether the right data was used and whether it is accurate [45]. Having a single view of customer data can be useful for all processes such as marketing, and sales and service, leading to a more customer-centric customer experience and improved retention levels. MDM also ensures the entire enterprise uses one unified model for all its primary master data objects. Enterprise-wide MDM significantly reduces the costs associated with organizational integration that are needed for any transformative strategy by removing organizational barriers that inhibit information reuse [31,46].

CONCLUSION

Big Data becomes a problem since a large amount of information and any type of data can come out from any digital resources continuing and expanding as users create new ways to process and handle data. Moreover, the evolution of revolution of technologies, with data replacement grantee, nowadays and in a few more years data will be available which has been collated before. It has become clear that the increase in data does not just mean more data available, but that more sets of different data will complicate the problem of Big Data more than it is today [46].

Today Facebook and Twitter, for example, and also other online social applications in platforms put in collectively around more than several tens of gigabytes of data per day, which is increasing every year and within a few years we will be facing the difficult challenges of Big Data. A technology that addresses this problem will ensure that the data will not be stored on one or few locations, not be formatted in one or few types of forms, and not be analyzed or processed by one or few analyzers or processors but data must be stored in many distributed systems storages, in many and different types of formations, and processed by many processing technologies. So as of now distributed data across multiple and parallel processing units improved the processing speeds also by using multiple layer architectures to acquire, load, analyze, and transform data ensuring that each layer can use the best of burst for its specific tasks and these layers supported by formatted application servers interface to friendly interface for users. Since the problem of Big Data storing and processing solved by distributed data systems, anew problems arise and it is how to make a searching relationship between different types of Big Data as in Google in web searching or as in Amazon. More research is required to overcome this problem or even to reduce the effect of Big Data problems.

REFERENCES

1. S. Crosier and J. Snow, *The London Cholera Epidemic of 1854*, Center for Spatially Integrated Social Science, University of California, Santa Barbara, 2007, http://www.csiss.org/classics/content/8. [Accessed 9th July 2014].
2. C. Ji, Y. Li, W. Qiu, U. Awada, and K. Li, Big data processing in cloud computing environments, *2012 International Symposium on Pervasive Systems, Algorithms and Networks*, IEEE, San Marcos, TX, 2012.
3. S. Kaisler, F. Armour, J. Alberto Espinosa, and W. Money, Big data: Issues and challenges moving forward, *46th Hawaii International Conference on System Sciences*, IEEE, Wailea, Maui, HI, 2013.
4. X. Zhou, J. Lu, C. Li, and X. Du, Big data challenge in the management perspective, *Communications of the CCF*, vol. 8, pp. 16–20, 2012.
5. D. Kossmann, T. Kraska, and S. Loesing, An evaluation of alternative architectures for transaction processing in the cloud, in *Proceedings of the 2010 International Conference on Management of Data*. ACM, 2010, pp. 579–590.
6. J. Dean and S. Ghemawat, Mapreduce: Simplified data processing on large clusters, *Communications of the ACM*, vol. 51, no. 1, pp. 107–113, 2008.
7. http://kosmosfs.sourceforge.net/ [Accessed 9th July 2014].
8. B. Cooper, R. Ramakrishnan, U. Srivastava, A. Silberstein, P. Bohannon, H. Jacobsen, N. Puz, D. Weaver, and R. Yerneni, Pnuts: Yahoo!'s hosted data serving platform, *Proceedings of the VLDB Endowment*, vol. 1, no. 2, pp. 1277–1288, 2008.

9. G. DeCandia, D. Hastorun, M. Jampani, G. Kakulapati, A. Lakshman, A. Pilchin, S. Sivasubramanian, P. Vosshall, and W. Vogels, Dynamo: amazon's highly available key value store, *ACM SIGOPS Operating Systems Review*, vol. 41, no. 6, pp. 205–220, ACM, 2007.

10. Y. Lin, D. Agrawal, C. Chen, B. Ooi, and S. Wu, Llama: Leveraging columnar storage for scalable join processing in the map reduce framework, in *Proceedings of the 2011 International Conference on Management of Data*. ACM, National University of Singapore, 2011, pp. 961–972.

11. M. Bramer, *Principles of Data Mining*, Springer-Verlag, 2013.

12. J. Han and M. Kamber, *Data Mining: Concepts and Techniques*, University of Illinois at Urbana-Champaign, Morgan Kaufmann Publishers by Elsevier Inc, 2006.

13. T.M. Mitchell, *The Discipline of Machine Learning*, Technical Report CMUML 06 108, Carnegie Mellon University, July 2006.

14. T.J. Billitteri, K. Koch, T.J. Colin, K. Jost, O.B. Davis, and M. Harris, Social media explosion: Do social networking sites threaten privacy rights? *CQ Researcher*, vol. 23, pp. 84–104, 2013.

15. B.H. Juang and L.R. Rabiner, *Automated Speech Recognition—A Brief History of the Technology Development*, October 8, 2004. http://www.ece.ucsb.edu/Faculty/Rabiner/ece259/Reprints/354_LALIASRHistoryfinal108.pdf [Accessed 9th July 2014].

16. *Where Speech Recognition Is Going*, Technology Review, May 29, 2012. http://www.kurzweilai.net/wherespeechrecognition [Accessed 9th July 2014].

17. M. Plenda, *Speech Recognition and 'Big Data' Research at Summer Speech Academy*, Friday, September 13, 2013. http://manchester.unh.edu/blog/campus-news/speech-recognition-and-big-data-research-summer-speech-academy [Accessed 9th July 2014].

18. R. Mokhtar and R.A. Saeed, Conservation of mobile data and usability constraints, in Z. Junaid and M. Athar (Eds.), *Cyber Security Standards, Practices and Industrial Applications: Systems and Methodologies*, Ch 03, pp. 40–55, IGI Global, USA, 2011, ISBN13: 978-1-60960-851-4.

19. A. Mislove, A. Post, B. Viswanath, and K.P. Gummadi, An analysis of social based network Sybil defenses, *ACM SIGCOMM Computer Communication Review, (SIGCOMM'10)*, New Delhi, India, August 30–September 3, p. 12, 2010.

20. L. Geetoor and E. Zheleva, Preserving the privacy of sensitive relationships in graph data, *Privacy, Security, and Trust in KDD*, vol. 4890, pp. 153–171, 2008.

21. L. Backstrom et al., Find me if you can: Improving geographical prediction with social and spatial proximity, *Proceedings of the 19th International Conference on World Wide Web*, North Carolina, USA, 2010.

22. http://www.mckinsey.com/insights/marketing_sales/were_all_marketers_now [Accessed 9th July 2014].

23. J. Manyika, M. Chui, B. Brown, J. Bughin, R. Dobbs, C. Roxburgh, and A.H. Byes. *Big Data: The Next Frontier for Innovation, Competition, and Productivity*, McKinsey Global Institute, 2011.

24. G. Navarro Arriba and V. Torra, Information fusion in data privacy: A survey, *Information Fusion*, vol. 13, no. 4, pp. 235–244, 2012.

25. B. Khaleghi et al., Multi-sensor data fusion: A review of the state of the art, *Information Fusion*, vol. 14, no. 1, pp. 28–44, 2013.

26. Google Inc. Bigtable: A Distributed Storage System for Structured Data. [Online] http://static.googleusercontent.com/external_content/untrusted_dlcp/research.google.com/en//archive/bigtable-osdi06.pdf [Accessed 10th Sept 2014].

27. Info Grid. Operations on a Graph Database. [Online] Available from: http://infogrid.org/blog/2010/03/operations-on-a-graph-database-part-4/ [Accessed 9th July 2014].

28. K. Boyer, Business Intelligence SaaS Pros and Cons, A DMG Federal eBook March 2013.

29. D. White, *Fast Affordable Agile the Case of SaaS BI*, Aberdeen Group Harte Hanks Company, Boston, MA, 2010.

30. M. Rittman, Director, Rittman Mead Consulting, Introduction to Master Data Management, https://s3.amazonaws.com/rmc_docs/Introduction%20to%20Oracle%20Master%20Data%20Management.pdf [Accessed 9th July 2014].

31. Master data management: The key to leveraging big data, Copyright IBM Corporation 2012, http://public.dhe.ibm.com/common/ssi/ecm/en/imw14652usen/IMW14652USEN.PDF [Accessed 9th July 2014].

32. D. Borthakur, The hadoop distributed file system: Architecture and design, *Hadoop Project Website*, vol. 11, 1–12, 2007.

33. C. Deng, L. Qian, and M. Xu, *Federated Cloud-Based Big Data Platform in Telecommunications*, Workshop on Cloud Services, Federation, and the 8th Open Cirrus Summit, San Jose, CA, pp. 1–5. September 21 2012.

34. A. Rabkin and R. Katz, Chukwa: A system for reliable large-scale log collection, in *USENIX LISA'10 Proceedings of the 24th International Conference on Large Installation System Administration*, California, San Jose, CA, 2010.

35. A.-S. Khan Pathan, R.A. Saeed, M.A. Feki, and N.H. Tran, Integration of IoT with future internet, *Journal of Internet Technology (JIT)*, vol. 15, no. 2, March 2014.

36. http://www-archive.xenproject.org/products/cloudxen.html [Accessed 9th July 2014].

37. http://www.osepa.eu/ [Accessed 9th May 2014].

38. http://net.pku.edu.cn/~webg/tplatform/ [Accessed 9th May 2014].

39. R.P. Limbole and G.P. Bhole, Infrastructure as a service and comparative study on open source cloud infrastructure solutions, *International Journal of Current Engineering and Technology*, vol. 4, no. 4, p. 5, Aug 2014.

40. R.A. Saeed, M. Al-Magboul, R.A. Mokhtar, *Machine-to-Machine Communication*, IGI Global, Encyclopedia of Information Science and Technology, Third Edition, DOI: 10.4018/978-1-4666-5888-2, pp. 6195–6206, July, 2014.

41. Telecom Cloud Standards Information Day, *OpenNebula Cloud Innovation and Case Studies for Telecom*, Hyatt Regency, Santa Clara, CA, USA 6–7 DSA-Research.org December, 2010. http://www.omg.org/news/meetings/tc/ca-10/special-events/pdf/5-2_Vazquez.pdf. [Accessed 9th May 2014].

42. L. Brégonzio-Rozier, F. Siekmann, and C. Giorio, First direct observation of secondary organic aerosol formation during cloud condensation-evaporation cycles in isoprene photo-oxidation reacting mixtures (CUMULUS project), *EGU General Assembly*, Vienna, Austria, 27 April–2 May, 2014.

43. D. Nurmi, R. Wolski, C. Grzegorczyk, G. Obertelli, S. Soman, L. Youseff, and D. Zagorodnov, Eucalyptus: An open-source cloud computing infrastructure, *Journal of Physics*, Conference Series, conference in University of California, Santa Barbara, vol. 180, no. 1, pp. 1–15, 2009.

44. M. Storch, R.N. Calheiros, and C.A.F. De Rose, *Virtual Machines Networking for Distributed Systems Emulation*, IX Workshop em Clouds, Grids e Aplicações http://sbrc2011.facom.ufms.br/files/workshops/wcga/ST01_3.pdf [Accessed 9th July 2014].

45. M.A. Vouk, *Creating a Cloud Computing Solution for NC State University*, https://www.ibm.com/ibm/cioleadershipexchange/us/en/pdfs/Vouk.pdf [Accessed 9th July 2014].

46. R. Jadhav, Big data: Challenges and opportunities for storage and management of data to be available and actionable for business survival and growth, *International Journal on Applied Information and Communication Technology* vol. 1, no. 3, 345–350, July 2014.

II

Networking Theory and Design for Big Data

CHAPTER 5

Moving Big Data to the Cloud

Online Cost-Minimizing Algorithms

Linquan Zhang, Chuan Wu, Zongpeng Li, Chuanxiong Guo, Minghua Chen, and Francis C. M. Lau

CONTENTS

CLOUD COMPUTING PROVIDES AGILE and scalable resource access in a utility-like fashion, especially for the processing of Big Data. An important open problem here is to efficiently move data from different geographical locations to a cloud for processing. This chapter examines two representative scenarios in this picture, and introduces online algorithms to achieve timely, cost-minimizing upload of Big Data into the cloud. First, we focus on uploading massive, dynamically generated, geo-dispersed data into a cloud encompassing disparate data centers, for processing using a centralized MapReduce-like framework. A cost-minimizing data migration problem is formulated, and two online algorithms are given: an online lazy migration (OLM) algorithm and a randomized fixed horizon control (RFHC) algorithm, for optimizing at any given time the choice of the data center for data aggregation and processing, as well as the routes for transmitting data there. Second, we discuss how to minimize the bandwidth cost for uploading deferral Big Data to a cloud, for processing by a (possibly distributed) MapReduce framework, assuming that the Internet Service Provider (ISP) adopts the MAX contract pricing scheme. We first analyze the single ISP case and then generalize to the MapReduce framework over a cloud platform. In the former, we review a Heuristic Smoothing algorithm whose worst-case competitive ratio is proved to fall between $2 - 1/(D + 1)$ and $2(1 - 1/e)$, where D is the maximum tolerable delay. In the latter, we employ the Heuristic Smoothing algorithm as a building block, and demonstrate an efficient distributed randomized online algorithm, achieving a constant expected competitive ratio.

BACKGROUND
Big Data and Cloud Computing

The cloud computing paradigm enables rapid on-demand provisioning of server resources (CPU, storage, bandwidth) to users, with minimal management efforts, as witnessed in Amazon EC2 and S3, Microsoft Azure, Google App Engine, Rackspace. The elastic and on-demand nature of resource provisioning makes a cloud platform attractive for the execution of various applications, especially computation-intensive ones [1,2]. More and more data-intensive Internet applications, such as Facebook and Twitter, and Big Data analytics applications, such as the Human Genome Project [3], are relying on clouds for processing and analyzing their petabyte-scale data sets, leveraging a computing framework such as MapReduce and Hadoop [4,5]. Facebook-like social media sites collect their web server logs, Internet click data and social activity reports from geographical locations over time, and parse them using MapReduce/Hadoop to discover usage patterns and hidden correlations, in order to facilitate decision making in marketing. In such data-intensive applications, a large volume of information (up to terabytes or even petabytes) is periodically transmitted between the user location and the cloud, through the public Internet. Parallel to utility bill reduction in data centers (computation cost control), bandwidth charge minimization (communication cost control) now represents a major challenge in the cloud computing paradigm [6,7], where a small fraction of improvement in efficiency translates into millions of dollars in annual savings across the world [8].

While substantial efforts have been devoted to designing better computing models for Big Data analytics, an important issue was largely left out in this respect: How does one move the massive amounts of data into a cloud, in the very first place? The current practice is to copy data into large hard drives for physically transportation to the data centers [9,10], or even to move entire machines [11]. Such physical transportation incurs undesirable delay and possible service downtime, while outputs of the data analysis are often needed to be presented to users in a timely fashion [11]. It is also less secure, given that hard drives are prone to infection of malicious programs and damages from road accidents. A safer and more flexible data migration strategy is desired, to minimize potential service downtimes.

Little existing work discussed such transfer of Big Data to the cloud. Cho et al. [12] designed Pandora, a cost-aware planning system for data transfer to the cloud provider, via both the Internet and courier services. The same authors [13] later proposed a solution to minimize the transfer latency under a budget constraint. These studies focus on static scenarios with a fixed amount of bulk data to transfer to a single cloud data center.

This chapter presents recent studies on online algorithms for moving dynamically and continuously produced data, for example, astronomical data from disparate observatories [14], usage data from different Facebook web servers, to a cloud consisting of multiple data centers. With dynamic data, efficient online algorithms are desired, for timely guiding of the transfer of data into the cloud over time.

Online Algorithm Basics

An online algorithm takes input gradually as they become available, and computes output on the fly. An offline algorithm is given complete information into the future, and generates a solution once in its entirety [15]. The competitive ratio is a widely adopted measure for the performance of an online algorithm. A deterministic minimizing online algorithm A is c-competitive if $\forall I, A(I) \leq cOPT(I)$, where I is a given sequence of input, $A(I)$ is the total cost to complete I by A, $OPT(I)$ denotes the cost to serve I by the optimal offline algorithm. Similarly, a randomized minimizing online algorithm A is c-competitive if $\forall I, E(A(I)) \leq cOPT(I)$.

A number of online algorithms were proposed to address different cloud computing and data center problems. For online algorithms without future information, Lin et al. [16] investigated energy-aware dynamic server provisioning, proposing a Lazy Capacity Provisioning algorithm with a three-competitive ratio. Mathew et al. [17] tackled the energy-aware load balancing problem in content delivery networks (CDNs) by an online Hibernate algorithm, which strikes a balance between energy consumption and customer service-level agreements (SLAs).

For online algorithms assuming a lookahead into the future, Lu and Chen [18] studied the dynamic provisioning problem in data centers, and designed future-aware algorithms based on the classic ski-rental online algorithm, where the competitive ratios can be significantly improved by exploiting the lookahead information up to the break-even interval. Lin et al. [19] investigated load balancing among geographically distributed data centers, applied a receding horizon control (RHC) algorithm, and showed that the competitive ratio can be reduced substantially by leveraging predicted future information, via relaxing the optimization variables.

MapReduce Framework

Typical MapReduce applications include two functions: *map* and *reduce*, both written by the users. *Map* processes input key/value pairs, and produce a set of intermediate key/value pairs. The MapReduce library combines all intermediate values associated with the same intermediate key *I* and then passes them to the *reduce* function. *Reduce* then merges these values associated with the intermediate key *I* to produce smaller sets of values. There are four stages in the MapReduce framework: *pushing, mapping, shuffling*, and *reducing*. The user transfers workloads to the mappers during the pushing stage. The mappers process them during the mapping stage, and deliver the processed data to the reducers during the shuffling stage. Finally, the reducers produce the results in the reducing stage. In a distributed system, mapping and reducing stages can happen at different locations. The system delivers all intermediate data from mappers to reducers during the shuffling stage, and the cloud providers may charge for interdata center traffic during the shuffling stage. Recent studies [20,21] suggest that the relation between intermediate data size and original data size depends closely on the specific application. For applications such as *n*-gram models, intermediate data size is much larger, and the bandwidth cost charged by the cloud provider cannot be neglected. We use β to denote the ratio of original data size to intermediate data size.

SYSTEM MODEL

A cloud user generates large amounts of data dynamically over time, and aims to transfer the data into a cloud comprising of geo-distributed data centers, for processing using a MapReduce-like framework. We show investigations of two representative scenarios in this big picture [22,23].

Timely Migration of Geo-Distributed Big Data into a Cloud

Consider a cloud consisting of K geo-distributed data centers in a set of regions [K]. A cloud user (e.g., a global astronomical telescope application) continuously produces large volumes of data at a set [Ξ] of multiple geographic locations (e.g., dispersed telescope sites). The user connects to the data centers from different data generation locations via virtual private networks (VPNs), with G VPN gateways at the user side and K VPN gateways each co-located with a data center. Let [G] denote the set of VPN gateways at the user side. An illustration of the system is in Figure 5.1. A private (the user's) network interconnects the data generation locations and the VPN gateways at the user side. Such a model reflects typical connection approaches between users and public clouds (e.g., Windows Azure Virtual Network [24]), where dedicated private network connections are established between a user's premises and the cloud, for enhanced security and reliability, and guaranteed interconnection bandwidth.

We aim to upload the geo-dispersed data sets to the best data center, for processing with a MapReduce-like framework. It is common practice to process data within one data center rather than over multiple data centers. For example, Amazon Elastic MapReduce launches all processing nodes of a MapReduce job in the same EC2 Availability Zone [25].

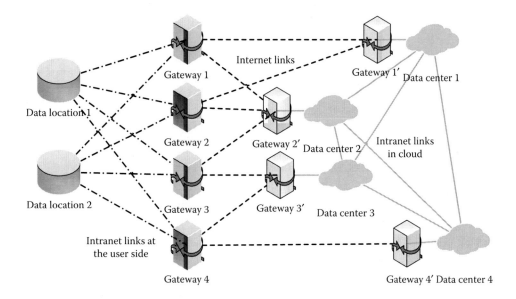

FIGURE 5.1   An illustration of the Big Data upload system: scenario 1.

Inter-datacenter connections within a cloud are dedicated high-bandwidth lines [26]. Within the user's private network, the data transmission bandwidth between a data generation location $d \in [\Xi]$ and a VPN gateway $g \in [G]$ is large as well. The bandwidth U_{gi} on a VPN link (g,i) from user side gateway g to data center i is limited, and constitutes the bottleneck in the system.

Assume the system executes in a time-slotted fashion [16,17] with slot length τ. $F_d(t)$ bytes of data are produced at location d in slot t, for upload to the cloud. l_{dg} is the latency between data location $d \in [\Xi]$ and user side gateway $g \in [G]$, p_{gi} is the delay along VPN link (g,i), and η_{ik} is the latency between data centers i and k. These delays, which can be obtained by a simple command such as *ping*, are dictated by the respective geographic distances. Given a typical cloud platform that encompasses disparate data centers of different resource charges, detailed cost composition and performance bottlenecks should be analyzed for efficiently moving data into the cloud.

Uploading Deferral Big Data to the Cloud

The next scenario we look at is to upload deferrable Big Data to a cloud by considering practical bandwidth charging models through the Internet, instead of assuming a VPN between the user and the cloud. Commercial Internet access, particularly the transfer of Big Data, is nowadays routinely priced by ISPs through a percentile charge model, a dramatic departure from the more intuitive total-volume-based charge model as in residential utility billing or the flat-rate charge model as in personal Internet and telephone billing [6,7,27,28]. Specifically, in a θ-th percentile charge scheme, the ISP divides the charge period, for example, 30 days, into small intervals of equal fixed length, for example, 5 min. Statistical logs summarize traffic volumes witnessed in different time intervals, sorted in ascending order. The traffic volume of the θ-th percentile interval is chosen as the charge volume. For example, under the 95th-percentile charge scheme, the cost is proportional to the traffic volume sent in the 8208-th (95% × 30 × 24 × 60/5 = 8208) interval in the list [7,27,28]. The MAX contract model is simply the 100-th percentile charge scheme. Such percentile charge models are perhaps less surprising when one considers the fact that infrastructure provisioning cost is more closely related to peak instead of average demand.

Toward minimizing bandwidth cost based on the percentile charge scheme, most existing studies examine strategies through careful traffic scheduling, multihoming (subscribing to multiple ISPs), and inter-ISP traffic shifting. They model the cost minimization problem with a critical, although sometimes implicit, assumption that all data generated at the user location have to be uploaded to the cloud immediately, without any delay [27,28]. Consequently, the solution space is restricted to traffic smoothing in the spatial domain only. Real-world Big Data applications reveal a different picture, in which a reasonable amount of uploading delay (often specified in SLAs) is tolerable by the cloud user, providing a golden time window for traffic smoothing in the temporal domain, which can substantially slash peak traffic volumes and hence communication cost. For instance, astronomical data from observatories are periodically generated at huge volumes but require no urgent attention. Another well-known example is human genome analyses [10], where data are also "big" but not time sensitive. We show a model and online algorithms that explore time deferral of the data upload to achieve cost efficiency.

We also assume the general case where the mappers and reducers may reside in geographically dispersed data centers. The Big Data can tolerate bounded upload delays specified in their SLA. We model a cloud user producing a large volume of data every hour, as exemplified by astronomical observatories. As shown in Figure 5.2, the data location is multihomed with multiple ISPs, for communicating with data centers. Through the

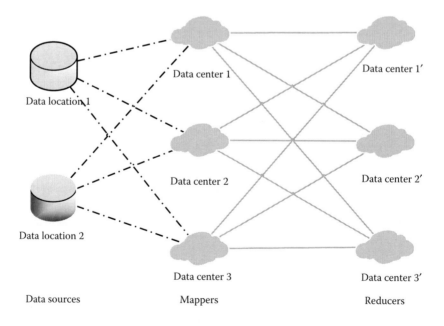

FIGURE 5.2   An illustration of the Big Data upload system: scenario 2.

infrastructure provided by ISP i, data can be uploaded to a corresponding data center DCi. Each ISP has its own traffic charge model and pricing function.

After arrival at the data centers, the uploaded data are processed using a MapReduce-like framework. Intermediate data need to be transferred among data centers in the shuffling stage. In a general model, multiple ISPs may be employed by the cloud to communicate among its distributed data centers, for example, ISP A for communicating between DC1 and DC2, and ISP B for communicating between DC1 and DC3. If two inter-DC connections are covered by the same ISP, it can be equivalently viewed as two ISPs with identical traffic charge models.

The system runs in a time-slotted fashion. Each time slot is 5 min. The charge period is a month (30 days). Assume there are M mappers and R reducers in the system. $[M]$ and $[R]$ denote the set of mappers and the set of reducers, respectively. Since each mapper is associated with a unique ISP in the first stage, we employ $m \in [M]$ to represent the ISP used to connect the user to mapper m. All mappers use the same hash function to map the intermediate keys to reducers [21]. The *upload delay* is defined as the duration between when data are generated to when they are transmitted to the mappers. We focus on uniform delays, that is, all jobs have the same maximum tolerable delay D, which is reasonable assuming data generated at the same user location are of similar nature and importance. We use W_t to represent each workload released at the user location in time slot t.

ONLINE ALGORITHMS FOR TIMELY MIGRATION OF BIG DATA INTO THE BEST CLOUD DATA CENTER

In this section, we present problem formulation as well as online algorithm design and analysis for cost-minimizing Big Data upload in the first scenario.

Problem Formulation

A cloud user needs to decide (i) via which VPN connections to upload its data to the cloud, and (ii) to which data center to aggregate data, for processing by a MapReduce-like framework, such that the monetary charges incurred, as well as the latency for the data to reach the aggregation point, are jointly minimized. The total cost C to be minimized has four components: bandwidth cost, aggregate storage and computing cost, migration cost, and routing cost.

Decision Variables
Two types of optimization variables are formulated:

1. Data routing variable $x_{d,g,i,k}(t), \forall d \in [\Xi], g \in [G], i \in [K], k \in [K]$ denotes the portion of data $F_d(t)$ produced at location d in t, to be uploaded through VPN connection (g,i) and then migrated to data center k for processing. $x_{d,g,i,k}(t) > 0$ indicates that the data routing path $d \to g \to i \to k$ is employed, and $x_{d,g,i,k}(t) = 0$ otherwise. Let $\vec{x}(t) = (x_{d,g,i,k}(t))_{\forall d \in [\Xi], g \in [G], i \in [K], k \in [K]}$, the set of feasible data routing variables are:

$$X = \left\{ \vec{x}(t) \middle| \sum_{g \in [G], i \in [k], k \in [K]} x_{d,g,i,k}(t) = 1 \text{ and } x_{d,g,i,k}(t) \in [0,1], \forall d \in [\Xi], g \in [G], i \in [K], k \in [K] \right\}$$

(5.1)

2. Binary variable $\vec{y}(t) = (y_k(t))_{\forall k \in [K]}$ indicates whether data center k is target of data aggregation in time slot t ($y_k(t) = 1$) or not ($y_k(t) = 0$). The current MapReduce framework often requires that at any given time, exactly one data center is chosen. Let $\vec{y}(t) = (y_k(t))_{\forall k \in [K]}$, the set of possible data aggregation variables are:

$$Y = \left\{ \vec{y}(t) \middle| \sum_{k \in [K]} y_k(t) = 1 \text{ and } y_k(t) \in \{0,1\}, \quad \forall k \in [K] \right\}$$

(5.2)

Costs
The costs incurred in time slot t, for uploading the data into the cloud and for processing the data at the selected data center, include the following components.

1. The overall *bandwidth cost* for uploading data via the VPN connections, where $\sum_{d \in [\Xi], k \in [K]} F_d(t) x_{d,g,i,k}(t)$ is the amount uploaded via (g,i), and c_{gi} is the charge for uploading one byte of data via (g,i), derived from bandwidth prices set by the cloud provider:

$$C_{BW}(\vec{x}(t)) = \sum_{g \in [G], i \in [K]} \left(c_{gi} \sum_{d \in [\Xi], k \in [K]} F_d(t) x_{d,g,i,k}(t) \right)$$

(5.3)

2. *Storage and computation costs* are important factors in choosing the data aggregation point. In a large-scale online application, processing and analyzing in t may involve data produced not only in t, but also from the past, in the form of raw data or intermediate processing results. For example, data analytics in social networks may rerun the data parsing flow when new data arrives, together using the new data and old data (or previous parsing results of the old data) [29]. Without loss of generality, let the amount of current and history data to process in t be $M(t) = \sum_{v=1}^{t} (\alpha_v \sum_{d \in [\Xi]} F_d(v))$, where $\sum_{d \in [\Xi]} F_d(v)$ is the total amount of data produced in time slot v from different data generation locations, and weight $\alpha_v \in [0,1]$ is smaller for older times v and $\alpha_t = 1$ for the current time t. The value of α_t is determined by specific applications and can be obtained through statistical data. Assume all the other historical data, except those in $M(t)$, are removed from the data centers where they were processed, since all needed information has been stored in the retained data. Let $\Psi_k(M(t))$ be a nondecreasing cost function for storage and computation in data center k in t (e.g.,

$\Psi_k(M(t)) = s_k M(t) + v_k M(t)$, if s_k and v_k are the per-byte per-time-slot costs for storing and processing in data center k, respectively. The value of s_k is determined by the cloud provider and the value of v_k depends on both the cloud provider and the specific application). The aggregate storage and computing cost incurred in the cloud in t is

$$C_{DC}(\vec{y}(t)) = \sum_{k \in [K]} y_k(t) \Psi_k(M(t)) \tag{5.4}$$

3. The best data center for data aggregation could differ in t than in $t-1$, due to temporal and spatial variations in data generation. Historical data needed for processing together with the new data in t, at the amount of $\sum_{v=1}^{t-1}(\alpha_v \sum_{d \in [\Xi]} F_d(v))$, should be moved from the former data center to the current. Let $\phi_{ik}(z)$ be the nondecreasing, convex migration cost to move z bytes of data from data center i to date center k, satisfying triangle inequality: $\phi_{ik}(z) + \phi_{kj}(z) \geq \phi_{ij}(z)$. The *migration cost* between time slot $t-1$ and time slot t is

$$C_{MG}^t(\vec{y}(t), \vec{y}(t-1)) = \sum_{i \in [K]} \sum_{k \in [K]} \left([y_i(t-1) - y_i(t)]^+ [y_k(t) - y_k(t-1)]^+ \phi_{ik}\left(\sum_{v=1}^{t-1} \alpha_v \sum_{d \in [\Xi]} F_d(v) \right) \right) \tag{5.5}$$

Here, $[a-b]^+ = \max\{a-b, 0\}$.

4. A *routing cost* can be used to model delays along the selected routing paths:

$$C_{RT}(\vec{x}(t)) = \sum_{d,g,i,k} L x_{d,g,i,k}(t) F_d(t)(l_{dg} + p_{gi} + \eta_{ik}) \tag{5.6}$$

where $x_{d,g,i,k}(t) F_d(t)(l_{dg} + p_{gi} + \eta_{ik})$ is the product of data volume and delay along the routing path $d \to g \to i \to k$. L is the routing cost weight converting $x_{d,g,i,k}(t) F_d(t)(l_{dg} + p_{gi} + \eta_{ik})$ into a monetary cost, reflecting how latency-sensitive the user is. L is a constant provided by the user *a priori*. The latency $l_{dg} + p_{gi} + \eta_{ik}$ is fixed in each time slot, but can change over time.

In summary, the overall cost incurred in t in the system is

$$C(\vec{x}(t), \vec{y}(t)) = C_{BW}(\vec{x}(t)) + C_{DC}(\vec{y}(t)) + C_{MG}^t(\vec{y}(t), \vec{y}(t-1)) + C_{RT}(\vec{x}(t)) \tag{5.7}$$

The Offline Optimization Problem

The optimization problem of minimizing the overall cost of data upload and processing over a time interval $[1,T]$ can be formulated as

$$\text{minimize} \sum_{t=1}^{T} C(\vec{x}(t), \vec{y}(t)) \tag{5.8}$$

subject to: $\forall t = 1, \ldots, T,$

$$\vec{x}(t) \in X \tag{5.8a}$$

$$\frac{\sum_{d \in [\Xi], k \in [K]} F_d(t) x_{d,g,i,k}(t)}{\tau} \leq U_{gi}, \quad \forall i \in [K], g \in [G] \tag{5.8b}$$

$$x_{d,g,i,k}(t) \leq y_k(t), \quad \forall d \in [\Xi], g \in [G], i \in [K], k \in [K] \tag{5.8c}$$

$$\vec{y}(t) \in Y \tag{5.8d}$$

Constraint (5.8b) states that the total amount of data routed via (g,i) in each time slot should not exceed the upload capacity of (g,i). Equation 5.8c ensures that a routing path $d \to g \to i \to k$ is used $x_{d,g,i,k}(t) > 0$, only if data center k is the point of data aggregation in t ($y_k(t) = 1$).

Two Online Algorithms
The Online Lazy Migration (OLM) Algorithm
The offline optimization problem in Equation 5.8 can be divided into T one-shot optimization problems:

$$\text{minimize} \, C(\vec{x}(t), \vec{y}(t)) \tag{5.9}$$

subject to Equations 5.8a through 5.8d.

A straightforward algorithm solves the above optimization in each time slot, based on $\vec{y}(t - 1)$ in the previous time slot. This can be far from optimal due to premature data migration. For example, assume data center k was selected at $t - 1$, and migrating data from k to j is cost-optimal at t according to the one-shot optimization (e.g., because more data are generated in region j in t); the offline optimum may indicate to keep all data in k at t, if the volume of data generated in k in $t + 1$ surges. We next explore dependencies among the selection of the aggregation data center across consecutive time slots, and design a more judicious online algorithm accordingly.

The overall cost $C(\vec{x}(t), \vec{y}(t))$ incurred in t can be divided into two parts: (i) migration cost $C_{MG}^t(\vec{y}(t), \vec{y}(t - 1))$ defined in Equation 5.5, related to decisions in $t - 1$; (ii) nonmigration cost that relies only on current information at t:

$$C_{-MG}^t(\vec{x}(t), \vec{y}(t)) = C_{BM}(\vec{x}(t)) + C_{DC}(\vec{y}(t)) + C_{RT}(\vec{x}(t)) \tag{5.10}$$

1: $t = 1$;

2: $\hat{t} = 1$;   //Time slot when the last change of aggregation data center happens

3: Compute data routing decision $\vec{x}(1)$ and aggregation decision $\vec{y}(1)$ by minimizing $C(\vec{x}(1), \vec{y}(1))$ subject to (8a) − (8d);

4: Compute $C^1_{MG}(\vec{y}(1), \vec{y}(0))$ and $C^1_{-MG}(\vec{x}(1), \vec{y}(1))$;

5: **while** $t \leq T$ **do**

6:     **if** $C^{\hat{t}}_{MG}(\vec{y}(\hat{t}), \vec{y}(\hat{t} - 1)) \leq \frac{1}{\beta_2} \sum_{\nu=\hat{t}}^{t-1} C^{\nu}_{-MG}(\vec{x}(\nu), \vec{y}(\nu))$ **then**

7:         Derive $\vec{x}(t)$ and $\vec{y}(t)$ by minimizing $C^t_{-MG}(\vec{x}(t), \vec{y}(t))$ in (10) subject to (8a) − (8d) and constraint $C^t_{MG}(\vec{y}(t), \vec{y}(t - 1)) \leq \beta_1 C^t_{-MG}(\vec{x}(t), \vec{y}(t))$;

8:         **if** $\vec{y}(t) \neq \vec{y}(t - 1)$ **then**

9:             Use the new aggregation data center indicated by $\vec{y}(t)$;

10:             $\hat{t} = t$;

11:         **end if**

12:     **end if**

13:     **if** $\hat{t} < t$ **then** //not to use new aggregation data center

14:         $\vec{y}(t) = \vec{y}(t - 1)$, compute data routing decision $\vec{x}(t)$ by solving (9) if not derived;

15:     **end if**

16:     $t = t + 1$;

17: **end while**

ALGORITHM 5.1 The Online Lazy Migration (OLM) Algorithm.

A *lazy migration* algorithm is given in Algorithm 5.1, whose basic idea is to postpone data center switching even if the one-shot optimum indicates so, until the cumulative non-migration cost has significantly exceeded the potential data migration cost.

At the beginning ($t = 1$), we solve the one-shot optimization in Equation 5.9, and upload data via the derived optimal routes $\vec{x}(1)$ to the optimal aggregation data center indicted by $\vec{y}(1)$. Let $\hat{t}$ be the time of the data center switch. In each following time slot t, we compute the overall nonmigration cost in $[\hat{t}, t - 1]$, $\sum_{\nu=\hat{t}}^{t-1} C^{\nu}_{-MG}(\vec{x}(\nu), \vec{y}(\nu))$. The algorithm checks whether this cost is at least β_2 times the migration cost $C^{\hat{t}}_{MG}(\vec{y}(\hat{t}), \vec{y}(\hat{t} - 1))$. If so, it solves the one-shot optimization to derive $\vec{x}(x)$ and $\vec{y}(x)$ without considering the migration cost, that is, minimizing C^t_{-MG} subject to Equations 5.8a through 5.8d and an additional constraint, that the potential migration cost, $C^t_{MG}(\vec{y}(t), \vec{y}(t - 1))$, is no larger than β_1 times the nonmigration cost $C^t_{-MG}(\vec{x}(t), \vec{y}(t))$ at time t (to make sure that the migration cost is not too excessive). If a change of migration data center is indicated ($\vec{y}(t) \neq \vec{y}(t - 1)$), the algorithm accepts the new aggregation decision, and migrates data accordingly. In all other cases, the aggregation data center remains unchanged from $t - 1$, while optimal data routing paths are computed given this aggregation decision, for upload of new data generated in t.

Algorithm 5.1 avoids aggressive switches of the aggregation data center, to prevent moving a large amount of data back and forth too often. Excessive "laziness" is also avoided. Parameters β_2 and β_1 control the "laziness" and "aggressiveness" of the algorithm: a large β_2 prolongs the interswitch interval, while a large β_1 invites more frequent switches.

Lemma 5.1

The overall migration cost in $[1,t]$ is at most $\max\{\beta_1, 1/\beta_2\}$ times the overall nonmigration cost in this period, that is,

$$\sum_{v=1}^{t} C_{MG}^{v}(\vec{y}(v), \vec{y}(v-1)) \le \max\left\{\beta_1, \frac{1}{\beta_2}\right\} \sum_{v=1}^{t} C_{-MG}^{v}(\vec{x}(v), \vec{y}(v))$$

Proof

Potential migration cost in t is at most β_1 times the nonmigration costs. For migration cost incurred in previous time slots, that is, $C_{MG}^{\hat{t}_i}(\vec{x}(\hat{t}_i), \vec{y}(\hat{t}_i))$ where $\hat{t}_i$ is the time of aggregation data center switch, $\forall i = 1,2,\ldots$, the nonmigration cost in the period from when this migration occurs to the time before the next migration, that is, in $[\hat{t}_i, \hat{t}_{i+1}-1]$, is at least β_2 times the migration cost. Hence we have:

$$\sum_{v=1}^{t} C_{MG}^{v}(\vec{y}(v), \vec{y}(v-1))$$

$$\le \frac{1}{\beta_2} \sum_{v=1}^{t-1} C_{-MG}^{v}(\vec{x}(v), \vec{y}(v)) + \beta_1 C_{-MG}^{t}(\vec{x}(t), \vec{y}(t))$$

$$\le \max\left\{\beta_1, \frac{1}{\beta_2}\right\} \sum_{v=1}^{t} C_{-MG}^{v}(\vec{x}(v), \vec{y}(v))$$

Lemma 5.2

The overall nonmigration cost in $[1,t]$ is at most ε times the total offline-optimal cost, that is,

$$\sum_{v=1}^{t} C_{-MG}^{v}(\vec{x}(v), \vec{y}(v)) \le \varepsilon \sum_{v=1}^{t} C(\vec{x}^*(v), \vec{y}^*(v))$$

where

$$\varepsilon = \max_{v \in [1,T]} \frac{\max_{\vec{y}(v) \in Y, \vec{x}(v):(8a)-(8c)} C_{-MG}^{v}(\vec{x}(v), \vec{y}(v))}{\min_{\vec{y}(v) \in Y, \vec{x}(v):(8a)-(8c)} C_{-MG}^{v}(\vec{x}(v), \vec{y}(v))}$$

is the maximum ratio of the largest over the smallest possible nonmigration cost incurred in a time slot, with different data upload and aggregation decisions.

Proof

By the definition of ε, at $v \in [1,t]$, the nonmigration cost of OLM is smaller than ε times the nonmigration cost incurred by the optimal offline algorithm, that is, $C^v_{-MG}(\vec{x}(v), \vec{y}(v)) \leq \varepsilon C^v_{-MG}(\vec{x}^*(v), \vec{y}^*(v))$. We have:

$$\sum_{v=1}^{t} C^v_{-MG}(\vec{x}(v), \vec{y}(v)) \leq \varepsilon \sum_{v=1}^{t} C^v_{-MG}(\vec{x}^*(v), \vec{y}^*(v))$$

$$\leq \varepsilon \sum_{v=1}^{t} \left\{ C^v_{-MG}(\vec{x}^*(v), \vec{y}^*(v)) + C^v_{MG}(\vec{y}^*(v), \vec{y}^*(v-1)) \right\}$$

$$\leq \varepsilon \sum_{v=1}^{t} C(\vec{x}^*(v), \vec{y}^*(v)) \qquad \text{Q.E.D.}$$

Theorem 5.1

The OLM algorithm is $\varepsilon(1 + \max\{\beta_1, 1/\beta_2\})$-competitive.

Proof

The overall cost incurred by the OLM algorithm in $[1,T]$ is $\sum_{v=1}^{T} \{C^v_{-MG}(\vec{x}(v), \vec{y}(v)) + C^v_{MG}(\vec{y}(v), \vec{y}(v-1))\}$. By Lemmas 5.1 and 5.2:

$$\sum_{v=1}^{T} \left\{ C^v_{-MG}(\vec{x}(v), \vec{y}(v)) + C^v_{MG}(\vec{y}(v), \vec{y}(v-1)) \right\}$$

$$\leq \left(1 + \max\left\{ \beta_1, \frac{1}{\beta_2} \right\} \right) \sum_{v=1}^{T} C^v_{-MG}(\vec{x}(v), \vec{y}(v))$$

$$\leq \varepsilon \left(1 + \max\left\{ \beta_1, \frac{1}{\beta_2} \right\} \right) \sum_{v=1}^{T} C(\vec{x}^*(v), \vec{y}^*(v)) \qquad \text{Q.E.D.}$$

The value of ε is mainly determined by data generation patterns over time, and is less involved with the system size, for example, the number of data centers. In empirical studies [22] with a typical astronomical data generation pattern, we have $\varepsilon = 1.7$. In this case, setting $\beta_1 = 0.5$ and $\beta_2 = 2$ leads to a competitive ratio of 2.55. The competitive ratio is the *worst-case* performance of the algorithm [15], assuming an adversary who knows the algorithm and chooses the "worst" input over time.

The Randomized Fixed Horizon Control (RFHC) Algorithm

In practical applications, near-term future data generation patterns can often be estimated from history, for example, using a Markov chain model or a time series forecasting model [30]. We next show an algorithm that exploits such predicted future information. Detail in the prediction module is treated as a black box, is free to vary, and is not of primary

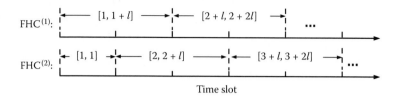

FIGURE 5.3   An illustration of different FHC algorithms with $l = 1$.

concern. The information in the lookahead window is assumed to be precisely predictable without error.

We divide time into equal-size frames of $l + 1$ time slots each ($l \geq 0$). In the first time slot t of each frame, assume information on data generation for the next l time slots, that is, $F_d(t), F_d(t + 1), \ldots, F_d(t + l), \quad \forall d \in [\Xi]$, are known. We solve the following cost minimization over time frame $[t, t + l]$, given the data aggregation decision of $\bar{y}(t - 1)$, to derive data routing decisions $\bar{x}(v)$ and aggregation decisions $\bar{y}(v), \forall v = t, \ldots, t + l$, using dynamic programing:

$$\text{minimize} \sum_{v=t}^{t+l} C(\bar{x}(v), \bar{y}(v)) \tag{5.11}$$

subject to Equations 5.8a through 5.8d

The method is essentially a *fixed horizon control* (FHC) algorithm, adapted from receding horizon control in the dynamic resource allocation literature [19]. Allowing the first time frame to start from different initial times $p \in [1, l + 1]$, we have $l + 1$ versions of the FHC algorithm (Figure 5.3). In particular, for an algorithm FHC$^{(p)}$ starting from a specific time slot p, the above optimization is solved at times $t = p, p + l + 1, p + 2(l + 1), \ldots$, for routing and aggregation decisions in the following $l + 1$ time slots. For each specific algorithm FHC$^{(p)}$, an adversary can choose an input with a surge of data produced at the beginning of each time frame, leading to a high migration cost. A randomized algorithm defeats such purposeful adversaries, by randomizing the starting times of the frames, achieving lower expected worst-case performance [15].

RFHC algorithm is given in Algorithm 5.2. At the beginning, the algorithm uniformly randomly chooses $p \in [1, l + 1]$ as the start of the first time frame of $l + 1$ slots, that is, it randomly picks one specific algorithm FHC$^{(p)}$ from the $l + 1$ FHC algorithms: at $t = 1$, it solves Equation 5.11 to decide the optimal data routing and aggregation strategies in the period of $t = 1$ to $p - 1$ ($p \neq 1$); then at $t = p, p + l + 1, p + 2(l + 1), \ldots$, it solves Equation 5.11 for optimal strategies in the following $l + 1$ time slots, respectively. An adversary, with no information on p, finds it hard to contrive specific inputs to degrade the performance of RFHC.

Lemma 5.3

The overall cost incurred by FHC$^{(p)}$ is upper-bounded by the offline-optimal cost plus the migration costs to move data from the aggregation data center computed by FHC$^{(p)}$ to the

---

1: $\vec{y}(0) = 0$;
2: $p = rand(1, l + 1)$;   //A random integer within $[1, l+1]$
3: **if** $p \neq 1$ **then**
4:     Derive $\vec{x}(1) \cdots \vec{x}(p - 1)$ and $\vec{y}(1) \cdots \vec{y}(p - 1)$ by solving (11) over the time window $[1, p - 1]$;
5: **end if**
6: $t = p$;
7: **while** $t \leq T$ **do**
8:     **if** $(t - p) \bmod (l + 1) = 0$ **then**
9:         Derive $\vec{x}(t), \dots, \vec{x}(t + l)$ and $\vec{y}(t), \dots, \vec{y}(t + l)$ by solving (11) over the time frame $[t, t + l]$;
10:     **end if**
11:     $t = t + 1$;
12: **end while**

ALGORITHM 5.2 The Randomized Fixed Horizon Control (RFHC) Algorithm.

offline-optimal one, at the end of the time frames. Let $\vec{x}^{(p)}$ and $\vec{y}^{(p)}$ be the solution derived by the FHC$^{(p)}$ algorithm and $\Theta_{p,t} = \left\{ \omega \mid \omega = p + k(l + 1), \quad k = 0, 1, \dots, \left\lfloor (t - p)/(l + 1) \right\rfloor \right\}$, we have for any $t \in [1, T]$,

$$\sum_{v=1}^{t} C(\vec{x}^p(v), \vec{y}^p(v)) \leq \sum_{v=1}^{t} C(\vec{x}^*(v), \vec{y}^*(v)) + \sum_{\omega \in \Theta_{p,t}} C_{MG}^{\omega}(\vec{y}^*(\omega - 1), \vec{y}^{(p)}(\omega - 1))$$

Proof

FHC$^{(p)}$ solves Equation 5.11 for locally optimal routing and aggregation decisions in the time frame $[\omega, \omega + l]$. Total cost incurred by FHC$^{(p)}$ in $[\omega, \omega + l]$ is at most that of any strategy with the same initial aggregation decision $\vec{y}^{(p)}(\omega - 1)$. Hence, the total cost incurred by FHC$^{(p)}$ in $[\omega, \omega + l]$ should be smaller than that of the following strategy: we first migrate the data from the data center specified by $\vec{y}^{(p)}(\omega - 1)$ to that specified by $\vec{y}^*(\omega - 1)$, and then operate data routing and aggregation in $[\omega, \omega + l]$ following the offline optimum solution in this time frame. We have

$$\sum_{v=1}^{t} C(\vec{x}^p(v), \vec{y}^p(v))$$

$$= \sum_{\omega \in \Theta_{p,t}} \sum_{v=\omega}^{\omega+l} (C_{-MG}^v(\vec{x}^{(p)}(v), \vec{y}^{(p)}(v)) + C_{MG}^v(\vec{y}^{(p)}(v), \vec{y}^{(p)}(v - 1)))$$

$$\leq \sum_{\omega \in \Theta_{p,t}} \left\{ \sum_{v=\omega}^{\omega+l} (C_{-MG}^v(\vec{x}^*(v), \vec{y}^*(v)) + C_{MG}^v(\vec{y}^*(v), \vec{y}^*(v - 1))) + C_{MG}^{\omega}(\vec{y}^*(\omega - 1), \vec{y}^{(p)}(\omega - 1)) \right\}$$

$$= \sum_{v=1}^{t} C(\vec{x}^*(v), \vec{y}^*(v)) + \sum_{\omega \in \Theta_{p,t}} C_{MG}^{\omega}(\vec{y}^*(\omega - 1), \vec{y}^{(p)}(\omega - 1)) \qquad \text{Q.E.D.}$$

Theorem 5.2

The RFHC algorithm is $1 + (1/(l + 1))(\kappa/\lambda)$-competitive, where

$$\kappa = \sup_{t\in[1,T], \vec{y}^1(t), \vec{y}^2(t)\in Y} \frac{C_{MG}^t(\vec{y}^1(t), \vec{y}^2(t))}{\sum_{v=1}^{t-1}(\alpha_v \sum_{d\in[\Xi]} F_d(v))}$$ is the maximum migration cost per unit data, and

$$\lambda = \inf_{t\in[1,T], \vec{x}(t), \vec{y}(t):(8a)-(8d)} \frac{C(\vec{x}(t), \vec{y}(t))}{\sum_{v=1}^{t-1}(\alpha_v \sum_{d\in[\Xi]} F_d(v))}$$ is the minimum total cost per unit data per time slot.

Proof

Let $C_{FHC^{(p)}} = \sum_{v=1}^T C(\vec{x}^p(v), \vec{y}^p(v))$ be the overall cost incurred by an $FHC^{(p)}$ algorithm, and $C_{OPT} = \sum_{v=1}^T C(\vec{x}^*(v), \vec{y}^*(v))$ be the offline-optimal cost. The expected cost of the RFHC algorithm is

$$E(\text{RFHC}) = \frac{1}{l+1}\sum_{p=1}^{l+1} C_{FHC^{(p)}} \le \frac{1}{l+1}\sum_{p=1}^{l+1}\left\{ C_{OPT} + \sum_{\omega\in\Theta_{p,t}} C_{MG}^\omega(\vec{y}^*(\omega-1), \vec{y}^{(p)}(\omega-1)) \right\}$$

$$= C_{OPT} + \frac{1}{l+1}\sum_{p=1}^{l+1}\sum_{\omega\in\Theta_{p,t}} C_{MG}^\omega(\vec{y}^*(\omega-1), \vec{y}^{(p)}(\omega-1))$$

The ratio of the above second term over C_{OPT} is

$$\frac{\sum_{p=1}^{l+1}\sum_{\omega\in\Theta_{p,t}} C_{MG}^\omega(\vec{y}^*(\omega-1), \vec{y}^{(p)}(\omega-1))}{C_{OPT}} = \frac{\sum_{v=1}^T C_{MG}^\omega(\vec{y}^*(v-1), \vec{y}^{(p)}(v-1))}{\sum_{v=1}^T C(\vec{x}^*(v), \vec{y}^*(v))} \le \frac{\kappa}{\lambda}$$

Therefore, we conclude that $(E(\text{RFHC})/C_{OPT}) \le 1 + (1/(l+1))(\kappa/\lambda)$.　　　　Q.E.D.

Theorem 5.2 reveals that the more future steps predicted (the larger l is), the closer the RFHC algorithm can approach the offline optimum. Values of κ and λ are related to system input including prices and delays, and are less involved with the data generation patterns and the number of data centers. In empirical studies [22] with a typical astronomical data generation pattern, we have $\kappa/\lambda \approx 0.69$, and even with $l = 1$, the competitive ratio is already as low as 1.34.

ONLINE ALGORITHMS FOR UPLOADING DEFERRAL BIG DATA TO THE CLOUD

Next we show the problem formulation as well as online algorithms designed for the second scenario, where we upload deferral Big Data to a cloud.

Problem Formation

Let $z_{d,t}^m$ be a decision variable indicating the portion of W_t assigned to mapper m at time slot $t + d$. The cost of ISP m is indicated by $f_m(V_m)$, where V_m is the maximum traffic that goes through ISP m from time slot 0 to T. To ensure all workload is uploaded into the cloud, we have: $0 \leq z_{d,t}^m \leq 1, \forall m \in [M]$ and $\sum_m \sum_{d=0}^D z_{d,t}^m = 1, \forall t$. Given the maximum tolerable uploading delay D, the traffic V_m^t between the user and mapper m is

$$V_m^t = \sum_{d=0}^D W_{t-d} z_{d,t-d}^m, \quad \forall m \in [M] \tag{5.12}$$

Let V_m be the maximum traffic volume of ISP m, which will be used in the calculation of bandwidth cost. V_m satisfies: $V_m - V_m^t \geq 0, \forall t$. We next assume that ISPs in the first stage, connecting user to mappers, employ the same charging function f_m; and ISPs in the second stage from mappers to reducers use the same charging function $f_{m,r}$. Both charging functions f_m and $f_{m,r}$ are nondecreasing and convex. We further assume that the first stage is nonsplittable, that is, each workload is uploaded through one ISP only.

The user decides to deliver the workload to mapper m in time slot t. Assume it takes a unit time to transmit data via ISPs. Let M_m^{t+1} denote the total data size at mapper m in time slot $t + 1$. M_m^{t+1} can be calculated as the summation of all transmitted workloads at time slot t: $M_m^{t+1} = \sum_{d=0}^D W_{t-d} z_{d,t-d}^m, \forall m \in [M]$. Assume the mappers take 1 time slot to process a received workload. Therefore the mappers will transfer data to the reducer in time slot $t + 2$. Notice that the MapReduce framework partitions the output pairs (key/value) of mappers to reducers using hash functions. All values for the same key are always reduced at the same reducer no matter which mapper it comes from. Moreover, we assume that data generated in the data locations are uniformly mixed, so we can calculate the traffic from mappers to reducers is in time slot $t + 2$:

$$V_{m,r}^{t+2} = \beta M_m^{t+1} h_r, \quad \forall m \in [M], r \in [R] \tag{5.13}$$

The maximum traffic volume of the ISP (m,r), $V_{m,r}$, satisfies: $V_{m,r} - V_{m,r}^{t+2} \geq 0, \forall t$.

The overall traffic cost minimization problem for the cloud user, under the MAX contract charge model, can be formulated as follows:

$$\text{minimize} \sum_m f_m(V_m) + \sum_{m,r} f_{m,r}(V_{m,r}) \tag{5.14}$$

subject to

$$V_m - V_m^t \geq 0, \quad \forall t, m \tag{5.14a}$$

$$V_{m,r} - V_{m,r}^{t+2} \geq 0, \quad \forall t, m, r \tag{5.14b}$$

$$\sum_{d=0}^{D} z_{d,t}^{m} = n_m, \qquad \forall t, m \tag{5.14c}$$

$$\sum_{m} n_m = 1 \tag{5.14d}$$

$$0 \leq z_{d,t}^{m} \leq 1, n_m \in \{0,1\}, \qquad \forall m \tag{5.14e}$$

where V_m^t and $V_{m,r}^{t+2}$ are defined in Equation 5.12 and Equation 5.13, respectively. n_m is a binary variable indicating whether ISP m is employed or not.

The Single ISP Case

We first investigate the basic case that includes one mapper and one reducer only, colocated in the same data center, with no bandwidth cost between the pairs. The online cost minimization for deferrable upload under percentile charging, even when defined over such a single link from one source to one receiver only, is still highly nontrivial, exhibiting a rich combinatorial structure, yet rarely studied before in the literature of either computer networking or theoretical computer science [6].

We show an online algorithm that incorporates a few heuristic smoothing ideas and is hence referred to as Heuristic Smoothing. Given a MAX charge model at the ISP, the online algorithm tries to exploit the allowable delay by scheduling the traffic to the best time slot within the allowed time window, for reducing the charge volume. This can be illustrated through a toy example: in $t = 1$, a job (100 MB, max delay = 9 time slots) is released; in the following time slots, no jobs are released. If the algorithm smooths the traffic across the 10 time slots, the charge volume can be reduced to 10 MB/5 min, from 100 MB/5 min if immediate transmission is adopted.

The Primal & Dual Cost Minimization LPs

We can drop the location index (m, r) in this basic scenario of one mapper and one reducer locating in the same data center. Note that the charging function f_m is a nondecreasing function of the maximum traffic volume. Minimizing the maximum traffic volume therefore implies minimizing the bandwidth cost. Consequently, the cost minimization problem in our basic single ISP scenario can be formulated into the following (primal) linear program (LP):

$$\text{minimize } V \tag{5.15}$$

subject to

$$\sum_{d=0}^{\min\{D,t-1\}} W_{t-d} z_{d,t-d} \leq V, \qquad \forall t \in [1, T] \tag{5.15a}$$

$$\sum_{d=0}^{D} z_{d,t} = 1, \qquad \forall t \in [1, T - D] \tag{5.15b}$$

$$z_{d,t} \geq 0, V \geq 0, \qquad \forall d \in [0, D], t \in [1, T - D] \tag{5.15c}$$

where $z_{d,t} = 0, \forall d \in [0, D], t > T - D$.

Introducing dual variable u and v to Constraint (5.15a) and Constraint (5.15b) respectively, we formulate the corresponding dual LP:

$$\text{maximize} \sum_{t=1}^{T-D} v_t \tag{5.16}$$

subject to

$$\sum_{t=1}^{T} u_t \leq 1 \tag{5.16a}$$

$$v_t - W_t u_{t+d} \leq 0 \qquad \forall t \in [1, T - D], d \in [0, D] \tag{5.16b}$$

$$u_t \geq 0 \qquad \forall t \in [1, T] \tag{5.16c}$$

$$v_t \text{ unconstrained} \qquad \forall t \in [1, T - D] \tag{5.16d}$$

The input begins with W_1 and ends with W_{T-D}, and $W_{T-D+1} = 0, \ldots, W_T = 0$ is padded to the tail of the input. Equation 5.15 is a standard linear program. For an optimal offline solution, one can simply solve Equation 5.15 using a standard LP solution algorithm such as the simplex method or the interior-point method.

Online Algorithms

The simplest online solution in the single ISP scenario is the *immediate transfer algorithm* (ITA). Once a new job arrives, ITA transfers it to mappers immediately without any delay. As we see in the aforementioned toy example, ITA is apparently not ideal, and may lead to high peak traffic and high bandwidth cost as compared with the offline optimum. Golubchik et al. [6] design a cost-aware algorithm that strikes to spread out bandwidth demand by utilizing all possible delays, referred to as the *Simple Smoothing Algorithm*. Upon receiving a new workload, Simple Smoothing evenly divides it into $D + 1$ parts, and processes them one by one in the current time slot and the following D time slots, as shown in Algorithm 5.3.

```
1: for τ = 1 to T − D do
2:     for d = 0 to D do
3:         z_{d,τ} = 1/(D + 1)
4:     end for
5: end for
```

ALGORITHM 5.3   The Simple Smoothing Algorithm.

Theorem 5.3

The competitive ratio of Simple Smoothing is $2 - 1/(D + 1)$ [6].

Theorem 5.3 can be proven through weak LP duality, that is, using a feasible dual as the lower bound of the offline optimal. Simple Smoothing is very simple, but guarantees a worst-case competitive ratio smaller than 2. Nonetheless, there is still room for further improvements, since Simple Smoothing ignores available information such as the hitherto maximum traffic volume transmitted, and the current "pressure" from backlogged traffic and their deadlines. Such an observation motivated our design of the more sophisticated Heuristic Smoothing algorithm for the case $D \geq 1$, as shown in Algorithm 5.4. τ is the current time slot, and H_d is the total volume of data that have been buffered for d time slots.

Theorem 5.4

The competitive ratio of Heuristic Smoothing is lower bounded by $2(1 - 1/e)$.

Proof

Consider the following input: $(W,W,\ldots,W,0,\ldots,0)$ whose first $D + 1$ time slots are W. The traffic demand V increases until time slot $D + 1$.

```
1: V_{max} = 0
2: W_τ = 0, ∀τ = T − D + 1, ..., T;
3: H_d = 0, ∀d = 1, ..., D;
4: for τ = 1 to T do
5:     V_τ = min { W_τ + Σ_{d=1}^{D} H_d, max{V_{max}, (W_τ)/(D+1) + (Σ_{d=1}^{D} H_d)/D } }
6:     if V_{max} < V_τ then
7:         V_{max} = V_τ;
8:     end if
9:     Transfer the traffic following Earliest Deadline First (EDF) strategy;
10:    Update H_d, ∀d = 1, ..., D;
11: end for
```

ALGORITHM 5.4   The Heuristic Smoothing Algorithm.

$$V_{D+1} = \frac{W}{D+1} + \frac{W}{D+1} + \frac{(D-1)W}{(D+1)D} + \cdots + \frac{(D-1)^{D-1}W}{(D+1)D^{D-1}} = \frac{W}{D+1}\left(1 + D\left(1 - \left(1 - \frac{1}{D}\right)^{D}\right)\right)$$

We can find a feasible primal solution that yields the charge volume $((D+1)/(2D+1))W$. This primal solution is an upper bound of the offline optimum. Therefore, the lower bound of the competitive ratio is

$$\frac{2D+1}{V_{D+1}(D+1)} = \frac{2D+1}{(D+1)^2}\left(1 + D\left(1 - \left(1 - \frac{1}{D}\right)^{D}\right)\right) \rightarrow 2\left(1 - \frac{1}{e}\right) \text{ as } D \rightarrow +\infty$$

Notice that $((2D+1)/((D+1)^2))(1 + D(1 - (1 - (1/D))^D))$ is a decreasing function for $D \in [1, +\infty)$, we further have the competitive ratio is at least $2(1 - 1/e)$. Q.E.D.

Theorem 5.5

The competitive ratio of Heuristic Smoothing is upper-bounded by $2 - (1/(D+1))$.

Proof

We take the Simple Smoothing algorithm as a benchmark, and we prove that $P_{\text{smooth}} \geq P_{\text{heuristic}}$, where P_{smooth} and $P_{\text{heuristic}}$ are the charged volume produced by the Simple Smoothing Algorithm and the Heuristic Smoothing Algorithm, respectively. The Heuristic Smoothing Algorithm will only increase the traffic demand when $(W_\tau/(D+1)) + \sum_{d=1}^{D} H_d/D$ exceeds $V_{\max}$. Therefore, we rearrange H_d to compute the maximum traffic demand. Let

$$V_{t+D} = \frac{W_{t+D}}{D+1} + \frac{W_{t+D-1}}{D+1} + \frac{(D-1)W_{t+D-2}}{(D+1)D} + \cdots + \frac{(D-1)^{D-1}W_t}{(D+1)D^{D-1}}$$

Then $P_{\text{heuristic}} = \max_t V_{t+D}$. Let $\tau = \text{argmax}_t V_{t+D}$ and we have

$$P_{\text{smooth}} = \max_t \sum_{i=t}^{t+D} \frac{W_i}{D+1} \geq \sum_{i=\tau}^{\tau+D} \frac{W_i}{D+1}$$

$$\geq \frac{W_{\tau+D}}{D+1} + \frac{W_{\tau+D-1}}{D+1} + \frac{(D-1)W_{\tau+D-2}}{(D+1)D} + \cdots + \frac{(D-1)^{D-1}W_\tau}{(D+1)D^{D-1}} = P_{\text{heuristic}}$$

Since the Simple Smoothing Algorithm is $2 - 1/(D+1)$-competitive, the competitive ratio of the Heuristic Smoothing Algorithm cannot be worse than $2 - 1/(D+1)$. Q.E.D.

From the proof above, we have following corollary.

Corollary 5.1

For any given input, the charge volume resulting from Heuristic Smoothing is always equal to or smaller than that of Simple Smoothing.

The Cloud Scenario

We next extend the single link case to a cloud scenario where multiple ISPs are employed to transfer Big Data dynamically. Data are routed from the cloud user to mappers and then reducers, both residing in potentially different data centers in the cloud. Heuristic Smoothing is applied as a plug-in module for achieving a distributed and randomized online algorithm with very low computational complexity.

Define $Cost_1 = \sum_m f_m(V_m)$, $Cost_2 = \sum_{m,r} f_{m,r}(V_{m,r})$, and adopt power charge functions by letting $f_m(x) = f_{m,r}(x) = x^\gamma, \gamma > 1$. The two-phase MapReduce cost optimization problem is defined in Equation 5.14, and is a discrete optimization with integer variables. Consequently, an offline solution that solves such an integer program has a high computational complexity, further motivating the design of an efficient online solution.

We present a distributed randomized online algorithm for Equation 5.14. For each workload, the user chooses ISPs uniformly at random to transfer the data to a randomly selected mapper. Formally, let *WA* be the randomized workload assignment allocating each workload to mappers. For each selected ISP, the user runs Heuristic Smoothing to guide one-stage traffic deferral and transmission, as shown in Algorithm 5.5.

Algorithm 5.5 can be analyzed by building a connection between the uploading scheme π and the randomized workload assignment *WA*. We combine π and *WA* to a new uploading scheme π_{WA}. Let $t_0 = 1 < t_1 \cdots < t_E = T$. During each interval $[t_i, t_i+1)$, each ISP is employed to transfer at most one workload in the uploading scheme π. If a workload is processed in $[t_i, t_i+1)$, then it cannot be finished before t_i+1. Due to the MAX charge model, the transfer speed for workload w in $[t_i, t_i+1)$ is a single speed, say $v_{i,w}$. If workload w is not processed in $[t_i, t_i+1)$, we set $v_{i,w} = 0$. Therefore, for any given i, there are at most M values of $v_{i,w} \neq 0$, where M is the number of mappers.

Assume there are n workloads, forming a set $[W]$, which contains all subsets of n workloads. Let $\Omega_m = \{w | \text{workload } w \text{ assigned to ISP } m\} \in [W]$. In scheme π_{WA}, the user transfers data at speed of $\sum_{w \in \Omega_m} v_{i,w}$ in time interval $[t_i, t_i+1)$. Let $\varphi_n(\Omega_m)$ be the probability that exactly the workloads Ω_m are allocated to ISP m. Then we have $\varphi_n(\Omega_m) = (1/M)^{|\Omega_m|}(1 - (1/M))^{n-|\Omega_m|}$. We next define function $\Lambda_n(\vec{x})$ where $\vec{x} \in \mathfrak{R}^n/\{0\}$:

1: Generate a randomized workload assignment WA which allocates each workload to a randomly selected mapper.
2: For each ISP m, apply the single ISP algorithm, *e.g.*, The The Heuristic Smoothing Algorithm to schedule the traffic.

ALGORITHM 5.5 Randomized Uploading Scheme.

$$\Lambda_n(\vec{x}) = M \sum_{\Omega_m \in [W]} \varphi_n(\Omega_m) \frac{(\sum_{w \in \Omega_m} x_w)^\gamma}{\sum_{w=1}^n x_w^\gamma}$$

Lemma 5.4

Given any uploading scheme π and a randomized workload assignment WA, we have a randomized uploading scheme π_{WA}, which satisfies:

$$E(\text{Cost}_1(\pi_{WA}) + \text{Cost}_2(\pi_{WA})) \leq \max_{\vec{x}} \Lambda_M(\vec{x})(\text{Cost}_1(\pi) + \text{Cost}_2(\pi))$$

Proof

Since the traffic pattern in ISP (m,r), $\forall r$ is exactly the same as ISP m, we only consider one stage. Let us consider scheme π first. In the first stage, the cost is

$$\text{Cost}_1(\pi) = \sum_{m \in [M]} \max_{i,w} (v_{i,w}^m)^\gamma \geq \max_i \Sigma_M^*(v_{i,w}^\gamma)$$

where $v_{i,w}^m$ indicates the transfer speed in ISP m during $[t_i, t_i+1)$ for workload w. $\Sigma_M^*(v_{i,w}^\gamma)$ is the sum of the largest M values of $v_{i,w}^\gamma$ when given i. The inequality holds because there are at most M nonzero speeds for any given duration $[t_i, t_i+1)$. The cost of the second stage is:

$$\text{Cost}_2(\pi) = \sum_m \sum_r \max_{i,w} (\beta h_r v_{i,w}^m)^\gamma = \beta^\gamma \sum_r h_r^\gamma \sum_m \max_{i,w} (v_{i,w}^m)^\gamma \geq \beta^\gamma \sum_r h_r^\gamma \max_i \Sigma_M^*(v_{i,w}^\gamma)$$

The cost of the first stage in π_{WA} is

$$E(\text{Cost}_1(\pi_{WA})) = \sum_{m \in [M]} \sum_{\Omega_m^{WA} \in [W]} \varphi_n(\Omega_m^{WA}) \max_i \left(\sum_{w \in \Omega_m^{WA}} v_{i,w} \right)^\gamma = M \max_i \sum_{\Omega_m^{WA} \in [W]} \varphi_n(\Omega_m^{WA}) \left(\sum_{w \in \Omega_m^{WA}} v_{i,w} \right)^\gamma$$

The second equality above holds because the assignment is uniformly random. Similarly, the cost of the second stage in π_{WA} is

$$E(\text{Cost}_2(\pi_{WA})) = M \sum_{\Omega_m^{WA} \in [W]} \varphi_n(\Omega_m^{WA}) \sum_r \max_i \left(h_r \sum_{w \in \Omega_m^{WA}} \beta v_{i,w} \right)^\gamma$$

$$= M\beta^\gamma \sum_r h_r^\gamma \max_i \sum_{\Omega_m^{WA} \in [W]} \varphi_n(\Omega_m^{WA}) \left(\sum_{w \in \Omega_m^{WA}} v_{i,w} \right)^\gamma$$

Again because for any $[t_i, t_i+1)$, there are at most M values of $v_{i,w} \neq 0$. We have

$$M \sum_{\Omega_m^{WA} \in [W]} \varphi_n(\Omega_m^{WA}) \frac{(\sum_{w \in \Omega_m^{WA}} v_{i,w})^\gamma}{\sum_M^*(v_{i,w}^\gamma)}$$

$$= M \sum_{\Omega_m^{WA} \in [W]} \varphi_n(\Omega_m^{WA}) \frac{(\sum_{w \in \Omega_m^{WA}} v_{i,w})^\gamma}{\sum_{w=1}^n (v_{i,w}^\gamma)} = \Lambda_n(\vec{v}) = \Lambda_M(\vec{v}')$$

where $\vec{v}'$ is an M-dimensional subvector of $\vec{v} \in \Re^n / \{0\}$, which contains all nonzero transfer speeds in $[t_i, t_i+1)$. Therefore, the ratio for the first stage is

$$E \frac{(\text{Cost}_1(\pi_{WA}))}{\text{Cost}_1(\pi)} \leq M \sum_{\Omega_m^{WA} \in [W]} \varphi_n(\Omega_m^{WA}) \max_i \frac{(\sum_{w \in \Omega_m^{WA}} v_{i,w})^\gamma}{\max_i \sum_M^*(v_{i,w}^\gamma)}$$

$$\leq M \sum_{\Omega_m^{WA} \in [W]} \varphi_n(\Omega_m^{WA}) \frac{(\sum_{w \in \Omega_m^{WA}} v_{i^*,w})^\gamma}{\sum_M^*(v_{i^*,w}^\gamma)} \leq \max_{\vec{x}} \Lambda_M(\vec{x})$$

where $i^* = \text{argmax}_i(\sum_{w \in \Omega_m^{WA}} v_{i,w})^\gamma$. Similarly, the ratio for the second stage is also bounded by $\max_{\vec{x}} \Lambda_M(\vec{x})$, that is, $E(\text{Cost}_2(\pi_{WA}))/\text{Cost}_2(\pi) \leq \max_{\vec{x}} \Lambda_M(\vec{x})$. This proves Lemma 5.4.

Let $S(\gamma, j)$ be the j-th Stirling number for γ elements, defined as the number of partitions of a set of size γ into j subsets [31]. Let B_γ be the γ-th Bell number, defined as the number of partitions of a set of size γ [31]. The Bell number is relatively small when γ is small: $B_1 = 1$, $B_2 = 2$, $B_3 = 5$, $B_4 = 15$. The definitions also imply: $\sum_j^\gamma S(\gamma, j) = B_\gamma$.

The following lemma is proven by Greiner et al. [32].

Lemma 5.5

$$\forall \gamma \in N \text{ and } \gamma \leq M, \quad \max_{\vec{x}} \Lambda_M(\vec{x}) = \sum_{j=1}^\gamma S(\gamma, j) \frac{M!}{M^j(M-j)!}$$

Theorem 5.6

Given a c-competitive algorithm with respect to cost for the single ISP case, then the randomized online algorithm is $cB_{\lceil \gamma \rceil}$-competitive in expectation.

Proof

Let π^* be the optimal uploading scheme, the corresponding randomized uploading scheme is π_{WA}^*. The algorithm we use is π_{WA}. Since the workloads in π_{WA}^* and π_{WA} are the same, we have: $E(\text{Cost}_1(\pi_{WA})) \leq cE(\text{Cost}_1(\pi_{WA}^*))$, since the algorithm is c-competitive. Similarly, we have: $E(\text{Cost}_2(\pi_{WA})) \le cE(\text{Cost}_2(\pi^*_{WA}))$, since the traffic pattern in ISP (m,r), $\forall r$ is exactly the same as in ISP m. Lemma 5.4 implies:

$$E(\text{Cost}_1(\pi^*_{WA}) + \text{Cost}_2(\pi^*_{WA})) \le \max_{\bar{x}} \Lambda_M(\bar{x})(\text{Cost}_1(\pi^*) + \text{Cost}_2(\pi^*))$$

Since $\Lambda_M(\bar{x})$ is a monotonically increasing function of γ, we use $\lceil \gamma \rceil$ as an upper bound of $\gamma > 1$, obtaining a corresponding upper bound of $\Lambda_M(\bar{x})$. Then we have the following expected cost of the randomized online algorithm:

$$\begin{aligned}
E(\text{Cost}_1(\pi_{WA}) + \text{Cost}_2(\pi_{WA})) &\le cE(\text{Cost}_1(\pi^*_{WA}) + \text{Cost}_2(\pi^*_{WA})) \\
&\le c \max_{\bar{x}} \Lambda_M(\bar{x})(\text{Cost}_1(\pi^*) + \text{Cost}_2(\pi^*)) \\
&= c \sum_{j=1}^{\lceil \gamma \rceil} S(\lceil \gamma \rceil, j) \frac{M!}{M^j(M-j)!}(\text{Cost}_1(\pi^*) + \text{Cost}_2(\pi^*)) \\
&\le c \sum_{j=1}^{\lceil \gamma \rceil} S(\lceil \gamma \rceil, j)(\text{Cost}_1(\pi^*) + \text{Cost}_2(\pi^*)) \le cB_{\lceil \gamma \rceil}\text{OPT} \quad \text{Q.E.D.}
\end{aligned}$$

Remark

For a single link, Heuristic Smoothing can be employed, whose competitive ratio is smaller than 2 with respect to maximum traffic volume. Then the competitive ratio of algorithm 5.4 is 2^γ in cost. Thus, algorithm 5.5 is $2^\gamma B_{\lceil \gamma \rceil}$-competitive in expectation. When $\gamma = 2$, the competitive ratio is 8, a constant independent of the number of mappers.

CONCLUSION

This chapter presents online algorithms for cost-minimizing upload of Big Data into a cloud platform, for processing using a MapReduce-like framework. We first show two efficient online algorithms for timely migration of geo-dispersed Big Data to the cloud: the OLM algorithm achieves a worst-case competitive ratio as low as 2.55 under typical real-world settings; the RFHC algorithm provides a decreasing competitive ratio with an increasing size of the lookahead window. Then we focus on a new, interesting percentile-based charge model used by ISPs. The model leads to new online algorithm design problems for minimizing the traffic cost incurred by uploading deferral Big Data to the cloud. A Heuristic Smoothing algorithm is proposed in the single link case, with proven better performance than the best alternative in the literature, and a smaller competitive ratio below 2. A randomized online algorithm is designed for the MapReduce framework, achieving a constant competitive ratio by employing Heuristic Smoothing as a building module.

As for the second scenario, the algorithms are designed to handle the uniform delays. Heterogeneous delays could be a future research direction since the discussed online algorithms in the chapter are still feasible and efficient is to be investigated. Another possible research direction is adopting the 95th-percentile charge model instead of the MAX contract charge model, as the former is widely employed by ISPs in the real world. The current system model, online algorithms as well as corresponding competitive analysis do not straightforwardly extend to the 95th-percentile cost model; new ideas and techniques may be required for this more realistic scenario.

We hope the algorithms in the chapter could help potential cloud users with massive amounts of data to embrace cloud computing with reduced cost, and help both industry and academia to get ready for the Big Data that is on the way.

REFERENCES

1. M. Armbrust, A. Fox, R. Grifth, A. D. Joseph, R. Katz, A. Konwinski, G. Lee, D. Patterson, A. Rabkin, I. Stoica, and M. Zaharia, *Above the Clouds: A Berkeley View of Cloud Computing*, EECS, University of California, Berkeley, Tech. Rep., 2009.
2. S. Pandey, L. Wu, S. Guru, and R. Buyya, A Particle Swarm Optimization (PSO)-based heuristic for scheduling workflow applications in cloud computing environment, in *Proceedings of IEEE AINA*, 2010.
3. *Human Genome Project*, http://www.ornl.gov/hgmis/home.shtml.
4. *Hadoop—Facebook*, http://www.facebook.com/note.php?note id=16121578919.
5. *Hadoop at Twitter*, http://www.slideshare.net/kevinweil/hadoop-at-twitter-hadoop-summit-201.
6. L. Golubchik, S. Khuller, K. Mukherjee, and Y. Yao, To send or not to send: Reducing the cost of data transmission, in *Proceedings of IEEE INFOCOM*, 2013.
7. H. Wang, H. Xie, L. Qiu, A. Silberschatz, and Y. Yang, Optimal ISP subscription for internet multihoming: Algorithm design and implication analysis, in *Proceedings of IEEE INFOCOM*, 2005.
8. S. Peak, Beyond bandwidth: The business case for data acceleration, *White Paper*, 2013.
9. *AWS Import/Export*, http://aws.amazon.com/importexport/.
10. E. E. Schadt, M. D. Linderman, J. Sorenson, L. Lee, and G. P. Nolan, Computational solutions to large-scale data management and analysis, *Nat Rev Genet*, 11(9), 647–657, 09 2010.
11. P. Yang, *Moving an Elephant: Large Scale Hadoop Data Migration at Facebook*, http://www.facebook.com/notes/paul-yang/moving-an-elephant-large-scale-hadoop-data-migration-at-facebook/10150246275318920.
12. B. Cho and I. Gupta, New algorithms for planning bulk transfer via internet and shipping networks, in *Proceedings of IEEE ICDCS*, 2010.
13. B. Cho and I. Gupta, Budget-constrained bulk data transfer via internet and shipping networks, in *Proceedings of ACM ICAC*, 2011.
14. R. J. Brunner, S. G. Djorgovski, T. A. Prince, and A. S. Szalay, Massive datasets in astronomy, in: J. Abello, P. M. Pardalos, and M. G. C. Resende (eds.) *Handbook of Massive Data Sets*. Norwell, MA, USA: Kluwer Academic Publishers, 2002, pp. 931–979.
15. A. Borodin and R. El-Yaniv, *Online Computation and Competitive Analysis*. Cambridge University Press, Cambridge, UK, 1998, vol. 2.
16. M. Lin, A. Wierman, L. L. Andrew, and E. Thereska, Dynamic right-sizing for power-proportional data centers, in *Proceedings of IEEE INFOCOM*, 2011.
17. V. Mathew, R. Sitaraman, and P. Shenoy, Energy-aware load balancing in content delivery networks, in *Proceedings of IEEE INFOCOM*, 2012.
18. T. Lu and M. Chen, Simple and effective dynamic provisioning for power-proportional data centers, in *Proceedings of IEEE CISS*, 2012.
19. M. Lin, Z. Liu, A. Wierman, and L. Andrew, Online algorithms for geographical load balancing, in *Proceedings of IEEE IGCC*, 2012.
20. S. Rao, R. Ramakrishnan, A. Silberstein, M. Ovsiannikov, and D. Reeves, *Sailfish: A Framework for Large Scale Data Processing*, Yahoo!Labs, Tech. Rep., 2012.

21. B. Heintz, A. Chandra, and R. K. Sitaraman, *Optimizing MapReduce for Highly Distributed Environments*, Department of Computer Science and Engineering, University of Minnesota, Tech. Rep., 2012.
22. L. Zhang, C. Wu, Z. Li, C. Guo, M. Chen, and F. Lau, Moving Big Data to the cloud: An online cost-minimizing approach, *IEEE Journal on Selected Areas in Communications*, 31(12), 2710–2721, 2013.
23. L. Zhang, Z. Li, C. Wu, and M. Chen, Online algorithms for uploading deferrable Big Data to the cloud, in *Proceedings of IEEE INFOCOM*, 2014.
24. *Windows Azure Virtual Network*, http://www.windowsazure.com/en-us/home/features/networking/.
25. *Amazon Elastic MapReduce*, http://aws.amazon.com/elasticmapreduce/.
26. *GoGrid*, http://www.gogrid.com/.
27. D. K. Goldenberg, L. Qiuy, H. Xie, Y. R. Yang, and Y. Zhang, Optimizing cost and performance for multihoming, in *Proceedings of ACM SIGCOMM*, 2004.
28. A. Grothey and X. Yang, Top-percentile traffic routing problem by dynamic programming, *Optimization and Engineering*, 12, 631–655, 2011.
29. D. Logothetis, C. Olston, B. Reed, K. C. Webb, and K. Yocum, Stateful bulk processing for incremental analytics, in *Proceedings of ACM SoCC*, 2010.
30. G. E. P. Box, G. M. Jenkins, and G. C. Reinsel, *Time Series Analysis: Forecasting and Control*, 4th ed. Wiley, Hoboken, NJ, USA, 2008.
31. H. Becker and J. Riordan, The arithmetic of Bell and Stirling numbers, *American journal of Mathematics*, 70(2), 385–394, 1948.
32. G. Greiner, T. Nonner, and A. Souza, The bell is ringing in speed-scaled multiprocessor scheduling, in *Proceedings of ACM SPAA*, 2009.

CHAPTER 6

Data Process and Analysis Technologies of Big Data

Peter Wlodarczak, Mustafa Ally, and Jeffrey Soar

CONTENTS

INTRODUCTION

Drowning in data yet starving for knowledge.

John Naisbitt, 1982

Mayer-Schonberger and Cukier define Big Data as "the ability of society to harness information in novel ways to produce useful insights or goods and services of significant value [1]." Throughout the current literature, Big Data is usually defined by the three Vs: volume, velocity, and variety. Volume refers to the large amount of data. "Large" ranges from gigabytes to petabytes. Typically, the volume increases, but the data itself does not change. Velocity refers to the speed at which the data volume grows. For instance, on Facebook more than 500 TB of data is created daily [2]. Variety describes the data types in Big Data. Big Data usually consists of structured, semistructured, and unstructured data. Big Data requires all 3 Vs to apply (Figure 6.1).

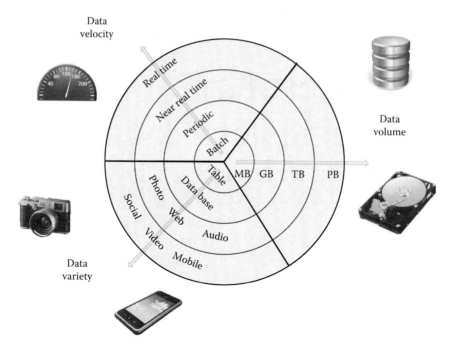

FIGURE 6.1 V-model for Big Data. (From D. Klein, P. Tran-Gia, and M. Hartmann, Big Data, *Informatik-Spektrum*, 36(3), 319–323, 2013.)

Other characteristics such as veracity and value have been added to the definition by other researchers [4]. Veracity refers to the fact that the data has to be credible, accurate, and complete as well as suitable for the task. Since Big Data comes from different sources outside the control of organizations such as social media, veracity has become a real issue. Fake posts or spam are widespread and make establishing trust a major challenge. Value refers to the fact that the data has to be of value to the business. It adds the commercial aspect to the technical aspects of Big Data.

Data sources include the Internet, mobile devices, social media, geospatial devices, sensors, and other machine-generated data. Big Data is used for reporting, diagnosing, and decision making.

Traditional technologies for structured data using SQL-based RDBMS and data warehousing are not suitable for Big Data with high volume, velocity, and variety [4]. That is why often for Big Data NoSQL databases are used. There is no common definition for NoSQL in the literature. In general NoSQL databases embrace schemaless data and run on clusters. NoSQL databases have less constraints than relational databases. Usually they do not support the Structured Query Language (SQL) for querying the database. They often use key-value pairs, tuples, and JavaScript Object Notation (JSON) format to persist data.

Frameworks such as Apache's Hadoop have been emerging to process very large datasets effectively. It aims to allow programmers to focus on building applications that deal with processing large amount of data, without having to handle other issues when performing parallel computations [5]. In the past years, the Hadoop ecosystem has become the de facto standard to handle so-called Big Data [6].

One of the biggest data sources for Big Data is social media. Not surprisingly some of the technologies have been developed at social media companies such as Twitter, LinkedIn, and Facebook to meet their needs for high volume data processing.

BIG DATA TECHNOLOGIES

From an application perspective, Big Data technologies fall into two categories: systems with operational capabilities for real time, interactive workloads where data is primarily captured and stored, for example, NoSQL databases, and systems that provide analytical capabilities for retrospective, complex analysis that may touch most or all the data, for instance massive parallel processing (MPP) database systems and MapReduce. In practice both are often combined. That is why in this chapter Big Data technologies are divided into three categories: how Big Data is stored, how Big Data is processed in a parallel and distributed way, and how Big Data is analyzed.

There are many proposed reference architectures for Big Data. There is no one-size-fits-all solution and every architecture has its advantages and disadvantages. A high-level layer view is shown in Figure 6.2. It does not provide a conclusive list and serves as a scaffold to exemplify where the components described in this chapter might fit into an overall architecture. Some layers such as the management, monitoring, and security layer are not shown.

The data layer is where the data is processed using frameworks such as Hadoop, and data is stored using NoSQL databases such as MongoDB.

The integration layer is where the data is preprocessed, relevance filtered, and transferred. For instance Sqoop is designed to transfer bulk data and Flume for collecting, aggregating, and moving large amounts of log data. Both, Sqoop and Flume, are projects of the Apache Foundation.

Once the data has been prepared, it is ready to be looked at by the analytic layer. The data is visualized and analyzed for patterns using dashboards with slice-and-dice and search functionality. Tools such as Pentaho or QlikView provide this functionality. Big Data analysis is typically exploratory and iterative by nature.

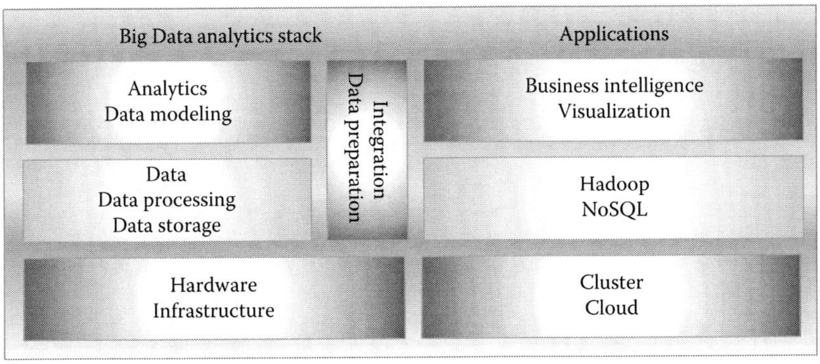

FIGURE 6.2 Big Data analytics stack.

Sometimes a predictive layer is added. Historic and real-time data is used to make predictions and identify risks and opportunities using machine learning techniques and business rules. In this chapter, it is considered part of the analytic layer.

This chapter describes the techniques and technologies of the data and the analytics layer. The hardware and integration layer are beyond the scope of this chapter.

NoSQL Databases

NoSQL databases are a form of non-relational database management systems. They are often schema-less, avoid joins, and scale easily. The term NoSQL is misleading since it implies that NoSQL databases do not support SQL. This is not necessarily true since some do support SQL-like query languages. NoSQL is thus sometimes referred to as "Not only SQL."

NoSQL databases are usually classified by their data model. There are different types of NoSQL databases. Some of the most widespread databases are

- Key-value store, for example, Dynamo, Riak, Scalaris, Voldemort

- Graph, for example, Neo4J, FlockDB, Allegro

- BigTable, for example, Accumulo, HBase, Hypertable

- Document, for example, CouchDB, ElasticSearch, MongoDB

Data Model
Key-value Store   Key-value pair databases are based on Amazon's Dynamo paper [7], for instance, Voldemort is a key-value pair database developed at LinkedIn. They store data as simple key-value pairs and data is retrieved when a key is known (Figure 6.3).

Key-value stores are one of the simplest forms of databases. They are often used as high performance in-process databases. For instance, a shopping cart at Amazon is stored in a key-value store.

Graph   The Graph DBs are inspired by the mathematical Graph theory and model data and their associations. Graph DBs contain nodes, properties and their relationships, the edges. A node can contain one to millions of values, called properties. Figure 6.4 shows nodes and their relations.

Key	Value
Name	Peter Wlodarczak
Occupation	Astronaut
Height	1.87 m

FIGURE 6.3   Key-value pair.

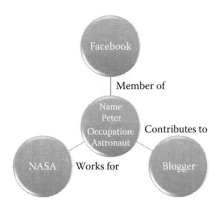

FIGURE 6.4   Graph database.

Nodes are organized with explicit relationships. The graph is queried with a traversal. An algorithm is traversing the graph from starting nodes to related nodes to answer questions of the form "what friends work for the same company like me."

Graph databases are optimized for highly connected data.

BigTable   BigTable or column families of DBs are based on Googles BigTable paper [8]. BigTable is a distributed storage system for managing structured data that is designed to scale to a very large size: petabytes of data across thousands of commodity servers [8]. A table in BigTable is a multidimensional map. In a cluster environment, it is distributed over the nodes. Data is organized in three dimensions, rows, columns, and timestamps. The basic storage unit is a cell, referenced by row key, column key, and timestamp. BigTable can have multiple timestamp version of data within a cell. Figure 6.5 shows a sample column family table.

BigTable can be regarded as a database with dynamic schemas.

Document Store   Document store databases such as MongoDB or CoucheDB store data as whole documents. A document can be almost in any form and most document-oriented databases accept different formats and encapsulate them in an internal format. XML and JSON are popular formats. A sample JSON is shown in Figure 6.6.

Column family: user

Rowid	Column name	Timestamp	Column value
u1	Name	v1	Peter
u1	Email	v1	peter@gmail.com
u1	Email	v2	peter@nasa.org
u2	Name	v1	John
u2	Phone	v1	640-43562

FIGURE 6.5   BigTable.

```
{
  "firstName": "Peter",
  "occupation": "Astronaut",
  "isAlive": true,
  "address": {
    "streetAddress": "22 Jump Street",
    "city": "New York",
  },
  "phoneNumbers": [
    {
      "type": "home",
      "number": "212 555-1234"
    },
    {
      "type": "office",
      "number": "646 555-4567"
    }
  ]
}
```

FIGURE 6.6   JSON sample.

The structure in a document database is usually flexible; a second JSON document in a database might have more or less entries. It can be processed directly by the application, no client-side processing is required.

Other Characteristics   NoSQL databases have a simpler design than RDBMS which makes them faster for certain operations. Accessing NoSQL databases is also easier since no complex SQL queries have to be submitted. They often support their own, simpler query language and offer application programming interfaces (APIs) for different programing languages such as Java or Python.

NoSQL databases are usually distributed across multiple nodes for high availability and scale horizontally. When one node fails, another node takes over without interruption or data loss. Most NoSQL databases usually do not support real ACID (Atomicity, Consistency, Isolation, Durability) transactions. They sacrifice consistency in favor of high availability and partition tolerance.

Hadoop

Hadoop MapReduce has become one of the most popular tools for data processing [9]. Hadoop is an open-source parallel distributed programming framework based on the popular MapReduce framework from Google [5]. Hadoop MapReduce has evolved to an important industry standard for massive parallel data processing and has become widely adopted for a variety of use-cases [10]. However, there are alternatives such as Apache Spark, HPCC Systems, or Apache Flink.

Hadoop, originally developed by Yahoo! [11], is used by Facebook [12], Amazon, eBay, Yahoo! [13], and IBM [14] to name a few.

Hadoop is normally installed on a cluster of computers [9]. Hadoop provides a distributed file system and a framework for the analysis and transformation of very large data

Hadoop V1	Hadoop V2
MapReduce Resource management Data processing	MapReduce Data processing
	YARN Resource management
HDFS Distributed redundant storage	HDFS Distributed redundant storage

FIGURE 6.7   Hadoop V1 versus Hadoop V2.

sets using the MapReduce paradigm [11]. The distributed file system, the HDFS, is at the storage level, MapReduce at the execution level.

MapReduce and the HDFS are the core components of Hadoop. Other components are Hadoop Common, the common utilities that support the other Hadoop modules and Hadoop YARN for job scheduling and cluster resource management [15].

With the release of version 2 of Hadoop, the workload management has been decoupled from MapReduce and Yet Another Resource Negotiator (YARN) has taken over this functionality. Figure 6.7 shows the two Hadoop versions.

MapReduce

MapReduce is based on a paper by Google [16]. MapReduce uses a "divide and conquer" strategy. A Hadoop job consists of two steps, a map step and a reduce step. There can be optionally steps before and between the map and reduce steps. The map step reads in data in the form of key/value pairs, processes it, and emits a set of zero or more key/value pairs. For example, in a text mining task, the parsing and preprocessing is done in the map step. The output is passed to the reduce step, where a number of reducers compute an aggregated, reduced set of data such as the word count and frequency, again as key/value pair. Figure 6.8 shows the Hadoop processing steps.

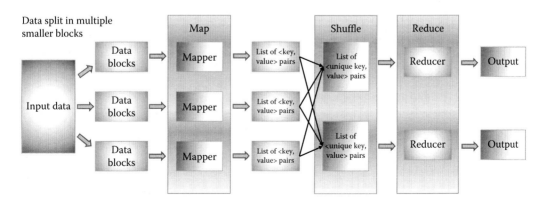

FIGURE 6.8   Hadoop processing steps.

YARN

Hadoop has undergone a major rework from version 1 to 2. The resource management has been separated out into YARN. YARN or MapReduce 2.0 consists of a global resource manager and a per-node slave, the node manager. The resource manager arbitrates the resources among all applications whereas the per-application Application Master (App Msr) negotiates the resource manager and works with the node manager to execute and monitor tasks.

The resource manager consists of an applications manager and a scheduler. The scheduler is responsible for allocating resources such as queues to the running applications. The applications manager accepts job-submissions, negotiates the first container for executing the Application Master and restarts it in case of failure.

The node manager is a per-machine agent. It is responsible for containers, monitoring their resource usage such as CPU, memory, and disk space and reporting to the resource manager and scheduler. Figure 6.9 shows the interactions of the YARN components.

Hadoop Distributed File System

HDFS is designed to store very large data sets reliably, and to stream those data sets at high bandwidth to user applications [11]. HDFS stores data across the cluster so that it appears as one contiguous volume. It also provides redundancy and fault tolerance. HDFS looks like a single storage volume and has been optimized for many serialized, concurrent reads of large files. HDFS supports only a single writer and random access is not really possible in an efficient way. There are replacement file systems that support full random-access read/

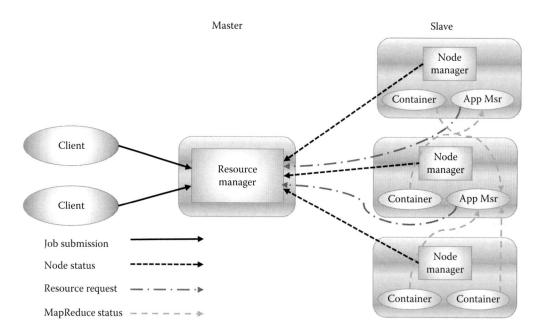

FIGURE 6.9 YARN. (Adapted from Thusoo, A. et al., Data Warehousing and Analytics Infrastructure at Facebook, in *Proceedings of the 2010 ACM SIGMOD International Conference on Management of Data*, Indianapolis, Indiana, USA, 2010, pp. 1013–1020.)

write functionality such as MapR Direct Access NFS [17] or IBM's General Parallel File System (GPFS) that can be used with Hadoop instead [18].

While the interface to HDFS is patterned after the UNIX file system, faithfulness to standards was sacrificed in favor of improved performance for the applications at hand [11]. Application data and file system metadata are stored separately. Application data is stored on DataNodes, metadata is stored on NameNodes. All nodes are connected and use TCP-based protocols to communicate among each other.

HDFS breaks files up into blocks and stores them on different file system nodes. Since the blocks are replicated across different nodes, failure of one node is a minor issue. HDFS re-replicates another copy of the block to re-establish the desired number of blocks.

The Hadoop ecosystem provides supporting analysis technologies that include the following:

- Apache Hive, a simple SQL-like interface

- Apache Pig, a high-level scripting language

- Apache Mahout, a data mining framework

The Apache ecosystem is shown in Figure 6.10. It is not a comprehensive list of Apache projects.

Hadoop is a complex system. It is difficult to program and needs skilled developers and data scientists to be properly used.

Big Data Analytics

There is no clear distinction between Big Data and data mining in literature. Data mining is the analytic process of exploring data to detect patterns and relationships and then applying the detected patterns to new data. Sometimes data mining is seen as focusing on the predictive rather than the descriptive side. However, data mining techniques such as association rule mining and sequential pattern mining also aim to understand relationships between data. Here, data mining is considered as an analytic step of Big Data.

Data Mining

Data mining is also called knowledge discovery in databases (KDD) [19]. Data mining is defined as the process of discovering patterns in data [20]. The data sources include

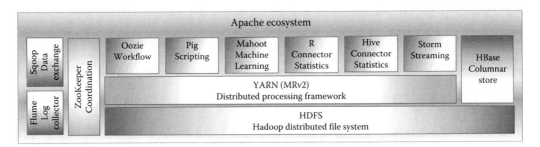

FIGURE 6.10   Apache ecosystem.

databases, the Web, texts, multimedia content, and machine-generated data such as sensor data. Examples of patterns are correlations between genomes and diseases to predict possible illnesses or seismic activities to detect new oil sources. Data mining is a multidisciplinary field in the areas of statistics, databases, machine learning, artificial intelligence, information retrieval, and visualization.

Data mining goes through several steps. They are divided into a data conditioning or data preprocessing phase and a data analysis phase. The data conditioning phase consists of a data collection and filtering step and a step where the predictor variables are elaborated. The analysis phase comprises a model selection step and a step where the performance of the model is evaluated. The data preprocessing techniques depend on the data that is being mined, whether it is text data, financial or sensor data and what it is being mined for. Text can be mined for instance for opinions or for spam to filter out junk mail. Sensor data can be mined for possible malfunctions or fatigue of parts that need to be replaced. Figure 6.11 shows the data mining process.

The data mining process usually starts with understanding the application domain and selecting suitable data sources for data collection and the target data.

The collected data is usually not in a suitable form for data mining. It has to go through a cleaning process. In the preprocessing step, irrelevant data such as stop words, noise, and abnormalities are removed and the attribute and features are selected. For instance, in opinion mining features can be frequencies of sentiment words like how often does a word such as "great" or "excellent" appear in a text? Preparing input for a data mining investigation usually consumes the bulk of the effort invested in the entire data mining process [20]. Data preprocessing is highly domain specific and beyond the scope of this chapter.

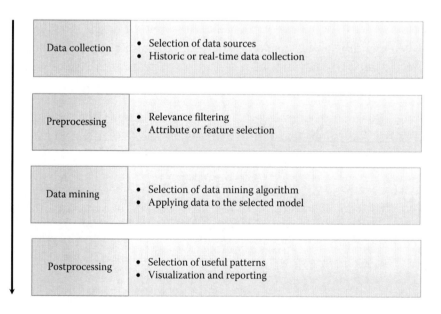

FIGURE 6.11   Data mining process.

In the data mining step, the preprocessed data is fed into a data mining algorithm. Usually, several algorithms are tested and the best performing one is being selected. The data mining step produces patterns or knowledge.

Postprocessing involves identifying the useful patterns for the application and visualizing the patterns for reporting and decision making.

There are many data mining techniques. Some of the more common ones are supervised and unsupervised learning, association rule mining, and sequential pattern. These techniques will be covered in the next chapters.

Supervised Learning   Analogous to human learning, machine learning can be defined as gaining knowledge from past experiences to perform better in future tasks. Since computers do not have experiences like humans, machine learning learns from data collected in the past. A typical application of machine learning are spam filters. They classify emails into legitimate and unsolicited bulk emails, "spam" or "junk mail." They have to adapt, to learn, to detect new forms of spam. Machine learning is a subfield of Artificial Intelligence. One form of machine learning is supervised learning.

Supervised learning is also called classification or inductive learning [19]. Supervised learning methods are used when the class label is known. For instance, text documents can be classified into different topics: politics, sciences, or arts. Here, the class is the topic and the class label are the values "politics," "sciences" and "arts." The classifier uses attributes as input. Attributes can be frequencies of words when classifying text documents or the age, income, and wealth of a person when classifying loan applications into "approved" or "rejected." Supervised learning is often used in predictive analysis, "namely, learning a target function that can be used to predict the values of a discrete class attribute" [19].

Given a data set D, which are described by a set of attributes $A = \{A_1, A_2, ..., A_{|A|}\}$, where $|A|$ denotes the number of attributes, and has a target attribute C, which is called the class attribute and has a set of discrete values, $C = \{c_1, c_2, ..., c_{|c|}\}$ where $|C|$ is the number of classes and $|C| \geq 2$, the objective is to find a function f to relate values of attributes in A and classes in C. f is the classification/prediction function or model or simply the classifier. The function can be of any form, for instance a Bayesian model, a decision tree, or a neural network. It is called supervised learning because the class labels C are provided in the data. In unsupervised learning, the classes are unknown and the learning algorithm needs to generate the classes.

For supervised learning methods, data is typically divided into training and test data. The training data is used to build the model. The model is trained using a training algorithm. Learning is the process of building the model. The test data is used to evaluate the trained models accuracy. To assess the model, the test data usually has class labels too.

Usually the training goes through several iterations until the classification accuracy converges. The resulting classifier is used to assign class labels to unseen data where the class label is unknown. The accuracy is defined as

$$\text{Accuracy} = \frac{\text{Number of correct classifications}}{\text{Total number of test cases}} \quad (6.1)$$

A correct classification means that the learned model predicts the same class label as the original class provided in the test data. Figure 6.12 shows the learning steps.

In the training step, a learning algorithm uses the training data to generate the classification model. In the testing step, the test data is used to evaluate the accuracy of the classification model. If it is satisfactory, it can be applied to real world, unseen, data. If it is not, a different learning algorithm can be chosen or the data can be preprocessed again (not shown in the figure). Experience shows that no single machine learning scheme is appropriate to all data mining problems [20]. For instance a different algorithm, k-nearest neighbor instead of naïve Bayesian is used or a different set of attributes A can be selected and the training and testing steps are performed again. Typically, a practical learning task goes through many iterations until a satisfactory result is achieved. It is possible that no satisfactory result can be achieved due to the poor quality of the data or the limitations of the learning algorithms.

Unsupervised Learning   Unsupervised learning is used when the class label is not known. Unsupervised learning methods generally are methods used to find patterns in the covariate or input landscape, irrespective of the outcome(s) of interest [21]. In supervised learning, attributes are related to class attributes, the class labels. Unsupervised techniques are used for data that has no class attributes. They are used if the user wants to understand the data and find some intrinsic structure in them. Clustering is a typical unsupervised learning technology. It organizes data instances into similarity groups, called clusters such that the data instances in the same cluster are similar to each other and data instances in different clusters are very different from each other [19]. Clustering provides a description of the data using some similarity criteria. Figure 6.13 shows a two-dimensional representation of three clusters.

In real-world applications, clusters are often not as well separated as in Figure 6.13 and automated techniques have to be used. Two popular methods are hierarchical clustering and k-means clustering. The basic concept is that of distance, how close or similar two instances are. Common measures of distances are the Euclidean distance, the Manhattan distance, and the Chebychev distance.

In hierarchical clustering, the data is progressively split into groups (divisive or top-down clustering) or incorporated into a group (agglomerative or bottom-up clustering) and typically represented by a dendrogram. In k-means clustering the number of groups is fixed a priori, the k in k-means.

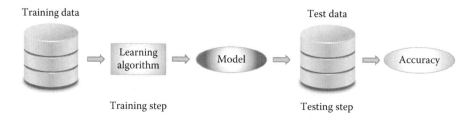

FIGURE 6.12   Learning process.

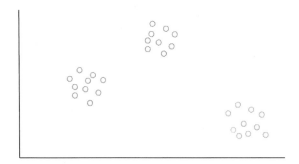

FIGURE 6.13   Clusters of data points.

Semisupervised Learning   Recently, researchers have begun to explore territory between the two, sometimes called semisupervised learning, in which the goal is classification but the input contains both unlabeled and labeled data [20]. In some cases a small set of labeled data and a large set of unlabeled data exist, for instance, text classification of Web pages where the labeling is typically done manually. This is a time-consuming task when the number of Web pages is large. Clustering can be used to some extent, but it does not guarantee the categorization results required. Unlabeled data such as online news articles can be classified using word frequencies. For instance, an article containing the words "Picasso" and "painting" several times can be classified into "art." The joint probability distribution over words is used to classify unlabeled data.

In semisupervised learning, the algorithm is trained with a small set of labeled data. First, a classifier such as the naïve Bayes classifier is trained using a set of labeled data. Second, the unlabeled data is applied to the trained model and labeled with class probabilities. As with supervised learning, a second algorithm can be trained and the results can be compared. Semisupervised learning is a combination of supervised and unsupervised learning. It works with any classifier and any iterative clustering algorithm. As with supervised and unsupervised learning, it typically goes through many iterations until the best results are achieved.

Association Rules and Sequential Patterns   Association rules are no different from classification rules except that they can predict any attribute, not just the class, and this gives them the freedom to predict combinations of attributes too [20]. Association rule mining finds strong associations between different attribute values. Its objective is to find all co-occurrence relationships, called associations, among data items [19].

A classic application of association rule mining is market basket analysis. Market basket analysis aims to discover how items purchased by customers are associated. Given a group of items $I = \{i_1, i_2, ..., i_n\}$, and transactions $T = \{t_1, t_2, ..., t_n\}$, where each transaction t_i is a set of items such that $t_i \subseteq I$, an association rule is an implication of the form:

$$X \rightarrow Y, \quad \text{where} \quad X \subset I, \quad Y \subset I, \quad \text{and} \quad X \cap Y = \varnothing$$

X and Y are an itemset. For example, an item can be an object purchased or an article read online. For a retailer, a transaction is a purchase of a customer or for a publisher a transaction is the group of articles read on a single visit. A rule would then be

$$\{peanuts, \ potato \ chips\} \Rightarrow \{beer\}$$

This rule says that customers who purchase peanuts and potato chips are likely also to be interested in buying beer. The strength of the rule is measured by its support and confidence. The support of the rule $X \rightarrow Y$ is the fraction of transactions T that contain X. It is expressed as the percentage of transactions in T that contain $X \cup Y$. The confidence of the rule $X \rightarrow Y$ is the percentage of transactions in T that contain X also contain Y.

Association rule mining is a very general model and can be used in many applications. It typically contains many rules. However, it does not consider the sequence in which items are purchased. That is what sequential rule mining is used for. For instance, it finds linguistic patterns from natural language texts or clickstreams from server logs. A sequential rule is an implication of the form $X \rightarrow Y$, where X is a subsequence of sequence Y. The support of sequence $X \rightarrow Y$ rule is the fraction of sequences in a sequence database S that contains Y. The confidence of a sequence rule is the proportion of sequences in S that contain X also contain Y.

Implementations   There are commercial as well as open source tools that implement Big Data analytics. IBMs SPSS data analysis tool is an industry independent solution for statistical data analysis and data management [22]. SPSS Modeler has implementations of all common data mining algorithms, statistical analysis and social network analysis and can be used for text and entity analytics, predictive analysis and to support decision making and optimization.

Similar functionality is provided by the SAS Enterprise Miner. It provides a graphical user interface for the SAS Programming Language for users without programming experience. It provides descriptive as well as predictive modeling capabilities to support decision making [23]. It has implementations of all common data mining algorithms such as decision trees, neural networks, and time series data mining and provides visualization and reporting functionality.

Implementations of data mining, statistics, data and predictive analytics, decision support, and visualization are also provided by Dell subsidiary StatSofts STATISTICA [24].

Partly open source, RapidMiner provides an integrated environment for data and text mining, machine learning, predictive and business analytics [25]. It supports all data mining steps including visualization and no programming is required.

There are also open source implementations such as Waikato Environment for Knowledge Analysis (WEKA) and Apache Mahout. WEKA is free open source software under the GNU General Public License [26]. WEKA has data preprocessing capabilities and implementations of most relevant machine learning algorithms. It can compare the performance of different learning methods so the best algorithm can be chosen. WEKA is suitable for Big Data. For large data sets, the work load can be distributed across multiple machines.

Apache Mahout is a machine learning tool that has implementations for classification, clustering, and collaborative filtering [27]. It can run on distributed systems and provides math functionality such as statistics and linear algebra. It runs on top of Apaches Hadoop using its map/reduce paradigm. However, it is not limited to Hadoop-based implementations and can run on other platforms.

FUTURE DEVELOPMENT

The data volumes created each year grow exponentially. They reached 2.8 zettabytes in 2012, a number that is as gigantic as it sounds, and will double again by 2015 [28]. The technologies to process these amounts of data have to scale and supercomputers have been emerging to provide the computing power needed. Also real-time data analysis is becoming increasingly important. Hadoop is batch oriented and a simple query might take minutes to return and thus is not suitable for real-time operations. The real-time computation system Storm, acquired by Twitter and now an open source project at the Apache Foundation, was developed to process unbounded streams of data and can be used with any programing language [29]. It is fault tolerant, scalable and can process one million tuples per second and node.

To provide the needed performance in-memory databases, also called memory resident databases, have been developed. They primarily use a computer's main memory for data storage rather than the slower disk storage subsystem. They are used for applications where response time is critical like in real-time analytics.

Similarly in-memory distributed data grids use data caching mechanisms to improve performance and scalability. For instance, the Hadoop MapReduce engine can be cached into memory for fast execution. New caching nodes can be added if more processing power is needed.

Complex Event Processing (CEP) is a method for tracking and analyzing data streams for events that are happening by combining data from multiple sources. It is used to identify events such as opportunities or threads. The large amounts of information about events available is called the event cloud. By analyzing and correlating events, complex events can be discovered. CEP is used in fraud detection, stock-trading, and business activity and security monitoring.

BigData has also been moving to the cloud offering data analysis in a data science as a service paradigm (DSaaS). DSaaS lets users focus on the analysis task without being concerned by the underlying platforms or technologies. One BigData cloud solution is Google's BigQuery [30]. It lets the user upload the data into BigQuery and analyze it using SQL-like queries. BigQuery can be accessed through the browser, a command-line tool or the Representational State Transfer Application Programming Interface (REST API) using the Java, PHP, or Python programming language.

As cloud computing has become a mainstream trend in computing, it is expected to see more cloud-based BigData solutions in the near future.

REFERENCES

1. V. Mayer-Schonberger, and K. Cukier, *Big Data: A Revolution That Will Transform How We Live, Work, and Think*, New York, USA: Houghton Mifflin Harcourt Publishing Company, 2013.
2. A. Twinkle, and S. Paul, Addressing big data with Hadoop, *International Journal of Computer Science and Mobile Computing*, 3(2), 459–462, 2014.

3. D. Klein, P. Tran-Gia, and M. Hartmann, Big Data, *Informatik-Spektrum*, 36(3), 319–323, 2013.

4. J. O. Chan, An architecture for big data analytics, *Communications of the IIMA,* 13(2), 1–13, 2013.

5. Y. S. Tan, J. Tan, E. S. Chng, B.-S. Lee, J. Li, S. Date, H. P. Chak, X. Xiao, and A. Narishige, Hadoop framework: Impact of data organization on performance, *Software: Practice and Experience,* 43(11), 1241–1260, 2013.

6. J. Dittrich, S. Richter, and S. Schuh, Efficient or Hadoop: Why not both? *Datenbank-Spektrum,* 13(1), 17–22, 2013/03/01, 2013.

7. G. DeCandia, D. Hastorun, M. Jampani, G. Kakulapati, A. Lakshman, A. Pilchin, S. Sivasubramanian, P. Vosshall, and W. Vogels, Dynamo: Amazon's highly available key-value store, *SIGOPS Operating Systems Review,* 41(6), 205–220, 2007.

8. F. Chang, J. Dean, S. Ghemawat, W. C. Hsieh, D. A. Wallach, M. Burrows, T. Chandra, A. Fikes, and R. E. Gruber, Bigtable: A distributed storage system for structured data, *ACM Transactions on Computer Systems,* 26(2), 1–26, 2008.

9. I. Tomasic, A. Rashkovska, and M. Depolli, Using Hadoop MapReduce in a multicluster environment. 36th International Convention on Information & Communication Technology Electronics & Microelectronics (MIPRO), http://ieeexplore.ieee.org/xpl/login. jsp?tp=&arnumber=6596280&url=http%3A%2F%2Fieeexplore.ieee.org%2Fxpls%2Fabs_all. jsp%3Farnumber%3D6596280, 345–350, 2013.

10. S. Richter, J.-A. Quiané-Ruiz, S. Schuh, and J. Dittrich, Towards zero-overhead static and adaptive indexing in Hadoop, *The VLDB Journal,* 23(3), 469–494, 2014/06/01, 2014.

11. K. Shvachko, K. Hairong, S. Radia, and R. Chansler, The Hadoop distributed file system. IEEE 26th Symposium on Mass Storage Systems and Technologies (MSST), http://ieeexplore.ieee.org/xpl/login.jsp?tp=&arnumber=5496972&url=http%3A%2F%2Fieeexplore.ieee.org%2Fxpls%2Fabs_all.jsp%3Farnumber%3D5496972, 1–10, 2010.

12. A. Thusoo, Z. Shao, S. Anthony, D. Borthakur, N. Jain, J. S. Sarma, R. Murthy, and H. Liu, Data warehousing and analytics infrastructure at facebook, in *Proceedings of the 2010 ACM SIGMOD International Conference on Management of data*, Indianapolis, Indiana, USA, 2010, pp. 1013–1020.

13. J. Vijayan, Hadoop works alongside RDBMS, *Computerworld,* 45(15), 5–5, 2011.

14. P. Zikopoulos, D. deRoos, K. Parasuraman, T. Deutsch, J. Giles, and D. Corrigan, *Harness the Power of Big Data: The IBM Big Data Platform*, McGraw-Hill Osborne Media, New York, USA, 2012.

15. "Welcome to Apache™ Hadoop®!," 19. September 2014, 2014; http://hadoop.apache.org/.

16. J. Dean, and S. Ghemawat, MapReduce: Simplified Data Processing on Large Clusters, *OSDI* 2004.

17. MapR. MapR Direct Access NFS, https://www.mapr.com/sites/default/files/mapr-tech-brief-direct-access-nfs-2.pdf.

18. W. Frings, and M. Hennecke, A system level view of Petascale I/O on IBM Blue Gene/P, *Computer Science—Research and Development,* 26(3–4), 275–283, 2011/06/01, 2011.

19. B. Liu, *Web Data Mining: Exploring Hyperlinks, Contents, and Usage Data,* 2nd ed., Heidelberg: Springer, 2011.

20. I. H. Witten, E. Frank, and M. A. Hall, *Data Mining,* 3rd ed., Burlington, MA, USA: Elsevier, 2011.

21. A. Dasgupta, Y. V. Sun, I. R. König, J. E. Bailey-Wilson, and J. D. Malley, Brief review of regression-based and machine learning methods in genetic epidemiology: The Genetic Analysis Workshop 17 experience, *Genetic Epidemiology,* 35(S1), S5–S11, 2011.

22. SPSS Modeler, 18 September, 2014; http://www-01.ibm.com/software/analytics/spss/products/modeler/.

23. SAS Enterprise Miner, 18 September, 2014; http://www.sas.com/en_us/software/analytics/enterprise-miner.html.
24. STATISTICA Features Overview, 18 September, 2014; http://www.statsoft.com/Products/STATISTICA-Features.
25. RapidMiner, 18 September, 2014; http://rapidminer.com/products/rapidminer-studio/.
26. Weka 3: Data Mining Software in Java, 18. September, 2014; http://www.cs.waikato.ac.nz/ml/weka/.
27. Mahout, 19 September, 2014; https://mahout.apache.org/.
28. P. Tucker, Has big data made anonymity impossible? *MIT Technology Review*, 116(4), 2013.
29. Storm, 19 September, 2014; https://storm.incubator.apache.org/.
30. Google BigQuery, 19 September, 2014; https://developers.google.com/bigquery/what-is-bigquery.

CHAPTER 7

Network Configuration and Flow Scheduling for Big Data Applications

Lautaro Dolberg, Jérôme François, Shihabur Rahman Chowdhury, Reaz Ahmed, Raouf Boutaba, and Thomas Engel

CONTENTS

INTRODUCTION

Big Data applications play a crucial role in our evolving society. They represent a large proportion of the usage of the cloud [1–3] because the latter offers distributed and online storage and elastic computing services. Indeed, Big Data applications require to scale computing and storage requirements on the fly. With the recent improvements of virtual computing, data centers can thus offer a virtualized infrastructure in order to fit custom requirements. This flexibility has been a decisive enabler for the Big Data application success of the recent years. As an example, many Big Data applications rely, directly or indirectly, on Apache Hadoop [11] which is the most popular implementation of the MapReduce programming

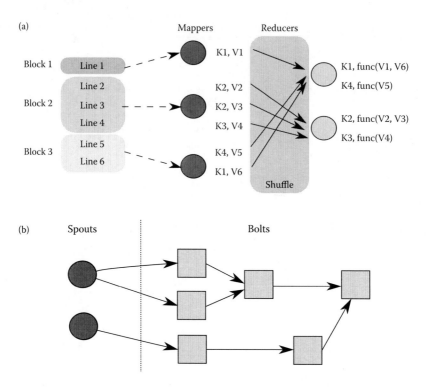

FIGURE 7.1 Big Data computational model and the underlying network traffic as plain arrows: (a) MapReduce with K as key and V as value; (b) Storm.

model [4]. From a general perspective, it consists in distributing computing tasks between mappers and reducers. Mappers produce intermediate results which are aggregated in a second stage by reducers. This process is illustrated in Figure 7.1a, where the mappers send partial results (values) to specific reducers based on some keys. The reducers are then in charge of applying a function (like sum, average, or other aggregation function) to the whole set of values corresponding to a single key. This architectural pattern is fault tolerant and scalable. Another interesting feature of this paradigm is the execution environment of the code. In Hadoop, the code is directly executed near the data it operates on, in order to limit the data transfer within the cluster. However, large chunks of data are still transferred between the mappers and reducers (shuffle phase) which thus necessitate an efficient underlying network infrastructure. It is important to note that the shuffle phase does not wait for the completion of the mappers to start as the latter already emits (key, value) pairs based on partial data it has read from the source (e.g., for each line). Since some failures or bottlenecks can occur, Hadoop tasks are constantly monitored. If one of the components (i.e., mappers or reducers) is not functioning well (i.e., it does not progress as fast as others for example), it can be duplicated into another node for balancing load. In such a case, this leads also to additional data transfers.

Storm [5] is another approach that aims at streaming data analytics, while Hadoop was originally designed for batch processing. Storm consists of spouts and bolts. Spouts read a data source to generate tuples and emit them toward bolts. Bolts are responsible for processing the tuples and eventually emit new tuples toward other bolts. Therefore, a Storm application is generally represented by a graph as shown in Figure 7.1b. The main difference between Storm and MapReduce is that data transfers occur all the time (streaming) and so are not limited to a specific phase (shuffle phase in Hadoop). As a result, among the diversity in Big Data applications, there are common problems, in particular optimizing the data transfer rate between host.

Therefore, while Big Data technological improvements were mainly highlighted by new computing design and approaches, like Hadoop, network optimizations are primordial to guarantee high performances. This chapter reviews existing approaches to configure network and schedule flows in such a context. In the following sections, we will cover the diverse optimization methods grouped according to their intrinsic features and their contributions. In particular, recent network technologies such as Software-Defined Networking (SDN) empowered the programmability of switching devices. Consequently, more complex network scheduling algorithms can be afforded to leverage the performance of MapReduce jobs. That is why this chapter focuses on SDN-based solutions but also introduces common networking approaches which could be applied as well as virtualization techniques. The latter are strongly coupled with the network design. For example, end-hosts in a data center are virtual machines (VMs) which can be assigned to different tasks and so would lead to various traffic types, which can be better handled if the network is adaptive and therefore easily reconfigurable.

This chapter is structured as follows:

1. *Optimization of the VM placement*: even if not dealing with network configuration, it has a significant impact on the same;

2. *Topology design*: it is an important topic as the way the machines are wired have an impact on performance;

3. *Conventional networking, in particular routing and Quality of Service (QoS) scheduling*: these might be customized to support Big Data as well.

4. *SDN*: this highlights recent approaches that leverage a global view of the network to implement efficient traffic management policies.

VM PLACEMENT FOR REDUCING ELEPHANT FLOW IMPACT

Very large flows, normally associated to long MapReduce jobs, are often called Elephant Flows [6]. Since any VM can be potentially hosted in any physical server, grouping VM that are involved in large data transfers can reduce the impact on the overall bandwidth usage of the network. This approach is based on the internal routing of Hypervisor systems used in virtualized data centers such as XEN [7], KVM [8], or VMWare [9] solutions. From a more general point of view, VMs can be colocated in a certain region of a network, even if on different physical machines. This is illustrated in Figure 7.2 where in the case of the original allocations (Figure 7.2a), the tasks of the same job are scattered in the network and so the traffic between them has to go through many hops eventually resulting in network

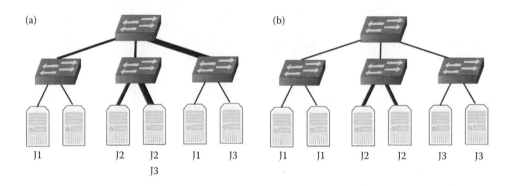

FIGURE 7.2   VM placement with three jobs (each job JI has two tasks). The width of a link represents its load. (a) Initial task allocation, and (b) optimized task allocation.

congestion. In Figure 7.2b, by moving only two tasks (one from J1 and one from J3), each job is isolated in a single rack (under a single switch) and so no congestion occurs at higher level switches while improving the data transfer efficiency between tasks of the same job since these are connected through a single switch.

VM placement is basically related to VM allocation problems, which are optimization problems under certain criteria. One of the criterion should be the usage of network resources. Because this is not the focus of this chapter, we recommend the reader to read Reference 10 for more details about network-aware VM placement.

The downside of existing network-aware VM placement approaches is that they lack the reactiveness. Normally, given the nature of MapReduce phases, it is not possible to exactly match in advance MapReduce jobs and needed network resources (e.g., how large the data transfer will be during the shuffle phase depends on the underlying data and applications). To cope with this practical issue, virtualized data centers may estimate the VM-to-VM traffic matrix but such a method works well with a known batch job only. Another solution is to migrate VMs during their execution, but this might be also resource consuming and negatively impact the finishing time of the Big Data jobs if this occurs too frequently.

TOPOLOGY DESIGN

Data-centers networks are usually organized in a tree topology [11,12] with three defined layers:

- *Core layer*: This layer is the backbone of the network where high-end switches and fibers are deployed. In this layer only L2 forwarding takes place without any packet manipulation. The equipment for this layer is the more expensive among the hierarchical network model.

- *Aggregation or distribution layer*: In this layer most of the L3 routing takes place.

- *Access layer*: This layer provides connectivity to the end nodes and so are located at the top of the racks. They perform the last step of L3 packet routing and packet manipulation. Normally, these are the cheapest devices in the hierarchical network model.

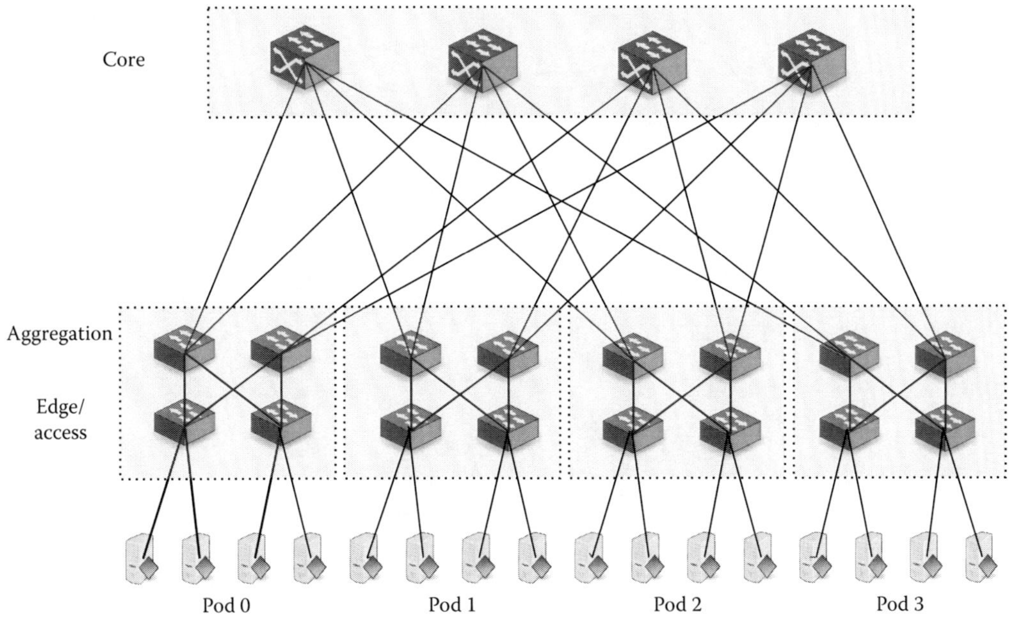

FIGURE 7.3 Example of a hierarchical network model: Multirooted network topology.

Thanks to this hierarchical model, a low latency is achieved for traffic between two nodes in the same rack. This explains why approaches like Hadoop leverage rack awareness to ensure fast replication of data by selecting nodes in the same rack for copying data (but also others out of the rack in order to guarantee data availability under a rack failure). In addition, this type of configuration supports a large number of ports at the access layer. A specific instance of the hierarchical model is the fat tree proposed in Al-Fares et al. [3] and illustrated in Figure 7.3, which enables fault-tolerance by ensuring redundant paths in a deterministic manner. The fat-tree or Clos topology was introduced more than 25 years ago [13] to reduce the cost of telephony-switched networks. The topology layout is organized as k-ary trees, where in every branch of the tree there are k switches, grouped in pods. Actually, a pod consists in $(k/2)^2$ end-hosts and $k/2$ switches. At the edge level, switches must have at least k ports connected as follows: half of the ports are assigned to end nodes and the other half is connected to the upper aggregation layer of switches. In total, the topology supports $(k^2/2)$ k-port switches for connecting host nodes.

DCell [14] is a recursively interconnected architecture proposed by Microsoft. Compared to a fat-tree topology, DCell is a fully interconnected graph in order to be largely fault tolerant even under several link failures. In fact, high-level DCell nodes are recursively connected to low level ones, implemented with mini switches to scale out as shown in Figure 7.4.

Experimental results have showed that a 20 nodes network can twice outperform a large data center used for MapReduce. As a downside, DCell requires a full degree of connectivity, making it in practice costly to maintain and deploy. To enhance network connectivity between servers, CamCube [15] is a torus topology where each server is interconnected to

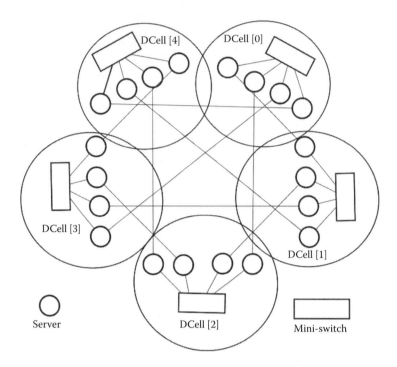

FIGURE 7.4 A DCell topology for five cells of level 0, each containing four servers. (From Guo, C. et al., in *Conference on Data Communication*, SIGCOMM, ACM, 2008.)

other six servers and all communications go through them, without any switch for internal communication. Finally, recent propositions like Singla et al. [16] promote a high flexibility by alleviating the need for a well-defined fixed graph structure, as the fat trees are, and do so by introducing some randomness in the topology bounded by some criteria.

CONVENTIONAL NETWORKING

Routing

Data-center network topologies like fat trees imply a large number of links leading to redundant paths. Therefore, routing algorithms can take that benefit to achieve a higher bandwidth. As an illustrative example in Figure 7.5a, the shortest path is used to route the traffic between the two tasks of the job J1. Unfortunately, it goes through a congested link. Hence, a redundant path can be used (Figure 7.5b) and even multiple of them conjointly (Figure 7.5a). Although these approaches have been proposed for routing in general, they are also used in data-centers to improve the performance of the Big Data applications. This is the reason why this section covers some propositions about how to use these principles in case of Big Data. However, the general issues are (1) to predict the traffic patterns and (2) to be able to rapidly change the configuration of the routing when the traffic suddenly changes, which is the case in a cloud infrastructure.

Nowadays, a major representative of such an approach is the equal cost multipath (ECMP) algorithm [17]. ECMP leverages the opportunity to route flows among multiple paths. Unlike traditional routing algorithms like OSPF which consider a single best path,

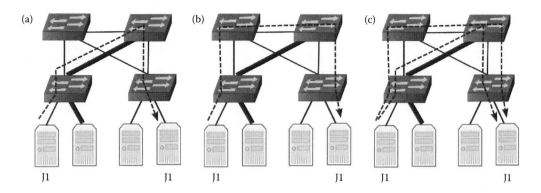

FIGURE 7.5 Routing decisions for one job with two tasks. The width of a link represents its load. (a) Shortest path routing, (b) high throughput, and (c) multipath routing.

ECMP considers all the best multipaths according to any metric (as, e.g., the number of hops) among which a single one is selected for a given flow through a load balancer. The number of multiple paths is dependent on the router implementation but is usually bounded to 16. Hence, this may yield a lower performance than expected for large data-centers. In fact, the amount of entries in the routing tables grows at an exponential rate, increasing the latency of the routing algorithm. Commercial solutions promoting multipath routing include FabricPath by Cisco Systems, BCube, VL2, and Oracle Sun data-center InfiniBand.

In addition to promoting the fat-tree topology usage for data-centers, Al-Fares et al. [3] proposed a dedicated routing algorithm based on an approach called Two-Level Routing Tables, where the routing tables are split into two hierarchical tables linked on the prefix length of the network address. A two layer table approach aims at leveraging the routing algorithm speed for establishing a route. This is possible because the authors introduced a private addressing system respecting a pre-established pattern like 8.pod.switch.host assuming a class A network. The first table index entries use a left-handed prefix length (e.g., 8.1.2.0/24, 8.1.1.0/24). The entries of the first table are linked to a smaller secondary table indexed by a right-handed suffix (e.g., 0.0.0.1/4, 0.0.0.4/4). For example, to find the route to the address 8.8.8.8, the algorithm will look up the first table, find the corresponding entry for the first part of the network address 8.8.8.0/24, then jumps to the secondary table and finds the remainder of the route. Since each switch of the aggregation layer in a fat-tree topology has always a $k/2°$ of connectivity to the access layer, Two-Level Routing Tables are bounded in the worst case to $k/2$ entries for suffixes and prefixes. Moreover, flows can be actually classified by duration and size. Then, the proposed algorithm in Al-Fares et al. [3] minimizes the overlap between the paths of voluminous flows. To achieve this, a central scheduler is in charge of keeping track of used links in the network in order to assign a new flow to a nonused path. From this perspective, it falls into the category of centralized networking (see section "Software-Defined Networks"), where a server acts as the controller by informing other ones about the link to use to forward specific packets of a flow.

The flow establishment is also leveraged by the previously described route lookup. In this approach, instead of routing traffic at a packet level, streams of data are grouped into flows and routed as a whole entity. One of the benefits of this approach is a faster route computation as it is reduced in a similar fashion as in circuit switching legacy technology. For example, if a host node requires to transfer a large data file as a part of a Big Data job, the whole stream will follow a pre-established route, reducing the latency of establishing a different route for each packet of the stream.

In order to enhance routing and network speed, hardware plays a core role. Therefore, there have been propositions to replace standard hardware. In particular, Farrington et al. [18] argue for a hybrid optical–electric switch as optical links achieve higher throughput but are not well adapted to bursty traffic. Combining both technologies thus helps in obtaining a good trade-off between accuracy and cost. Moreover, the technological availability of programmable circuits also leads to the possibility of implementing switching devices, especially in the aggregation and core layer using ASIC and FPGA devices. Lu et al. [19] propose an approach for implementing switching cards with a PCI-E interface. A recent proposal [20] addresses dynamic routing by replacing the traditional dynamic host configuration protocol (DHCP) address configuration by an another automated address configuration system. In this approach, the network is automatically blue printed as a graph. Then, by interpreting a set of labels assigned to each computing node, the system tries to find an isomorphism that minimizes the traffic at the aggregation layer. From the preliminary results, this approach has yielded promising results. However, it actually runs only over BCube or DCell because they have a fully connected topology.

Flow Scheduling

Network operators perform various traffic engineering operations in order to provide different network services on a shared network. This consists in classifying the traffic according to the intrinsic characteristics of each service or application using the network. For example, it is possible to define policies to specially treat Big Data applications. Similarly, the IPv6 Traffic Class includes the possibility of injecting information specific to applications in the packet stream. Other types of support for enabling network infrastructure to perform management of traffic are proposed in request for comments (RFCs) [21] and [22]. The first (DiffServ) proposes a protocol for differentiating services and its network behavior. The latter, Resource Reservation protocol (RSVP), specifies also a protocol that enables applications to reserve network resources in advance of initiating a data transfer.

As highlighted in the introduction, Big Data applications include both batch processing and streaming analytics, which are different by nature. In particular, batch processing jobs are more prone to use the network heavily during certain phases while streaming uses the network constantly with various rates. Therefore, the apparition of a batch job (Hadoop) may suddenly impact the network and so the other underlying applications. Dogar et al. [23] have proposed to schedule flows from BigData applications in a data center using a variation of first-in first-out (FIFO) scheduling that allows some level of multiplexing between the flows. The authors propose to schedule flows in the order of arrival with a certain degree of freedom and allow multiplexing over a limited number of flows which in turn allows small flows to be processed alongside large flows. This approach allows the co-execution of batch and streaming Big Data applications.

Limitations

It is worth mentioning that, in traditional data center networks, only aggregation and core layer switches have the capability of scheduling flows. This is a limitation imposed by the hardware. To be able to exploit the full potential of flow scheduling, an additional network function is required. This is often implemented in a central controller, this way allowing core and aggregation switches to be replaced by simple switches. One of the main advantages of using this approach is the reduced cost of switching and forwarding (L2) devices.

Another disadvantage of traditional networking is that the network configuration remains static and so impacts on the maintenance cost of the infrastructure because any modification of the topology must be wired manually by the network administrators. Virtualized networks come into play for coping with the lack of flexibility in traditional networks, and have become popular over the last years, thanks to the emerging virtualization technologies and computing power to support them. As a result, data-center owners offer their clients not only VMs (known as Virtual Private Servers [VPS]) but also virtual network infrastructure. This allows VPS users to create customized topologies. Virtual LANs (VLAN) have been popular in the past decades for splitting large organizational networks into smaller ones. However, this approach fails to segregate application traffic because of the coarse routing granularity inside a VLAN. A possible solution to this issue is to use a dynamic topology that adapts to the specific needs of each application. In such a scope, the section "Software-Defined Networks" covers emerging technologies facilitating dynamic network configuration using a centralized control plane implemented in software.

SOFTWARE-DEFINED NETWORKING

This section covers both theoretical approaches as well as practical implementations. Solutions highlighted in the following paragraphs combine three aspects: computational patterns present in most of Big Data services, data-centers network architectural improvements such as hierarchical topologies (e.g., fat trees) and dynamic routing algorithms leveraged by the adoption of technologies such as SDN. These three aspects combined together allow the adaptation of the network configuration from the core to the aggregation infrastructure layer to better suit Big Data application needs.

Routing and scheduling decisions rely on the traffic matrix. Such a matrix can be observed in real-time at the network level but can also be predicted in order to plan next course of action. The traffic matrix usually reflects the flow's size, duration and frequency for each pair of nodes and eventually application instances or even between multiple tasks of a single job. Alternatively, Big Data applications can interact with a central controller to expose their current usage and needs. These two types of approaches are differentiated in Figures 7.6a and 7.6b. In every cases, there is a Big Data application controller or manager (e.g., the job-tracker or the resource manager in Hadoop), which is in charge of triggering and monitoring the tasks. In Figure 7.6a, a monitoring service gathers traffic from forwarding devices and sends the information to the network controller itself which is in charge of taking routing decisions. The monitoring can even be done by OpenFlow as an OpenFlow controller can request such statistics from OpenFlow switches [24]. In this case, both the monitor and

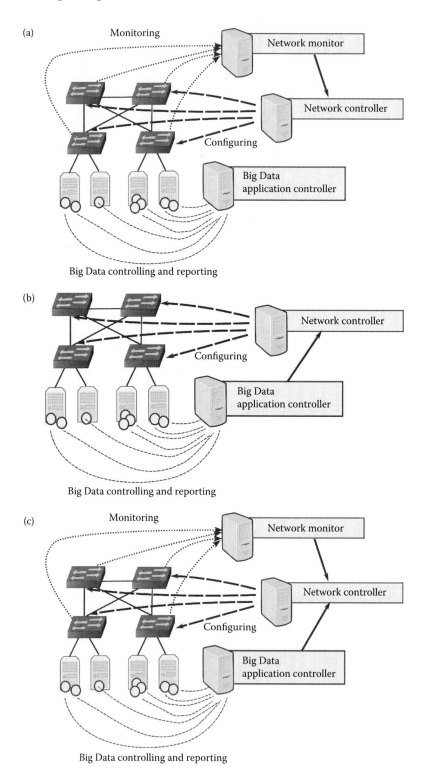

FIGURE 7.6 The different type of *-aware networking (small circles represent a task of a Big Data process). (a) Traffic-aware networking, (b) application-aware networking, and (c) hybrid awareness.

controller are merged in a single entity. In a second scenario (Figure 7.6b), the Big Data controller itself sends information about the running jobs to the network controller which can thus take proper configuration actions. Finally, it is also possible to imagine a hybrid approach (Figure 7.6c) where both types of information are made available to the controller. It might be useful if the level of details from the Big Data controller is coarse-grained.

To summarize, the different methods covered in the following subsections are actually similar to conventional networking (select better paths, minimize congestion, etc.), but they rely on a higher and more dynamic coupling between the network configuration and applications (or the corresponding traffic).

Software-Defined Networks

In recent years, SDN emerged introducing a new layer of abstraction for more flexible network management. Under this approach, switches are just forwarding devices while most of the control (e.g., routing decisions) is performed in a central controller. As a result, a network can be built with merchant silicone and can be programmatically controlled by the central control plane. This eventually results in reduction of both capital expenditures (CAPEX) and operation expenditures (OPEX).

SDN decouples the data and the control plane as shown in Figure 7.7, where

- *Control plane*: The concept of the control plane is to have a dedicated communication channel for exchanging signalization messages among forwarding and management devices. Most of the available products for SDN expose a North Bound application programming interface (API) for applications to subscribe to real-time statistics and service usage.

- *Data plane*: This layer, also referred as the forwarding plane, performs the actual switching/forwarding of the network traffic. The traffic in this plane is accounted and measured but not interpreted by any decisional algorithms.

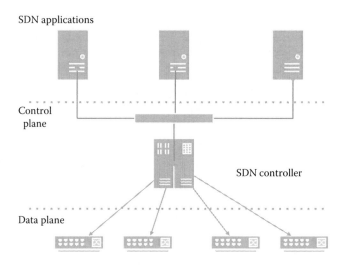

FIGURE 7.7 SDN architecture example.

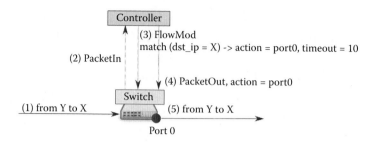

FIGURE 7.8   SDN with open flow rules.

Additionally, the application layer is composed of custom-made applications. The latter subscribe to the North Bound API of the SDN controller to enable extra functionality not provided by the out of the box controller. For example, these applications might be security oriented [25] or for routing purposes [26]. OpenFlow [27] is adopted as de facto standard control protocol. OpenFlow acts as the communication protocol between switches and controllers (e.g., NOX, Floodlight, POX). An OpenFlow rule consists of two parts: a match field, which filters packet headers, and instructions, indicating what actions to take with the matched packets. Upon arrival of a packet at a switch, the controller decides on the route of the packet and sends the corresponding rule to the switch. This event is known as FlowMod. Finally, the packet is sent (PacketOut). Figure 7.8 illustrates an example where a routing action is taken upon arrival of a packet with destination X and source Y. Additionally, a controller can provision switches with flow tables entries in advance. Hence, a PacketIn message is not required to emit an event FlowMod. The rules also have soft (last seen packet) and hard (maximum absolute value) timeouts, and after expiration of these timeouts the rule is removed.

While originally proposed for campus networks, the modification proposed by Curtis et al. [28] consists of reducing the overhead induced by OpenFlow to enable a more efficient flow management for Big Data analytics applications networking through the extensive use of wildcard rules within the switches to avoid invoking the OpenFlow controller for each new flow. However, the extensive use of wildcards on OpenFlow might cause loss of granularity in the statistics derived from the counters on the controller and evidently on routing and scheduling decisions. As mentioned in Curtis et al. [28], DevoFlow aims to devolve control by cloning rules whenever a flow is created using wildcards. The cloned rule will replace the wildcard fields using the clone's specific information. Additionally, DevoFlow enriches OpenFlow rules by including local routing actions (without relying on the OpenFlow controller), such as multipath routing. This last feature allows to rapidly reconfigure the route for a given flow leveraging the flow scheduling.

Traffic-Aware Networking

The Topology Switching approach [29] proposes to expose several adaptive logical topologies on top of a single physical one. It is similar to the allocations problem in VM placement introduced in section "VM Placement for Reducing Elephant Flow Impact" by trying to assign every individual flow to a specific path to optimize an objective. The optimization objectives can be multiple in case of Big Data applications, the most important one is the total capacity, that is, trying to use the available bandwidth as much as possible in order to reduce the job completion time. For example, considering a fat-tree topology as showed in Figure 7.3, every MapReduce typical bisection traffic is considered as a separate routing task. Thus, each task runs an instance of a particular routing system. For every routing system, a pre-allocated bandwidth is established in the physical topology to maximize the bandwidth. Topology Switching is implemented in a central topology server, responsible for allocating resources but also for subtracting unused resources and collecting metrics. The two metrics used in this approach are the bisection bandwidth and the all-to-all transfer. Bisection bandwidth is used to measure the topology ability to handle concurrent transfers at the physical layer. The all-to-all metric is used to evaluate how the logical topologies react under a worst case scenario. Based on both metrics, the Topology Switching approach runs an adaptive algorithm for readjusting the logical configurations for the virtual networks. Topology Switching offers an alternative to "one-size fit all" data-center design, providing a good trade-off between performance and isolation.

Hedera [30] scheduler assigns the flows to nonconflicting paths similarly to Al-Fares et al. [3], especially by aiming at not allocating more than one flow on routes that cannot satisfy its network requirements in terms of aggregate bandwidth of all flows. Hedera works by collecting flow information from the aggregation layer switches, then computing nonconflicting paths, and reprogramming the aggregation layer to accommodate the network topology in order to fulfill the MapReduce jobs requirements. More especially, bottlenecks can be predicted based on a global overview of path states and traffic bisection requirements in order to change the network configuration.

Application-Aware Networking

The methods described in this section improve the network performance by scheduling flows according to application-level inputs and requirements. At the transport layer, flows are not distinguishable from each other but groups of computing nodes in Big Data Application usually expose an application semantic. For example, an application can be composed of several shuffle phases and each of them corresponds to a specific set of flows. Furthermore, a Big Data application can evaluate its current stage. For instance, in a MapReduce task, the mapper status (completion time) is computed from the proportion of the data, from the source, which has been read and such a completion time can approximate the remaining data to transfer. Therefore, a mapper having read 50% of its data source and having already sent 1GB of data should send approximately another 1GB. This is an approximation and it cannot be guaranteed that the mapper will send as much information for the remaining data it has to read. For example, a usual example where a mapper sends a <key,value> pair for each read line can also apply some filtering and so may emit nothing based on the input data.

Therefore, some methods build a semantic model reflecting Big Data application needs. The semantic model used for these approaches associates the network traffic to be managed with the characteristics and the current state of the application it originates from. This model might differ among the different proposed works but generally aims at assessing the state of the Big Data applications and their related flows.

In this context, Ferguson et al. [31] propose to optimize network performance by arranging QoS policies according to application requests. Host nodes running Big Data applications can exchange messages within their proposed framework called PANE to submit QoS policies similarly to what can be done with conventional networks (see section "Flow Scheduling"). Naturally, this approach will lead to traffic oversubscription under high traffic demand circumstances. To solve this issue, users have also to provide conflict resolution rules for each QoS rule they submit into the system. Also, this approach can be employed for implementing security policies such as denial of service prevention by setting a top hierarchy policy triggered at the SDN controller.

OFScheduler [32] is a scheduler which assesses the network traffic while executing MapReduce jobs and then load-balances the traffic among the links in order to decrease the finishing time of jobs based on the estimated demand matrix of MapReduce jobs. OFScheduler assumes that MapReduce flows can be marked (e.g., by Hadoop itself) to distinguish those related to the shuffle from those related to the load balancing (when a task is duplicated). The scheduling first searches for heavily loaded links and then selects flows to be offloaded by giving the preference to (1) load-balancing flows, and (2) larger flows in order to limit the impact on performance (cost of the offloading due to OpenFlow rule installation). The reason for (1) is that it corresponds to a duplicated task the original of which may finish somewhere else in the data-center unlike the others. The rationale behind (2) is to minimize the global cost of offloading and so by moving big flows, there are more chances to remedy the problem of the link load without rescheduling additional ones.

Assuming optical links, Wang et al. [33] describe an application-aware SDN controller that configures optical switches in real time based on the traffic demand of Big Data applications. By enabling the Hadoop Job Scheduler to interact with the SDN controller, they propose an aggregation methodology to optimize the use of optical links by leveraging intermediate nodes in the aggregation. In the simplest case, when a single aggregate has to gather data through N switches whereas the number of optical links is lower, it has to go through multiple rounds (optical switching) in order to complete the job. The other switches only using a single connection to the aggregating switch can also be connected together to act as intermediate nodes to form a spanning tree rooted in the aggregator and so to avoid the multiple rounds. Such a principle (many to one) is extended toward general case with any to many jobs or when multiple single aggregation overlaps (e.g., different sources overlap their aggregators). This requires more complex topologies such as torus. Other data center network topologies discussed in this chapter such as DCell or CamCube also make use of high redundancy to build similar shaped topologies. Building a torus topology is more complicated than a tree because the search space for suitable neighbors is larger, a greedy heuristic is used to support the traffic demand as much as possible. The routing algorithm within the torus topology is meant to exploit all possible optical paths. Authors also propose to assign weights to the optical links for load-balancing purposes on the torus topology.

FlowComb [34] is a combination of proactive and reactive methods for flow scheduling. It allows the Hadoop controller to specify requirements but also promotes the use of a statistic-based method that predicts based on the network load of previous runs. Hence, this approach lies between application-aware and traffic-aware. Based on that, any routing or scheduling approach described in section "Traffic-aware Networking" could be applied, especially Hedera [30] which has been chosen by the authors. The central decision engine gathers all the job pertinent data and creates a set of Open Flow rules to be installed temporarily and erased after job completion. However, the main drawback of the proactive method using estimation is that about 30% of jobs are detected after they start, and 56% before they finish.

Coflow [35] proposes a full reactive method, which only after receiving the Hadoop Job Scheduler network requirements is able to yield results. Its implementation exposes an API for declaring flows at application level. This API can be used, for example, from the Hadoop Job Scheduler as it is mentioned by the authors to express on demand bandwidth requirements at the different phases of a MapReduce job. Actually, CoFlow introduced an abstraction layer to model all dependencies between flows in order to schedule an entire application, that is, a set of flows, and not only a single flow.

In contrast with the methods described previously, Dixit et al. [36] propose an approach for routing on a packet basis by splitting the flows in chunks similarly to TCP. These chunks are distributed to the available ports of a switch using different strategies: random, round robin, and counter based. However, the main limitation of this approach is the necessity to reorder the chunks.

CONCLUSIONS

Big Data applications are a major representative in today's cloud services, which have also guided the network design and configuration for performance purposes. For example, the fat-tree network topology is a popular choice among data-centers hosting Big Data applications. Also, the usage of ECMP as a routing algorithm leverages the notion of flow routing for a better efficiency in redundant-linked networks. Complementary to the fat-tree approach, the DCell and BCube design patterns propose a high degree or almost full connectivity between the nodes of the data-center. The usage of these kind of topologies is tightly related to the type of applications running over the network. Therefore, one size (network architecture/topology) does not fit all applications and some will experience degraded performance. To cope with this situation, alternatives in the field of dynamic routing and flow scheduling have been proposed.

The network topology can be adapted dynamically to meet the application bandwidth needs in terms of data transfer but also to reduce the latency and improve the Big Data job's finishing time. Many of the solutions proposed in this field consist in regrouping application nodes (VMs) that concentrate a high volume of data to be transferred.

Programmable networks are more flexible in having a central controller that can take a lead role in flow scheduling. Many Big Data applications have an observable traffic pattern which is exploited by several works to propose specific scheduling to make more efficient network usage (e.g., load balancing, traffic management, and resources allocation).

In this direction, several authors have highlighted the notion of "network awareness". In general, two kinds of application state-full controllers and network architectures have been proposed: Passive application controllers (traffic-awareness) are those that take the traffic matrix as input; on the active controllers, there is an interface that allows the application, for instance the Hadoop Job Scheduler, to interact with the network controller about the job status.

Furthermore, applications can also leverage network awareness such that they adapt themselves to network conditions like for instance bandwidth usage and topology. This has been demonstrated in Chowdhury et al. [37] for different types of applications including Big Data ones.

In summary, network awareness seems to be a very promising direction for Big Data applications and its early adoption has already shown improvements. Programmable networks are a fundamental enabler for leveraging the statefulness of the controllers, and accordingly provide customized support for Big Data applications.

REFERENCES

1. Armbrust, M., Fox, A., Griffith, et al. A view of cloud computing. *Communications of the ACM* 53 (4), 2010, 50–58.
2. Kavulya, S., Tan, J., Gandhi, R., and Narasimhan, P. In *International Conference on Cluster, Cloud and Grid Computing*, CCGrid, IEEE/ACM, Illinois, USA.
3. Al-Fares, M., Loukissas, A., and Vahdat, A. A scalable, commodity data center network architecture. *SIGCOMM Computer Communication Review* 2008, vol. 38, ACM, New York, NY, USA, pp. 63–74.
4. Lee, K.-H., Lee, Y.-J., Choi, H., Chung, Y. D., and Moon, B. Parallel data processing with mapreduce: A survey. *SIGMOD Record* 40 (4), 2012, 11–20.
5. Toshniwal, A., Taneja, S., Shukla, A., Ramasamy, K., Patel, J. M., Kulkarni, S., Jackson, J. et al. Storm@twitter. In *SIGMOD International Conference on Management of Data* 2014, ACM, Utah, USA, p. 18.
6. Pandey, S., Wu, L., Guru, S. M., and Buyya, R. A particle swarm optimizationbased heuristic for scheduling workflow applications in cloud computing environments. In *International Conference on Advanced Information Networking and Applications* 2010, AINA, IEEE, Perth, Australia, pp. 400–407.
7. Barham, P., Dragovic, B., Fraser, K., Hand, S., Harris, T., Ho, A., Neugebauer, R., Pratt, I., and Warfield, A. XEN and the art of virtualization. *ACM SIGOPS Operating Systems Review* 37 (5), 2003, 164–177.
8. Kivity, A., Kamay, Y., Laor, D., Lublin, U., and Liguori, A. KVM: The Linux virtual machine monitor. In *Proceedings of the Linux Symposium*, Ottawa, Canada, 2007, vol. 1, pp. 225–230.
9. Rosenblum, M. VMWare's virtual platform. *In Proceedings of Hot Chips*, Palo Alto, CA, USA 1999, 185–196.
10. Yao, Y., Cao, J., and Li, M. A network-aware virtual machine allocation in cloud datacenter. In *Network and Parallel Computing, vol. 8147 of Lecture Notes in Computer Science*. Springer, New York, USA, 2013.
11. Cisco Data Center Infrastructure 2.5 Design Guide. 2008. http://www.cisco.com/c/en/us/td/docs/solutions/Enterprise/Data_Center/DC_Infra2_5/DCI_SRND_2_5a_book.html.
12. Niranjan Mysore, R., Pamboris, A., Farrington, N., Huang, N., Miri, P., Radhakrishnan, S., Subramanya, V., and Vahdat, A. Portland: A scalable fault-tolerant layer 2 data center network fabric. In *Conference on Data Communication* 2009, SIGCOMM, ACM, Barcelona, Spain, pp. 39–50.

13. Leiserson, C. E. Fat-trees: Universal networks for hardware-efficient supercomputing. *IEEE* C-34 (10), 1985, 892–901.
14. Guo, C., Wu, H., Tan, K., Shi, L., Zhang, Y., and Lu, S. DCell: A scalable and fault-tolerant network structure for data centers. In *Conference on Data Communication* 2008, SIGCOMM, ACM, Seattle, WA, USA.
15. Abu-Libdeh, H., Costa, P., Rowstron, A., O'Shea, G., and Donnelly, A. Symbiotic routing in future data centers. *Computer Communication Review* 40 (4), 2010, 51–62.
16. Singla, A., Hong, C.-Y., Popa, L., and Godfrey, P. B. Jellyfish: Networking data centers randomly. In *Conference on Networked Systems Design and Implementation* 2012, NSDI, USENIX Association, San Jose, California.
17. Iselt, A., Kirstadter, A., Pardigon, A., and Schwabe, T. Resilient routing using MPLS and ECMP. In *Workshop on High Performance Switching and Routing* 2004, HPSR, IEEE, Arizona, USA, pp. 345–349.
18. Farrington, N., Porter, G., Radhakrishnan, S., Bazzaz, H. H., Subramanya, V., Fainman, Y., Papen, G., and Vahdat, A. Helios: A hybrid electrical/optical switch architecture for modular data centers. In *SIGCOMM* 2010, ACM, New Delhi, India, pp. 339–350.
19. Lu, G., Guo, C., Li, Y., Zhou, Z., Yuan, T., Wu, H., Xiong, Y., Gao, R., and Zhang, Y. Serverswitch: A programmable and high performance platform for data center networks. In *Conference on Networked Systems Design and Implementation* 2011, vol. 11 of NSDI, USENIX, San Jose, California, pp. 15–28.
20. Chen, K., Guo, C., Wu, H., Yuan, J., Feng, Z., Chen, Y., Lu, S., and Wu, W. Dac: Generic and automatic address configuration for data center networks. *Transactions on Networking* 20 (1), 2012, 84–99.
21. Blake, S., Black, D., Carlson, M., Davies, E., Wang, Z., and Weiss, W. RFC 2475: An Architecture for Differentiated Service, IETF, California, USA, 1998.
22. Braden, R., Zhang, L., Berson, S., Herzog, S., and Jamin, S. RFC 2205: Resource ReSerVation Protocol (RSVP)—Version 1 Functional Specification, September 1997.
23. Dogar, F. R., Karagiannis, T., Ballani, H., and Rowstron, A. Decentralized task-aware scheduling for data center networks. In *SIGCOMM* New York, NY, USA, 2014, ACM.
24. Chowdhury, S. R., Bari, M. F., Ahmed, R., and Boutaba, R. PayLess: A low cost network monitoring framework for software defined networks. In *Network Operations and Management Symposium* 2014, NOMS, IEEE/IFIP, Krakow, Poland, p. 16.
25. Roschke, S., Cheng, F., and Meinel, C. Intrusion detection in the cloud. In Dependable, Autonomic and Secure Computing, 2009. DASC'09. *Eighth IEEE International Conference on* 2009, IEEE, Chengdu, China, pp. 729–734.
26. Dinh, H. T., Lee, C., Niyato, D., and Wang, P. A survey of mobile cloud computing: Architecture, applications, and approaches. *Wireless Communications and Mobile Computing* 13 (18), 2013, 1587–1611.
27. McKeown, N., Anderson, T., Balakrishnan, H., Parulkar, G., Peterson, L., Rexford, J., Shenker, S., and Turner, J. Openflow: Enabling innovation in campus networks. *SIGCOMM Computer Communication Review* 38 (2), 2008, 69–74.
28. Curtis, A. R., Mogul, J. C., Tourrilhes, J., Yalagandula, P., Sharma, P., and Banerjee, S. Devoflow: Scaling flow management for high-performance networks. In *Computer Communication Review* 2011, vol. 41, ACM SIGCOMM, Toronto, ON, Canada, pp. 254–265.
29. Webb, K. C., Snoeren, A. C., and Yocum, K. Topology switching for data center networks. In *Hot Topics in Management of Internet, Cloud, and Enterprise Networks and Services* 2011, Hot-ICE, USENIX, Boston, MA.
30. Al-Fares, M., Radhakrishnan, S., Raghavan, B., Huang, N., and Vahdat, A. Hedera: Dynamic flow scheduling for data center networks. In *Symposium on Networked Systems Design and Implementation*, NSDI, USENIX, San Jose, California.

31. Ferguson, A. D., Guha, A., Liang, C., Fonseca, R., and Krishnamurthi, S. Participatory networking: An api for application control of SDNS. In *SIGCOMM* 2013, ACM, Hong Kong, China, pp. 327–338.
32. Li, Z., Shen, Y., Yao, B., and Guo, M. *Ofscheduler: A Dynamic Network Optimizer for Mapreduce in Heterogeneous Cluster*. Springer, New York, USA, pp. 1–17.
33. Wang, G., Ng, T. E., and Shaikh, A. Programming your network at run-time for big data applications. In *First Workshop on Hot Topics in Software Defined Networks* 2012, HotSDN, ACM, Helsinki, Finland, pp. 103–108.
34. Das, A., Lumezanu, C., Zhang, Y., Singh, V., Jiang, G., and Yu, C. Transparent and flexible network management for big data processing in the cloud. In *Workshop on Hot Topics in Cloud Computing*, Berkeley, CA, 2013, USENIX.
35. Chowdhury, M. and Stoica, I. Coflow: A networking abstraction for cluster applications. In *Workshop on Hot Topics in Networks*, 2012, HotNets, ACM, Redmond, WA, USA, pp. 31–36.
36. Dixit, A., Prakash, P., and Kompella, R. R. On the efficacy of fine-grained traffic splitting protocolsin data center networks. In *SIGCOMM* 2011, ACM, Toronto, ON, Canada.
37. Chowdhury, M., Zaharia, M., Ma, J., and Jordan. Managing data transfers in computer clusters with orchestra. In *SIGCOMM Computer Communication Review* 2011, vol. 41, ACM, Toronto, ON, Canada, pp. 98–109.

CHAPTER 8

Speedup of Big Data Transfer on the Internet

Guangyan Huang, Wanlei Zhou, and Jing He

CONTENTS

INTRODUCTION

The trend of computing technology is that everything is merged into the Internet [1–3] and "Big Data" are integrated to comprise complete information for collective intelligence. Sensors and human beings become two major contributors for Big Data. With the advance of low cost data capturing devices and storages, most of data are collected via sensors [4]. Human-generated data on the web has become even more popular in the recent years. The top five biggest data in 2014 come from archives, government websites, social media, the media, and business apps [5]; all these data record human behaviors and social activities. Data is generated in a way exceeding the human limits to use them [6]; 90% of the data in the world was created in the past few years alone [1] and the amount of data is doubling every year in every science domain [7]. The big-sized data exceeds the ability of general information technologies to capture, store, manage, and process within a tolerable elapsed time [8]. Therefore, Big Data is defined as "high-volume, high-velocity, and/or high-variety information assets that require new forms of processing to enable enhanced decision making, insight discovery and process optimisation" [9].

There are three types of data collectors [10] on the Internet: Internet-based navigation sites (e.g., Google, Yahoo, and Bing); social networking and mobile applications (e.g., Facebook, Google+, Twitter, and Yelp); and third-party marketing providers (e.g., Gmail, KBM, Acxiom, and Equifax). These data collectors always use data centers (i.e., clouds), such as Amazon CloudFront [11], to store the data and provide services to end users. For example, a collector server uses a web crawler to collect web pages from various geographically dispersed websites (i.e., all-to-one gather) and distributes massive data replicas to several edge locations for faster data delivery to local end users (i.e., one-to-all broadcast).

However, the speed limitation of transporting data on the Internet has become one of the key difficulties for Big Data collectors. Cloud computing technology developed unexpectedly quickly—"Each of today's cloud datacenters contains more computing and storage capacity than the entire Internet did just a few years ago". But, the communication performance lags far behind on the Internet. For example, broadband cable currently supports speeds of around 30 megabits per second; that is, we may remotely transmit 30 megabits data within a second but we cannot transport 3 terabyte data over 1 day and 1 petabyte data over 1 year.* Communication bandwidth never catches up with the blast data, such as video, real-time data stream, and a huge number of web pages on the Internet. Furthermore, the bandwidths for moving data in and out of the clouds are very limited compared to the speed of computing data, since the performance improvements of wide-area networking are lower than all other IT hardware [12]. For very limited bandwidths between two nodes, physically sending disks or even whole computers via overnight delivery services to send a huge amount of data may be the most efficient method [13].

By 2014, there were several breakthroughs in hardware technologies for Big Data transfer. For example, 43 terabits per second achieved by a single optical fiber[†]; wireless transmission of 40 gigabits per second at 240 GHz over a distance of 1 km[‡]; 10 Gbps Li-Fi (light fidelity) for wireless data transfer[§]; Huawei achieved a data transfer rate of 10.53 Gbps on 5 GHz frequency.[¶] However, when these advanced technologies will be used in real life cannot be predicted; the 10.53 Gbps bands will be available from 2018 with the assumption that industry standards can be agreed upon and there is sufficient chipset availability. Thus, the basic infrastructure of the Internet cannot be totally replaced by advanced hardware due to unpredictable time to reach the market; and even when they are available, due

---

* Similar information can be found in [7] based on a lower data transfer speed.
† See http://www.gizmag.com/dtu-world-record-data-transmission-43tbps/33214/.
‡ See http://phys.org/news/2013-05-gbits-ghz-world-wireless-transmission.html.
§ See http://www.gizmag.com/li-fi-wireless-technology/32968/.
¶ See http://www.gizmag.com/huawei-10-gbps-wi-fi-transmission/32308/.

to their high cost, we may only take them as rare resources to deploy at some key locations to help us efficiently use the current Internet infrastructure.

The more practicable solution for improving data transfer speeds is to optimize network and system. Google pushes development of 10 Gbps Internet speeds*; a technique that improves data transfer speed up to 10 times of TCP/IP by smarter and more adaptable network coding[†]; that is, each node elaborate packets as needed by re-routing or re-encoding them. But network and system level solutions suffer from distance limitations and high network cost [14].

The original web data are distributed everywhere but lack a suitable format to satisfy various application purposes. Once we develop more data collectors for different purposes, the need for Big Data transportation will become more critical. Comparing the status of Internet data to the status of our society resources (e.g., oil, coal, iron ore), we can imagine that, in the future, the Internet infrastructure for Big Data transport will be improved by adding "Big Data freeways," "Big Data pipe system," and "Big Data railway" to the already existing low-speed connection (like "average roads"). But we have observed that "average roads" are still major connections in the current traffic networks. So, it is still important for us in the current Internet infrastructure to improve the speed of transporting Big Data.

In this chapter, we present two classes of techniques for efficient Big Data transfer on the Internet. The first class is to optimize throughputs, including data segmentation for multipathing and parallel TCP streams, multihop path splitting, and hardware-supported dynamic bandwidth control. The second class is to improve bandwidths, such as BitTorrent. Also, we apply and extend these techniques to two basic data transfer patterns for Big Data collection and use on the Internet: all-to-one gather and one-to-all broadcast.

The rest of this chapter is organized as follows. In the section "The Protocols of Internet Data Transfer," we introduce Internet data transfer protocols and the challenges for transporting Big Data. In the section "Efficient Big Data Transfer," we detail four techniques of efficient Big Data transfer. We present all-to-one gather of Big Data in section "All-to-One Gather of Big Data" and one-to-all broadcast of Big Data in section "One-to-All Broadcast of Big Data." Section "Conclusion" concludes this chapter.

THE PROTOCOLS OF INTERNET DATA TRANSFER

Two basic protocols for data transfer on the Internet are TCP and File Transfer Protocol (FTP). TCP ensures reliable data transfer and fair use of bandwidth on the Internet, while FTP is designed for transporting files using TCP connections. Both are not originally designed for Big Data transfer.

The Mechanism of TCP

Most data transmitting on the Internet uses TCP, which works with the Internet Protocol (IP) to send packets of data between computers over the Internet through the following three steps.[‡]

---

* See http://www.zdnet.com/google-pushes-development-of-10gbps-internet-speeds-7000026351/.
[†] See http://www.gizmag.com/random-linear-network-coding/33038/.
[‡] See http://searchnetworking.techtarget.com/definition/TCP.

Step 1: The TCP program layer in the sender computer segments a file into small packets, numbers them, and forwards the packets individually to the IP layer.

Step 2: The IP layer routes packets through different paths toward the same IP address destination.

Step 3: The TCP program layer in the receiver computer reassembles all the packets into the original file format and forwards the file to the receiving application.

The change of data formats is shown in Figure 8.1.

TCP is used to reduce high bandwidth delay, to decrease packet loss rates, and to maximize throughputs by exploiting multipathing and parallel pipeline streams and dynamically increasing TCP window size (the larger congestion window size, the higher the throughputs [15]). TCP employs its window size as the congestion control technique for fairness and a single TCP connection process gives good results with all sized files with no severe packet loss. The default TCP settings on most hosts are configured to deliver reasonable data transfer performance other than optimal performance, both on Ethernet local area networks (LANs) and on wide area networks (WANs) [14].

File Transfer Protocol (FTP)

Ninety percent of data today are file-based, unstructured, or with a mix of file sizes [16]. FTP is the most common protocol used for bulk data transfer on the Internet. FTP is an application protocol that uses the Internet's TCP/IP protocols to transmit files.[2] FTP makes intelligent use of available paths for parallel streams to maximize the achievable bandwidth. A data stream is either a data file or a directory listing. FTP protocol mandates a separate TCP connection for a control session and a new TCP connection for every data stream, as shown in Figure 8.2.

The Challenges of Big Data Transfer on the Internet

Four metrics are used to measure the performance of Big Data movement on the Internet: bandwidth (bits per second), throughput, round-trip time (RTT), and packet loss rate [14]. Bandwidth indicates the capacity of the communication links and throughput measures the average rate of successful message delivery over a communication channel. RTT

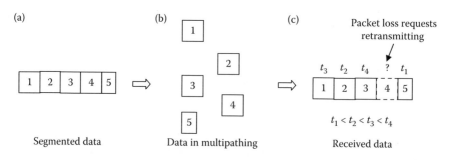

FIGURE 8.1   The change of data formats in a TCP connection.

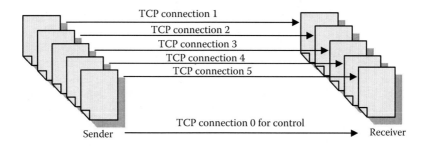

FIGURE 8.2   The standard FTP for bulk files.

is to measure the time delay of transmission times between two nodes in the network. Bandwidth and throughput are used for measuring data transfer speed, while RTT and packet loss rates are two major factors that impact on the throughputs. Bandwidth is the theoretical maximum throughput of the system and throughput means the bandwidth consumption.

However, TCP and TCP-based FTP are unsuitable for moving massive datasets across networks, particularly for WANs. First, TCP incurs high-speed connections with long delays [17]. Also, TCP performance degrades with distance; that is, throughput bottleneck becomes more severe with increased latency and packet loss [16]. Moreover, TCP does not scale with bandwidth, since TCP is designed for low bandwidth and thus adding more bandwidth does not improve throughput [16]. The last but not the least, the packet loss or the worse path for routing a packet (when no packet loss) impacts the data transmission speed, especially for Big Data. When the original data is very big, TCP needs to segment it to more packets, that means the possibility of packet loss increases; and when the distance between the sender and the receiver is longer, it is more possible that longer delay occurs and retransmitting takes longer time.

Therefore, two schemes are very critical to remotely transport Big Data through TCP:

- We should limit the data package size for every session (e.g., segmenting a Big Data block into small pieces), since one packet loss will delay a complete set of data on a TCP connection.

- We should reduce the transmitting distance for each transfer (e.g., using multiple hops to route data), since once a transmission on a long-distance TCP connection fails, it is more time consuming for retransmission.

EFFICIENT BIG DATA TRANSFER

We present four methods for speedup of Big Data transfer: data segmentation for multipathing and parallel TCP streams (in section "Data Segmentation for Multipathing and Parallel TCP Streams"), multihop path splitting (in section "Multihop Path Splitting"), hardware-supported dynamical bandwidth control for reducing delay and packet loss rate (in section "Hardware-Supported Dynamic Bandwidth Control: Aspera FASP") and BitTorrent, improving Big Data transfer speed by making the best use of the bandwidth resources available on the Internet (in section "Optimizing Bandwidth: BitTorrent"). The first three methods optimize throughputs and the last method increases bandwidths for improving Big Data transfer.

Data Segmentation for Multipathing and Parallel TCP Streams

Segmenting a Big Data block into small pieces is the basis for both multipathing and parallel TCP streams. Multiple streams may route data pieces through multiple paths to achieve different levels of parallelism; that is, one path may be used by more than one stream in different time.

Multipathing

Moving Big Data in and out of the data center becomes a challenge, since existing transport technology cannot fully utilize the end-to-end capacity provided by the underlying hardware platform, particularly over a wide area [18]. According to Aspera [19], leading web search companies, such as the Hadoop File system (HDFS), Google file system (GFS), and Amazon Dynamo, often adopt object storage architectures that organize file data and associated metadata as an "object." They assume the file data is written into the storage system in small "chunks"—typically 64–128 MB and stored redundantly across many physical disks. For example, writing a 1 Terabyte file requires dividing it into more than 10,000 64 MB-chunks. So, the cloud storage systems use HTTP to PUT and GET each object chunk. So, multipathing employs multiple independent routes to simultaneously transfer disjoint chunks of a file to its destination for efficiency [20].

Parallel TCP Streams

Parallel TCP streams, for example, in bbFTP [21] and GridFTP [22], use multiple flows in parallel to address the problem of large file transfers [23]. The relationship among throughput, number of streams, packet loss rate, and RTT is critical to optimize the throughput of multiple concurrent transfers of files [24]. For example, the optimal number of concurrent threads at runtime may speedup data transfers, the packet loss, and delay may greatly impact the throughputs of FTPs and a mixed system using different FTPs (i.e., bbFTP for single big files and GridFTP for bulk small files) may satisfy various Big Data applications.

The bbFTP protocol [21], an open source file transfer software, implements its own transfer protocol optimizing for large files (larger than 2 GB) using parallel TCP streams [25]. The main strength of bbFTP is the ability to use Secure Shell (SSH) and certificate-based authentication, data compression on-the-fly, and customizable time-outs [26]. As shown in Figure 8.3a, the bbFTP protocol segments a Big Data file into n smaller subfiles and opens m ($m \leq n$) FTP connections depending on the number of streams required. Since m often is less than n, bbFTP reopens data connections for transfer of each subsequent file and thus it sends files of small or medium size at a low throughput. Also, bbFTP uses fixed TCP window size and tries to flexibly balance the stable settings for the number of parallel streams and TCP window sizes used for different applications; and the usage of fixed TCP window size may benefit high packet loss scenarios [27].

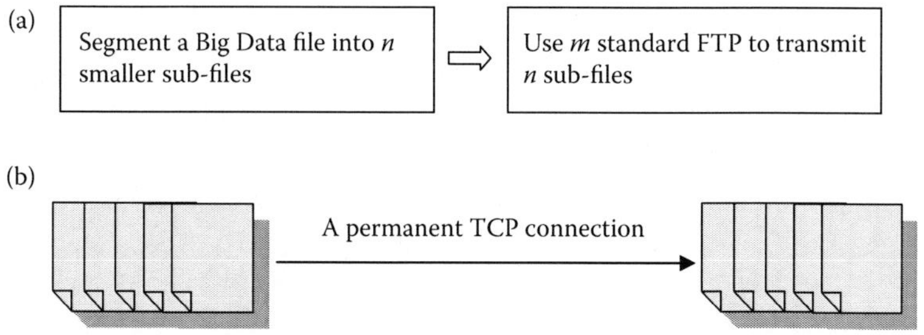

(a)

| Segment a Big Data file into *n* smaller sub-files | ⟹ | Use *m* standard FTP to transmit *n* sub-files |

(b)

A permanent TCP connection →

FIGURE 8.3 A comparison of two FTPs: (a) bbFTP for A Big File and (b) GridFTP for Bulk Small Files.

The GridFTP protocol opens permanent data connections that can be reused to transfer multiple files as shown in Figure 8.3b, and thus allows achieving higher throughput with small files; for files bigger than what can be sent within one TCP window, GridFTP utilizes parallel transfer of a single file over several streams—a feature common with bbFTP [27]. So, GridFTP is highly suited for medium and large file transfer on WANs with no packet loss. But in case of packet loss on the network, GridFTP decreases throughputs.

Also, parallel TCP streams can be used to increase throughput by multiplexing and demultiplexing data blocks. But the side effect is that significant data block reordering occurs due to differences in transmission rate between individual TCP streams when applications use the obvious round robin scheduling algorithm for multiplexing data blocks. This forces the demultiplexing receiver to buffer out-of-order data blocks, consuming memory and potentially causing the receiving application to stall [28]. So, a new adaptive weighted scheduling approach is provided in Hacker et al. [28] for multiplexing data blocks over a set of parallel TCP streams. Compared with the scheduling approach used by GridFTP, it reduces reordering of data blocks between individual TCP streams, maintains the aggregate throughput gains of parallel TCP, and consumes less receiver memory for buffering out-of-order packets.

Multihop Path Splitting

Multihop path splitting [29] replaces a direct TCP connection between the source and destination by a multihop chain through some intermediate nodes. A split-TCP connection may perform better than a single end-to-end TCP connection. First, the RTT on each intermediate hop is shorter as compared to the direct end-to-end path. The congestion control mechanism of TCP would sense the maximum throughput quickly thereby attaining steady state, wherein it will give maximal possible throughput until a congestion event occurs. Second, any packet loss is not propagated all the way back to the source but only to the previous intermediate hop.

If the bandwidth on each of the intermediate hops is higher than the direct path, the overall throughput can be improved; an example is shown in section "One-to-All Broadcast of Big Data." Based on pipelining parallelism scheduling in He et al. [30], Theorem 8.1 proves that multihop is more efficient than single hop.

Theorem 8.1

We assume that R ($R \geq 1$) Gigabytes data on the source node is split into k pieces with the same size and the greatest bandwidth is less than f ($f \ll k$) times of the smallest bandwidth. Using pipelining parallelism to move data, multihop ($w \ll k$ hops) is more efficient than single hop if the smallest bandwidth on multihop is greater than the bandwidth on single hop.

Proof

We analyze the pipelining time shown in Figure 8.4. Suppose the multihop path has $w - 1$ hops shown in Figure 8.4a, bandwidths sorted from low to high are $b_1, b_2, \ldots, b_w$, and thus $t_1 = (1/b_1) > t_2 = (1/b_2) > \cdots > t_w = (1/b_w)$. The pipelining time is

$$T_{\text{pipelining}} = kT + \Delta T \tag{8.1}$$

where $T = (R/kb_1)$ and $\Delta T = \left(R/k \sum_{i=2}^{w}(1/b_i)\right) \leq (w - 1/kb_2)$. Due to $f \ll k$ and $w - 1 \ll k$, $(w - 1/(kb_2)(w-1)f)/kb_1 \ll (1/b_1)$, so $kT \gg \Delta T$. Thus,

$$T_{\text{pipelining}} \approx kT = \frac{R}{b_1} \tag{8.2}$$

For single hop, if the bandwidth $b < b_1$, then $T_{\text{pipelining}} = (R/b_1) < T_{\text{singlehop}} = (R/b)$. This proves Theorem 8.1.

Hardware-Supported Dynamic Bandwidth Control: Aspera FASP

Aspera FASP [16] uses a hardware-supported dynamic bandwidth control to significantly improve throughput, compared to standard FTP and TCP transfers, to transfer large files whatever the impaired long delay links and high loss rates occur or not [31].

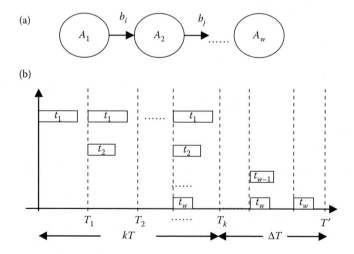

FIGURE 8.4 Pipelining time analysis of (a) $t_1 (= 1/b_1) > t_2 (= 1/b_2) > \cdots > t_w (= 1/b_w)$ and (b) $kT \gg \Delta T$.

The Mechanism of Aspera FASP

A limitation of the WAN transport is that the round-trip latency and packet loss are sufficient to limit the achievable throughput to <100 Mbps and over international WANs to limit the throughput to <10 Mbps at a WAN [19]. Aspera FASP provides a dynamic bandwidth control with hardware support, which manages priority and bandwidth control, sacrifices TCP's coupling of rate control and reliability, and may bring congestions; and therefore achieves higher efficiency and bandwidth utilization.

Aspera's FASP is limited only by the available network bandwidth and the hardware resources at both ends of the transfer, and it enables transfer speeds between 100 and 1000 times faster than standard TCP over the same conditions [16].

According to Munson [16], Aspera FASP achieves 10GBps+ transfers over global WAN through leveraging Intel® Xeon® processor E5-2600 product systems and Aspera's FASP transport. The support hardware components include

- "Intel® Data Direct I/O Technology (Intel® DDIO), which allows Intel® Ethernet controllers to route I/O traffic directly to the processor cache."

- "Built-in support for Single-Root I/O Virtualization (SR-IOV), which allows virtual machine platforms to bypass the hypervisor in order to directly access resources on the physical network interface."

The Performance of Aspera FASP

In transfer throughput test with FASP [31], when transferring larger files, the packet loss and delay do not impact the throughput very much; only high loss rates impact the throughput. Also, the bigger the data, the worse the delay and packet loss rate; for example, the packet loss is increased from 5% (50GB) to 10% (100 GB) and round-trip delay (RTD) also climbs from 120 ms (50 GB) to 240 ms (100 GB).

We present the throughput test of transferring a 2 GB file on FASP and FTP provided in Keltsch and Hammer [31] in Table 8.1. FTP only reaches an average throughput of 172 Mbps with no delay and loss environment while FASP reaching 930 Mbps. But with 120 ms delay and 0% packet loss, FTP only reaches an average throughput of 320 Kbps while FASP still keeping about 930 Mbps. With 5% packet loss and no delay, the FTP throughput is 120 Kbps and the FASP throughput is 880 Mbps. This test validates that packet loss impacts the throughput more than delay, since packet loss in TCP connections means an unknown delay as shown in Figure 8.1.

TABLE 8.1 FASP versus FTP

	Throughput	
Test Environment	**FASP**	**FTP**
No delay and 0% packet loss	930 Mbps	172 Mbps
120 ms delay and 0% packet loss	930 Mbps	320 Kbps
No delay and 5% packet loss	880 Mbps	120 Kbps

TABLE 8.2   FASP versus TCP

	Throughput		
Test Environment	**FASP**	**1 TCP Session**	**4 TCP Sessions in Parallel**
120 ms RTD and no packet loss	948 Mbps	500 kbps	—
40 ms RTD and no packet loss	—	—	930 Mbps
40 ms RTD and no packet loss	465 Mbps[a]	—	465 Mbps[a]

[a] Estimated.

In a test where Aspera FASP and standard TCP transfer a 2 GB file in parallel over the same link, the comparison is illustrated in Table 8.2 according to results from Keltsch and Hammer [31]. With 120 ms RTD and no loss, TCP session reaches 500 Kbps while FASP reaches 948 Mbps. In the second test with 40 ms RTD and no loss, four TCP sessions were run simultaneously instead of one, the four TCP sessions reached a total throughput of around 930 Mbps. In the third test (40 ms RTD, no loss), the Aspera FASP was initiated first reaching 930 Mbps, then four TCP sessions were started in parallel and FASP left almost half of the available bandwidth for the TCP transfer.

Optimizing Bandwidth: BitTorrent

BitTorrent [32] is a peer-to-peer file sharing protocol like FTP in client/server paradigm, which aggregates available bandwidth between data centers. BitTorrent is simple, widely used, and effective at most cases. BitTorrent uses a simple tracker to coordinate the complex participating nodes and tries to utilize the underlying network bandwidth as much as possible [14]; as we analyzed, its performance depends on the size and behavior of the group of downloaders [33]. BitTorrent [32] is widely used to transmit massive files by changing the data source from one to a distribution of multiple sources; this actually increases the involved bandwidth resources in the network.

We plot the main technique of BitTorrent [14] in Figure 8.5. In Figure 8.5a, a static file with the extension .torrent is put on an ordinary web server. The .torrent contains information about the file, its length, name, and hashing information and the URL of a tracker. BitTorrent cuts files into pieces of fixed size (e.g., 1/4 MB) and the SHA1 hashes of all the pieces. Trackers help downloaders to find each other. Trackers and downloaders use a simple protocol layered on top of HTTP (HTTP runs over TCP*). The downloader sends information about what file it is downloading, what port it is listening on, and so on and tracker responds with a list of contact information for peers which are downloading the same file. Downloaders then use this information to connect to each other. In Figure 8.5b, a downloader that has the complete file is called a seed. A seed must send out a complete copy of the original file. BitTorrent transfers data over TCP to achieve pipelining parallel streams, BitTorrent breaks pieces (e.g., 256 KB) further into subpieces (e.g., 16 KB). BitTorrent adopts various piece selection schemes, such as subpieces from the same piece have higher priority, random first piece, and rarest first.

---

* Tim Berners-Lee, The Original HTTP as defined in 1991, World Wide Web Consortium. http://www.w3.org/Protocols/HTTP/AsImplemented.html.

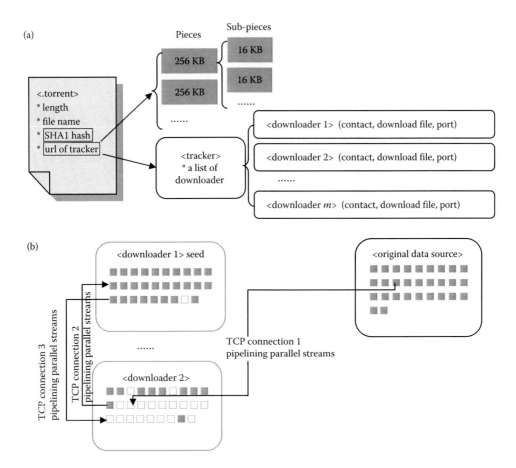

FIGURE 8.5 BitTorrent for broadcast data (a) A <.torrent> file and (b) parallel data transmissions.

ALL-TO-ONE GATHER OF BIG DATA

It is a challenge to automatically gather all of the data from geographically dispersed data sources through Internet, mobile, and sensors (e.g., GPS) due to the limited transmitting speeds of the wire and wireless communication channels. For example, if we try to collect a complete set of daily news about 157 countries for world-wide event analysis [34], suppose there are 10 million URLs, the challenge is how to efficiently access the geographically dispersed web pages. It is time consuming to access all URLs from a centered server.

We provide a new Distributed FTP (dFTP) protocol, which is different from the standard FTP in that TCP connections share the same receiver but have different senders at different URLs. The receiver checks if a complete set of URLs of a cluster of senders is collected and the missing URL content is retransmitted for a reasonable number of times. Based on dFTP, we propose a Gathering Distributed Bulk Small Files (GDBSF) application to collect data from geographically dispersed URLs.

Step 1. Group nearer URLs into clusters.

Step 2. For each cluster, choose a nearest data center to upload a collector.

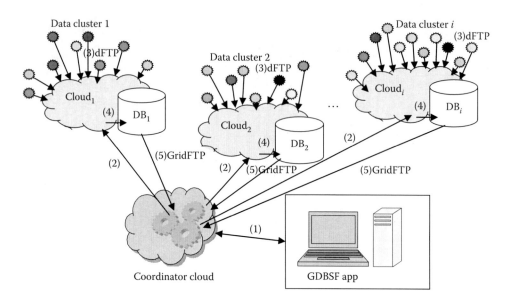

FIGURE 8.6   All-to-one gather of distributed bulk small files.

Step 3. Each collector uses a dFTP protocol to collect data.

Step 4. For each URL in the failure list, set a retransmitting rule, for example, all are retransmitted once.

Step 5. A coordinator is used to request data of clusters from different datacenters. The massive data of each cluster is transmitted by GridFTP.

A practical solution is to utilize several cloud datacenters that are nearer to URLs, as shown in Figure 8.6 and the data flows are explained as follows:

1. GDBSF app groups a set of URLs into clusters and allocates a crawler and a cloud data center for each cluster; clusters of URLs and crawlers are sent from GDBSF app to a nearest cloud as a coordinator.

2. The coordinator sends a crawler and a cluster of URLs to a related data center.

3. The crawler uses the new dFTP to collect web pages from a set of distributed URLs.

4. A cluster of webpage files are stored into database.

5. A bulk of files are transferred to the coordinator using GridFTP.

ONE-TO-ALL BROADCAST OF BIG DATA

Broadcast is one of the most common practical data transfer problems in a distributed environment [35,36]. Data moving between two clouds through the Internet, where the routing protocols always choose a route with minimal hops to optimize the performance of the whole network. Broadcasting Big Data to multiple datacenters in a clouds environment is time consuming, since bandwidths interdatacenters for moving data are limited. Most of existing solutions that focused on improving the performance of data transmission between the sender and the receiver, such as FTP and its variations, as well as Aspera FASP, cannot be used to this application, very common in scientific computing, where multiple receivers request the same data. Although BitTorrent actually handles the broadcast of Big Data to multiple receivers, it only can be used for unauthorized Big Data sharing on the Internet [14].

To broadcast Big Data on the Internet, we first present our previous Replace the Smallest Bandwidth Edge (RSBE) algorithm [36] and then develop an Improved Algorithm based on Pipelining Parallelism (IAPP) to improve RSBE further.

In RSBE, we build an initial flat tree, which is composed of edges from the vertex A to every replica vertex B_i. For the edge (A, B_s) with smallest bandwidth, w_{AB_s} in the tree, the B_s is scheduled to receive data at time $t_s = 1/w_{AB_s}$. Try to replace it by an edge (B_k, B_s), where $k \neq s$ and $t_s > t_{ks}$, where t_{ks} is the earliest time that the B_s obtained the data from A through any B_k to B_s. Repeat replace the smallest bandwidth on unused edges until no replace happens.

A pipelined broadcast is more effective than other broadcast schemes [37]. IAPP is different from RSBE in that, in addition to find a multihop path to replace a single hop path with smallest bandwidth, IAPP uses pipelining parallelism for broadcasting data along a series of nodes on the multihop path based on Theorem 8.1. In IAPP, only the smallest bandwidth on a path determines the broadcast completion time of each node and the smallest bandwidth of the whole spanning tree determines the total broadcast completion time in IAPP; while all the bandwidths on a path determine the broadcast completion time of each node and the longest broadcast completion time of nodes is the total broadcast completion time.

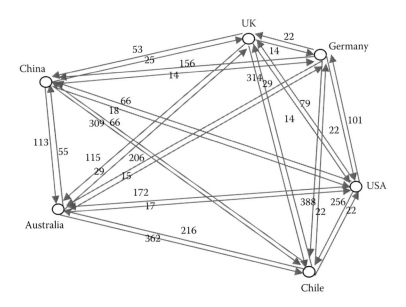

FIGURE 8.7 Bandwidths provided in He et al. [36].

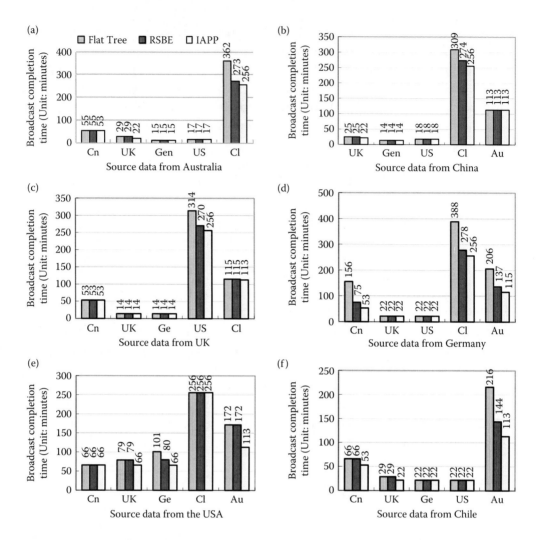

FIGURE 8.8 Broadcast completion time.

We check the download speeds of several Google datacenters (or clouds)* located in different countries from a set of other non-Google clouds in different locations around the world by using a URL check tool.† Based on download speeds, we simulated the bandwidths of a real-world clouds network as shown in Figure 8.7, which is used to evaluate RSBE and IAPP. We have done six experiments to evaluate the effectiveness of our proposed algorithms; in each experiment, one cloud is chosen as the source cloud to broadcast 1 Gigabytes data to the other five clouds.

Figure 8.8 shows the time efficiency of broadcasting achieved by IAPP compared to those achieved by the flat-tree method and RSBE. Figure 8.8 shows that IAPP reduces the total completion time of broadcasting (the highest value) in Figure 8.8a through f.

---

* Google Data Center FAQ, http://www.datacenterknowledge.com/archives/2008/03/27/google-data-center-faq/.
† Checks website performance from multiple locations around the world, http://internetsupervision.com/scripts/url-check/check.aspx.

For example, in Figure 8.8f, the completion time achieved by IAPP is 113 min (1.9 h), which is more efficient than 216 min (3.6 h) achieved by the flat-tree method; the time spent by IAPP is nearly reduced to 52% of the time spent by the flat-tree method. We also observe that more than half of the clouds achieved better broadcast completion time in Figure 8.8a, c through f. In Figure 8.8e, the broadcast completion time of three clouds in the United Kingdom, Germany, and Australia has obviously improved, though the total broadcast completion time is the same. Both RSBE and IAPP use multihop to replace single hop in the flat-tree method for better time efficiency; and IAPP is more effective than RSBE.

In summary, we use a flat tree as the initial optimal tree and then improve it by replacing each arc by using a multihop path that has greater bandwidth. The replacement starts from the destination cloud and we observe that the number of hops from the source to the destinations is limited to a small value in this application; so, IAPP and RSBE run efficiently in most cases.

CONCLUSION

With the increasing size of Big Data, the techniques of transmitting data on the Internet have advanced ahead from TCP, to FTPs for bulk data, to BitTorrent and Aspera FASP. This chapter presents practical optimization for high-speed Big Data transfer on the Internet. Four techniques about improving bandwidths and optimizing throughputs on the Internet are introduced; and they are also applied and extended to two basic data transfer patterns for Big Data collection and use on the Internet: all-to-one gather and one-to-all broadcast.

REFERENCES

1. D. A. Reed, D. B. Gannon, and J. R. Larus, Imagining the future: Thoughts on computing, *Computer*, 25–30, 2012.
2. G. Huang, J. He, and Y. Zhang, Web services for things, *Advanced Web Services*, 605–629, 2014.
3. J. He, Y. Zhang, G. Huang, and J. Cao, A smart web service based on the context of things, *ACM Transactions on Internet Technology*, 11(3), 13:1–13:23, 2012.
4. A. Szalay, Science in an exponential world, *Australiasia eResearch Conference*, Brisbane, Australia, 2007.
5. L. Alton, 5 Biggest Big Data in 2014, June 2014. http://spinnakr.com/blog/data-2/2014/06/5-biggest-big-data-2014/.
6. S. H. Muggleton, 2020 computing: Exceeding human limits, *Nature*, 440, March 2006, 409–410.
7. A. Szalay and J. Gray, Science in an exponential world, *Nature*, 440, 413–414, 2006.
8. A. Mukherjee, J. Datta, R. Jorapur, R. Singhvi, S. Haloi, and W. Akram, Shared disk big data analytics with Apache Hadoop, *the 19th International Confernece on High Performance Computing (HiPC)*, Pune, India, 2012.
9. M. A. Beyer and D. Laney The importance of "big data": A definition, 2008. http://www.gartner.com
10. A. Ferris, D. Moore, N. Pohle, and P. Srivastava, Big Data: What is it? How is it collected and How might life insurers use it? *The Actuary Magazine*, 10(6), 28–32, 2014.
11. CloudFront. http://aws.amazon.com/cloudfront/.
12. J. Gray, Distributed computing economics, *Queue*, 6(3), 63–68, 2008.
13. J. Gray and D. Patterson, A conversation with Jim Gray. *ACM Queue*, 1(4), 8–17, 2003.
14. A. Kaplan, Collaborative Framework for High-Performance P2P-Based Data Transfer in Scientific Computing, *PhD Thesis*, the Department of Computer Science, Indiana University, 2009.
15. Y. Zhang, E. Yan, and S. Dao, A measurement of TCP over long-delay network. *Proceedings of 6th International Conference on Telecommunication Systems, Modelling, and Analysis*, 1998.

16. M. Munson, Aspera high-speed transfer software—Moving the world's data at maximum speed. https://www.caudit.edu.au/system/files/uploads/Aspera%20Overview%20for%20RDSI%20final.pdf

17. R. X. Wu and A. A. Chien, GTP: Group Transport Protocol for Lambda-Grids, in Cluster Computing and the Grid, 2004. *CCGrid 2004,* Chicago, Illinois, USA, 2004.

18. Aspera, Aspera White Paper, Big Data Technologies for Ultra-High-Speed Data Transfer and Processing—Using technologies from Aspera and Intel to achieve 40 Gbps WAN/LAN data transfer/speeds, 2013.

19. Aspera, Aspera Direct-to-Cloud Storage, *Whitepaper,* April, 2014.

20. C. Raiciu, C. Pluntke, S. Barre, A. Greenhalgh, D. Wischik, and M. Handley, Data center networking with multipath TCP, *Proceedings of the 9th ACM SIGCOMM Workshop on Hot Topics in Networks,* Hotnets-IX, Monterey, California, USA, pages 10:1–10:6, 2010.

21. bbFTP—Large files transfer protocol 2005. http://doc.in2p3.fr/bbftp/index.html.

22. W. Allcock (editor), GridFTP Protocol Specification (Global Grid Forum Recommendation GFD.20), March 2003.

23. D. M. Lopez-Pacheco and C. Pham, Enabling large data transfers on dynamic, very high-speed network infrastructures, *International Conference on Networking, International Conference on Systems and International Conference on Mobile Communications and Learning Technologies,* Morne, Mauritius, 2006.

24. T. J. Hacker, B. D. Noble, and B. D. Atley, The end-to-end performance effects of parallel TCP Sockets on a Lossy Wide Area Network, *IPDPS'02,* Marriott Marina, Florida, pp. 314. 2002.

25. H. Sivakumar, S. Bailey, and R. L. Grossman, PSockets: The case for application-level network striping for data intensive applications using high speed wide area networks, *Proceedings of the 2000 ACM/IEEE conference on Supercomputing (CDROM),* Dallas, Texas, USA, 2000.

26. C. A. Mattmann, S. Kelly, D. J. Crichton, J. S. Hughes, S. Hardman, P. Ramirez, and R. Joyner, A classification and evaluation of data movement technologies for the delivery of highly voluminous scientific data products. *Proceedings of the NASA/IEEE Conference on Mass Storage Systems and Technologies College Park,* 2006. Maryland, USA.

27. L. Truksans, E. Znots, and G. Barzdins, File transfer protocol performance study for EUMETSAT meteorological data distribution, *Scientific Papers,* University of Latvia, 770, 56–67, 2011.

28. T. J. Hacker, B. D. Noble, and B. D. Athey, Adaptive data block scheduling for parallel TCP streams. *Proceedings of 14th IEEE International Symposium, HPDC'05,* pp. 265–275. IEEE Computer Society, 2005, North Carolina, USA.

29. G. Khanna, U. Catalyurek, T. Kurc, R. Kettimuthu, P. Sadayappan, I. Foster, and J. Saltz, Using overlays for efficient data transfer over shared widearea networks, *Proceedings of the 2008 ACM/IEEE conference on Supercomputing (SC'08),* Austin, Texas, USA, pp. 47:1–47:12, 2008.

30. J. He, Y. Zhang, G. Huang, and C. Pang, A novel time computation model based on algorithm complexity for data intensive scientific workflow design and scheduling, *Concurrency and Computation: Practice and Experience,* 21(16), 2070–2083, 2009.

31. M. Keltsch, and M. Hammer, Transfer testing of aspera FASP solution—Phase 1, *Project Report,* Institut für Rundfunktechnik GmbH, Aug. 28, 2014.

32. B. Cohen, Incentives Build Robustness in BitTorrent, 2003. http://www.bittorrent.org/.

33. K. Li, W. Zhou, S. Yu, and B. Dai, A parallel downloading algorithm for redundant networks, *Proceedings of the 7th International Conference on Computer and Information Technology,* Fukushima, Japan, pp. 177–182, 2007.

34. G. Huang, J. He, Y. Zhang, W. Zhou, H. Liu, P. Zhang, Z. Ding, Y. You, and J. Cao, Mining streams of short text for analysis of world-wide event evolutions, *World Wide Web Journal,* http://dx.doi.org/10.1007/s11280-014-0293-1, 2014.

35. K. Takahashi, H. Saito, T. Shibata, and K. Taura, A stable broadcast algorithm, *Proceedings of 8th IEEE International Symposium on Cluster Computing and the Grid (CCGrid'08),* Lyon, France, pp. 392–400, 2008.

36. J. He, Y. Zhang, G. Huang, Y. Shi, and J. Cao, Distributed data possession checking for securing multiple replicas in geographically dispersed clouds, *Journal of Computer and System Sciences*, 78(5), 1345–1358, 2012.
37. P. Patarasuk, A. Faraj, and X. Yuan, Pipelined broadcast on ethernet switched clusters, *Proceedings of IEEE International Parallel and Distributed Processing Symposium (IPDPS'06)*, Rhodes Island, Greece, 2006.

CHAPTER 9

Energy-Aware Survivable Routing in Ever-Escalating Data Environments

Bing Luo, William Liu, and Adnan Al-Anbuky

CONTENTS

D ATA EXPLOSION HAS BEEN a continuous trend since the 1970s and the Internet has grown along with this data explosion, as well as has indeed greatly contributed to it. The three Vs (volume, variety, and velocity) from today's Big Data however are unprecedented. Our world is generating data at a speed faster than ever before. In 2010, 5 exabyte (10^{18} bytes, or 1 billion gigabytes) of data were created every two days, exceeding the total amount of information that was created by human beings from the dawn of civilization to 2003 [1]. Till 2020, over 40 zettabytes (10^{21} bytes) of data is to be created, replicated, and consumed [2]. With the overwhelming amount of data pouring into our lives, from anywhere, anytime, and any device, we are undoubtedly entering the era of Big Data.

In general, "Big Data" are stored in data warehouses and processed in powerful data centers with massive interconnected server nodes. There are some significant studies [3] that introduced the knowledge discovery and mining over the data and high-performance parallel computing tools for Big Data (e.g., MapReduce). But Big Data also needs to be transmitted from a variety of sources and utilized at a variety of destinations for broad purposes. Generation, collection, aggregation, processing, and application delivery are the basic stages of Big Data flow [4]. First of all, the data are generated by and collected from geographically distributed devices, then they are aggregated to Big Data and processed in data centers, finally the data knowledge or service is distributed to interested users. It goes without saying that networks are playing a critical role in bridging the different stages, and there is a strong demand to create a fast and reliable digital highway for the Big Data to flow freely on it. This network highway [5] concerns not only just one segment of data delivery, but rather the whole series of segments for the life cycle of Big Data, from access networks [6], to the Internet backbone [7], and to intra- and inter-data-center networks [8].

BACKGROUND

In recent years, the requests for green networking in Big Data networks' design have become increasingly important due to its environmental impact [9,10] and potential economic benefits [11,12]. First, the various studies such as [13–15] have started highlighting the devastating effects of massive green house gas (GHG) emissions and their consequences on climate change. It is reported that the volume of GHG emissions produced by the telecommunication sector alone accounts for approximately 2% of total man-made emissions [16]. Moreover, by considering the rapid development of telecommunication services, the situation could become even worse in the near future [17,18]. As the ITU-T Technology Watch Reports [19] point out, the energy usage of the telecommunication sector will grow steadily over time, and therefore it is important that the industry takes solid steps to curb and ultimately reduce its carbon emission as soon as possible. Second, as far as economic aspects are concerned, energy-efficient networks could help telecom companies to reduce operational expenditures. Normally, telecom companies spend a large amount of money on energy consumption due to their huge scale of network infrastructure. A research study [20] has reported that the power consumption of telecommunication networks is not negligible. Taking Telecom New Zealand limited as an example, as shown in its official website [21], it is one of the top 15 electricity users in New Zealand, and approximately 85% of its energy consumptions is related to running the network.

However, the architectures of existing telecommunication networks are often designed to endure peak loads and degraded conditions, which leave a large space for energy savings since they are under-utilized in normal operations [22] for most of the time. Besides, the current network operational approach is also energy unaware, for example, balancing the traffic as evenly as possible on the network links [23], or minimizing the bandwidth and maximizing the shareability of backup wavelengths [24], which do not consider the operational energy consumption of network resources for example, nodes and links. Therefore, by considering all the current research studies above, there is an urgent need to apply energy efficient approaches to our telecommunication network design. In recent years, we have seen great progress in green networking technologies that enable telecommunication systems to reduce energy expenditure from different network layers such as adaptive link rate applied in Data Link layer [25], Interface Proxying used in Application and Network layers [26], and also the Energy-Aware Application applied in Transport layer [27].

Green technology is improving rapidly according to recent research studies, while the current green approaches take little consideration of the network survivability aspect. The definition of network survivability [28] is the capability of a system to fulfil its mission, in a timely manner, in the presence of threats such as attacks or large-scale natural disasters. In other words, network survivability refers to that when local failures happen, such as fiber cuts, key components malfunction, or router hardware/software failures, the global information carrying ability of the network should not be jeopardized. The popular mechanisms to increase network survivability are protection mechanism, and device utilization restriction.

The protection mechanism [29] uses extra redundancy resources to protect critical network components so as to guarantee the network services in the event of failure. When the primary path fails, the backup path can be used to resume services immediately so that the quality of service would not be influenced. Moreover, the device utilization restriction is to limit the usage level of network devices. In the real world, the network operators set a threshold [30] as common practice to limit the load of the devices to enforce Quality of Service (QoS) and robustness in their networks.

However, applying network survivable approaches lessen the potential of energy saving in green networks due to the nature of the network survivability strategy, which is to provide extra backup resources. Our motivation is to study the trade-off problems between energy reduction and network survivability when designing the network highway to accommodate the Big Data requirements. From the saving energy aspect, first, we apply energy-aware routing, to aggregating traffic flows over a subset of the network devices and links. Then those non-working nodes and links will be switched into sleeping mode. In addition, the energy consumption of network elements is configured to several energy levels according to the volumes of its actual data traffic load. For guaranteeing network survivability requirements, we introduce protection mechanisms into the routing algorithms.

RELATED WORKS

Considering both energy reduction and service resiliency requirements, we propose to synthesize several novel mechanisms into our energy-efficient survivable network designing approaches. For saving energy, we apply energy-aware routing to aggregate data flows over an essential subset of network nodes and links. Then those inactive nodes and links can be switched into sleeping mode. In addition, the energy consumption of network elements is configured to several energy levels based on its workload. For service resilience, we embed protection mechanisms into these routing algorithms.

Energy-Aware Routing

The energy-aware routing approach has been first evoked in the position paper [9], which aims at aggregating data flows over a subset of the network devices and links, allowing other links and interconnection devices to be switched off or in sleep status [31]. The main idea can be briefly illustrated as shown in Figure 9.1. The three data flows highlighted in black can be aggregated into one working path colored in red, which is shown on the right-hand side of Figure 9.1, therefore, those network elements (i.e., links and nodes) that are not used can be turned into sleep state or shut down.

The energy-aware routing could be a promising solution [32] to address the problem of energy waste in Big Data networks. It can be used to more efficiently route traffic data demands and switch off the unused network nodes and links to save unnecessary energy consumption [33,34]. Recently, the potential energy-saving capacity of energy-aware routing was analyzed by some studies, for example, the work of [35] proposed an energy profile aware-routing algorithm, which is assuming the network nodes capable of adapting their performance according to the actual data load. By applying it, a reduction in energy consumption of over 35% can be achieved. The study in [36] introduces a novel energy-aware routing protocol (EARP) that is based on the autonomic network-routing protocol. In this study, energy metrics, QoS metrics and the number of hops are

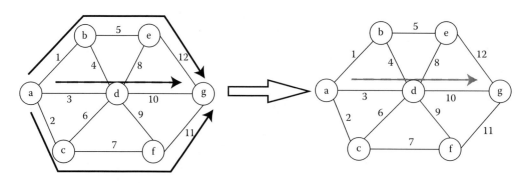

FIGURE 9.1 An illustration of energy-aware routing approach.

considered. The result shows that the EARP achieves overall reduction of power consumption on average throughout the network. However, most of the recently studies have not taken the network survivability into consideration. For guaranteeing the network performance [18,30,37], just set a parameter between 0 and 1 to limit the maximum of link utilization. It clearly cannot avoid the packet loss if the working path (as shown in red in Figure 9.1) fails.

In summary, the energy-aware routing could be a promising approach to reduce the energy usage of Big Data networks. However, the existing solutions of energy-aware routing normally sacrifice network robustness in order to achieve maximum energy reduction [38]. Therefore, our objective is to use energy-aware routing to achieve energy reduction but also to maintain the same level of network survivability performance.

Sleeping Mode

The sleeping mode is a subclass of adaptive link rate strategies, which often refers to network devices or a part of them that can turn themselves to enter very low-energy states, while all their functionalities are frozen. Thus, the sleeping/standby states can be considered as deeper idle states, characterized by higher energy saving and much larger wake-up times. The sleeping mode is a state-of-the-art technology, which is still not widely applied to existing Big Data networks. Because, today's networking devices are commonly designed to be fully available all the time, due to telecom companies putting more priority on service resiliency rather than energy saving. Therefore, there is a basic problem that needs to be addressed: when a device is sleeping, how do we maintain its network connectivity? To address this problem, the work in [39] proposes to add a "proxy," namely Network Connectivity Proxy (NCP), between the sleeping device and the network. This NCP will process the low-level network presence tasks during the idle time. Some other works such as [40] use a shadow port to handle the synchronizing signal on behalf of a cluster of sleeping ports, also use a buffer in the device's interface to store the packets received during the sleeping intervals, and then process them when it wakes up.

In this study, how to implement the sleeping mode in hardware is out of our scope. Here, we hypothesize that the hardware supports sleeping mode. Moreover, we assume the sleeping mode in our new routing algorithms is similar to the literature [41], where the network components can be reactivated within a short time in case a failure occurs.

Energy Consumption Rating Strategy

The studies in Refs. [42,43] have showed that energy consumption on the current network device is largely independent of its utilization. In practice, even during the off-peak period, devices are still working on their full power no matter how low the actual load is. Therefore, the energy consumption of a device largely depends on its configuration rather than the actual load of the device. To saving wasted energy during the low utilization period, some works in [44,45] advocate using the transmission rate-switching approach. They define several transmission rates, from 10 Mbit/s to 10 Gbit/s. There is a non-negligible difference in the interface energy consumption, across the different data rates. When a device is at a certain load, the interface will automatically choose a suitable rate to achieve energy saving. Other works such as [30] proposed a fully proportional model for network elements, in which the energy consumption is exactly proportional linearly according to the ratio of actual load/capacity usage. This model represents an ideal case where energy consumption varies linearly with the device utilization, ranging between 0 and full power. However, in the real world, it is difficult to implement this design requirement with current hardware technology.

In our work, the energy consumption rating strategy is inspired by rate switching. We propose that the energy consumption of network components such as nodes and links is basically based on the actual traffic load passing them, which is similar to the assumption in [46]. Figure 9.2 illustrates the six energy-consuming rates in our scheme. For any network element a (a node or a link), the minimum value of energy expenditure is E_0, which represents its turning on status, and the maximum value is E_m, which represents its maximized energy consumption. In addition, the value of E_m E_{sa} represents the energy consumption when a network element is in sleeping state. The energy consumption E_a can be configured as the following six levels:

i. $E_a = 0$, represents the energy consumption as the device is switched off;

ii. $E_a = E_{sa}$, represents the energy consumption as the device is set to a sleeping state;

iii. $E_a = 25\% (E_{ma} - E_{0a}) + E_{0a}$, represents the energy consumption as its traffic load is less than or equal to 25% of its capacity;

iv. $E_a = 50\% (E_{ma} - E_{0a}) + E_{0a}$, represents the energy consumption as its traffic load is greater than 25%, but less than or equal to 50% of its capacity;

v. $= 75\% (E_{ma} - E_{0a}) + E_{0a}$, represents the energy consumption as its traffic load is greater than 50%, but less than or equal to 75% of its capacity;

vi. $= E_{ma}$, represents the energy consumption as its traffic load is greater than 75% of its capacity, and operates at its full power.

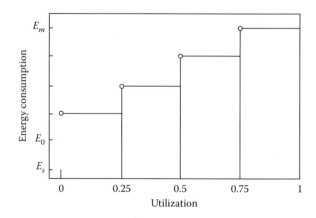

FIGURE 9.2 The six energy consumption levels of network devices.

Network Survivability Approaches

Network survivability is the ability of the network to provide and maintain an acceptable level of service in the case of various failures in the normal operation. It reflects the ability of a network to continue to function during and after failures. Nowadays, network failures are frequent [47], including fiber cuts, key components malfunction, or router hardware/software failures. When an element of the network fails, all the traffic data passing through this element is lost (i.e., at least during the recovery procedure), which can really decrease the QoS perceived by all the users of the network, especially for green networking approaches, in which the traffic flows tend to be aggregated to several high capacity links. If one of these active links fails, this may lead to a more significant data loss. For this reason, there is a critical need to apply a protection scheme that will allow the network to quickly recover from any failure it may encounter. In on-line traffic engineering, the network must be able to compute and establish a path from an ingress router to an egress one and to protect it against failures, based on the requested bandwidth and QoS requirements of the traffic low. In general, there are three kinds of backup protection mechanisms such as 1+1 backup protection scheme, 1:1 backup protection scheme, and shared backup protection scheme.

1+1 Backup Protection

In the 1+1 backup protection scheme [29], for each traffic flow, it needs to compute two completely disjointed paths from the ingress to the egress nodes, one is the primary path, and the other is the backup path. Both paths are used simultaneously: all packets are duplicated at the ingress nodes and sent on both paths to the egress nodes. The egress node continuously monitors both inputs and selects the "best" one to receive and process [48,49].

Figure 9.3 illustrates 1+1 backup protection scheme. WP1 and WP2 are working paths for two traffic flows, which are from node a to node g, each with the traffic volume of 1 unit. PP1 and PP2 are the protection paths corresponding to WP1 and WP2, respectively. The egress node g may choose to receive WP1 or PP1, and WP2 or PP2, depending on the received signal quality. This approach of protection has the advantage of fast receiver-driven

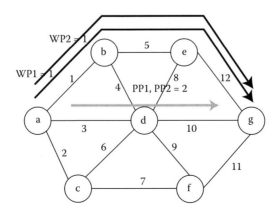

FIGURE 9.3 An illustration of 1+1 backup protection scheme.

recovery upon failure but is of course very costly in terms of bandwidth and energy consumption. Because 1+1 backup is the dedicated scheme, therefore no backup capacity can be shared. Moreover, both primary and backup path are working at the same time, the sleeping mode cannot be applied into the backup path so as to reduce energy expenditure.

1:1 Backup Protection
In the 1:1 scheme, only the primary path is used to forward packets while the backup path can be configured in sleeping mode. If a failure occurs in the primary path, a message is sent to the ingress node which swaps the traffic to the backup path from the primary path. Obviously, the 1:1 protection induces more delay than the 1+1 scheme. The failure has to be detected, and a message must propagate to the ingress node to trigger the recover actions.

The 1:1 backup protection scheme is shown in Figure 9.4. Different from 1+1 backup protection, for the two traffic demands, the egress node g receives data from the primary paths WP1 and WP2. If failure happens on the primary path a–b–e–g (WP1 and WP2), the working path will swap to a–d–g (PP1 and PP2). The advantage of the 1:1 solution is that a significant energy saving can be realized [50,51]. Indeed if we assume that only a single failure may happen in the network at any given time, not all backup paths can be activated simultaneously. The reserved network resources for independent backup paths can thus be switched into sleeping mode [52]. For example, PP1 and PP2 could be turned into sleep state in Figure 9.4.

Shared Backup Protection
In the shared backup scheme [53], only when the two traffic flows' primary paths are completely disjointed, the bandwidth can be shared in the overlapped backup links. The reserved capacity will be the larger one of the two, rather than the total amount of the two.

Figure 9.5 illustrates the shared backup protection scheme. Because the two traffics' primary paths WP1 and WP2 are disjointed, and their backup path PP1 and PP2 are overlapped, therefore the two traffics can share the backup bandwidth on backup path a–d–g. If WP1 or WP2 fails, the working path can switch to the backup path. In our thesis, we

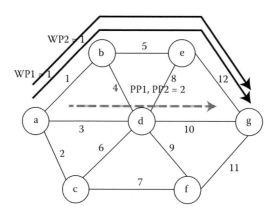

FIGURE 9.4 An illustration of 1:1 backup protection scheme.

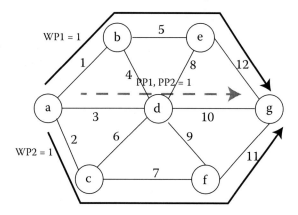

FIGURE 9.5 An illustration of shared backup protection scheme.

assume there is only one failure happening at a time. In other words, WP1 and WP2 would not fail at the same time.

The shared backup protection mechanism can effectively reduce the capacity consumption, however it may consume more energy than the other two, because to separate two traffic flows' primary path in disjointedness may need more working nodes and links. The backup links can be switched into sleeping mode in order to save energy expenditure.

Comparison of Different Protection Mechanisms
Figure 9.6 illustrates the difference among the 1+1 backup scheme, 1:1 backup scheme, and the shared backup scheme in (a), (b), (c), respectively. We assume there are two working traffic flows, that is, WP1, WP2 are the primary paths and each has 1 unit of capacity requirement. The PP1 and PP2 represent the protection paths for WP1 and WP2, respectively.

The diagram (a) shows how the 1+1 backup scheme works, the backup paths PP1 and PP2 are working with the primary paths WP1 and WP2. Therefore, the network needs to turn on 5 nodes and 5 links, with the total capacity of 10 units to meet the traffic

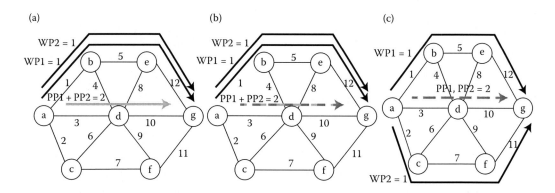

FIGURE 9.6 Comparison of the three backup protection schemes: (a) 1+1 backup scheme, (b) 1:1 backup scheme, and (c) shared backup scheme.

TABLE 9.1   Energy and Capacity Demands of the Three Protection Schemes

	Energy Consumption		Bandwidth Reservation
	Working	**Sleeping**	
1+1 backup scheme	5 nodes 5 links	N/A	10 units
1:1 backup scheme	4 nodes 3 links	1 node 2 links	10 units
Shared backup scheme	6 nodes 6 links	1 node 2 links	8 units

demand. For 1:1 backup scheme (b), the backup resources can be switched into sleeping mode. From the aspect of energy consumption, there are 4 nodes and 3 links in working mode, 1 node and 2 links in sleeping mode. For the capacity usage aspect, the system still needs to reserve 10 units of bandwidth in total for the two traffic flows. Figure 9.6c shows the solution of the shared backup scheme. To meet the requirements of backup sharing, the two primary paths of WP1 and WP2 have to be disjointed completely. In this scheme, the network turns 6 nodes and 6 links in working mode, and 1 node and 2 links in sleeping mode. However, from the capacity point of view, it just needs 8 units of capacity in total. Table 9.1 compares the three protection mechanisms in detail, both from energy consumption and bandwidth reservation aspects. From the table, it can be seen that the 1:1 backup scheme can be the best approach to save energy, while the shared backup can reserve the least bandwidth but need the most nodes and links in working mode.

ENERGY-AWARE SURVIVABLE-ROUTING ALGORITHMS

The problems of trade-off between energy efficiency and network survivability can be modeled using Integer Linear Programming (ILP) formulations [54]. In this chapter, first, we introduce the background knowledge on ILP modeling, and then present the notations used in our models. Following that, we propose the formulations for our new three energy-aware survivable-routing models: Energy-Aware 1+1 Backup Protection (EABP 1+1), Energy-Aware 1:1 Backup Protection (EABP 1:1), and Energy-Aware Shared Backup Protection (EASBP).

Introduction on ILP Modeling

The integer linear programming plays an important role in algorithm design. Lot of combinatorial optimization problems can be formulated as integer linear programming problems. But it is NP-Complete [55]. One potential solution is to solve ILP problems in polynomial time using linear programming with the technique of LP relaxation [56]. Thus, linear programming and the concepts of rounding and duality are very useful tools in the design of approximation algorithms for many NP-Complete problems.

In integer linear programming, our aim is to find an assignment that maximizes or minimizes the objective while also satisfying all the constraints [57]. Typically, the constraints are given in the form of inequalities. For example, the standard form of minimize integer linear programming instance looks like:

$$\text{Minimize} \quad c_1 x_1 + c_2 x_2 + \cdots + c_n x_n$$

Subject to

$$a_{11} x_1 + a_{12} x_2 + \cdots + a_{1n} x_n \geq b_1$$
$$a_{21} x_1 + a_{22} x_2 + \cdots + a_{2n} x_n \geq b_2$$
$$\cdots$$
$$a_{m1} x_1 + a_{m2} x_2 + \cdots + a_{mn} x_n \geq b_m$$
$$\forall i, x_i \geq 0$$

Any assignment of values for variables x_i which can satisfy the constraints is called a feasible solution. The challenge in integer linear programming is to find a feasible solution that can also maximize or minimize the objective function. In our work, we tackle the trade-off optimization problem between network energy efficiency and network survivability by using energy-aware survivable-routing approaches. This sort of trade-off problem falls in the category of capacitated multi-commodity minimum cost flow problems (CMCF). In other words, the problem in which multiple commodities have to be routed over a graph with constraints [58]. Generally speaking, this problem is also categorized as combinatorial optimization, which can be precisely modeled using ILP formulation [16]. ILP can be used for determining a way to achieve the best outcome (such as maximum profit or lowest cost) in a given mathematical model for a list of requirements and constraints represented as linear relationships [59]. In this research, we have proposed the ILP models to tackle our optimization problems.

Notation

The notation used for the ILP formulations in this thesis is defined by the following indexing rules:

- (s, d) which represents the node pair of the source and destination nodes for a connection request;

- (x, y) and (m, n) are the node pairs representing the links in the network topology traversed by primary and backup routes, respectively.

To describe the mathematical model and problem formulation, the following notations are further introduced for parameters and variables.

Given parameters

- G (N, L): A network topology consisting of a set of N nodes and a set of L links.

- a: Network element, either a node or a link. For example, a is i which means that a represents node i; if a is ij, it means that a represents the link between node i and node j.

- l_a: The total traffic load of primary path of a. That is, l_i and l_{ij} stand for the total amount of capacity usage of node i and link ij for providing primary paths.

- l'_a: The total traffic load of backup path of a. That is, l_i and l_{ij} stand for the total amount of capacity usage of node i and link ij for providing backup paths.

- C_a: The capacity of a, which indicates its maximum capacity.

- α: An arbitrary value to preserve QoS, which is a configurable utilization threshold of network elements. Nowadays, network operators adopt as common practice to limit the load of the links to enforce QoS and robustness in their networks, α is between 0 and 1.

- E_{ma}: The maximum energy consumption of network element a when it is turned on. It indicates the full power of a network element.

- E_{0a}: The minimum energy consumption of network element a when it is turned on. It indicates the minimum power to maintain a network element in working status.

- E_{sa}: The energy consumption of network element a when it is in sleeping mode. It represents the sleeping status' power consumption of a network element.

- M: Constant value used in the big-M constraints. M is a "big" number (i.e., greater than twice the maximum nodes capacities).

- T_i: The request traffics matrix. i is the index of the matrix. That is, T_1 is the first line of the traffic demands, and it could be from node i to node j with the volume of x Gbit.

Variables

- p^{sd}_{xy}: Number of path requests from s to d which passes through link (x, y) in their primary path.

- ∂^{sd}_{mn}: Number of path requests from s to d which passes through link (m, n) in their backup path.

- k_a: A binary variable. If $k_a = 1$, network element a is in working status.

- s_a: A binary variable. It indicates whether a network element in sleeping mode or not. If $s_a = 1$, network element a is in sleeping state for backup protection. If $s_a = 0$, network element a is either in primary path or has no load at all.

- $z1_a$: A binary variable. If $z1_a = 1$, network element a adapts to the first working level of energy expenditure.

- $z2_a$: A binary variable. If $z2_a = 1$, network element a adapts to the second working level of energy expenditure.

- $z3_a$: A binary variable. If $z3_a = 1$, network element a adapts to the third working level of energy expenditure.

- $z4_a$: A binary variable. If $z4_a = 1$, network element a adapts to its maximum power.

- E_a: The total energy consumption of network element a.

- k_{L,T_i}: A binary variable. If $k_{L,T_i} = 1$, link L is used as a primary link by a connection request T_i. If $k_{L,T_i} = 0$, link L is not used as a primary link by a connection request T_i.

- $k1_{L,T_i}$: A binary variable. If $k1_{L,T_i} = 1$, link L is used as a backup link by a connection request T_i. If $k1_{L,T_i} = 1$, link L is not used as a backup link by a connection request T_i.

- $p0_{T_1,T_2}$: A binary variable. If $p0_{T_1,T_2} = 1$, the primary paths of T_1 and T_2 have overlapped link, which means T_1, T_2 cannot share backup. If $p0_{T_1,T_2} = 0$, the primary paths of T_1 and T_2 are disjointed, which means T_1, T_2 may share backup capacity.

- $p1_{L,T_1,T_2}$: A binary variable. If $p1_{L,T_1,T_2} = 1$, the link L used as backup paths for both T_1 and T_2, which means T_1, T_2 may share backup in L. On the other hand, if $p1_{L,T_1,T_2} = 0$, the link L used as backup paths for either T_1 or T_2, and also may not be used as backup for T_1 and T_2. In this case, T_1 and T_2 cannot share backup resource in L.

- $p2_{L,T_1,T_2}$: A binary variable. If $p2_{L,T_1,T_2} = 1$, T_1 and T_2 can share backup in link L. If $p2_{L,T_1,T_2} = 0$, T_1 and T_2 cannot share backup in link L.

- C_{L,T_1,T_2}: The amount of backup capacity can be shared by T_1 and T_2 in link L. In other words, this amount can be saved.

Energy-Aware 1+1 Backup Protection (EABP 1+1)

First, we propose the 1+1 backup protection scheme is embedded in EABP 1+1, so that the backup path will transmit the duplicated information simultaneously as the primary path. Based on this protection scheme, the nodes and links on the backup path cannot be switched into sleeping mode. Our goal is to minimize the whole network's overall energy consumption, which includes the energy consumption of nodes and links. Therefore EABP 1+1 will aggregate traffic flows to a small subset of the network, then turn off those unloaded network elements to achieve energy saving. The ILP formulations of EABP 1+1 are listed as follows:

Objective
Minimize

$$\sum_{n \in N} E_n + \sum_{(x,y) \in L} E_{xy} \tag{9.1}$$

The objective function (9.1) is to minimize the total energy consumption of active nodes and links in the network.

Constraints

$$\sum_{x\in N}p_{xk}^{sd}+\sum_{y\in N}p_{ky}^{sd}=\begin{cases}\gamma_{sd}, & k=d\\-\gamma_{sd}, & k=s, \quad \forall k,s,d\in N\\0, & k\neq s,d\end{cases} \tag{9.2}$$

$$\sum_{m\in N}\partial_{mk}^{sd}+\sum_{n\in N}\partial_{kn}^{sd}=\begin{cases}\gamma_{sd}, & k=d\\-\gamma_{sd}, & k=s, \quad \forall k,s,d\in N\\0, & k\neq s,d\end{cases} \tag{9.3}$$

Constraints (9.2) and (9.3) are flow conservation constraints for routing γ_{sd} number of connection requests from node s to d for primary and backup paths, respectively. For a traffic request T_i, if k is a destination node, there are the volume of T_i inflow to it; if k is a source node, there are the volume of T_i outflow from it; if k is an intermediate node, the total inflows should be equal to the outflows.

$$\partial_{mn}^{sd}=0\,\forall(s,d)\in N \quad \forall(m=x,n=y)\in L \tag{9.4}$$

Constraint (9.4) guarantees link disjointedness of a failure in primary from the backup path which assures that if a link (x, y) fails, the connection from s to d cannot be routed through link (x, y).

$$\sum_{s,d\in N}p_{xy}^{sd}=l_{xy}, \quad \forall(x,y)\in L \tag{9.5}$$

$$\sum_{s,d\in N}\partial_{mn}^{sd}=l_{mn}', \quad \forall(m,n)\in L \tag{9.6}$$

l_{xy} is the total traffic load of link (x, y) using primary paths. l_{mn}' is the total traffic load of link (m, n) using backup paths. Therefore, traffic load of primary paths on link (x, y) is defined in constraint (9.5). Traffic load of backup paths on link (m, n) is defined in constraint (9.6).

$$\sum_{(i,n)\in L}l_{in}+\sum_{(n,i)\in L}l_{ni}=l_n, \quad \forall n\in N \tag{9.7}$$

$$\sum_{(i,n)\in L}\ell_{in}'+\sum_{(n,i)\in L}\ell_{ni}'=l_n', \quad \forall n\in N \tag{9.8}$$

We assume node load to be the direct sum of the traffic entering and leaving the node, therefore, constraints (9.7) and (9.8) define traffic load of primary paths and backup paths converge to node n, respectively.

$$\alpha C_{xy} \geq l_{xy} + l'_{xy}, \quad \forall (x, y) \in L \tag{9.9}$$

$$\alpha C_n \geq l_n + l'_n, \quad \forall n \in N \tag{9.10}$$

Constraints (9.9) and (9.10) are to preserve QoS, no links or nodes should reach 100% utilization or more in general, an arbitrary value that the network operator considers safe enough. C_{xy} and C_n are the capacity of link and node, respectively. The α is in the range of 0 to 1. In our experiments, it has been set as 0.8.

$$Mk_{xy} \geq l_{xy} + l'_{xy}, \quad \forall (x, y) \in L \tag{9.11}$$

$$Mk_n \geq l_n + l'_n, \quad \forall n \in N \tag{9.12}$$

Constraints (9.11) and (9.12) define the value of decision variables according to whether a link or a node is used or not. k_a is a binary variable. Its value will be 1 when a is used in working status, otherwise it equals to 0. M is a "big" number (i.e., greater than twice the maximum nodes' capacities) used to force the variable k_a to take the value 1 when a has a load greater than 0, and the value 0 when $l_a = 0$.

$$k_n \geq z1_n + z2_n + z3_n + z4_n, \quad \forall n \in N \tag{9.13}$$

$$(l_n + l'_n)/C_n \geq 25\% z1_n + 50\% z2_n + 75\% z3_n + z4_n, \quad \forall n \in N \tag{9.14}$$

$$E_n = (25\% z1_n + 50\% z2_n + 75\% z3_n + z4_n)(E_{mn} - E_{0n}) + k_n E_{0n}, \quad \forall n \in N \tag{9.15}$$

In the previous chapter, we have introduced the six levels of energy consumption for network elements. The first level is when network element a has no load, the energy consumption is none. The second level is when network element a is in sleeping mode, its energy usage is E_{sa}. The remaining four levels represent a in working status according to its load. If a network element's load less than or equal to 25% of its capacity, a is working on the first working level controlled by $z1_a$. If its load greater than 25%, but less than or equal to 50% of its capacity, the network device a is working on the second working level controlled by $z2_a$. Similarly, $z3_a$ and $z4_a$ decide the network element a working on the third or the fourth working level.

The combination of constraints (9.13), (9.14), and Equation 9.15 ensures each node can be assigned to the proper energy consumption level according to their load. Constraint

(9.13) let node n can be only working on one of the four working levels. Because k_n is binary, thus $z1_n$, $z2_n$, and $z4_n$ are no more than one $z3_n$ of them can be set to value 1. Constraint (9.14) means the working level of node n will be decided by the actual load. We can see the ratio of load divided by node's capacity is in the range of 0–1. If the ratio is no more than 1/4, the node is working on level 1; if the ratio is from 0.25 to 0.5, the node is working on level 2; if the ratio is no more than 0.75, the node is working on level 3; if the ratio is larger than 0.75, the node is working on full power. Equation 9.15 calculates the energy consumption of node n, E_{0n} is the minimum energy consumption of node n when it is turned on.

$$k_{xy} \geq z1_{xy} + z2_{xy} + z3_{xy} + z4_{xy}, \quad \forall(x, y) \in L \tag{9.16}$$

$$(l_{xy} + l'_{xy})/C_{xy} \geq 25\%z1_{xy} + 50\%z2_{xy} + 75\%z3_{xy} + z4_{xy}, \quad \forall(x, y) \in L \tag{9.17}$$

$$E_{xy} = (25\%z1_{xy} + 50\%z2_{xy} + 75\%z3_{xy} + z4_{xy})(E_{mxy} - E_{0xy}) + k_{xy}E_{0xy}, \quad \forall(x, y) \in L \tag{9.18}$$

Similarly, constraints (9.16), (9.17), and Equation 9.18 are for links' energy consumption rate assignment constraints, which ensure each link is allocated to the proper energy consumption leve according to their workload. In addition, the energy consumption of link (x, y) is calculated by Equation 9.18.

Energy-Aware 1:1 Backup Protection (EABP 1:1)

Second, we propose the EABP 1:1 model which integrated the 1:1 backup protection scheme. The backup path will be only active when a node or link failure occurs in the primary path. Therefore, the sleeping mode could be introduced into the network components in backup path. Our goal is to minimize the energy expenditure of the whole network. Basically, we develop EABP 1:1 by introducing sleeping mode into EABP 1+1. Since sleeping mode or turn-off status consumes significantly less energy than working status, the EABP 1:1 model tends to aggregate traffic flows to existing working devices, then switch off as many as possible unloaded elements and turn backup resources into sleeping mode. Therefore, the EABP 1:1 model is highly expected to consume less energy than EABP 1+1. The ILP formulations of EABP 1:1 are as follows:

Objective
Minimize

$$\sum_{n \in N} E_n + \sum_{(x,y) \in L} E_{xy} \tag{9.19}$$

The objective (9.19) is to minimize energy consumption of nodes and links, which includes network element used by primary path and in sleeping state.

Constraints: (9.2) through (9.10)

Because EABP 1:1 is based on EABP 1+1, thus constraints (9.2) through (9.10) can be shared.

$$Mk_{xy} \geq l_{xy}, \quad \forall (x, y) \in L \tag{9.20}$$

$$Mk_n \geq l_n, \quad \forall n \in N \tag{9.21}$$

Constraints (9.20) and (9.21) define the value of decision variables according to whether a link or a node is used by any primary path. M has big value, therefore if l_a is greater than 0, k_a will be set as 1.

$$k_n + s_n \leq 1, \quad \forall n \in N \tag{9.22}$$

$$l'_n - Ml_n \leq Ms_n, \quad \forall n \in N \tag{9.23}$$

Constraints (9.22) and (9.23) define that a node is used in primary path or switched into sleeping mode. s_a is a binary variable, which indicates whether a network element is in sleeping mode or not. If $s_a = 1$, network element a is in sleeping state for backup protection. If $s_a = 0$, network element a is either in primary path or has no load at all. Constraint (9.22) restricts node n cannot be in both working status and sleeping status. Constraint (9.23) sets node n in sleeping mode only when this node is not used as primary by any connection request T_i.

$$k_{xy} + s_{xy} \leq 1, \quad \forall (x, y) \in L \tag{9.24}$$

$$l'_{xy} - Ml_{xy} \leq Ms_{xy}, \quad \forall (x, y) \in L \tag{9.25}$$

Similarly, constraints (9.24) and (9.25) define links used by primary path or switched into sleeping mode.

$$k_n \geq z1_n + z2_n + z3_n + z4_n, \quad \forall n \in N \tag{9.26}$$

$$l_n / C_n \geq 25\% z1_n + 50\% z2_n + 75\% z3_n + z4_n, \quad \forall n \in N \tag{9.27}$$

$$E_n = (25\% z1_n + 50\% z2_n + 75\% z3_n + z4_n)(E_{mn} - E_{0n}) + k_n E_{0n} + s_n E_{sn}, \quad \forall n \in N \tag{9.28}$$

Constraints (9.26), (9.27) and Equation 9.28 ensure each node is allocated to the proper energy consumption level according to their load. Constraint (9.26) forces node n can be working on only one of the four working levels. It confines only one of $z1_n$, $z2_n$, $z3_n$, and $z4_n$, could be set to value 1. Constraint (9.27) means the working level of node n will be decided by the actual load, but it is different to the previous model. Here only the capacity of primary working path will be taken into calculation, because the backup resources are just reserved not actually transmitted as EABP 1+1. We can see the ratio of load divided by the node's capacity is in the range of 0 to 1. If the ratio is less than or equal to 1/4, the node is on the first working level; if the ratio is larger than 1/4, and less than or equal to 1/2, the node is on working level 2; if the ratio is larger than 1/2, and less than or equal to 3/4, the node is on working level 3; if the ratio is above 3/4, the node is working on full power. Equation 9.28 calculates the energy consumption of node n. In comparison to the previous model, here we add a new term $s_n E_{sn}$, which means when node n is in sleeping mode, energy consumption of n will be equal to E_{sn}. E_{sn} is the energy consumption of node n when it is in sleeping mode.

$$k_{xy} \geq z1_{xy} + z2_{xy} + z3_{xy} + z4_{xy}, \quad \forall (x, y) \in L \tag{9.29}$$

$$l_{xy}/C_{xy} \geq 25\%z1_{xy} + 50\%z2_{xy} + 75\%z3_{xy} + z4_{xy}, \quad \forall (x, y) \in L \tag{9.30}$$

$$E_{xy} = (25\%z1_{xy} + 50\%z2_{xy} + 75\%z3_{xy} + z4_{xy})(E_{mxy} - E_{0xy}) + k_{xy}E_{0xy} + s_{xy}E_{sxy}, \quad \forall (x, y) \in L \tag{9.31}$$

The power expenditure of links is confined by constraints (9.29), (9.30), and Equation 9.31. The three formulations ensure each link is allocated to the proper energy consumption level according to their load. The energy consumption of each link L will be calculated out by Equation 9.31. The difference between EABP 1+1 model and EABP 1:1 model is that the sleeping mode is introduced in the latter. Thus for switching off unnecessary network elements and turning backup resources into sleeping mode, the routing strategy of EABP 1:1 may differ from EABP 1+1. However, the backup resources of EABP 1:1 should consume considerably less amount of energy compared with that of EABP 1+1.

Energy-Aware Shared Backup Protection (EASBP)

In the third model, we have proposed the EASBP algorithm which applied the shared backup protection scheme. In this model, we are trying to make the capacity in the backup path shared as much as possible under a single failure scenario. The backup paths are reserved in case of the primary path break down, and the sleeping mode is used for the backup links. The goal of EASBP is to minimize the energy usage as well as making the backup bandwidth share to a large extent. Because two disjointed traffic flows may share a backup path, thus EASBP cannot aggregate too much traffic into high capacity links and nodes. This model may not achieve as much energy reduction as EABP 1:1, but it could save capacity consumption compared with the other two. The ILP formulations of EASBP are as follows:

Objective

Minimize

$$\left(\sum_{n \in N} E_n + \sum_{(x,y) \in L} E_{xy} \right) + \Sigma \left(\sum_{(x,y) \in L} l_{xy} + \sum_{(x,y) \in L} l'_{xy} \right) \qquad (9.32)$$

Objective (9.32) here is to minimize the total energy consumption as well as capacity consumption, where Σ is a scale factor to make these two metrics in the similar range.

Constraints: (9.2) through (9.5), (9.7) through (9.10), (9.20) through (9.31)

EASBP can share the common constraints (9.2) through (9.5), (9.7) through (9.10) from EABP 1+1. In addition, it has applied sleeping mode for backup resources, therefore it can share constraints (9.20) through (9.31) from EABP 1:1. The difficulties of developing EABP are how to separate those connection requests' primary paths to achieve backup sharing and how to calculate the shareable amount.

$$p0_{T_1,T_2} \geq k_{L,T_1} + k_{L,T_2} - 1, \quad \forall T_1, T_2 \in T_i \qquad (9.33)$$

Constraint (9.33) checks whether the primary path of T_1 and T_2 is disjointed or not. Here k_{L,T_i} is a binary variable. If $k_{L,T_i} = 1$, link L is used as a primary link by a connection request T_i. If $k_{L,T_i} = 0$, link L is not used as a primary link by a connection request T_i. The variable $p0_{T_1,T_2}$ equals to 1 when the primary paths of T_1 and T_2 have overlapped links, which make T_1 and T_2 unable to share any backup capacity due to their primary paths not being disjointed. If $p0_{T_1,T_2} = 0$, the primary paths of T_1 and T_2 are disjointed, so that they have the potential to share the backup capacity.

$$p1_{L,T_1,T_2} \geq k1_{L,T_1} + k1_{L,T_2} - 1, \quad \forall T_1, T_2 \in T_i \qquad (9.34)$$

Then constraint (9.34) checks whether T_1 and T_2 have overlapped links or not on their backup path. These overlap links have the potential to be shared. $k1_{L,T_i}$ is a binary variable. If $k1_{L,T_i} = 1$, link L is used as a backup link by a connection request T_i. If $k1_{L,T_i} = 0$, link L is not used as a backup link by a connection request T_i. The variable $p1_{L,T_1,T_2}$ equals to 1 when the backup paths of T_1 and T_2 have overlapped in link L, in this case, T_1 and T_2 may share backup in link L.

$$p2_{L,T_1,T_2} \geq p1_{L,T_1} - p0_{T_1,T_2}, \quad \forall T_1, T_2 \in T_i \qquad (9.35)$$

Constraint (9.35) defines $p2_{L,T_1,T_2}$ which is an indicator to show whether the backup resources of T_1 and T_2 can be shared or not. Only when $p1_{L,T_1,T_2} = 1$ and $p0_{T_1,T_2} = 0$, then $p2_{L,T_1,T_2}$ equals to 1, which shows that T_1 and T_2 can share backup in link L. Otherwise, $p2_{L,T_1,T_2} = 0$, means T_1 and T_2 cannot share backup bandwidth.

$$C_{L,T_1,T_2} = p2_{L,T_1,T_2} * \min(T_1, T_2), \quad \forall T_1, T_2 \in T_i \tag{9.36}$$

Equation 9.36 ensures that the possible sharable capacity C_{L,T_1,T_2} will be the smaller one of the two traffics T_1 and T_2. In other words, the capacity of the large one has been reserved in link L.

$$l'_{mn} = \sum_{s,d \in N} \partial_{mn}^{sd} - 0.5^* \sum_{T_1,T_2 \in T} C_{L,T_1,T_2}, \quad \forall (m,n) \in L, \quad \forall T_1, T_2 \in T_i \tag{9.37}$$

The total backup bandwidth on link (m, n) that needs to be reserved is defined in Equation 9.37, which means the reserved backup capacity on link L equals to the total backup of all volumes of T_i minus the amount of shared capacity. Since T_1 and T_2 both belong to T_i, when we calculate the total shared part, it will be twice as much as it should be. Therefore, the overall shared capacity needs to be multiplied by 0.5.

CASE STUDIES IN CPLEX OPTIMIZATION STUDIO

To validate and evaluate the performance of our proposed three models, we have conducted extensive case studies. The main goal is to show that, for a given static traffic demand, it is possible to turn off some network elements to advance energy efficiency but still guarantee network survivability. We have used the Optimization Programming Language (OPL) [60] and IBM ILOG CPLEX Optimization Studio [61] to conduct these case studies. OPL + CPLEX is a popular and powerful combination to solve optimization problems. In our case study, we first use Optimization Programming Language to model the three energy-aware survivable-routing algorithms of the previous chapter. Then the three models are solved in the IBM ILOG CPLEX Optimization Studio.

IBM ILOG CPLEX Optimization Studio

IBM ILOG CPLEX Optimization Studio is a consolidation of the OPL integrated development environment (IDE) and the CPLEX and CP Optimizer solution engines in a single product. CPLEX Optimization Studio provides the fastest way to build efficient optimization models and state-of-the-art applications for the full range of planning and scheduling problems. With its integrated development environment, descriptive modeling language and built-in tools, it supports the entire model development process. CPLEX, a feature of IBM ILOG Optimization Studio, offers state-of-the-art performance and robustness in an optimization engine for solving problems expressed as mathematical programming models.

Figure 9.7 shows the GUI of CPLEX Optimization Studio. It is divided into four main areas: 1. OPL projects have been set up in the left hand side; 2. The center is where we place OPL programs; 3. The right-hand side lists all the variables and their type; 4. The experimental result can be obtained from the bottom.

There are two features that need to be introduced in details. Figure 9.8 shows the OPL project window, each fold is an existing OPL project. There are two types of file, one is .mod

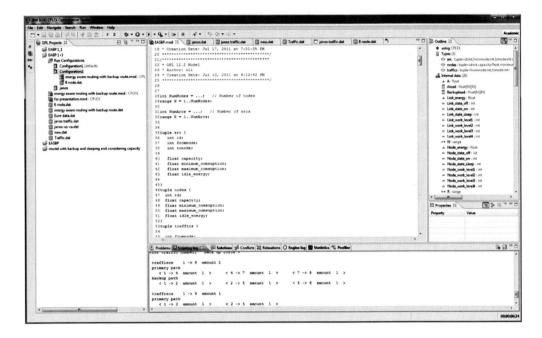

FIGURE 9.7   GUI of IBM ILOG CPLEX Optimization Studio.

and the other is .dat, which represent model and data, respectively. In this studio, model and data are independent. One model can be tested by different data set in quite an easy way. In other words, our three energy-aware survivable-routing models can be validated by different topologies and traffic loads.

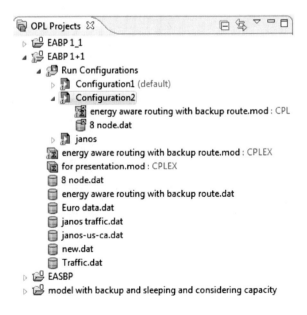

FIGURE 9.8   OPL Projects Window of CPLEX Optimization Studio.

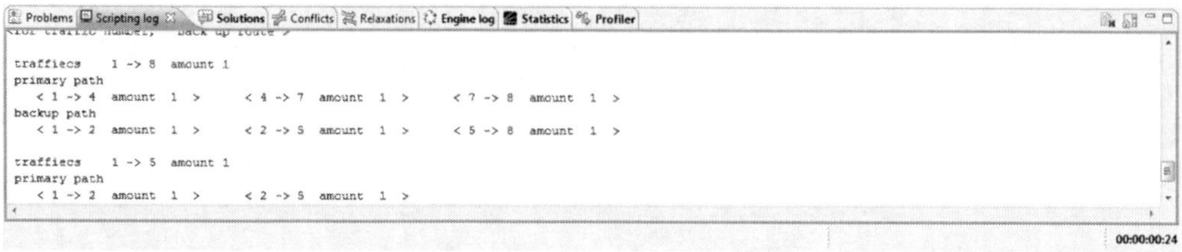

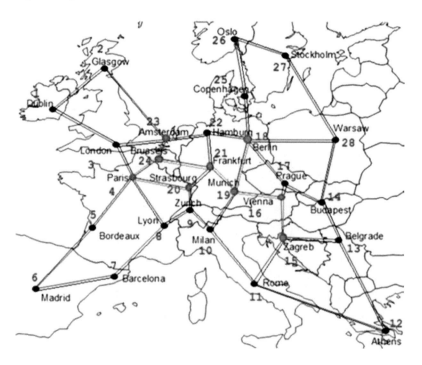

Problems
Scripting log
Solutions
Conflicts
Relaxations
Engine log
Statistics
Profiler
traffiecs 1 -> 8 amount 1
primary path
< 1 -> 4 amount 1 > < 4 -> 7 amount 1 > < 7 -> 8 amount 1 >
backup path
< 1 -> 2 amount 1 > < 2 -> 5 amount 1 > < 5 -> 8 amount 1 >
traffiecs 1 -> 5 amount 1
primary path
< 1 -> 2 amount 1 > < 2 -> 5 amount 1 >
00:00:00:24

FIGURE 9.9 Script Log Window of CPLEX Optimization Studio.

The experimental result can be checked in Script Log Window (Figure 9.9), such as energy expenditure, bandwidth usage, working level of network elements. Moreover, we also wrote some code to print out both primary path and backup path of every traffic demand. In this way, for every traffic demand, we can identify all the links and nodes used by its primary and backup path.

Case Study: The COST266 Network

In the case study, our models are implemented in the COST266 network. Their performance is compared through different perspectives, such as energy consumption, capacity utilization and network devices' working status. Figure 9.10 shows the COST266 network topology.

The traffic data in this case study is listed in Table 9.2. We set the traffic demands between the long distance nodes pair so that more optional and intermediate nodes and links can be involved. There are four scenarios of traffic demands, which are 30, 60, 90, and 120 Gbit, respectively.

Oslo
26
27
25
2
Glasgow
23
22
Warsaw
28
London
3
21
Frankfurt
17
Prague
Paris
4
20
19
14
Vienna
16
5
Lyon
9
Bordeaux
8
Milan
10
Belgrade
13
Zagreb
15
7
6
Barcelona
Madrid
11
12

FIGURE 9.10 The COST 266 network topology.

TABLE 9.2   Data Traffic Scenarios of 30, 60, 90, 120 Gbit in the COST 266

	30 Gbit	**60 Gbit**	**90 Gbit**	**120 Gbit**
Node 1→Node 12	10	10	10	15
Node 4→Node 28	10	10	10	15
Node 6→Node 26	10	10	10	15
Node 9→Node 27	0	10	10	15
Node 11→Node 22	0	10	10	15
Node 12→Node 2	0	10	10	15
Node 14→Node 4	0	0	10	10
Node 28→Node 23	0	0	10	10
Node 26→Node 9	0	0	10	10

Energy Consumption

Detailed results obtained for the three routing models are summarized in Table 9.3. It shows that links consume significantly less energy than nodes in both networks. This means that the energy saving is achievable by switching off links, but there is less contribution to the total energy saving than by switching off nodes. Moreover, we notice that it is interesting that the total energy consumption of the EASBP model is always higher than EABP 1:1. The reason for this is that the total capacity saving needs more energy usage to be compromised. In other words, for achieving the efficient capacity consumption using backup paths sharing, the primary paths of traffic demands need to be disjointed, therefore, more nodes and links are turning into working mode which causes energy expenditure to rise significantly. Moreover, EABP 1+1 consumes more power than the other two in every scenario of traffic demands.

Figure 9.11 gives a graphic view of the behaviors of total energy consumption of the three models according to various traffic demands in COST266. It clearly shows that EABP 1+1 model always consumes more power compared with the other two models. The main reason is that EABP 1+1 does not have sleeping technology. In addition, EABP 1:1 is the most energy efficient model among the three. This is because it can switch backup resources into sleeping mode, and yet not need to disjoint primary path for some connection requests

TABLE 9.3   Energy Consumption (Watts) for Links and Nodes of Different Models in Various Connect Requests of the COST266

		Connect Requests = 30 Gbit	**Connect Requests = 60 Gbit**	**Connect Requests = 90 Gbit**	**Connect Requests = 120 Gbit**
EABP 1+1	Links	1311.1	2023.6	2510.3	3183.2
	Nodes	129,081	159,816	190,551	255,394
	Total	130,392.1	161,839.6	193,061.3	258,577.2
EABP 1:1	Links	674.1	1158.2	1686.5	1927.7
	Nodes	63,063	100,366	115,733.5	131,101
	Total	63,737.1	101,524.2	117,420	133,028.2
EASBP	Links	1147.5	1856.4	2215.2	2870.7
	Nodes	105,709.4	137,522	143,017.5	152,375
	Total	106,856.9	139,378.4	145,232.7	155,245.7

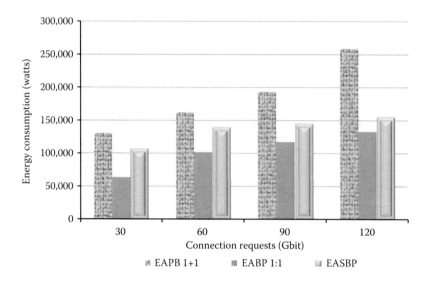

FIGURE 9.11   Total energy consumption vs. traffic scenarios for the three models in the COST266.

to achieve backup resource sharing. Furthermore, along with the increase of connection requests, there is a trend that the gap of energy consumption between EABP 1:1 and EASBP is shortened. It is because when traffic demands increase to certain amount, more nodes will be working state and less can be switched off or in sleep mode, thus the advantage of EABP 1:1 on energy saving is not so obvious compared to EASBP.

From the findings above, we come to the following three conclusions: First, EABP 1+1 is the most energy-hunger model in the three energy-aware survivable-routing models. Because EABP 1+1 is the only model that has not applied sleeping technology, therefore it confirms that sleeping mode is a promising approach to reduce energy cost. The main difference between EABP 1+1 and EABP 1:1 is that the latter's backup paths can be switched into sleeping mode while the former's backup paths are always occupied for transmitting exactly the same data as primary path. Therefore by comparing EABP 1+1 and EABP 1:1, we will see how much energy can be saved by sleeping mode. In COST266, when traffic demand is 30 Gbit, the energy usage of EABP 1:1 is 48.8% of that of EABP 1+1. Therefore, sleeping mode could save up to half the power expenditure in this topology.

Second, EABP 1:1 algorithm is our most energy efficient model due to the energy-aware routing, energy consumption rating and sleeping mode strategies. By comparing this with the traditional approach, the energy-saving figure can be found. The traditional telecommunication routing strategy, that is, the Multi Commodity Flow (MCF) algorithm, is that energy consumption is independent of traffic loads [58] and tries to balance the traffic as evenly as possible on the network link [59] for the sake of network survivability. In other words, the traditional MCF algorithm is trying to get more links and nodes involved in order to lower the utilization level, and it does not have the energy scaling strategy and the sleeping mode. Therefore, in our two networks, we assume MCF sets every link and node into working status with full power. Hence, by calculating 28 nodes and 82 links working on full power, we can get the energy consumption of the MCF is 692,852 Watts in the

COST266. Compared to the worst-case scenario, our most energy efficient model—EABP 1:1, could save up to 90% of power expenditure when connect requests are 30 Gbit.

Last but not least, when traffic demands increase, the value of energy consumption of EASBP will draw near to that of EABP 1:1. In other words, when traffic demands of network are high, the advantage of EABP 1:1 will become less obvious compared with EASBP on energy saving because more and more network elements have to be switched on to support various traffic demands.

In summary, nodes can consume significantly more energy than links, therefore switching off or putting unnecessary nodes into sleep mode could contribute to more energy saving than doing the same with links. In addition, the sleeping technique is a promising approach to reduce energy wasting; it could save up to half the power expenditure in certain network topology and traffic demands. Moreover, as compared with the traditional MCF algorithm, our most energy efficient model, that is, EABP 1:1 could save up to 90% of energy cost when a network is lightly loaded. This is due to combinational using of energy-aware routing, energy consumption rating strategy, and sleeping mode technology. Finally, when traffic demands in a network are high, the advantage of the EABP 1:1 on energy saving will become less obvious compared to EASBP.

Capacity Consumption

In this session, we will look into the capacity usage requirements of the three algorithms. Figure 9.12 reveals the difference of their capacity usage behavior in the topology of COST266.

It can be seen from the bar graph that EABP 1:1 shown as red bars always consumes more capacity than the other two models. It shows that more energy saving requires more capacity to be sacrificed. For minimizing the total energy consumption, EABP 1:1 model tends to reserve the backup path in existing sleeping links and nodes, which may need to detour

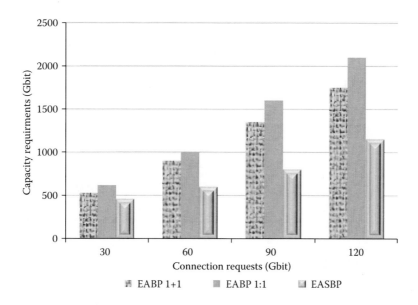

FIGURE 9.12   Total capacity consumption vs. traffic scenarios for the three models in the COST266.

primary or backup route, which causes the increase of the total amount of capacity usage. As for EABP 1+1 shown in blue, it does not apply sleeping mode, hence it will select the shortest path for both primary and backup paths in order to get less network devices allocated. This is why it needs less capacity than EABP 1:1. For EASBP, it will search for potential shareable backup paths for traffic flows to save capacity usage, which makes it as the most capacity aware model among the three. Furthermore, it is noticeable that the gap between the red bar and the green bar, which represent EABP 1:1 and EASBP, is widened along with the increasing of connection requests. This is because alongside the increase of traffic requests, there are more links and nodes that can be shared for backup in the EASBP model. In detail, the capacity consumption of EASBP is approximately 63% of EABP 1:1 when connection requests are equal to 60 Gbit, and this value drops to about 53% when requests increase to 120 Gbit.

In summary, by analyzing the three models' capacity performance in the COST266 topologies, two conclusions can be reached. First, EABP 1:1 model consumes more capacity among the three, because it needs to use relatively more capacity to achieve energy saving. Second, as the traffic demands go up, the capacity consumption gap between EABP1:1 and EASBP becomes larger. In other words, as the traffic demands increase, the advantage of EASBP becomes even more noticeable.

The State of Network Elements
When the traffic demands are relatively large, the states of network elements (i.e., links and nodes) are shown in Figure 9.13. It is interesting to see that EABP 1:1 is trying to switch more nodes into sleeping or power-off state to achieve energy saving, because nodes consume much more energy compared to links. EABP 1:1 has 10 nodes working in low energy consumption status (either in power-off or sleeping), while EABP 1+1 and EASBP have

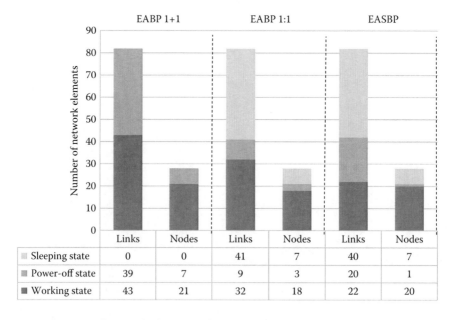

	EABP 1+1		EABP 1:1		EASBP	
	Links	Nodes	Links	Nodes	Links	Nodes
Sleeping state	0	0	41	7	40	7
Power-off state	39	7	9	3	20	1
Working state	43	21	32	18	22	20

FIGURE 9.13 The state of network elements when connection requests = 120 Gbit in the COST266.

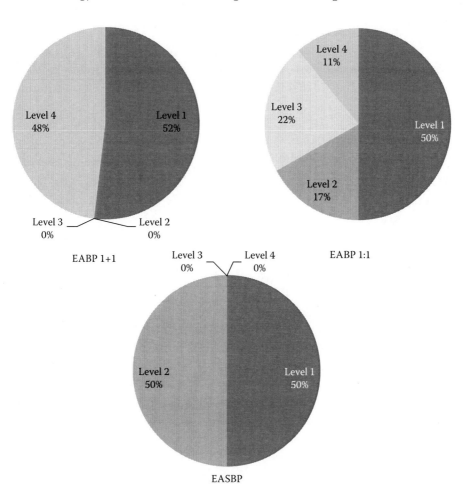

FIGURE 9.14 The working level of nodes of different models when connection requests = 120 Gbit in COST266.

7 nodes and 8 nodes, respectively. That is the reason why EABP 1:1 is the most energy efficient model among the three.

Figure 9.14 illustrates the energy level of working nodes in the three models when connection requests equal to 120 Gbit. It shows that EABP 1+1 has 48% of nodes which are working on the highest level, while EABP 1:1 has 22% nodes working on the third level and 11% nodes on the fourth level. These highly loaded nodes may become obstacles when network's traffic demands increase further. On the other hand, the EASBP model has no nodes working on the third and the highest level, which indicates that EASBP has much better network capacity compared to the former two models when the traffic demands become larger.

SIMULATION OF ENERGY-AWARE SURVIVABLE-ROUTING MODELS IN TOTEM TOOLBOX

As CPLEX + OPL development environment can only produce numerical results, it is more useful and informative to implement the three models in a network simulator, which can better visualize the results and also show how the models work. For visualizing the results, we have developed and embedded the three energy-aware survivable-routing models into a simulation toolbox—TOTEM [62,63], which stands for TOolbox for Traffic Engineering Methods. In this chapter, we present how we develop TOTEM to primarily integrate our new three energy-aware survivable-routing models in detail. Then the simulation results are analyzed and compared.

Integrate Energy-Aware Survivable-Routing Models into TOTEM

The TOTEM toolbox has been designed to facilitate the integration of new algorithms by providing different generic network simulation components. It provides topology information (nodes, links, LSPs, etc.) to the algorithm to be integrated. It also provides multiple scenarios execution functionalities.

In our work, we have primarily integrated our three energy-aware survivable-routing algorithms in TOTEM, then modified its Topology Manager, Algorithms Repository and Native Interfaces. First, we have modified its GUI file, such as adding a drop-down list for our three algorithms, and also introducing a new link status of turn off, which is indicated by the color yellow when the utilization of these links equals to zero (see Figure 9.15). In this condition, we assume these links have no loads which could be turned off. Then, we have built our ILP models using AMPL [64], which is a modeling language similar to OPL. These models are placed in totem\src\resources\modelAMPL, so that they can be called by TOTEM main function. The last step is to modify the Java core functions so that the models can be called, and the results can be transferred and interpreted into GUI to be visualized in diagram.

Simulation in the COST266 Network

We have conducted simulation studies of these three models in the COST266 network. All parameters of network configuration are identical to the previous chapter. We have chosen

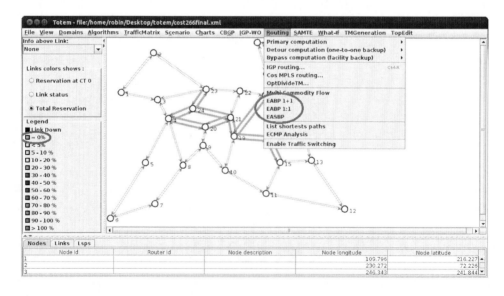

FIGURE 9.15 Modification on TOTEM GUI.

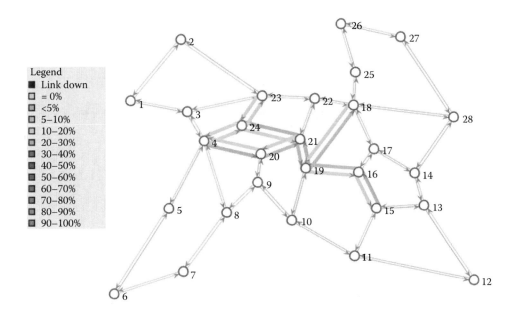

FIGURE 9.16   Simulation results of MCF in the COST266.

the large connection requests (120G) as our simulation traffic matrix. Moreover, the MCF algorithm is used here as a benchmark algorithm.

Figure 9.16 demonstrates the simulation results of the MCF algorithm in the COST266 network. The thick lines are the high capacity links with the volume of 320 Gbit/s, while the thin lines are links with the capacity of 80 Gbit/s. As we can see from Figure 9.16 that the colors of links mostly are green or light green, which indicates that links carry very low traffic load (below 10%) when using the MCF algorithm. However, the MCF does not apply any energy-aware strategy, which means all nodes in MCF are in working status. Thus MCF is a good model to balance the link utilization but sacrifices extra energy consumption for diversity.

The simulation of EABP 1+1 can be found in Figure 9.17. Here we can see that node 24 and node 15 could be shut down, because all links connected to it are in yellow, which means no traffic loads. Compared with MCF, nearly half of the working links of EABP 1+1 are in higher utilization rate, shown in blue or purple. It may not be as advanced as MCF on balancing links' utilization, but by shutting two possible nodes down and applying the energy consumption rating strategy, it can reduce more energy than MCF (Figure 9.18).

The EABP 1:1 model's simulation result is shown in Figure 9.19. First, we notice that there are two nodes that could be shut down, node 24 and node 19. Second, in the core of the network, most of the links have no traffic loads or in light loads, shown in yellow or in green. However, on the edge, the links have almost formed a "purple ring" which indicates the links' capacity is highly utilized over 60%. The reason is that since the edge nodes are the terminals of traffic demands, most of the edge nodes and links have to be turned on, therefore EABP 1:1 tries to aggregate the traffic flows into the already working edge nodes and links. In other word, EABP 1:1 avoids as much as possible to turn on core nodes or

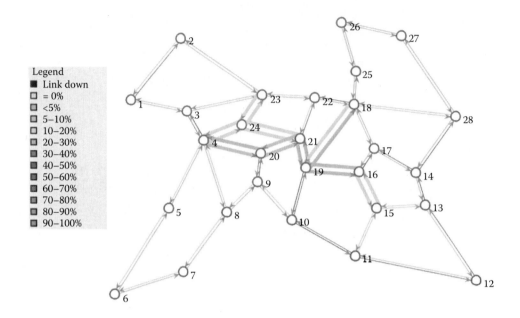

FIGURE 9.17   Simulation results of EABP 1+1 in the COST266.

links to save energy. It will turn off some of the core nodes and aggregate the backup capacity to the rest core nodes, which could be switched into sleeping mode.

Figure 9.19 shows the situation of the EASBP algorithm simulating in the COST266 network. It also has two nodes that could be shut down: the node 20 and node 15. Compared to EABP 1:1, most of the working links of EASBP have not reached high utilization levels.

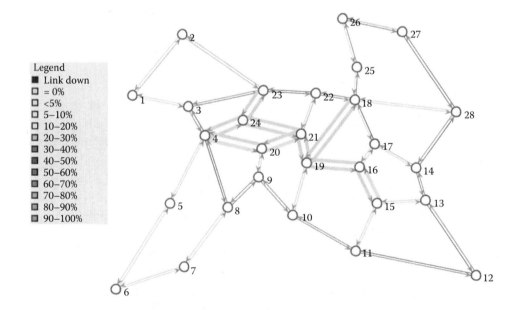

FIGURE 9.18   Simulation results of EABP 1:1 in the COST266.

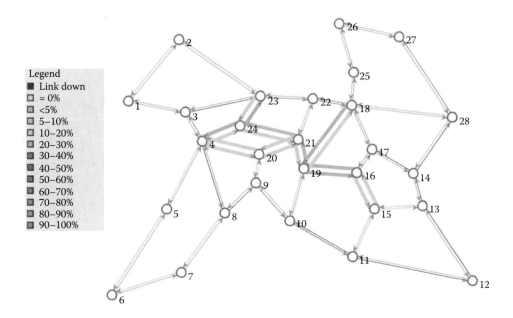

FIGURE 9.19   Simulation results of EASBP in the COST266.

It can be seen that there are just a few links in purple, which reflects that EASBP has an advantage over EABP 1:1 on lowering the utilization of links.

Moreover, Figure 9.20 compares the link utilization of these four models' capacity behavior. It can be seen that all the red bars, which represent the MCF algorithm, are in the first two utilization intervals, which confirms that MCF is targeting to load balancing

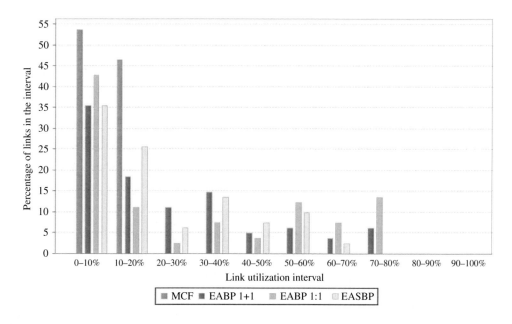

FIGURE 9.20   Link utilization distribution of the four models in the COST266.

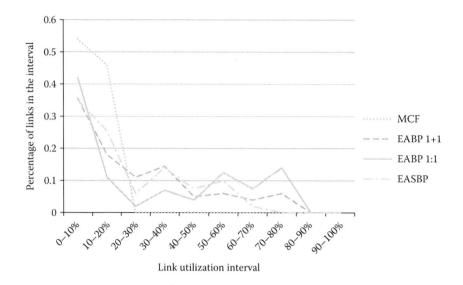

FIGURE 9.21   Link usage states of the four models in the COST266.

and thus no link goes over 20% of its capacity. While for EABP 1+1 represented as blue bars, more than 17% of its links reach 50% utilization or higher. This figure for EABP 1:1 is even worse, approximately 35% of its links are in more than 50% utilization. However, EASBP shown as yellow bars has only 12% half loaded and no one link reaches utilization of 70%. Figure 9.21 further illustrates the utilization comparison among the four models. It also showed that, when the utilization of links is above 50%, EABP 1:1 highlighted with solid green lines is above all other models, while EASBP (purple lines) is below the other two. This interesting finding again proves that EASBP has better performance of lowering links' utilization, while EABP 1:1 and EABP 1+1 aggregate traffic flows which increase the burden of links.

From the overall findings in the COST266 network, we can draw three conclusions. First, MCF has the best performance on lowering links' utilization. The reason for that is MCF sets most of the nodes and links in working state to share traffic load. Second, EABP 1:1 aggregates traffic flow into edge nodes and links, and avoids as much as possible turning on core nodes or links to save energy. It is the most energy efficient model among the four, yet has the highest link utilization. Last but not least, the EASBP has the best performance of lowering the utilization of links among our models.

CONCLUSION AND FUTURE WORK

The main target of this study was to find a possible approach to tackle the trade-off between energy reduction and network survivability in the design of the Big Data network highway. There are three main contributions: first, three energy-aware survivable-routing algorithms have been proposed, which not only consider energy reduction, but also take network survivability into account. In energy-saving aspects, we integrate several green technologies into the algorithms, such as energy-aware routing, sleeping mode, and energy consumption rating strategy. For network survivability concern, EABP 1+1, EABP 1:1, and EASBP are embedded with 1+1 backup protection, 1:1 backup protection, and shared backup protection, respectively. Moreover, we develop the ILP formulations for each of them.

Then the ILP models of three routing algorithms have been implemented in IBM ILOG CPLEX Optimization Studio and solved by the CPLEX 11.1 Solver. By collecting the numerical results, the performance of the three routing algorithms is extensively studied and compared. The results show that when designing the Big Data network highway, EASBP could be the best approach to tackle the trade-off between energy reduction and network survivability. This model consumes significantly less capacity but a small increase in energy expenditure, especially under the condition of large traffic demands. Furthermore, to visualize the results, we develop and embed the three energy-aware survivable-routing models into the TOTEM simulator. Among our models, EASBP consumes less capacity and has the advantage of limiting the utilization of the links. Besides, when traffic demands increase to a large number, the performance of EASBP will be comparable to the most energy efficient model—EABP 1:1 on the energy reduction aspect.

This study has initiated an interesting research direction to explore the combined impact on network performance such as network survivability in Big Data network design. Considering the work covered in the study and the development of future networks, it would be useful to highlight some future areas of investigation. More extensive studies on the optimization between capacity efficiency, energy efficiency in more complex topologies and traffic patterns should be explored. In this research, it is hoped to find the relationship among network topology, traffic demand, energy reduction, and network survivability. In other words, for improving our models' advantages, how to modify network topology according to traffic demand, that is, adding nodes or links. Moreover other QoS metrics such as delay, and control data overhead could be taken into consideration for the purpose of network survivability. It is possible to add a delay factor into our models' ILP formulations. In addition, there are energy expenditures when switching the node between working mode and sleeping mode in data center networks. Therefore it is worthy to consider switching overheads in our models.

REFERENCES

1. H. Hu, Y. Wen, T.-S. Chua, X. Li, Toward scalable systems for big data analytics: A technology tutorial, *Access*, IEEE, vol. 2, pp. 652, 687, 2014.
2. J. Zhang, Y. Chen, T. Li, Opportunities of innovation under challenges of big data, in *Fuzzy Systems and Knowledge Discovery (FSKD), 2013 10th International Conference on*, pp. 669, 673, July 23–25, 2013.
3. S. Pandey and V. Tokekar, Prominence of MapReduce in big data processing, in *Communication Systems and Network Technologies (CSNT), 2014 Fourth International Conference on*, pp. 555, 560, April 7–9, 2014.
4. X. Cheng, C. Hu, Y. Li, W. Lin, H. Zuo, Data evolution analysis of virtual DataSpace for managing the big data lifecycle, *Parallel and Distributed Processing Symposium Workshops & PhD Forum (IPDPSW), 2013 IEEE 27th International*, pp. 2054, 2063, May 20–24, 2013.
5. X. Yi, F. Liu, J. Liu, H. Jin, Building a network highway for big data: Architecture and challenges, *Network*, IEEE, vol. 28, no. 4, pp. 5, 13, July–August 2014.
6. A. Katal, M. Wazid, R.H. Goudar, Big data: Issues, challenges, tools and good practices, in *Contemporary Computing (IC3), 2013 Sixth International Conference on*, pp. 404, 409, Aug. 8–10, 2013.

7. F. Tekiner, J.A. Keane, Big data framework, in *Systems, Man, and Cybernetics (SMC), 2013 IEEE International Conference on*, pp. 1494, 1499, Oct. 13–16, 2013.

8. Z. Liu, P. Yang, L. Zhang, A sketch of big data technologies, in *Internet Computing for Engineering and Science (ICICSE), 2013 Seventh International Conference on*, pp. 26, 29, Sept. 20–22, 2013.

9. M. Webb, SMART 2020: Enabling the low carbon economy in the information age, *The Climate Group*. London, vol. 1, p. 1.1, 2008.

10. P. Chowdhury et al., Towards green broadband access networks, in *Global Telecommunications Conf., 2009. GLOBECOM 2009*. IEEE, Honolulu, Hawaii, USA, pp. 1–6, 2009.

11. W.D. Nordhaus, To slow or not to slow: The economics of the greenhouse effect, *The Economic Journal*, vol. 101, pp. 920–937, 1991.

12. D. Pamlin and K. Szomolányi, Saving the climate@ the speed of light. First roadmap for reduced CO_2 emissions in the EU and beyond, *European Telecommunications Network Operators' Association and WWF*, 2006, http://www.pamlin.net/new/?publication=saving-the-climate-the-speed-of-light.

13. N. Wang et al., An overview of routing optimization for Internet traffic engineering, *Communications Surveys & Tutorials*, IEEE, vol. 10, pp. 36–56, 2008.

14. C. Lange, Energy-related aspects in backbone networks, in *Proc. 35th European Conf. on Optical Communication (ECOC 2009), (Wien, AU)*, Vienna, Austria, 2009.

15. K.J. Christensen et al., The next frontier for communications networks: Power management, *Computer Communications*, vol. 27, pp. 1758–1770, 2004.

16. C. Cavdar et al., Energy-efficient design of survivable WDM networks with shared backup, in *Global Telecommunications Conf. (GLOBECOM 2010)*, IEEE, Miami, Florida, USA, pp. 1–5, 2010.

17. Y. Agarwal et al., Somniloquy: Augmenting network interfaces to reduce PC energy usage, in *Proc. 6th USENIX Symp. Networked Systems Design and Implementation*, Boston, Massachusetts, USA, pp. 365–380, 2009.

18. L. Chiaraviglio et al., Reducing power consumption in backbone networks, in *Communications, 2009. ICC'09. IEEE Int. Conf.*, Dresden, Germany, pp. 1–6, 2009.

19. T. Kelly and S. Head, ICTs and climate change, *ITU-T Technology, Tech. Rep*, 2007.

20. L. Chiaraviglio et al., Energy-aware networks: Reducing power consumption by switching off network elements, in *FEDERICA-Phosphorus Tutorial and Workshop (TNC2008)*, Bruges (Belgium), 2008.

21. *Energy Management: Telecom New Zealand Limited Web Page*, http://www.telecom.co.nz/content/0,8748,203942-203113,00.html.

22. R. Bolla et al., Energy efficiency in the future Internet: A survey of existing approaches and trends in energy-aware fixed network infrastructures, *Communications Surveys & Tutorials*, IEEE, vol. 13, pp. 223–244, 2011.

23. E. Gelenbe and C. Morfopoulou, Routing and G-networks to optimise energy and quality of service in packet networks, *Energy-Efficient Computing and Networking*, vol. 54, pp. 163–173, 2011.

24. E. Yetginer and G.N. Rouskas, Power efficient traffic grooming in optical WDM networks, in *Global Telecommunications Conf., 2009. GLOBECOM 2009*. IEEE, Honolulu, Hawaii, USA, pp. 1–6, 2009.

25. S. Nedevschi et al., Reducing network energy consumption via sleeping and rate-adaptation, in *Proc. the 5th USENIX Symp. Networked Systems Design and Implementation*, Salt Lake City, Utah, USA, 2008.

26. C. Gunaratne et al., Managing energy consumption costs in desktop PCs and LAN switches with proxying, split TCP connections, and scaling of link speed, *Int. Journal of Network Management*, vol. 15, pp. 297–310, 2005.

27. L. Irish and K.J. Christensen, A "Green TCP/IP" to reduce electricity consumed by computers, in *Southeastcon'98. Proc. IEEE*, pp. 302–305, 1998, http://ieeexplore.ieee.org/xpl/articleDetails. jsp?tp=&arnumber=673356&queryText%3DA+%E2%80%9CGreen+TCP%2FIP%E2%80 %9D+to+reduce+electricity+consumed+by+computers.

28. D. Chen et al., Network survivability performance evaluation: A quantitative approach with applications in wireless ad-hoc networks, in *Proc. the 5th ACM Int. Workshop on Modeling Analysis and Simulation of Wireless and Mobile Systems*, Newport Beach, California, USA, pp. 61–68, 2002.

29. S. Balon et al., A scalable and decentralized fast-rerouting scheme with efficient bandwidth sharing, *Computer Networks*, vol. 50, pp. 3043–3063, 2006.

30. A.P. Bianzino et al., Energy-aware routing: A reality check, in *GLOBECOM Workshops (GC Wkshps)*, IEEE, pp. 1422–1427, 2010.

31. S. Henzler et al., Sleep transistor circuits for fine-grained power switch-off with short power-down times, in *Solid-State Circuits Conf., 2005. Dig. Tech. Papers. ISSCC. 2005 IEEE Int.*, pp. 302–600, 2005.

32. M. Baldi and Y. Ofek, Time for a "Greener" Internet, in *Communications Workshops, 2009. ICC Workshops 2009. IEEE Int. Conf.*, pp. 1–6, 2009.

33. A. Bianzino et al., Energy-awareness in network dimensioning: A fixed charge network flow formulation, in *1st Int. Conf. Energy-Efficient Computing and Networking (e-Energy 2010), Extended Abstract*, Passau, Germany, 2010.

34. A. Kansal and F. Zhao, Fine-grained energy profiling for power-aware application design, *ACM SIGMETRICS Performance Evaluation Review*, vol. 36, pp. 26–31, 2008.

35. J.C.C. Restrepo et al., Energy profile aware routing, in *Communications Workshops, 2009. ICC Workshops 2009. IEEE Int. Conf.*, pp. 1–5, 2009.

36. E. Gelenbe and T. Mahmoodi, Energy-aware routing in the cognitive packet network, in *ENERGY 2011, The 1st Int. Conf. Smart Grids, Green Communications and IT Energy-Aware Technologies*, Venice, Italy, pp. 7–12, 2011.

37. W. Fisher et al., Greening backbone networks: Reducing energy consumption by shutting off cables in bundled links, in *Proc. 1st ACM SIGCOMM Workshop on Green Networking*, pp. 29–34, 2010.

38. M. Allman et al., Enabling an energy-efficient future Internet through selectively connected end systems, in *6th ACM Workshop on Hot Topics in Networks (HotNets)*, Atlanta, Georgia, USA, pp. 1–6, 2007.

39. G. Ananthanarayanan and R.H. Katz, Greening the switch, in *Proc. HotPower*, 2008.

40. K. Bilal et al., A survey on Green communications using Adaptive Link Rate, *Cluster Computing*, pp. 1–15, 2012.

41. K.J. Nowka et al., A 32-bit PowerPC system-on-a-chip with support for dynamic voltage scaling and dynamic frequency scaling, *Solid-State Circuits, IEEE Journal of*, vol. 37, pp. 1441–1447, 2002.

42. H. Hlavacs et al., Energy consumption of residential and professional switches, in *Computational Science and Engineering, 2009. CSE'09. Int. Conf.*, pp. 240–246, 2009.

43. P. Mahadevan et al., A power benchmarking framework for network devices, *NETWORKING 2009*, pp. 795–808, 2009.

44. S. Paget-McNicol et al., The Plasmodium falciparum var gene switching rate, switching mechanism and patterns of parasite recrudescence described by mathematical modelling, *Parasitology*, vol. 124, pp. 225–235, 2002.

45. J. Boch et al., The use of a dose-rate switching technique to characterize bipolar devices, *Nuclear Science, IEEE Transactions on*, vol. 56, pp. 3347–3353, 2009.

46. C. Gunaratne et al., Reducing the energy consumption of Ethernet with adaptive link rate (ALR), *Computers, IEEE Transactions on*, vol. 57, pp. 448–461, 2008.

47. A. Markopoulou et al., Characterization of failures in an IP backbone, in *INFOCOM 2004. Twenty-third Annu. Joint Conf. IEEE Computer and Communications Societies*, pp. 2307–2317, 2004.

48. K. Kar et al., Routing restorable bandwidth guaranteed connections using maximum 2-route flows, *Networking, IEEE/ACM Transactions on*, vol. 11, pp. 772–781, 2003.

49. M. Kodialam and T. Lakshman, Minimum interference routing with applications to MPLS traffic engineering, in *INFOCOM 2000. 19th Annu. Joint Conf. IEEE Computer and Communications Societies. Proc. IEEE*, pp. 884–893, 2000.

50. M. Kodialam and T. Lakshman, Dynamic routing of locally restorable bandwidth guaranteed tunnels using aggregated link usage information, in *INFOCOM 2001. 20th Annu. Joint Conf. IEEE Computer and Communications Societies. Proc. IEEE*, pp. 376–385, 2001.

51. G. Li et al., Efficient distributed path selection for shared restoration connections, in *INFOCOM 2002. 21st Annu. Joint Conf. IEEE Computer and Communications Societies. Proc. IEEE*, pp. 140–149, 2002.

52. Q. Chunming and X. Dahai, Distributed partial information management (DPIM) schemes for survivable networks.1, in *INFOCOM 2002. 21st Annu. Joint Conf. IEEE Computer and Communications Societies. Proc. IEEE*, vol. 1, pp. 302–311, 2002.

53. D.A. Mello et al., A matrix-based analytical approach to connection unavailability estimation in shared backup path protection, *Commun. Lett., IEEE*, vol. 9, pp. 844–846, 2005.

54. A.M. Koster et al., Towards robust network design using integer linear programming techniques, in *Next Generation Internet (NGI), 2010 6th EURO-NF Conf.*, pp. 1–8, 2010.

55. R.M. Karp, Reducibility among combinatorial problems, *50 Years of Integer Programming 1958–2008*, pp. 219–241, 2010.

56. J. Könemann et al., From primal-dual to cost shares and back: A stronger LP relaxation for the Steiner forest problem, *Automata, Languages and Programming Lecture Notes in Computer Science*, vol. 3580, pp. 930–942, 2005, http://link.springer.com/chapter/10.1007%2F11523468_75.

57. M.S. Bazaraa et al., *Linear Programming and Network Flows*, vol. 2, Wiley Online Library, 1990.

58. S. Ricciardi et al., Energy-aware RWA for WDM networks with dual power sources, in *Communications (ICC), 2011 IEEE Int. Conf.*, pp. 1–6, 2011.

59. A. Vahdat et al., Every joule is precious: The case for revisiting operating system design for energy efficiency, in *Proc. 9th workshop on ACM SIGOPS European Workshop: Beyond the PC: New Challenges for the Operating System*, pp. 31–36, 2000.

60. P. Van Hentenryck, *The OPL Optimization Programming Language*, The MIT Press, Cambridge, Massachusetts, 1999.

61. G. Pérez Sainz de Rozas and M. A. Garín Martín, On downloading and using CPLEX within COIN-OR for solving linear/integer optimization problems, *Biltoki*, 2011, http://www.researchgate.net/publication/254410538_On_Downloading_and_Using_CPLEX_within_COIN-OR_for_Solving_LinearInteger_Optimization_Problems.

62. J. Lepropre, S. Balon, and G. Leduc, Totem: A toolbox for traffic engineering methods, *Poster and Demo Session of INFOCOM'06*, April 2006.

63. G. Leduc et al., An open source traffic engineering toolbox, *Computer Communications*, vol. 29, pp. 593–610, 2006.

64. R. Fourer et al., *The AMPL Book*, Duxbury Press, Pacific Grove, 2002.

III

Networking Security for Big Data

CHAPTER 10

A Review of Network Intrusion Detection in the Big Data Era

Challenges and Future Trends

Weizhi Meng and Wenjuan Li

CONTENTS

INTRODUCTION

Intrusions such as virus, malware, and Trojans are a big challenge for current network security. An intrusion can be defined as any set of actions that attempt to compromise the integrity, confidentiality, or availability of a resource [1]. In order to mitigate this problem, intrusion detection systems (IDSs), especially network intrusion detection systems (NIDSs), are widely implemented in different network environments aiming to defend against various network attacks. These systems can be roughly classified as signature-based NIDSs and anomaly-based NIDSs. Specifically, a signature-based NIDS like Snort [2] detects an attack mainly based on its stored signatures where a signature is an expert knowledge-based description of known attacks and exploits. On the other hand, an anomaly-based NIDS like Bro [3] aims to identify an anomaly by comparing pre-established normal profiles with current network events. A profile can be used to represent a normal network connection.

Network intrusion detection primarily focuses on the identification of potential network attacks and anomalies. For example, these systems could detect and alert when an attacker has successfully compromised a network system and then report the incident to security administrators. In particular, signature-based detection is very effective in detecting known threats but is ineffective in detecting previously unknown threats [4]. For example, a signature searching for "ddos.exe" could not match "ddos2.exe." In contrast, anomaly-based detection is very effective at detecting previously unknown threats, since an anomaly usually performs significantly different from the established normal profiles for a specific network. However, in practice, the signature-based NIDSs are more widely used in an organization than the anomaly-based NIDSs. The main reason is that the false alarm rate, which indicates the possibility of generating an alarm when there is no intrusion, incurred by the former is significantly lower than that by the latter [5].

In a traditional network, overload network packets are already a challenging issue for network intrusion detection, in which the number of network packets would greatly exceed the maximum processing capability of an IDS [6,7]. With the rapid development of the Internet, data volumes during communication have become significantly large. This situation is even more complex than that in a traditional network [8]. Thus, the term *Big Data* developed, which describes data that is difficult to be managed efficiently by on-hand techniques, tools, and devices. For instance, every day, 2.5 quintillion bytes of data are created and 90% of the data in the world today were produced within the past 2 years [9].

Compared to the overload packets in a traditional network, Big Data makes the situation more complicated and involves more characteristics. For example, Big Data can be represented by a mathematical relationship among three independent variables: volume, velocity, and variety [10]. Using these variables, we can define Big Data as such a situation: when the volume, variety, and velocity of the data are increased, rendering current techniques and technologies unable to handle storage and processing of the data. The situation above can be defined as Big Data, that is, network traffic in Big Data can show high volume of data with large varieties of traffic types arriving at high velocity. In these cases, an IDS would be greatly affected since detection is time-sensitive and requires highly efficient techniques. In the era of Big Data, many issues of network intrusion detection would become even worse. In order to survive an IDS in such an environment, it is critical to take appropriate countermeasures to improve detection performance.

In the literature, there are more research works paying attention to Big Data, but still not many articles discussing intrusion detection under Big Data. In this chapter, we focus on the impact of Big Data on network intrusion detection and our motivation is to provide an overview regarding potential challenges and promising solutions. The contributions of the chapter can be summarized as below:

- We begin by providing a brief introduction related to the background of Big Data (e.g., characteristics) and intrusion detection (e.g., work flow).

- We then identify major challenges and issues regarding intrusion detection in the era of Big Data, describe potential solutions, and present related research studies in the literature.

- We later present a study by employing an additional mechanism to improve the performance of network intrusion detection under Big Data volumes and point out the future trends in this area.

The remaining parts of this chapter are organized as follows. Section "Background" introduces the background of Big Data and network intrusion detection. Section "Challenges and Issues for Network Intrusion Detection in the Era of Big Data" identifies major challenges and issues for network intrusion detection in the era of Big Data and section "Potential Solutions and Research Studies" presents potential techniques and existing research efforts which aim to tackle the issues caused by Big Data. In section "Our Study and Future Trends," we conduct a study and point out future trends. Finally, section "Conclusion" makes a conclusion.

BACKGROUND

Intrusion detection has been developed for over 30 years, while the notion of Big Data is relatively new. In order to better understand these topics, in this section, we attempt to introduce the background of Big Data and intrusion detection.

Big Data

There are few works in literature regarding Big Data in network intrusion detection. Before introducing these existing approaches, a basic question is what Big Data is. Intuitively, this term implies that this kind of data is somewhat small or that the only challenge is its sheer size. In short, Big Data applies to information where the data cannot be processed or analyzed using traditional processes or tools [10]. In other words, it is a collection of large and complex data sets that is difficult to process using on-hand database management tools.

Current organizations are facing more and more Big Data-related problems. For instance, a company has access to a wealth of information, but it may not know how to get value from the information. The main reason is that the information is in a raw format or semistructured format or unstructured format. Thus, it is hard to decide whether the information is worth keeping. To tackle this issue, we require exceptional technologies to efficiently process large quantities of data within tolerable elapsed times. Some technologies are being applied to Big Data including massively parallel-processing (MPP), data-mining grids, search-based applications, distributed file systems and databases, and cloud-based infrastructure.

In particular, Big Data can be represented using three independent variables (or characteristics): volume, velocity, and variety [10]. In Figure 10.1, we present these characteristics from a view of IBM. These new characteristics create the need for a new way to provide better control over the existing knowledge domain and the ability to act on them.

- *Volume.* In the year of 2000, about 800,000 petabytes (PB) of data were stored in the world, but most of the data has not been analyzed. By the year of 2020, this number is expected to reach 35 zettabytes (ZB). Take Twitter as an example, it may generate 7 terabytes (TB) of data every day [10]. As shown in Figure 10.1, it is visible that data volumes have changed from terabytes to perabytes with an inevitable shift to zettabytes. In addition, it is imaginable that the percentage of data that can be processed by an organization is decreasing while the amount of data is on the rise. Therefore, some data cannot be analyzed in time or even will not be analyzed. For this gap between

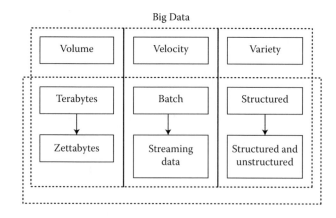

FIGURE 10.1   IBM characterizes Big Data by its volume, velocity, and variety.

the increased data volumes and the relatively decreased processing capability, it is hard to know the possible consequences.

- *Variety.* With a lot of collaboration technologies, data in an organization has already become complex as it contains not only traditional relational data, but also raw, semistructured and unstructured data from other sources such as web pages, email messages, sensor data, search indexes, and so on. As shown in Figure 10.1, variety represents all types of data: a fundamental shift in analysis requirements from traditional structured data to include raw, semistructured, and unstructured data. As a result, traditional analytic platforms cannot handle this new characteristic of data volume.

- *Velocity.* Traditionally, the term of velocity mainly considers how quickly the data arrives and is stored and what the rates of retrieval are. In the era of Big Data, velocity has extended its definition: that is, data in motion. For instance, current organizations usually deal with petabytes of data instead of terabytes and the increasing information streams have made a constant flow of data at a pace at which a traditional system finds it hard to handle [10]. Figure 10.1 shows a shift from merely batch insight to streaming insight. Thus, handling the data requires performing analytics against the volume and variety of data while it is still in motion.

Big Data brings new challenges in the aspects of security and privacy [11]. Regarding intrusion detection, these new variables and characteristics make Big Data become a more challenging issue than the data management problems before. For example, with the advent of Big Data, it is easily to collect more logs and information than before; however, more data does not always mean more understanding. Thus, developing techniques to tackle this issue has become very critical for intrusion detection.

Intrusion Detection

Intrusion detection is the process of monitoring the events occurring in a computer system or network and analyzing them for signs of possible *incidents*, which are violations or imminent threats of violation of computer security policies, acceptable use policies, or standard security practices [4]. Incidents can have many causes, such as malware such as worms, spyware, attackers gaining unauthorized access to systems from the Internet, and authorized users of systems who misuse their privileges or attempt to gain additional privileges. Based on this, an IDS is a kind of software that automates the intrusion detection process. For example, IDSs can be configured with firewall rules, allowing them to identify network traffic that violates the security policies of an organization. In real-world applications, these systems can be complementary to current security mechanisms.

In addition to identifying undesirable activity by monitoring and analyzing current events, all types of IDS technologies typically perform the following functions:

- *Recording information.* To record related useful information is very important for expert analysis. Information can be usually recorded locally, and may also be sent to a separate system such as centralized logging servers and enterprise management systems.

- *Notifying administrators.* The notification (also called *alert*) occurs when any intrusions are detected. An alert typically includes only basic information about an observed event, thus, security administrators have to access the IDS log for additional information.

- *Producing reports.* An IDS can be set to produce reports periodically according to specific demands.

According to the specific deployment, there are two basic types of IDSs: network intrusion detection systems (NIDSs) and host intrusion detection systems (HIDSs). The former monitors network traffic for particular network segments or devices and analyzes network, transport, and application protocols to identify suspicious activity, such as distributed denial of service (DDoS) attacks, certain forms of malware. By contrast, a host-based system aims to monitor the characteristics of a single/local host and the events occurring within that host for suspicious activity.

According to the different detection techniques, IDSs can be classified into two categories: signature-based detection and anomaly-based detection.

- *Signature-based detection* is the process of comparing signatures against observed events to identify possible incidents. It is very effective at detecting known threats but largely ineffective at detecting previously unknown threats, and many variants of known threats. For example, if an attacker modified the malware name to "freepics2.exe," then a signature looking for "freepics.exe" would not match it.

- *Anomaly-based detection* is the process of comparing definitions of what activity is considered normal against observed events to identify significant deviations. The key point for an anomaly-based detection system is to build an accurate normal profile. The normal profiles are usually developed by monitoring the characteristics of typical activity over a period of time. For example, profiles can be built for many behavioral attributes, such as the number of e-mails sent by a user, the number of failed login attempts for a host, and the level of processor usage for a host in a given period of time.

In Figure 10.2, we illustrate the work flow for a typical IDS. When network traffic arrives, the signature-based detection would perform differently from the anomaly-based detection.

- Signature-based detection will extract the packet payloads and compare them to the stored signatures. We call this process as signature matching (or signature comparison). If an accurate match is detected, then an alarm or several alarms will be produced.

- Anomaly-based detection will compare the current observed events with the prebuilt normal profile (called profile comparison). If the extracted feature values of current events exceed a normal threshold, then an alarm will be generated.

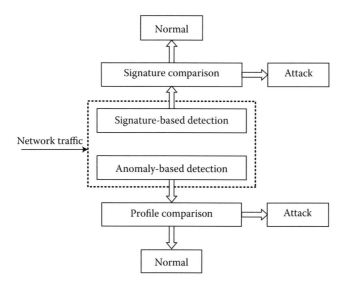

FIGURE 10.2   The work flow for a typical IDS.

Practical Case

Snort [2,12] is an open-source lightweight signature-based NIDS, which has the ability to perform real-time traffic analysis and packet logging on Internet Protocol (IP) networks by performing protocol analysis, content searching, and content matching.

In Figure 10.3, we illustrate the workflow of Snort. There are mainly four modules: *packet decoder, preprocessor, detection engine,* and *alarm generation.* Specifically, the packet decoder examines the structure of network packets and ensures that their constructions are in line with the specification. The preprocessor is mainly used to normalize traffic to

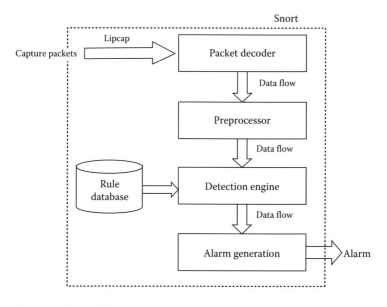

FIGURE 10.3   The work flow of Snort.

make sure that both packet data and signatures can be recognized. The detection engine is responsible for examining incoming packets and detecting potential attacks by launching signature matching. Finally, the alarm generation aims to report results and output alarms during the detection.

CHALLENGES AND ISSUES FOR NETWORK INTRUSION DETECTION IN THE ERA OF BIG DATA

In the era of Big Data, data volumes would become extremely large so that it is very difficult, or impossible for a traditional NIDS to handle such huge data sets. In the area of network intrusion detection, the Big Data problem has its own characteristics, that is, the large number of data can cause a chain reaction regarding the performance of NIDSs. The main challenges and issues regarding network intrusion detection under Big Data can be summarized in Table 10.1.

The table shows that the *volume* of Big Data can cause the traffic overloaded and simply exceed the processing capability of NIDSs. In other words, this characteristic makes the processing capability slower as compared to the size of incoming data volumes. The *velocity* of Big Data may cause a large number of packets to come within a unit time, which makes NIDSs hard to handle in real time and thus miss or drop many packets. Finally, the *variety* of Big Data makes data even complex so that it is very hard to select and extract suitable features during network intrusion detection. In addition, due to the complexity, traditional machine-learning techniques are not applicable under such situations.

Challenges and Issues regarding Large Data Volume

The intrusion detection task is very sensitive to time consumption. In a traditional network like a large-scale distributed network, overload network packets have already become a big problem for NIDSs when dealing with large data sets [6,7]. Taking Snort as an example, it usually spends about 30% of its total processing time in comparing its signatures with incoming packets, but the time consumption can reach more than 80% in a heavy traffic environment [13].

Big Data indicates the situation that data cannot be efficiently processed using on-hand tools. For NIDSs, the processing burden can be treated as a constant. When the incoming traffic significantly exceeds its processing capability, a large number of packets will be dropped or not be examined. In this case, a lot of security issues will be caused under such

TABLE 10.1 Main Challenges and Issues of Big Data in Network Intrusion Detection

Big Data Variables	Description	Challenges and Issues in Intrusion Detection
Volume	The size of data sets	1. Overload traffic 2. Making the processing capability low
Velocity	The speed of data arriving	1. Hard to handle traffic in real time 2. Missing packets
Variety	The complexity of data	1. Hard to select and extract features 2. Not applicable for traditional machine-learning techniques

a network environment (i.e., missing potential attacks). With the increasing data volumes, Big Data always can bring a heavy (or unaffordable) burden to existing solutions such as Network Traffic Recording System (NTRS), Hadoop Distributed File System (HDFS), and Cloud Computing Storage System (CCSS). For instance, bandwidth and latency are two major network features that will affect the communication between the clients and the cloud server. The data volumes of Big Data can greatly exhaust bandwidth and cause huge delays. In these cases, traditional intrusion detection techniques would not be effective in the era of Big Data.

Challenges and Issues regarding Real-Time Requirement

The early detection of an attack can provide a cost-effective strategy for organizations to limit and reduce loss. Thus, real-time detection is an important requirement for an efficient NIDS. However, in the era of Big Data, streaming data can continuously go through NIDSs (either signature-based or anomaly-based), which can exhaust the processing capability of a system more quickly than in a traditional network environment. Under Big Data, both detection methods are hard to meet the real-time requirement in a traditional way.

- For signature-based detection, the process of signature matching is a key limiting factor to hinder the performance of detection, in which the matching burden is at least linear to the size of an input string [14]. In the era of Big Data, more packets can arrive per unit time so that the process of signature matching becomes a crucial bottleneck. In order to meet the real-time requirement, more efficient signature matching is desirable.

- For anomaly-based detection, it is a hard job to analyze and manage such a large volume of incoming traffic in time. For example, it is difficult for this system to extract and establish event models from incoming data due to too many packets arriving within a unit time. With the restricted processing capability, the real-time requirement is difficult to achieve.

Challenges and Issues regarding Feature Selection and Extraction

As shown in Figure 10.2, either signature-based detection or anomaly-based detection requires extracting features from network traffic. Then, a pattern can be constructed using these features. However, in the era of Big Data, it is a difficult task for both detection methods to extract features effectively.

- Signature-based NIDSs need these features to create signatures (or rules) that can be used in the process of signature matching. But the *variety* of Big Data makes data more complex so that it is a challenging problem to select and extract appropriate features to represent such data.

- Anomaly-based NIDSs are usually based on machine-learning techniques, which can transform the original characteristics of the data to another single domain to improve detection accuracy, reduce computational complexity, and increase processing speed. However, the *variety* of Big Data requires multidomain due to its large and growing data domain. Therefore, it becomes a big challenge for selecting and extracting features for anomaly-based detection.

Challenges and Issues regarding Machine-Learning Techniques

Machine-learning techniques are a powerful tool for NIDSs, especially for anomaly-based NIDSs. However, the three major problems shown below make the traditional machine-learning techniques inappropriate for Big Data classification [15]:

- A machine-learning classifier is mainly trained on a particular labeled data set or data domain, and it may not be suitable for another data set or data domain. In this case, a traditional machine-learning algorithm cannot handle *variety* since it may not be robust over different data sets and data domains.

- In order to train a machine-learning classifier, a certain number of class types are required. But under Big Data, a large variety of class types can be dynamically growing which would lead to inaccurate classification results.

- In addition, traditional machine-learning technique is developed for a single learning task, thus it may be not suitable for multiple learning tasks and transfer requirements of Big Data analytics.

Challenges and Issues regarding Data Analysis in Intrusion Detection

Analyzing logs, network flows, and system events for intrusion detection has been a problem for the information security community for decades. Under Big Data, it is definitely inefficient for IDSs to perform analytics and complex queries on large, unstructured data sets with incomplete and noisy features [16]. For example, several popular security information and event management (SIEM) tools were not designed to analyze and manage unstructured data and were rigidly bound to predefined schemas. The most fundamental challenge for Big Data applications is to explore the large volumes of data and extract useful information or knowledge for future actions [17].

The management of large data warehouses has traditionally been expensive, and their deployment usually requires a strong business case. Therefore, developing new applications and schemes to handle Big Data is a big challenge for intrusion detection.

Challenges and Issues regarding Benchmark in Intrusion Detection

In the area of intrusion detection, the DARPA data set [18] is the only well-documented and widely available data set for testing the performance of an IDS. It was produced by MIT Lincoln Laboratory and Air Force Research Laboratory in 1998 and 1999. But McHugh [19] has conducted an evaluation on the DARPA data set and pointed out that this data set suffers from many issues associated with its design and execution. For example, many questions remain unsettled regarding the use of synthetic data to estimate a real-world system.

In the era of Big Data, this issue becomes much worse as it is extremely hard to collect and organize such a benchmark for testing the performance of an IDS. There are mainly two reasons:

- One is that collecting a Big Data–related dataset is time-consuming and requires large storage space.

- The other reason is that it is hard to control the environment to collect such a data set (i.e., large data volumes that are collected from a real environment may include sensitive information).

Challenges and Issues regarding False Alarms

It is noted that the signature-based detection can generate fewer false alarms (false positives) than the anomaly-based approach. However, due to the complexity of current network traffic, a signature-based NIDS would still produce many false alarms in real-world applications. The large number of false alarms can greatly reduce the effectiveness of detection and significantly increase the burden on analyzing the alarms produced. Even worse, false alarms can have a negative effect on the analysis of detection outputs [20]. Therefore, false alarms are regarded as a key limiting factor in impeding the performance of a signature-based NIDS [21].

In a traditional network, an IDS may produce thousands of alarms a day. However, in the era of Big Data, the data volumes may cause an IDS to generate even larger false alarms (i.e., over hundreds of thousands of alarms a day). This number of alarms cannot be handled by a security expert. Therefore, it is a big challenge to handle these alarms in an efficient way.

POTENTIAL SOLUTIONS AND RESEARCH STUDIES

In the era of Big Data, the performance of NIDSs will be significantly affected by the challenges and issues mentioned above. Thus, Big Data has become a hot topic in network intrusion detection. In this section, we describe some potential solutions in mitigating the challenges above and introduce several research studies in the literature.

Potential Solutions

To enhance the performance of an IDS in the Big Data era, more appropriate and stronger techniques should be developed. In this section, we aim to discuss several potential solutions in general situations.

To Tune Big Data for Intrusion Detection

Big Data has provided many new characteristics to the traditional network, thus it is necessary to tune this notion in the area of intrusion detection. That is, we should better understand the features of Big Data and make them proper and clear in the context of intrusion detection.

For example, it is noted that Big Data can be represented using three variables such as volume, velocity, and variety. In practice, these characteristics should be tuned based on specific intrusion detection problems.

To Develop New Features for Intrusion Detection

Traditionally, an IDS can perform detection with predefined features. However, in the era of Big Data, the *variety* of Big Data makes data even complex. Thus, based on traditional features, it is necessary to design new features in intrusion detection. For example, we can develop several dynamic parameters in IDS signatures, which make signature matching more flexible.

To Improve Machine-Learning Techniques

Machine-learning techniques suffer from many issues in the era of Big Data, but they are a powerful and essential tool for anomaly-based intrusion detection. In this case, developing stronger machine leaning techniques is very crucial for Big Data [22]. In many situations, the process of knowledge extraction has to be very efficient and close to real time because storing all observed data is almost infeasible. The unprecedented data volumes require an effective data analysis and prediction platform to achieve fast response and real-time classification.

Therefore, novel machine-learning techniques should be developed. For example, machine-learning algorithms with appropriate evaluation metrics should be designed, which are able to handle the large data volumes in an effective way.

To Enhance Analysis Techniques

With the increasing data volumes, it is very difficult for a traditional IDS to perform detection under Big Data. Moreover, large incoming packets would cause lots of alarms generated, which are hard to deal with for security experts. These alarms may also cause the difficulty in identifying relationships among various alarms. New Big Data technologies such as the Hadoop ecosystem (including Pig, Hive, Mahout, and RHadoop), stream mining, complex-event processing, and NoSQL databases are enabling the analysis of large-scale, heterogeneous data sets at unprecedented scales and speeds. Thus, it is a promising way to develop more efficient analysis techniques in the area of intrusion detection [23].

To Employ Additional Mechanisms for Intrusion Detection

In a traditional network, the performance of an IDS can be enhanced by employing new detection algorithms or using hardware techniques. However, it is a hard task to improve the performance of an IDS under Big Data.

In order to achieve this goal, another promising solution is to employ additional mechanisms in intrusion detection such as packet filter and alarm filter. These added mechanisms can help reduce the number of target packets and alarms, which could decrease the workload of IDSs and increase the effectiveness of analysis. In the section "Our Study and Future Trends," we present a study which aims to explore the effect of employing a filter mechanism for an IDS.

Related Research Studies

This section introduces some research efforts and approaches in the field of intrusion detection in the literature related to the above challenges and issues.

To Refine Characteristics of Big Data for Intrusion Detection

Suthaharan [15] identified that the first challenging problem is the current definition of Big Data. They assume a dataset has n number of zeros, n number of ones, n number of twos, and continuously growing to infinity, then the three Vs (volume, velocity, and variety) may suggest it as Big Data, but a sampling will simply suggest it as small data. Thus, they proposed three new variables (simply called three Cs) to represent Big Data: cardinality, continuity, and complexity.

In particular, they argued that the term of *cardinality* defines the number of records in the dynamically growing data set at a particular instance. The term of *continuity* defines two aspects: representation of data by continuous functions, and continuous growth of data size with respect to time. Finally, the term of *complexity* defines three aspects: large varieties of data types, high dimensional data set, and the high speed of data processing.

Discussions. This work aims to refine the characteristics of Big Data for intrusion detection. Unfortunately, no proof was given in Suthaharan [15] so that it is hard to identify the specific advantages of the three new Cs over the three Vs. More analyses and future work should be conducted.

To Improve Machine-Learning Techniques for Big Data Classification

In fact, network intrusion detection is a classification problem of identifying incoming traffic as normal or abnormal. However, as mentioned above, many problems make the traditional machine-learning techniques inappropriate for Big Data classification such as *data domains, class types,* and *learning tasks.*

To solve these issues, Suthaharan [24] proposed a single-domain, representation-learning technique to characterize the geometric representation properties of the network intrusion traffic using the concept of the unit-circle algorithm. This approach, called the unit-ring machine (URM), can identify network intrusion and regular traffic from incoming traffic, since it can compute the distribution similarity using the unit-circle representation and determine the distribution with unit-rings, in which a unit-ring contains a collection of unit-circles.

The URM is to represent the data by unit-rings and classify the data by classifying the unit-rings. It can use two feature variables denoted by X and Y to construct unit-rings. The normalized observation can be represented by xi and yi respectively, and they satisfy the following equation:

$$R = \{(xi, yi) \mid 0 \leq \sqrt{(xi^2 + yi^2)/2} \leq 1, i = 1, 2, \ldots, n\} \tag{10.1}$$

The URM approach can further divide R into k unit-rings with equal widths, so that regular traffic class and intrusion traffic class can be decided by Equations 10.2 and 10.3 respectively (t is a threshold used to distinguish regular and intrusion traffic):

$$C_1 = \cup R_j, \text{ where } 0 \leq j \leq t \tag{10.2}$$

$$C_2 = \cup R_j, \text{ where } t \leq j \leq k \tag{10.3}$$

Discussions. In the experiment, this approach was evaluated using visual tools only and the work argues that this can provide sufficient information to understand and assess the performance of the proposed representation-learning model. The simulation results using a subset of the NSL-KDD dataset showed that this approach is feasible to manage Big Data classification tasks. Although the idea here is very interesting, the main problem is that no real data was used and this approach is based on a single domain (i.e., Big Data can leverage data to multidomain).

Big Data Security Analytics in Intrusion Detection

Bowers et al. [25] identified that Big Data security analytics is an emerging approach for intrusion detection, since it involves a combination of automated and manual analysis of security logs and alerts from a wide and varying array of sources such as IDSs and syslog, in which these are called Security Analytics Sources (SASs). In addition, security analytics are only as good as the data being analyzed to that an attacker can undetectably suppress or tamper with SAS messages to conceal attack evidence. To mitigate this issue, they proposed *PillarBox*, a tool for securely relaying SAS messages in a security analytics system to secure SAS messages against tampering, even against an attacker that controls the network and compromises a message-generating host.

Discussions. In the experiment, they presented an implementation of *PillarBox* and showed that it had minimal overhead and is practical for real-world Big Data security analytics systems. Their results also showed that *PillarBox* could achieve integrity protection on alert messages even in the worst case, but a major weakness is that they did not prove the used data volumes to be applicable under Big Data.

OUR STUDY AND FUTURE TRENDS

In this section, we perform a study of employing additional mechanisms for an IDS and present the future trends in this area.

Our Study of Additional Mechanisms

To mitigate the Big Data problem in intrusion detection, we advocate that employing additional mechanisms can help enhance the performance of an IDS. Based on our previous efforts, we conducted a study by proposing an approach which consists of two major components: *character frequency-based exclusive signature matching* and *context-aware list-based packet filter*. The former aims to speed up the process of signature matching while the latter attempts to reduce the number of target packets. We present the detailed architecture of our approach in Figure 10.4.

In the architecture, the context-aware list-based packet filter would be deployed in front of NIDSs so that it can handle the incoming network traffic. If the traffic meets some criteria, that is, the source IP matches the record in the list, then the module of the character

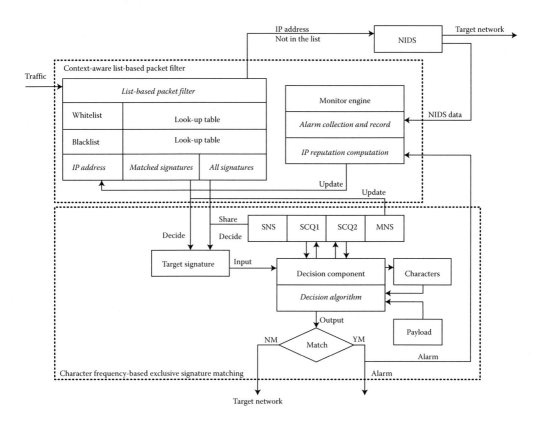

FIGURE 10.4   The detailed architecture of our approach combining context-aware list-based packet filter and character frequency-based signature matching.

frequency-based exclusive signature matching can speed up the process of signature matching. These two specific components are introduced next.

Character Frequency-Based Exclusive Signature Matching

The key idea is to decide if an input string contains all fixed-size bit strings of a signature string without considering the bit-string sequence [26]. In Meng and Li [27], we focused on improving the signature-matching issue in a distributed network intrusion detection and developed an adaptive character frequency-based exclusive signature-matching scheme for a signature-based NIDS. It is mainly composed of four statistical tables: the table of stored NIDS signatures (denoted SNS), two tables of character frequency (denoted SCQ1, SCQ2), the table of matched NIDS signatures (denoted MNS), and a decision component. These four tables are responsible for calculating character frequency and recording relevant statistical data while the decision component is responsible for determining and outputting characters for signature matching. The experimental results demonstrate that the scheme can encouragingly reduce the time consumption of signature matching in the range from 11.2% to 37.6%.

To explore this matching scheme in a cloud environment, we further proposed a cloud-based parallel exclusive signature-matching model (called CPESMM) [28]. In the evaluation, the experimental results indicate that our approach can reduce the time consumption by near 50%. In the era of Big Data, efficient signature matching is greatly desirable, so we consider this scheme a potential solution for network intrusion detection.

Context-Aware List-Based Packet Filter

In our previous work [29], we developed a context-aware list-based packet filter by integrating both blacklist and whitelist techniques. There are mainly three components in the packet filter: *a whitelist-based packet filter, a blacklist-based packet filter,* and *a monitor engine.* More specifically, the blacklist-based packet filter is responsible for filtering out network packets and comparing packet payloads with NIDS signatures in terms of their IP addresses. The blacklist generation is based on a statistic-based method. The function of the whitelist-based packet filter is similar to the blacklist-based filtering but the look-up tables are different. The monitor engine is used to calculate IP confidence through collecting network data such as the produced alarms from both the NIDS and the blacklist-based packet filter. The details of the blacklist-based packet filter can be referred to Meng and Kwok [30].

In the experiment, the results demonstrate that the packet filter can provide over 30% packet reduction for NIDSs like Snort. It is also found that the reduction rate can be further increased by fine-tuning the number and content of the lists. In the era of Big Data, reducing the target number of packets for NIDSs is a promising way to reduce the workload and protect normal operations. Thus, we consider it a potential solution to handle the Big Data problem in intrusion detection.

Evaluation. In order to evaluate the performance of our proposed approach, as a study, we implemented our approach in a small data center. The data in this data center can be treated as heavy traffic. We define "heavy traffic" as the situation that the packet rate of the monitored network exceeds the handling capability of the matching scheme. In Table 10.2, we provide statistical information about the packet rate within this center.

Results and Analysis. We explore two situations: one is without our implementation and the other is with our implementation. We employ Snort as the NIDSs in the evaluation. The deployment is described in Figure 10.5.

By comparing the performance of Snort1 and Snort2, we can estimate the effect of our approach. The experiment was conducted for 12 h and the results show that our approach can reduce the workload of Snort in the range between 28% and 42%. It is considered that our approach can help reduce the burden of IDSs and improve its performance in a heavy traffic environment. Although it is hard to imply that the heavy traffic environment is equal to a Big Data scenario, our study presents that our approach is feasible to improve the performance of an IDS under large data volumes.

TABLE 10.2   The Packet Rate in the Data Center

Levels	Packet Rate (Packets/Sec)
Main router level	17,000–18,500
Server level	6500–13,500

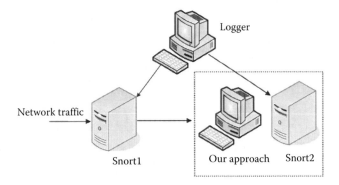

FIGURE 10.5 The network deployment in the study.

Future Trends

Big Data is an emerging hot topic for many areas, but most of the work focusses on business, on the application, and information-processing level. In network intrusion detection, there are only few works conducted in the literature so that many topics can be explored in both academia and industry such as

- Handling large data volumes.

- Developing more efficient schemes to meet real-time requirement.

- Designing standards to select and extract appropriate data features.

- Proposing more appropriate and robust machine-learning algorithms for anomaly-based detection.

Several technologies have been proposed to handle Big Data including massively parallel-processing (MPP) databases, data-mining, distributed file systems and databases, and cloud-based infrastructure. There are mainly two objectives for using any of these tools in network intrusion detection: one is to improve the processing speed or enhance the processing capability of an IDS while the other is to reduce or filter out the target packets for processing.

In future, these existing technologies can be fine-tuned in the area of network intrusion detection to meet the above objectives and definitely more research work should be undertaken to solve issues like Big Data-based NIDSs. In addition, NIDSs can also be used to identify security issues for the above technologies when dealing with Big Data in a cloud environment.

CONCLUSION

In this chapter, we mainly focus on the impact of Big Data on network intrusion detection. In particular, we begin by introducing the background and characteristics of Big Data and intrusion detection. We then identify major challenges and issues caused by Big Data for an IDS, describe potential solutions and present several existing research efforts in handling the Big Data problem. In addition, we conduct a study of employing an additional mechanism to improve the detection performance under heavy traffic, which consists of a context-aware list-based packet filter and a module of character frequency-based signature matching. The study reveals that employing additional mechanisms is a promising solution for enhancing an IDS. Finally, we point our future trends regarding Big Data in intrusion detection. To the best of our knowledge, this chapter is an early work to provide an overview of Big Data in network intrusion detection. Our effort attempts to stimulate more research studies to these challenges and issues in this area.

REFERENCES

1. Heady, R., Luger, G., Maccabe, A. and Servilla, M. 1990. The architecture of a network level intrusion detection system, Technical Report, Department of Computer Science, University of New Mexico.
2. Snort. Lightweight network intrusion detection system. Homepage: http://www.snort.org/
3. Bro. Network Security Monitor. Homepage: http://www.bro.org/.
4. Scarfone, K. and Mell, P. 2007. Guide to Intrusion Detection and Prevention Systems (IDPS), Information Technology Laboratory, National Institute of Standards and Technology, February.
5. Sommer, R. and Paxson, V. 2010. Outside the closed world: On using machine learning for network intrusion detection, in *Proceedings of the IEEE Symposium on Security and Privacy*, pp. 305–316.
6. Meng, Y., Kwok, L.F. and Li, W. 2012. Towards designing packet filter with a trust-based approach using bayesian inference in network intrusion detection, in *Proceedings of the SECURECOMM*, LNICST, Springer, pp. 203–221.
7. Papadogiannakis, A., Polychronakis, M. and Markatos, E.P. 2010. Improving the accuracy of network intrusion detection systems under load using selective packet discarding, in *Proceedings of the EUROSEC*, pp. 1–7.
8. Mervis, J. 2012. U.S. Science Policy: Agencies rally to tackle big data, *Science*, 336(6077), 22.
9. IBM What Is Big Data: Bring Big Data to the Enterprise, http://www-01.ibm.com/software/data/bigdata/, IBM, 2012.
10. Zikopoulos, P.C., Eaton, C., deRoos, D., Deutsch, T. and Lapis, G. 2012. *Understanding Big Data—Analytics for Enterprise Class Hadoop and Streaming Data*, McGraw-Hill.
11. Lu, R., Zhu, H., Liu, X., Liu, J.K. and Shao, J. 2014. Toward efficient and privacy-preserving computing in big data era, *IEEE Network*, 28(4), 46–50.
12. Roesch, M. 1999. Snort: Lightweight intrusion detection for networks, in *Proceedings of the Usenix LISA Conference*, pp. 229–238.
13. Meng, Y. and Kwok, L.F. 2011. Adaptive context-aware packet filter scheme using statistic-based blacklist generation in network intrusion detection, in *Proceedings of the IAS*, pp. 74–79.
14. Dreger, H., Feldmann, A., Paxson, V. and Sommer, R. 2004. Operational experiences with high-volume network intrusion detection, in *Proceedings of the ACM CCS*, pp. 2–11.
15. Suthaharan, S. 2013. Big data classification: Problems and challenges in network intrusion prediction with machine learning, in *Proceedings of the Big Data Analytics Workshop*.
16. Cardenas, A.A., Manadhata, P.K. and Rajan, S.P. 2013. Big data analytics for security, *IEEE Security & Privacy*, 11(6), 74–76.
17. Rajaraman, A. and Ullman, J. 2011. *Mining of Massive Data Sets*, Cambridge University Press, United Kingdom, http://www.cambridge.org/us/academic/subjects/computer-science/knowledge-management-databases-and-data-mining/mining-massive-datasets.
18. DARPA intrusion detection dataset. http://www.ll.mit.edu/mission/communications/cyber/CSTcorpora/ideval/data/

19. McHugh, J. 2000. Testing intrusion detection systems: A critique of the 1998 and 1999 DARPA intrusion detection system evaluations as performed by Lincoln laboratory, *ACM Trans Information System Security*, 3(4), 262–294.

20. Pietraszek, T. 2004. Using adaptive alert classification to reduce false positives in intrusion detection, in *Proceedings of the Recent Advances in Intrusion Detection (RAID)*, pp. 102–124, 2004.

21. Axelsson, S. 2000. The base-rate fallacy and the difficulty of intrusion detection, *ACM Trans. on Information and System Security*, 3(3), 186–205.

22. Wu, X., Zhu, X., Wu, G.-Q. and Ding, W. 2014. Data mining with big data, *IEEE Transactions on Knowledge and Data Engineering*, 26(1), 97–107.

23. Yen, T.-F., Oprea, A., Onarlioglu, K., Leetham, T., Robertson, W., Juels, A. and Kirda, E. 2013. Beehive: Large-scale log analysis for detecting suspicious activity in enterprise networks, in *Proceedings of the ACSAC*, pp. 199–208.

24. Suthaharan, S. 2013. A single-domain, representation-learning model for big data classification of network intrusion, in *Proceedings of the MLDM*, pp. 296–310.

25. Bowers, K.D., Hart, C., Juels, A. and Triandopoulos, N. 2013. Securing the Data in Big Data Security Analytics, IACR Eprint.

26. Meng, Y., Li, W. and Kwok, L.F. 2012. Single character frequency-based exclusive signature matching scheme, in *Proceedings of the IEEE ICIS*, Studies in Computational Intelligence, Springer, pp. 67–80.

27. Meng, Y. and Li, W. 2012. Adaptive character frequency-based exclusive signature matching scheme in distributed intrusion detection environment, in *Proceedings of the TrustCom*, IEEE, pp. 223–230.

28. Meng, Y., Li, W. and Kwok, L.F. 2013. Design of cloud-based parallel exclusive signature matching model in intrusion detection, in *Proceedings of the HPCC*, pp. 175–182.

29. Meng, Y. and Kwok, L.F. 2012. Enhancing list-based packet filter using IP verification mechanism against IP spoofing attack in network intrusion detection, in *Proceedings of the NSS*, pp. 1–14.

30. Meng, Y. and Kwok, L.-F. 2014. Adaptive blacklist-based packet filter with a statistic-based approach in network intrusion detection, *Journal of Network and Computer Applications*, 39, 83–92.

Toward MapReduce-Based Machine-Learning Techniques for Processing Massive Network Threat Monitoring

Linqiang Ge, Hanling Zhang, Guobin Xu, Wei Yu, Chen Chen, and Erik Blasch

CONTENTS

INTRODUCTION

Networking technology has greatly changed the way that our society functions as a whole, leading to a new era of e-business, social interaction, and virtual organizations. There is an omnipresent need for security and robust detection schemes to protect critical network infrastructures. Cyber-threats are significantly more dangerous than they have ever been and are growing in number and sophistication. Due to the widespread nature of cyber-threats (e.g., malware propagation), large-scale traffic monitoring across networks has become an essential part of effectively detecting and defending against contemporary cyber-attacks. Nonetheless, large-scale threat monitoring over distributed networks leads to extremely Big Data from monitored end-hosts and network devices [1].

Effectively processing of threat-monitoring data from both end-hosts and network devices will better facilitate the detection of cyber-threats as well as help security administrators respond to cyber-threats in a timely manner. In our previous work, the development of effective threat-monitoring systems to defend against cyber-attacks was established [2–6]. Nonetheless, Big Data poses serious challenges for cyber operations because an ever-growing large and complex threat-monitoring system from a large computer network needs to capture, store, manage, and process Big Data [7]. With continuous, unbounded, rapid, and time-varying data streams generated by end-hosts and network devices, the complexity of storing and processing big network data will significantly increase. As such, there is an urgent need to develop efficient techniques to process and transform these complex, often vast unstructured, amounts of network threat-monitoring data into manageable, useful, and exploitable information.

To address big cyber data, we develop an efficient threat-monitoring system with an objective of monitoring and processing the real-time data streams generated by threat-monitoring agents, which monitors the statuses of end-hosts or networks and then detects suspicious activities. To ensure that the threat detection methods are efficient, MapReduce-based machine-learning (MML) schemes efficiently deal with threat monitoring over Big Data. The core idea of the MML system is to speed up the machine-learning (ML) process using cloud computing. The first step is to collect the characteristics of traffic flows (e.g., flow duration and average bytes per packet of the flow, average bytes per seconds of the flow). To accurately and rapidly detect traffic anomalies, two MML schemes are developed to profile the dynamic characteristics of traffic flows and then to detect anomalies based on learned classifiers: logistic regression (LR) and naïve Bayes. In the proposed MML schemes, the computational burden of the learning process is spread across multiple machines. The learned computational results from multiple machines are then integrated into one single learned classifier. Finally, the learned classifier will then be used to recognize whether a new traffic flow is either normal or abnormal (benign or malicious).

Using real-world data sets consisting of both botnet and normal traffic, we develop a cloud computing testbed and conduct experiments to evaluate the effectiveness of the developed MML schemes in terms of learning accuracy, training set size, and training and detection processes overhead. The experimental data shows that the proposed MML schemes rapidly detect anomalous traffic flows with the same accuracy as standard ML schemes without using MapReduce.

The remainder of the chapter is organized as follows: section "Background" highlights background research. Section "Our Approach" develops the MML approach in detail. Section "Performance Evaluation" lists experimental results to validate the MML effectiveness. Finally, section "Conclusion" provides conclusions.

BACKGROUND

In this section, we review the background, including network security, Big Data in network security, and cloud computing and MapReduce framework.

Network Security

In recent years, computer networks have become more complex and the size of networks is continually increasing. Cyber-attacks pose a great threat to computer networks and affect people daily. For example, JPMorgan Chase was attacked by hackers and a massive amount of sensitive data was stolen, affecting 76 million households and 7 million small businesses [8]. Similarly, Home Depot was compromised by a similar style cyber-attack, which caused the account information of 56 million cardholders to be leaked [9]. Cyber-adversaries may hack into computer network entities (e.g., routers, servers, and others) to disrupt network operations, resulting in serious damage. The emerging cyber-attacks include false data injection attacks [10], denial-of-service attacks [11], worm/malware propagation attacks [12], botnet attacks [13], as well as many others. Taking botnet attacks as an example, the adversary can exploit different types of viruses (e.g., Trojan viruses [14], TDL-4 [15], and others) or system vulnerabilities to compromise a user's computer to achieve control over infected computers. As such, the adversary may take control of thousands, tens of thousands, or even millions of computers to form a large zombie network, which is also called a botnet. Once the attack control is complete, the adversary can take advantage of these zombie computers to conduct other malicious activities, which include: denial-of-service attacks, spam-mail propagation, and many others. With the popularity of mobile phones, mobile botnet attacks also become a new version of this serious threat. For example, Karim et al. [16] investigated mobile botnet attacks when exploring attacking vectors and presenting thematic taxonomy. Abdullah et al. [17] studied how to efficiently detect mobile botnet attacks. With the many variations of attacks over many computers, a new phenomenon is emerging of big to massive data analytics.

Big Data in Network Security

To defend against cyber-attacks, an effective cyber threat-monitoring system becomes critical, and it should be able to characterize, track, and mitigate security threats in computer networks in a timely manner. To detect these attacks, a large amount of threat-monitoring and detection tools, including the Advanced Intrusion Detection Environment (AIDE) (http://aide.sourceforge.net/), OSSEC (http://www.ossec.net/) and others, have been developed with the intention to monitor behavioral changes on end-hosts and network devices. By leveraging these tools, massive data (e.g., system logs, security logs, application logs, traffic logs, and others) generated by end-hosts (e.g., computers, mobile devices, and others) and network devices (e.g., routers, firewalls, and others) can be collected for the purpose of cyber-threat situational awareness. In addition to passively logging the activities associated with attacks, honeypots can directly and actively interact with attacks and collect more insightful data from these attacks. For a large computer network, the collected threat-monitoring-related data will be massive and is featured by a high volume of data size, a high velocity of data transmission, and a high variety of data types [18]. For example, about a gigabyte of data per day needs to be gathered for further analysis [18]. In addition, data collected from different monitoring systems have different data formats, which can be structured or unstructured. How to effectively process and analyze massive threat monitoring-related data becomes a challenging issue.

Cloud Computing and MapReduce Framework

The acceleration of data generation requires new technologies to analyze massive data. With large data storage space, high computational capacity, and low infrastructure investment, cloud computing can offer a platform for massive data analysis. Cloud computing can support different service models, including Infrastructure as a Service (IaaS), Platform as a Service (PaaS), and Software as a Service (SaaS) [19]. In this way, a large number of distributed servers can be used for data access, computation, and storage.

MapReduce is a parallel programming model primarily designed for batch-processing Big Data in a distributed-computing environment [9]. MapReduce is designed using the concept of divide-and-conquer and follows the master/slave computing paradigm, consisting of the map function and the reduce function [20]. The purpose of the map function is to split and distribute data sets to different servers for processing whereas the purpose of the reduce function is to collect the results for data sets and generate the final result.

As shown in Figure 11.1, the workflow of MapReduce is detailed as follows:

- *Step 1. Functions definition:* In this step, programmers need to define both the map and the reduce functions, which will be used by MapReduce to implement data analysis;

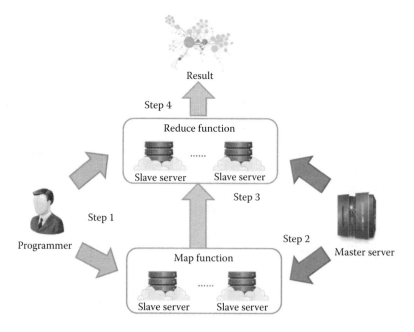

FIGURE 11.1 The MapReduce workflow.

- *Step 2. Data split and distribution*: For large size data sets, the master server will split them into several relatively small-sized data sets and distribute these data sets to map slave servers for computation;

- *Step 3. Data computation*: With the defined map function, the map slave servers can concurrently process small data sets and generate intermediate results; and

- *Step 4. Data resolving*: After collecting intermediate results, based on the defined reduce function, the reduce slave servers will resolve and aggregate the intermediate results to produce the final result.

It is worth noting that MapReduce has a built-in fault-tolerant feature, through which data can be duplicated and assigned to different servers for processing. The working status of slave nodes shall be periodically reported to the master node. If a slave node does not reply to the request in a given time, it will be considered as a failure node. Then, the task that the failure node was initially assigned to process will be reassigned to other nodes.

OUR APPROACH

In this section, we first introduce the design rationale of our approach and then present our MML schemes in detail.

Design Rationale

To defend against cyber-attacks, anomaly-based intrusion detection systems (IDSs) have been widely developed. Anomaly-based detection refers to the issue of finding patterns in data that do not conform to an expected behavior [21]. In anomaly detection, the system administrator commonly defines the baseline (i.e., normal) measures to qualify normal system behavior (e.g., network traffic volumes). The threat-monitoring and detection system monitors various system segments and compares their states to defined profiles. If the observed states are beyond the defined profiles, anomaly alerts will be issued.

Due to the widespread nature of threats such as malware propagation, a large-scale traffic monitoring system across networks has become essential. Such threat-monitoring systems can lead to extremely large amounts of data collected from monitored end-hosts and network devices. In the realm of cyber security, Big Data refers to the management and analysis of large-scale information, which exceeds the capabilities of traditional data-processing technology. With the continuous, unbounded, rapid, and time-varying data streams generated by end-hosts and network devices, the complexity to store and process big network data will significantly increase. Hence, the effective processing of threat-monitoring data from both end-hosts and network devices will facilitate the detection of cyber-threats and help security administrators respond to cyber-threats in a timely manner. In this chapter, the key focus is on the network-based IDS, which analyzes network traffic in order to identify the presence of malicious traffic flows. Using traffic flows as an example to demonstrate our idea, we begin with the following collection of traffic flow characteristics: flow duration, average bytes per packet of the flow, average bytes per second of the flow, and so on. To accurately detect traffic anomalies, we then implement the

MML schemes to profile the characteristics of traffic flows and to detect traffic anomalies based on a learned classifier.

To make the threat detection capability efficient, how to make ML schemes efficiently deal with big network data for threat monitoring is critical. The main idea is to speed up the ML process by using the cloud computing system. Our developed MML schemes will distribute the computational task of the learning process across multiple physical machines. The detection system consists of both the offline training and the online detection phases. In the *offline training phase*, we use a training set, where collected network traffic flows consist of both normal flows and attack flows. The subsets of the training set are then assigned to different computers to conduct the training process independently. The computational results of the learning phase from different computers are then integrated into one single learned classifier. In the *online detection phase*, the use of the learned classifier is then set in place to determine whether a traffic flow in question is either normal or malicious. The detail of the algorithm design and the detection workflow will be introduced in the following sections.

Algorithm Design

Being one of the most dangerous network-based attacks, botnets can be massive. Coordinated groups of compromised hosts have the ability of conducting malicious activities such as spamming, Distributed Denial-of-Service (DDoS) attacks, and so on. To accurately and rapidly learn the anomalous behavior of malicious traffic associated with botnets, we develop two MML schemes: LR and naïve Bayes in a cloud computing environment.

MapReduce-Based LR ML Scheme

Logistic regression is a type of probabilistic statistical classification model, which is commonly used for binary classification problems [22–25]. We implement the traditional LR algorithm in the MapReduce framework to carry out the learning process in parallel. In our detection system, we first collect the characteristics of traffic flows. Each characteristic is considered as one feature of observed data and each feature has its own numerical value. The detailed feature definition and extraction process will be introduced in section "Implementation." Because each flow is either normal or malicious, we consider each flow as one observation which can be represented as (X, Y), where $X = (x_1, x_2,..., x_n)$ is the feature value vector and $Y \in (0, 1)$ is the class value. For *LR* ML, we take our input features x_i multiply each one by the regression coefficient $\theta = (\theta_0, \theta_1,..., \theta_n)$ and then add them up as $z = (\theta_0 x_0 + \theta_1 x_1, + \cdots + \theta_n x_n)$. The result z will be put into the logistic (sigmoid) function [26]. In this way, we will obtain a number between 0 and 1. We then consider input observations >0.5 as class 1 and input observations ≤0.5 as class 0. In this way, the LR classifier is a probability estimate process. The detailed principle of the LR algorithm can be found in Harrington [22].

During the training process, it is critical to determine the best regression coefficients. Suppose we train a dataset with m observations, $(X_1, y_1), (X_2, y_2),...,(X_m, y_m)$ and each observation has n features $X = (x_1, x_2,..., x_n)$. We implement the gradient descent as an optimization method to find the best regression coefficients. *Gradient descent* can be used for most ML schemes to update parameters iteratively in order to minimize the cost function [27]. In LR, the gradient descent rule is

$$\theta_i = \theta_i - \alpha \frac{\partial L(\theta)}{\partial \theta} = \frac{\alpha}{m} \sum_{i=1}^{m} (h(\theta^T X_i) - y_i) X_i \qquad (11.1)$$

where α is the arbitrary learning rate that determines the step size, $L(\theta)$ is the cost function, and h is the sigmoid function. With a training set input, the parameter θ will be iteratively updated based on Equation 11.1.

It is worth noting that in the parameter updating process of gradient descent, all iterations need to visit all the training samples for a given parameter. It is challenging to develop an efficient mechanism to process and transform complex, large amounts of data into useful detection information. In an attempt to remediate this, we apply the MapReduce framework to distribute the computational task to multiple nodes in the cloud. Recall that MapReduce is a parallel programming model primarily designed for batch-processing Big Data in a distributed-computing environment [9]. MapReduce is designed using the concept of divide-and-conquer and follows the master/slave computing paradigm. The master node receives the computational training task and sends the subset to the slave nodes to separately conduct different training processes. Eventually, the computational results will be combined together as learned classifier. Figure 11.2 illustrates the main idea of this process.

Using the MapReduce framework, we implement gradient descent for the LR learning scheme and update the parameters iteratively. Suppose that we have large-scale data, which contains 1 million observations (1 million traffic flows in our performance evaluation), then we need to conduct the gradient descent as

$$\theta_i = \theta_i - \alpha \frac{\partial L(\theta)}{\partial \theta} = \theta_i - \frac{\alpha}{1,000,000} \sum_{i=1}^{1,000,000} (h(\theta^T X_i) - y_i) X_i \qquad (11.2)$$

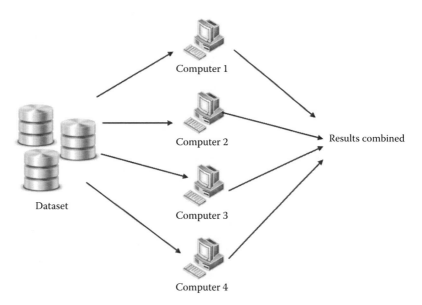

FIGURE 11.2   ML-based on MapReduce framework.

Then, we use MapReduce to distribute the data set to four different computers. Computer one uses subset $((X_1, y_1), (X_2, y_2),...,(X_{250,000}, y_{250,000}))$ to carry out gradient descent. Similarly, computers 2, 3, and 4 also get their respective subsets. In doing so, we can derive the computational process as

$$
\left.
\begin{array}{l}
((X_1, y_1),(X_2, y_2),..,(X_{250,000}, y_{250,000}))\,tmp1 = \dfrac{\alpha}{250,000}\displaystyle\sum_{i=1}^{250,000}(h(\theta^T X_i) - y_i)X_i \\[2em]
((X_1, y_1),(X_2, y_2),..,(X_{250,000}, y_{500,000}))\,tmp2 = \dfrac{\alpha}{250,000}\displaystyle\sum_{i=1}^{500,000}(h(\theta^T X_i) - y_i)X_i \\[2em]
((X_1, y_1),(X_2, y_2),..,(X_{500,000}, y_{750,000}))\,tmp3 = \dfrac{\alpha}{500,000}\displaystyle\sum_{i=1}^{750,000}(h(\theta^T X_i) - y_i)X_i
\end{array}
\right\}
\begin{array}{l}
\theta_i = \theta_i - \dfrac{\alpha}{1,000,000}\\[1em]
(tmp1 + tmp2\\[0.5em]
\quad + tmp3 + tmp4)
\end{array}
$$

$$
((X_1, y_1),(X_2, y_2),..,(X_{750,000}, y_{100,000}))\,tmp4 = \frac{\alpha}{100,000}\,i = 1,100,000(h(\theta^T X_i) - y_i)X_i \tag{11.3}
$$

In our MapReduce-based LR scheme, each iteration has a map phase and a reduce phase. Figure 11.3 illustrates the MapReduce-based framework for conducting this parallel ML process. As we can see, the MapReduce framework is based on key/value tuples and relies on two built-in functions: a map function and a reduce function. Suppose that we have data samples $(A_1, A_2,..., A_m)$ collected from threat monitors on end-hosts and network devices. Each data sample contains values of predefined features (e.g., system logs, source and destination addresses, and others). In the map function, the map workers visit the training samples in parallel and perform key matching to list associated key/value pairs. Visiting one training sample generates n key/value pairs. The keys are 1 to n and the values in the gradient descent algorithm are $(h_\theta(x^{(i)}) - y^{(i)})x_j^{(i)}$. Then, we can obtain intermediate results such as $K_1 \to \{a_{11}^{(1)}, a_{12}^{(1)},..., a_{1m}^{(1)}\}$, where $a_{1m}^{(1)}$ represents the value of key K_1 from sample m computed by map worker 1. In the reduce phase, the values of the same key are added up to yield $\sum_{i=1}^{m}(h_\theta(x^{(i)}) - y^{(i)})x^{(i)}$ and the parameters are updated by $\theta_j = \theta_j - (\alpha/m)\sum_{i=1}^{m}(h_\theta(x^{(i)}) - y^{(i)})x_j^{(i)}$. Then, the aforementioned process will be further validated in our developed cloud computing test bed until convergence of the subtasks, where the learned model is ready for use.

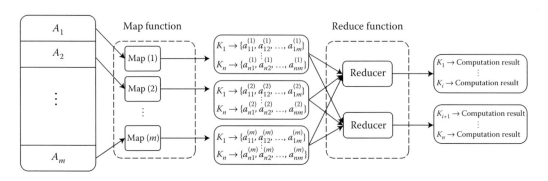

FIGURE 11.3 MapReduce-based framework for parallel ML.

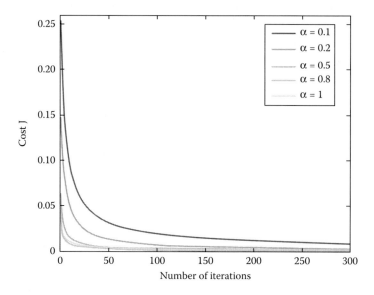

FIGURE 11.4   Cost of gradient descent using MapReduce.

We use real-world data to evaluate the performance of our parallel ML scheme. Based on the cost function of LR ML, we collected the cost of gradient descent in the MapReduce process shown in Figure 11.4. As we can see from Figure 11.4, the computational cost of gradient descent declines as the number of iterations increases. This demonstrates that our LR MML scheme can speed up the learning process. In addition, we compared the cost of different arbitrary learning rates α. We can see that the higher the arbitrary learning rate, the cost declines at a higher speed. Hence, we conclude that with a big arbitrary learning rate, the gradient descent algorithm can quickly locate the optimal point in a function. Next, we explore another common MML technique of naïve Bayes.

MapReduce-Based Naïve Bayes ML Scheme
The other ML algorithm we implement is the naïve Bayes classifier. Generally speaking, the naïve Bayes classifier is a probabilistic classifier based on applying Bayes' theorem [28]. The naïve Bayes can construct a classifier given a set of training data with class labels. In our system, the training data is the observation of features determined by features associated with traffic flows and the class falls into two categories: 1 (a positive one when the monitored data is normal) and 0 (a negative one when the monitored data is malicious).

Denote $X = (x_1, x_2, ..., x_n)$ to be one observation of E, where x_n is the value of feature n. Then, the probability of observation E in this category c is $P(c|x_1, x_2, ..., x_n)$. Using Bayes theorem, we have

$$P(c|x_1, x_2, ..., x_n) = \frac{P(c)P(x_1, x_2, ..., x_n)}{P(x_1, x_2, ..., x_n)}$$

(11.4)

Then, we can define two types of parameters for the naïve Bayes model: $q(c)$ for $c \in \{1, 0\}$, where $P(c) = q(c)$ and $q_i(x_i|c)$ with $P(x_i|c) = q_i(x_i|c)$. Then, we have the naïve Bayes model as

$$P(c|x_1, x_2, \ldots, x_n) = q(c)\prod_{i=1}^{n}q_i(x_i|c) \qquad (11.5)$$

The naïve Bayes model learns the probability of classes when each feature is given. The naïve Bayes model analyzes all features and combines them to form the probability of each class. After that, whenever a new observation appears, the classifier then distinguishes the class according to the value of each feature. The detailed principle of the naïve Bayes model can be found in Chelba and Acero [28].

Similar to LR, we can use the maximize likelihood estimate (MLE) method to learn the optimal parameters. Suppose we are given a training set that contains m observations $(X_1, y_1), (X_2, y_2), \ldots, (X_m, y_m)$ and each observation has n features of $X = (x_1, x_2, \ldots, x_n)$. Based on the log-likelihood function [26] of the naïve Bayes model, we then apply gradient descent to maximize the likelihood. The rule is similar to LR as

$$\theta_i = \theta_i - \alpha\frac{\partial L(\theta)}{\partial\theta} = \frac{\alpha}{m}\sum_{i=1}^{m}(q(c) + q_i(X_i|c_i)) \qquad (11.6)$$

where $q(c) = \Sigma_{i=1}^{m}[c_i = c]/n = count\,(c)/n$, and $q_i(X_i|c) = \Sigma_{i=1}^{m}[c_i = c$ and $X = X_i]/\Sigma_{i=1}^{m}[c_i = c] = count\,(X_i|c_i)/count\,(c)$. Hence, in the naïve Bayes algorithm, we need to conduct only one iteration to optimize the parameter θ_i. We also apply the MapReduce framework to improve the learning efficiency of naïve Bayes to train the data set in parallel. The mechanism is similar to the LR learning scheme. Each computer receives a subset of the training data and then computes $q(c)$ and $q_i(X_i|c)$. In the following subsection, we introduce the procedures to implement the parallel ML scheme in the MapReduce framework.

Implementation

Figure 11.5 illustrates the workflow of the offline training process. In this process, we first extract and select the useful information from traffic flows as samples. Then, we define the

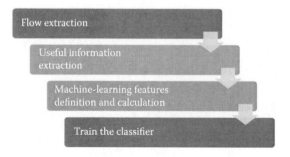

FIGURE 11.5   Detection work flow.

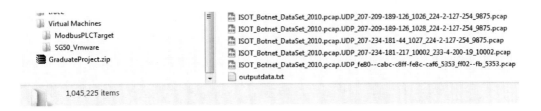

FIGURE 11.6   Flow extraction.

features for ML and give the features a value for each sample. Finally, we conduct the training process for the classifier.

The detailed steps are illustrated as follows:

- *Step 1. Flow extraction*: To conduct network traffic monitoring, we collect a large volume of traffic data. Recall that in common practice, data will be stored in packet capture (PCAP) format and a large number of flows will be stored in one PCAP file. Therefore, we need to extract traffic flows from each PCAP file and separate each traffic flow into a single file. Figure 11.6 illustrates what was extracted from 1,045,225 traffic flows to form a large data set.

- *Step 2. Useful information selection:* The trace file of each traffic flow consists of massive packets. As shown in Figure 11.7, in each packet, there is plenty of data recorded and most of this data is useless and redundant. In this step, we propose to select the most useful information, which will be used for our ML process. The tool *TSHARK* (https://www.wireshark.org/docs/man-pages/tshark.html) is used to extract and select the useful information from each flow in the sample. Figure 11.8 shows an example flow output file through this step, where each row represents one packet in this flow. Note that each column contains one characteristic of packets, where the selected characteristics include: the time, the size of the packet (bytes), the type of network, and the destination media access control (MAC) address. For a destination MAC address, when the MAC address is of the format *aa:aa:aa:aa:aa:aa*, it can be regarded as an instance of malicious traffic. We can see that only small amounts of data in packets are selected so that the size of the input data is then placed into the ML algorithms, which are used to largely reduce the data size and to help speed up the data processing.

```
<field name="frame.encap_type" showname="Encapsulation type: Ethernet (1)" size="0" pos="0" show="1"/>
<field n. 2010 18:0  2010 18:05:38.958596000"/>
<field name="frame.offset_shift" showname="Time shift for this packet: 0.000000000 seconds" size="0" pos="0" show="0.000000000"/>
<field name="frame.time_epoch" showname="Epoch Time: 1286402738.958596000 seconds" size="0" pos="0" show="1286402738.958596000"/>
<field name="frame.time_delta" showname="Time delta from previous captured frame: 0.000000000 seconds" size="0" pos="0" show="0.000000000"/>
<field name="frame.time_delta_displayed" showname="Time delta from previous displayed frame: 0.000000000 seconds" size="0" pos="0" show="0.000000000"/>
<field name="frame.time_relative" showname="Time since reference or first frame: 0.000000000 seconds" size="0" pos="0" show="0.000000000"/>
<field name="frame.number" showname="Frame Number: 1" size="0" pos="0" show="1"/>
<field name="frame.len" showname="Frame Length: 62 bytes (496 bits)" size="0" pos="0" show="62"/>
<field name="frame.cap_len" showname="Capture Length: 62 bytes (496 bits)" size="0" pos="0" show="62"/>
<field name="frame.marked" showname="Frame is marked: False" size="0" pos="0" show="0"/>
<field name="frame.ignored" showname="Frame is ignored: False" size="0" pos="0" show="0"/>
<field name="frame.protocols" showname="Protocols in frame: eth:ip:tcp" size="0" pos="0" show="eth:ip:tcp"/>
```

FIGURE 11.7   The information of a data packet.

```
Oct  6, 2010 18:23:57.992603000 62     65535   Ethernet II, Src: aa:aa:aa:aa:aa:aa
Oct  6, 2010 18:23:57.992834000 62     5840    Ethernet II, Src: aa:aa:aa:aa:aa:aa
Oct  6, 2010 18:23:57.993173000 60     65535   Ethernet II, Src: aa:aa:aa:aa:aa:aa
Oct  6, 2010 18:24:08.038100000 103    5840    Ethernet II, Src: aa:aa:aa:aa:aa:aa
Oct  6, 2010 18:24:08.052309000 105    65486   Ethernet II, Src: aa:aa:aa:aa:aa:aa
Oct  6, 2010 18:24:08.052466000 54     5840    Ethernet II, Src: aa:aa:aa:aa:aa:aa
Oct  6, 2010 18:24:08.052566000 76     5840    Ethernet II, Src: aa:aa:aa:aa:aa:aa
Oct  6, 2010 18:24:08.254036000 60     65464   Ethernet II, Src: aa:aa:aa:aa:aa:aa
Oct  6, 2010 18:24:08.556363000 68     65464   Ethernet II, Src: aa:aa:aa:aa:aa:aa
Oct  6, 2010 18:24:08.556633000 68     5840    Ethernet II, Src: aa:aa:aa:aa:aa:aa
Oct  6, 2010 18:24:08.757903000 60     65450   Ethernet II, Src: aa:aa:aa:aa:aa:aa
```

FIGURE 11.8 An example of data selection output.

TABLE 11.1 Description of Extracted Features

Duration	Defined as the Total Time Duration of the Flow
bpp	Defined as average bytes per packet of the flow
bps	Defined as the average bytes per second of the flow
pps	Defined as the average packets per second of the flow
VarIAT	Defined as the variance of packet interarrival time of the flow
VarBpp	Defined as the variance of bytes-per-packet of the flow
tws	Defined as the average TCP window size of the flow
VarTws	Defined as the variance of TCP window size of the flow

- *Step 3.* ML *features definition and computation:* Based on the output data of Step 2, we define and compute the features for the ML process for each sample. In our study, we consider eight features during the training stage, which are shown in Table 11.1.

  Figure 11.9 shows a screenshot of the computed input data for the LR classifier. In this screenshot, each row represents one observation and each column stands for each computed feature value. For example, in the first observation, the value of *Average Bytes per Packet* is 90.1429 and the value of *Average Bytes per Second* is 194.15. In addition, the last column represents the class of data, either 0 or 1, meaning that the observation is either nonmalicious or malicious traffic, respectively. Similarly, we can compute feature values as input for naïve Bayes, which is shown in Figure 11.10.

1	13000.0	90.14285714285714	194.15384615384616	2.1538461538461537	29263.62962962963	13973.622448979591	39607.75	8.912148347589285E8	1
1	13000.0	94.5	203.53846153846155	2.1538461538461537	40698.07407407407	19332.678571428572	39578.28571428572	8.931365509897959E8	1
1	13000.0	92.96428571428571	200.23076923076923	2.1538461538461537	36136.88888888889	17189.534438775514	39613.53571428572	8.908382220344385E8	1
1	13000.0	94.39285714285714	203.30769230769232	2.1538461538461537	40370.96296296296	19179.024234693883	39575.392857142855	8.933260871670092E8	1
1	13000.0	92.53571428571429	199.30769230769232	2.1538461538461537	34912.88888888889	16614.177295918365	39600.67857142857	8.916741190752553E8	1
1	9000.0	62.0	20.666666666666668	0.3333333333333333	0.0	0.0	65535.0	0.0	1
1	13000.0	93.07142857142857	200.46153846153845	2.1538461538461537	37145.7037037037	17677.923469387755	39624.25	8.901437457589285E8	1
1	13000.0	89.53571428571429	192.84615384615384	2.1538461538461537	26442.222222222223	12618.39158163265	39570.83571428572	8.936774483915817E8	1
1	13000.0	90.39285714285714	194.69230769230768	2.1538461538461537	28850.88888888889	13757.381377551017	39601.857142857145	8.915973804795921E8	1
1	13000.0	96.03571428571429	206.84615384615384	2.1538461538461537	46092.81481481482	21877.105867346934	39624.57142857143	8.901229410306121E8	1
1	9000.0	62.0	20.666666666666668	0.3333333333333333	0.0	0.0	65535.0	0.0	1
1	13000.0	87.78571428571429	189.07692307692307	2.1538461538461537	24126.59259259259	11506.882653061222	39539.392857142855	8.956964274528061E8	1
1	13000.0	90.75	195.46153846153845	2.1538461538461537	30131.925925925927	14367.544642857143	39548.17857142857	8.951159590752553E8	1
1	13000.0	89.35714285714286	192.46153846153845	2.1538461538461537	27006.962962962964	12985.515306122443	39578.28571428572	8.931365509897959E8	1
1	13000.0	94.35714285714286	203.23076923076923	2.1538461538461537	40999.03703703704	19488.943877551028	39581.17857142857	8.929471542895410E8	1
1	13000.0	93.14285714285714	200.6153846153846	2.1538461538461537	37967.62962962963	18076.62244897959	39554.17857142857	8.947202809323981E8	1
1	13000.0	96.53571428571429	207.92307692307693	2.1538461538461537	48663.92592592593	23102.53443877551	39645.78571428572	8.887536361683674E8	1
1	13000.0	88.42857142857143	190.46153846153845	2.1538461538461537	24747.85185185185	11841.17346938776	39547.642857142855	8.951513166581633E8	1
1	13000.0	94.10714285714286	202.69230769230768	2.1538461538461537	39712.14814814815	18873.738520408166	39569.607142857145	8.937055779528059E8	1
1	13000.0	91.03571428571429	196.07692307692307	2.1538461538461537	30978.37037037037	14767.677295918369	39557.82142857143	8.944803405038265E8	1
1	13000.0	96.42857142857143	207.69230769230768	2.1538461538461537	46589.03703703704	22094.316326530603	39628.42857142857	8.898734180020410E8	1
1	0.0	106.08333333333333	9.9999999E7	9.9999999E7	65338.17391304348	30208.74305555556	33457.333333333336	8.653305469722223E8	1

FIGURE 11.9 Screenshot of feature values computing for LR.

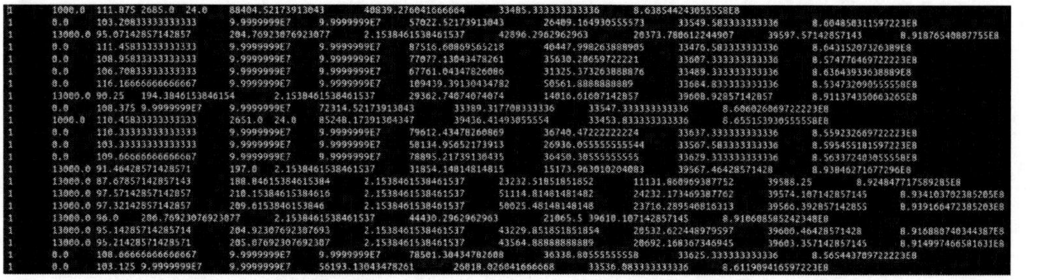

FIGURE 11.10   Screenshot of feature values computing for Bayes ML.

- *Step 4. Train the classifier:* After Step 3, we have the input data ready for the ML schemes. We input the data to the Hadoop Distributed File System (HDFS) using the command: "*sudo -u hdfs hadoop fs -put train.txt/inputs/*", which means that the input data is train.txt and we store it in the/inputs folder on the HDFS. We train the input data with our ML schemes with the command: "*sudo -u hdfs hadoop jar BigData-1.0-SNAPSHOT.jar bigdata.towson.edu.BigDataCC/inputs/train.txt/output,*" where our executable java program is called *BigData-1.0-SNAPSHOT.jar*, and *bigdata.towson. edu.BigDataCC* is the class name. Then, the trained model will be generated under the/output folder on the HDFS, which can be used for the offline detection process. For the online detection process, similar to the offline training process, we use our data preprocessing program to obtain the input file and then use the classification program to classify the input test data based on the trained model.

PERFORMANCE EVALUATION

To validate the effectiveness of our proposed approach, we developed a cloud testbed and used it to conduct experiments. In the following, we first present the evaluation methodology and then show the experimental results.

Evaluation Methodology

As shown in Figure 11.11, we built a cloud computing testbed with one master node and three slave nodes. Each slave node can act as both a map node and a reduce node. Each node is a DELL Optiplex 9010 computer with Intel Core i7 3.40 GHZ 8 processors with 16 GB RAM and 2 TB hard drive. We use the Cloudera Manager [29] as the central interface to perform management tasks such as configurations, management, and monitoring of the designed system. We downloaded *cloudera-manager-installer. bin* from the Cloudera website. The executable permission was configured by using the command "*chmod u + x cloudera-manager-installer.bin*". Then, the installer can be executed with the command "*sudo./cloudera-manager- installer.bin*" to install the Cloudera Manager. To install the Cloudera Manager on hosts in the cloud, the Cloudera Manager Admin Console is used to install and configure Cloudera Distribution including Apache Hadoop (CDH).

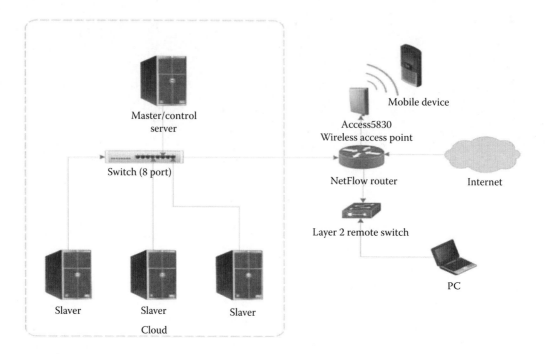

FIGURE 11.11   A cloud computing testbed.

To evaluate the effectiveness of our developed system, we obtained the ISOT data set [30] from http://www.uvic.ca/engineering/ece/isot/datasets to conduct our experiments. The ISOT data set is the combination of several publicly available malicious and nonmalicious data sets. Specifically, the ISOT data set contains 1,675,424 total traffic flows, which consists of 55,904 (3.33%) malicious traffic flows and 1,619,520 (96.66%) nonmalicious traffic flows.

For the accuracy of detection, we expect that with a number of training samples, the ML schemes will have more information for the training process, leading to higher detection accuracy. To validate this hypothesis, we define the following evaluation metrics: (i) *Detection rate:* It is defined as the probability of correctly classifying the malicious traffic flows and is the ratio of the number of malicious traffic flows correctly classified versus the total number of malicious traffic flows. (ii) *False-positive rate.* It is defined as the probability of falsely classifying nonmalicious traffic flows and is the ratio of the number of nonmalicious traffic flows falsely classified as malicious traffic flows versus the total number of nonmalicious traffic flows. In our experiments, we show the correlation between these metrics and the number of traffic flow samples used for the training process.

Experimental Results

We select 20,000 test samples (10,000 malicious traffic flows and 10,000 nonmalicious traffic flows) from the data set, which are not used in the training process. In terms of the training samples, in each group of samples, the number of malicious flows and the number of nonmalicious flows are equal. For example, when we use 100 samples for training, 50 are malicious traffic flows and 50 are nonmalicious traffic flows.

TABLE 11.2   Detection Accuracy of the Naïve Bayes ML Scheme

Training Samples Numbers	Detection Rate	False-Positive Rate
20	78.19%	28.68%
100	99.31%	0.18%
140	99.30%	0.69%
200	99.19%	0.81%
1000	99.92%	0

TABLE 11.3   Detection Results of LR Scheme

Training Samples Numbers	Detection Rate	False-Positive Rate
20	99.48%	0.14%
100	99.55%	0.12%
140	99.99%	0.02%
200	99.48%	0.14%
1000	1	0

Table 11.2 illustrates the relationship between the detection accuracy of the naïve Bayes ML scheme and the number of samples used for the training process. As we can see, the naïve Bayes ML scheme can achieve a high detection accuracy. The detection rate from using 20 samples is 78.91%. Starting from 100 samples, the detection rate of each scenario is close to 100%, meaning that all malicious traffic flows can be accurately identified. In addition, the false-positive rate is near 0, meaning that very few numbers of nonmalicious flows are falsely classified as malicious flows. Table 11.3 shows the detection accuracy of the LR ML scheme. In comparison with the naïve Bayes ML scheme, when there are 20 training samples, the LR ML scheme can achieve a high detection accuracy near 99% and a low false-positive rate near 0%.

In addition to the detection accuracy, the time efficiency of the MML schemes is also measured. The metric we used is the *training time*, which is defined as the time taken for

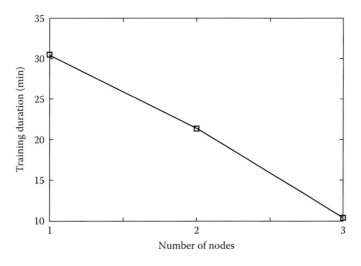

FIGURE 11.12   Time cost versus number of nodes for naïve Bayes.

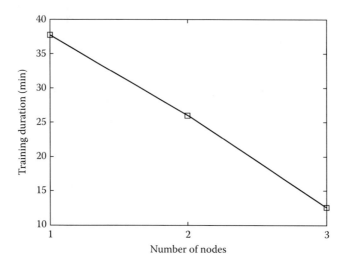

FIGURE 11.13   Time cost versus number of nodes for LR.

the training process. Figure 11.12 illustrates the relationship between the training time of the naïve Bayes ML scheme and the number of slave nodes used in the training process. As we can see, the training duration declines when the number of nodes increases. When we use three nodes to carry out the training process, it takes only 10.35 min to complete the training process. If we only use one node, it will take 30.58 min. Similarly, in the LR-based ML scheme, the training time can be significantly reduced when more slave nodes are used (Figure 11.13).

CONCLUSION

In this chapter, we addressed the issue of detecting malicious traffic flows from a large scale of monitored traffic data. To make threat detection efficient, we developed LR and naïve Bayes MML schemes to deal with big amounts of threat-monitoring data. The main contribution is to speed up the ML process using the MapReduce framework in a cloud computing environment. We demonstrated our MML schemes in a cloud computing environment with a variety of existing structures of data flows, detection techniques, and implementation protocols. Using a real-world traffic data set consisting of both botnet traffic and normal traffic, we conducted experiments and evaluated the effectiveness of our developed MML schemes. Our results verify the accuracy and efficiency of our proposed MML detection schemes to detect malicious traffic.

ACKNOWLEDGMENT

This work was supported in part by US Department of Defense (DoD) under grant: H98230-13-1-0445, and US National Science Foundation (NSF) under grants: CNS 1117175 and 1350145. Any opinions, findings and conclusions, or recommendations expressed in this material are those of the authors and do not necessarily reflect the views of the funding agencies.

REFERENCES

1. R. V. Zicari, Big data: Challenges and opportunities, in *Big Data Computing*, Akerkar, R. (Ed.), Chapman and Hall/CRC, 103–128, 2013.
2. D. Zhang, W. Yu, R. Hardy, A distributed network-sensor based intrusion detection framework in enterprise networks, in *Proceedings of the IEEE Military Communication (MILCOM)*, May 2011.
3. W. Yu, Z. Chen, G. Xu, S. Wei, N. Ekedebe, A threat monitoring system for smart mobiles in enterprise networks, in *Proceedings of the 2013 Research in Adaptive and Convergent Systems (RACS)*, October 2013.
4. L. Ge, D. Zhang, R. Hardy, H. Liu, W. Yu, R. J. Reschly, On effective sampling techniques for host-based intrusion detection in MANET, in *Proceedings of the IEEE MILCOM—Track 3: Cyber Security and Trusted Computing—Cyber Security and Trusted Computing*, October 2012.
5. G. Xu, W. Yu, Z. Chen, H. Zhang, P. Moulema, X. Fu, C. Lu, A cloud computing based system for cyber security management, *International Journal of Parallel, Emergent and Distributed Systems (IJPEDS)*, 30(1), 29–45, 2015.
6. W. Yu, H. Zhang, L. Ge, R. Hardy, On behavior-based detection of malware on android platform, in *Proceedings of the IEEE Global Communications Conference (GLOBECOM)*, December 2013.
7. J. Manyika, M. Chui, B. Brown, J. Bughin, R. Dobbs, C. Roxburgh, A. H. Byers, Big Data: The next frontier for innovation, competition, and productivity, *McKinsey Global Institute*, 2011.
8. J. Sliver-Greenberg, M. Goldstein, N. Perlroth, JPMorgan Chase hacking affects 76 million households, available at http://dealbook.nytimes.com/2014/10/02/jpmorgan-discovers-further-cyber-security-issues/?_php=true&_type=blogs&_r=0, 2014.
9. N. Perlroth, Home Depot says data from 56 million cards was taken in breach, available at http://bits.blogs.nytimes.com/2014/09/18/home-depot-says-data-from-56-million-cards-taken-in-breach/, 2014.
10. J. Lin, W. Yu, X. Yang, G. Xu, W. Zhao, On false data injection attacks against distributed energy routing in smart grid, in *Proceedings of the ACM/IEEE Third International Conference on Cyber-Physical Systems (ICCPS)*, April 2012.
11. J. Mirkovic, P. Reiher, A taxonomy of DDoS attack and DDoS defense mechanisms, *ACM SIGCOMM Computer Communication Review*, 34(2), 39–53, April 2004.
12. D. Moore, C. Shannon, J. Brown, Code-red: A case study on the spread and victims of an internet worm, in *Proceedings of the 2rd Internet Measurement Workshop (IMW)*, November 2002.
13. G. Gu, R. Perdisci, J. Zhang, W. Lee, BotMiner: Clustering analysis of network traffic for protocol- and structure-independent botnet detection, in *Proceedings of the 17th USENIX Security Symposium*, August 2008.
14. P.-M. Annegret, G. Raposo, M. Marsh, Endosomes, exosomes and Trojan viruses, *Trends in Microbiology*, 12(7), 310–316, 2004.
15. V. Dave, S. Guha, Y. Zhang, Measuring and fingerprinting click-spam in Ad networks, *ACM SIGCOMM Computer Communication Review*, 42(4), 175–186, August 2012.
16. A. Karim, S. A. A. Shah, R. Salleh, Mobile botnet attacks: A thematic taxonomy, *New Perspectives in Information Systems and Technologies*, 2, 153–164. *Springer International Publishing*, 2014.
17. Z. Abdullah, M. M. Saudi, N. B. Anuar, Mobile botnet detection: Proof of concept, in *Proceedings of the IEEE Control and System Graduate Research Colloquium (ICSGRC)*, August 2014.
18. S. Marchal, X. Jiang, R. State, T. Engel, A big data architecture for large scale security monitoring, in *Proceedings of the IEEE 2014 International Conferences on Big Data (BigData Congress)*, June–July 2014.
19. D. Leaf, Overview: NIST Cloud Computing Efforts, NIST Senior Executive for Cloud Computing, Available at: http://csrc.nist.gov/groups/SNS/cloud-computing/documents/forumworkshop-may2010/nist_cloud_computing_forum-leaf.pdf, 2010.
20. J. Dean, S. Ghemawat, MapReduce: Simplified data processing on large clusters, *Communications of the ACM*, 51(1), 107–113, January 2008.

21. V. Chandola, A. Banerjee, V. Kumar, Anomaly detection: A survey, *ACM Computing Survey*, 41(3), Article 15, July 2009.

22. P. Harrington, *Machine Learning in Action*, Manning Publications Co., Greenwich, CT, USA, 2012.

23. J. Liu, J. Chen, J. Ye, Large-scale sparse logistic regression, in *Proceedings of the 15th ACM SIGKDD International Conference on Knowledge Discovery and Data Mining (KDD)*, June–July, 2009.

24. B. Quanz, J. Huan, Aligned graph classification with regularized logistic regression, in *Proceedings of the 2009 SIAM International Conference on Data Mining*, April/May 2009.

25. Y. Nardi, S. E. Fienberg, R. J. Hall, Achieving both valid and secure logistic regression analysis on aggregated data from different private sources, *Journal of Privacy and Confidentiality*, 4(1), Article 9, 2012.

26. R. Garg, A. L. Varna, M. Wu, A gradient descent based approach to secure localization in mobile sensor networks, in *Proceedings of the 2012 IEEE International Conference on Acoustics, Speech and Signal Processing (ICASSP)*, 1869–1872, March 2012.

27. J. Zhang, C. Chen, Y. Xiang, W. Zhou, Y. Xiang, Internet traffic classification by aggregating correlated naive Bayes predictions, *IEEE Transactions on Information Forensics and Security*, 8(1), 5–15, January 2013.

28. C. Chelba, A. Acero, *Conditional Maximum Likelihood Estimation of Naive Bayes Probability Models Using Rational Function Growth Transform*, Tech Report, Microsoft Research, pages 12, 2004.

29. K. Marcel, J. Erickson, Cloudera Impala: Real-Time Queries in Apache Hadoop, for Real, Available at: http://blog.cloudera.com/blog/2012/10/cloudera-impala-real-time-queries-in-apache-hadoop-for-real/, 2014.

30. A. Shiravi, H. Shiravi, M. Tavallaee, A. A. Ghorbani, Toward developing a systematic approach to generate benchmark datasets for intrusion detection, *Computers & Security*, 31(3), 357–374, May 2012.

CHAPTER 12

Anonymous Communication for Big Data

Lichun Li and Rongxing Lu

CONTENTS

INTRODUCTION

Anonymous Communication

Anonymous communication has received considerable attention to protect privacy in many applications such as anonymous web browsing [1,2], email [3], and voting [4]. Depending upon the applications, anonymous communication may hide one or more kinds of the following information from adversaries: (1) the linkage between messages and their senders/recipients; (2) the linkage between two communication parties; (3) activities of sending or/and receiving messages. Anonymous communication can protect privacy and the right of free speech/opinion. It can be utilized to access censored contents as well [5].

In this chapter, we focus on anonymous communication for Big Data especially the collection and sharing of data. In the Big Data era, collecting and sharing data are becoming more and more prevalent. It forms the cornerstone of collaboration, and is vital for individuals, industry, governments, and organizations. Consequently, while collecting data and sharing data are indispensable ways of obtaining up-to-date information, they also pose a threat to the privacy of data contributors/users. For example, in a mobile healthcare application, patients upload their vital data for medical research. They want to hide the linkage between their data and network addresses, which can be linked to their identities. For another example, a successful investor retrieving records of interested companies from a public database may wish to keep his/her identity or the retrieved records' identities private. Sometimes, even seemingly harmless information (e.g., one's interests in music or movies) may reveal personal information [6] that may need protection.

Preserving anonymity can encourage data contributors/users to contribute/use data. For data collection, preserving anonymity can improve the accuracy and usability of collected data as well. Without anonymity, data perturbation techniques, which add controllable noises to data, may be applied to data contributors' data. Data perturbation needs to carefully balance privacy and data usability. Weak noises may not protect data contributors' privacy, while strong noises may make the accuracy and usability of data too low. Without anonymity, some data contributors may even report some fake data, which also lower the accuracy and usability.

System Model of Big Data Collection/Sharing

The system model considered in this chapter is shown in Figure 12.1. In data collection, there is a database owner and multiple data contributors. Data contributors send their private data to the database owner. The database owner may collect data for his/her own use. For example, the database owner may perform data mining tasks on the data to obtain some interesting findings or knowledge. The database owner may collect data on behalf of some data users. In data sharing, there is a database owner and multiple data users. Data users retrieve some data from the database for their own uses. The data in the database may be generated by the database owner or collected from data contributors.

To protect the privacy of data contributors/users, we want to (1) hide the linkage between a data contributor and the data he or she sends to the database in data collection; (2) hide the linkage between a data user and the data he or she retrieves from the database in data

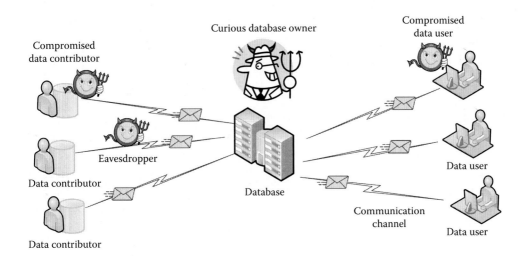

FIGURE 12.1   Data collection and sharing.

sharing. In this chapter, we focus on the anonymity preserving during data transfer instead of anonymizing data. For example, we care about concealing the network address of a data item's contributor/user from adversaries. Network addresses need protection because the location of the data contributor/user can be determined easily through his or her network address, which may narrow down the set of potential data contributors/users to very few or even one contributor/user. The Internet Service Provider (ISP) of the data contributor/user usually knows the linkage between network addresses inside its network and the identities of the people using the addresses. By compromising the ISP, a powerful adversary can learn the identity through network address. Besides anonymous communication, anonymizing data may be needed to protect privacy. In data collection, we assume that any data item received by the database owner does not contain the identity of the data item's contributor or information linking to the identity. Before the database owner receives these data items, data may be anonymized to remove such identities and information [7,8]. Such anonymizing is out of the scope of this book because we focus on anonymous communication.

The adversaries include the database owner, some data contributors/users, and third parties. They may collude together, and they try to learn the linkage between data and data contributors/users for different reasons. For example, the database owner wants to learn more information about data contributors/users for economic incentives; criminals want to gather information of potential victims; governments want to carry out mass surveillance. The adversaries may try to learn the linkage by means like observing the database and network traffic. The database owner is considered semitrusted and curious. The database owner wants to collect data from data contributors, and honestly returns the requested data to data users. However, the database owner also tries to learn the linkage between data and data contributors/users. Even if the database owner is fully trusted, the database may be open to everyone or many users so that an adversary can easily learn the data and the change of the database. In addition, an adversary may be able to observe some or all network traffic related to data collection/sharing.

Terminology

In this chapter, we mainly follow the terminology document of anonymity [9] maintained by Andreas Pfitzmann and Marit Hansen. We use the following definition of anonymity from Pfitzmann and Hansen [9].

Anonymity and Anonymity Set

Anonymity of a subject from an adversary's perspective means that the adversary cannot sufficiently identify the subject within a set of subjects, the anonymity set.

In the context of anonymous communication, subjects are senders and recipients. Senders send messages to recipients. A subject can have a higher level of privacy if the anonymity set is bigger. Again, we use the following definitions of sender anonymity and recipient anonymity from Pfitzmann and Hansen [9].

Sender Anonymity and Recipient Anonymity

Anonymity of a sender (resp. recipient) from an adversary's perspective means that the adversary cannot sufficiently identify the sender (resp. recipient) within a set of potential senders (resp. recipients), the sender (resp. recipient) anonymity set.

Anonymity can be achieved through unlinkability or unobservability. Their meanings in the context of anonymous communication are explained as follows.

Unlinkability and Unobservability

Sender (resp. recipient) unlinkability means the unlinkability between senders (resp. recipients) and sent (resp. received) messages, while sender (resp. recipient) unobservability means that it is undetectable whether any sender (resp. recipient) within a set of senders (resp. recipients) sends (resp. receives). Unobservability implies unlinkability, and the anonymity achieved through unobservability is stronger than the one through unlinkability.

In the context of data collection/sharing, we want to protect the privacy of data contributors/users. Data contributors/users play both the roles of senders and receivers. In data collection, data contributors send data to the database owner, and may receive replies from the database owner. In data sharing, data users send data requests to the database owner, and receive data from the database owner. The same as common anonymous communication, anonymity in data collection/sharing can be achieved through unlinkability or unobservability. We define unlinkability or unobservability in the context of data collection/sharing as follows.

Unlinkability and *Unobservability* in data collection/sharing. In the context of data collection/sharing, unlinkability means the unlinkability between contributed/retrieved data and data contributors/users, while unobservability means whether any data contributor/user within a set of contributors/users who contributes/retrieves data or not is undetectable from an adversary's perspective.

Traditionally, anonymity is regarded as a property of a subject, which is also implied in Pfitzmann and Hansen [9]'s definition of anonymity shown above. In this chapter, we define object anonymity and data anonymity for the "anonymity" achieved by Private Information Retrieval (PIR) [10]. PIR usually is not regarded as an anonymous communication technique because it is used in database access only and the achieved "anonymity" is different. However, PIR can achieve unlinkability in data sharing. In addition, PIR can be used with other anonymous communication techniques, which will be discussed later in this chapter. In this chapter, we regard PIR as a nontraditional anonymous communication technique, and refer to the other techniques as traditional techniques. The definition of object anonymity we have given below is very similar to Pfitzmann and Hansen [9]'s definition of anonymity. When discussing these two kinds of anonymity, we also refer to Pfitzmann and Hansen [9]'s anonymity as subject anonymity.

Object Anonymity

Anonymity of an object from an adversary's perspective means that the adversary cannot sufficiently identify the object within a set of objects, the anonymity set. The object in the data sharing context is data item. We define data anonymity as below.

Traditional anonymous communication techniques require an anonymity set of senders/recipients. Different from traditional techniques, PIR requires an anonymity set of data items instead. The anonymity set contains all data items in the database.

Data Anonymity

Anonymity of a data user's retrieved data item from an adversary's perspective means that the adversary cannot sufficiently identify the data item within a set of potential data items, the data anonymity set.

Organization

In this chapter, we focus on two traditional anonymous communication techniques, relay and Dining Cryptographer's network (DC-network) [11], and one nontraditional technique for data sharing, PIR. In the remainder of this chapter, we introduce these techniques, and discuss their usages and challenges in the Big Data context one by one. Then, we analyze the differences between traditional and nontraditional techniques as well as their complementarities. Finally, we conclude with a discussion of possible future research directions.

RELAY-BASED ANONYMOUS COMMUNICATION

There are already very good surveys on relay-based anonymous communication [12–14]. Therefore, we briefly introduce all three kinds of relay-based anonymous communication: mix networks, low-latency relay networks, and single relay. Then, we discuss their usages and challenges in the context of Big Data collection/sharing. For more information about relay-based anonymous communication, please refer to Edman and Yener [12], Danezis et al. [13], and Ren and Wu [14].

High-Latency Relay Networks: Mix Networks

In 1981, Chaum first introduced the idea of using a network of mixes (one kind of relay nodes) for anonymous communication [15]. Chaum's original mix network is mainly designed for high-latency applications like email. All high-latency relay networks are variants of Chaum's original mix networks, and mix is the building block of mix networks.

As shown in Figure 12.2, a mix is a relay node (relay for short) forwarding messages for message senders. To hide the linkage between input messages and output messages, a mix reorders and transforms the messages it forwards. To hide the linkage, dummy messages may be added by the mix and/or senders. Reordering messages prevents passive observers from detecting the linkage by correlating the input order and output order of messages. Transforming messages achieves bitwise unlinkability of input and output messages. Transforming could be done by encryption, decryption, or re-encryption. Padding may be required in transforming in order to make the size of all output messages the same.

Using a single mix is a single point of failure and trust. If the mix is compromised, anonymity cannot be preserved. To increase the level of security, a sender could use a cascade of mixes to forward a message to the recipient. Based on the ways to choose cascades, mix networks can be divided into two kinds: predefined mix networks and freely connected mix network. As illustrated in Figure 12.3, in predefined mix networks, for example, [1,4], there are a set of one or more predefined mix cascades, and a sender chooses one cascade to send a message. Freely connected mix networks, for example, [3] allow a sender to choose all mixes in the path freely by its will. As shown in Figure 12.4, any mix could forward messages to any mix in such mix networks. Some mix networks like Gulcu and Tsudik [16] further allow intermediate mixes to add more mixes to the routing path chosen by the sender. To do that, a mix adds one or more mixes in the path from itself to the original next-hop mix chosen by the sender. Freely connected mix networks make adversaries hard to find out a message's routing path, while verifiable mix networks, for example, [4] can be realized with predefined mix networks. A verifiable mix network allows senders and/ or mixes to detect misbehavior in the routing like substituting messages. (If the compromised mix(es) substitutes all messages of noncompromised senders with dummy messages

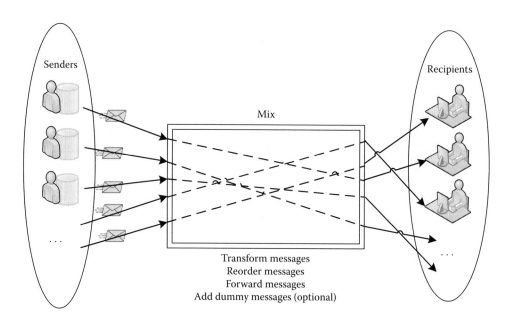

FIGURE 12.2 Anonymous communication based on a mix.

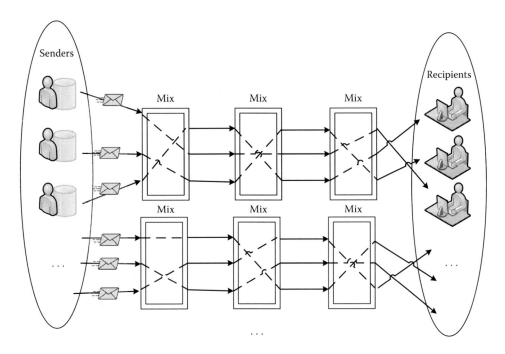

FIGURE 12.3 Predefined mix network.

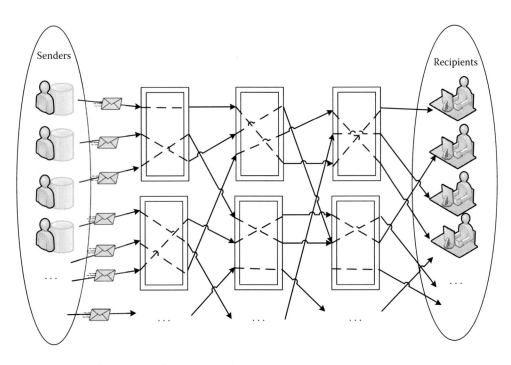

FIGURE 12.4 Freely connected mix network.

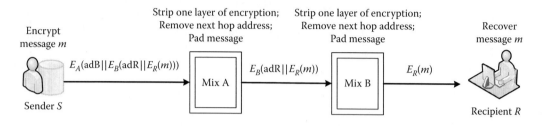

FIGURE 12.5   A message transform scheme generalized from Chaum's original mix network.

except the message of one noncompromised sender, the adversary is able to tell the sender's message output from the mix network.) If misbehavior is detected, the protocol will be aborted. If there are at least two noncompromised senders and at least one noncompromised mix in the mix cascade, verifiable mix networks can detect misbehavior, and make every noncompromised sender anonymous in the set of noncompromised senders.

There are quite a number of variants of Chaum's original mix network and transforming schemes. We show only a scheme generalized from Chaum's original mix network as follows. Please refer to Edman and Yener [12], Danezis et al. [13], and Ren and Wu [14] for more mix network designs and their transforming schemes. Suppose a sender S wants to send a message m to a recipient R via a series of mixes. The sender first encrypts m with the public keys of R and all these mixes, and obtains a ciphertext having multiple layers of encryptions. The addresses of the next hops are also embedded during the encryption so that one address can be recovered by stripping one layer of encryption except for the innermost layer. The sender sends the encrypted message to the first mix. Each mix receiving the encrypted message transforms the message by stripping one layer of encryption with its private key, removing the next hop's address, and padding the message to keep the message size unchanged. Then, the mix forwards the transformed message to the next hop. Finally, R receives the encrypted message, and strips the last layer of encryption to obtain the plaintext message m. An example is shown in Figure 12.5. In the example, the intermediate mixes are A and B. EA(), EB(), and ER() are the functions of encrypting with the public keys of A, B, and R, respectively. adA, adB, and adR are the addresses of A, B, and, R respectively.

Low-Latency Relay Networks and Single Relay

In mix-networks, to reorder forwarded messages, a mix has to delay messages for a long time if message arriving rate is low. To meet the need of real-time communication applications, low-latency relay networks only delay messages for a short time or even do not delay messages at all. Low-latency relay networks still can be viewed as variants of the (high-latency) mix networks. Different from mix networks, a relay in low-latency relay networks changes message order a little or does not change the order at all. This makes low-latency relay networks more vulnerable to traffic analysis attacks [17–19]. Using a single relay also reduces latency. As discussed earlier, a single relay is a single point of trust. So, both low-latency relay networks and single relay sacrifice security are to achieve a low latency.

Using Relay for Big Data

Unlinkability in data collection and sharing can be achieved by using relay networks and single relay. A big challenge of using relay for Big Data and some other applications is preserving anonymity while supporting authentication and fine-grained accounting. Data become more valuable in the Big Data era. Many databases are accessible to authorized data users only, and we need to prevent attackers from contributing fake data to pollute the database. Therefore, there is a need to authenticate contributors/users. In addition, a contributor/user may be awarded/changed based on the amount of contributed/retrieved data.

To prevent unauthorized access, a natural way is to enforce access control of the mix network: only authorized nodes can be mixes, and only authorized contributors/users can send/receive messages via the mix network. For example, mix network-based anonymous data collection protocols [20–22] enforce such access control. All senders and mixes are data contributors in these protocols. Such a mix network is used for the data collection/sharing of one database only and the number of mixes and senders is smaller than that in a mix network for multiple applications or databases. Therefore, it is easier for a powerful adversary to compromise a high ratio of mixes and data contributors/users. As mentioned earlier, verifiable mix networks are resilient to up to all but one compromised mixes and all but two compromised senders. Verifiable mix networks are used in Yang et al. [20], Brickell and Shmatikov [21], and Ashrafi and Ng [22] to counter the powerful adversary.

Blind signature [23] can be used to verify data items/requests from legitimate data contributors/users anonymously. Blind signature allows a message's author to obtain the signer's signature for the message without the signer knowing the content of the message. Laskari et al. [24] propose an anonymous data collection solution using blind signature and mix network. In the solution, a data contributor first blinds his/her data item with a random blinding factor (a random number selected with a certain rule depending on the blind signature scheme). In other words, the blinded item is computed from the original item and a random number. The data contributor signs the blinded item with a standard signature scheme, and sends the blinded item along with the signature to the database owner directly. The database owner verifies the data contributor's signature, and signs the blinded message with the database owner's private key. A blind signature scheme is used here. Then, the data owner's signature on the blinded message is sent to the data contributor. The data contributor verifies the database owner's signature, and removes the blinding factor to get the signature on the original data item. At last, the data contributor sends the data item to the database owner via the mix network, and the database owner verifies the signature. Similarly, an anonymous data sharing solution can be built using blind signature and mix network.

Group signature [25] and ring signature [26] may be used to verify data items/requests anonymously as well. Both group signature and ring signature allow a member of a group to anonymously sign a message on behalf of the group. To a verifier's perspective, any member could be a signature's producer. A major difference between group signature and ring signature is that there is a group manager in a group signature scheme. The manager is in charge of adding group members, and has the ability to reveal a signature's signer. Data contributors/users can sign their data items/requests with a group or ring signature scheme. Unlike blind signature, the signing here does not require interacting with the database owner. Though group/ring signature stops unauthorized nodes from creating valid messages, a malicious authorized data contributor/user still can create a lot of valid messages to abuse the system. In contrast, blind signature allows the database owner to control the number of messages signed for each data contributor/user.

Pseudonymity may be needed in some data collection applications so that the database owner can distinguish different contributors' data. For example, the database owner collects data from some anonymous patients periodically. The linkage between patients' network addresses and their contributed data items should be kept secret from the database owner. However, the database owner needs to know which data items come from the same patient. All data contributors may generate their pseudonyms and the corresponding key pairs by their own. Then, each data contributor reports his/her pseudonym and the public key to the database owner anonymously. (The public key itself can also be the pseudonym.) Alternatively, pseudonyms and key pairs could be generated and assigned by the database owner anonymously. To make sure each data contributor sends/receives only one pseudonym, verifiable mix networks can be used for the reporting/assigning. After the reporting/assigning, each data contributor should sign every data item with the private key associated with his/her pseudonym.

DINING CRYPTOGRAPHER'S NETWORK (DC-NET)

In 1988, Chaum proposed the dining cryptographer's problem and DC-net to solve the problem [11]. In this problem, some cryptographers are having dinner together. The waiter informs them that the bill has been paid anonymously. They suspect that one of them or the National Security Agency (NSA) paid the bill. They want to find out which is the case with a communication protocol. This protocol allows the cryptographer who paid the bill (if exists) to inform others about his/her payment anonymously. DC-net is such a protocol. In the protocol, each cryptographer chooses a secret random bit, 1 or 0, by tossing a coin, and shares the random bit with the one to his/her right. Each one computes a bit by XORing some bits. If a cryptographer did not pay the bill, he/she XORs his/her own random bit and the random bit received from the one to his/her left. Otherwise, the cryptographer XORs these two random bits and a "1." Everyone sends his/her computing result to all the other cryptographers. By XORing all cryptographers' computing results, everyone learns if one of them paid the bill or not. Because each random bit is shared by two cryptographers, XORing all cryptographers' computing results will cancel out all the random bits. If none of the cryptographers paid the bill, the result of this XORing is 0. Otherwise, the result is 1. Therefore, through this protocol, the cryptographer who paid the bill can broadcast the 1 bit message to others anonymously. If the adversary compromises a cryptographer's neighbors, the adversary can learn whether the cryptographer paid the bill or not. To make the protocol more secure, a cryptographer can share distinct random bits with more cryptographers. A cryptographer not paying the bill XORs all the random bits he/she knows to compute his/her result. Similarly, the cryptographer paying the bill XORs all known random bits and a "1."

DC-net achieves sender anonymity through sender unobservability. DC-net allows only one participant to send a message in one round of communication, whether a participant sending a message or not is unobservable to the adversary. In situations where multiple participants need to send messages, an anonymous time-slot reservation protocol should be run in advanced to determine which participant sends a message in which round of communication. Multiple reservation protocols have been proposed in the original DC-net and its variants [27–29].

DC-net can be applied to the case of sending a multibit message in one round of communication. The message length of each communication round can be shared with all participants via the anonymous reservation protocol too. In the case of sending an l-bit message, two participants share a random l-bit string instead of a random bit, and each participant XORs bit strings instead of bits. To reduce the communication cost of sharing random strings, instead of directly sharing the strings, Chaum [11] proposes to share keys of a cryptographically secure pseudo-random number generator (CSPRNG). A pair of participants sharing the same key can use the CSPRNG to generate shared random strings for multiple rounds of communication.

In the dining cryptographer's problem, the message is intended to all participants, and every participant broadcasts his/her computing result. DC-net can be used in the case that the message is intended to only a participant or a node outside the DC-net. If the message is intended to a participant and recipient anonymity is required, every participant still needs to broadcasts his/her computing result. Otherwise, if recipient anonymity is not required, every participant sends his/her computing result to the recipient (a participant or a node outside DC-net) instead of all participants. By XORing all received results, the recipient can recover the message. Figure 12.6 shows a toy example of sending a message to an outside node via DC-net. In the example, Sender 4 is the one sending the message, and other senders send cover traffic.

Using DC-Net for Big Data

A set of data contributors/users can form a DC-net. In one round of communication, a data contributor/user sends a data item/request to the database owner via DC-net. This set of data contributors/users are the possible senders to the adversary, that is, the anonymity set. The database owner may need to response a message back to the sender. For example, the database owner may send the data contributor a notification about receiving his/her data item, or send the data user the data item corresponding to his/her data request. Not knowing the sender, the data owner can simply broadcast the response message to all members of the DC-net. To keep the content of the response confidential from other data contributors/users, the sender can attach a session key in the message sent to the database owner, and the response message sent by the database owner is encrypted with the key.

The limitation of using DC-net is its low scalability. In a DC-net of N participants, $N-1$ participants send cover traffic in every round of communication. If using DC-net to send an l-bit message to a node outside the DC-net, the total traffic is $N \times l$ bits. Due to the high

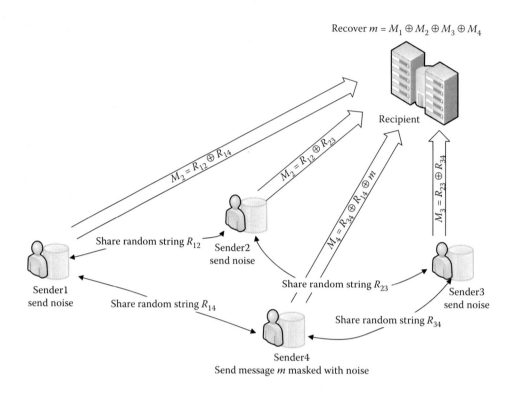

FIGURE 12.6 Send a message m to an outside node via DC-net. m: the real message; R_{ij}: the random string shared by sender i and sender j; M_i: the noise or message masked with noise sent by sender i. Random strings can be shared via sharing the keys of CSPNRG.

traffic, the number of participants, which is also the size of the anonymity set, cannot be very big. Reliability also affects DC-net's scalability. If a participant fails before sending its computing result or a malicious participant sends a wrong computing result, the message cannot be recovered successfully by the recipient(s). More participants in a DC-net can cause a higher change of unsuccessfully recovering. Despite the disadvantage in scalability, compared with relay network, DC-net can achieve a lower latency for low-speed communication. In DC-net, there is no latency caused by relay. If DC-net's communication traffic does not cause network congestion, DC-net's latency could be lower. Therefore, DC-net is suitable for low-speed communication.

Other Solutions Achieving Unobservability

Some other solutions [30,31] not based on DC-net can also achieve unobservability. However, they are designed for many-to-many communication. When applying them to many-to-one communication such as data collection/sharing, their communication costs are higher than DC-net's. Also, in Beimel and Dolev [30]'s solution, a sender is anonymous to third-parties but not the corresponding recipient. This does not meet our requirement. When a data contributor/user sends a data item/request to the database owner, we want the data contributor/user to remain anonymous to both the database owner and third-parties.

PRIVATE INFORMATION RETRIEVAL

PIR was first proposed by Chor et al. [10] to protect user interest privacy in accessing shared databases. PIR allows a user to retrieve a data item from a database without letting the database server know which item is being retrieved. Direct application of PIR allows querying a data item by the item's ID. Here, an item could be a record of a relational database, a file, a file chuck, and so on. Based on PIR, advanced privacy-preserving queries such as queries by keywords [32] and SQL-like queries over relational databases [33] are realized. This privacy primitive has been used in diverse settings including patent databases [34], pharmaceutical databases [34], email systems [35], e-commerce [36], P2P file sharing systems [37], and so on.

Broadly, there are two kinds of PIR techniques—information-theoretic PIR (itPIR) and computational PIR (cPIR), providing unconditional and computational hardness-based privacy, respectively. The privacy in cPIR is guaranteed subject to computational bounds on the server, while all communication efficient itPIR schemes are multiserver based, and assume that not all the servers collude together.

Information-Theoretic PIR

There is no single-server itPIR scheme apart from the trivial one, that is, downloading the whole database. Efficient multiserver itPIR schemes can be built under the conditions that each server holds a replication of the database and not all servers collude. A multiserver itPIR scheme is called a t-private k-server itPIR scheme if it requires k ($k > 1$) database servers and resists up to t ($k > t \geq 1$) colluding servers. Suppose a database has n data items, a t-private k-server itPIR works in the following way: (1) the user's PIR client uses the ID(s) of the wanted data item(s) to generate k questions, and sends each server a question; (2) each server computes an answer using its received question and $O(n)$ data items in the database, and sends the answer to the client; (3) the client recovers the wanted data item(s) from received answers. Any t or fewer servers together cannot learn any nontrivial information of any wanted data item's ID from their received questions.

Beimel et al. [38,39] find that secret sharing and share conversion are the key techniques used implicitly or explicitly by most existing itPIR schemes, and summarized the common underlying mechanism of these schemes. Li et al. [40] generalize this mechanism to cover also new PIR schemes using ramp secret sharing [40,41]. The generalized mechanism is as follows:

- First, the user uses a t-private secret-sharing scheme to break a secret (or a set of secrets) containing the ID(s) of the retrieved data item(s) (we call it input secret) into shares, and sends each share (or a set of different secrets' shares) to a server as a question.

- Second, each server converts the received question to an answer locally with an elaborately chosen/designed function, and sends the answer to the user. Each answer is a share of a secret containing the value(s) of the retrieved data item(s) (we call it output secret) under a t-private secret-sharing scheme, which may not be identical to the scheme used to break up the input secret.

- Third, the user recovers the output secret, that is, the data item(s) to retrieve, from the answers.

Many itPIR schemes use a perfect threshold secret sharing-scheme like Shamir [42], while Li et al. [40] and Henry et al. [41] apply ramp secret-sharing [43] instead. In this chapter, we say that a secret sharing scheme is a t-private scheme if it has a threshold t and any nontrivial information of the secret cannot be learned from t or less shares. In perfect threshold secret sharing, for example, Shamir's secret sharing [42], the entire secret can be learned from more than t shares. In ramp secret sharing, for example, [44,45], there are two thresholds t and K. Any nontrivial information of the secret cannot be learned from t or less shares; partial information can be learned from $t + 1$ to $K - 1$ shares; the entire secret can be learned from K or more shares. The t-private property of secret sharing assures the t-private property of itPIR schemes. In other words, the security of multiserver itPIR schemes depends on the security of their underlying secret-sharing schemes.

Example: Chor's t-private (t + 1)-server itPIR from Additive Secret Sharing
To illustrate the above mechanism, we show an itPIR scheme proposed by Chor [10] and the secret-sharing scheme used in it.

Trivial Additive Secret Sharing   A secret s is represented by a vector over F_2. Suppose the vector length is h. Then $\in F_2^h$. The user breaks s into $t + 1$ additive shares by generating t uniform random vectors $V[1], V[2], V[3], \ldots, V[t] \in F_2^h$ and an additional vector $V[t + 1] = s - \sum_{i=1}^{t} V[i]$. Then $V[1], V[2], V[3], \ldots, V[t + 1]$ are additive shares of s, and $s = \sum_{i=1}^{t+1} V[i]$. Any t shares reveal no information about the secret. Please note that the addition/subtraction operations over the field F_2 are XOR operations.

Suppose the database has n data items and each item's size is l bits. There are $k = t + 1$ servers indexed from 1 to k, each of which holds a replication of the database. Let $X[1]$, $X[2], \ldots, X[n]$ be the data items in the database. Suppose the PIR client wants to retrieve the i-th data item $X[i]$. Simply put, in this scheme, the PIR client asks each server to return the XOR of a random set of data items. Any t sets look random to servers, but XORing all $t + 1$ sets of data items can recover the wanted item. A toy example is shown in Figure 12.7, and a formal description of the scheme is given as below.

The i-th data item $X[i] \in F_2^l$ can be evaluated with the following linear function over field F_2. Here, Y_j is the j-th component of the vector Y. This function actually adds/XORs data items, and the items being added/XORed are indicated by the Y. A data item $X[j]$ is added/XORed, only if the j-th bit in the n-bit string Y is 1.

$$P(Y) = \sum_{j=1}^{n} X[j] \times Y_j, \quad X[j] \in F_2^l \text{ and } Y \in F_2^n \tag{12.1}$$

Note that $X[i] = P(e_i)$ for any $i \in \{1, 2, \ldots, n\}$, where e_i is a unit vector in F_2^n and only the i-th component is 1. Therefore, the retrieval of $X[i]$ can be reduced to an evaluation of the function $P(Y)$ on a point e_i where the servers hold $P(Y)$ and the user holds i. This scheme

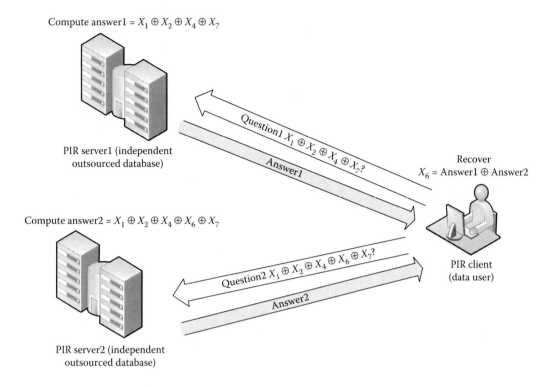

Compute answer1 = $X_1 \oplus X_2 \oplus X_4 \oplus X_7$

PIR server1 (independent
outsourced database)

Question1 $X_1 \oplus X_2 \oplus X_4 \oplus X_7$?

Answer1

Recover
X_6 = Answer1 $\oplus$ Answer2

Compute answer2 = $X_1 \oplus X_2 \oplus X_4 \oplus X_6 \oplus X_7$

Question2 $X_1 \oplus X_2 \oplus X_4 \oplus X_6 \oplus X_7$?

Answer2

PIR client
(data user)

PIR server2 (independent
outsourced database)

FIGURE 12.7   A toy example of Chor's itPIR scheme.

uses additive secret sharing to prevent up to t colluding servers to recover the secret e_i. The user retrieves a data item $X[i]$ by following steps:

- Using the trivial additive secret sharing, the user breaks the input secret e_i into a set of k additive shares $V[1]$, $V[2]$, $V[3]$, ..., $V[k]$. So $e_i = \sum_{j=1}^{k} V[j]$.

- The user sends the vector $V[j]$ to the j-th server as a question for every $j \in \{1, 2, ..., k\}$. The question length is n.

- The j-th server uses its received vector to compute $P(V[j])$, and returns the result to the user as an answer. k servers compute and return k answers in total. Each answer's length is l.

- The user reconstructs data item $X[i]$ (i.e., the output secret) with the answers using the equation below, where S_i is the set of e_i's additive shares.

$$X_i = P(e_i) = P\left(\sum_{j=1}^{k} V[j]\right) = \sum_{h=1}^{n} X(h) \times \left(\sum_{j=1}^{k} V[j]\right)_h$$
$$= \sum_{j=1}^{k} \left(\sum_{h=1}^{n} X(h) \times V[j]_h\right) = \sum_{j=1}^{k} P(V[j])$$

(12.2)

Computational PIR

The first cPIR scheme [46] is a 1-private 2-server scheme and also the only multiserver cPIR scheme. Chor and Gilboa [46]'s scheme uses a 1-private 2-server itPIR scheme as a building block, and achieves a much lower communication cost by utilizing a cryptographically secure pseudo-random number generator (CSPRNG) in the generation of itPIR's questions. All the other cPIR schemes are single-server schemes. In a single-server cPIR scheme, a PIR client retrieves a data item by the following steps:

- The client encrypts the data item's ID, say i. (Please note that cPIR schemes usually do not encrypt data item's ID in standard ways.)

- The client sends the encrypted ID as a question to the database server.

- The database server computes the ciphertext of the i-th data item using the encrypted ID and all the data items in the database. The server is not aware of the ID of the encrypted data item during the computation.

- The database server returns the ciphertext of the i-th data item as the answer to the client's query.

- The client decrypts the received answer to obtain the i-th data item.

Most cPIR schemes are constructed from customized group-homomorphic encryption schemes [47]. Such an encryption scheme is also probabilistic. Ostrovsky and Skeith [47] gave a general cPIR construction from such an encryption scheme. To make cPIR easy to understand, in this chapter, we demonstrate only one special cPIR construction from an additive homomorphic encryption scheme.

Preliminary: Additive Homomorphic Encryption
Homomorphic encryption is one kind of encryption, which allows one or more kinds of plaintext operations (e.g., addition and multiplication) to be carried out on ciphertext. If the addition operation is allowed in an encryption scheme, this scheme is an additive homomorphic scheme. More specifically, as shown below, an additive homomorphic scheme allows the encrypted result of adding two numbers $m1$ and $m2$ to be obtained with some kind of computation "•" on their ciphertexts. Their ciphertexts are not decrypted during the computation, and the decryption key is not required. Let $E()$ and $D()$ be the encryption and decryption functions, respectively. An additive homomorphic encryption scheme also allows to obtain $E(m1 \times m2)$ by doing $m2$ times of "•" computation on $E(m1)$, which is notated by $E(m1)^{\bullet m2}$ in this chapter.

$$E(m1 + m2) = E(m1) \bullet E(m2)$$

$$E(m1 \times m2) = E(m1)^{\bullet m2} = E(m1) \bullet E(m1) \bullet E(m1) \cdots \bullet E(m1)$$

For example, Paillier's encryption scheme [48] is an asymmetric encryption scheme with an additive homomorphic property. Given $E(m1)$, $E(m2)$ and only the public key used in encryption, one can compute $E(m1 + m2)$ by doing a modular multiplication of $E(m1)$ and $E(m2)$. Modular multiplication is the "•" computation in Paillier's encryption scheme. Similarly, given $E(m1)$, $m2$ and the public key, one can compute $E(m1 \times m2)$ by doing a modular exponentiation $E(m1)^{m2}$.

cPIR from Additive Homomorphic Encryption

Let $X[1]$, $X[2]$, ..., $X[n]$ be the data items in the database. Suppose a PIR client wants to retrieve the i-th data item $X[i]$. Using an additive homomorphic encryption scheme, the PIR client retrieves $X[i]$ from the database by the following steps:

- Question generation and transfer.

  - The PIR client generates n ciphertexts $C_1, C_2, ..., C_n$ as the question, and sends it to the PIR server. For each j in $[n]$, $C_j \leftarrow E(1)$ if $j = i$. Otherwise, $C_j \leftarrow E(0)$.

    Remark: The secret data item ID i is encrypted using n ciphertexts. The encryption scheme is probabilistic, and any two ciphertexts of the same or different plaintexts look different with overwhelming probability. The adversary cannot tell which ciphertext is the encryption of 1.

- Answer computing and transfer.

  - The PIR server computes the answer *Ans* with following formula, and sends it to the client.

$$Ans = C_1^{\bullet X_1} \bullet C_2^{\bullet X_2} \cdots \bullet C_n^{\bullet X_n} \tag{12.3}$$

    Remark: The above formula computes the ciphertext of $\sum_{j=1}^{n} I_j \times X_j$, where $I_j = 1$ if $j = i$, and $I_j = 0$ otherwise. So the answer is $E(X_i)$.

- Data recovery.

  - The PIR client recovers the data item X_i by decrypting the received answer $E(X_i)$.

A cPIR scheme of above construction can be used iteratively to reduce question communication traffic (traffic from client to server). Let us take a two-level iterative retrieval as an example. Before the retrieval, the original database is divided into $\sqrt{n}$ small databases, each of which has $\sqrt{n}$ data items. Suppose the item to be retrieved is in the $i1$-th item in the $i2$-th database denoted by $X[i1, i2]$. First, the PIR client sends one PIR question for retrieving the $i1$-th item of each small database. Second, based on the question, the PIR server computes an answer for each small database, and keeps the answer locally instead of sending it to the client. So $\sqrt{n}$ answers, $E(X[i1, 1])$, $E(X[i1, 2])$, ..., $E(X[i1, \sqrt{n}])$, are generated, which are viewed as a new database. The j-th item of the new database is the ciphertext of

$i1$-th data item of the j-th small database. Third, the PIR client sends another PIR question for retrieving the $i2$-th item of the new database, and the PIR server sends the answer $E(E(X[i1, i2]))$ to the client. Finally, the client decrypts the received answer to recover $X[i1, i2]$. Please note that two PIR questions can be sent together to the server, and only one round of communication is required. The server's computational cost is almost the same as that without iteration. The client needs to do one more decryption operation but much less encryption operations. The question communication traffic is also much lower. The answer communication traffic (traffic from server to client) may be higher because the answer has one more layer of encryption.

Barriers of PIR's Use in Big Data

Since the invention of PIR, the biggest barriers for PIR's practical use are its high communication and computational costs, which increase as the database size increases. Much work has been done to reduce the costs. Most itPIR works of reducing communication cost like Beimel et al. [38, 49] and Yekhanin [50] all focus on question communication cost, that is, the traffic from PIR client to PIR server. Two recent works [40,41] reduce itPIR's answer communication cost, that is, the traffic from server to client, which is very important for databases with Big Data items. Early cPIR works like Lipmaa [51] and Gentry and Ramzan [52] pay more attention to communication cost, and Gentry and Ramzan [52]'s single-server cPIR scheme is able to achieve a very low communication cost. However, later works [53,54] discover that Gentry and Ramzan [52]'s computational cost is unsustainable and reducing computational cost is much more important for a single-server cPIR's practical use.

To compute a PIR answer, in a single-server PIR scheme, a PIR server uses the whole database such that the retrieved data item is hidden among the whole database. Similarly, in a multiserver server scheme, a server uses $O(n)$ data items. The first multiserver itPIR and cPIR schemes [10,46] are the most computationally efficient schemes. They require only XOR operations on the database to compute answers. As for a single-server cPIR, efforts have been taken to design more and more computationally efficient schemes. Originally, single-server cPIR schemes were considered impractical for normal database sizes [54] due to their high computational costs. Sion and Carbunar [54]'s experiments show that downloading the whole database is faster using single-server PIR schemes. Subsequently, more efficient cPIR schemes were invented and considered computationally practical for restricted database sizes [53,55,56]. Reference [56]'s experiments show that PIR is faster than downloading the whole database and itPIR's latency is at least one order lower than that of a single-server cPIR. Recently, cPIR and itPIR schemes exploiting parallelization of cloud/cluster computing [57,58] or GPU [59] were proposed to make them practical for huge databases. Though the computation cost is not reduced, parallelization can reduce the time to compute a PIR answer.

In the Big Data era, huge databases are not rare. The biggest concern of using PIR today is still communication and computational costs, and there are still urgent needs to design better PIR schemes and better solutions to relieve the impacts of these costs. Nevertheless, using PIR for Big Data is becoming practical especially for databases with Big Data items. Under many settings of data item sizes and data item counts especially the settings of Big

Data item sizes, the latency of some PIR schemes is acceptable and lower than the latency of downloading the whole database [56,58], and the bandwidth usage is only a few times higher than or even close to that of trivially downloading the data item [40,58].

To use PIR, a few things regarding costs should be considered. A good PIR scheme must be chosen carefully considering both communication and computational costs, which are affected by factors such as data item size, data item count, the number of PIR servers, and security requirement. Parallelization of cloud/cluster computing or GPU could be utilized to reduce the latency caused by high computational cost. The impacts of high communication and computational costs may be relieved by shifting some costs offline [60,61] as well. At last, we may relax the privacy requirement to reduce costs. If hiding the retrieved data item's ID among a portion of the database is enough to protect privacy, we can simply apply the PIR scheme to only a portion instead of the whole of the database. The portion is viewed as a new and smaller database, and the communication and computation costs are lower.

SUBJECT ANONYMITY VIA RELAY/DC-NET AND DATA ANONYMITY VIA PIR

Though relay, DC-net and PIR all can be used for anonymous data sharing, PIR's philosophy is quite different from that of the other two. As mentioned in the Terminology section, the "anonymity" PIR provides does not fit the well-accepted definition given by Pfitzmann and Hansen [9]. However, unlinkability can be achieved via PIR. PIR protects privacy by hiding the identities of retrieved data items, while traditional techniques (relay and DC-net) achieve anonymity by hiding the identity of any retrieved data item's requester. PIR and traditional techniques achieve object anonymity and subject anonymity, respectively. As discussed below, PIR and traditional techniques are complementary to each other, and sometimes they can be used in different parts of an anonymous communication system or be even combined together to achieve better privacy.

Different philosophies make the situations of using PIR and traditional techniques different. They all could be applied in some situations, while only PIR or traditional techniques could be applied in some other situations. For the situations of data users requesting some complicated queries or data mining tasks on the database, using PIR is inefficient or even infeasible. It is better to use relay or DC-net. For the two kinds of situations below, relay and DC-net are not suitable, and PIR offers better privacy than relay and DC-net do.

- Privacy breach via overall interest. Relay and DC-net cannot hide the overall interest of all data users (e.g., the access time and frequency of a sensitive record), which itself may contain sensitive information. On the other hand, if one or a few data item(s) are queried by most data requests in a short period, the adversary can link these data with the active data users in this period with high confidence.

- Too small anonymity set. If the database or a portion of the database is authorized to only one or very few data users, the anonymity set is too small to protect privacy of the data user(s). Also, if the adversary knows which users are online and there are very few online users, the anonymity set still could be too small.

At least two works [35,62] use PIR and relay together in their anonymous communication systems. In Mittal et al. [62]'s anonymous communication system, a user joining the system uses PIR to retrieve the information of some relays from directory servers, which manage the information. The user will use these relays to route his/her messages, and these relays must be kept secret from the adversary. In other systems, a user usually downloads the information of a lot of relays to hide the ones he/she will use. Mittal et al. [62] shows that using PIR instead is more efficient in many cases. Sassaman et al. [35] have a pseudonymous email system, which utilizes mix network to send emails and PIR to retrieve emails. Sassaman et al. [35] use PIR instead of mix network to retrieve emails because previous pseudonymous email systems are not secure or reliable enough.

A more interesting thing is that PIR schemes can be built from relay, and combining PIR with relay offers better privacy than using PIR or relay alone. Trostle and Parrish [55] and Ishai et al. [63] utilize relay to transmit PIR messages. This approach turns a t-private k-server itPIR scheme to a single-server cPIR scheme. In the original itPIR scheme, to retrieve a data item, a PIR client sends each of the k servers a question. If more than t servers collude together, they can recover the requested data item's identity from the PIR questions they receive. In the cPIR scheme, there is only one PIR server. All clients' questions are sent to the server anonymously, and the PIR server cannot distinguish one client's questions from another's. The server may recover data requests by trying different combinations of questions received in a short time window. When t and the number of querying clients are big enough, recovering data requests becomes computationally infeasible. Different from sending plain data requests via relay, sending PIR questions via relay hides the data item retrieved by a data user among the whole database instead of the items retrieved by all users. Compared with the other PIR schemes, the schemes built from relay may hide a data user's activity of retrieving data if the adversary cannot observe all network traffic. Other than these PIR schemes built from relay and itPIR, it is also possible to send the messages of cPIR schemes via relay to enjoy the above benefits.

CONCLUSION

In the Big Data era, the prevalence of data collection and sharing poses a threat to privacy. In this chapter, we have introduced two kinds of anonymous communication techniques to protect privacy in the context of data collection and sharing. The first kind is traditional anonymous communication techniques relay and DC-net, which can be used in both data collection and sharing. The second kind is a nontraditional anonymous communication technique PIR, which is used for data sharing only. These techniques' usages and challenges in the Big Data context have been discussed. Though there are quite a few works on the topic of anonymous Big Data collection and sharing, there are seldom deployed anonymous systems/prototypes. Attracting people to use such a system is very important as more people mean a bigger anonymity set. It is still an open issue to balance the privacy, performance and usability of anonymous Big Data collection and sharing. Another interesting direction-requiring attentions is the combination of anonymous communication techniques and data-anonymizing techniques (e.g., k-anonymizing).

REFERENCES

1. Berthold, O., Federrath, H. and Köpsell S. 2001. Web mixes: A system for anonymous and unobservable internet access, *International Workshop on Designing Privacy Enhancing Technologies*, Springer, pp. 115–129.
2. Dingledine, R., Mathewson, N. and Syverson, P. 2004. Tor: The second-generation onion router, *DTIC Document*, Tech. Rep.
3. Danezis, G., Dingledine, R. and Mathewson, N. 2003. Mixminion: Design of a type iii anonymous remailer protocol, in *Proceedings of the IEEE S&P* 2003, pp. 2–15.
4. Neff, C. A. 2001. A verifiable secret shuffle and its application to e-voting, in *Proceedings of the ACM CCS' 2001*, pp. 116–125.
5. Clarke, I., Sandberg, O., Wiley, B. and Hong, T. W. 2001. Freenet: A distributed anonymous information storage and retrieval system, *International Workshop on Designing Privacy Enhancing Technologies*, Springer, pp. 46–66.
6. Chaabane, A., Acs, G. and Kaafar, M. A. 2012. You are what you like! Information leakage through users' interests, in *Proceedings of the Internet Society NDSS' 2012*.
7. Zhang, L. and Zhang, W. 2008. Generalization-based privacy-preserving data collection, *Proceedings of Springer DWKD' 2008*, pp. 115–124.
8. Zhong, S., Yang, Z. and Chen, T. 2009. k-anonymous data collection, *Information Sciences*, 179(17), 2948–2963.
9. Pfitzmann, A. and Hansen, M. 2010. A terminology for talking about privacy by data minimization: Anonymity, unlinkability, undetectability, unobservability, pseudonymity, and identity management, available at http://dud.inf.tu-dresden.de/literatur/Anon_Terminology_v0.34.pdf
10. Chor, B., Goldreich, O., Kushilevitz, E. and Sudan, M. 1995. Private information retrieval, in *Proceedings of the IEEE FOCS' 1995*, pp. 41–50.
11. Chaum, D. 1988. The dining cryptographers problem: Unconditional sender and recipient untraceability, *Journal of Cryptology*, 1(1), 65–75.
12. Edman, M. and Yener, B. 2009. On anonymity in an electronic society: A survey of anonymous communication systems, *ACM Computing Surveys*, 42(1), 1–35.
13. Danezis, G., Diaz, C. and Syverson, P. 2009. Systems for anonymous communication, *Handbook of Financial Cryptography and Security, Cryptography and Network Security Series*, pp. 341–389.
14. Ren, J. and Wu, J. 2010. Survey on anonymous communications in computer networks, *Computer Communications*, 33(4), 420–431.
15. Chaum, D. L. 1981. Untraceable electronic mail, return addresses, and digital pseudonyms, *ACM Communications*, 24(2), 84–90.
16. Gulcu, C. and Tsudik, G. 1996. Mixing e-mail with babel, in *Proceedings of the Internet Society NDSS' 1996*, pp. 2–16.
17. Shmatikov, V. and Wang, M. H. 2006. Timing analysis in low-latency mix networks: Attacks and defenses, in *Proceedings of the Springer ESORICS' 2006*, pp. 18–33.
18. Serjantov, A. and Sewell, P. 2003. Passive attack analysis for connection-based anonymity systems, in *Proceedings of the Springer ESORICS' 2003*, pp. 116–131.
19. Danezis, G. and Clayton, R. 2007. Introducing traffic analysis. In *Digital Privacy: Theory, Technologies, and Practices*. Auerbach Publications, Taylor & Francis Group.
20. Yang, Z., Zhong, S. and Wright, R. N. 2005. Anonymity-preserving data collection, in *Proceedings of the ACM SIGKDD' 2005*, pp. 334–343.
21. Brickell, J. and Shmatikov, V. 2006. Efficient anonymity-preserving data collection, in *Proceedings of the ACM SIGKDD' 2006*, pp. 76–85.
22. Ashrafi, M. Z. and Ng, S. K. 2009. Collusion-resistant anonymous data collection method, in *Proceedings the of ACM SIGKDD' 2009*, pp. 69–78.
23. Chaum, D. 1984. Blind signature system, in *Proceedings of* the *Springer CRYPTO' 1984*, pp. 153–153.

24. Laskari, E. C., Meletiou, G. C., Tasoulis, D. K. and Vrahatis, M. N. 2005. Privacy preserving electronic data gathering, *Mathematical and Computer Modelling*, 42(7), 739–746.
25. Chaum, D. and Van Heyst, E. 1991. Group signatures, in *Proceedings of the EUROCRYPT' 1991*, pp. 257–265.
26. Rivest, R. L., Shamir, A. and Tauman, Y. 2001. How to leak a secret, in *Proceedings of the Springer ASIACRYPT' 2001*, pp. 552–565.
27. Goel, S., Robson, M., Polte, M. and Sirer, E. 2003. Herbivore: A scalable and efficient protocol for anonymous communication, *Cornell University, Tech. Rep.*
28. Corrigan-Gibbs, H. and Ford, B. 2010. Dissent: Accountable anonymous group messaging, in *Proceedings of the ACM CCS' 2010*, pp. 340–350.
29. Neikes, M. 2014. Efficiency of large-scale DC-networks, *Bachelor thesis, Radboud University*.
30. Beimel, A. and Dolev, S. 2003. Buses for anonymous message delivery, *Journal of Cryptology*, 16(1), 25–39.
31. Sherwood, R., Bhattacharjee, B. and Srinivasan, A. 2005. P5: A protocol for scalable anonymous communication, *Journal of Computer Security*, 13(6), 839–876.
32. Chor, B., Gilboa, N. and Naor, M. 1997. Private information retrieval by keywords, Technical report, TR CS0917, Department of Computer Science, Technion, 1997.
33. Reardon, J., Pound, J. and Goldberg, I. 2007. Relational-complete private information retrieval, University of Waterloo, *Tech. Rep. CACR 34.*
34. Asonov, D. 2001. Private information retrieval: An overview and current trends, in *Proceedings of the ECDPvA Workshop*, Informatik.
35. Sassaman, L., Cohen, B. and Mathewson, N. 2005. The pynchon gate: A secure method of pseudonymous mail retrieval, in *Proceedings of the 2005 ACM Workshop on Privacy in the Electronic Society*, 2005, pp. 1–9.
36. Mane, S. B., Sawant, S. T. and Sinha, P. K. 2012. Using private information retrieval protocol for an e-commerce application, in *Proceedings of the CUBE International Information Technology Conference*. ACM, pp. 659–663.
37. Miceli, M. 2011. Private information retrieval in an anonymous peer-to-peer environment, *University of New Orleans Theses and Dissertations*. Paper 1331.
38. Beimel, A., Ishai, Y. and Kushilevitz, E. 2005. General constructions for information-theoretic private information retrieval, *Journal of Computer and System Sciences*, 71(2), 213–247.
39. Beimel, A., Ishai, Y., Kushilevitz, E. and Orlov, I. 2012. Share conversion and private information retrieval, in *Proceedings of the IEEE CCC' 2012*, pp. 258–268.
40. Li, L., Militzer, M. and Datta, A. 2014 rPIR: Ramp secret sharing based communication efficient private information retrieval. *IACR Cryptology ePrint Archive*, 2014, 44.
41. Henry, R., Huang, Y. and Goldberg, I. 2013 One (block) size fits all: PIR and SPIR over arbitrary length records via multi-block PIR queries, in *Proceedings of the Internet Society NDSS' 2013*.
42. Shamir, A. 1979. How to share a secret, *ACM Communications*, 22(11), 612–613.
43. Blakley, G. R. and Meadows, C. 1985. Security of ramp schemes, in *Proceedings of the Springer CRYPTO' 1985*, pp. 242–268.
44. Kurihara, J., Kiyomoto, S., Fukushima, K. and Tanaka, T. 2009. A fast (k,l,n)-threshold ramp secret sharing scheme, *IEICE Transactions on Fundamentals of Electronics, Communications and Computer Sciences*, 92(8), 1808–1821.
45. Yamamoto, H. 1986. Secret sharing system using (k, l, n) threshold scheme, *Electronics and Communications in Japan (Part I: Communications)*, 69(9), 46–54.
46. Chor, B. and Gilboa, N. 1997. Computationally private information retrieval, in *Proceedings of the ACM SOTC' 1997*, pp. 304–313.
47. Ostrovsky, R. and Skeith, W. E. III. 2007. A survey of single-database private information retrieval: Techniques and applications, in *Proceedings of the Springer PKC' 2007*, pp. 393–411.

48. Paillier, P. 1999. Public-key cryptosystems based on composite degree residuosity classes, in *Proceedings of the IACR EUROCRYPT' 1999*, pp. 223–238.
49. Beimel, A., Ishai, Y., Kushilevitz, E. and Raymond, J.-F. 2002. Breaking the $O(n^{1/(2k-1)})$ barrier for information-theoretic private information retrieval, in *Proceedings of the IEEE FOCS' 2002*, pp. 261–270.
50. Yekhanin, S. 2008. Towards 3-query locally decodable codes of subexponential length, *Journal of the ACM*, 55(1), 1, 1–16.
51. Lipmaa, H. 2005. An oblivious transfer protocol with log-squared communication, in *Proceedings of* the *Springer ISC' 2005*, pp. 314–328.
52. Gentry, C. and Ramzan, Z. 2005. Single-database private information retrieval with constant communication rate, in *Proceedings of the Springer ICALP' 2005*, pp. 803–815.
53. Aguilar-Melchor, C. 2007. A lattice-based computationally-efficient private information retrieval protocol, in *Proceedings of the WEWORC' 2007*.
54. Sion, R. and Carbunar, B. 2007. On the computational practicality of private information retrieval, in *Proceedings of the Internet Society NDSS' 2007*.
55. Trostle, J. and Parrish, A. 2011. Efficient computationally private information retrieval from anonymity or trapdoor groups, in *Proceedings of* the *Springer ISC' 2011*, pp. 114–128.
56. Olumofin, F. and Goldberg, I. 2012. Revisiting the computational practicality of private information retrieval, in *Proceedings of the Springer FC' 2012*, pp. 158–172.
57. Devet, C. 2013. Evaluating private information retrieval on the cloud, *Technical report, CACR 2013-05, University of Waterloo*.
58. Mayberry, T., Blass, E.-O. and Chan, A. H. 2013. PIRMAP: Efficient private information retrieval for mapreduce, in *Proceedings of the Springer FC' 2013*, pp. 371–385.
59. Melchor, C. A., Crespin, B., Gaborit, P., Jolivet, V. and Rousseau, P. 2008. High-speed private information retrieval computation on GPU, in *Proceedings of the IEEE SECURWARE' 2008*, pp. 263–272.
60. Di-Crescenzo, G., Ishai, Y. and Ostrovsky, R. 1998. Universal service-providers for database private information retrieval, in *Proceedings of the ACM PODC' 1998*, pp. 91–100.
61. Beimel, A., Ishai, Y. and Malkin, T. 2004. Reducing the servers' computation in private information retrieval: PIR with preprocessing, *Journal of Cryptology*, 17(2), 125–151.
62. Mittal, P., Olumofin, F. G., Troncoso, C., Borisov, N. and Goldberg, I. 2001. PIR-TOR: Scalable anonymous communication using private information retrieval, in *Proceedings of the USENIX Security' 2011*, pp. 475–490.
63. Ishai, Y., Kushilevitz, E., Ostrovsky, R. and Sahai, A. 2006. Cryptography from anonymity, in *Proceedings of the IEEE FOCS' 2006*, pp. 239–248.

CHAPTER 13

Flow-Based Anomaly Detection in Big Data

Zahra Jadidi, Vallipuram Muthukkumarasamy,
Elankayer Sithirasenan, and Kalvinder Singh

CONTENTS

INTRODUCTION

Every day, a large amount of new data is produced by high-speed networks. This Big Data can be created from many sources, for example, sensors for climate information, social media sites and on-line purchases. Therefore, Big Data has a large volume of data and an extraordinary diversity of data, and an effective analytical method is very essential [1,2].

In respect to security, the traffic of high-speed networks needs to be analyzed, as the ever-increasing number of anomalies has a destructive effect on confidentially and availability of information. Intrusion detection systems (IDSs) need to be scaled into modern large networks and be able to process these Big Data sets. Scalability is a challenging problem for traditional packet-based IDSs because they inspect every individual packet [3,4].

Flow-based analysis is widely used for monitoring and traffic management of high-speed networks. NetFlow is proprietary to Cisco and it is used in routers to generate flow records. In the last decade, the research community has been considering flow-based anomaly detection for large data sets in high-speed networks. This method is based only on packet headers and it processes less traffic compared with packet-based systems. Therefore, this scalable method is more efficient in terms of required memory and processing time. In addition, due to the absence of packet payloads, flow-based anomaly detection decreases privacy concerns. An important challenging issue in packet-based systems is increasing encrypted protocols. The merit of flow-based methods is that they are not affected by encrypted protocols. However, the attacks related to packet payloads are not detectable by flow-based anomaly detectors. These systems can detect volume-based anomalies which cause changes in flow traffic volume, for example, denial of service (DoS) attacks, distributed DoS (DDoS) attacks, worms, scans and botnets. Therefore, network administrators will have hierarchical anomaly detection in which flow-based systems are used in earlier stages of high-speed networks while packet-based systems may be used in small networks. Recently, a variety of methods have been proposed to improve the accuracy of flow-based anomaly detection. These methods are considered in this chapter.

Flow-based methods significantly reduce the amount of data that needs to be examined. However, there is still a high volume of flow traffic in high-speed networks. The size of flow data sets generated from high-speed networks can be in terabytes. The analysis of this volume of data is time consuming. Sampling is a solution method to reduce the size of data [1]. Sampling methods are widely used in flow-based management tools. However, as flow-based anomaly detection is new, traditional sampling methods often have a negative impact on performance. Two important categories of sampling methods are packet sampling and flow sampling. Packet sampling is easier to implement and is used in NetFlow. Flow sampling preserves the characteristics of the traffic better than packet sampling but it needs more memory. In this regard, several methods have been proposed to reduce memory requirements of flow sampling, such as smart sampling and sample-and-hold sampling methods. However, these methods affect anomaly detection negatively. Therefore, a number of methods improve anomaly detection in sampled traffic such as selective sampling. Packet sampling and flow sampling methods and their impact on anomaly detection are considered in this chapter.

BIG DATA

In recent years, the explosion of Big Data sets has attracted the attention of researchers in data mining. A large number of these Big Data sets are generated over high-speed networks. Big Data are large, diverse, complex, and distributed data sets which are generated from different resources such as sensors, video, and email. Some of the major problems in Big Data are data collection, storage, data mining and anomaly detection [4]. The processing of large data sets in Big Data needs scalable analyzing methods. Anomaly detection in Big Data is particularly crucial because of the velocity and volume of the data sets. In addition, traditional anomaly detection methods have many difficulties for Big Data.

Anomaly detection in Big Data sets consists of finding patterns that have abnormal behavior. In this regard, various papers have been published. For example, Adaptive Stream Projected Outlier deTector (A-SPOT) [3] is an outlier detection technique for anomaly detection in large data sets. A-SPOT uses a novel adaptive subspace analyzing method to detect anomalies in network data sets.

Volume and velocity are two problems of Big Data. In this regard, a flow-based analyzer addresses these problems by reducing the volume of traffic in large data sets collected in high-speed networks. Artificial intelligence (AI) methods in flow-based analysis provide effective data mining and anomaly detection in Big Data sets. These methods will be discussed further in the following sections. In this chapter, flow-based analysis is considered as a suitable solution for Big Data. This method is helpful for the detection of some anomalies because flow traffic contains the main features of the original traffic [3,4].

FLOW TRAFFIC AND ITS APPLICATIONS

Computer networks should be able to provide quality Internet services. An IDS is an important mechanism to protect these networks from malicious activities. Nowadays, the networks are constantly growing in speed and hence, IDSs should be able to handle existing high volumes of data. In this way, flow-based solutions can help to solve the problem by the reduction of data and processing time, opening the way to high-speed detection in Big Data.

A flow is defined as a group of unidirectional IP packets, which have some common properties and pass a monitoring point in a specified time interval [5]. Flow-based tools such as NetFlow are useful for monitoring, troubleshooting and anomaly detection. NetFlow-based monitoring is capable of processing high volumes of data. There are different flow-based monitoring tools such as FlowMon probe and nProbe, which are suitable for Gigabit speed networks [6]. On the other hand, flow-based anomaly detection can be deployed for early detection of a number of particular attacks. This method is complementary to traditional packet-based methods.

There are two intrusion detection methods: anomaly detection and misuse detection. The anomaly-based method detects activities deviating from established patterns. This method has a high false alarm rate, but it is able to detect unknown attacks. On the other hand, the misuse-based IDS compares user activities with existing signatures [7]. This IDS can accurately detect known attacks, but it cannot detect unknown attacks.

Various methods have been proposed to examine both misuse and anomaly detection methods in large amounts of data. High-speed IDSs should analyze traffic in real time. In this chapter, flow-based analysis is considered to address anomaly detection in a high volume of traffic. This method uses only packet headers, and hence it reduces the amount of traffic to be analyzed. Flow-based analysis, which can be enabled on most routers, decreases the concern about privacy issues because of the lack of packet payloads.

The artificial neural network or ANN-based flow anomaly detection is a method considered in [7,8]. A light-weight Multilayer Perceptron (MLP) neural network is used to detect malicious flows. To improve the detection rate, the MLP model is optimized with meta-heuristic algorithms. Then, two flow-based data sets are used to evaluate the optimized flow-based anomaly detectors. The results show the effectiveness of flow-based anomaly detection in Big Data sets.

NETFLOW

NetFlow, which is a Cisco proprietary protocol, is an example of a flow generator which is enabled in Cisco routers to provide network flows [5]. Service providers use NetFlow for the prediction of network growth, resource management, intrusion detection, accounting and billing, traffic engineering and data mining.

NetFlow has three components: NetFlow cache, NetFlow exporter and NetFlow collector. Headers of packets which pass an observation point are extracted by the NetFlow Exporter. Afterwards, the exporter turns this data into flow records. Initially, flow records are in NetFlow cache. These flows are sent to NetFlow collector after they have expired. A collector receives this data for further analysis such as anomaly detection (see Figure 13.1).

There are rules for flow record expiry. Expired flow records are grouped into NetFlow datagrams to be exported through the device with enabled NetFlow. NetFlow uses User Datagram Protocol (UDP) to export data to a NetFlow collector. The collector then sends flow records to a flow analyzer. There are different flow-based applications which do more processing, such as intrusion detection or monitoring systems. There are five versions of NetFlow export data: Version 9, Version 8, Version 7, Version 5, and Version 1. Version 9 and Version 5 are the most important versions.

Versions 5 and 9 have some common fields in their flow records such as: source/destination IP address, source/destination Transmission Control Protocol (TCP)/UDP application port, next hop router IP address, input physical interface index, output physical interface index, packet count for each flow, byte count for each flow, start of flow timestamp, end of flow timestamp, IP protocol (for example, TCP = 6; UDP = 17), Type of Service byte, TCP Flags, source Autonomous System (AS) number, destination AS number, source subnet

NetFlow exporter   NetFlow collector   Flow analyzer

FIGURE 13.1   NetFlow generates flow records.

mask, and destination subnet mask. These fields are common between Versions 5 and 9 but Version 9 can also have other flow fields. NetFlow Version 5 has a fixed export format so it cannot be extended and cannot support new features. Up to 30 flow records can be included in a NetFlow Version 5 export datagram. NetFlow Version 9 is an extensible format that supports new features [9].

FLOW-BASED ANOMALY DETECTION

A Network IDS (NIDS) monitors data exchanged over a network. Traditional packet-based NIDSs analyze every packet but recent high-speed networks put a heavy computational load on traditional NIDSs. Examining all packets captured in the network is very time consuming, therefore, NIDSs should be able to process faster with lower false alarms. Thus, high-speed networks need alternative solutions to traditional methods [5,7,10,11].

All high-speed IDSs are classified into two main groups: packet-based methods and flow-based methods (see Figure 13.2). Several packet-based methods for high volume of data have been proposed such as hardware-based methods and distributed methods. These packet-based methods, which analyze both packet header and packet payload, are very time consuming. However, they can detect all attack types.

Recently, researchers have used flow traffic to detect anomalies. This method has several advantages over packet-based methods [12,13]:

- A flow-based anomaly detection method is based only on packet headers. Therefore, it processes a lower number of flows in comparison to the number of packets in a packet-based method. For instance, in the University of Twente network, the ratio between packets exported by NetFlow and packets on the network was 0.1.

- A flow-based method is more efficient computationally in terms of memory and time.

- Flow-based analysis also decreases privacy concerns in comparison with the packet-based method, due to the absence of payload.

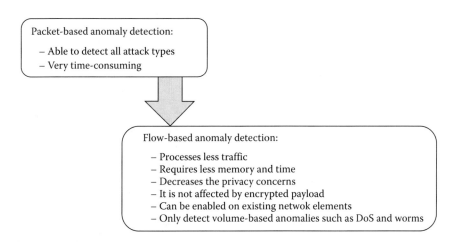

FIGURE 13.2 Anomaly detection methods.

- The spread of encrypted protocols is a challenging issue for packet-based systems, and it is addressed in flow-based methods.

- Moreover, a flow-based method is supported by routers and relies on existing network elements.

As a flow-based method cannot detect attacks related to payloads, it is not a replacement for packet-based IDSs [5]. A network administrator can use a flow-based method to have hierarchical anomaly detection and to reduce the computational load on high-speed networks.

ATTACKS

A flow-based NIDS can be implemented in high-level routers to complement packet-based intrusion detection [5]. In an ideal world, the attacks detected by a flow-based NIDS should also be detectable by a packet-based NIDS. However, in the real world this is not applicable to Big Data sets in high-speed networks, mainly because of limitations such as the high resource requirement of a packet-based NIDS. These different NIDSs can cover different categories of attacks in the real world [14]. The flow-based method is applicable only for volume-based anomalies such as DoS, scans, worms and botnets, which cause volume changes in the traffic. These anomalies change the distribution of a number of flow features such as the flow size, source/destination IP and source/destination port (see Table 13.1). Several studies consider flow-based intrusion detection [15,16]. A brief description about attacks detectable in flow-based methods is as follows [5]:

- DoS attacks: deny authorized users from using the resources.

- Probing attacks: scan networks and collect information about some specified valid IP addresses to find vulnerabilities to use for future attacks.

- Botnets: are a number of computers which are infected with malicious programs. These computers may operate against their owners' intentions.

- Worms: programs that replicate and can propagate.

TABLE 13.1 Flow Features Affected by Anomalies

Anomaly Label	Definition	Traffic Feature Distribution Affected
DoS	Denial of Service attack (distributed or single-source)	Destination IP, destination port
Flash Crowd	A large amount of unusual demand to a single destination	Slightly changes source IP/port, destination IP/port, flow size
Port Scan	Send probe packets to a large number of ports on a host to find the available services	Mainly source IP/port, and destination IP Slightly affects destination port and flow size
Worms	Infecting other systems to exploit a vulnerability	Mainly source IP and destination port Slightly affects destination IP, source port, and flow size

Volume-based anomalies such as DDoS, worms, and port scan activities have small-sized flows. In addition to malicious flows, some unusual activities in the network also cause changes in the features of flow traffic. For example, Flash Crowd is defined as a large demand for a specific service on a server (see Table 13.1) [17]. These activities have large sized flows and they affect the destination IP/port. The sampling methods, which will be discussed in the Section "Data sets," might be proposed based on these flow features.

EFFECT OF DDoS ATTACKS ON FLOW-BASED ANALYSIS

DDoS attacks affect both the flow exporter and the flow-monitoring system. In DDoS attacks, the flow exporter uses a number of rules to manage its internal memory. However, in extreme cases, for systems analyzing the flows, such as IDSs, there are various problems. The behavior of flow-monitoring applications under DDoS attack is investigated in [18] using a simple queuing model. The paper [18] assumed that the flow exporter can process all packets after an attack, and it is assumed that there are no problems for the flow collector. The focus of [18] is the effect on flow-monitoring applications since they are susceptible to anomalies causing lots of flows like DDoS attacks.

There are two types of DoS attacks: semantic and brute-force attacks. Some types of brute-force attacks, causing a great change in flow traffic, have an impact on the monitoring application. Since a DDoS attack uses several attackers, it generates a high volume of SYN packets and causes a great change in the flows. In this attack type, the attacker can exhaust the flow cache, which is the internal memory, and which is very fast. In DDoS attacks, each SYN packet generates a flow record so the flow cache will be full.

The paper [18] assumes that when adding a new flow record to the flow cache is required, an existing flow record has to have expired. It also considers the changes of flow traffic when there is a DDoS attack. A simple queuing model is proposed to describe the behavior of a flow-monitoring application under DDoS attack. Finally, this chapter examines the behavior of a flow-monitoring application with real traffic, collected at the University of Twente. The results show that the changes in the flow traffic affect flow monitoring. This affects both attack and normal flow traffic. DDoS attacks also affect some flow features. For instance, the DDoS flow record will be smaller and shorter, and the number of aggregated packets in a flow record will also be decreased in DDoS traffic. These changes in flow characteristics affect monitoring applications.

To give a better explanation, this chapter divides flow records into two groups: first, flow records to/from attacked host; second, flow records to/from others. Each SYN packet generates a flow record so the number of exported flow records related to the first group increases greatly. In a DDoS attack, there is also a growth in the rate of flow records exported by other hosts (second group). In total, DDoS attacks can generate a high volume of flow records and change some flow metrics. Beside the changes in the attack rate, this attack also affects the rate of normal flow data. This can affect flow-monitoring applications such as an IDS.

EXISTING FLOW-BASED IDSs

Some flow-based IDSs are described in this section.

HiFIND

There are two methods to evade an IDS: (i) using a DoS attack; and (ii) fooling the IDS to generate a lot of false positives. The higher the rate of false-positive alarms, the more the ignored real alerts. Current IDSs are vulnerable to DoS attacks. In this regard, the resiliency of IDS against attacks is very important. A High-speed Flow-level Intrusion Detection System (HiFIND) is proposed in [19]. HiFIND is an online DoS resilient system for high-speed networks.

Sketches are used in this system to record flow-level traffic. The recorded traffic is the basis for statistical intrusion detection. A sketch is a one-dimensional hash table used for storing information. It records traffic for specific keys. HiFIND uses two-dimensional (2D) sketches which hash a set of flow-derived fields for each dimension. 2D sketches are employed in HiFIND to distinguish between different types of attacks. This method is employed to detect SYN flooding and port scans. Compact sketches from multiple routers are aggregated to detect intrusion. In HiFIND, the traffic is recorded in each router using sketches. The sketches over multiple routers are aggregated into a new sketch. Then, time series are applied and forecast sketches are obtained. Forecast sketches give a forecast error which is the key metric for detection. HiFIND can be used as a black box and can connect to the high-speed routers of ISPs without any negative impact. In [19], two parts are included: the recording stage and the detection stage. First, attacks are detected using reversible sketches. 2D sketches are used in the second step to reduce the false positives for port scans introduced by a SYN flooding attack. Finally, the heuristics are utilized to reduce the false-positive rate of SYN flooding attacks. The chapter claims that HiFIND is resilient against negative effects of attack and uses a small amount of memory. For instance, in respect to attack resiliency, one possible attack is creating a collision in hash tables of sketches to introduce false-positive or false-negative errors. Reverse engineering of hash functions of sketches is required to create collisions. However, inferring the parameters from input and output of sketches is difficult because the interval parameters of hash functions, which are used by sketches, and the functionality sketches, which are archived, are independent. Consequently, attacks on HiFIND are very difficult.

Artificial Intelligence-Based Methods

Flow-based methods can learn the behavior of normal traffic to provide high performance and detect new attacks. Therefore, intelligent flow-based analysis is a valuable method for a high volume of traffic. Different intelligent, flow-based anomaly detection methods have been proposed, such as statistical methods, data-mining methods and Support Vector Machines (SVMs). Statistical techniques are used for flow-based anomaly detection in a controlled environment which represents consistent patterns of network activities [16]. This is used for the prediction of future activities and any deviation from the forecast is an anomaly. According to the results, the proposed method can be used in real-time anomaly detection. Five learning algorithms, such as SVMs and C4.5, are used in [20] to classify SSH-based and Skype-based encrypted traffic using flow-based features. According to the results, C4.5 has the best classification performance. The performance of different intelligent methods in flow-based anomaly detection is compared using centralized analysis.

Various artificial intelligence methods are deployed in intrusion detection, for example [21–23], ANNs, fuzzy logic and genetic algorithms (GA), and evolutionary fuzzy neural networks and evolutionary neural networks-based IDSs. However, these intelligent systems are not suitable for high-speed networks. Several researchers have considered the application of intelligent methods in Big Data sets [24].

Different AI methods have been used in flow-based intrusion detection such as: the hidden Markov model (HMM) [25] and data mining and visualization [26]. An HMM-based IDS has a low false-positive rate and a high detection rate, but it spends a long time modeling normal behavior. The privileged transition flows are used in an improved HMM-based IDS, which reduces computational costs and improves performance [25]. In the second example, a combination of data mining and an optimized visualization technique is used to increase the detection rate of botnets in flow-based traffic [26]. The next study considers the application of three algorithms—Bayesian networks, decision trees and MLP—in the classification of flow-based traffic [27].

ANNs provide important classifiers due to their impressive properties such as accuracy, adaptability, ability to generalize and learning capability. Supervised ANNs use labeled data sets. Training is necessary in ANN as it is responsible for adjusting weights and biases to minimize errors. A well-known training algorithm is back-propagation (BP). Sometimes, the convergence of BP is to the points which are the best solutions locally (local minima) not globally (global minimum). When local minima happens, ANN methods give suboptimal solutions [7].

Several metaheuristic algorithms have been proposed to solve the problem of local minima. In ANN, these algorithms can be employed in terms of the optimization of the structure such as neuron numbers. Furthermore, metaheuristic algorithms are useful for training ANNs to avoid local minima. Most metaheuristic algorithms such as GA, Firefly Algorithm, Ant Colony Search Algorithm, Particle Swarm Optimization (PSO), Gravitational Search Algorithms (GSA), and Cuckoo Algorithm are inspired by nature [28]. GSA [29], which is based on Newtonian gravity, is employed in [7] to optimize the interconnection weight of the MLP. Then, the optimized MLP is used to detect malicious flows. This study [7] compares the performance of the GSA with PSO, and three gradient descent algorithms. The results show that the GSA is more efficient for the flow-based IDS compared to PSO and gradient-based algorithms.

Modified GSA-based methods are also used to train ANN-based anomaly detectors in [8,30]. The results show improvement in flow-based anomaly detection compared to GSA. These intelligent anomaly detectors are evaluated using four metrics: true positive (t_p), true negative (t_n), false positive (f_p) and false negative (f_n). To evaluate the efficiency of the flow anomaly detector, it is necessary to define the four following metrics (Equations 13.1 through 13.4) [8].

$$\text{Accuracy} = \frac{t_p + t_n}{t_p + t_n + f_p + f_n} \tag{13.1}$$

$$Error\_Rate = \frac{f_n + f_p}{t_p + t_n + f_p + f_n} \qquad (13.2)$$

$$Miss\_Rate = \frac{f_n}{t_p + f_n} \qquad (13.3)$$

$$False\_Alarm\_Rate = \frac{f_p}{t_n + f_p} \qquad (13.4)$$

The first public labeled flow-based data set is generated in [31] for the evaluation of flow-based NIDSs. Winter [12] modified this data set and used it to train a One-Class SVM (OC-SVM) to detect malicious flows. This public data set includes flows defined according to NetFlow Version 5. This data set is also used in [7,8,30] for the evaluation of the proposed methods.

Hardware-Based Flow Anomaly Detection

An improved block-based neural network (BBNN), which is an intelligent learning algorithm, is integrated with a high-frequency field-programming gate array (FPGA) in [32]. This combination provides flexibility to learn and detects unknown attacks with a high detection rate and a low number of false alarms. A flow-based DARPA data set is also generated in [32]. This data set is used to evaluate the proposed hardware-based IDS. The results show that it has real-time intrusion detection.

DATA SETS

Studies about IDSs suffer from inaccurate evaluation due to the lack of a reliable public data set. The existing data sets are unable to give an adequate evaluation of an IDS. A suitable public data set should be realistic and capable of covering evolving intrusions. Using a common data set helps researchers to provide comprehensive comparison with other methods. Some public packet-based data sets are listed below (see Figure 13.3) [33]:

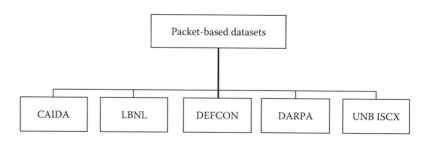

FIGURE 13.3   A number of existing packet-based data sets.

- CAIDA: these data sets are anonymized with respect to their payloads and sometimes protocol information and destination, etc. Most of CAIDA data sets include only specific attacks or events.

- The Internet Traffic Archive (Lawrence Berkeley National Laboratory): these data sets are also anonymized and important packet information is eliminated.

- DEFCON: this is not a very useful data set since it includes only intrusive traffic.

- DARPA: due to privacy concerns, many public data sets eliminate payload information and even some header information. DARPA 99 data set addresses this issue. However, this data set is very old.

- UNB ISCX: a new labeled data set called UNB ISCX Intrusion Detection Evaluation Data set is proposed in [33] to address the problems of the data sets above.

A real labeled network trace, which includes a comprehensive set of intrusions, is a suitable method for the evaluation of a proposed IDS. Concern for privacy is the main reason that researchers do not share their data sets. This limits the evaluation and comparison of studies about intrusion detection methods. Some data sets are anonymized and remove the whole payload. Most of the aforementioned data sets are unlabeled. The UNB ISCX data set, DARPA and DEFCON have several attack scenarios. All of the aforementioned data sets are captured in a realistic network configuration except for DEFCON. All of the mentioned data sets are packet-based. However, while flow-based intrusion detection is an important issue, there are only few public flow-based data sets. Therefore, for the evaluation of a flow-based IDS, we can either use the existing flow-based data set or extract flows from the aforementioned packet-based data sets. Some flow-based data sets are discussed below.

First Labeled Flow-Based Data Set

The first public labeled flow-based data set [31], which we call the Sperotto data set, was captured through monitoring a honeypot in the University of Twente network. Three services, SSH (OpenSSH) service, FTP and Apache Web server, were installed in this honeypot [31]. There are a large number of flows in this data set; therefore, the training phase will be time consuming for intelligent flow-based methods. To address this problem, Winter [12] modifies this data set and provides a smaller one. The modified data set only contains 22,924 malicious flows. Each flow record in the Winter data set has seven features (see Table 13.2). All flow records in the Sperotto data set are malicious but the benign flows are also necessary for the evaluation. Therefore, in the modified data set, Winter [12] provides a combination of malicious and benign flows. Table 13.2 presents the flow features of the Winter data sets.

DARPA Flow-Based Data Set

The Winter data set is suitable for the evaluation of anomaly detectors, but it has some weaknesses. In this data set, the number of malicious flows is highly overrepresented

TABLE 13.2   Feature Set of Winter Data Set

Feature Name	Description
Packets/flow	Number of packets carried by the flow
Octets/flow	Number of bytes carried by the flow
Duration	The duration between start and end time of the flow
Source port	Source port number of the flow
Destination port	Destination port number of the flow
TCP flags	TCP flags in the flow
IP protocol	IP protocol number of the flow

compared to benign flows. In the real networks, the number of malicious flows is very small compared to the overall flows. When the number of malicious flows increases, it may affect the results of anomaly detection. In addition, The Winter data set is not comprehensive because it includes only HTTP and SSH services. A comparison between the Winter data set and the DARPA data set is shown in Table 13.3 [32]. The flow-based DARPA data set is extracted from existing packet-based DARPA in [32] using Softflowd and Flowd software. Figure 13.4 shows different components of the paper [32].

Softflowd [34] and Flowd [35] are open-source softwares, which simulate NetFlow exporters and collectors, respectively [32]. Softflowd [34] can generate flow records by reading a packet-based captured file. Then, these flow records are sent to a NetFlow collector, Flowd [35]. Flowd has a tool called Flowd-reader. This tool reads the following NetFlow fields: source/destination IP, source/destination port, packets, octets, start and end time, flags and protocol. Softflowd can export as a NetFlow Version 1, Version 5 and Version 9 exporter. It is able to track and report on IPv6 traffic since NetFlow version 9 is IPv6 capable. Softflowd can also listen to the traffic. Softflowd is developed on Linux and OpenBSD [34]. Flowd is a secure NetFlow collector. It understands NetFlow protocols (Versions 1, 5,

TABLE 13.3   Distribution of Winter and DARPA Data Sets

		Training Data Set	Testing Data Set	Description
Winter Data set	Benign flows	962	942	• Few benign flows compared to malicious flows
	Malicious flows	15,236	7688	• Malicious flows are generated based on the concept of honeypot
	Total traffic	16,198	8630	• Limited attack types • Format: NetFlow
Flow-based DARPA Data set	Benign flows	59,980	45,053	• There are enough of both malicious and benign flows
	Malicious flows	5952	18,586	• Malicious flows are generated manually
	Total traffic	65,932	63,639	• Various attack types • Format: TCPdump

Source: Jadidi, Z., Muthukkumarasamy, V., and Sithirasenan, E., Metaheuristic Algorithms Based Flow Anomaly Detector, in *Communications (APCC), 2013 19th Asia-Pacific Conference on*, 2013, pp. 717–722.

Note: The DARPA data set contains various attack types. In the generated flow-based DARPA data set, the statistical features of flows can be different for different hosts [32]. However, this data set focuses only on the flows sent to host 172.16.112.50, which receives most attacks.

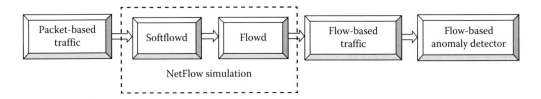

FIGURE 13.4   NetFlow simulation.

7 and 9), hence, it can support both IPv4 and IPv6 flows. NetFlow exporter can be either hardware-based like routers or software-based such as Softflowd. Flowd can work with both of these exporters [35].

SAMPLING

Network administrators need to monitor and analyze network traffic to manage it and to ensure that it operates reliably. There are a large number of flows on high-speed links, and hence, storing and processing all flows with limited resources is a challenging issue. In this regard, sampling methods provide a suitable solution to collect statistical information about flows. In sampling methods, the conclusion about the behavior of the whole traffic is drawn using partial observation of the traffic. The sampling helps routers to decrease the measurement overhead in their CPU, memory and bandwidth. Sampling techniques are deployed at different routers such as Cisco's NetFlow [36] and Juniper's Traffic Sampling [37] to cope with increasing link speed. Each flow has several features. The size of a flow is vital in sampling.

Anomalies may affect different flow features. For example, DoS attacks change the distribution of destination ports/IPs. Therefore, a suitable sampling method should take important features into consideration. In other words, a sampling method should not affect anomaly detection significantly [17]. To make the sampling method scalable and accurate, information loss should be minimized. Inaccurate sampling can lead network administrators to react inappropriately. Several studies consider sampling issues within high-speed networks. Based on the sampling point, there are two categories [38]:

- *The online method:* this is performed at the flow exporter and it samples at routers when they capture packets; the online method reduces memory requirements at routers. The data communication from the router to the collector is decreased in this method.

- *The offline method:* this method samples flows at flow collectors after receiving flows from flow exporters. The offline method reduces the data communication from the collector to the analyzing points and, hence, they reduce the processing and memory requirements.

In addition, based on types of sampling, there are two groups: packet-based sampling which samples network packets, and flow-based sampling in which traffic is aggregated into network flows first and sampling is then applied to the flows. Different types of sampling methods are described below (see Figure 13.5) [5,39].

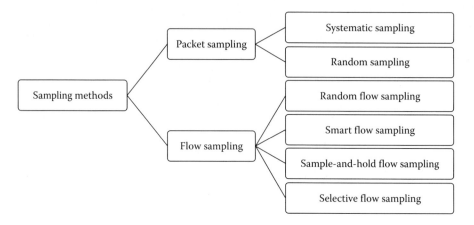

FIGURE 13.5   Categories of sampling methods.

Packet Sampling

Two important types of packet sampling methods are discussed as follows:

- *Systematic packet sampling*: with this method, a time interval or a sequence of packet arrivals is used to sample a packet.

- *Random packet sampling*: this method uses the probability distribution function as the basis of its sampling. NetFlow, which is used for Cisco routers, uses the random packet sampling method. There are two types of random sampling:

  - *n*-in-*N* sampling, in which n packets are sampled out of a sequence of *N* packets. This method is used in Cisco's NetFlow [5].

  - Probabilistic sampling, which assigns a probability to each packet.

Random packet sampling is described in Figure 13.6 [39]. The impact of random packet sampling on the blaster worm anomaly is investigated in [40]. The results show that the effect of sampling on entropy-based metrics is less than on volume-based metrics. Therefore, entropy-based metrics are more appropriate for anomaly detection purposes.

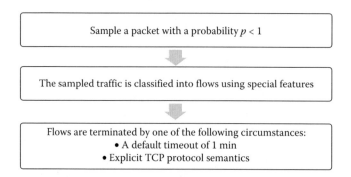

FIGURE 13.6   Random packet sampling.

Flow Sampling

A flow-based traffic has heavy-tailed distribution for packets and bytes [41]. In this distribution, the majority of flows have a small size, and a few of them have a large size (called elephant flows which carry a large number of packets). On the other hand, although there are a large number of small flows, called mice, they carry little Internet traffic [42]. Due to the unbalanced number of small and large flows, most sampling methods provide a biased output. Many sampling methods have bias toward elephant flows, as they are vital for efficient bandwidth management.

However, these sampling methods can corrupt anomaly detection because anomalies mostly have a small size. In this way, a sampling method which is able to sample small flows with a higher priority improves anomaly detection. Most studies about sampling methods focus on effective network traffic accounting, and not on anomaly detection. The reason is that sampling methods have been widely used for traffic engineering. However, sampling has been used recently in flow anomaly detection methods. Flow-based anomaly detection has attracted many researchers who proposed several methods to improve its accuracy. However, only a few papers have considered flow-based anomaly detection with sampled NetFlow traffic. Some important flow sampling methods are discussed as follows:

- *Random flow sampling*: random probability is used in random flow sampling to select flows. First, random flow sampling classifies packets into flows. Then, each flow is sampled with a probability ($p < 1$) [39].

- *Smart sampling*: a random flow sampling method seems to be an ideal option for traffic engineering and anomaly detection, but it has poor scalability and heavy resource requirements. This is why administrators avoid the widespread deployment of this method. In this regard, smart sampling, which requires fewer resources, is proposed [43]. Probabilistic sampling is one type of sampling in which each flow is sampled with a certain probability. Smart sampling is an important type of probabilistic flow sampling and is a size-dependent flow selection algorithm. Smart sampling is a type of flow-based sampling that focuses on the selection of large flows because omitting large flows can cause substantial errors in network administrators' estimations of original traffic behavior. If $S = \{x_i : i = 1,\ldots,n\}$ is a set of flow sizes, x is a flow size in bytes, and z is a threshold, the probability of each flow is $p(x)$. The probability is defined according to Equation 13.5.

$$p(x) = \begin{cases} x/z & x < z \\ 1 & x \geq z \end{cases} \tag{13.5}$$

According to Equation 13.5, flow sizes larger than z are sampled with a probability of 1. On the other hand, flow sizes smaller than the threshold are sampled with a probability proportional to their size.

Researchers have realized that the distribution of traffic features is changed in sampling procedures. This negatively affects the flow-based anomaly detection. Smart sampling concentrates on large flows which carry more information than small flows. Therefore, it is a suitable method for traffic monitoring. As most malicious flows have small sizes, smart sampling is not applicable for anomaly detection [17,39].

- *Sample-and-hold*: with this method, a flow table lookup is performed for each incoming packet to check whether a flow entry exists for it [44]. The procedure of this method is shown in Figure 13.7. In spite of random packet sampling, the sample-and-hold method updates a flow entry using all the subsequent packets when it is created. Therefore, flow table lookups for all of the incoming packets are needed. This method decreases the memory size for the flow table because it is biased toward large flows [39].

- *Selective flow sampling*: it is shown that small flows are often the source of many network anomalies such as DDoS, port scan, and worm propagation [17]. Flow sampling improves estimation accuracy of flow statistics and hence it is more suitable for anomaly detection purposes. To address the poor anomaly detection of smart sampling, selective sampling, which targets small flows, is proposed [45]. The selective sampling method has a probability, $p(x)$, for each individual flow, as shown in Equation 13.6:

$$p(x) = \begin{cases} c & x \leq z \\ z/n \cdot x & x > z \end{cases} \tag{13.6}$$

where x is the flow size in packets, $0 < c \leq 1$, $n \geq 1$ and z is a threshold (measured in packets). According to Equation 13.6, flow sizes smaller than z are sampled with a constant

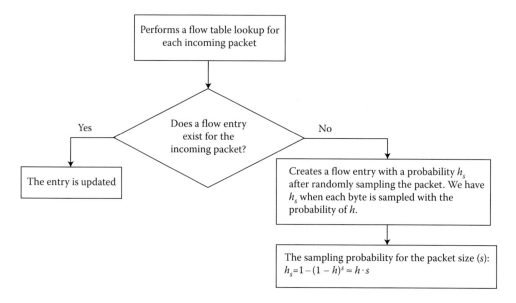

FIGURE 13.7 Sample-and-hold sampling method.

probability, c. On the other hand, flow sizes larger than z are sampled with a probability inversely proportional to their size. Using an appropriate value for the parameter c helps to sample a significant proportion of small flows without decreasing anomaly detection effectiveness. In addition, an increase in the value of parameter n further decreases the selection of large flows.

Selective sampling and its impact on a sequential non-parametric change-point anomaly detection method are studied in [45]. According to the results, even with a small sampling rate the performance of the anomaly detection method is better than random flow sampling and smart sampling. In addition, for DDoS attacks, worms, botnets and port scans, selective sampling is valuable and it can preserve the changes in the entropy of small flows [17].

Sampling Rate

Different methods have been proposed to determine sampling rate, for example [5,46]:

1. *Static sampling*: it takes the worst traffic conditions into consideration to set the sampling rate.

2. *Adaptive sampling*: it is proposed to overcome the problem of static methods. This method is a popular method in which the packet sampling rate is periodically adjusted to network conditions. An Adaptive NetFlow (ANF) performs according to the following order [47]: (i) sampling packets; (ii) collecting flow aggregate in a table; (iii) reducing the packet sampling rate for the future when the memory becomes full; and (iv) updating all flow entries at the same time (renormalization procedure). This method is beneficial because it chooses a new sampling rate based on traffic conditions. Therefore, the fraction of discarded flows corresponds to the traffic distribution. According to the second step, there is a table of active flows in the adaptive NetFlow, which decreases the sampling rate when this table is full and then updates the table entries.

In NetFlow, the operator needs to specify a fixed (static) sampling rate which is selected based on the worst situation. Therefore, adaptive sampling is a solution for this tool. However, Cisco's NetFlow still uses static sampling because of two problems: (i) adaptive sampling uses complex algorithms and data structures which are difficult to implement in hardware; (ii) in addition, it uses a large amount of CPU.

FLOW-BASED ANOMALY DETECTION IN SAMPLED TRAFFIC

Researchers have proposed various sampling methods most of which concentrate on preserving the volume characteristics of the monitored traffic such as the number of transferred bytes, packets and flows. The impact of sampling on monitoring is a mature area of study, however, the effect of sampling methods on anomaly detection has only been considered in recent years. Therefore, the impact of sampling methods on anomaly detection is an open issue [39,41].

There are few papers which investigate flow anomaly detection with sampled data. In fact, sampling severely harms the effectiveness of anomaly detection and data analysis algorithms. Pattern recognition and statistical traffic analysis are the basis of the analysis algorithms. Therefore, the distortion of traffic features can enhance the error rate by changing the traffic characteristics, which were the assumption of underlying methods. Traffic statistics such as the mean rate and the flow size distribution are affected by sampling methods. Traditional sampling methods are biased toward large flows. However, these methods can corrupt anomaly detection because anomalies often have flows with small sizes [17]. Flow sampling is more suitable for anomaly detection purposes than packet sampling. However, it still has a negative impact on the performance of anomaly detection. Selective sampling is proposed [45] to address this problem, but it only focuses on small flows.

The effect of four sampling methods on the performance of a wavelet-based volume anomaly detection method and two portscan detection algorithms is investigated in [39]. The results show the negative impact of sampling on anomaly detection.

Table 13.4 shows a comparison of four sampling methods [39,43,44]. It is shown in [48] that the random packet sampling method distorts traffic features, which are important for various port scan detection methods.

The sampling methods in Table 13.4 use different parameters for sampling. The authors in [39] use resource consumption, such as CPU and memory usage, as metrics to provide comparisons. The paper sets the parameters of these four sampling methods to sample the same number of sampled flows because the anomaly detection results related to different sampling methods are comparable if the total numbers of sampled flows are the same.

IDEAL SAMPLING TECHNIQUE

The characteristics of an ideal sampling method for anomaly detection are described as follows [41]:

1. Using this method, the samples of the input flows should be at the maximum rate allowed by the available memory budget.

2. The selection of the number of samples and their distribution in an ideal model should cause minimum loss of information. Therefore, the sampled traffic should have similar information to the original traffic (as much as possible).

3. Each flow has five basic features: source/destination IP address, source/destination port and protocol. Also, there is additional information such as timestamp, number of bytes, etc. These features are the input for the detection procedure. The statistics of the features are computed using anomaly detection methods. Therefore, these statistics have to be preserved in sampling methods as much as possible.

The authors in [39] compare different sampling methods. The comparison shows that the majority of sampling methods focuses on traffic monitoring and does not pay sufficient attention to preservation of the traffic features for anomaly detection. In their paper [39], the authors also consider the impact of sampling methods on the performance of anomaly

TABLE 13.4   Comparison of Different Sampling Methods

	Effect on Anomaly Detection	**Advantages/Disadvantages**
Random packet sampling	Negative	*Advantages*: Easiest method to implement. Low CPU power and memory requirements. *Disadvantages*: According to [39], the flow shortening effect of this method causes a high number of false positives in port scan detection. This method is inaccurate for inference of flow statistics such as the original flow size distribution.
Random flow sampling	Negative	*Advantages*: The flow sampling method could improve accuracy compared to packet sampling. Among flow sampling methods, random flow sampling has the least distortion of the important traffic features for volume-based anomaly detection. The aim of proposing this method was improvement in the estimation accuracy of flow statistics. This method seems to be an ideal option for both traffic engineering and anomaly detection. *Disadvantages*: The main problems of this method are poor scalability and heavy resource requirement. These reasons are why administrators avoid the widespread deployment of this method.
Smart sampling	Negative	*Advantages*: This method requires less resources than random flow sampling. *Disadvantages*: In terms of anomaly detection, this method performs poorly. This method cannot capture small-sized flows, which are the source of a large number of attacks.
Sample and hold	Negative	*Advantages*: Similar to smart sampling, this method requires less resources than random flow sampling. *Disadvantages*: In terms of anomaly detection, this method, similar to smart sampling, performs poorly.

Note: A packet sampling method is proposed in [49]. The proposed method tries to decrease the impact of sampling on anomaly detection. Therefore, it samples malicious packets with higher probability. Packet-based sampling causes a bias in flow statistics.

detection algorithms. The results show that packet sampling introduces bias and decreases detection rates. Flow sampling is suitable for anomaly detection because it improves the estimation accuracy of flow statistics (see Table 13.5) [41].

To investigate the existing sampling methods and propose a more suitable method, it is necessary to gain knowledge about traffic distribution. There are various distribution types, which may show the characteristics of flow traffic. According to Kahe and Jahangir [50], the flow inter-arrival time generally has Weibull distribution. When the network becomes larger, the distribution will have Poisson distribution. Finally, short-lived flows on high-speed links have Gaussian distribution.

A number of anomalies can change the distribution. Therefore, suitable sampling for anomaly detection should preserve the distribution as much as possible. An entropy value

TABLE 13.5   Impact of Different Sampling Methods on Anomaly Detection

Sampling Method	Preservation of Traffic Volume	Preservation of Traffic Distribution	Anomaly Detection
Random flow sampling	Suitable	Particularly suitable	Particularly suitable
Sample and Hold sampling	Suitable	Not suitable	Not suitable
Smart sampling	Suitable	Not suitable	Not suitable
Selective flow sampling	Not suitable	Not suitable	Suitable

Note: Sampling methods distort traffic characteristics and the distribution of a number of important flow features is changed. This negatively affects different anomaly detection methods. Table 13.5 compares the performance of four sampling methods. Sampling methods which take different flow features into consideration may have less distortion of flow features.

can examine the distribution of flow features to identify any changes in the distribution. The entropy value of $H(x)$ is as Equation 13.7, when the data set is $X = \{x_1, x_2, \ldots, x_N\}$ [17].

$$H(x) = -\sum_{i=1}^{N} p_i \log_2 (p_i) \tag{13.7}$$

Data set X has N numbers of elements; p_i is the probability. In fact, the randomness of a data set is calculated in entropy value. When an entropy value is high, it shows more dispersed probability distribution. On the other hand, the concentration of a distribution is shown by a low entropy value. The normalization of Equation 13.7 is shown in Equation 13.8.

$$H(x) = -\frac{\sum_{i=1}^{N} p_i \log_2 (p_i)}{\log_2 N} \tag{13.8}$$

The entropy value is a valuable method to investigate the changes in the distribution of flow features. Distribution of each feature has a specific meaning, which can be used by different methods to detect anomalies.

CONCLUSION

Intrusion detection is a significant issue in computer networks. Nowadays, the networks deal with a high volume of traffic and data, and analyzing all packets decreases the quality of the service. Previous methods were often packet-based methods in which both packet header and packet payload are analyzed. Packet-based IDSs face different limitations. For example, they have privacy concerns because of analyzing payloads which contain private data. The flow-based method addresses these problems. It is a promising method because: (1) flow-based IDS analyzes considerably lower traffic; (2) unlike packet-based methods, flow-based IDSs are not affected by encrypted protocols; (3) flow-based IDSs decrease the privacy concern because they only analyze packet headers; (4) flows are monitored by specific existing modules in routers. Therefore, the flow-based method is considered in this chapter as a suitable method for large data sets.

One limitation in the evaluation of the flow-based anomaly detection method is the lack of public data sets. This chapter introduced a number of packet-based data sets, which can be used to generate flow-based data sets.

Another issue in large packet-based data sets is the limitation of processing resources. Therefore, analyzing the whole data set is very difficult and reducing the number of packets is required. While flow-based methods can reduce the data, analyzing these large numbers of flows is still very time consuming and needs large memory. In this regard, sampling is an important solution. As monitoring is an important task in networks, traditional sampling methods usually aim to provide suitable information for monitoring, while they affect anomaly detection negatively. Therefore, investigating the impact of sampling on anomaly detection performance is an open issue, and it is investigated in this chapter. In this regard, a number of sampling methods are introduced in this chapter in which some methods improve the performance of anomaly detection with sampling.

REFERENCES

1. X. Zhou, M. Petrovic, T. Eskridge, and M. Carvalho, *Exploring Netfow Data Using Hadoop*, ASE BIGDATA/SOCIALCOM/CYBERSECURITY Conference, Stanford University, May 27–31, 2014.
2. Y. Lee and Y. Lee, Toward scalable internet traffic measurement and analysis with hadoop, *ACM SIGCOMM Computer Communication Review*, vol. 43, pp. 5–13, 2013.
3. J. Zhang, H. Li, Q. Gao, H. Wang, and Y. Luo, Detecting anomalies from big network traffic data using an adaptive detection approach, *Information Sciences*, vol. 318, pp. 91–110, 2015.
4. W. Wang, D. Lu, X. Zhou, B. Zhang, and J. Mu, Statistical wavelet-based anomaly detection in big data with compressive sensing, *EURASIP Journal on Wireless Communications and Networking*, vol. 2013, pp. 1–6, 2013.
5. A. Sperotto, G. Schaffrath, R. Sadre, C. Morariu, A. Pras, and B. Stiller, An overview of IP flow-based intrusion detection, *Communications Surveys & Tutorials, IEEE*, vol. 12, pp. 343–356, 2010.
6. M. Forconesi, G. Sutter, S. Lopez-Buedo, and J. Aracil, Accurate and flexible flow-based monitoring for high-speed networks, in *Field Programmable Logic and Applications (FPL), 2013 23rd International Conference on*, IEEE, Portugal, September 2013, pp. 1–4.
7. Z. Jadidi, V. Muthukkumarasamy, E. Sithirasenan, and M. Sheikhan, Flow-based anomaly detection using neural network optimized with GSA algorithm, in *Distributed Computing Systems Workshops (ICDCSW), 2013 IEEE 33rd International Conference on*, IEEE, USA, July 2013, pp. 76–81.
8. Z. Jadidi, V. Muthukkumarasamy, and E. Sithirasenan, Metaheuristic algorithms based flow anomaly detector, in *Communications (APCC), 2013 19th Asia-Pacific Conference on*, Indonesia, August 2013, pp. 717–722.
9. NetFlow Configuration Guide, Cisco IOS Release 12.4, http://www.cisco.com/en/US/docs/ios-xml/ios/netflow/configuration/12-4t/nf-12-4t-book.html
10. P. Barford and D. Plonka, Characteristics of network traffic flow anomalies, in *Proceedings of the 1st ACM SIGCOMM Workshop on Internet Measurement*, ACM, USA, November 2001, pp. 69–73.
11. B. Li, J. Springer, G. Bebis, and M. H. Gunes, A survey of network flow applications, *Journal of Network and Computer Applications*, vol. 36, no. 2, pp. 567–581, 2013.
12. P. Winter, Inductive Intrusion Detection in Flow-Based Network Data using One-Class Support Vector Machines, MSc Thesis, 2010.
13. A. Sperotto and A. Pras, Flow-based intrusion detection, in *Integrated Network Management (IM), 2011 IFIP/IEEE International Symposium on*, IEEE, Ireland, May 2011, pp. 958–963.

14. G. Schaffrath and B. Stiller, Conceptual integration of flow-based and packet-based network intrusion detection, in *Resilient Networks and Services*, Springer, Berlin, Heidelberg, 2008, pp. 190–194.

15. N. Muraleedharan, A. Parmar, and M. Kumar, A flow based anomaly detection system using chi-square technique, in *Advance Computing Conference (IACC), 2010 IEEE 2nd International*, IEEE, India, February 2010, pp. 285–289.

16. M. J. Chapple, T. E. Wright, and R. M. Winding, Flow anomaly detection in firewalled networks, in *Securecomm and Workshops*, IEEE, USA, 2006, pp. 1–6.

17. G. Androulidakis, V. Chatzigiannakis, and S. Papavassiliou, Network anomaly detection and classification via opportunistic sampling, *Network, IEEE*, vol. 23, pp. 6–12, 2009.

18. R. Sadre, A. Sperotto, and A. Pras, The effects of DDoS attacks on flow monitoring applications, in *Network Operations and Management Symposium (NOMS), 2012 IEEE*, IEEE, USA, April 2012, pp. 269–277.

19. Z. Li, Y. Gao, and Y. Chen, HiFIND: A high-speed flow-level intrusion detection approach with DoS resiliency, *Computer Networks*, vol. 54, pp. 1282–1299, 2010.

20. R. Alshammari and A. N. Zincir-Heywood, Machine learning based encrypted traffic classification: Identifying SSH and Skype, in *Computational Intelligence for Security and Defense Applications, 2009. CISDA 2009. IEEE Symposium on*, IEEE, Canada, July 2009, pp. 1–8.

21. S. X. Wu and W. Banzhaf, The use of computational intelligence in intrusion detection systems: A review, *Applied Soft Computing*, vol. 10, pp. 1–35, 2010.

22. V. Engen, Machine learning for network based intrusion detection: An investigation into discrepancies in findings with the KDD cup'99 dataset and multi-objective evolution of neural network classifier ensembles from imbalanced data, PhD dissertation, Bournemouth University, 2010.

23. V. Chandola, A. Banerjee, and V. Kumar, Anomaly detection: A survey, *ACM Computing Surveys (CSUR)*, vol. 41, p. 15, 2009.

24. Z. Jadidi, V. Muthukkumarasamy, and E. Sithirasenan, Based intrusion detection techniques, in *The State of the Art in Intrusion Prevention and Detection*, CRC Press, p. 285, 2014.

25. S.-B. Cho and H.-J. Park, Efficient anomaly detection by modeling privilege flows using hidden Markov model, *Computers & Security*, vol. 22, pp. 45–55, 2003.

26. A. Shahrestani, M. Feily, R. Ahmad, and S. Ramadass, Architecture for applying data mining and visualization on network flow for botnet traffic detection, in *Computer Technology and Development, 2009. ICCTD'09. International Conference on*, IEEE, USA, 2009, pp. 33–37.

27. M. Soysal and E. G. Schmidt, Machine learning algorithms for accurate flow-based network traffic classification: Evaluation and comparison, *Performance Evaluation*, vol. 67, pp. 451–467, 2010.

28. X.-S. Yang, *Engineering Optimization: An Introduction with Metaheuristic Applications*. John Wiley & Sons, 2010.

29. E. Rashedi, H. Nezamabadi-pour, S. Saryazdi, GSA: A gravitational search algorithm, *Information Sciences*, vol. 179, pp. 2232–2248, 2009.

30. M. Sheikhan and Z. Jadidi, Flow-based anomaly detection in high-speed links using modified GSA-optimized neural network, *Neural Computing and Applications*, vol. 24, pp. 599–611, 2014.

31. A. Sperotto, R. Sadre, F. van Vliet, and A. Pras, A labeled dataset for flow-based intrusion detection, in *IP Operations and Management*. Springer, Heidelberg, Berlin, 2009, pp. 39–50.

32. Q. A. Tran, F. Jiang, and J. Hu, A real-time NetFlow-based intrusion detection system with improved BBNN and high-frequency field programmable gate arrays, in *Trust, Security and Privacy in Computing and Communications (TrustCom), 2012 IEEE 11th International Conference on*, 2012, pp. 201–208.

33. A. Shiravi, H. Shiravi, M. Tavallaee, and A. A. Ghorbani, Toward developing a systematic approach to generate benchmark datasets for intrusion detection, *Computers & Security*, vol. 31, pp. 357–374, 2012.

34. http://www.mindrot.org/projects/softflowd/.
35. http://www.mindrot.org/projects/flowd/.
36. Cisco IOS Software NetFlow. http://www.cisco.com/warp/public/732/Tech/nmp/netow/.
37. Juniper Networks: JUNOS 7.2 Software Documentation. http://www.juniper.net/techpubs/software/junos/junos72/index.html.
38. S. Fernandes, C. Kamienski, J. Kelner, D. Mariz, and D. Sadok, A stratified traffic sampling methodology for seeing the big picture, *Computer Networks*, vol. 52, pp. 2677–2689, 2008.
39. J. Mai, C.-N. Chuah, A. Sridharan, T. Ye, and H. Zang, Is sampled data sufficient for anomaly detection?, in *Proceedings of the 6th ACM SIGCOMM Conference on Internet Measurement*, 2006, pp. 165–176.
40. D. Brauckhoff, B. Tellenbach, A. Wagner, M. May, and A. Lakhina, Impact of packet sampling on anomaly detection metrics, in *Proceedings of the 6th ACM SIGCOMM Conference on Internet Measurement*, 2006, pp. 159–164.
41. K. Bartos and M. Rehak, Towards efficient flow sampling technique for anomaly detection, in *Traffic Monitoring and Analysis*. Springer, Heidelberg, Berlin, 2012, pp. 93–106.
42. L. Guo and I. Matta, The war between mice and elephants, in *Network Protocols, 2001. Ninth International Conference on*, IEEE, USA, 2001, pp. 180–188.
43. N. Duffield, C. Lund, and M. Thorup, Properties and prediction of flow statistics from sampled packet streams, in *Proceedings of the 2nd ACM SIGCOMM Workshop on Internet Measurement*, ACM, France, November 2002, pp. 159–171.
44. C. Estan and G. Varghese, New directions in traffic measurement and accounting, *ACM*, vol. 32, no. 4, pp. 323–336, 2002.
45. G. Androulidakis and S. Papavassiliou, Improving network anomaly detection via selective flow-based sampling, *Communications, IET*, vol. 2, pp. 399–409, 2008.
46. J. Sanjuaas-Cuxart, P. Barlet-Ros, N. Duffield, and R. Kompella, Cuckoo sampling: Robust collection of flow aggregates under a fixed memory budget, in *INFOCOM, 2012 Proceedings IEEE*, IEEE, USA, March 2012, pp. 2751–2755.
47. C. Estan, K. Keys, D. Moore, and G. Varghese, Building a better NetFlow, *ACM SIGCOMM Computer Communication Review*, vol. 34, no. 4, pp. 245–256, 2004.
48. J. Mai, A. Sridharan, C.-N. Chuah, H. Zang, and T. Ye, Impact of packet sampling on portscan detection, *Selected Areas in Communications, IEEE Journal on*, vol. 24, pp. 2285–2298, 2006.
49. S. Ali, I. U. Haq, S. Rizvi, N. Rasheed, U. Sarfraz, S. A. Khayam, and F. Mirza, On mitigating sampling-induced accuracy loss in traffic anomaly detection systems, *ACM SIGCOMM Computer Communication Review*, vol. 40, pp. 4–16, 2010.
50. G. Kahe and A. H. Jahangir, On the Gaussian characteristics of aggregated short-lived flows on high-bandwidth links, in *Advanced Information Networking and Applications Workshops (WAINA), 2013 27th International Conference on*, IEEE, Spain, 2013, pp. 860–865.

IV

Platforms and Systems for Big Data Applications

Mining Social Media with SDN-Enabled Big Data Platform to Transform TV Watching Experience

Han Hu, Yonggang Wen, Tat-Seng Chua, and Xuelong Li

CONTENTS

INTRODUCTION

Microblog services have emerged as an essential platform for people managing interpersonal relationships with friends, posting updates about daily activities, publishing and exploring messages of their personal interest. Twitter [1], one of the largest worldwide microblog service platforms, has 1 billion registered users, and over 200 million active users send 400 million microblogs per day [2]. Due to the open data policy and abundant application programming interfaces (APIs), researchers and companies can crawl data from these platforms and conduct analysis for their own purpose. Actually, microblog services have become a manifold Big Data [3] source for analyzing people's relationships, daily thoughts, comments, and interactions on particular concerns, like TV programs. As reported by Nielsen [4], a third of active Twitter users tweeted about TV-related contents during June 2012, which refers to an increase of 27% from the beginning of that year. Mining social media contents associated with TV programs, resulting in a novel paradigm of social TV analytics [5], can extract many insights to fulfill multiple purposes, such as offering targeted advertisements, interactive program composing, user marketing, and so on. Inspired by the commercial success of Bluefine and Trendrr [6], it has been widely known that social TV analytics can benefit the whole TV ecosystem, from TV content producers, TV channel operators, advertisement agencies, to audiences. Therefore, building a Big Data platform for social TV analytics attracts more and more attention from both academia and industry.

However, owing to the uniqueness of social media, designing a scalable Big Data platform for social TV analytics faces a series of technical challenges, including the following:

- *Microblog data collection*: There are millions of microblogs being posted every day, the length of which is limited (commonly less than 140 words). Besides, slang and abbreviations are often used in the microblogs. It is difficult to elicit adequate microblogs about TV programs in real time under access constraints set by most OSNs.

- *Massive data storage and processing*: The data format of microblog messages includes number, text, image, social relationship, and so on. Furthermore, microblog stream is generated continuously. The Big Data platform needs to organize these diversity data in an efficient way for fast retrieval and analyzing.

- *Analytics metrics and approaches*: Few works have been devoted to study how to benefit the TV stakeholder by analyzing social media. We should determine various analysis metrics by jointly considering the analysis complexity and potential users, and implement corresponding algorithms to achieve the analysis goal.

These technological challenges demand an overhauling re-examination of current data collection and management systems, ranging from their architectural principles to implementation details.

As collecting a large scale of high-quality social media data plays the paramount role in social network-related researches and applications, there are many data collection methods to tackle the first challenge, which can be categorized into stream-based, user-based, and search-based. The stream-based methods rely on the platform to push posts according to a given set of keywords. The user-based strategies track the information related to specific users. The search-based methods query the given keywords to acquire posts. However, all these methods depend on APIs provided by social media platforms. To effectively manage and process a huge amount of microblogs, several revolutionary technologies have been considered as the fundamental building blocks, including cloud computing, Hadoop [7], and SDN. As a novel computing and service paradigm, cloud computing abstracts physical resources into a unified resource pool, and dispatches them via virtual machines in an on-demand pattern. With the fast growth of data volume, Hadoop, an open-source implementation of Google MapReduce [8], has been widely deployed as the prominent platform in the area of data-intensive computing. It is noted that Hadoop only provides a concise framework, involving two major types of tasks, Map and Reduce, to implement various applications. Therefore, there are great opportunities for performance optimization. For example, the shuffle phase is a major component of task completion time [9,10]. Recently, the emergence of SDN provides a chance for more dynamic and flexible network operation. The core idea is to decouple the data plane and the control plane. Compared with the traditional network model, only the data plane resides on the switch, and the control logic is separately placed on logically centralized controllers. Through status query and flow table modification from the controllers, the application can dynamically sense and operate the underlying network to gain better performance.

Inspired by these research efforts, we focus on building a unified Big Data platform for social TV analytics. In particular, we design and implement a cloud-centric SDN-enabled platform, which integrates the virtualization technology and the OpenFlow [11] tool together. Leveraging the platform, we customize our social TV analytics solution, involving three key components, a data crawler system, an SDN-enabled Big Data-processing system, and a microblog analytics system. The data crawler system consists of two modules, including program descriptor and distributed crawler. The program descriptor generates a set of keywords and social users to represent a specific TV program. The distributed crawler is deployed in a collection of nodes distributed in different IP segmentations. These nodes collaborate to crawl data from online social networks, while preventing being blocked by requested sites. The SDN-enabled Big Data process system is built on Hadoop, and exploits the network control with Openflow to accelerate the processing rate. The microblog analytics system mines social response associated with TV programs. Our analysis metrics can be categorized into statistical analysis and semantic analysis, which are able to benefit the whole TV value chain, from TV audience, TV channel operator, to TV content producer. Our prototype system has been implemented on top of a private cloud at NTU to demonstrate the concept and evaluate its performance. Some preliminary results are presented to illustrate the benefits of our data-crawling strategy, the SDN-enabled Big Data-processing platform, and deep analytics from microblog messages.

The rest of this article is organized as follows. Section "Related Work" outlines related work. Section "A Generic Big Data Platform for Social TV Analytics" introduces the Big Data value chain and presents a generic Big Data system architecture for social TV analytics. Section "Distributed Data Crawler," "SDN-Enabled Data-Processing Platform," and "TV Program-Related Microblog Analytics" describe the actual implementation of a proof of the concept demo, which highlights data crawler, SDN-enabled Big Data processing and microblog analytics. Section "Evaluation" discusses performance evaluation for data gathering and Big Data processing. In addition, some microblog analysis results on a trial TV program are also provided. Section "Conclusion" summarizes this article.

RELATED WORK

Social TV analytics is an interdisciplinary field at the intersection of social media collection, Big Data computing, and social media analysis. In the following, we will conduct literature investigation on these three research fields.

Social Media Collection

Since social media data offers a broad range of potential applications, including brand tracking, social marketing, and consumer relationship management, numerous organizations have started to collect social media data through APIs provided by social media platforms. Unlike traditional web search, the social media collection is carried out through multiple calls to APIs, and therefore data-crawling strategies highly rely on API types and access constraints. Currently, there are three main data collection strategies, including stream-based, user-based, and search-based. The stream-based strategies use the Stream API, from which the platform pushes the real-time microblogs according to the given keyword set. The user-based data collection strategies track the microblogs from the selected user set. The search-based strategies first set a number of keywords, and then search these words through the Search API. All these methods start from a predefined keyword/user set. Hence, the effectiveness of data collection methods depends on the completeness and representativeness of keyword/user set. The similar issue is addressed by query suggestion and query expansion [12] in the traditional information retrieval domain, which can dynamically extend the search results to enhance precision and recall. In this work, we combine the search-based and user-based methods together to crawl microblogs. Moreover, similar to query expansion in the information retrieval domain [12], we exploit keyword/user expansion to automatically generate representative keywords/users.

Big Data Computing

Currently, the research community and industry have proposed various solutions for Big Data systems in an ad-hoc manner. Cloud computing [13,14] can be deployed as the infrastructure layer for Big Data systems to meet certain infrastructure requirements, such as cost-effectiveness and elasticity. Distributed file systems and NoSQL databases are suitable for persistent storage and management of massive scheme free data sets. Although NoSQL databases are attractive for many reasons, unlike relational database systems, they do not support declarative expression of the joint operation and offer limited support of querying and analysis operations. The programming model is critical to implementing application logics and facilitating data analysis applications. Recently, MapReduce [8] has become the dominant batch-processing model. The core idea of MapReduce is that data are first divided into small chunks. Next, these chunks are processed in parallel and in a distributed manner to generate intermediate results. The final result is derived by aggregating all the intermediate results. The start point for the streaming processing paradigm is the assumption that the potential value of data depends on data freshness. Hadoop, the de-factor implementation of MapReduce, integrates data storage, data processing, system management, and other modules to form a powerful system-level solution, which is becoming the mainstay in handling Big Data challenges. It is noted that Hadoop only provides a concise framework, involving two major types of tasks, Map and Reduce, to implement various applications. Therefore, there are great opportunities for performance optimization. For example, the shuffle phase is a major component of task completion time [9,10]. Fortunately, the emergence of SDN provides a chance for a more dynamic and flexible network operation. The core idea is to decouple the data plane and the control plane. Compared with the traditional network model, only the data plane resides on the switches, and the control logic is separately placed on logically centralized controllers. Through status query and flow table modification from the controllers, the application can dynamically sense and operate the underlying network to gain better performance. Wang et al. [10] exploited the centralized control feature of both SDN and Hadoop, and combined the SDN controller and Hadoop scheduler to achieve intelligent data flow routing.

Social Media Analysis

With the wide popularity of online social networks, research on analyzing social media to assist decision making in other domains has gained much interest. Topic detection of live microblog streams has been applied to earthquake detection [15], political election outcomes prediction [16], controversial topics discovery [17], and so on. By analyzing health-related messages in Twitter or Facebook, the forecasting models have been built to provide early warning of several epidemics, including H1N1 [18] and influenza [19]. Since there are large amounts of shared images and videos reflecting social habits and preferences, mining such visual media, along with the associated text and metadata, can reveal fashion trends, and even recommend clothing styles [20]. Our previous works [21,22] on social TV aims to integrate social functions into the traditional video-watching experience. Although these applications are distinct in different levels with social TV analytics, they may share some fundamental analysis methods.

A GENERIC BIG DATA PLATFORM FOR SOCIAL TV ANALYTICS

In this section, we discuss the functional requirements of Big Data systems from a data value chain perspective, and then present a generic architecture for social TV analytics, associating some leading technologies, including cloud computing, Hadoop, and SDN, in this domain.

Big Data Value Chain

A Big-Data system is complex, providing functions to deal with different phases in the digital data life cycle, ranging from its birth to its destruction. At the same time, the system usually involves multiple distinct phases for different applications. In this case, we adopt a system-engineering approach [23], which has been well accepted in industry, to decompose a typical Big-Data system into four consecutive phases, including a data generation phase, a data acquisition phase, a data storage phase, and a data analytics phase. The details for each phase are explained as follows:

- *Data Generation*: deals with how Big Data are generated. In this paper, we focus on the online social networks, which produce massive user-generated contents (UGCs) every minute or even second. In general, UGCs are trivial, noisy, and sparse, positing overwhelming technical challenges in collecting, processing, and analyzing them, beseeching new solutions that would embrace the latest advances in the ICT domain.

- *Data Acquisition*: refers to the process of obtaining information, which is the basis of the subsequent data-processing phase. This process is tightly coupled with data sources. According to the physical characteristics and application environment, we need to adopt appropriate data collection methods or equipment to collect data, integrate them with necessary preprocessing, including data cleansing, redundancy elimination, and so on, and emit them into the storage-sustaining system on the fly to preserve data freshness.

- *Data Storage*: organizes the collected information in a convenient way for fast access and analysis. It can be divided into two parts, that is, the storage infrastructure and the data management strategy. The storage infrastructure refers to physical storage devices, such as random access memory (RAM), hard disk, solid-state drive, and storage networks that connect these devices to meet the capacity, access rate, and reliability requirements. On the basis of the storage infrastructure, the data management strategy deals with how to effectively store and process the collected data. Typical technologies include distributed file systems, databases, and programming models.

- *Data Analytics*: leverages analysis methods or tools to inspect, transform, and model data with the goal of extracting concealed value. Data visualization, statistical analysis, data mining, and machine learning are widely employed to achieve different goals. The methods adopted in this phase range from descriptive analysis, predictive analysis, to prescriptive analysis, depending on the given data characteristic and application.

A Generic Platform for Social TV Analytics

To fulfill the aforementioned functional requirements, we customize a generic Big Data platform for social TV analytics, as illustrated in Figure 14.1. The anatomy of this proposed architecture consists of four fundamental components, including an infrastructure layer, a distributed data crawler layer, a data storage and processing layer, and a data analytics layer, from a layered perspective. Each of them is elaborated as follows:

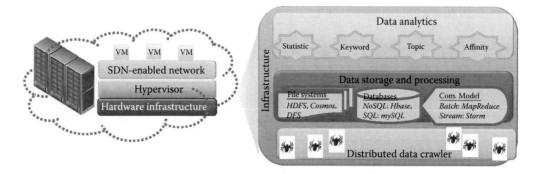

FIGURE 14.1   A generic architecture for social TV analytics, consisting of four layers, that is, infrastructure, distributed data crawler, data storage and processing, and data analytics.

Infrastructure

By using the cloud computing paradigm, raw ICT resources, including CPU, storage, bandwidth, and so on, are abstracted into a resource pool, and provided in the form of virtual machines (VMs). The capacity of VMs can be dynamically tailored in a fine granular manner to adapt to the changing resource demand. Furthermore, SDN-enabled switches can be exploited to construct the data center network. Using the cloud computing and SDN features, the system administrator can monitor the utilization of VMs and network dynamics, and then dynamically adjust the network flow path via flow rerouting or bandwidth reservation. In this way, we can optimize resource allocation and simultaneously prevent network congestion.

Distributed Data Crawler

The distributed data crawler aims to gather adequate social media data, which can guarantee data coverage, relevance, and representativeness. It consists of two core modules, including program descriptor and distributed crawler. The program descriptor generates a set of keywords and key users to represent a specific TV program. These keywords and key users will be mapped into different crawling tasks, which invoke the search-based and user-based crawling strategies. The distributed crawler is deployed in a collection of nodes distributed in several IP segmentations. One node will be elected as the scheduler to dispatch the crawling tasks to other crawler nodes. Each crawler node adopts multiple threads to crawl data.

Data Storage and Processing

The data storage and processing layer provides a unified scheme to effectively manage and process microblogs. In this work, we build our solution on two emerging Big Data analytics platforms, that is, Hadoop and Storm. Hadoop integrates the Hadoop distributed file system (HDFS), NoSQL database (HBase), and batch-style programming model (MapReduce). To accelerate the processing rate, we implement a two-layer SDN-enabled data analysis architecture based on Hadoop, which enables shuffling the intermediate data across distributed data centers or computing clusters. With the network traffic knowledge from the SDN controller and the estimation of the intermediate data size, our scheduling algorithm will calculate the approximate transmission time and processing time, and determine the optimal data center or computing cluster to execute the final phase.

Data Analytics

By leveraging the Big Data platform, data analytics aims to provide different levels of analysis results, from statistical analysis to semantic analysis. These analysis results can assist understanding social perception on TV programs for different types of potential users. For instance, when end users are watching a TV program, our system will crawl live microblogs related to this program, rank these messages according to length, topic, social friendship, and other factors, and push these messages to users to make them know what other audiences are saying about this program. In addition, our system can also calculate the discussion degree, user geo-distribution, topic, and keywords to help TV operators/producers to analyze social response and create an advertisement strategy. In this way, the whole TV ecosystem, from dramatists, TV producers, TV operators, to advertisement agencies, can benefit from data analytics.

In the following sections, we highlight our social TV analytics system in the proposed generic system architecture by introducing three key components, including a distributed data crawler component, an SDN-enabled data-processing component, and a TV program-related microblog analytics component.

DISTRIBUTED DATA CRAWLER

The distributed data crawler aims to gather representative data with respect to TV programs through APIs provided by social media platforms. It is the basis for data storage and data analysis. However, the data-crawling strategy faces the following fundamental challenges:

- *Huge Volume:* Different TV programs attract distinct volumes of social response, that is, microblogs, comments, and reposts. For some breaking programs, the volume of relevant microblogs may be huge. For example, in 2013, the Super Bowl tallied up 30.6 million social media comments (Twitter, public Facebook data, and GetGlue check-ins), 2.5 times last year's social activity of 12.2 million. It is a great challenge to collect adequate data to guarantee coverage within a short time.

- *Missing Data:* Microblogs are typically short, consisting of no more than 140 characters, and informal. There are many typos, abbreviations, phonetic substitutions, and ungrammatical structures. Many relevant microblogs may not contain the predefined keywords, and hence cannot be found by issuing variants of API searches using the fixed keyword set.

- *API Restriction:* Most live microblog services set limits on the amount and frequency of data that can be acquired. Taking Sina Weibo, the largest microblogging platform with over 500 million users in China, as an example, the primary account is authorized to request 150 times per hour via the official APIs, and the response to an HTTP query (corresponding to one keyword) only contains the first 50 pages, that is, accounts for 1000 tweets at most.

To tackle these issues, we design a novel strategy to obtain more microblogs rapidly. There are two main parts in our strategy. First, to collect more microblogs, we design a program descriptor to dynamically generate keywords and key users. These keywords and key users will be mapped to crawling tasks. Second, we implement a distributed crawling mechanism to accelerate the crawling rate.

Program Descriptor

A program descriptor is a keyword and user set used to issue search requests to APIs provided OSNs. The keywords and social users in this set have the contextual relationship with a TV program. For example, given a TV program, the title can be a keyword, and the official social account can be the social user. In this work, we design four types of items to represent a TV program, that is, fixed keywords, known accounts, dynamic keywords, and dynamic users, as shown in Figure 14.2. The generation procedure works as follows:

- *Step 1*: Given a TV program, we first manually select a few keywords that uniquely identify the TV program, such as the name of the TV program, character name, famous actor lines, and so on. Then, we identify a set of program-related accounts. These are typically official accounts of this TV program on the microblog platform that often post relevant microblogs about the TV program. We use both the fixed keywords and known accounts to issue search requests to crawl microblogs, viewed as the relevant data set.

- *Step 2*: To elicit a more live and diverse set of relevant microblogs about the TV program, typically those do not contain the fixed keywords or posted by unknown

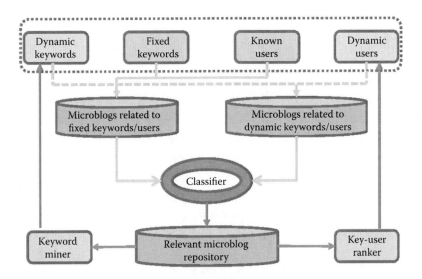

FIGURE 14.2 Program descriptor generating procedure: the program descriptor relates to a keyword and use set. This set is first determined by manually selected keywords and known social users, and then iteratively enriched with dynamic keywords and users.

accounts. Based on the microblog repository, we extract a list of temporally emerging terms as dynamic keywords. In addition, we extract social accounts that post relevant microblogs, and rank them to identify the dynamic key users. These dynamic keywords and users are further used to crawl microblogs, which are potentially relevant to the TV program.

- *Step 3*: The data collected from these four items are a mix of relevant and irrelevant microblogs to the TV program. In order to filter out noisy data, we employ the standard two-class SVM classifier. For the training data, we regard all the microblogs from the fixed keywords and known accounts as relevant.

Since the aired time of a TV program may range for several weeks or months, we can divide the time into slots (e.g., 1 day or 1 hour), and iteratively execute the step 2 and step 3 to generate dynamic keywords and users.

Distributed Crawler

Given the program descriptor, we can issue the items to the OSN APIs to gather microblogs. However, most live microblog services set limits on the amount and frequency of data that can be acquired. In general, there are three types of restriction:

- *Account*: Every account can only send a limited number of search requests within a time duration.
- *IP*: The request rate from the same IP address is restricted.
- *Amount*: For an API search to a keyword, we can only get the best or latest 1000 or 1500 microblogs.

To break through the first and second restrictions, our system maintains a resource pool, consisting of OSN accounts and IP/proxy addresses, and exploits the distributed mechanism to utilize this resource to crawl microblogs. To address the amount restriction, our system will automatically divide a search query into several subqueries when the microblog number to this query exceeds the threshold. For example, we can constrain the query in a smaller time period. In this way, a regular query can be split into many subqueries within a time slot or a region, like "keyword = k, time = 0:00–1:00, region = r."

Figure 14.3 presents the architecture of our proposed distributed data crawler. Each TV program is depicted by a program descriptor, consisting of four types of items that can be dynamically expanded. Since a microblog is a mixture of different types of data, including user profile, microblog contents, reposts, comments, associated users' profile, and so on, the data to be gathered depends on the analysis purpose. For example, to study audience sentiment, we only need to crawl the microblog contents, whereas we need to crawl the user social relationship and associated users' profile for analyzing audience social structure. Therefore, we design different task queues for different types of data. For instance, the live queue is for gathering live microblogs to a given keyword; the friendship queue

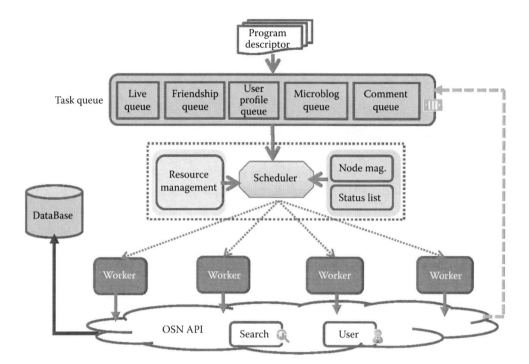

FIGURE 14.3 Architecture of the distributed data crawler. It is comprised of four key components, that is, a program descriptor, task queues, a request scheduling, and execution nodes. For each program of interest, we have a corresponding program descriptor, the items in which will be mapped to multiple crawling tasks inserted to task queues. The request scheduling dispatches these tasks to distributed execution nodes with the consideration of request rate and resource utilization, as well as load balance.

is for gathering social relationships to a given social account. For each item in the program descriptor, our system will map it to the corresponding task queues according to the analysis purpose. The scheduler fetches the crawling task from these queues to gather data. Considering the access constraint, we implement a resource pool to management accounts and IP/proxy addresses. In addition, we exploit Zookeeper [24] to monitor the running status of all machines. According to the system status, the scheduler will dispatch the tasks combined with the account information to the execution nodes in a load-balance way. When the allocated task is accomplished successfully, the execution node will notify the status to the resource pool. In some cases, one successful execution will generate extra tasks to other task queues. For example, when we have crawled a microblog to a keyword and we want to know the comments, the execution node will insert this task into the comment queue. Once Zookeeper detects one node is down, the allocated task will be rescheduled to another active node. In the end, all the data are stored in our storage system.

SDN-ENABLED DATA-PROCESSING PLATFORM

As described in the previous section, our system exploits a set of nodes distributed in different IP segmentations to prevent being blocked by OSNs. Once we collect adequate microblogs, we can merge them to a specific cluster and employ Hadoop for analysis. However, this method incurs significant network traffic and analysis-delay. An improved method is to analyze data locally, and merge the intermediate data to generate the final result. The benefit comes from two aspects: (1) In many cases, intermediate data is much smaller than the raw data; (2) Network traffic in the shuffle stage is in waves, while sustained in the previous method, leading to higher possibility of network congestion. Unfortunately, current Hadoop does not support cross-site shuffle.

In this work, by leveraging the flow forwarding feature provided by SDN, we implement an SDN-enabled Hadoop framework to combine the SDN controller with the Hadoop job scheduler to tackle this issue [25], as depicted in Figure 14.4. The framework consists of two layers, that is, a local layer and a global layer. The local layer is comprised of a collection of data centers located at different IP segmentations. The data center network is organized in fat tree or other network topologies using OpenFlow-enabled switches. One centralized local controller is installed to monitor and configure the network flow, so that local shuffles can be moved to other data centers. The distributed data centers are interconnected via upper layer switches that are controlled by a logically centralized global controller. Local controller has the insight of local network traffic, while the global controller has the full view of network traffic among data centers, enabling global traffic engineering. All local controllers are connected to a global controller. Moreover, they can exchange and share network views.

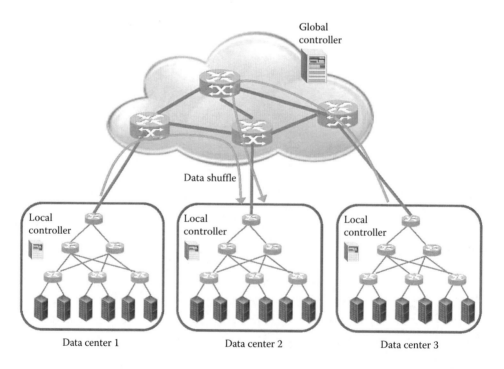

FIGURE 14.4 Two-layer architecture for SDN-enabled Hadoop platform. The lower layer consists of a set of data centers located at different IP segmentations. The upper layer has a centralized controller, which monitors and configures the network flow.

On this platform, we can shuffle the intermediate data cross sites. However, the volume of intermediate data produced by different data centers is distinct, and the choice of the central data center where to execute the final step will greatly affect the system performance. We solve this problem by two steps. First, all map tasks run the same map function. Hence, their intermediate data volume will be similar when the input size to the mappers is consistent. With the historical knowledge, the job scheduler can predict the traffic demand. Second, based on this estimation, we can use graph structure to model the problem, and make decisions in the global controller. Given a topology, $G = (V, E)$ where $V = \{v_n \mid n = 1,2,...\}$ is the set of data centers, and E is the set of links among them. For each data center, the processing capacity and intermediate data volume are c_n and I_n, respectively. Hence, this problem is transformed to the following optimization problem:

$$\arg\min_n \left(\sum_{n'} \mathbf{pr}\left(\mathbf{l}_{n'}, \, \mathbf{c}_n\right) + \max_n \mathbf{tr}\left(\mathbf{c}_n, \mathbf{n}\right) \right)$$

where $\mathbf{tr}(\mathbf{c}_{n'}, \mathbf{n})$ is the time cost of transmitting the intermediate data $\mathbf{c}_{n'}$ from node $\mathbf{n'}$ to $\mathbf{n}$, $\mathbf{pr}(\mathbf{c}_{n'}, \mathbf{l}_n)$ represents the time cost of processing intermediate data $\mathbf{c}_{n'}$ using the resource $\mathbf{I}_n$ in node $\mathbf{n}$. The goal is to find a node that minimizes the sum of transmission time and processing time.

TV PROGRAM-RELATED MICROBLOG ANALYTICS

Microblog services provide an essential platform for users to publish messages, which contain everyday thoughts, opinions, and experiences. Parts of these UGCs reflect their interests, concerns, and criticisms about TV programs. The aim of social TV analytics is to associate public perception with the TV programs. Currently, we provide different levels of analysis results, from statistic analysis to semantic analysis, for TV audience, TV operators, and TV producers.

Statistics

We set a collection of statistic metrics to reveal public interest on a particular TV program [21], including the following:

- *Microblog volume per hour*: casts the microblog volume on an hourly basis, which can reflect the audience discussion degree to a TV program. Higher microblog volume indicates that there are more discussions.

- *Microblog volume in different locations*: calculates the microblog distribution over geolocations, which reveals the hot degree in different geographical locations.

- *User behavior over week*: indicates the microblog volume at different times on the weekly basis. We can find the hot duration of this program.

- *Gender distribution*: demonstrates the distribution of social users.

These general metrics can benefit the whole TV ecosystem.

Live Microblog Ranking

When audiences watch TV programs, some of them may post messages to share their real-time opinions to TV programs. Live microblog ranking aims to rank live microblogs according to their "interestingness" and present them to the audience on the fly. This function can enhance the watching experience, promote information sharing, and aid screenwriters in assessing the social response to a story. In this work, we represent "interestingness" from two levels:

- *Message level*: refers to informativeness, opiniatedness, popularity, and authority. An interesting microblog should contain informative, opinionated and popular messages referring to TV programs. Furthermore, the messages should be written mostly by users who have authority.

- *Set level*: includes diversity. An interesting ranking should contain microblogs that are diverse in contents.

The ranking scheme is illustrated in Figure 14.5: first, at each time slot, our system takes as input a TV program as well as all the live microblogs referring to this TV program; second,

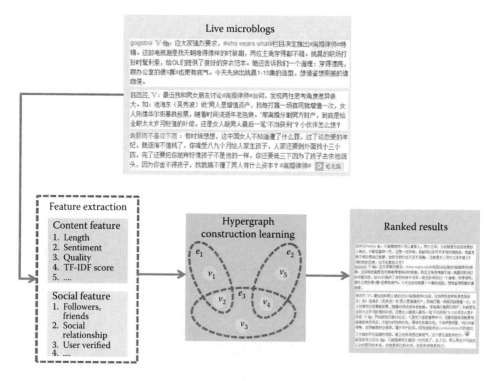

FIGURE 14.5 Hypergraph-based live microblog ranking. At each time slot, we can gather a set of relevant microblogs to a TV program. Each microblog is represented by two types of features, that is, content feature and social feature. These features will be used to construct the hyperedges, resulting in a hypergraph to describe the connection of all the microblogs. Finally, graph-based learning will be employed to rank these microblogs according to interestingness.

each microblog is then represented by two types of features, including the content feature and the social feature. The content feature captures the linguistic aspects that indicate how interesting, informative, and opinionated a microblog is, and the social feature represents the level of diffusion of a microblog and the topical authority in the social network; third, a hypergraph is constructed, in which the vertices denote the microblog for ranking, and each feature generates a hyperedge. During the learning process, all the features will be jointly considered; finally, the live microblogs will be outputted according to the interestingness level.

Dynamic Keywords and Key User Identification

Keywords are words which occur in the microblogs more often than we would expect to occur by chance alone. They can act as a reference for TV programs. Key-users are those who influence the information prorogation. Roughly speaking, we can know who are talking about what on TV programs from keyword and key-user sets. In the previous section, we set four types of items, fixed/dynamic keyword, and known/dynamic key-user. Dynamic keywords and key-users are extracted from the dataset identified by fixed keywords and known accounts. The generation of these two items is detailed as follows:

- *Dynamic Keyword Generation*: Considering a time slot t (e.g., one day), we can construct two microblog sets S_t and S_{t-}, where S_t refers to the relevant microblogs in the current time slot; while S_{t-} covers all the microblogs sent during the time period $[t - T,t]$, T is the predefined time interval, for example, 1 day or 1 week. The vocabulary sets of these two microblog sets are denoted as $W_t = \{W_1,W_2,...\}$ and $W_{t-} = \{w'_1, w'_2,...\}$. Our goal is to identify the terms that have distinctively distributions in S_{t-} and S_t. Those terms with rising frequencies are the potentially emerging keywords, whereas those with decreasing frequencies will gradually disappear. In this work, we use the chi-square test [26] to compare the two distributions due to its efficiency and ability to handle rapidly evolving microblog contents.

- *Key User Generation*: At time slot t, given a time interval T, we get a user set U_t who post at least one relevant microblog in the time window. For user $u_n \in U_t$, his activity is measured by the ratio of relevant microblogs sent by himself during the time window. Considering the information propagation pattern, a user's score is calculated by incorporating the activity of all his followers. We then rank users in U_t by their scores, and the top N users are selected as the key users.

Topic Modeling

As for topic modeling, we need to handle the live and large volume of microblogs to detect the topics without any prior knowledge of the number of topics. Since the topics are constantly evolving and growing in size, we employ a single-pass incremental clustering algorithm [27] with a threshold τ. At each time slot t, we obtain all the microblogs S in a time order. The clustering algorithm considers each microblog s_i in turn and calculates the similarity $(S_i, Center_j)$ with existing cluster C_j. If the maximum similarity value is greater than τ, the microblog will be distributed to the cluster, and the clustering center will be updated; otherwise, a new cluster will be generated for this microblog. The details of this algorithm are shown in Figure 14.6.

Algorithm 1 Topic Detection Algorithm

INPUT:
  Microblog set S, and threshold τ.
OUTPUT:
  topic cluster set C, and cluster center $Center$;
  1: Random select N microblogs from S and add into C and $Center$.
  2: **for** $s_i \in S$ **do**
  3:   calculate the similarity sim with between s_i and all the clusters;
  4:   find the maximum of sim_k and the corresponding cluster k;
  5:   **if** $sim_k > \tau$ **then**
  6:     distribute s_i to cluster k, and update its center;
  7:   **else**
  8:     create a new cluster and center, insert s_i to this cluster, and add this cluster and center to cluster set and center set;
  9:   **end if**
  10: **end for**
  11: **return** C and $Center$

FIGURE 14.6   Topic detection algorithm.

EVALUATION

In this section, we first describe our testbed built on a private data center. Following that, we conduct a performance comparison to demonstrate the efficiency of our microblog-crawling mechanisms and SDN-enabled Big Data platform. Finally, we present some preliminary results on social TV analytics.

System Setup

We build our system on top of a modular data center at NTU, which consists of 10 racks. Each rack contains up to 30 HP servers and 2 Gigabit Cisco switches. The data center can provide an ICT capacity of 25 TB disk space, 1200 GB memory space, and 600 CPUs. We utilize CloudStack to virtualize physical machines into a collection of virtual machines in the infrastructure layer.

Microblog-Crawling Performance

Since microblog crawling plays the fundamental role in social media analysis, we first show the effectiveness of our proposed mechanism. We choose three famous Chinese TV series programs, "Lan Ling Wang," "Longmen Express," and "Best Time" (represented by program 1, program 2, and program 3, respectively), for trial. For each program, the initial program descriptor consists of five fixed keywords and five social accounts. The default crawling strategy only uses the given keywords and social accounts to crawl microblogs. We have presented the comparison between our proposed mechanism and the default method in Table 14.1. From the table, we can observe that our proposed mechanism can collect more than 10 times as many relevant microblogs in comparison with the default

TABLE 14.1   Effectiveness of Microblog-Crawling Strategy

	Microblog # (Default)	Microblog # (Proposed)	Microblog # Relevant	Precision	Increase
Program 1	3020	41,168	32,918	0.79	10.9×
Program 2	4751	80,050	58,437	0.73	12.3×
Program 3	5142	124,403	77,130	0.62	15.0×

method, which is an amazing improvement. In addition, we also find that more potential relevant microblogs lead to lower relevant precision.

Performance Evaluation for SDN-Enabled Big Data Platform

In order to evaluate the performance of our Big Data platform, we exploit three racks to build a two-layer architecture, as shown in Figure 14.7a. The numbers of servers in three racks are 10, 8, and 5, respectively. All servers in a rack are connected to the corresponding SDN switch via the ToR switch with the link capacity of 500 Mbps. We configure three racks into different IP segmentations. The link capacity between two SDN switches is 1 Gbps. The Java-based OpenFlow Controller, Floodlight [28], is instaled to setup flow entries in the OpenFlow switches. We use the Hadoop Sort program to run as the job under test. Each server has to process 5 GB microblogs. We compare two types of solutions, that is, traditional method (TM-) and SDN scheme (SDN-). For each type of solutions, we can either move the raw data to one of the three racks to process (marked as TM-R1, TM-R2 or TM-R3), or only shuffle the intermediate data (marked as SDN-R1, SDN-R2, or SDN-R3).

Figure 14.7b shows the execution time for different methods. When we choose the same rack to process the intermediate data or raw data, our scheme can finish the task with less time. Moreover, the shortest execution time of our scheme is much less than that of the traditional methods. In our experimental configuration, the processing capability of rack 1 is larger than the other two racks, hence moving the data to rack 1 will lead to less execution time.

Social Perception for TV Programs

Social TV analytics aims to discover the social perception of TV programs in the context of social media. Such information is determined by statistical analysis and semantic analysis. In Figure 14.8, we present several statistics for the TV series *Longmen Express*, a hot TV program aired from 31/Jul/2013 to 14/Aug/2013, including microblog number in the aired days, microblog geographical distribution, microblog time distribution, and gender distribution.

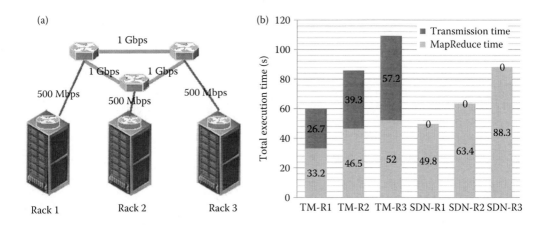

FIGURE 14.7 Performance evaluation for SDN-enabled Big Data platform. (a) Testbed architecture, consisting of three racks connected via three SDN switches; (b) Total execution time for two types of strategies, traditional method, and SDN-enabled architecture.

We crawled 315,337 microblogs from Sina Weibo, involving 240,465 unique users. Figure 14.8a presents the degree of interest over time, including the number of microblogs, reposts, and comments, respectively. During the broadcasting period, audience posted more microblogs on this program, and cumulated to a peak during the aired time of the final episode. Figure 14.8b shows the geographical distribution of our data set. According to the

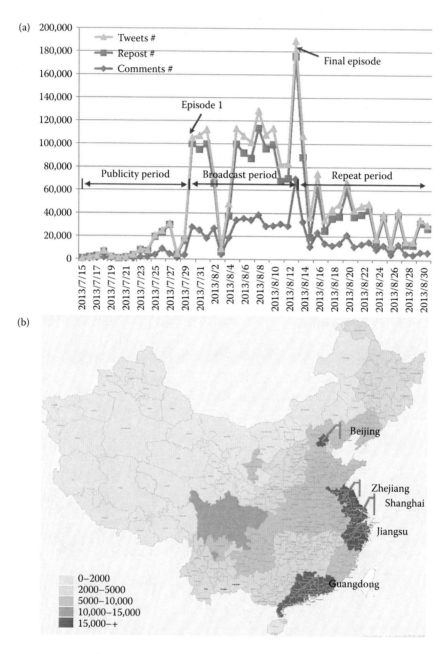

FIGURE 14.8 Statistics for the TV series *Longmen Express*. (a) Microblog number on different days, (b) Microblog geographical distribution, (c) Microblog distribution over time, (d) Gender distribution.

(Continued)

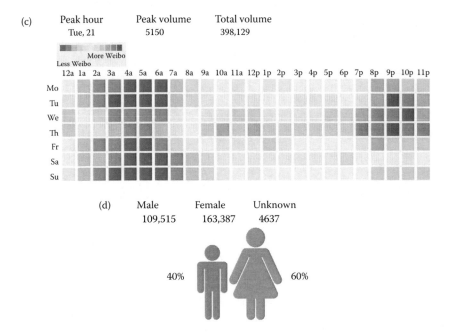

FIGURE 14.8 (*Continued*)   Statistics for the TV series *Longmen Express*. (a) Microblog number on different days, (b) Microblog geographical distribution, (c) Microblog distribution over time, (d) Gender distribution.

color depth, we can see that audience in Guangdong, Beijing, and Shanghai published more microblogs than that published by viewers in other regions. Figure 14.8c reveals the habits of audience posting microblogs. During the live broadcasting period, audiences are accustomed to watch TV and publish their opinions simultaneously. Figure 14.8d illustrates the gender distribution of all the social users, who posted at least one relevant microblog. The keyword cloud and topics are shown in Figures 14.9 and 14.10, respectively.

FIGURE 14.9   Keyword cloud for the TV series *Longmen Express*.

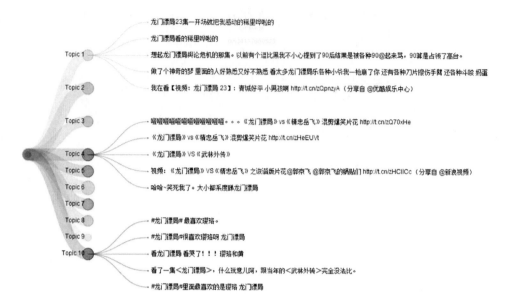

FIGURE 14.10   Topic graph for the TV series *Longmen Express*.

CONCLUSION

In this chapter, we proposed a cloud-centric Big Data platform for social TV analytics, aiming to mine social perception on TV programs from social media. Our system consists of three key components, that is, the distributed data crawler, the Big Data processing, and the social TV analytics. The distributed data crawler collects the microblogs from online social networks, and then stores them in the Big Data platform. Using the Big Data-processing paradigm, the social TV analytics implements different levels of analysis on the collected microblogs. A proof-of-concept demo has been built on top of a private cloud at NTU. Feature verification and performance comparison demonstrate the feasibility and effectiveness of our innovative system. For future work, we will further study the affinity between TV audience and brands and social media-assisted video tagging.

REFERENCES

1. Twitter. [Online]. Available: http://twitter.com.
2. Digital Marketing Ramblings. [Online]. Available: http://expandedramblings.com/index.php/march-2013-by-the-numbers-a-few-amazing-twitterstats/#.U855Wfm4WjA.
3. H. Hu, Y. Wen, T.-S. Chua, and X. Li. 2014. Toward scalable systems for big data analytics: A technology tutorial, *Access, IEEE*, 2, 652–687.
4. Nielsen. 2012. State of the media: The social media report, http://www.nielsen.com/content/dam/corporate/us/en/reports-downloads/2012-Reports/The-Social-Media-Report-2012.pdf.
5. H. Hu, J. Huang, H. Zhao, Y. Wen, C. W. Chen, and T.-S. Chua. 2014. Social TV analytics: A novel paradigm to transform tv watching experience, *Proceedings of the 5th ACM Multimedia Systems Conference*, Singapore, pp. 172–175.

6. M. Proulx and S. Shepatin. 2012. *Social TV: How Marketers can Reach and Engage Audiences by Connecting Television to the Web, Social Media, and Mobile*, New York: John Wiley & Sons.

7. T. White. 2012. *Hadoop: The Definitive Guide*, Sebastopol: O'Reilly Media, Inc.

8. J. Dean and S. Ghemawat. 2008. MapReduce: Simplified data processing on large clusters, *Communications ACM*, 51(1), 107–113.

9. M. Hammoud, M. S. Rehman, and M. F. Sakr. 2012. Center-of-gravity reduce task scheduling to lower mapreduce network traffic, *Cloud Computing (CLOUD), 2012 IEEE 5th International Conference on IEEE*, Hawaii, USA, pp. 49–58.

10. G. Wang, T. Ng, and A. Shaikh. 2012. Programming your network at run-time for big data applications, *Proceedings of the First Workshop on Hot Topics in Software Defined Networks. ACM*, Helsinki, Finland, pp. 103–108.

11. N. McKeown, T. Anderson, H. Balakrishnan, G. Parulkar, L. Peterson, J. Rexford, S. Shenker, and J. Turner. 2008. Openflow: Enabling innovation in campus networks, *ACM SIGCOMM Computer Communication Review*, 38(2), pp. 69–74.

12. C. Carpineto and G. Romano. 2012. A survey of automatic query expansion in information retrieval, *ACM Computing Surveys (CSUR)*, 44(1), 1.

13. Y. Jin, Y. Wen, and H. Hu. 2013. Minimizing monetary cost via cloud clone migration in multi-screen cloud social tv system, *Global Communications Conference (GLOBECOM), 2013 IEEE*, Atlanta, USA, pp. 1747–1752.

14. H. Hu, Y. Wen, T.-S. C. Chua, Z. Wang, J. Huang, W. Zhu, and D. Wu. 2014. Community based effective social video contents placement in cloud centric CDN network, *Multimedia and Expo (ICME), 2014 IEEE International Conference on*, Chengdu, China, pp. 1747–1752.

15. T. Sakaki, M. Okazaki, and Y. Matsuo. 2010. Earthquake shakes twitter users: Real-time event detection by social sensors, *Proceedings of the 19th International Conference on World Wide Web. ACM*, pp. 851–860.

16. A. Tumasjan, T. O. Sprenger, P. G. Sandner, and I. M. Welpe. 2010. Predicting elections with twitter: What 140 characters reveal about political sentiment, *ICWSM*, 10, 178–185.

17. A.-M. Popescu and M. Pennacchiotti. 2010. Detecting controversial events from twitter, *Proceedings of the 19th ACM International Conference on Information and Knowledge Management*, Toronto, ON, Canada, pp. 1873–1876.

18. J. Ritterman, M. Osborne, and E. Klein. 2009. Using prediction markets and twitter to predict a swine flu pandemic, *Proceedings 1st International Workshop on Mining Social Media*, Sevilla, Spain, pp. 1–9.

19. A. Culotta. 2010. Towards detecting influenza epidemics by analyzing twitter messages, *Proceedings of the First Workshop on Social Media Analytics*, Washington DC, USA, pp. 115–122.

20. S. Liu, Z. Song, G. Liu, C. Xu, H. Lu, and S. Yan. 2012. Street-to-shop: Cross-scenario clothing retrieval via parts alignment and auxiliary set, *Computer Vision and Pattern Recognition (CVPR), 2012 IEEE Conference on*, Providence, Rhode Island, pp. 3330–3337.

21. H. Hu, Y. Wen, H. Luan, T.-S. Chua, and X. Li. 2014. Toward multiscreen social tv with geolocation-aware social sense, *MultiMedia, IEEE*, 21(3), 10–19.

22. H. Hu, Y. Jin, Y. Wen, T.-S. Chua, and X. Li. 2014. Toward a biometric-aware cloud service engine for multi-screen video applications, *Proceedings of the 2014 ACM conference on SIGCOMM*, pp. 581–582.

23. F. Gallagher. 2012. The big data value chain [Online]. Available: http://fraysen.blogspot.sg/2012/06/big-data-value-chain.html.

24. P. Hunt, M. Konar, F. P. Junqueira, and B. Reed. 2010. Zookeeper: Wait-free coordination for internet-scale systems, *Proceedings of the 2010 USENIX Conference on USENIX Annual Technical Conference*, Boston, USA, 8, pp. 145–148.

25. H. Hu, Y. Wen, Y. Gao, T.-S. Chua, and X. Li. 2015. Towards SDN-enabled big-data platform for social TV analytics, *Network, IEEE*, in press.

26. H. O. Lancaster and E. Seneta. 1969. *Chi-Square Distribution*, New York: John Wiley & Sons, Inc.

27. Y. Chen, H. Amiri, Z. Li, and T.-S. Chua. 2013. Emerging topic detection for organizations from microblogs, *Proceedings of the 36th International ACM SIGIR Conference on Research and Development in Information Retrieval*, Dublin, Ireland, pp. 43–52.

28. Floodlight. 2013. [Online]. Available: http://www.projectfloodlight.org/floodlight/.

CHAPTER 15

Trends in Cloud Infrastructures for Big Data

Yacine Djemaiel, Boutheina A. Fessi, and Noureddine Boudriga

CONTENTS

INTRODUCTION

Cloud computing is a promising and widely used technology in several domains, such as business, education, and healthcare. This technology provides different benefits that allow people to increasingly adopt it. In fact, it is worth mentioning that the cloud is primarily used as a storage technique that overcomes the limitations of traditional tools in storing huge amounts of data as well as complex data. Over time and due to the importance of such a technique to provide more than a storage task, developers enhance and introduce new features that provide and exploit common and measured services, and share easy access to stored data thanks to broad network access and rapid elasticity. However, some constraints should be considered when employing this technology, related mainly to the security of data, its management, and its processing.

On the other hand, cloud computing is used as an analytic and a storage tool that copes with the Big Data paradigm. This is an emergent concept representing the heterogeneity and the increasing growth of data that should be accurately managed and processed to extract pertinent information needed to drive the best decisions. This data explosion is due to the materialization of new and modern information technology coupled with the additional information derivable from the analysis of information or flowing within the information system. A number of developments have been conducted to address Big Data problems, related either to major processing data activities or to Big Data dimensions (5V), which represent different data properties. Enhanced techniques to deal with such problems have also been considered, such as data mining, parallel processing, virtualization, and cloud computing, but none of them provides full coverage of the identified issues.

In this context, it is noted that cloud infrastructures present useful platforms and provide solutions to address important issues that have been identified for Big Data-based environments, such as storage, management, and access to huge volumes of data. In addition, they allow reducing run time, response time, and different costs.

The proposed chapter aims at presenting the trends in cloud infrastructures for Big Data focusing on the provided solutions to the determined Big Data issues, and surveys the achieved works on the cloud for Big Data. It also discusses the major challenges and opportunities of handling Big Data on cloud. In addition, the chapter presents a set of applications that process huge and complex data sets including heterogeneous data on cloud.

These applications should respect at least a set of security measures in order to ensure the protection of confidentiality, integrity, and availability of Big Data on cloud. Furthermore, the management and processing of Big Data on cloud are detailed. These tasks are significant since they allow the extraction of pertinent information from a large volume of data using several techniques. Finally, the chapter discusses a set of unresolved issues for the management of Big Data oncloud and states future directions that could be investigated to improve developed models.

Limits and Challenges of Cloud Infrastructures

As it is described in Figure 15.1, Big Data gathers all types of data from structured to unstructured such as text files, databases, videos, and audio files; and could use different analytics, namely, cloud, data mining, parallel processing, and virtualization to process them. The use of these analytics drives us to ask different questions related to management, processing, services, and security of cloud environments for Big Data.

In fact, the application of analytics is needed for the following reasons:

1. *Data volumes*: With the increasing advances in new information and communication technologies, organizations are accumulating continually high volumes of data that should be stored and managed. Traditional tools could not deal with these data effectively since they are of several types and thus the use of multiple techniques at the same time could be inappropriate. The application of the analytics could exploit any types of data, even unstructured, fast-changing data that breaks the relational databases and the conventional models.

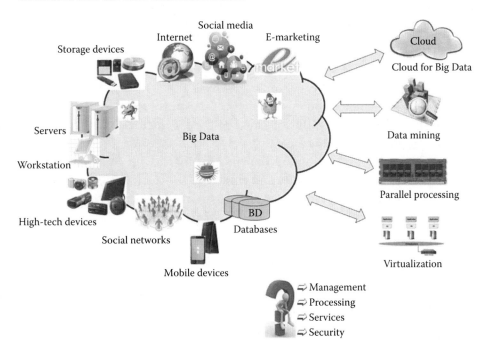

FIGURE 15.1 Big Data requirements.

2. *Business value*: The collected data helps organizations to enhance their business processes and decision-making by taking values from the analyzed information. Thus, collecting more and more data allows mining additional patterns and insights by the analytics that would provide a forward looking view for the organization. A recent book by Judah Phillips [1] examines the importance of applying and adopting analytics to help businesses in developing and managing streamed and digital data; to either generate new or incremental profitable revenue; and/or to reduce costs.

3. *Sustainable advantage*: The information and intelligence are harnessed by the applied analytics. Indeed, organizations see Big Data analytics as one of the last frontiers of achieving competitive advantage, by considering them as a service that carries on significant activities (make sense out of vast quantities of data and help management make better decisions) made previously by skilled staff. Therefore, organizations could take advantage of the outputs of the analytics' application on Big Data to anticipate and to execute the opportunities of the future.

These analytics operate according to top-down or bottom-up approaches depending on the type of treatment to be processed on historical data: exploration and analysis or prediction and optimization. Techniques from several fields, such as data mining and data visualization tools, parallel processing, virtualization, and cloud are thus applied. Each technique has its advantages and limits and is specified to support certain tasks.

In this context, the proposed chapter focuses on the deployment of the cloud to support and to manage Big Data. This use provides diverse benefits affecting various aspects. It allows the improvement of collaboration and information sharing, through the access of team members to the same centralized data sources or to data stored in multiple clouds [2]; and the reduction in hardware infrastructure, IT operating, and effort costs since data are stored in the same accessible resources. Thus, there is a decrease in the number of required and used physical hardware resources as well as a reduction in IT maintenance and management costs as processes can be automated; the reduction of response and run time, because of the specificities of the cloud to reduce network latency via globally dispersed instances and to reduce processing time via a high degree of parallel processing [3]; the effective increase of storage capacity as the cloud is characterized by its flexibility and elasticity. The capacity could grow as a business requires and scale back as soon as this excess capacity is no longer needed; and there is easy access to Software as a Service (SaaS) application. The user is not involved with management, security, availability, and performance of the application, which are provided by the application providers. The user simply needs an Internet connection to access it via the cloud infrastructure.

It is crucial to note that the primary and the most known advantage of adopting the cloud for Big Data is the storage of huge volumes of data from different types (structured, semistructured, and unstructured). However, this task causes critical issues that should be carefully considered to efficiently manage, process, and protect the stored data, in order to provide appropriate and secured services.

As the cloud infrastructure includes huge data sets, conventional computing solutions (e.g., relational databases) are increasingly not capable of handling these data or of being scalable to Big Data proportions. In addition, traditional query languages are not sufficient to find and extract the required information, so that there is a need to define an appropriate query language for information search. This insufficiency has an effect on the data velocity feature where the processing time and information speed are increased. In some instances, the search of pertinent information will require additional processing time to be performed since it would parse huge data sets to extract them. In other cases, this time depends on the type of the executed processes, such as catching fraud, where Big Data must be used as it streams into the enterprise in order to maximize its value.

The diversity of the stored data on cloud could also present issues related mainly to storing different data types (e.g., photographs, audio, video, 3D models) in many corporate data silos. The analysis of these data requires preprocessing and data cleansing before being processed.

Another issue that could be highlighted is related to the data quality (veracity). In fact, as the variety and the number of data sources grow, the rate of uncertainty increases and therefore the extraction of confident data will be a serious and difficult problem to solve. Techniques that deal with reducing uncertainty would be effective to determine the needed information and to establish trust in Big Data.

For the security aspect, the outlined limits affect mainly access control to stored data. In fact, when using a cloud platform there is less control over who has access to the stored information and little knowledge of where it is stored. In addition, the cloud infrastructure is a big target for malicious users and different security risks could be identified and affect stored data, since the access to these data could be performed through an unsecured Internet connection.

Therefore, despite the add-on benefits provided by the cloud for Big Data, it is noted that several researches have to be done to solve the remaining issues.

CLOUD BIG DATA APPLICATIONS

Several applications have been developed to process large, heterogeneous, and complex data sets. They target different fields including healthcare, social networks, military, and financial and marketing services. These available applications make use of various approaches, such as optimization methods, statistics, data mining, machine learning, visualization, and social network analysis [4]. In this section, we focus only on the applications that use cloud computing as an analytic to deal with Big Data.

Data Management

Xu et al. [5] proposed a semantic-based model that issues the importance of parsing and organizing the content in video Big Data. The proposed Video Structural Description (VSD) model allows the detection and the analysis of the related surveillance events, on the basis of the definition of various concepts (e.g., person, vehicles, and traffic signs) and their spatial and temporal relations. The presented video structural description aims at parsing video content into text information, using spatiotemporal segmentation, feature selection, object recognition, and semantic web technology.

Moreover, a dedicated modeling language for the description of performance models, including applications based on the MapReduce paradigm, is presented in Barbierato et al.'s paper [6]. The proposed language exploited the Apache Hive query language for NoSQL databases, which is built over Apache Hadoop MapReduce infrastructure. The use of this language proves its efficiency in the modeling process that becomes easier to perform. Furthermore, it is noted that the presented work allowed Big Data application designers and system administrators to evaluate their choices and experiments by means of vertical multi-formalism modeling.

In this line of research, Garcia et al. [7] have focused on assisting Big Data developers in working with extremely large datasets without preprocessing or importing them into a repository, by analyzing available tools and techniques. The parsing and querying tasks are performed on raw data sets using Hadoop and Amazon cloud services to mine data. The latter are among a list of suitable technologies that solve Big Data challenges [8]. The presented work used Amazon cloud services to store large RDF files in the Amazon simple storage service and then used Hadoop to answer the required queries through running the parsers using the Amazon Elastic MapReduce (EMR). Therefore, this work has provided a rich set of information about tackling Big Data and semantic web challenges thanks to the combination of Hadoop and Amazon technologies.

It is noted that these technologies are widely used when dealing with flooded data. In fact, Issa et al. [9] used the Amazon cloud infrastructure as a basis for a streaming-based scheme to support data-intensive cloud-based sequence analysis. The proposed model processes the data while it is transferred. It provides a framework based on the client–server model, and is composed of a set of modules for constructing and managing a computer cluster in the cloud and executing analysis jobs on it. The proposed model overcomes the problem of the data transfer latency of the large size of the next-generation sequencing and saves both time and cost of computation.

Healthcare

For the healthcare field, it is noted that several works have been conducted related essentially to the involvement of the patient in medical programs and the improvement of health decisions and patient care. In fact, Lin et al. [10] proposed a cloud-based framework for implementing a self-caring service, named Home-diagnosis, to allow users to get diagnosis assistance by themselves at home. The developed framework is based on an offline Hadoop cluster and an online distributed search cluster that parses massive historical medical records to provide highly concurrent and scalable online medical record retrieval, data analysis, and privacy protection functions. The Home-diagnosis model provides efficient primary detailed diagnosis for submitted user's queries through a disease-symptom lattice as well as through medical records with privacy processing. It also serves as a means of assistance to provide disease precaution knowledge for various user groups, especially for older adults and individuals with chronic diseases.

Costa [11], in the other hand, reviewed the major breakthroughs achieved in combining omics and clinical health data applied to personalized medicine. The author highlighted the importance of the new wave of technologies applied to biomedical research in successfully developing large-scale sequencing projects and in analyzing the related information using Big Data analytics solutions through presenting two examples of developed projects. Moreover, Costa stresses the appropriateness of cloud computing as a storage solution that can deal with huge medical and scientific data. However, the continued increase in the amounts of omics data, health information, and emerging technologies generates several challenges related to storage, transfer, security, and privacy of the detected volumes of data that should be deeply considered.

Another work, outlined in Lusher et al.'s paper [12], described the involvement of medicinal chemistry to the area of Big Data. In fact, the increasing growth in data volumes on medicinal chemists coupled with the increase in the diversity and the specialization of technologies embedded within the process of drug discovery require new approaches to be applied to improve decision making and to uncover the meaningful relationships and patterns in available data for these research projects. The authors discuss the Big Data challenges in medicinal chemistry according to Big Data dimensions. They also stress on the different factors that show the need to undertake Big Data approaches: the access and the requirement to manage large amounts of data; the requirement for all researchers to become data scientists; the increased complexity of research projects; and the need to work effectively in larger teams with colleagues from multiple disciplines and at multiple locations.

Therefore, medicinal research should consider the technological advances and use them efficiently to successfully address the Big Data problems that may occur in the future, namely, the storage and management of real-time streamed data and the assurance of the security of stored and processed data.

Public Safety

Cloud computing is used more and more to manage public safety. This technique proves its efficiency as a good infrastructure to support and to exploit huge amount of data that are scattered on large networks. Public safety aims to protect the public and to keep them safe. It could be related to national security, military, airport security surveillance, or surveillance of critical infrastructure, where multiple distributed sensors are deployed to collect heterogeneous types of data from diverse sources (private or public).

An actual example of such public safety application is the US federal communication commission (FCC), which is created "for the purpose of the national defense" and "for the purpose of promoting safety of life and property through the use of wire and radio communications" [13]. In fact, the FCC is moving toward cutting-edge architectures based on cloud computing to deliver quality services quickly to the citizens that depend on them [14]. The integration of such techniques may raise privacy and security concerns for consumers. This should be considered and expected to be ensured by the cloud provider.

BIG DATA MANAGEMENT IN CLOUD

This section details the management process of Big Data in cloud environments. The latter represents an important task, involving the organization, administration, and governance of large volumes of heterogeneous and variable arrivals data, as described in Figure 15.2. In the following, we present the requirements for designing data management systems for

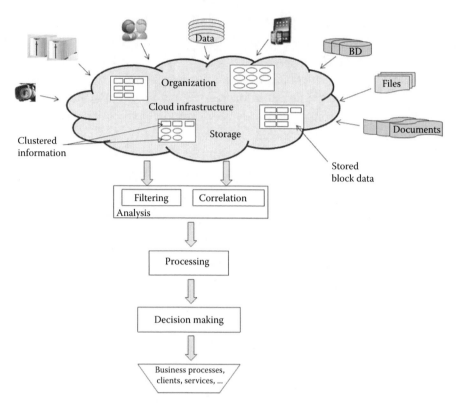

FIGURE 15.2   Managing Big Data on cloud.

Big Data in cloud environments. Then, we describe a proposed framework developed for managing Big Data in cloud environments.

Designing Data Management Systems Principles

The shift of a large number of services to the cloud in addition to the huge volumes of data to be handled in this case, has opened up the challenge for designing data management systems that provide consistency guarantees at a granularity larger than single rows and keys. In this context, we discuss the design choices that allowed modern scalable data management systems to achieve higher levels of scalability compared to traditional databases in the presence of Big Data. The following set of design choices that ensure scalable design for data management systems are detailed in Aminzadeh et al. [15].

Segregate System and Application State

It is required to deal differently with the system components rather than viewing them as a cohesive whole. The system state is critical and needs stringent consistency guarantees. In addition, the application state requires varying degrees of consistency and operational flexibility, and hence it can use different means for ensuring these requirements.

Limit Interactions to a Single Physical Machine

The management system should have the ability to horizontally partition and to balance the load as well as the data. Moreover, the failure of certain system components does not affect the functioning of the remaining components. As a consequence, the use of a single machine also obviates distributed synchronization and the associated cost.

Limited Distributed Synchronization
Distributed synchronization can be used in a scalable data management system. The system design should limit distributed synchronizations to the minimum, but eliminating them altogether is not necessary for a scalable design. The above-mentioned design principles will form the basis for the management systems for scalable data stores in cloud environments.

A Framework for the Management of Big Data on Cloud

In order to deal with Big Data on cloud in an efficient manner, a management framework is required. In this context, a recent network management framework, called FlowComb, is proposed in Federal Communications Commission [16]. This framework enables Big Data-processing applications, such as Hadoop, to achieve high utilization and low data-processing times. FlowComb predicts application network transfers based on the use of software agents installed on application servers. It resolves basically three problems: (1) how to anticipate the network demand of the running services; (2) how to schedule detected transfers; and (3) how to enforce the schedule in the network.

The proposed framework is built on a set of components that are needed to ensure management. The main component of this framework is a centralized decision engine that collects data from each agent, processes them in order to maintain network topology and utilization information. The decision engine checks for another path with sufficient available bandwidth when a pending or current transfer creates congestion. To obtain information about data transfers without modifying Hadoop, agents are installed on each server in the cluster. An agent performs two basic tasks: (1) periodically scans Hadoop logs and queries Hadoop nodes to determine which map tasks have been accomplished and which transfers have been initiated (or already finished), and (2) sends this information to

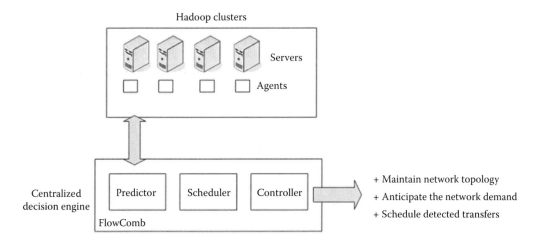

FIGURE 15.3   FlowComb architecture.

FlowComb's flow scheduling module. Three components are available that ensure respectively: the flow prediction, flow scheduling, and flow control, as illustrated in Figure 15.3.

The proposed management scheme is effective when the network is congested. This is more likely to occur for network-heavy MapReduce jobs, where the ratio of map input to output is close to 1, and for large Hadoop clusters, with little data locality.

BIG DATA-PROCESSING ON CLOUD

The processing of Big Data is among the issues that should be well investigated to ensure an acceptable level of quality of service dealing with related Big Data constraints and generated structures. Cloud, as a powerful computation and storage platform, proves its suitability for processing and analyzing Big Data. However, current typical techniques of big graph data processing, such as MapReduce, may introduce high computation cost. In this context, several research works have been proposed to enhance the processing Big Data on cloud. As an example, Amazon EC2 infrastructure as a service is considered as a cloud-based distributed system for Big Data processing. In addition, MapReduce is used as a programming model for several research works dealing with the processing of Big Data over cloud computing such as the work detailed in Costa [17]. This model has been revised in Lee et al. [18] from a batch-processing framework into a more incremental one to analyse huge-volume incremental data on cloud. A stream as you go approach is proposed in Kienzler et al. [19] to access and process incremental data for data-intensive cloud applications.

Big Graph Data Processing

The management of Big Data requires the processing of big graph data that is expensive on cloud, in most cases, and that may introduce memory bottlenecks, deadlocks, and so on. In order to prevent such degradations, a technique is proposed in Yang et al. [20] to effectively process big graph data on cloud. By exploring spatial data correlation, a graph data set is partitioned into clusters. For a cluster, the workload can be shared by the inference based on time series. The proposed technique reduces the quantity and the processing time of Big Data sets by performing the following steps: (1) input a Big Data set to cloud platform; (2) filter the Big Data set using the proposed data compression algorithms. During the compression, the spatiotemporal correlations between data are used. The clustering and the order compression are combined together for better suppression effect when processing data sets using different distributions. The third step is to partition and distribute the filtered and compressed data/graph data on cloud according to the proposed scheduling algorithm for further data processing as service providing.

Analysis of Big Streaming Data

The analysis of large scale streaming data represents a processing issue that is well investigated. In fact, incremental feature extraction is an effective technique that facilitates data mining from large-scale streaming data. Partial Least Squares (PLS) is among the feature extraction techniques for the classification of traditional data. It enables the modeling of the relations between blocks of observed variables using latent variables. Moreover, PLS is built on the assumption that the observed data are generated by a system or a process that is driven by a small number of latent (not directly observed or measured) variables. Therefore, PLS aims to find uncorrelated linear transformations (latent components) of the original predictor variables that have high covariance with the response variables. Based on these latent components, PLS predicts the response variables and reconstructs the original matrix.

The technique introduced in Zeng and Li [21] is based on the incremental feature extraction, where a dimension reduction algorithm called Incremental PLS (IPLS) is proposed. The extraction process of the proposed approach is composed of two stages. During the first stage, the PLS target function updates the historical mean to extract the leading projection direction. In the second stage, the leading PLS projection vector is computed incrementally. It should be noted that PLS is a supervised feature extraction method, therefore it is efficient when all of the samples do not belong to the same class, since, in the other case, the covariance of the label vector relative to any other variable is zero. As a consequence, the projection directions computed by IPLS are considered as invalid in this situation.

Big Data Classification

The Use of a Hybrid Decision Tree Induction Scheme for Big Data Classification

Learning from Big Data is required in many fields such as machine learning, pattern recognition, image processing, etc. The major difficulties in learning from huge volumes of data include the following aspects: (1) it is difficult to accomplish computation on a single computer within an acceptable time; (2) the efficiency of the learning algorithm may be affected by the high-dimensional and multimodal features; and (3) the transformation of learning concepts is hard to perform since the data volume increases in a dynamic manner. In order to overcome such insufficiencies, the parallelization of sequential classification algorithms is adopted. The use of Decision Tree (DT) induction is considered among the promising classification algorithms for parallelization due to its simple implementation, the use of few parameters, and the low computation load. The generalization capability of a DT is among the required features during the processing of Big Data. This feature is largely influenced by the scale of the tree that may be affected by the degree of over-partitioning during the induction process and the selection of heuristic measure for splitting nodes. In order to resolve the over-partitioning problem, a hybrid DT induction scheme, called Extreme Learning Machine Tree (ELM-Tree), is introduced in Wang et al. [22]. An ELM-Tree differs from a DT model, since the leaf nodes are ELMs for an ELM-Tree model and they are linear regression functions for a DT model. The ELMs in the ELM-Tree have a fast-training speed feature, which helps learning from Big Data. This model uses the uncertainty reduction heuristics and embeds ELMs as its leaf nodes when the information gain ratios of all the cut-points are smaller than a given uncertainty coefficient. According to the ELM-Tree model, ELMs are embedded as the leaf nodes when a number of conditions are met. In an ELM, the input weights are randomly assigned and the output weights are analytically determined via the pseudo-inverse of the hidden layer output matrix [23]. The generation of ELM-Tree starts by splitting a nonleaf node, then determining an ELM leaf node. To deal with Big Data constraints, a parallel ELM-Tree model is proposed for Big Data classification to reduce computation time. This parallelization of the ELM-Tree is possible since the computations of information gain and gain ratio for different cut-points are all independent.

Representation of Classification Functions on Big Data

The classification of Big Data needs the organization of the data as graphs, which can often be reorganized according to a tree that should be processed. In Cohen [24], an orthogonal system is defined based on a local filtration, that is, the sub tree of a filtration comprising a vertex and its children. The different orthogonal systems constructed at the vertices at each level are then combined into a single orthogonal system by means of a special enumeration scheme, which is denoted as Leave Left Out (LLO) scheme. Thus, the construction method has a built-in self-similarity as well as a localization at different vertices of the filtration.

Low Data-Processing Approaches

A bottleneck for data analysis is observed due to the gap between computation and I/O capacity on processing units. Since different data-processing strategies have different impact on performance and cost, there is a need for flexibility in the location of data analytics. In this context, several potential data-analytics placement strategies along the I/O path are explored. To find out the best strategy to reduce data movement in a given situation, a flexible data analytics (FlexAnalytics) framework is proposed in Zou et al. [25]. Based on this framework, a FlexAnalytics prototype system is developed for analytics placement. The FlexAnalytics system ensures data pre-processing, runtime data analysis and visualization. It is also useful for large-scale data transfer and enhances the scalability and the flexibility of current I/O stack on processing platforms. According to experimental results, the FlexAnalytics framework increases data transition bandwidth and improves the end-to-end transfer performance at the application level.

SECURITY OF BIG DATA ON CLOUD

To efficiently ensure the processing and managing of Big Data on cloud infrastructures, a set of security measures should be deployed. This section outlines the security services and mechanisms required to ensure the protection of a set of security properties (confidentiality, integrity, and availability) for Big Data on cloud. Before introducing these measures, major common threats targeting Big Data on cloud will be discerned.

Threats for Big Data on the Cloud

There are several types of threats that target Big Data and the set of resources that are needed to ensure its storage, processing, and management. These threats may have an impact on the aforementioned three security properties. Application layer Denial-of-Service (DoS) attacks are among these threats targeting the availability of web services. These attacks aim at consuming resources by sending Simple Object Access Protocol (SOAP) requests that contain malicious XML content. These requests may bypass deployed intrusion detection and filtering techniques at the network or on the transport (TCP/IP) layer since they are considered as legitimate packets. Moreover, HTTP flooding with legitimate requests may result in a denial of service. Based on these attacks, the communication channel of the running server on cloud may be exhausted. Moreover, distributed denial of service attacks is more used by intruders compared to simple DoS as the probability of attack success is greater than a DoS using a unique malicious agent. This threat is more appropriate for cloud infrastructures since the processing is distributed over several malicious agents. Using cloud infrastructures, the main weakness in this case is related to the Cloud Broker as detailed in Varalakshmi and Selvi [26]. The users have to issue requests targeting this broker in order to receive the needed services. Making the broker unavailable may engender the unavailability of the entire service of the cloud system. This single point of failure may be the target of several attacks that may be tested using an attack generating tool as proposed in Vissers and Selvi [27]. Confidentiality may be affected by malicious activities basically for public cloud infrastructures or for private cloud infrastructures when attacks may be performed by internal users. In addition, the integrity of exchanged Big Data may be altered if malicious users have access to exchanged Big Data or to problems occurring during the data transfer.

Intrusion Detection

Intrusion detection is a security mechanism that helps detecting performed attacks on cloud infrastructures. Intrusion detection could be performed by anomaly or misuse-based techniques.

Anomaly-based classification may not be applied if attacks originate from multiple machines at lower speed, such as the scenario of Peer-to-Peer Botnets. In Singh et al. [28], the authors provide a scalable implementation of a quasi-real-time intrusion detection system based on the progress of open source tools like Hadoop, Hive, and Mahout. The proposed system provides a distributed framework using Hive for collecting exchanged network traffic and processing network traces enabling extraction of dynamic network features. It uses the parallel-processing power of Mahout to build a Random Forest-based Decision Tree model, which is applied to the detection of Peer-to-Peer Botnet attacks.

Big Data Confidentiality Assurance

The extraction of pertinent information from large volumes of data is an important task that should be efficiently protected in order to prevent intruders from learning extracted knowledge or even accessing stored Big Data. To solve the above problems, a new identity-based generalized signcryption scheme is proposed in Wei et al. [29]. This scheme that considers Big Data constraints is characterized by its ability to work only as an encryption scheme, a signature scheme or for both operations as a signcryption scheme. This scheme has a straightforward certificate management compared to the traditional cryptographic schemes.

Secure and Reliable Big Data Transmissions in Wireless Networks

Wireless networks are currently used in several fields, such as the military, governmental, and financial communications. Such networks are exposed to a set of attacks for wired networks in addition to some specific attacks that exploit wireless communications particularities. In order to deal with these threats, cooperative jamming, as a physical layer technique, has been developed to provide security for wireless networks. The work detailed in Shen and Zhang [30] is based on the aforementioned technique and proposes a two-hop transmission protocol to ensure secure and reliable Big Data transmissions in wireless networks with multiple eavesdroppers. The proposed protocol can provide flexible control of security, reliability, and energy balance performance, which characterizes how energy consumption for forwarding messages is balanced among all the relays.

Integrity Checking for Big Data Over Cloud

Integrity is a significant security property that should be ensured especially when dealing with huge volumes of data. This feature enables the detection of data alteration and helps to ensure the consistency of the stored data on cloud. In this context, a model for integrity checking on cloud computing is introduced in Barbierato et al. [31]. This model supports a Third Party Auditor (TPA), which is an entity used to ensure the integrity of Big Data, using the digital signature technique. The proposed model proves its efficiency for a number of situations that are performed by unauthorized attackers.

FUTURE PERSPECTIVES

We discuss in this section a set of unresolved issues for the management of Big Data on cloud, and we present the most interesting challenges related to the optimization of the management, processing, and security of Big Data on cloud in the presence of emergent technologies (e.g., mobile technologies). Several future research directions have been discussed in Attas and Batrafi [32] among a set of identified open issues.

The Use of Mobile Technologies as Sources of Big Data in Cloud Infrastructures

The extensive use of mobile devices in various critical domains, particularly healthcare, disaster recovery, and education, has enabled the generation of huge volumes of data. Mobile Cloud Computing (MCC) is developed to increase mobile storage by leveraging infinite cloud resources to provide storage capabilities with energy-dissipation prevention. Several MCC aspects and their related challenges have been already surveyed by researchers in addition to the Mobile Storage Augmentation (MSA) approaches. In Attas and Batrafi [32], an investigation is provided for the main MSA issues in three domains of mobile computing, cloud computing, and MCC. Moreover, it examines several credible MSA approaches and mechanisms in MCC and presents a classification of characteristics of cloud-based storage resources.

Security Assurance

The security of cloud infrastructures used to store and to process Big Data could be improved thanks to the centralization of Big Data and increased security-focused resources and mechanisms. Additional issues should be considered that are related to the loss of control over certain sensitive data and the lack of security for the stored kernels entrusted to cloud providers. In addition, several issues need special processing for private clouds, including unbalanced resources utilization, managing the security of the provided services, and operating over secure virtual private networks without isolating the private cloud infrastructure. Trust in clouds infrastructures is typically processed in a centralized manner which has the negative consequence of amplifying potential damage from node compromises, leaving such clouds vulnerable to numerous attacks.

Quality of Service Requirements

Applications generating Big Data and exploiting cloud infrastructures for their processing are characterized by Quality of Service (QoS) requirements, such as timeliness, scalability, high availability, trust, and security as specified in the so-called Service Level Agreements (SLAs). Current cloud technology is not fully tailored to comply with possible SLAs. In addition, to ensure that an application SLA is not violated, a resource overprovision policy is often adopted. This policy might lead to largely suboptimal use of hosting environment resources and energy overconsumption.

A QoS-aware hybrid cloud should be able to dynamically change the amount of resources made available to the applications it hosts to guarantee that the relevant SLA is satisfied. Furthermore, trust should be deployed as a multilevel service that takes into consideration varying users, requests, and IT infrastructures. This makes the QoS provision hard to achieve for time-constraining requests related to a service. In addition, failure-aware resource provisioning schemes capable of providing scalable users' QoS are among the needs that should be satisfied.

In addition, the architecture proposed should consider the constraints for private clouds, where resource management may become critical if a number of resources are shared among several available services. In public cloud infrastructures, the secure usage of the shared public cloud is more challenging compared to private clouds, since trust is an important issue to be provided and where multiple users' profiles should be appropriately handled.

Novel Dynamic Payment Schemes

The most common model employed in cloud computing is the "pay-as-you-go" model, where users ensure the payment of a fixed price per unit of use. In addition, several models for cloud computing pricing have been introduced, but they show limited applications in hybrid cloud architectures integrating private clouds. Moreover, pricing models currently used by cloud providers do not reflect dynamic resource prices due to changes in supply and demand. Dynamic pricing schemes suitable for allocating resources on hybrid clouds should be developed. In federated clouds, users request more than one type of resource from different infrastructures. In this case, pricing models can be developed for hybrid clouds based on specific game theories taking into consideration customer and provider behavior, the quality of available IT infrastructure, or using specific financial option theories considering cloud resources as assets to capture their realistic values.

Energy-Awareness

Energy is one of the resources that should be conserved in mobile computing, cloud computing, and MCC domains. The limitation of resources, processing, storage, and battery life of mobile devices can be prevented through rich cloud-based resources. In order to ensure energy conservation in mobile devices, energy-awareness using lightweight mobile augmentation frameworks and communication-aware approaches are required. The use of lightweight solutions may be among the solutions to be considered for offloading overheads related to processing.

Data Integrity

There are several storage services provided by varied cloud vendors where each running service has particularities that may lead to a data integrity issue. In order to deal with this problem, some solutions have been proposed such as the provided uniform interface, detailed in Mao et al. [33], that enables the access to various cloud storage services by exploiting middleware, SOA, and domain specific language approaches. Cryptographic functions should be defined to ensure the verification of data integrity taking into consideration Big Data and cloud infrastructures particularities. Big Data migration is also another issue that may affect integrity. It should be considered for the design of a unified standard storage infrastructure and management of heterogeneous resources.

Trust

Establishing trust is among the needs for end-users accessing deployed services that are provided through cloud infrastructures. Several studies have focused on trust in cloud resources such as the client-based privacy manager, proposed in Mowbray and Pearson [34], that helps reducing the risk related to data leakage and loss of privacy if sensitive data is processed on cloud. Encryption and decryption techniques have been used in Zhou and Huang [35] to protect user data, in addition to authorization and authentication services. Furthermore, new lightweight trust establishment techniques should be developed, similar to the proposed model in Wang et al. [36], with respect to the limited resources of mobile devices and wireless communication in cloud-based environments.

CONCLUSION

The huge amount of data generated continuously by running services, emerging technological devices and infrastructures, and the increasing growth of information systems represent big challenges for enterprise to store and manage these data efficiently. The deployment of cloud computing for Big Data has proved its usefulness and has been widely used for different types of applications in several areas. It is noted that it is also infused as a promising technique for critical fields, especially public safety. However, several constraints and issues should be considered and resolved to provide efficient services.

In this chapter, an overview of the different features of cloud environments for Big Data has been presented, followed by the challenges and limits around Big Data management in addition to the benefits of deploying cloud infrastructure. Moreover, this chapter has focused on the management and the processing of Big Data on cloud infrastructure, and has examined the security issues and requirements related to such environments.

REFERENCES

1. J. Phillips. *Building a Digital Analytics Organization: Create Value by Integrating Analytical Processes, Technology, and People into Business Operations.* Pearson FT Press, US, 2013.
2. B.M. Thuraisingham, V. Khadilkar, J. Rachapalli, T. Cadenhead, M. Kantarcioglu, K.W.Hamlen, L. Khan, and M.F. Husain. Cloud-centric assured information sharing. In Michael Chau, G. Alan Wang, Wei Thoo Yue, and Hsinchun Chen, editors, PAISI, volume 7299 of Lecture Notes in Computer Science, pages 1–26. Springer, Kuala Lumpur, Malaysia, 2012.

3. J. Weinman. As time goes by: The law of cloud response time. April 12, 2011.

4. C.K. Chui, F. Filbir, and H.N. Mhaskar. Representation of functions on big data: Graphs and trees. *Applied and Computational Harmonic Analysis*, 38(3): 489–509, 2014.

5. Z. Xu, Y. Liu, L. Mei, C. Hu, and L. Chen. Semantic based representing and organizing surveillance big data using video structural description technology. *The Journal of Systems and Software*, 102:217–225, 2015.

6. C.L.P. Chen and C.-Y. Zhang. Data-intensive applications, challenges, techniques and technologies: A survey on big data. *Information Sciences*, 275:314–347, 2014.

7. T. Garcia and T. Wang. Analysis of big data technologies and method—Query large web public rdf datasets on amazon cloud using Hadoop and open source parsers. *2013 IEEE Seventh International Conference on Semantic Computing (ICSC)*, pages 244–251, Irvine, California, September 16–18, 2013.

8. J. Manyika, M. Chui, B. Brown, J. Bughin, R. Dobbs, C. Roxburgh, and A. Hung Byers. *Big Data: The Next Frontier for Innovation, Competition, and Productivity*. McKinsey & Company, USA, June 2011.

9. S.A. Issa, R. Kienzler, M. El-Kalioby, P.J. Tonellato, D. Wall, R. Bruggmann, and M. Abouelhoda. Streaming support for data intensive cloud-based sequence analysis. *BioMed Research International*, 2013:1–16, 2013.

10. W. Lin, W. Dou, Z. Zhou, and C. Liu. A cloud-based framework for home-diagnosis service over big medical data. *Journal of Systems and Software*, 102:192–206, 2015.

11. A. Das, C. Lumezanu, Y. Zhang, V. K. Singh, G. Jiang, and C. Yu. *The 5th USENIX Workshop on Hot Topics in Cloud Computing (HotCloud'13)*, pages 1–6, San Jose, CA, USA, June 25–26, 2013.

12. S.J. Lusher, R. McGuire, R.C. van Schaik, C.D. Nicholson, and J. de Vlieg. Data-driven medicinal chemistry in the era of big data. *Drug Discov Today*, 19(7):859–868, July 2014.

13. D. Agrawal, A. El Abbadi, S. Antony, and S. Das. Data management challenges in cloud computing infrastructures. In *Proceedings of the 6th International Conference on Databases in Networked Information Systems*, DNIS'10, pages 1–10, Berlin, Heidelberg: Springer-Verlag, 2010.

14. S. VanRoekel. Moving fcc.gov into the cloud. Technical report, Federal Communications Commission, Washington, DC, USA, October 20, 2010.

15. N. Aminzadeh, Z. Sanaei, and S.H. Ab Hamid. Mobile storage augmentation in mobile cloud computing: Taxonomy, approaches, and open issues. *Simulation Modelling Practice and Theory*, 50:96–108, 2015.

16. Federal Communications Commission 2008. Performance and accountability report. Technical report, US: Federal Communications Commission, pages 1–173, SW, Washington, DC, USA, 2008.

17. F.F. Costa. Big data in biomedicine. *Drug Discovery Today*, 19(4):433–440, April 2014.

18. K.-H. Lee, Y.-J. Lee, H. Choi, Y.D. Chung, and B. Moon. Parallel data processing with mapreduce: A survey. *SIGMOD Record*, 40(4):11–20, January 2012.

19. R. Kienzler, R. Bruggmann, A. Ranganathan, and N. Tatbul. Stream as you go: The case for incremental data access and processing in the cloud. In *IEEE ICDE International Workshop on Data Management in the Cloud (DMC'12)*, pages 159–166, Washington, DC, USA, April 2012.

20. C. Yang, X. Zhang, C. Zhong, C. Liu, J. Pei, K. Ramamohanarao, and J. Chen. A spatiotemporal compression based approach for efficient big data processing on cloud. *Journal of Computer and System Sciences*. Special Issue on Theory and Applications in Parallel and Distributed Computing Systems, 80(8):1563–1583, December 2014.

21. X.-Q. Zeng and G.-Z. Li. Incremental partial least squares analysis of big streaming data. *Pattern Recognition*, 47:3726–3735, June 2014.

22. R. Wang, Y.-L. He, C.-Y. Chow, F.-F. Ou, and J. Zhang. Learning elm-tree from big data based on uncertainty reduction. *Fuzzy Sets and Systems*, 258:79–100, 2015.

23. G.-B. Huang, H. Zhou, X. Ding, and R. Zhang. Extreme learning machine for regression and multiclass classification. *IEEE Transactions on Systems, Man, and Cybernetics*, Part B, 42(2):513–529, 2012.

24. J. Cohen. Graph twiddling in a MapReduce world. *Computing in Science and Engineering*, 11(4):29–41, July 2009.

25. H. Zou, Y. Yu, W. Tang, and H.-W.M. Chen. Flexanalytics: A flexible data analytics framework for big data applications with i/o performance improvement. *Big Data Research*, 1:4–13, 2014.

26. P. Varalakshmi and S. Thamarai Selvi. Thwarting ddos attacks in grid using information divergence. *Future Generation Computer Systems*, 29(1):429–441, 2013.

27. T. Vissers, S. Thamarai Selvi, L. Pieters, K. Govindarajan, and P. Hellinckx. Ddos defense system for web services in a cloud environment. *Future Generation Computer Systems*, 37:37–45, 2014.

28. K. Singh, S.C. Guntuku, A. Thakur, and C. Hota. Big data analytics framework for peer-to-peer botnet detection using random forests. *Information Sciences*, 278:488–497, March 2014.

29. G. Wei, J. Shao, Y. Xiang, P. Zhu, and R. Lu. Obtain confidentiality or/and authenticity in big data by ID-based generalized signcryption. *Information Sciences*, 2014, in press.

30. Y. Shen and Y. Zhang. Transmission protocol for secure big data in two-hop wireless networks with cooperative jamming. *Information Sciences*, 281:201–210, June 2014.

31. E. Barbierato, M. Gribaudo, and M. Iacono. Performance evaluation of NoSQL big-data applications using multi-formalism models. *Future Generation Computer Systems*, 37:345–353, July 2014.

32. D. Attas and O. Batrafi. Efficient integrity checking technique for or securing client data in cloud computing. *International Journal of Electrical & Computer Sciences* (IJECS-IJENS), 11(5):43–48, October 2011.

33. H. Mao, N. Xiao, W. Shi, and Y. Lu. Wukong: A cloud-oriented file service for mobile Internet devices. *Journal of Parallel and Distributed Computing*, 72(2):171–184, February 2012.

34. M. Mowbray and S. Pearson. A client-based privacy manager for cloud computing. In *Proceedings of the Fourth International ICST Conference on COMmunication System softWAre and middlewaRE*, COMSWARE '09, pages 1–8, New York, NY: ACM, 2009.

35. Z. Zhou and D. Huang. Efficient and secure data storage operations for mobile cloud computing. In *Proceedings of the 8th International Conference on Network and Service Management*, CNSM '12, pages 37–45, Laxenburg, Austria, Austria, 2013. International Federation for Information Processing.

36. W. Wang, Z. Li, R. Owens, and B. Bhargava. Secure and efficient access to outsourced data. In *Proceedings of the 2009 ACM Workshop on Cloud Computing Security*, CCSW '09, pages 55–66, New York, NY: ACM, 2009.

CHAPTER 16

A User Data Profile-Aware Policy-Based Network Management Framework in the Era of Big Data

Fadi Alhaddadin, William Liu, and Jairo A. Gutiérrez

CONTENTS

D URING THE LAST DECADES, the flow of data has been rapidly increasing due to the continuous growth of computational power and the associated ability to compute data on a larger scale. For example, recent advances in web technologies have made it easy for users to provide and consume data content of any form, and this has created a critical need for a paradigm shift in current computing architectures and large-scale data-processing mechanisms [1]. Consequently, the concept of Big Data has emerged as a widely recognized trend, and it refers to very large data sets that are orders of magnitude bigger in volume, and more diverse that traditional data flows. They also include structured and semistructured data [2]. Big Data is defined as the high-velocity, and high-variety information assets that require new forms of processing to enable enhanced decision making, insight discovery, and process optimization [3]. In other words, it is the emergence of applications and services that generate massive collections of data. To process these high volumes of data in a cloud computing environment requires management frameworks that support a large number of applications, each of which has a small data footprint [4]. Cloud computing provides service to users via three popular paradigms: Infrastructure as a Service (IaaS), Platform as a Service (PaaS), and finally Software as a Service (SaaS), however, it can be extended to add another paradigm called Database as a Service (DaaS) in which database management systems (DBMS) can be accommodated on the cloud and accessed on a pay-as-you-go model as well as requiring low upfront investment at the user side [5]. Therefore, scalable DBMS are considered a critical part of the cloud infrastructure and play an important role in ensuring the smooth transition of applications from traditional enterprise infrastructures to next generation cloud infrastructures, which can handle this emerging Big Data trend. Today, cloud computing technology is regarded as an important trend toward future's distributed and ubiquitous computing services offered over the global internet [6]. It is also gaining a great deal of attention and popularity in our current society due to the benefits that it can flexibly offer to its users with various applications such as accommodating DBMS and other various applications for various purposes within the context of a pay-as-you-go model.

BACKGROUND

Despite the great benefits that cloud computing technology returns such as handling Big Data processes, the spread of cloud computing data centers has led to establishing huge-scale data centers, which comprise of thousands of computing nodes and consume massive amounts of electrical energy [7]. Power consumption is considered one of the main issues related to the success of cloud computing especially with the management of Big Data sets. Due to the ever-growing number of large cloud computing data centers and the continuously increasing scale of databases being handled, the electrical energy consumed by hardware facilities and cooling systems has increased notably. Greenpeace estimated that the total energy consumption of cloud systems including data centers and telecommunications was up to 622.6 billion KWh (Kilo Watt per Hour) in 2007 [8]. A research conducted in 2010 showed that cloud computing data centers in 2010 were responsible of 1.1%–1.5% of the total power consumed in the world [9]. As a consequence to the huge amount of energy consumed by cloud computing data centers, Gartner in 2007 estimated that the information and communication technologies (ICT) industry generates approximately 2% of the total global CO_2 emissions which is equal to that of the aviation industry [10]. Surprisingly, the main reason behind the huge amount of power consumption that cloud computing is responsible for is not only the quantity of computing resources or the inefficiency in power consumption of hardware devices, but rather lies in the inefficient usage of these resources.

One of the major causes of energy inefficiency in data centers is the idle power wasted when servers run at low utilization. Even at a very low CPU load or utilization, the power consumed is over 50% of the peak power [11]. A research which involved collecting data from more than 5000 production servers in a period of 6 months has shown that although servers usually are not idle, their utilization rarely approaches 100% as most of the time they operate at 10%–50% of their full capacity, and this leads to extra expenses on over-provisioning and thus extra total cost of acquisition (TCA) [12]. Thus, keeping servers underutilized contributes to a great inefficiency from the perspective of power consumption, which is today considered as a critical problem in the field of cloud computing.

RELATED WORK

Although cloud computing has been widely adopted in various fields in today's industry, the research on cloud computing is still at an early stage as many existing issues have not been yet fully addressed [13,14]. There are many threats and challenges in cloud computing that are currently being targeted by researchers and Big Data-processing applications that are seen to be significant contributors toward these issues such as data confidentiality, integrity and availability, as well as the huge processing power that these applications need which cause extra energy consumption in data centers. The processing of data in cloud computing requires a management framework that supports a large number of applications, each of which has a small data footprint. An example of Big Data is the DZero1 system which typically generates more than one terabyte of data per day, or famous social network websites such as Facebook which serves 570 billion page views per month, stores 3 billion new photos, and manages 25 billion pieces of content every month [5]. These figures illustrate the increasing growth of the size of data and data processing, which require efficient DBMS in order to be efficiency managed.

Moreover, due to the fact that cloud computing provides strong storage, computation, and distribution abilities, the International Data Corporation (IDC) estimates that 40% of data will be touched by cloud computing by the year 2020 [15]. This points toward a strong need for an efficient cloud management framework that handles the management of Big Data processing with a particular consideration to the energy efficiency of the cloud data center. In addition, there is a need for a more efficient data-processing mechanism that can handle the large-scale data flows in order for them to be smoothly processed by complex computing environments such as those configured for cloud computing. Several studies have been conducted with the goal of overcoming the issue of managing the Big Data processes with respect to cloud computing technology. In Das et al. [16], the authors have proposed a network management platform for Big Data-processing applications that is transparent to the application yet is able to quickly and accurately detect changes in their demand patterns. The platform is called FlowComb and it uses application domain knowledge to detect network transfers between the components of applications and often before they even start. It also uses software-defined networking to change the associated network paths to support these transfers. Experimental results showed that FlowComb could potentially reduce the process time of data by 35% of the time needed to process the same data flow without employing FlowComb.

However, the major issue in cloud computing technology today is energy efficiency, and this means that focusing on the issue from one perspective such as Big Data-processing applications might not be sufficient toward overcoming the issue of energy inefficiency. It is highly important to design a management framework for cloud computing infrastructure that can manage and handle applications such as data-processing applications and other applications in a more energy efficient way. The widespread use of cloud computing services is expected to increase rapidly the power consumed by ICT equipment in cloud computing environments [17]. The study in Zyga [18] has conducted research to investigate the use of cloud computing for three different services: storage services, software services, and processing services in public and private systems. Their results have shown that cloud computing is not always the greenest option in terms of power consumption. The increasing demand on cloud computing infrastructures and services has become a major environmental issue due to the amount of power it requires. Hence, the major aim of this study is to propose a solution for the problem of inefficient energy consumption in cloud computing. One of the major causes of energy inefficiency in cloud computing is the idle power wasted when data centers and servers run at low utilization rates.

Recently, a study in Gong Chen et al. [19] has identified a need for collaboration among servers, communication networks, and power networks in order to reduce the total power consumption by the entire ICT equipment in a cloud computing environment. Since the reliability of computing resources is one of the characteristics of cloud computing, the underutilization of computing resources has become a major issue and root cause of the inefficiency of energy consumption in those computing configurations. Servers may run on 10% utilization while they consume energy at their maximum consumption capabilities.

Data center energy savings can come from both hardware and software through accurate resource management. In Kuribayashi [17], the researcher gives an example of where accurate management of computing resources is needed for both processing time and network speed where both of them have strong impact on the energy consumption rates. They have found that slowing the processing of a server to reduce its power consumption rate can prolong not only its processing time, but also the bandwidth holding time in the network, this increases the power consumed by the network. Conversely, raising the processing speed of a server increases its power consumption but reduces the processing time, and consequently reduces the power consumed by the network. Similarly, the issue of underutilization of computing resources requires an accurate computing resources management framework in order to achieve efficient levels of energy consumption rates without negatively affecting the Quality of Service (QoS) delivered.

Service Level Agreements (SLA) Metrics

The QoS is a very important matter in the field of cloud computing and thus meeting its requirements and maintaining it is an essential requirement for the management of any cloud-based environment. In Firoiu et al. [20], the QoS of a network is defined in a variety of ways and includes a diverse set of service requirements such as performance, availability, reliability, security, and so on. All these service requirements are important aspects of a comprehensive network QoS service offering. The QoS refers to the capability of a network in providing better service to selected network traffic over various technologies such as Ethernet networks, and IP-routed networks which may use any or all of these underlying technologies [21]. The QoS is normally delivered in the context of an agreed SLA which can be specified in terms of many characteristics such as minimum throughput, availability, or maximum response time delivered by the deployed system. In Szigeti and Hattingh [22], it has stated that a successful QoS deployment includes three key phases: strategically defining the business objectives to be achieved via QoS, analyzing the service-level requirements of the traffic classes, and designing and testing QoS policies. The study in Tiso [23] argues that the network infrastructure must be designed to be highly available in order to successfully implement QoS, and the target for high availability of service is 99.999% up time. In other words, only 5 min of downtime is permitted per year. The transmission quality of the network is determined by three factors: loss, delay, and delay variation (i.e., jitter). Loss is a relative measure of the number of packets that were not received compared to the total number of packets transmitted. In order to obtain the highest availability of a network, losses during periods of noncongestion would be essentially zero. Delay is defined as the predetermined amount of time that a packet requires to reach the endpoint after being transmitted from the sending endpoint. Delay variation is the difference in the end-to-end delay between packets.

However, QoS requirements in cloud computing are normally delivered in a form of an SLA. SLA characteristics can then vary according to various applications domains and for cloud computing. It is necessary to define independent workload metrics to be used for evaluating the performance of the virtual machines (VMs) that are running in an IaaS configuration. The work in Beloglazov and Buyya [7] was on virtualization in cloud computing, which involved a competitive analysis and proven competitive ratios of optimal online deterministic algorithms for single VM migration and dynamic VM consolidation problems. They defined two workload independent metrics that can be used to evaluate the SLA delivered to any VM under IaaS. The first was the percentage of time during which active hosts have experienced CPU utilization of 100% (SLATAH), and the second dealt with the degradation of performance caused by VM migration (PDM). For this research, we have used two major SLA metrics (i.e., SLATAH and PDM) proposed in Beloglazov and Buyya [7].

SLA Violation Time per Active Host (SLATAH)
The first metric we choose for our research is the percentage of time in which active hosts have experienced a CPU utilization of 100%. This SLA metric is considered suitable to use because it helps toward validating our proposed approach that involves VM migrations and consolidation processes. The consolidation approach involves migrating VMs from a host to another, for the goal of switching off the "home" physical host to a power-saving mode to save energy. This requires selecting VMs to migrate, and further choosing a "new physical" host to accommodate them. Moreover, VM migrations serve toward balancing the load on physical servers (hosts). For that, the SLATAH metric has been chosen for our work because it observes and indicates to the host that it is experiencing 100% CPU utilization. When a host CPU capacity is being 100% utilized, VMs on this particular host might not be fully provided with the required performance level, this leads to performance degradation of VMs and hence SLA violations. The SLATAH is calculated as shown in Equation 16.1:

$$\text{SLATAH} = \frac{1}{N} + \sum_{i=1}^{N} \frac{Ts_i}{Ta_i} \tag{16.1}$$

where N indicates the number of hosts; Ts_i is the total time during which the host i has experienced the utilization of 100% leading to an SLA violation, Ta_i indicates the total time during which host i is in the active state (serving VMs). The SLATAH metric refers to the violation degree/level to the SLA in terms of controlling and monitoring the status of a particular host. If SLATAH is high, this means the host often reaches the maximum capacity utilization which leads to a violation in the agreed upon SLA.

Performance Degradation due to Migration
The second metric is the degradation of performance caused by VM migration (PDM). The reason for choosing the PDM as an SLA metric for our work is due to the nature of the study, as VM migration processes might have a negative impact on the performance of the VMs. When a VM is going through a migration process from a host to another, there is a period of time during the process in which the VM goes down. The downtime of the VM has a negative effect on the QoS delivered and therefore on its SLA terms. The PDM metric is calculated mathematically as shown in Equation 16.2.

$$\text{PDM} = \frac{1}{M} + \sum_{j=1}^{M} \frac{Cd_j}{Cr_j} \qquad (16.2)$$

where M indicates the number of VMs, Cd_j is the estimate of the performance degradation of the VM j caused by migration, Cr_j is the total CPU capacity requested by the VM j during its lifetime, which is estimated as 10% of the CPU utilization in Million Instructions per Second (MIPS) during all migrations of the VM j. Since both the SLATAH and PDM metrics have similar importance in terms of the level of SLA violation by the infrastructure, they can be combined into one SLA Violation (SLAV) metric, which is calculated as shown in Equation 16.3.

$$\text{SLAV} = \text{SLATAH} \times \text{PDM} \qquad (16.3)$$

Heuristic Algorithms for Dynamic VM Consolidation

The term "Heuristic" was initially created by the Greeks and its original meaning is discover. Algorithms that either give nearly the right answer or provide partial solutions are called heuristic algorithms. Heuristic algorithms' validation and complexity is one of the most important topics in the field of computer science today [24]. Heuristic algorithms are used in computer science to quickly solve complex problems and perform challenging tasks. In order to understand the concept of heuristic algorithms, the Travelling Salesman problem [25] is one of the classic enigmas in computer science for which heuristic algorithms have found many solutions. More information about heuristic algorithms can be found in Kokash [24]. Since the beginning of Genetic Algorithms (GA) and heuristic algorithms research in general, it has become known that parameters and operators have significant impact on the optimization process and the efficiency of such algorithms [26]. Due to the nature of this study, in order to obtain the best results from heuristic algorithms, it is essential to define parameters and operators which are closely linked to our research target problem.

For our research, the nature of the problem is fully related to VM migration and consolidation processes hence, choosing suitable heuristic algorithms and defining suitable parameters and operators is highly important to solve this problem.

In Beloglazov and Buyya [7], the researchers have proposed unique adaptive heuristics that are based on analysis of historical data on the resource usage for performance and energy efficient dynamic consolidation of VMs. They have proposed five host overloading detection algorithms: Static Threshold VM allocation policy (THR), Inter Quartile Range (IQR), Median Absolute Deviation (MAD), Local Regression (LR), Local Regression Robust (LRR), and three VM selection algorithms; Minimum Migration Time (MMT), Random Selection (RS), and Maximum Correlation (MC). Table 16.1 illustrates the characteristics of these different algorithm combinations (median values). All combinations of host overloading detection algorithms and selection algorithms have been extensively simulated on large-scale experimental setups with the goal of comparing their efficiencies in terms of the trade-offs between power consumption and QoS violations (SLAV).

TABLE 16.1   Simulation Results of the Best Algorithm Combinations and Benchmark Algorithms

Policy	ESV ($\times 10^{-3}$)	Energy kWh	SLAV ($\times 10^{-5}$)	SLATAH (%)	PDM (%)	VM migr. ($\times 10^{3}$)
NPA	0	2419.2	0	0	0	0
DVFS	0	613.6	0	0	0	0
THR-MMT-1.0	20.12	75.36	25.78	24.97	0.10	13.64
THR-MMT-0.8	4.19	89.92	4.57	4.61	0.10	17.18
IQR-MMT-1.5	4.00	90.13	4.51	4.64	0.10	16.93
MAD-MMT-2.5	3.94	87.67	4.48	4.65	0.10	16.72
LRR-MMT-1.2	2.43	87.93	2.77	3.98	0.07	12.82
LR-MMT-1.2	1.98	88.17	2.33	3.63	0.06	11.85

Based on the results illustrated in Table 16.1, the difference in efficiency among all the proposed consolidation algorithms in terms of SLA violations and power consumption ratios is clear. The dynamic VM consolidation algorithms (NPA and DVFS) significantly perform better than static allocation policies; however, they lead to greater power consumption rates in comparison to all other consolidation algorithms. There is also a proportional relationship between the number of VM migrations and the SLATAH metric for all the static allocation policies. The reason behind the variation of efficiency levels lies on the details of each algorithm and the metrics that each algorithm uses to select and allocate VMs from one host to another. According to the results in Table 16.1, LR-MMT-1.2 produces the best trade-off between power consumption and SLA violations due to the relatively small number of VM migrations, while the efficiency in terms of the same trade-off decreases by going up in the table as LRR-MMT-1.2 is the second best algorithm followed by MAD-MMT-2.5, and so on. In this research, we intend to employ the top three static allocation policies which are LR, LRR and MAD, one dynamic VM consolidation algorithm (DVFS), and MMT as the VM selection policy proposed by Beloglazov and Buyya [7]. We aim at using these policies for the goal of designing our proposed system model and validate it toward overcoming the issue of underutilized computing resources in cloud-based environments and to eventually reduce the amount of energy consumed without violating the SLA.

Static Allocation Policies
Local Regression (LR)   The main idea behind the LR algorithm is fitting simple models to localized subsets of data for the goal of building up a curve that approximates the original data. LR is based on the Loess method proposed in Cleveland [27]. The observations (x_i, y_i) are assigned neighborhood weights using the *tricube weight* function presented in Equation 16.4

$$T(u) = \begin{cases} (1-|u|^3)^3 & \text{if } |u| < 0 \\ 0 & \text{otherwise} \end{cases}$$

(16.4)

Assuming that $\Delta i = (x) = |x_i - x|$ is the distance between x and x_i and $\Delta i(x)$ denotes these distances ordered from shortest to longest, then the neighborhood weight for the observation (x_i, y_i) is calculated using Equation 16.5 below.

$$w_i(x) = T\left(\frac{\Delta i(x)}{\Delta_{(q)}(x)}\right) \tag{16.5}$$

For x_i such that $\Delta i(x) < \Delta_{(q)}(x)$ where q denotes to the number of observations in the subset of data localized around x, the size of the subnet is then defined by a parameter of the method called bandwidth. For example, if the degree of the polynomial fitted by this method is 1, then the parametric family of functions is $(y) = (a) + (bx)$. The line is fitted in the observations subset using the weighted least squares method with weight $w_i(x)$ at (x_i, y_i). The values of (a) and (b) can be calculated by Equation 16.6.

$$\sum_{i=1}^{n} w_i(x)(y_i - a - bx_i)^2 \tag{16.6}$$

This approach is used to fit the trend polynomial and find the last k observations of the CPU utilization where $(k) = q/2$. The polynomial is fit for one single point and the last observation of the CPU utilization is the right boundary (x_k) of the data set. In Cleveland [27], all fitted polynomials of the degree 1 typically distort peaks in the interior of the configuration of observations, whereas polynomials of degree 2 remove the distortion but result in higher biases at boundaries. This is the reason behind choosing polynomials of the degree 1 as it reduces the bias at the boundary. Assuming that (x_k) is the last observation, and (x_1) is the $(k\text{th})$ observation from the right boundary. For that, (x_i) is assumed to satisfy $(x_1) \le (x_k) \le (x_k)$, then $(x_k) = \Delta i(x_k) - (x_i)$, and $0 \le (\Delta i(x_k)/\Delta 1(x_k)) \le 1$. Hence, the function of the tricube weight can be simplified as $T^*u = (1 - u^3)^3$ for $0 \le u \le 1$, and the weight function can be formulated as shown in Equation 16.7:

$$w_i(x) = T^*\left(\frac{\Delta i(x_k)}{\Delta 1(x_k)}\right) = \left(1 - \left(\frac{x_k - x_i}{x_k - x_1}\right)^3\right)^3 \tag{16.7}$$

In LR, with consideration to the explained method which is deried from Loess, we find new trend line $\hat{g}(x) = \hat{a} + \hat{b}_x$ where each new observation is used to estimate the next observation $\hat{b}(x_k + 1)$. The algorithm therefore decides whether the host is overloaded and there is a need for VM migration or not with consideration to the following inequalities shown in Equation 16.8:

$$s \cdot \hat{g}(x_k + 1) \ge 1, \quad x_k + 1 - x_k \ge t_m \tag{16.8}$$

where $s \in R^+$ is the safety parameter; and t_m denotes to the maximum time required for a migration of any of the VMs allocated to the host.

Local Regression Robust (LRR) The Robust local regression (RLR) is an extension to the LR described in the previous subsection. Since the (LR) described in the previous section is considered vulnerable to outliners and extreme readings due to leptokurtic or heavy-tailed distribution, the authors in Cleveland [27] have proposed the addition of the robust estimation method *bisquare* to find the "*least squares*" for more accurate parametric fitting in the entire distribution of observations. The starting fitting process is done with weights defined by the tricube weight function mentioned earlier. The fit then gets evaluated at the x_i to get the fitted values $\widehat{y}_i$, and the residuals $\widehat{\in}_i = y_i - \widehat{y}_i$. In the next step, every observation (x_i, y_i) is assigned an additional robustness weight r_i, whose value depends on the magnitude of $\widehat{\in}_i$. Every observation is assigned the weight $r_i w_i(x)$, where r_i is defined as shown in Equation 16.9:

$$r_i = B\left(\frac{\widehat{\in}_i}{6_s}\right) \tag{16.9}$$

where "s" denotes to the MAD for the least-square fit or subsequent weighted fit as shown in Equation 16.11, and $B(u)$ denotes to the bisquare weight function shown in Equation 16.10.

$$B(u) = \begin{cases} (1 - u^2)^2 & \text{if } |u| < 1 \\ 0 & \text{otherwise} \end{cases} \tag{16.10}$$

$$s = \text{median}\left|\widehat{\in}_i\right| \tag{16.11}$$

The next observation is then estimated using the estimated trend line, by applying the method described in previous section for the goal of deciding whether the host is overloaded or not with consideration to the inequalities shown in Equations 16.8.

Median Absolute Deviation (MAD)   One way of deciding whether there is a need for VM migration can be based on the utilization threshold of the physical host. This can be done by simply setting upper and lower utilization thresholds for hosts and keeping the total utilization of the CPU by all the VMs between these thresholds. If the utilization of a host falls below the lower threshold, all VMs have to be migrated from this host in order to switch it off to save energy. If the utilization exceeds the upper threshold, VMs have to be migrated to another host to avoid potential violations to the SLA. However, due to the fact that fixed threshold values are not suitable for environments with dynamic and unpredictable workloads, there is a need for other techniques that can automatically adjust the utilization threshold of hosts based on statistical analysis of historical data collected during the life time of the VMs. One solution toward overcoming the issue of setting up threshold values for hosts is relying on the strength of deviation of the CPU utilization. When the deviation is high, the value of the upper utilization threshold is low because CPU utilization is vulnerable to reach the maximum utilization value and therefore cause an SLA violation.

The MAD can be defined as a measure of statistical dispersion. Its estimates scale more robustly than the sample variance or standard deviations as it interacts more accurately with a distribution without a mean or variance, such as the Cauchy distribution [28]. The MAD is a robust statistic; it is more resilient to outliers in data sets than the standard deviation. With standard deviations, distances from the mean are squared hence, large deviations are weighted more heavily, and thus this statistic can be greatly influenced by outliers. In the MADs measure, the distances magnitude of a small number of outliers is not relevant.

For instance, if we assume a data set of $(X_1, X_2, X_3, X_4, \ldots, X_n)$, the MAD is defined as the median of the absolute deviations from the data set's median as shown in the following equation:

$$\text{MAD} = \text{median}_i \left(|X_i - \text{median}_j(X_j)| \right) \tag{16.12}$$

In other words, the MAD is defined as the median of the absolute values of a data set. Hence, the upper utilization threshold can be calculated using the following equation:

$$T_u = 1 - s \cdot \text{MAD} \tag{16.13}$$

where $s \in R^+$ the parameter of the method that defines how aggressively the system consolidates VMs. Moreover, the parameter s facilitates the adjustment of the safety of the method; the lower "s" decreases the energy consumption but causes higher SLA violation due to aggressive consolidation of VMs.

Dynamic VM Consolidation Algorithm
Dynamic Voltage Frequency Scaling (DVFS)   DVFS is a commonly used technique to save power on a wide range of computing systems, from embedded, laptop and desktop systems to high-performance server-class systems [29]. DVFS is a very popular power management technique where the clock frequency of a processor is decreased to allow a corresponding reduction in the supply voltage. DVFS offers great opportunities to dramatically reduce energy consumption by adjusting both the voltage and frequency levels of a system according to the changing characteristics of its workloads [30]. DVFS is able to reduce the power consumption of complementary metal-oxide-semiconductor (CMOS) integrated circuits [31], such as those used in modern computer processors by reducing the frequency at which it operates as shown in the following equation:

$$P = CfV^2 + P_{\text{static}} \tag{16.14}$$

where C is the capacitance of the transistor gates which depends on feature size, f denotes the operating frequency, and V denotes the supply voltage.

The main idea of the DVFS technique is to intentionally scale down the CPU performance, when it is not fully utilized, by decreasing the voltage and frequency of the CPU. The

DVFS algorithm can be applied in various applications, however, due to the nature of this study, and its research objectives which are fully related to VM migration, we here present the four major processes that DVFS performs in order to reduce energy consumption under the umbrella of VM migration in virtualized environments. The DVFS algorithm adjusts the hosts' energy consumption according to their CPU utilization. There are four main processes that DVFS performs in order to reduce the total energy consumed in a data center:

- The first step involves getting signal acquisition of the system load (CPU utilization).

- The system load is then used to predict the amount of energy it requires in the next period of time.

- The predicted amount of energy is then transformed into the desired frequency, and therefore the clock from the chip set is changed accordingly.

- Finally, the new frequency is used to calculate the new voltage, and then the power management module gets notified to adjust the voltage of the CPU.

- More information on the DVFS algorithm can be found in Agrawal et al. [1].

VM Selection Policy
Minimum Migration Time (MMT)   The MMT policy migrates VMs according to the length of time they require to complete their migration processes. MMT works by listing all VMs and sorting them according to the time they require to complete their migration. The VM that requires the minimum time to complete its migration is selected for migration. The first step an MMT algorithm takes in its operation is listing VMs that are running in one host and are eligible for migration. Once all VMs are listed for migration, the algorithm looks for VMs which require the least time to complete their migration process and selects them for migration to another host. The process of finding the VM migration time is fully related to the RAM utilized by the VM. The migration time for a VM is estimated as the amount of RAM utilized by a VM divided by the spare network bandwidth available for the home host. Let us assume that host j is currently allocated a number of VMs running on it, and V_j is the set of VMs running on host j. The MMT algorithm selects the VM that satisfies the conditions formalized in the following equation:

$$\mu \in V_j \left| \forall_a \in V_j, \frac{RAM_\mu(\mu)}{NET_j} \le \frac{RAM_\mu(a)}{NET_j} \right. \tag{16.15}$$

where $RAM_\mu(\mu)$ is the amount of RAM that is currently utilized by the VM a, and NET_j is the spare network bandwidth available for host j.

Issues with the Current Systems
One of the main advantages that cloud computing offers to users is the pay-as-you-go elasticity [2]. Cloud computing allows users to pay for what they actually use based on time,

storage capacity, and other factors that can be agreed on between the cloud provider and users instead of paying for what they can potentially use. However, the current implementation of virtualized cloud computing environments is not yet efficient due to the issue of underutilization of computing resources. The underutilization of computing resources causes extra energy consumption and therefore increases the operating cost of computing resources in the cloud. Nevertheless, the underutilization of computing resources can also be a disadvantage for cloud clients; for example, clients may demand the highest available QoS from the cloud provider for a certain time window during the day, while they do not need the same QoS at other time window. According to the current system model, for clients, in order to satisfy their requirements during the time window in which the highest available QoS is needed, they need to purchase the highest available QoS throughout the day hence overpaying for the required services.

THE UDP-PBNM FRAMEWORK

Policy-Based Management (PBM)

PBM is one of the active research topics that has been driven by the great complexity inherent in the administration and management of today's networking and telecommunications systems [32]. It is today attracting considerable research focus as an empowering technology for managing large scale, heterogeneous information systems and communications infrastructure [33]. The PBM has attracted significant attention both from industry and the academic research community in recent years, and it has been recognized that PBM can effectively provide good means to solve the puzzle of integrated IP/telecom management [34]. PBM is based on defining a set of global rules, according to which a network or distributed system must operate [35]. In Berto-Monleon et al. [36], PBM is defined as the technology that provides the tools for an automated management of networks. It focuses on delivery of services to users and applications rather than devices and interfaces, and thus enables a holistic management of the network.

A research conducted in Agrawal et al. [37] aimed to provide an overview of how the policy management for autonomic computing (PMAC) platform works and manages networked systems. The researchers intended to demonstrate the concept and the technical issues associated with the management model on networked systems such as cloud computing systems. The outcomes of the study revealed the ability of policy-based network management (PBNM) to reduce the burden on the human administrator in such networks by providing systematic means to create, modify, distribute, and enforce policies for managed resources [37]. In Verma [38], a research was conducted on the PBM system and its usability for network administration purposes. The main objective of the study was to demonstrate how a network administration can be simplified using a PBM system. It also intended to express the main framework-related issues encountered and those that need to be considered when developing PBM systems such as the critical issue of policy conflicts. The policy conflict issue occurs when two or more policies are due to be enforced simultaneously due to satisfactory conditions for both of them at the same time. The outcome of the research indicated that the PBM framework can be greatly beneficial toward simplifying the management of networks hence achieving more accuracy in network management.

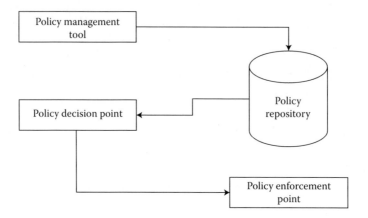

FIGURE 16.1   The IETF/DMTF policy framework.

PBM Architecture

The general PBM framework we present is considered as an adaptation of the Internet Engineering Task Force (IETF) policy framework [39]. IETF is an open international community of network designers, operators, vendors, and researchers concerned with the evolution of internet architecture and the smooth operation of the internet, more information on IETF is available in Davies et al. [40]. The IETF framework for Distributed Management Task Force (DMTF) is shown in Figure 16.1, which consists of four main elements: policy management tool, policy repository, policy decision point (PDP), and policy enforcement point (PEP). Components of the DMTF framework all work together toward managing a particular distributed system by enforcing policies.

Policy Management Tool

The policy management tool is defined as the component of the framework which allows defining policies to be enforced within the network. Due to the fact that a policy management tool is not defined by the IETF standards, in this study, we focus on this component in terms of how it can leverage the power of policies to simplify the provisioning and configuring of the different devices within the network. The policy management tool simplifies the management functions of a network via two elements of the policy management tool and the policy architecture: centralization and business-level abstraction [38].

Centralization is the process of defining all the device provisioning and configuration at a single point (policy management tool) rather than provisioning and configuring each device itself. This reduces the manual efforts that an administrator puts to configure and provision devices especially in large-scale networks. With a policy management tool, the network administrator inputs the policies needed for network operation into the management tool that populates the repository component, which is discussed further in the section. For example, in a network that comprises 1000 devices, on average, the administrator needs 10 min to configure each of these devices hence he/she needs over a week to complete the configuration work for all devices within the network, while with the policy-based solution, the network administrator requires 15 min to populate the repository with appropriate policies, and other components of the framework such as the PDP and the PEP will take care of the rest.

Business-level abstraction simplifies the job of the policy administrator by defining the policies in terms of a language closer to the business needs of an organization rather than in terms of the technical language needed for its deployment. For example, we assume a case of a network operator that needs to define two levels (high and low) of risk. With the business-level abstraction, it is very simple for an administrator to identify each risk level and to define which level they may map to. The business-level abstractions fully depend on the business needs and the technology that the policies are being defined for, as the business needs of an organization may be satisfied by many different technologies. For example, business needs such as an SLA can be satisfied by technologies such as capacity planning [41] or content distribution [42], while a business need such as establishing a secure virtual private network may be satisfied using IP Security (IPSec) [43] or TLS protocol [44].

Policy Repository

The policy repository is the component where policies, which have been created by the policy management tool, are stored. In order to ensure interoperability across products from different vendors, information and policies stored in the repository must correspond to an information model specified by the Policy Framework Working Group [38]. The policy repository may have many different interfaces enabled, in order to allow different types of users to manipulate the contents of the policy database [45].

Policy Decision Point

PDP is the component of the framework that is responsible for interpreting the policies stored in the repository and communicating them to the PEP, which is discussed in the following subsection. PDP works by translating a policy into a form that is understandable to network devices. PDP is an intermediary point between the point that is responsible for enforcing policies on devices within the network (PEP), and the repository where polices are stored in the system.

Policy Enforcement Point

PEP is the component in which policies are actually enforced; decisions are actually enforced; policy decisions are primarily made at the PDP [45]. The PEP is responsible for starting the interaction between the components of the entire system, in other words, in case of an event, the PEP formulates a request for a policy decision and sends it to the PDP, and hence the PEP is the component that detects events and request decisions to be made from the PDP. As soon as a request is formulated and sent to the PDP, the PDP decides which policy to enforce and then forwards it to the PEP to enforce it on the network devices.

User Data Profile-Aware Differentiated Services Architecture

In response to the issue of power consumption caused by insufficient usage of computing resources in cloud-based environments, this research presents a new approach that aims at tackling these issues and producing an efficient trade-off between energy consumption and

QoS. The key concept of the proposed management framework is the consolidation processes toward better utilization efficiency of computing resources. Consolidation processes are done in virtualized cloud environments via migrating VMs from a host to another. The consolidation processes involve switching off physical nodes after migrating VMs from them to other hosts in a particular data center. The processes of VM migration are fully dependent on certain criteria, which will be discussed further in this section. The User Data Profile-aware Policy-based Network Management (UDP-PBNM) framework involves a dynamic UDP-aware policy management mechanism that can manage cloud resources in a virtualized-cloud environment. The main goal of the UDP-PBNM framework is to reduce the extra energy consumption caused by an inefficient usage of computing resources without aggressively impacting on the QoS provided to users. The proposed approach also aims at improving the cloud infrastructure in terms of business for both cloud provider and cloud clients by reducing the operating costs of the cloud infrastructure (data centers) as well as facilitating more options for users in order to better manage their ICT costs hence creating more means of elasticity in the field of cloud computing. In order to successfully achieve the objectives of this research, there are several terms that have to be carefully considered when dealing with a problem related to cloud computing such as QoS. QoS is a broad topic in distributed systems such as cloud computing and is often referred to as the resource reservation control mechanisms in place to guarantee a certain level of performance and availability of service [46].

The UDP-PBNM Framework

The main contribution of this study is to propose a new framework for managing a group of green VMs migration policies in a virtualized cloud environment, with the goal of overcoming the issue of underutilization of computing resources which causes inefficiency in power consumption while still satisfying user requirements in cloud data centers. In order to design an accurate management framework for any cloud-based environment, we propose a new system model that uses several adaptive heuristic algorithms for dynamic VMs consolidation as proposed by [7] and that can be managed using a PBM framework. The objective of our proposed system model is twofold; first, it addresses the issue of underutilized computing resources by dynamically consolidating VMs, hence reducing the power consumption. Second, it involves users in the management of their own profiles and facilitates more flexibility in terms of service schemes that a cloud provider can offer to users; this helps users decide what and how a cloud service can best suit and satisfy their organizations' or individuals' needs with consideration to costs and time benefiting both cloud users and cloud providers.

The main feature of our UDP-PBNM framework is that it allows users to choose the QoS level that they need for a particular time-window in their UDP. The system allows users to switch from a particular QoS mode to another. For example, a user might demand the highest available QoS during business hours and the lowest available QoS with cheaper costs after business hours with the goal of minimizing the costs of their cloud data usage. Enabling users to manage their required QoS can vastly contribute toward addressing the issue of resources underutilization, because it decreases the operating costs of the cloud by eliminating the energy consumed due to underutilized resources. In order to illustrate our proposed system model, we introduce an example of a cloud network which provides four data service schemes to users at four different price levels. Each service scheme has a different QoS level; hence each service scheme has a different price for users. The differentiation between service schemes happens according to the SLA metrics defined and discussed in previous section. The price of the service scheme is inversely correlated with the SLA violation. In other words, the service scheme that provides QoS with a higher SLAV has relatively cheaper price than other service schemes providing service with a lower SLAV metric. The reason behind the low cost of any service scheme that provides QoS with SLAV is due to the low cost of producing it on the cloud infrastructure end, because the higher SLAV indicates higher VMs consolidation rates and therefore less power consumption. This is unlike previous models in which cloud providers paid high power bills just for delivering the highest available QoS to users who did not necessarily need it.

Each service scheme is generated using an adaptive heuristic consolidation algorithm proposed in Beloglazov and Buyya [7]. We opt to design our proposed system with three service schemes that provide QoS with SLAV on different levels, and another scheme which provides the highest possible QoS without any degradation of service. The process of deciding the SLA for each service scheme happens through simulating the heuristic algorithm used for that scheme to find out the percentage of performance degradation caused by the algorithm due to aggressive VMs consolidation processes. Based on the QoS degradation percentage, SLA terms are set and the price for that particular service scheme is decided accordingly. For example, a particular service scheme denoted as Service C provides service with 8% performance degradation, while another service scheme denoted as Service B provides service with 4% performance degradation. The purchasing price for Service C will be relatively cheaper than the price for Service B. This allows users to minimize the cost of their IT services during the time when QoS is not a big concern for them. For example, a customer might not demand high QoS during the night time; they might only demand email service, hence, a delay of service or any sort of performance degradation might not have an impact on their business. Therefore, a cheaper price for their cloud service is beneficial to them in terms of business as it reduces their business operating costs. On the other hand, the cloud provider obtains the benefit of reducing the amount of power consumed by data centers. The consolidation processes that take place due to the heuristic algorithm (policy) leads to a reduction of power consumption as seen in Table 16.1; this eventually generates significant savings in terms of power consumption and operating costs.

Policy-Based Management
Once all service schemes are decided (heuristic algorithms), it becomes compulsory to employ a management framework that enables cloud users to switch from a service scheme to another without the necessity of having a manual administration at the cloud provider end. For that, we propose the adoption of a PBNM framework that can automatically switch policies according to the SLA signed between cloud service provider and cloud users. PBNM is a promising solution for managing heterogeneous networks. It addresses the requirements for providing flexible and dynamic management and deals with the

escalating size and complexity of modern systems. PBNM aims at simplifying the complex management tasks of large-scale systems, since the system based on a number of policies monitors the network and automatically enforces appropriate actions [3]. As discussed, the PBNM framework consists of four main components namely: policy management tools, a policy repository, PDPs, and finally PEPs. Policy management tools are used by the administrator to define policies to be enforced within the network [3].

User Data Profile

In order to implement our proposed system model, we propose a new architectural component called the UDP, which is a database that contains instructions that a user chooses for the management of his/her profile in order to satisfy their needs. The UDPs refer to the sequence of policies that are to be used according to time, work load, or other metrics decided by users within the available options offered by the cloud provider. For example, a user can decide to purchase Service A during business hours (from 8 a.m. to 5 p.m.), switching to Service B for the rest of the day; these requirements are coded into the system by users via a user interface supplied by the cloud service provider. A UDP decides the SLA terms agreed on between the cloud provider and the user. The policy repository component stores all policies produced by the policy management tool in the system. All UDPs are also stored in the policy repository. The cloud system deals with each user according to their profiles. Each rule in a UDP has a policy code in the repository to comply with. For example, at 5 p.m. the system automatically invokes a policy from the repository to be enforced by the PEP to switch the user from Service A to Service B as per our previous example, and at 8 a.m. another policy switches the user from Service B to Service A, and so on. Figure 16.2 illustrates how a UDP can be generated.

The PEP is the component that is responsible for enforcing policies throughout the network (cloud system). The PEP uses the PDP as an intermediary in order to communicate with the repository. The PDP is responsible for interpreting the policies stored in the repository and communicating them to the PEP.

	User Details	
User ID :		7767758
User Name:		ABC
User Type:		Business
	Service Scheme Sequence	
Start		End
8am	to	5pm ---- Service (A)
5pm	to	8am ---- Service (B)
	Usage Meter	
240 Hours ------- Service (A)		
720 Hours ------- Service (B)		

FIGURE 16.2   Example of a UDP.

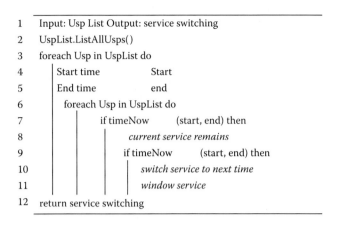

```
1    Input: Usp List Output: service switching
2    UspList.ListAllUsps( )
3    foreach Usp in UspList do
4    │  Start time          Start
5    │  End time            end
6    │    foreach Usp in UspList do
7    │    │      if timeNow       (start, end) then
8    │    │      │   current service remains
9    │    │      │   if timeNow       (start, end) then
10   │    │      │   │  switch service to next time
11   │    │      │   │  window service
12   return service switching
```

FIGURE 16.3   UDP-aware policy switching (UDP-PS).

To solve the problem of policy switching, we propose the UDP-aware Policy Switching (UDP-PS) algorithm presented in Figure 16.3. The metric used in our proposed algorithm is time; however, the same algorithm can be used with other metrics such as work load, utilization or just by modifying metrics in the algorithm and stating the preferred one. In steps 2–4, the scheduler sets the parameters as metrics to be used. The key parameters according to our proposed algorithm are the start time and the end time. The start time indicates the start time of a particular time window for a particular service scheme according to the UDP of each cloud user, while the end time indicates the end time of the same particular time window.

Using the same example mentioned earlier in the chapter, a user might decide to purchase Service A from 8 a.m. to 5 p.m., the start time for Service A for this particular user is 8 a.m., while the end time for the same service for the same user is 5 p.m.; therefore this particular user during this particular time window (8 a.m. to 5 p.m.) should be provided with Service A. Using the parameters defined in steps 2–4, and in steps 5–7, for each UDP, the scheduler checks if the current real time falls within between the start time and end time for the current service (time window) provided for a particular user at that particular moment. If the current time falls in that time window, the scheduler lets the current service continue without switching it. In steps 8–11, if the scheduler finds that the current real time does not fall within the current time window for the service being provided to a particular user, it looks for the second time window in which the current real time falls within, and then switches the current provided service to the service for the proper time window such as Service B.

An Example of the Proposed Framework

In order to illustrate our proposed system architecture, we find it useful to draw an example scenario of a cloud service provider with two major clients: a university and a bank. The cloud provider has two major architectural units which are part of the PBM framework namely policy management tool and repository, both are connected to the main policy distribution point (PDP), which belongs to the cloud provider's system architecture, it is also called the mother PDP. The main role of the mother PDP is deciding policies to be invoked from the policy repository unit to be distributed and enforced in further steps in the system. Each client, in order to manage their own network, has an internal PDP as a gateway between them and the cloud service provider. The clients' main PDP is connected to the mother PDP in order to communicate with the cloud provider system and receive policies to be further distributed to the internal PDPs within their own network. In our example scenario, the bank receives policies from the mother PDP through its local main PDP which is as mentioned earlier considered as the gateway to the cloud service provider. The main local PDP in the bank has another policy repository that is created internally by the bank in order to store policies on the local system/ network; however, it was not drawn on the figure with the goal of simplifying the example and to better illustrate the main concept of our proposed system architecture. The main local PDP forwards policies to another PDP within the local system that is responsible for distributing these policies to users according to their UDPs. Each user has a PEP assigned to it, in other words, each user receives services and works according to policies delivered to it through its assigned PEP. In our example, a user can be a local network or a group of computers connected within one network that can be a particular branch in the bank or a department, and so on. Policies enforced on each user are decided by the PDP according to the user's UDP.

As seen in Figure 16.4, each user has a PEP and UDP in order to be part of the system. Each device runs an instance of PEP and its corresponding UDP. The PEP reads instructions from the UDP and communicates with the PDP accordingly. The PDP retrieves policies from the policy repository and sends them to the PDP. The PDP responds to the PEP and supplies the PEP with the policies to be enforced on its particular user. The second client in our example in Figure 16.4 is a university. The reason for having two PDPs after the main local PDP is due to the fact that a university (as a big enterprise) usually has more than one operating environment or platforms running within its networks, moreover, it is common for such enterprise to have more than one location (campuses/offices), hence, we aimed to draw our example with two PDPs to show the flexibility that our proposed system model provides in terms of satisfying requirements that any network system might demand.

CASE STUDIES
Simulation Setup

In this section, we present extensive simulation studies which we have conducted on our proposed cloud computing system model and architecture. We have chosen the CloudSim toolkit [47] as a simulation platform. The proposed cloud system model is studied and validated through different network scenarios, for the goal of testing its efficiency in terms of energy consumption reduction, as well as its ability toward adding more elasticity to the technology of cloud computing in the context of provider–client business relations. For the validation of our proposed system model, two SLA metrics were defined to be used: SLATAH and PDM which were proposed in Beloglazov and Buyya [7], and the simulation processes involved investigating and employing several

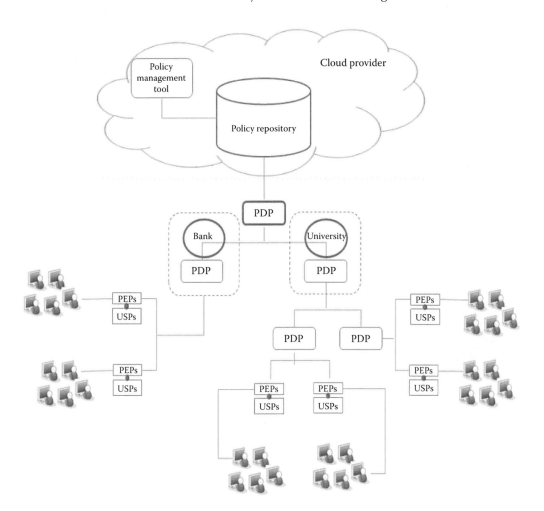

FIGURE 16.4   Proposed system architecture.

heuristic algorithms proposed by other researchers for the goal of validating the proposed system model. The validation of our proposed system model is done based on defined SLA metrics in different network scenarios. The proposed system model has proved ability in handling several heuristic algorithms in the context of a PBM framework. The proposed system model has shown contributions in the field of cloud computing: first, it contributes toward decreasing the energy consumption in datacenters; second, it gives clients the facility of managing their own service schemes according to the needed service. The simulation studies were conducted in several stages; the first stage involved simulating cloud scenarios according to the current system model, and next simulating the same cloud scenario according to the proposed system model. The proposed system model has proved to provide improvements in energy efficiency, and showed more elasticity that cloud clients can enjoy in terms of budget control on their ICT services as well as convenience in changing the scheduling of their service schemes according to their needs and requirements.

CloudSim Simulator

Since our targeted system is an IaaS configuration which is a cloud computing environment that is supposed to create a view of unbounded computing resources to users, we find it very important to evaluate the proposed approach on a large-scale experiment on real infrastructure. However, it is obviously very difficult to conduct repeatable experiments on such large-scale cloud infrastructure, hence, we opt to simulate the configuration under study in order to validate and test the efficiency of the proposed system model. For that, we have chosen the CloudSim toolkit [47] as the simulation platform for this research. The CloudSim toolkit is considered a modern simulation framework aimed at cloud computing environments and it is widely used. The CloudSim toolkit permits the modeling of virtualized environments and supports on-demand resource provisioning and management. It also facilitates simulating energy-aware models; this makes it more useful for our simulation than alternative simulation toolkits such as GangSim [48] and SimGrid [49]. More information on CloudSim simulator is available in Rodrigo et al. [47].

For accurate results and successful system validation in this research, we intend to run our simulation of cloud scenarios on similar network hardware configurations. This enables us accurately compare results of both simulation runs (current system model vs. proposed system model) and therefore allows accurate validation. Similar to the simulation scenario built in Beloglazov and Buyya [7], our simulation scenarios for this research involved running a data center that comprises 800 heterogeneous physical nodes, half of them are HP ProLiant ML110 G4 servers, and the other half are HP ProLiant ML110 G5 servers. The CPU frequency for each server is mapped onto MIPS ratings: 1860 MIPS for each core of the HP ProLiant ML110 G5 servers and 2660 MIPS for each core of the HP ProLiant ML110 G5 servers. The network bandwidth for each server is 1 GB. VMs characteristics correspond to Amazon EC2 instance types with the only exception that all the VMs are single-core.

Simulation Studies Structure

To validate our proposed approach which aims at overcoming the issue of inefficiency of energy consumption in cloud computing, our simulation studies involved two main stages in which the current system model and our proposed system model are both simulated (Figure 16.5). The results of both simulation stages are recorded for the goal of comparing them against each other to find out the efficiency of the proposed system model in terms of energy consumption. For the validation of our proposed approach, we opt to use two different scenarios in which each one has different cloud client requirements in terms of needed service schemes. For accurate results and fair results comparison in this study, we have chosen to run the simulation for all clients' scenarios under similar network hardware configurations; this assures fairness and accuracy in the final comparison and validation of results.

Case Studies

For this research, in order to validate our proposed approach, we opt to design two cloud scenarios in which two clients have different requirements in terms of SLA. The cloud scenarios in this research are simulated according to the same network configurations discussed in the previous section of this section. The main goal of creating cloud scenarios is

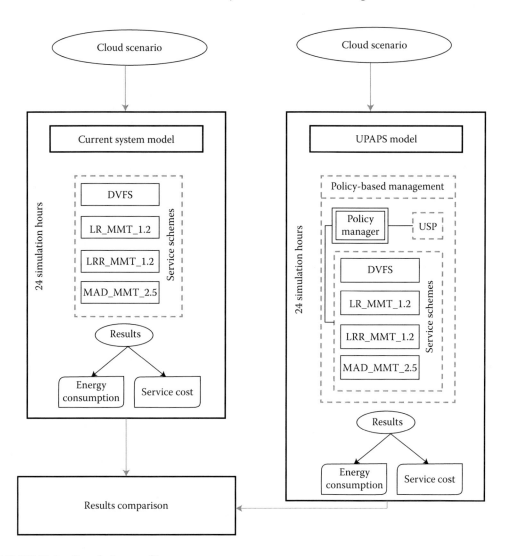

FIGURE 16.5 Simulation studies structure.

to test our proposed approach against the current system model. Both cloud scenarios are dedicated to one assumed cloud provider scenario, in which there are many service schemes offered to clients. Service schemes in our cloud provider scenario vary according to the SLA provided and therefore priced to end consumer (clients). Our client scenarios are based on assumption about users' IT service preference with particular consideration to their daily usage of the cloud service. Each client scenario is simulated according to both: current system model and proposed system model. This allows testing the efficiency of the proposed system model and validating it by comparing the results obtained for both systems. For the rest of the section, the three client scenarios are denoted as Scenario 1, and Scenario 2.

Cloud Provider's Scenario

For this research, we assume a scenario of a cloud provider that provides services to clients based on their IT service preferences with particular consideration to their daily usage of

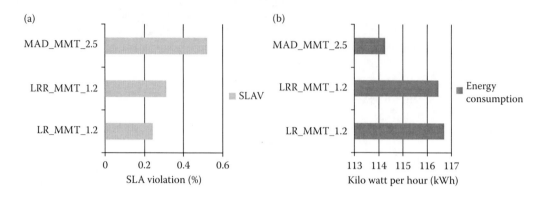

FIGURE 16.6 Simulation results of the selected heuristics.

the cloud service as mentioned earlier. In our cloud provider scenario, there are four available service schemes offered by the cloud provider in which each service scheme is priced differently according to the QoS (SLA) offered in each scheme.

In order to generate our service schemes for this research, we opt to simulate the chosen heuristic algorithms discussed in previous section to find their efficiency levels in terms of energy consumption and SLAV. For that, we have run a full day simulation on each heuristic algorithm and results were recorded to be put on the comparison bench. Results of this simulation are presented Figure 16.6a and b.

As seen in Figure 16.6a, the dynamic consolidation algorithm (DVFS) outperformed the heuristic algorithms in terms of the SLAV metric. The energy consumption rate caused by DVFS in one full simulation day was 803.91 kilo watt per hour (kWh), which is much higher than the energy consumed by the heuristic algorithms. However, results indicated zero SLA violations caused by DVFS while the heuristic algorithms produced violations due to their use of aggressive VMs consolidations.

In Figure 16.6b, the power consumption rates varied among algorithms. The LR_MMT_1.2 algorithm produced the highest energy consumption rate which was 116.71 (kWh), followed by LRR_MMT_1.2 which produced 116.48 (kWh), finally, MAD_MMT_1.2 produced an energy consumption rate of 114.27 (kWh). However, the efficiency of each heuristic algorithm does not only rely on the power consumption, but on the SLAV metric. Comparing the results shown in Figure 16.6a and b, it is clear there is an inverse relationship between the power consumption and the SLAV metric. This is justified by aggressive consolidation of VMs that causes less energy consumption. For instance, MAD_MMT_2.5 with SLAV of 0.524% appears to produce the best results in terms of energy consumption, while in fact, the reason behind this energy efficiency is the high violation to the SLA due to its aggressive consolidation processes.

Based on the results in both Figures 16.6a and b, the heuristic algorithms can be categorized according to the SLAV (violations) they cause. None of these algorithms can be efficient when used on their own. The SLAV metric is considered very important in the field of cloud computing, even though all heuristic algorithms contribute toward saving energy, they are still not efficient to be applied practically due to the SLAV that they cause.

TABLE 16.2   Price Plan for Service Schemes

Service Scheme	Price (Per Hour)
Service A	$NZ 0.34
Service B	$NZ 0.27
Service C	$NZ 0.20
Service D	$NZ 0.13

Moreover, although the DVFS algorithm does not cause violation to the SLA, the energy consumption rate that it causes is considered relatively high according to the target consumption rate in our proposed approach. Nevertheless, applying the DVFS algorithm on its own would put cloud users in a position to pay for high QoS all the time even if they do not actually need it.

For our cloud scenario in this research, we opt to categorize service schemes according to the SLAV metric that each heuristic algorithm produces. These service schemes are: service scheme "A" which provides the highest SLA due to its use of the DVFS algorithm, service scheme "B" which has the second highest SLA due to the LR-MMT-1.2 algorithm, service scheme "C" which provides lower SLA which is generated using the LRR-MMT-1.2 algorithm, and finally service scheme "D" which offers the lowest SLA due to MAD-MMT-1.2 algorithm. Table 16.2 presents service schemes prices according to our cloud provider scenario. Also, we here assume the cost of 1 kilo watt of power is equal to $NZ 0.17, which is part of the cloud operating costs.

Cloud Users' Scenarios

For this study, as mentioned earlier, we assume three cloud clients scenarios in which each client has different requirements of service schemes according to their needs. The first client is a bank, the second client is a university, and finally, the last client is an individual office manager who requires cloud service for his office network.

Scenario 1 (Bank)

The first client scenario represents a bank branch that requires the highest available QoS during business hours, and the second highest QoS outside business hours. The bank branch manager specifies a great need of high internet connection speed during business hours due to the high workload on the bank intranet, while having a lower need to that outside their business hours due to less workload on the intranet of the bank.

Current System Model   According to the current system model, only one policy (algorithm) can be enforced. In order to achieve 0.0 SLAV, service scheme "A" is the proper service scheme to be offered as it satisfies the need of the bank by providing the highest available SLA level, this is due to the need of high QoS during business hours hence lower QoS can violate the SLA between the cloud provider and the bank during business hours. Service scheme "A" is generated using DVFS algorithm, we here run our simulation for one full simulation day (24 h). The energy consumption rate as per CloudSim simulator for DVFS algorithm is 52.98 kilo watt per hour (kWh), and the price of the service as per our assumption in Table 16.2 equals to NZ$0.34. The total energy consumption in one full day using DVFS as per CloudSim simulator is calculated as follows:

$$803.91*24 = 19,293.84 \text{ KW}$$

While the price of service scheme "A" in one full day is calculated as follows:

$$0.34*24 = 8.16 \text{ NZ\$}$$

Due to the fact that the current system is only using one dedicated scheme which does not allow flexibly switching policies/service schemes according to the dynamic user needs, the service scheme "A" is provided to the bank throughout the full working day. This makes the bank pay for such service during outside business hours without an actual need for it.

The UDP-PBNM System Model   In our proposed system model, the adoption of PBM facilitates more elasticity in managing service schemes according to the actual need of them. According to the bank scenario, the bank has the facility of choosing service schemes from a pool of service schemes according to what is needed with consideration to time windows. In this scenario, the bank requires the service scheme that provides service with the highest available QoS. The bank requirements can be summarized as the following:

From 8 a.m. to 4:59 p.m., service scheme "A"

From 5 p.m. to 7:59 a.m., service scheme "B"

The bank's requirements can be satisfied by our proposed system model by designing the bank UDP according to them. Figure 16.7 presents the bank's UDP as per our proposed

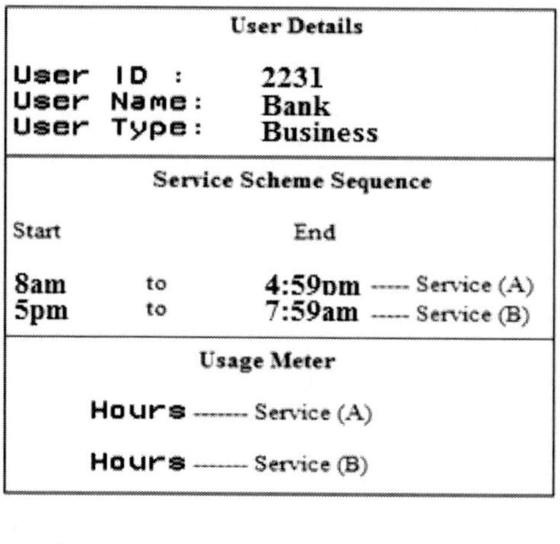

FIGURE 16.7   UDP for the bank.

system model. This UDP is used by the cloud provider in order to set their service schemes schedule according to the required services and time windows. Moreover, in the proposed system model, users can also be part of the management for their own service schemes by modifying their service schemes using the user interface which is connected to the Policy Repository.

As seen in Figure 16.7, service schemes can be modified and set according to time windows as per the bank needs. The first part of the UDP includes user details such as ID, name, and user type, while the second part involves the service schemes schedule in which the bank itself (client) can modify and set it according to its needs. The third part involves the usage meter in which each service scheme is measured hourly and priced accordingly. This means, UDP allows the bank to set up its service schemes schedule according to the required service as well as eliminating the costs of the ICT service provided by the cloud service provider. Figure 16.8 presents the energy consumption rate in one full simulation day according to the UDP of the bank.

As seen in Figure 16.8, during business hours, service scheme "A" is applied, which is generated using the DVFS algorithm, while outside business hours, service scheme "B" is applied. The total energy consumed in 1 full business day according to Figure 4.6 can be calculated as follows:

12 a.m. to 8 a.m. service scheme "B"	8 Hours	(116.71*8) = 933.68 Kw
8 a.m. to 4 p.m. service scheme "A"	8 Hours	(803.91*8) = 6431.28 Kw
4 p.m. to 12 a.m. service scheme "B"	8 Hours	(116.71*8) = 933.68 Kw

Therefore the total energy consumed in one full business day = 8298 KW.

The price that the bank has to pay for 1 full business day service as per its UDP is also calculated as follows:

16 Hours of service scheme "B" + 8 Hours of service scheme "A"
16*NZ$ 0.27 + 8*NZ$ 0.34

Therefore, the total cost for one full business day is NZ$ 7.04.

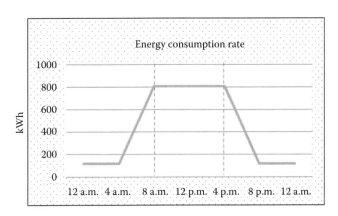

FIGURE 16.8   Energy consumption in 1 full business day.

Results Discussion

Results of both simulation stages (current system model and proposed UDP-PS system model) indicate significant reduction in the energy consumption using our proposed system model, as well as significant savings in terms of service costs that the bank has to pay the cloud provider. Figure 16.9a presents the total reduction of energy consumption by our proposed system model, while Figure 16.9b presents the cost reduction of cloud service using the proposed system model.

As seen in Figure 16.9a, the results of simulations indicate to a significant energy consumption reduction in our proposed system model. The total energy consumed in the current system model equals to 19,293.84 KW in one business day, while according to the proposed system model, the energy consumed is reduced to 8298 KW. This proves the efficiency of our proposed system model in terms of energy consumption as the total energy saved is 19,293.84 − 8298 = 10,995.84 KW, which is 57% of the total energy consumed in the current system model and saved without violating the SLA that the bank requires.

Moreover, according to the simulation of the bank scenario, results also point to significant cost reductions of the cloud service provided to the bank. As seen in Figure 16.9b, the cost of the service for one full day is reduced by 8.16 − 7.04 = 1.12 NZ$, which is around 13% of the total cost in the current system model; hence, this also proves the cost efficiency of our proposed system model in comparison to the current one.

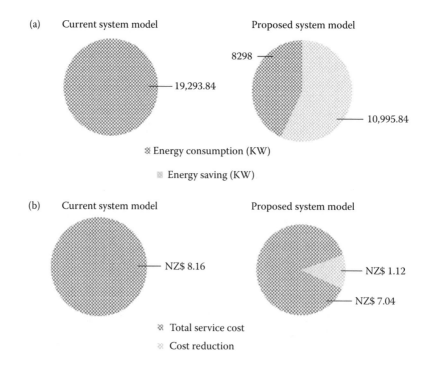

FIGURE 16.9   (a) Energy consumption reduction. (b) Service cost reduction (NZ$).

Scenario 2 (University Office/Department)

Similarly, the second scenario represents an office manager, who requires cloud services for her office ICT. The manager of the office decides to reduce the costs of ICT by choosing service schemes according to their demand. The service schemes required by the office manager are not fully dependent on the opening hours of the branch, but rather on the working time and workload (number of computers that are sharing the network bandwidth in the office at each particular time window of the day). The requirements of the office manager are more complex that the bank in our previous scenarios. These requirements include 3 service schemes which are scheduled according to both working time and workload. The manager of the office requires the highest available QoS during business hours, due to the need for fast internet connection and voice and video communications that usually take place during working hours. During outside business hours, due to the nature of the office work, there is always a possibility that some of the staff members are doing overtime work in order to accomplish tasks when needed. This means that the workload of the office network is unpredictable during outside business hours. For that, the manager of the office requires scheduling service schemes according to the number of running computers on the office network. In other words, when the number of computers running is more than 3, the workload is considered high, and if the number of running computers on the office network is less than 3, the workload is considered low, and so on. The number of computers influences the speed of the internet as each computer shares the internet bandwidth with the other running computers on the office network. The following represents the office requirements in terms of service schemes.

Current System Model   According to the current system model, in order to satisfy the office manager's requirements, and due to the need for service scheme "A" during business hours and possibly after business hours when workload is considered high, the simulation results will not differ from the simulation results of the previous scenario (the bank), because service scheme "A" is generated using the DVFS algorithm which consumes energy at the rate of 903.91 Kilo Watt per hour, which means in one full day, the total energy consumption can be calculated as follows:

$$803.91*24 = 19{,}293.84 \text{ KW}$$

However, the current system model does not support such requirements because only one service scheme can be provided throughout the day and therefore no complexity of requirements can be handled.

UDP-PS System Model   In order to satisfy the client's requirements, these requirements have to be included in the UDP of the client as a set of policies. This set of policies plays the key role in the process of scheduling the service schemes provided to the client (office). This is because of the unpredictable workload that the office network might encounter after business hours. According to the requirements of the office manager, the service scheme required during business hours is service scheme "A," while after business hours, there is a need to create a set of policies that can automatically handle the scheduling and the switching processes of the service schemes without violating the QoS required. This can be done by adopting the PBM framework. Policies can be switched from one to another depending on the workload metric decided by the office manager, which is the number of running computers on the network. The following presents the set of policies, which are to be included in the UDP of the office:

During Business Hours	→	Service scheme "A"

Outside Business Hours
1. If number of working computers = 0	→	Service scheme "D"
2. If number of working computers > 0, ≤3	→	Service scheme "B"
3. If number of working computers > 3	→	Service scheme "A"

Figure 16.10 presents the client's UDP in which the set of policies above is included in order to satisfy the requirements of the office manager.

As seen in Figure 16.10, service schemes are provided to the office network according to both metrics of time and workload. During business hours, only one service scheme is provided which is service scheme "A," while after business hours, there are three different service schemes, which can be provided according to the workload of the network at any particular time outside business hours. This reflects the flexibility that the proposed

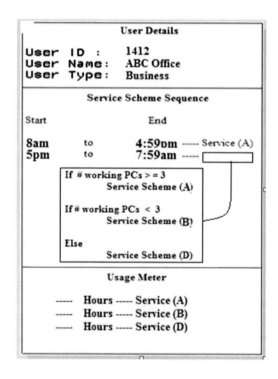

FIGURE 16.10 UDP for the university office.

approach, along with the PBM framework, provides. Moreover, the advantage of the PBM framework also resides in the simplification of the management of the cloud network as switching from a service scheme to another does not require human effort once policies are set and enforced in the system.

Policy Conflicts and Resolutions

Policy conflicts occur due to the satisfaction of conditions of two or more policies in the system at the same time. The adoption of PBM framework can often encounter policy conflicts that can be a barrier toward the adoption of such management framework. In our office scenario, policies were set up and designed to be enforced according to two metrics: time and network workload therefore, there is no occurrence of policy conflicts, however, on larger scales, there is always a potential for policy conflicts that take place due to more requirements to be satisfied and higher demand on a greater number metrics in various applications or client type scenarios. For example, let us assume that the design of our policies set in the office scenario was different in a way that Service Scheme "B" was to be provided during outside business hours unless there is a workload on the network, and other service schemes are to be provided according to the size of the workload on the network. In this case, in order to overcome the issue of policy conflicts, we would set up a unique priority value for each policy with its service scheme. For example, the policy for service scheme "A" has the priority of "3," policy for service scheme "B" has the priority of "2" and policy for service scheme "D" has the priority of "1." According to that, outside business hours, Service "D" is supposed to be provided, but when the workload metric starts to increase, the priority therefore would be for the other policy that has higher priority value such as policy "B." Similarly, if the workload metric increases to satisfy the condition of the policy for the service scheme "A," the priority for the policy for service scheme "A" is higher therefore, service "A" is to be enforced, and so on.

Prioritizing policies in the PBM framework helps toward avoiding policy conflicts and therefore obtaining the best of what such a management framework can offer. For our simulation, we opt to further create a subscenario derived from the office scenario for the goal of validating our proposed system model in terms of energy consumption and costs. For that, we assume that during outside business hours, the workload on the office network was as follows.

From 5 p.m. to 8 p.m., three computers were running due to three staff members who were performing overtime work in the office. From 8 p.m. to 9 p.m., the manager of the office was doing some work in the office using one computer of the office network. After 9 p.m., the office network was not occupied and none of the office computers were running. According to the mentioned subscenario, the workload of the office network after business hours according to the UDP of the office can be summarized as the following:

1. 3 hours of service scheme "A"

2. 1 hour of service scheme "B"

3. 11 hours of Service scheme "D"

According to the simulation runs on the assumed subscenario of the office branch, the total energy consumption for each of the above time windows is calculated as the following:

3 hours of service scheme "A" → 3*(103.09 kWh) → 309.27 KW
1 hour of service scheme "B" → 1*(5.34 kWh) → 5.34 KW
11 hours of service scheme "D" → 11*(55.08 kWh) → 605.88 KW
Total Energy consumed = 309.27 + 5.34 + 605.88 = 920.49 KW

The total cost of the cloud scenario according to our subscenario is calculated as the following:

3 hours of service scheme "A" → 3*(0.34 NZ$) → 1.02 $NZ
1 hour of service scheme "B" → 1*(0.27 NZ$) → 0.27 $NZ
11 hours of service scheme "D" → 11*(0.13 NZ$) → 1.43 $NZ
The total cost of the cloud service = 1.02 + 0.27 + 1.43 = 2.72 $NZ

Results of both simulation stages (current system model and UDP-PS system model) indicate a significant reduction in the energy consumption using our proposed system model, as well as significant savings in terms of service costs that the office is required to pay to the cloud provider. Figure 16.11a presents the total reduction of energy consumption by our proposed system model, while Figure 16.11b presents the cost reduction of cloud service using the proposed system model.

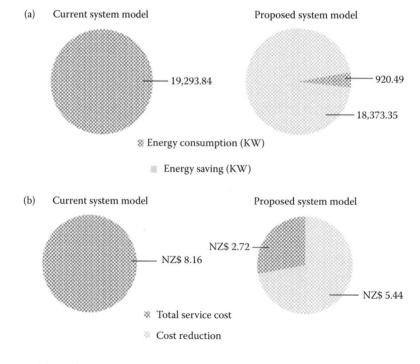

FIGURE 16.11 (a) Total energy consumption. (b) Service cost reduction.

As seen in Figure 16.11a, there is a significant reduction in the total energy consumed by running the cloud scenario according to the client's UDP under the proposed system in comparison to the current system model. The total energy reduction due to the model is 19,293.84 − 920.49 = 18,373.35 KW, which makes around 95% of the total energy consumed according to the current system model. This indicates better efficiency in terms of energy consumption without violation to the QoS required by the office branch. Moreover, the cost of service appears to be significantly reduced according to the proposed system model as seen in Figure 16.11b. The total reduction of the cost of service according to the UDP-PS model is 8.16 − 2.72 = 5.44 NZ$, this indicates significant reduction of service cost which is around 66% of the total costs of service according to the current system model.

The proposed system model involves the adoption of the PBNM framework concept in which a group of heuristic algorithms can be managed toward the reduction of the energy consumption in the field of cloud computing without violation to the QoS required. The proposed system model and cloud architecture which involves the two proposed architectural components (UDP and UDP-PS) work together toward better management of cloud networks as well as providing more means of elasticity in the field of cloud computing under the umbrella of the pay-as-you-go model.

CONCLUSIONS AND FUTURE WORK

In this book chapter, first we conducted an extensive survey of the state of the art in network management for Big Data. After that, we proposed an innovative UDP-aware PBNM (UDP-PBNM) framework to exploit and differentiate UDPs to achieve better power efficiency and optimized resource management. The framework facilitates the achievement of those two goals while guaranteeing the quality of their services. The proposed UDP-PBNM framework enables more flexible and sustainable expansion in resource management when using data center networks to handle Big Data requirements. The simulation results have shown significant improvements on the performance of the infrastructure in terms of power efficiency and resource management while fulfilling the QoS requirements and cost expectations of the users. In addition, the proposed framework has proven abilities in effectively managing a group of policies, and in resolving policy conflicts for VM allocation and migration. This is done by employing new architectural components such as the UDP-Aware Policy Switching (UDP-PS) unit and the UDP unit that cater for both customer data service requirements and providers' energy efficiency concerns. In our future work, we aim at enhancing the UDP-aware PBM framework to handle more complex cases of increasing demanding and finer user needs.

REFERENCES

1. D. Agrawal, S. Das and A. E. Abbadi, Big data and cloud computing: New wine or just new bottles? *PVLDB*, 3 (2), pp. 1647–1648, 2010.
2. I. I. Center, Big data in the cloud: Converging Technologies, Big data in the cloud, 2014.
3. Gartner, IT glossary: Big data, *Gartner Research*, p. 578, 2013. [Online]. Available: http://www.gartner.com/it-glossary/big-data/. [Accessed 2014 September 13].
4. D. Agrawal, S. Das and A. E. Abbadi, Big data and cloud computing: Current state and future opportunities, *Proceedings of the VLDB Endowment*, Lausanne, Switzerland, 2010.

5. C. Ji, Y. Li, W. Qiu, U. Awada and K. Li, Big data processing in cloud computing environments, *2012 International Symposium on Pervasive Systems, Algorithms and Networks*, San Marcos, TX, pp. 17–23, 2012.

6. J. M. Pedersen, M. Riaz, J. C. Junior, B. Dubalski, D. Ledzinski and A. Patel, Assessing measurements of QoS for global cloud computing services, *IEEE Ninth International Conference on Dependable, Autonomic and Secure Computing*, Sydney, Australia, pp. 682–689, 2011.

7. A. Beloglazov and R. Buyya, Optimal online deterministic algorithms and adaptive heuristics for energy and performance efficient dynamic consolidation of virtual machines in cloud data centers, *Concurrency and Computation: Practice and Experience*, 24, pp. 1–24, 2011.

8. Greenpeace, *Cloud Computing and its Contribution to Climate Change*, Greenpeace International, Amsterdam, 2010.

9. J. G. Koomey, A report by Analytics Press, completed at the request of *The New York Times*, Stanford University, USA, 2011.

10. S. Rivoire, M. A. Shah, P. Ranganathan and C. Kozyrakis, Joulesort: A balanced energy-efficiency benchmark, *ACM SIGMOD International Conference on Management of Data*, Beijing, China, 2007.

11. S. Srikantaiah, A. Kansal and F. Zhao, Energy aware consolidation for cloud computing, in *HotPower*, 10, 2008.

12. L. A. Barroso and U. Hölzle, The case for energy-proportional computing, *Computer*, 40, pp. 33–37, 2007.

13. Q. Zhang, L. Cheng and R. Boutaba, Cloud computing: State-of-the-art and research challenges, *Journal of Internet Services and Applications* 2010, pp. 7–18, 2010.

14. D. Agrawal, S. Das and A. E. Abbadi, Big data and cloud computing: New wine or just new bottles?, in *Proceedings of the VLDB Endowment*, Singapore, 2010.

15. J. Gantz and D. Reinsel, *The Digital Universe in 2020: Big Data, Bigger Digital Shadows, and Biggest Growth in the Far East—United States*, IDC, USA, 2013.

16. A. Das, C. Lumezanu, Y. Zhang, V. Singh, G. Jiang and C. Yu, Transparent and flexible network management for big data processing in the cloud, in *HotCloud'13*, San Jose, CA, 2013.

17. S.-i. Kuribayashi, Reducing total power consumption method in cloud computing environments, *International Journal of Computer Networks & Communications*, 4, pp. 69–84, 2012.

18. L. Zyga, How energy-efficient is cloud computing? 8 October 2010. [Online]. Available: http://phys.org/news205737760.html. [Accessed 11 August 2012].

19. W. H. Gong Chen, J. Liu, S. Nath, L. Rigas, L. Xiao and F. Zhao, Energy-aware server provisioning and load dispatching for connection-intensive internet services, *5th USENIX Symposium on Networked Systems Design and Implementation*, San Francisco, CA, USA, pp. 337–350, 2008.

20. V. Firoiu, J.-Y. L. Boudec, D. Towsley and Z.-L. Zhang, Theories and models for internet quality of service, in *Proceedings of the IEEE*, 2002, DOI : 10.1109/JPROC.2002.802002.

21. Cisco, Quality of service networking, in *Internetworking Technologies Handbook*, Cisco Press, Indianapolis, pp. 1–31, 2004.

22. T. Szigeti and C. Hattingh, *End-to-End QoS Network Design: Quality of Service in LANs, WANs and VPNs*, Cisco Press, 2004.

23. J. Tiso, Enterprise QoS solution reference network design guide, in *Designing Cisco Network Service Architectures (ARCH) Foundation Learning Guide*, Cisco Press, USA, 2005.

24. N. Kokash, *An Introduction to Heuristic Algorithms*, Department of Informatics and Telecommunications, University of Trento, Italy, 2012.

25. F. Greco, *Travelling Salesman Problem*, In-Teh, Vienna, Austria, 2008.

26. G. Winter, B. Galvn, S. Alonso and B. n. G. alez, *Solving Economic and Environmental Optimal Control of Dumping of Sewage with a Flexible and Parallel Evolutionary Computation*, Institute of Intelligent Systems and Numerical Applications in Engineering, Evolutionary Computation and Application Division, University of Las Palmas De gran Canaria, pp. 244–247, 2000.

27. W. S. Cleveland, Robust locally weighted regression and smoothing scatterplots, *Journal of Statistical American Association*, 74, pp. 829–836, 1979.
28. C. Walck, *Hand-Book on Statistical Distributions for Experimentalists*, Particle Physics Group, Fysikum, University of Stockholm, Stockholm, Sweden, 2007.
29. E. L. Sueur and G. Heiser, Dynamic voltage and frequency scaling: The laws of diminishing returns, in *HotPower'10 Proceedings of the 2010 International Conference on Power Aware Computing and Systems*, USA, 2010.
30. V. Spiliopoulos, S. Kaxiras and G. Keramidas, Green governors: A framework for continuously adaptive DVFS, in *Green Computing Conference and Workshops (IGCC), 2011 International*, Orlando, FL, 2011.
31. E. Vittoz and J. Fellarath, CMOS analog integrated circuits based on weak inversion operation, *IEEE Journal of Solid-State Circuits*, 12, pp. 224–231, 1977.
32. K. C. Feeney, D. Lewis and V. P. Wade, Policy based management for internet communities, in *Fifth IEEE International Workshop on Policies for Distributed Systems and Networks*, Ireland, 2004.
33. R. Chadha, G. Lapiotis and S. Wrighi, Policy-based networking, *IEEE Network*, 2, 8–9, 2002.
34. T. Hamada, P. Czezowski and T. Chujo, Policy-based management for enterprise and carrier IP networking, *Fujitso*, 2, pp. 128–139, 2000.
35. M. Dam, G. Karlsson, B. S. Firozabadi and R. Stadler, A research agenda for distributed policy-based management, *International Journal of P2P Network Trends and Technology*, 3, pp. 116–122, 2013.
36. R. Berto-Monleon, E. Casini, R. v. Engelshoven, R. Goode, K.-D. Tuchs and T. Halmai, Specification of a policy based network management architecture, *The 2011 Military Communications Conference, Track 3, Cyber Security and Network Operation*, Baltimore Convention Center, Baltimore, MD, USA, pp. 1393–1398, 2011.
37. D. Agrawal, K.-W. Lee and J. Lobo, Policy-based management of networked computing systems, *IEEE Communications Magazine*, 43, pp. 69–75, 2005.
38. D. C. Verma, *Simplifying Network Administration Using Policy-Based Management*, IBM Thomas J Watson Research Cente, IEEE Network, IEEE Press, Piscataway, NJ, USA, pp. 20–26, 2002.
39. RIPE, Internet Engineering Task Force, 10 August 2012. [Online]. Available: http://www.ripe.net/internet-coordination/internet-governance/internet-technical-community/ietf.
40. M. Davies, C. Clark and D. Legare, *Proceedings of the Twenty-Fourth Internet Engineering Task Force*, Twenty-Fourth Internet Engineering Task Force, Cambridge, 1992.
41. J. Rich and J. Hill, How to do capacity planning, *TeamQuest*, 2013.
42. Y. J. Song, V. Ramasubramanian and E. G. Sirer, *Optimal Resource Utilization in Content Distribution Networks*, Dept. of Computer Science, Cornell University, Ithaca, 2006.
43. A. Balchunas, Overview of IPSEC, 2007. http://www.routeralley.com/guides/ipsec_overview.pdf.
44. H. L. McKinley, *SANS Institute InfoSec Reading Room*, Sans Institute, Singapore, 2003.
45. J. Follows and D. Straeten, *Application-Driven Networking: Concepts and Architecture for Policy-Based Systems*, International Technical Support Organization, IBM, USA, 1999.
46. D. Armstrong and K. Djemame, Towards quality of service in the cloud, in *Proceedings of the 25th UK Performance Engineering Workshop*, UK, 2009.
47. R. R. Rodrigo, N. Calheiros, A. Beloglazov, C. A. F. D. Rose and R. Buyya, CloudSim: A toolkit for modeling and simulation of cloud computing environments and evaluation of resource provisioning algorithms, *Practice and Experience (SPE)*, 41, pp. 23–50, 2011.
48. M. Bsoul, I. Phillips and C. Hinde, MICOSim: A simulator for modelling economic scheduling in Grid computing, World Academy of Science, Engineering and Technology, pp. 1298–1301, 2012.
49. A. Legrand, M. Quinson, H. Casanova and K. Fujiwara, The SimGrid Project, Simulation and Deployment of Distributed Applications, 2006.

CHAPTER 17

Circuit Emulation for Big Data Transfers in Clouds

Marat Zhanikeev

CONTENTS

INTRODUCTION

Big Data has several distinct incarnations in clouds. It can be chunks of data stored in HDFS/Hadoop clusters for analysis. Or it can be virtual machine images migrating within or across data centers (DCs). Or it can be backup of data sent from one place to another over the network. Regardless of contents, recently it has become clear that intra-DC and inter-DC networking are subjected to tough throughput (or performance in general) requirements at level with that inside physical boxes. For example, there is already research that views *over-the-network storage* as an extension of local hard disk drive (HDD)/solid state drive (SSD) environment, which is put into action when local storage or processing capacity are exceeded [1]. This means that there is already some demand for high-volume communications within services running both inside DCs as well as across multiple DCs.

In the meantime, the world has completed the transition to the so-called *all-IP* technology, where most of the traffic is packetized and carried over IP networks. Note that both Ethernet and optical—the two widespread kinds of networks today—fit this description. However, with the *Big Data networking* problem, the old *circuits versus packets* argument is back on the table [2]. This chapter shows that *sharing the bandwidth* by having multiple flows send packets concurrently is detrimental the each flow's throughput. Assuming that the flows carry Big Data (another term in this chapter is *bulk transfer*), the ON–OFF statistical model for such flows is very different for what is considered *conventional* by the all-IP technologies. Obviously, Big Data flows strive to have longer ON periods and very short or even ideally zero length OFF periods. This chapter discusses the *hotspot* model [3] as an alternative to the traditional ON–OFF sources. The hotspot model is used to model the so-called *heavy hitters*—the flows which carry most of the traffic on a link. Big Data flows are obviously heavy hitters.

This chapter presents the concept of *circuits-over-packets* emulation. Circuits are simply defined as *exclusive line access for a single flow*. Emulation means that circuits are not physical (like in the old analog phone systems) but are emulated using packets in all-IP networks. Another way to present the main proposal in this chapter is to state that it *discusses the special case of networking tailored for Big Data*.

The proposed technology is multifaceted. It involves the full awareness of how modern switches operate, specifically the cut-through versus store-and-forward modes [4,5]. The proposal also applies end-to-end (e2e) Quality of Service (QoS) concepts both at Layer 2 (L2) and Layer 3 (L3) of networks [6], thus making sure that circuits can function e2e. This chapter discusses optimization techniques and practical designs that can implement circuits in practice. The optimization framework is related to the traditional Traffic Engineering (TE) problem, specifically, the Open Shortest Path First (OSPF) formulation [7]. As an example, this chapter proposes a brand new networking technique called *the Tall Gate model* which is a combination of topology control, realistic optimization targets, and practical algorithms.

One of the strong opinions expressed in this chapter is that the common Ethernet, in its cheapest possible form, can be used for circuit emulation. In fact, there are already examples in practice where such a choice was made even for supercomputers—see the discussion of K Computer [8] further on. This chapter also discusses the alternatives, where Fiber Channel over Ethernet (FCoE) is arguably the most popular technology [9] and even the subject of DC- and cloud-specific standards process [10]. This chapter also discusses optical networks [11] and virtual networking with the cost it imposes [12] by formulating the related models and using them for analysis and comparison.

This chapter has the following structure. Section "Data Centers and Clouds" is an introduction to hardware and software networking environments found in clouds and DCs, with the focus on network performance. Section "End-to-End QoS Basics" is fully dedicated to e2e QoS technology. Section "Bulk Transfer Methods and Technologies" discusses the specifics of bulk transfer from hardware level and up to e2e networking. Section "Bulk Transfer Methods and Technologies" also introduces the Tall Gate model for the first time. Section "The Circuits-over-Packets Emulation" contains the core proposal of circuits-over-packets emulation but discusses and formulates models for other technologies as well. Section "Implementation and Practice" is fully dedicated to implementation and practical designs. Section "Summary" summarizes the chapter.

DCs AND CLOUDS

DC networking is an urgent problem. More and more services spread their resources across multiple DCs or even cloud providers and start imposing strict performance requirements on migration of resources across physical locations [13]. Migration of virtual machines as well as resources in general can also be triggered by the cloud provider, where ecological (green clouds) grounds are far from the least [14].

DC networking is conducted at least at three distinct layers:

- Inside racks or small hardware clusters
- IntrAnets inside DCs
- IntErnets across DCs

This section discusses networking and performance management methods at all these layers. Special attention is paid to *virtual networking*, which claims to be a singular solution to all the problems at all these layers.

Racks and Hardware Clusters

Let us walk a DC based on a recent example of the *K supercomputer* [8]. There is no bias in this particular choice—this author is in no way affiliated with the project. The choice is due to the fact that K computer came up with several interesting solutions, which are just as useful for DCs. Note that the link between supercomputing (HPC: High Performance Computing) and DCs already exists since Amazon commenced its HPC service. K computer is a recent project and is very well publicized. All the details below can be found in several of its white- or research papers in [8]. This chapter's interest in the project focuses on its networking technology, specifically the fact that it runs on common 10 Gbps Ethernet.

Note that this chapter also proposes a technology that is supposed to run effectively on cheap Ethernet networks.

K supercomputer is assembled in one huge room, just like any DC, in rows of racks of equipment. Apparently, ventilation (or air-conditioning) is better when performed in one large space.

Racks normally have three kinds of hardware:

- Switching equipment

- Computing modules (computers, CPUs, etc.)

- Storage modules

Racks also have intricate cooling systems and can have original layouts that may improve cooling. Networking inside racks can be very intricate with semimesh or full-mesh connections among modules inside the rack. It is not rare when high-end switches are used inside racks, indicating that network performance inside racks is very important.

It is common to use non-Ethernet technology inside racks. In fact, it is more common to use technologies like FCoE and eSCSI inside racks rather than outside [9], mostly to connect storage with computing modules. Note that K computer uses Ethernet both outside and inside racks.

DCs can have multiple clusters of hardware. It is common in Japan for DCs to host separate hardware clusters for different businesses. For example, there can be a Hadoop cluster with data coming from and analyzed by a given client (service provider). K computer is one huge cluster, obviously because of the HPC purpose of the hardware. To simplify, it is fair to call clusters *mini-DCs* and apply the same set of considerations to them as to full-size DCs. Intercluster networking then becomes functionally identical to DC–DC networking.

Intra-DC (inside DC) networking used to be simple. Nowadays, it can be as complex and dynamic as that in the greater Internet. For example, optical networks and FCoE can be used [9]. There are examples of using virtual networking at this level as well [15].

As was mentioned before, the sole unique feature of K computer is that it uses common 10 Gbps Ethernet at all networking levels. The only technology simplifies networking as there is no need to convert between two or more incompatible networking layers. That said, it should be noted that K computer uses special NICs which come with special MTU, and are delay and priority optimized, which, in fact, covers some of the territory specified in the recent standards on FCoE [10]. K computer solutions do not go as far as a standard, instead fixing only the specific problems that affect network performance.

One of the unique networking features of K computer is the *6-way connections* for each rack, including edges of rows and corners. This greatly improves topological flexibility of internal networking. This layout apparently also helps to transfer large bulks across racks by allowing for more nonoverlapping routes.

Ethernet versus Nonethernet Networking

Returning again to the K supercomputer [8], this chapter also assumes that the common Ethernet is used while circuit emulation in particular and higher e2e performance in general are achieved via robust topologies and efficient control algorithms.

One of the popular alternatives to Ethernet is optical networking [11]. Specifically, Optical Burst Switching (OBS) is obviously more suitable for Big Data transfer. However, it is widely recognized that dynamic routing is a difficult task. Specifically to OBS, difficulty also comes from the fact that many sources have to compete for their *bursts*, which are implemented as sessions of access to lightpaths [16]. When topology grows more complex, the argument shifts more toward *lightpaths versus wavelength routing* [17]. Lightpaths are defined, simply put, as *same wavelength end-to-end*, while wavelength routing obviously involves switching between different wavelengths (wavelength conversion) at intermediate nodes. Obviously, the latter technology offers more flexibility and therefore higher capacity, but is proportionally more difficult to manage. This argument relates to a general discussion of connection-oriented networking (circuits) [11]. This chapter returns to this argument many times throughout the rest of the text.

FCoE is a solution to the problems experienced by pure optical networks. It is a recent development by the INCITS T11 standardization body [10] and is defined in several normative documents. Specifically the following three documents are key to FCoE technology. Qau [18] defines *congestion notification* which facilitates *contention sensing*—the concept which is also part of the proposed Tall Gate model in a slightly modified form. Qaz [19] is a protocol used for bandwidth sharing across multiple flows. This document is basically a connection between optical (the original FC) and Ethernet (FCoE) domains and defines how to emulate wavelengths (or lightpaths) on top of the otherwise single Ethernet cable line. Qbb [20] defines flow control, which is also a necessity given the *bandwidth-sharing* environment of the Ethernet.

FCoE is a very popular technology in DC networking today [9]. FCoE-aware and capable devices are manufactured by several providers. For example, one can refer to HP [21] and Cisco [22] whitepapers on the subject.

Note that this chapter is not in contradiction to the optical or FCoE technologies. This chapter can be viewed as a scientific approach to the same problem tackled by existing technologies. Solutions are discussed in form of optimizational and technical frameworks, where the only fixed component is that all solutions are expected to be implemented over common Ethernet. *Common Ethernet* here means that devices and control are expected to be traditional rather than the modified versions like those found in FCoE standards.

In other words, this chapter can be viewed as a process in which black boxes like FCoE are opened up for scrutiny, details that relate to network performance under Big Data transfers are analyzed, and solutions are presented as *methods* rather than standards. Specifically, the level of complexity (and the overhead it results in) found in the control layer of FCoE is found to be detrimental to the overall throughput in the later sections of this chapter. Moreover, this chapter will show that when viewed from the viewpoint of overhead from excessive control complexity, network virtualization has many similarities to FCoE.

Switches and Practical Performance

From this point on, let us assume that Ethernet is the default technology unless specified otherwise. The other default assumption is that the discussed network is used for *bulk transfer*, which is the same as *BigData networking*.

There is a gap between the following three topics in research literature:

- Performance of packet processing in switches [4], where *cut-through mode* stands out as the preferred choice [5].

- QoS technology both in individual switches (CoS/QoS) as well as e2e [6], where AF [23] and EF [24] modes of packet forwarding are specifically important and are well defined both at Layer 2 (CoS header) and Layer 3 (DSCP header) [25]; note that penetration rate of these standards in practical use is fairly low, which results in poor overall e2e QoS support in networks today [6,26–28].

- Practical DC-specific technology applied to both intra- and inter-DC networking [9], which today mostly ignores the above two topics and mostly focuses on FCoE [21,22].

Most of the literature also ignores the simplest possible way to view bulk transfers—the congestion problem. This chapter will use both *congestion* and *contention* to describe what happens in switches when multiple flows access the link in parallel.

Figure 17.1 is a simple way to visualize the *congestion* problem. It occurs when two or more sources *contend* for a single outgoing port (left). This brings back the old argument of *circuits versus packets* [2], where the currently widely accepted resolution is that packets are better. This resolution is based on the results of statistical analysis of interaction among multiple flows generated by ON/OFF sources. Note that the OFF periods in ON/OFF cycles are normally larger possibly because such analysis was first done on conversations between people over the phone. This resolution led to the global initiative to switch over to *all-IP* networks. Note that this argument was resolved a long time before the *cut-through mode* in modern switches or, for that matter, advanced QoS-aware forwarding modes became available in switching equipment.

Also note that, as Figure 17.1 shows, the congestion problem cannot be resolved by having multiple incoming and outgoing ports. Such many-to-many cases can be generalized

FIGURE 17.1 A simple way to visualize switches in respect to the congestion problem. The right side can be generalized as several overlayed many-to-one switches (left).

into several many-to-one overlays, which indicate that the problem is not resolved. The case where each outgoing port is used only by one unchanging incoming port is not considered because this would render the switch itself unnecessary.

Figure 17.2 presents a very simple proof of the existence of the congestion problem. It is based on a small experiment conducted on a small isolated 1 Gbps Ethernet setup with two sources and one destination. The two sources send the same large file to the same destination using one of the following two methods. *Method 1: circuit emulation* is when two transmissions happen in sequence, which takes a bit of synchronization but is not too difficult to implement. The other is *Method 2: packets in contention*, where both sources start sending the file at the same time. A simple and obvious performance measure is the completion time of both transmissions, or whichever ends the last in case of Method 2.

Figure 17.2 shows the results which indicate that circuits perform reliably better because it always takes less time to complete both transfers when they are sequential and do not complete with each other for bandwidth. The distribution is two legged because the balance between two sources during transmission often shifts considerably in favor of one or the other. Note that file transfer in this experiment was done over the imperfect (and probably unfit for Big Data) TCP protocol, the setup is valid because practical alternatives to TCP are very rare in clouds today. Even if optical or FCoE connections are used for transfer, TCP is still the protocol used by applications.

The above experiment reveals that the biggest effect on e2e throughput is inflicted by the inability to use the *cut-through* mode of transfer, which is possible only when a flow gets exclusive line access. As far as bulk transfers are concerned, while packets might be better for general use, it looks like DCs might benefit from a return to the old technology of circuits. This argument is unfolded further in this chapter.

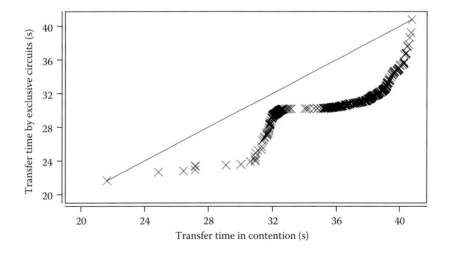

FIGURE 17.2   Results of a simple test where two large flows are transmitted over the same switch from two sources in *parallel* (in contention) versus *sequential* manner.

Virtual Networking

The antiterm for *virtual* is *physical* regardless of the fact that both are processed by software prior to entering the physical domain—the Ethernet line in this chapter. Virtual is *not physical* because virtual resource represents something other than the physical resource. For example, one can have a virtual configuration which would make one 100 Mbps physical link appear to be 2×50 Mbps links. Virtualization incurs *per-packet overhead*, which can also be referred to as the *cost* of virtualization. Since one cannot stop using virtualization in the middle of a flow, the cost is per-packet. Literally, when virtualization is used, every packet is inspected by virtualization software to make routing and other decisions.

The added cost can be made visible by studying *throughput* and specifically its packets-per-second (pps) metric. e2e delay is another independent metric, which could tell us about the per-packet lag added by virtualization. However, one-way delay is extremely hard to measure without precise synchronization.

Based on years of experience one might have had with L2/L3 VLAN setup in Linux (and on specialized network equipment), one might expect Software-Defined Network (SDN) software (an umbrella term for network visualization) to follow the example and exist as an option. That would mean that SDN could be switched on and off whenever necessary. Alternatively, one might want to use SDN only for a portion of traffic while the rest would be unaffected. Instead, the reality of SDN software today is that one can use either the traditional network stack or whatever the SDN stack one chooses to install.

As Figure 17.3 shows, the de-facto standard SDN software OpenVSwitch [29] installs as a kernel module that appears to operate side by side with the traditional network stack. Yet, in reality OpenVSwitch is using traditional network stack for routing rather than bypassing it and implementing its own routing function. At the level of user-space applications, one can use only one or the other stack at a given point of time. In fact, experience shows that switching from one technology to another requires a cold restart of the OS, which makes it very difficult to create control software which would switch between the two at runtime.

Finally, OpenFlow controller exists in user space and uses OpenVSwitch commands to configure the network in accordance with OpenFlow protocol. The case of OpenFlow + OpenVSwitch is also a rigid configuration. Once one sets OpenVSwitch to

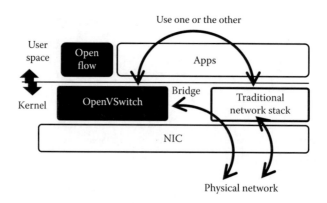

FIGURE 17.3　Reality of virtual networking on Linux boxes today.

use OpenFlow controller, the base SDN functionality provided by OpenVSwitch comes under full control of the controller unless the controller itself severs its connection. In OpenVSwitch this is referred to as *fallback*. SDN, in any form, results in per-packet processing cost, as was found in an earlier study by Zhanikeev [12] and confirmed by other existing literature [30,31].

There is another way to approach analysis of per-packet processing cost in general and that of virtual networking in particular. There is a recent discipline called *network calculus* [32], which studies *curve response* of e2e paths to packet trains. The curve is normally formed by plotting delay for the sequence of packets in a train, but metrics other than delay (throughput, etc.) can also be used.

High per-packet cost under virtual networking is a known problem. There are attempts to build virtualization frameworks which would overcome this problem. For example, Click Router is a good alternative to OpenVSwitch [33] because it has the notion of batch routing, which is used to minimize per-packet cost [34]. In fact, Click Router seems to be moving toward the cut-through mode complacency—the mode itself is discussed later in this chapter. PICA8 is another popular alternative with the same goal of minimizing per-packet processing cost [35].

There is also research into a platform-independent method for improving route lookup for extremely large (virtual) tables, with a practical target of a billion pps [36]. Some literature develops APIs for network I/O without much attention spent on processing delays [37,38]. The same applies to research that develops better software for management of network slices (virtual e2e capacity channels) [39] rather than concentrating on performance. Note that the majority of such research does not even consider hardware modes of packet transfer and is therefore unaware of the benefits of the cut-through mode. A separate subsection further in this chapter is entirely dedicated to transfer modes.

There are also hardware-level frameworks of network virtualization, which might be somewhat faster yet still suffer from the same fundamental problems listed above [40].

e2e QoS BASICS

The QoS problem has a long history, with the last major standards effort dating back to the Next Generation Networks (NGN) process in 2006. QoS was part of the NGN process, but was never actually implemented when country after country declared that it now fully complied with NGN.

However, the QoS process was continued. For example, robust large-scale QoS frameworks are now part of CCNA certification at Cisco [41]. It is now a well-defined framework [6,42], with well-defined packet forwarding classes like AF and EF at both Layer 2 (L2) and Layer 3 (L3) of networking. These classes can also be part of an intricate technology that puts them together with policies at network edge, traffic shaping, and so on. As was mentioned before, these issues are not considered in existing literature on DC networks [9].

Negotiating versus Planning Routes

IntServ versus DiffServ argument [43] is somewhat similar to the one on packets vs sockets. However, IntServ and DiffServ are not always rivals but are closer to the two elements of a larger QoS technology [44]. They can also be viewed as bottom-up versus top-down process in e2e path establishment [6].

IntServ is a top-down approach because e2e paths are negotiated on the fly. It is suitable for dynamic AS-AS QoS routing [6]. A good practical example is the Session Initiation Protocol (SIP), which is not in itself a QoS technology but defines a protocol for negotiating and provisioning of a given level of QoS in and after negotiations [44,43].

DiffServ is the bottom-up technology [44,43]. e2e paths are predefined and preconfigured in switching equipment. The routing along the path is performed by each switch based on packet headers, where QoS mapping can happen at either L2 or L3. DiffServ is a subject of the well-known TE problem, where OSPF is a popular TE formulation [7].

In practice, technologies are often a mixture of IntServ and DiffServ approaches. For example, in virtual networking OpenFlow is a control protocol (IntServ-like) while OpenVSwitch is a DiffServ-like routing engine [15]. The same goes for optical networks with lightpaths or wavelength switching [11], where sources negotiate their paths based on demand while the entire topology is optimized taking into consideration the total demand. Notably, DC networking has to be a mixture in order to make sure that Big Data transfer sessions are optimized for throughput and, therefore, minimized for time. Demand in form of Big Data transfer requests is crucial when configuring topology is such a way that all Big Data transfers are optimized, even at the cost of poorer quality on all other connections.

CoS and HSCP Packet Headers

L2 QoS is implemented in 802.1Q protocol, which allows for three-bit CoS info, which makes it possible to define 7 QoS (CoS) classes (meaning that one combination stands for no QoS). The L2 solution is completely independent from the L3 solution because different headers are used. This means that both solutions can be used in the same device or even in the same header. In case both headers are used, the CoS header requests a crude QoS class while the L3 header specifies a more detailed requirement.

L3 QoS is defined through the DSCP header [45] and is the main focus of the DiffServ standard [46]. A longer header allows for 64 classes of QoS. However, the L3 routers can only send traffic between themselves, since L2 devices cannot handle L3 headers. Without an L2 solution present as well, queuing at the input of the L3 router may be a problem since no priority queuing can be implemented before traffic is classified and marked.

Queuing and packet forwarding modes are layer-independent and are the same for both layers. Two major Packet Handling Behaviors (PHBs) are standardized: AF [23] and EF [24]. Logically, only one EF queue can exist on the same port simply because processing logic is unclear in cases when multiple EF classes are attached on the same port. In this case queues either function as one EF queue or the selection logic between the two is undefined. Following the *simple is better* rule of thumb [47], it is recommended to have only one EF per port.

Sub-Best Effort (SBE) class is commonplace in practice and has recently been standardized in [48]. It is common to select heavy hitters (Big Data are definitely heavy hitters) from the best effort traffic and mark it as SBE, unless such flows are specifically picked as EF or

AF class. AF queues serving SBEs are traditionally set to very low upper capacity limits, normally around 1%. This means that rogue heavy hitters end up with very low capacity.

AF class [24] itself is more general and allows the setup of any upper capacity limit on the aggregate traffic for that class. Note that this limit is applied to the aggregate traffic rather than individual flows, which means that it is not a target policy. If you are looking for target policies, you need to use EF and classify a narrow set of flows.

Practical Network QoS Technology

Cisco recommendations in QoS delivery are often used in practice today [47,49]. Both references contain recommendations for both L2 and L3 QoS solutions. Also, the topic of queuing is paid special attention, especially since queuing itself is separate from the QoS layer-ness. Basically, these references provide the toolkit that network administrators can use to develop their own QoS delivery solutions. Since the intended audience is campus network administrators, most of the subjects discussed in the references are extremely practical.

QoS provisioning is not only about EF/AF/SBE classes, but also about policies at domain edge which map unclassified traffic to these classes and performs traffic shaping, if necessary. This combination of solutions guarantees that a well-configured network can fully support the QoS classes and forwarding modes it is configured to handle. A more general textbook-style overview of QoS technologies and their relation to physical technologies used in networking can be found in Perros [11]. A good share of the book is spent on optical networks.

Theoretical aspects of QoS provisioning can be found in Wang [44] and Chang [43]. These books feature a more scientific approach to QoS delivery and contain many optimization problems related to both queuing and topology. All the network setups discussed in this chapter can be found in one of these two books.

Finally, there is the relatively new concept of *network calculus* [32], whose entire premise is based on a new algebra which simplifies analysis of network performance. The unit of analysis in network calculus is a sequence of packets, which is represented as a function, referred to as *response curve*. The curve is affected by each hop along e2e path.

Figure 17.4 shows an example QoS setup for a network domain. The setup has the following targets:

- Maximize throughput for Big Data transfers—those are also heavy hitters but are treated as Premium Class traffic

- Minimize throughput for all other heavy hitters

Non-BigData heavy hitters are separated and mapped to the SBE class (in practice defined as AF with upper limit of 1% of capacity). The actual Big Data flows are sampled (a job for an edge switch/router, e.g., a gate in/out of a DC) and mapped to the EF class. The rest of the traffic remains unchanged and is mapped to the FIFO class, which normally means that it will get all the capacity that is left over from EF.

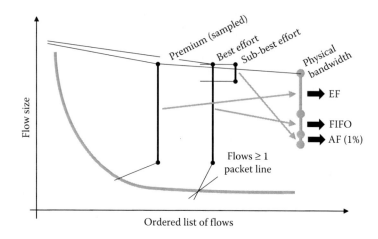

FIGURE 17.4   An example configuration for how heavy hitters can be mapped to various forwarding classes to provide a suitable distribution of QoS across traffic.

Note that this setup creates a solid image that seems to work for Big Data transfers. However, the contention problem is not solved. In fact, all the above classes apply to the store-and-forward mode of packet transfer, where EF is the best class but is still 10–15 times worse than the cut-through mode on the same device.

L2 versus L3: Problems and Solutions

Motivation for the search of the best QoS design between L2 and L3 comes primarily from the GRNET project [26] in its various stages of development [27,28]. GRNET development follows a very basic premise that L3 can benefit from the underlying L2 component in QoS provisioning. GRNET originally used L3 only QoS solution implemented by DiffServ. When it was discovered that QoS guarantee was not sufficient, the project manager considered implementing L2 QoS together with L3 QoS [42]. The tangible outcome of the endeavor is the ANS tool [50], which has the following features:

- It implements the L2 QoS solution based on the L3 QoS requests from users; while traditionally only L3 configurations were created based on user request, in its new form the tool also generates the L2 solution and distributes it across the network;

- Has specific algorithmic TE solutions for the ring topology used within the project.

GRNET discovered that L3-only solutions without L2 solutions suffered from one major flaw in the input queue of an L3 router. By definition, L3 QoS solution starts from the ingress L3 router. The problem is that without L2 QoS implemented by the L3 router, QoS of flows is impaired simply because input queue into the L3 router is not prioritized. With L3 only solution, in fact, the input queue cannot be prioritized since L3 headers are necessary to discriminate between L3 QoS classes. GRNET administrators discovered that some of the flows suffered major delay and jitter inside the input queue into the ingress L3 router simply because priority traffic would be mixed with best effort and all other traffic in the same queue.

GRNET example is a very specific case, which features very unique hardware implementation and relatively few, mostly academic, clients. As for real large-scale implementation, beyond GRNET, there is little to no evidence that GRNET-like L2 and L3 technology tandems are used in commercial networks.

General features of a large-scale network are

- Around 20% of nodes in the grid have L3 capability, which reflects the business reality of common network providers fairly well;

- There are almost twice as many L2 ingress nodes than L3 ingress nodes;

- Each L3 device has a single best path to any other L3 device, which simplifies routing decisions among L3;

- For the L2 only case (all L3 devices are L2 devices at this level), there is enough richness in the topology between ingress and egress nodes, with a certain level of randomness in e2e paths, so that TE optimizations can produce nontrivial results.

These motivations were explored further in Zhanikeev and Tanaka [6] and translated into a set of recommendations and practical designs. Given the above argument on L2/L3 QoS versus the cut-through mode, this chapter goes further by stating that circuits are best when used in the pre-QoS form which can be implemented by making sure that circuits are handled in cut-through mode e2e. The main notion at this level is whether or not the access to the uplink is exclusive or not.

BULK TRANSFER METHODS AND TECHNOLOGIES

The first step toward understanding bulk transfer is to understand how Big Data sources (heavy hitters, big flows, etc.) are different from flows defined by the traditional ON/OFF model [3]. First, Big Data sources themselves might still follow the ON/OFF model, but the point is that not all such sources are made equal. This chapter presents the *hotspot model* that defines distribution in various metrics across heavy hitter flows [3]. Another way to refer to such traffic statistically is to call it *workload*.

The second step is, having understood the nature of the workload, to create management platforms for various technologies, where this chapter focuses on optical, optical-over-Ethernet (FCoE), and pure Ethernet. The main workload in this chapter is created by Big Data transfers. The workload is still a distribution since not all Big Data is equally "big." *Heavy hitter* is the synonymous term from flow terminology [3]. In terms of workload, there will be one added level of complexity in form of *Flash events* occurring for some of the heavy hitters.

Topology is also important. This section discusses the *backbone-and-spokes* topology specifically as well as the general notion of aggregation and grouping of nodes. Note that this subject is very closely related to the Virtual Network Embedding (VNE) problem [51,52].

Hotspot Distribution for Big Data Sources

Hotspot method is used to generate realistic workloads of various types, of which flows and packets are the most popular. The overall idea of hotspots was first published in Bodk et al. [53] and further developed and adopted for flow and packet traffic in Bodk et al. [53]. Synthesis process can be split into two parts:

- Volume in one of its popular forms (packets, flows, etc.)

- Popularity of destinations

Both the above metrics are important for e2e QoS as well as bulk transfer. For example, if we assume that two concurrent circuits cannot have overlapping paths, then the second metric, distribution of popularity across destinations, is just as important as distribution of volume.

The basic idea behind the *hotspot* model is that the timeline of the synthetic workload (trace, etc.) has two epochs, generated in two separate steps:

- *Step 1* is to generate the hotspots themselves by using the Stick-Breaking (SB) random process

- *Step 2* is to generate a Flash event for a subset of hotspots using Dirichlet distribution

Flash events [3] are times when some hotspots suddenly experience a sudden further (much above their baseline) increase in popularity. Terms such as *viral content*, and so on, describe similar events in real life. In Big Data transfer the concept also finds a natural representation—Big Data sources (or destinations) are already hotspots based on their average activity, but their impact on the total traffic is extremely high when they initiate a bulk transfer session. Naturally, only a subset of Big Data sources are part of a Flash event at any given point of time.

The volume distribution is generated using the following process. The generation is done using two processes in parallel—Beta distribution and the SB process. The process has only one setup parameter—the value of d used to generate Beta distributions at each step of the generation process. Values of d approaching zero will produce final distributions almost identical to the underlying Beta distributions. With values approaching 1, the resulting distribution will be completely independent of the underlying beta distribution and will exhibit acute randomness. Figure 17.5 shows the outcome of the generation for $d = 0.5$. The SB distribution is based on the underlying Beta distribution and shows some similarities but is otherwise completely different. The process produces a distribution of flow size across all flows. Alternatively, the same method can be used to synthesize aggregate (sum of all flows) packet or byte count or substitute per-flow packet count for size.

Mathematical details of the synthesis can be found in Zhanikeev and Tanaka [3]. This section only describes the process in general terms and reveals only as much as is necessary for performance analysis further in this chapter.

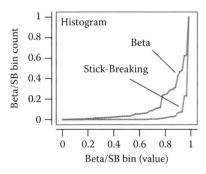
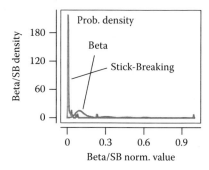

FIGURE 17.5   Results of the *hotspot* method used to generate relative difference across flows.

Synthesis of one hotspot model is configured by the following tuple of parameters:

$$<n, m, k, t_1, t_2, t_3, t_4, a, f_n, f_m, f_v> \tag{17.1}$$

where *n, m, k* are numbers of all sources, hotspots sources, and sources that experience a Flash event, respectively. Timeline is configured using t_1, t_2, t_3, t_4 which define *start of Flash event, peak (plato) of Flash event, end of peak of Flash event (start of decline), end of Flash event*, while the timeline before t_1 and after t_4 defines a period of normal function of sources. The *a* parameter is used for Beta distribution and by extension the SB process. Finally, f_n, f_m, f_v are *number, max magnitude,* and *variance* for the synthesized Flash event.

Synthesis of popularity across destinations can be *zipfian* for most practical cases [3], but can be tailored into a specific model which would fit Big Data sources exchanging information among each other. It is likely that the resulting distribution would have a much smoother distribution of popularity across destinations than is normally expected.

A practical scenario that uses such a synthesis process is described and applied in analysis further in this chapter.

The Importance of the Cut-Through Mode

It is hard to overestimate the cut-through mode in Ethernet switches. It is a well-publicized feature in all modern switches, including even the cheapest possible 1 Gbps Ethernet ones [4,5]. It is possible that this mode is the sole reason why the K computer [8] chose Ethernet over a relatively more expensive FCoE or other Ethernet alternatives.

Although simple in concept, explanation of its physical functionality involves a certain level of detail. The simplest possible definition is as follows. *The switch is in the cut-through mode when the packet is forwarded immediately after only the first six bytes of its header are read.* However, modern versions of the cut-through mode are much more advanced. High-end switches implement a form of optimization tradeoff, where +x bytes on top of the baseline of 6 bytes are allowed as long as it translates into a tangible benefit in routing flexibility [4]. Basically, one can easily see that this mechanism reminds one of virtual networking but with the minimum of per-packet processing cost. In fact, the cost in case of the cut-through mode is only 6 plus 1–2 additional bytes per packet, while traditional virtual networking has to read the entire packet prior to making a forwarding decision.

The big issue is whether or not the e2e form of cut-through is possible. By definition, it is possible as long circuits are provided on e2e basis. In this case, the e2e delay on such paths is literally the speed of light plus the processing speed of 6 bytes per hop. Technically speaking, these are very fast e2e paths. This chapter will show further on how e2e circuits can be implemented in practice.

Figure 17.6 shows a model that can be used to represent all the possible delays a packet can encounter inside a switch. Although this chapter cannot accommodate a full statistical analysis of such a model, the reader is encouraged to keep it in mind when attempting to visualize processing overhead. Single-letter codes in the figure can be used to encode processing sequences.

The *C* path is the most desired mode because it is the fastest possible mode a switch can offer. *SF* is the second best—the entire packet is read and stored but it is forwarded immediately after that, limiting the cost to the reading and writing of the packet length of bytes from/into the line. *CQF* adds more processing cost because the packet now has to queue up and is not processed immediately. All the QoS classes discussed earlier apply in this case, where the EF class is the best choice for high-priority traffic because the queue will always process such packets first regardless of their position in queue. Finally, if the queue is congested beyond its storage capacity (or configurations of EF/AF classes), the packet can also be dropped in the *SQD* path, which is the worst case scenario because it will normally trigger a retransmission procedure, thus, further decreasing e2e throughput.

On the practical side, both technical specifications of modern switches and benchmarks in existing literature show that the difference in throughput (in packets or bytes) between the *C* and *SF* modes is between 10 and 15 times. This is a huge difference if one takes into consideration the practical benefits for Big Data transfers where we are talking 10–15 times shorter transfers of bulk.

The Optical Solution

There is the old OPS versus OBS (packets vs. bursts) argument [11], which is not unlike the circuits versus packets argument [2]. The basics of optical networks are simple. Light does

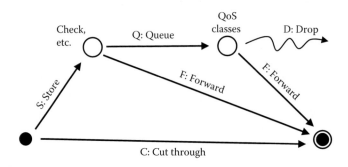

FIGURE 17.6 Modeling the delay encountered by individual packets in Ethernet switches.

not allow for storage, where Optical Delay Line (ODL) technology does exist but can only offer very short delays. In fact, ODL can only be used with packets as even short bursts immediately exceed physical capacity of existing ODLs. With the short delays in ODLs, the optical version of the store-and-forward mode is not too different from the cut-through mode. On the other hand, the benefits from using ODLs are relatively small as is the added capacity. Other basic information about optical networks is that one line in optical network is in fact several lines, each for a separate wavelength. This chapter will return to this argument when the proposed Tall Gate model is generalized between Ethernet and optical implementations.

The easiest routing solution for a complex optical topology is to use *lightpaths* [17], which are defined as the same wavelength (same color of light) at each hop on an e2e path. The simplicity of such a solution comes at the price of small capacity.

A better routing solution is to use *wavelength routing/switching* [16]. Wavelengths for an e2e path can now change at every hop. This change is performed by optical converters which shift the light spectrum of a wavelength, thus effectively changing one wavelength into another.

Regardless of the approach, both the lightpath and wavelength switching solutions are TE problems and can easily be written in the OSPF form. In this respect, the optical solution can be compared with Ethernet networks as long as optimization formulations are similar. This chapter will do just that further on.

Network Topology and Practical Designs

Topology is extremely important for intra- and inter-DC networks [9]. In fact, virtual networks are possibly so popular nowadays specifically because they offer much more flexible control over topology at various levels (inside racks, across racks, across DCs, etc.), even if this flexibility comes with a noticeable per-packet processing cost.

The best formulation of the topology problem to the day is the VNE [51]. The formulation is simple. There is one underlying physical network topology—normally written/handled as a graph. There are also multiple overlaying virtual networks on top of it. The system is dynamic along the timeline, where virtual networks can be added and removed on request. Note that this is a major shift of paradigm compared to the traditional OSPF (TE) formulation, which is traditionally based on the demand matrix which is comprised of multiple source–destination (SD, another name is OD: Origin–Destination) flows as unit demands [7]. In VNE, the complexity increases because each unit demand is an entire topology—hence the name of the problem/formulation.

The response to this increase in complexity has been to simplify the topology itself. Existing research on VNE is converging to some form of logical grouping in nodes [51,52]. Research in Houidi et al. [51] talks about the *hub-and-spokes* topology specifically, or a backbone in the physical topology (core and edges) as a general approach. Obviously, such grouping helps by decreasing the computational complexity of TE optimization problems. It also helps with more straightforward algorithms.

Figure 17.7 presents the basic notions of the Tall Gate model, which is based on the experience from VNE research. The main players/components of the model are *(Big Data)*

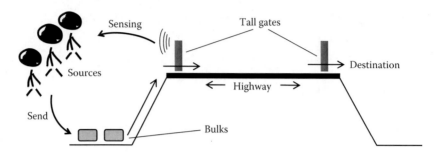

FIGURE 17.7 The Tall Gate model suitable for communications across DCs or even for hardware clusters (or even racks) inside DCs.

sources, *bulks*, and *Tall Gates* that allow access to a highway (backbone) heading toward remote destinations. The core idea of the model in terms of topology is to use a mixture of fixed and dynamic networks. The highway (backbone) part is the fixed component and is not expected to change frequently. The dynamic part is all the network used to access Tall Gates and can change frequently depending on local environments and control algorithms. Note that the parallel with road traffic is intentional because it is expected that there is a cost for a flow to use the highway which should serve as a filter between bulk transfer that can bear this cost and all the other transfers which either cannot or do not want to pay for the access to the highway. Naturally, the cost here is not monetary and is used only as an illustration while in practice the cost is just a weight or a threshold that helps separate priority traffic from the rest.

The sensing part in Figure 17.7 is a means toward *asynchronous multiparty access* to the highway from multiple Big Data sources. It is similar to what is used in OBS networks for contention resolution [54]. Note that contention resolution today exists in optical and wireless networks where some basic fundamental methods are the same. This chapter will return to the sensing part of the Tall Gate model with a new fundamental method, distinct from those found in optical and wireless networks.

Figure 17.8 shows the Tall Gate in practice. In fact, this model represents a current project in which two small educational clouds (DCs) are connected via the Japan Gigabit Network (JGN). The figure is a rough representation of the JGN topology. JGN is a ring network but the physical topology is not actually a ring—instead, all the optical fibers in the trunk are split into two clusters where one is used as uplink and the other as downlink. The Tall Gate model takes a very logical form in such a topology. There are two access points, links between which are in full duplex (in fact, physically separated) mode. This means that the gates do not have to synchronize or negotiate access between each other. Instead, access to Gate A is controlled by the intra-DC management software located at Gate A, and the same happens at Gate B. Of course, with three or more gates some form of syncing between the gates should also be implemented. However, as will be revealed further in this chapter, this depends on the overhead. If overhead from such a synchronization is too high, it can potentially be more beneficial to represent N-gate rings as pairs of two gates with an automatic relay mechanism for multihop transfers.

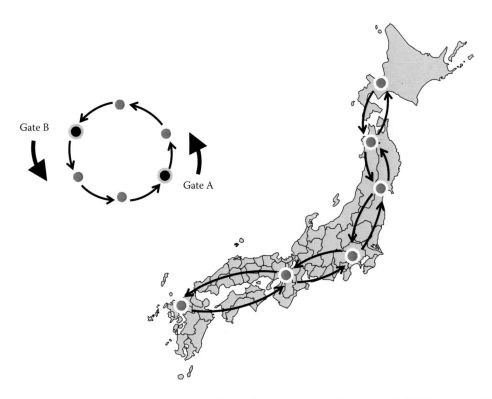

FIGURE 17.8   A rough representation topology of the Japan Gigabit Network (JGN) operated by NICT in Japan. Two DCs can be connected via two gates (in the Tall Gate model) to communicate in both directions.

THE CIRCUITS-OVER-PACKETS EMULATION

Returning back to the core topic—the *circuits*, it should be reminded that circuits have to be engineered because they are an emulation on top of packets. This is the TE problem where OSPF [7] is the most popular formulation, possibly with the exception of the very recent VNE formulation. This section presents the basic OSPF but also proposes a new notation that helps when various technical solutions are compared for performance further in the next section. Finally, the last part of this chapter introduces an interesting optimizational technique which is not part of the traditional TE but can be very helpful when trying to maximize throughput of bulk transfers.

Related Problems (OSPF, etc.)

OSPF sounds like a path establishment method, but it is actually the most popular formulation of the TE problem. In this respect, OSFP is more of an umbrella term for various TE methods than a specific method.

Figure 17.9 shows the baseline approach of most OSPF methods. Traditional input is a demand matrix, where each cell defines an OD (origin-destination) flow. There can be multiple flows between the same source and destination in which case they are usually aggregated into one. The output is a mapping for each OD flow onto an e2e path. The

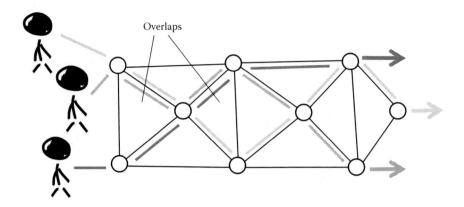

FIGURE 17.9 A simple diagram representing the common goal of all TE methods.

mapping is achieved via weight setting at each node in such a way that the intended path is achieved. Note that this formulation also suits virtual networking where routing decision can be made by each node at the cost of per-packet processing overhead. In OSPF practice, routing is normally accomplished via a static routing table.

The quality of mapping is estimated applying the concept of utility of some form. Utility obviously depends on a particular practical objective. Traditional utilities are used to maximize throughput on all flows, or minimize the number of nodes participating in routing (energy minimization). In case of circuits, it is important to minimize or even completely avoid overlaps across e2e paths.

OSPF is traditionally written as a linear problem [7] but various solvers such as Linear Programming (LP), Generic Algorithm (GA), or Memetic Algorithm (MA) can be used. A traditional OSPF linear problem goes as follows. The sum of costs on all links is to be minimized. The cost is put in direct relation to congestion on each line by increasing the cost (often exponentially) with increasing traffic volume. A solution to such a problem normally results in dispersing traffic smoothly across the entire topology, thus, minimizing e2e cost for individual flows. Obviously, this is not the only formulation in practice, but this problem is arguably among the easiest OSPF illustrations.

While many utility functions are the same across different technologies, some of the constraints are often different. Roughly standard constraints across different formulations are *e2e path consistency*, which simply says that all demand items should get a valid e2e path, and *flow conservation* which says that each node except for source and destination should get as much traffic in as comes out. Others are not as standard. For example, the *limited capacity constraint* is uncommon because link cost (in turn based on congestion) takes care of limiting traffic volume on each link. As will be shown further on, circuits may also be in need of uncommon constraints to achieve the intended utility.

The TE Problem for Circuits

It is difficult to compare OSPF formulations across different technologies, mostly because formulations of utility functions are different. This section presents a new notation for OSPF problems, which emphasizes the mapping part without focusing on the utility function. This helps by making it possible to compare OSPF problems in various practical implementation scenarios while the utility definition and algorithms used to find the optimal solution are placed outside of the notation.

Let us define a *unit demand* as source s, destination d, volume v, time t, and sometimes optical wavelength λ. The demand tuple for demand item i can be written as

$$T_i = <s, d, v, t> \tag{17.2}$$

Repeating the earlier statement, the points of this notation is to define the mapping between demand and path mapping while the utility function remains undefined in this new notation. However, all the below formulations can be solved using the standard OSPF problem in Fortz and Thorup [7].

Based on the above demand tuple, the core formulation is in the form of *in/demand tuple → path mapping* and retains this form for all the distinct technologies below.

Traditional Ethernet formulation is the most standard case written as

$$T_i = <s, d, v> \rightarrow <s, a, b, ..., d> \tag{17.3}$$

where a, b,... are intermediate nodes. Note that demand tuple lacks the time t which is because traditional OSPF is not aware of time. In practice, such optimizations are conducted at regular time intervals, changing configurations for each switch based on the new mapping.

Optical Networks without Switching is possibly the simplest notation written as

$$T_i = <s, d, v> \rightarrow <s, \lambda> \tag{17.4}$$

where λ is the wavelength of the lightpath. Again, this formulation does not take time into consideration. Also, it should be obvious from notation that the capacity of such networks is fairly low. For example, with 24 or 48 wavelengths, depending on the hardware, there can only be 24 or 48 concurrent flows.

Optical Networks with Switching can solve the problem of low capacity by introducing wavelength switching:

$$T_i = <s, d, v> \rightarrow <s, \lambda_s, \lambda_a, \lambda_b, ...> \tag{17.5}$$

where λ_a, λ_b are different wavelengths assigned at intermediate nodes along the path. Obviously, this has a great potential to increase the overall capacity of the network.

Finally, the *Tall Gate* model can be written as

$$T_i = <s, d, v, t_1, t_2> \rightarrow <s, \lambda, t> \tag{17.6}$$

where t_1 and t_2 define the intended time frame for a circuit and t is the time that comes from the best solution and guarantees exclusive access to the line. The mapping without λ applies to Ethernet networks. In fact, this shows how optical lines are simply multiple Ethernet lines from the viewpoint of this formulation. Also, as far as the Tall Gate model is concerned, this is exactly the case. In fact, the Tall Gate model completely guarantees exclusive access because lines on the highway do not overlap or interact with any other lines, by definition.

Distributed versus Centralized Designs and Topologies

There are two ways to look at large-scale management of circuit emulation:

- Distributed versus centralized process

- Whether or not separate networks (segments) are used for control and data planes

Specifically, the second parameter is extremely important for burst optical switching and FCoE because both technologies heavily rely on intensive data exchange in the control plane.

Figure 17.10 shows the important points from both these parameters in two specific designs. The design on the left side is largely conventional, where the same network segment is used for both control and data planes. The design on the right side is more interesting because each storage node (traffic source) can now support a control protocol over one network segment while sending bulk over another. In practice this is easily accomplished by using machines with at least two network cards (NICs). In virtual network, the same design can be accomplished by using isolated slices but this, again, is accomplished at the added per-packet overhead.

Note that the two designs in Figure 17.10 are not the centralized versus distributed classification. Both distributed and centralized methods can be implemented in both these designs. However, it should be clear that the two-network design is more suitable for distributed methods. As this chapter will show further on, distributed methods require substantially more overhead for circuits, FCoE-like protocols, optical bursts, and so on.

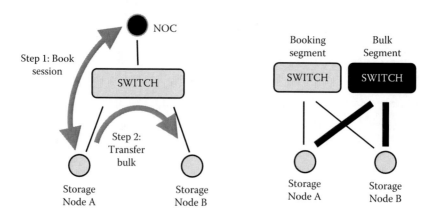

FIGURE 17.10 Two fundamental designs for circuit emulation.

As part of the Tall Gate model, this chapter will discuss a practical implementation of *sensing* based on two network segments. Note that the two areas which actively use sensing—OBS and wireless networks—both implement sensing inside the same network domain which is used for data transfers.

Contention via Sensing

This section talks about contention methods and specifically sensing with the main focus on the Tall Gate model.

As was mentioned before, contention and/or sensing methods exist in both optical [11,54] and wireless networks [55]. Note that both assume that sensing is performed on the same network that is used for bulk transfers.

However, a two-network design of sensing is not very difficult to achieve in practice. All we need is some form of feedback on the status of the data plain fed via an independent network back to traffic sources. This reminds one of the parallel with road traffic where congestion on roads does not necessarily have to be revealed to drivers when they arrive at the gate, but can be communicated to them via signs or electronically at considerable distances away from the gate.

Since isolation between the data network and the feedback network is preferred, an SNMP-like solution is obvious. The status of line(s) on a switch is made available (or is pushed via broadcast) to traffic sources. Sources can then use the standard technique (used at wireless MAC today) of trying to grab the line and backing off with random (and possibly exponentially increasing) intervals on collision.

If randomness and backoff periods appear to affect performance in a major way, one can consider having a Network Operations Center (NOC) that would poll the status, collect requests from traffic sources, solve the related OSPF problem, and distribute good mappings to all sources in a centralized manner. Obviously, this method will change the technology from *async and fully distributed* to *synced and centralized*. The choice between the two should be up to a given setup in real life. It depends on the number of sources, irregularity of bulks (syncing across data transfers is not good for distributed methods), and the size of bulk transfers.

The bottom line here is that the experience from optical and wireless sensing can be very helpful if you decide to create a fully distributed environment in which sources would not have to sync their bulk transfers with each other.

Bulk Aggregation and Dynamic Performance Tradeoffs

Even with the Tall Gate model, all the above formulations roughly stayed within the OSPF framework. This section also discussed network designs with high level of distribution where async distribution might be preferred because it assumes that sources sort out access to the line (gate) by themselves without having to build an NOC. In fact, NOCs are often called Single Points of Failure (SPOFs) because failure of such a node can easily stall the whole network.

So, assuming we prefer a distributed async design, the next problem we have to solve is the *strategy* for individual sources. The simple strategy was described above—on collision

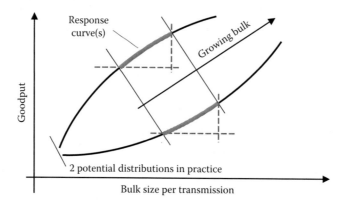

FIGURE 17.11 The concept of bulk aggregation and the related tradeoffs.

sources are advised to backoff at random intervals, increasing the range of random variables exponentially on each sequential collision (exponential backoff).

With Big Data transfers, a new set of strategies can be defined. Figure 17.11 is a visualization of one such strategy, called *aggregation tradeoff*.

The assumptions for such source are as follows. Each source is expected to have a range of Big Data sizes—those are simply the history of past bulk transfers or a preset distribution. The history (or sampled projections) can be either convex or concave distributions (assuming straight line is concave). The *aggregation tradeoff* strategy is simply when a source makes a decision on whether or not to keep aggregating its bulk as long as it can get better throughput in the future. *Better throughput* in Figure 17.11 is simply higher throughput for a larger bulk of data but in practice it can be the benefit of obtaining one larger circuit versus two smaller ones, from the optimizational point of view.

As this chapter shows further on, there is more complexity to such tradeoffs. For example, from the viewpoint of the entire DC, it might be easier to optimize and handle fewer large circuits rather than very many relatively small ones. This rule of thumb is obviously true for the Tall Gate mode, where the overhead from sensing and negotiating circuits can be reduced by having fewer but larger sessions.

IMPLEMENTATION AND PRACTICE

This section assembles all the above technologies, models, and formulations, and compares them across several practical configurations from the viewpoint of performance. The proposed Tall Gate model is one of the configurations. In order to achieve a comprehensive comparison, a fairly simple analytical framework is proposed first, and then translated into each unique practical configuration. Performance analysis is performed for hotspot/Flash sources at various ranges of Big Data with 10 Mbyte to 100 Gbyte bulks.

Basic Models

The configuration tuple for the hotspot/Flash model was discussed above. Setting the time frame apart and assuming that number of sources f_n participating in a Flash event is a fixed parameter, the main tuning parameters are a for Beta/SB process, f_m for the max magnitude during Flash event, and f_v for variance in magnitude across sources during Flash event. Many combinations with these parameters are possible producing interesting environments. Note that a system is expected to work well under both normal hotspots and when they are in Flash events (nightly backups, intensive transfer, etc.).

Observing space limitation of this chapter, Figure 17.12 shows one of the arbitrarily picked combinations—those when magnitude is tested at 2 and 10. The difference between the two configurations is obvious in the range between normal and extreme (Flash) states of most hotspots in the synthetic trace. The other parameters were fixed at $f_n = 15$ (half of all hotspots participate in Flash event), $f_v = 2$ (relatively small variance across hotspots). The only variance parameter that translates into two separate configurations is $f_m = \{2, 10\}$. Note that there is no simulation along the timeline. Simulations are simply four distributions—normal/Flash for each value of f_m. Performance for each design below is calculated as average of the values obtained for these four configurations.

Let us list some assumptions on traffic handling and then formulate a set of technical designs. First, let us assume that our DC is aware of the hotspot model and has verified that its own traffic is explained by the model. The DC wants to create a special environment for Big Data sources. Based on the hotspot model, our DC decides to draw a clean separation line, classifying non-hotspot sources as normal traffic and hotspot sources as priority traffic. The DC makes sure that normal traffic is handled by an isolated network so that its interference with Big Data sources is minimized. The DC is also aware that, in accordance with the hotspot model, such sources can experience sudden surges of traffic (Flash events).

Table 17.1 presents six models classified in the following three metrics:

- *Interference* indicates how much bulk transfers interact with control traffic—naturally, two-network design has zero interference, by definition;

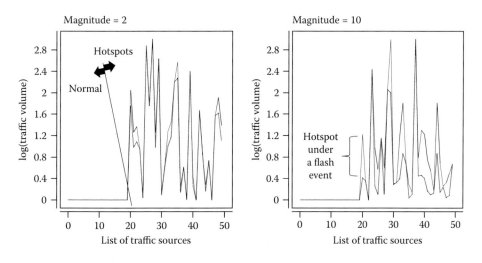

FIGURE 17.12   Example trace where stress is placed on the magnitude *m* of a Flash event that further enhances a subset of hotspots (heavy hitters).

TABLE 17.1 Six Basic Models and Their Rough Evaluation Based on the Three Metrics that Directly Affect Throughput

	Interference	Overhead	Isolation
Do Nothing	HIGH	ZERO	NO
Network Virtualization	HIGH	HIGH	NO (store-and-forward)
Traditional Scheduler	LOW	HIGH	YES
P2P × 1N (1 networks)	HIGH	VERY HIGH	YES
P2P × 2N (2 networks)	ZERO	VERY HIGH	YES
Tall Gate (sensing)	LOW	HIGH	YES

- *Overhead* measures the relative volume of control traffic necessary for servicing bulk transfers;

- Finally, *isolation* is mostly a binary metric defining whether or not bulk transfers are isolated with each other; circuits in the Tall Gate model are completely isolated, by definition.

Table 17.1 only has three metrics, which is clearly too small a number. There can be other metrics. For example, *fairness* can be used to measure how well QoS classes are supported or technically implemented. However, too many metrics will complicate the analysis. On the other hand, the analysis below will show that the three metrics in the table are the bigger contributors to overall performance.

This analysis will ignore TCP/UDP argument for now. The use of TCP clearly results in performance impairment, which grows with increasing delay and delay variation. This means that the technology that has the smallest e2e delay suffers the least from using TCP, which should result in additional difference among the models in the table. However, it is expected that such difference is much smaller than the one created by the above three metrics.

Let us define each design in Table 17.1.

Do Nothing design is when hotspot traffic is isolated from the rest but nothing else is done to the Ethernet network. Big Data sources have to compete for bandwidth in the traditional way—simply by starting TCP connections and trying to push as much bulk through them as currently available bandwidth allows. The good news is that there is zero overhead from the complete absence of control traffic but interference is high and there is not isolation.

Network Virtualization represents the existing technology when virtual slices (segments) are created on top of physical infrastructure. As was discussed before, network virtualization cannot provide the actual physical isolation for flows simply because the switch has to be in the store-and-forward mode. Control traffic runs on top of the data network, which creates high interference and requires substantial overhead for each source to negotiate a virtual connection.

Traditional Scheduler is also about circuits but is otherwise traditional. Since the target of the design is to provide isolated circuits, it requires the cut-through mode in switches, that is, perfect isolation. However, since the same network is used for control and data traffic, there is a minor interference with existing circuits. Also, in order to make sure that circuits are valid and are fair across all traffic sources, considerable overhead should be dedicated to negotiate the schedule.

P2PxN1 is the fully distributed (P2P: peer-to-peer) design with one network segment (1N). The design is also used for circuits and therefore benefits from near-complete isolation. However, the one network segment is a major hurdle for isolation. First, because of the fully distributed method, the overhead of negotiating an optimal schedule is high. Second, the high intensity control chatter interferes with existing circuits, where interference is much higher in relative terms when compared to, for example, the Traditional Scheduler.

P2PxN2 is the two-network version of the *P2PxN1* design. The overhead from negotiating the total schedule is still very high, but zero interference is achieved because control chatter now happens over a separate network.

Finally, the *Tall Gate* design follows the guidelines discussed above. It uses second network for sensing, due to which the overhead is still high but not as high as that of P2P design. Some small interference is possible simply because the design does not rely on centralized scheduling but instead uses sensing, which does not completely eliminate probability of collisions—hence this design suffers from a low level of interference.

Basic Middleware

This chapter cannot accommodate discussion of all possible middleware but will concentrate on the modules which proved to be useful when implementing the Tall Gate model between two clouds in Japan (see the description of the project earlier in text).

Some modules are obvious. For example, most of the designs defined in the previous chapter had a scheduling component. This software is simple. One defines, either in centralized or distributed manner, a schedule shared by all traffic sources. The schedule is then implemented, where each source knows its own starting time and commences its own bulk transfer accordingly. Issues related to runtime corrections to the schedule, if one of the sources falls behind the schedule, are also part of this module.

One particular software component that was found extremely useful is shown in Figure 17.13. As was mentioned before, the Tall Gate model depends on two networks. Each traffic source has two NICs. It was discovered that machines under all common operating systems emitted regular traffic even though the traffic source itself had nothing to send. This is because modern OSes have too many components that use (or try to use) Internet connections automatically as part of their background operation. The important part of the middleware is therefore to turn off the NIC connected to the data network when traffic source is idle. Figure 17.13 shows the stats from an NIC that was turned off. The switch still sends packets—mostly broadcasts (bytes sent—by the switch), but the machine itself does not emit any traffic. At the same time, this machine can use the other NIC to negotiate circuits or perform sensing on other sources' circuits. Obviously, it is crucial that machines have at least 2 NICs.

HTTP APIs (RESTfull APIs) are probably the best—and cloud-like—way to implement protocols for circuit emulation. Some high-end switches already implement such APIs while older equipment may only allow access over SNMP or implement their own web

Port Statistics

Port	Bytes Received	Bytes Sent	CRC Error Packets
01	761	3280	0
02	580	3461	0
03	0	0	0
04	0	0	0
05	0	0	0
06	0	3818	0
07	0	0	0
08	0	4041	0

FIGURE 17.13   Ability to cut off traffic sources from the network can create well-managed scheduling environments, provided the machines can get instructions on another port.

service for maintenance functions. Note that if the equipment already has a web interface, it is very easy for the manufacturer to implement a web API as part of the interface. The biggest difference between web interface and web API is that the latter can be used for automation. Software automation is crucial for circuit emulation.

In the Tall Gate project, it was discovered that it is not common for high-end optical switches to have advanced web APIs. It is a stark contrast with, for example, modern virtual networking equipment which all have very good and flexible APIs both for active and passive functions. The experience with optical switches showed that the benefits of having an API are so great that it pays to install a separate *translation* machine whose whole purpose is to implement a web API while at the same time communicating with optical switches over SNMP.

Performance Analysis

This subsection compares performance across all the practical designs defined at the beginning of this section. A single 10 Gbps Ethernet line is accessed by multiple traffic sources in all models. Traffic sources themselves are defined using the hotspot model with two configurations and four sets of distributions, explained above. Each distribution is first randomized and passed to each design for decision making on how to perform the bulk transfer. The single metric on the output is the total time it takes for all traffic sources to complete bulk transfers.

Practical numeric setup is as follows. Big Data size ranges (maps hotspots to this range) are *10M..100M, 10M..100M, 100M..500M, 100M..1G, 1G..10G, 10G..50G,* and *10G..100G,* all in bytes. The ranges are picked by hand as representative of various environments. The three metrics in the table above have to be put to numeric form. Interference is represented by the set {10, 20, 30, 40, 50}, representing percentage of decrease in throughput.

Zero interference is translated as 0%, low is selected from values below 30% inclusive, and high is selected from values above 30% inclusive. Overhead is selected from the set {10 ms, 100 ms, 1 s, 10 s, 30 s}, defining the time period it takes to negotiate and establish a circuit. Similarly to interference, zero is the special case of 0 ms, and high and very high are selected from values up to or above 1 ms, both inclusive. Isolation is selected from the set {20, 40, 60, 80, 100} representing percentage of decrease in throughput. Again, *no interference* is the special case of 0% while *yes* translates into selection of one of the values from the entire set. All the selections from the above sets (or subsets when low, high, or very high) are done randomly.

Note that these values are compiled from raw logs observing each configuration metric in practice. Granted the split in each set is arbitrary and was performed by hand, the range of values comes from practical experience.

The only result metric is the *duration* of all bulk transfers from a given hotspot distribution. Randomness in configuration parameters and order of bulks in hotspot distributions is removed by having 1000 runs for each design, each with a new hotspot distribution (but same configuration). Since each run results in four values for four sets of hotspot distributions, each run is represented by the average over the four duration values. Avoiding crowded plots (1000 runs = 1000 points), the resulting values for each method are listed in decreasing order and converted into 10 points for each design, where each point is an average of 100 points. The result of this procedure is a 10-point curve for each design on each plot.

Figure 17.14 shows the results of analysis. Plots are generated using the above method, while each plot represents a separate size range. We can see that the *Do Nothing* design does well until the bulk exceeds 1 Gbyte range. *Network Virtualization* also does relatively well up to 1 G past which it performs about the same as *Do Nothing*. The *Tall Gate* model is second best up to 1 Gbytes and the best for all the size ranges above that.

Note that in 1 G–50 G range (to bottom plots), the Tall Gate model results in an interesting curve in which we can find sources at both extremes (much better and much worse) while the majority of sources experience the average performance. Given that vertical scales on all plots are logs, this range indicates a big difference between the two extremes. This is potentially a good indicator that the distribution of results under the Tall Gate model reflected the distribution of bulk in the hotspot model. The issue here is fairness, where it is desirable that fairness across traffic sources would be distributed in accordance with their relative bulk.

The remaining designs all resulted in bad performance, which did not improve even for large size ranges. Note that it did not help much for the P2P design to have a separate network for control traffic because the time delay itself from negotiating the circuits made a non-negligible contribution to the overall duration.

Granted the results in Figure 17.14 are fuzzy (e.g., performance for some models suddenly improves for the biggest size range) due to randomness and irregularity in size ranges, the overall performance as well as the effect of bulk size on performance is evident. The take-home lesson here is that performance varies depending on the size range of Big Data. This means that, for some cases, it might even be better not to implement circuits—the

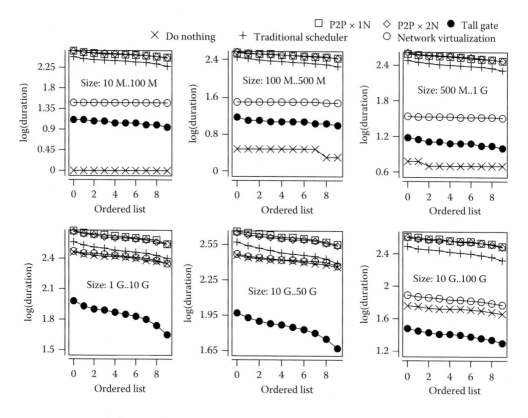

FIGURE 17.14 Performance for all models, separated in separate charts for each size range. The Tall Gate models is marked as filled-in bullets.

case for all the small size ranges. On the other hand, if we know that our sources have to exchange considerable bulk, it might be beneficial to implement one of the circuit designs and benefit from increased throughput.

The difference in performance depending on bulk size brings us back to the discussion of the *aggregation tradeoff*. Although it was not part of the performance analysis above, it is clear from the results that sources can potentially benefit from a process in which each source aggregates bulk up to a given level and then triggers bulk transfer. The benefit here would be better throughput from a larger bulk than for several smaller bulks.

SUMMARY

This chapter discusses circuit emulation. Circuits can be emulated over common Ethernet using cheapest switching equipment available today, which means that circuit emulation can compete with more expensive technology like FCoE.

The Tall Gate model was proposed as a practical design that can implement circuits in practice. The current implementation of the model is in form of two DCs connected over a high-capacity optical backbone. A gate is installed at the switches on each end and the Tall Gate model implements an access protocol through which traffic sources on each side can get exclusive access—that is, the circuit—to the backbone. Note that the optical implementation does not contradict the earlier statement about cheapest Ethernet switches. In fact, this chapter clearly shows that the method is independent of the underlying technology and will work in exactly the same way in Ethernet or optical domains. In fact, this chapter goes as far as to state that, as far as the Tall Gate model is concerned, optical backbone is the same as several e2e Ethernet lines.

The Tall Gate model can be implemented between racks or hardware clusters as well. As performance analysis shows, the choice should be made based on the range of bulk size rather than on the physical tier. If very large bulks are transferred within a single rack, it makes sense to implement a circuit emulation within that rack. In this respect, the applicability realm of the model is just as broad as that of virtual networking today which, due to its flexibility, is applied to networks inside racks, between racks, and between DCs, using roughly the same designs at all these tiers.

The key advantage of circuits is that they aim at the cut-through mode in Ethernet switches (in optical domain this is a natural mode). This chapter builds the full priority list of technologies, where cut-through is the best option, followed by L2 and L3 QoS modes, and ending with virtual networking. In all cases, including the cut-through mode, it was discussed how all these modes can be implemented e2e, even the cut-through mode. In fact, the Tall Gate model makes the e2e part relatively easy to implement—one simply has to make sure that e2e path between gates allows for exclusive line access. The exclusivity of access outside of the gates is ensured by the sensing part of the Tall Gate model, which brings the probability that circuits are interfered with to a minimum.

Setting the Tall Gate model aside, this chapter reviewed the traditional TE problem and specifically the OSPF formulation. A different notation was proposed and used for several unique formulations describing a range of practical technologies, including fully distributed storage networks, optical networks, and the Tall Gate model. Yet, it was shown that Big Data networking is more than just the TE problem. In order for circuit emulation to work in practice, such a network also has to incorporate a scheduling problem where problems such as time overlap, and interference, of bandwidth sharing among circuits do not occur. Exclusive line access is extremely important to guarantee that switching equipment on e2e paths remains in the cut-through mode during the Big Data transfers. This is why TE formulation for the Tall Gate model focuses on the schedule, while time as a parameter is missing from all the conventional formulations.

This chapter argues that Big Data sources should be treated as *special traffic sources*. Along this line of thought, this chapter discussed the concept of *strategy* for individual traffic sources. A practical example called *aggregation tradeoff* was discussed, where each source would monitor its past bulks and make decisions on whether to send current bulks immediately or aggregate them to send bigger bulks in the future. The tradeoff makes sense when the history of past bulks indicates that bigger bulks can enjoy higher average throughput.

The work on the topics in this chapter will continue. Source strategy is an interesting topic, which will be pursued further in future work. The unusual sensing technique discussed in this chapter will be improved and brought to the level of hardware and software maturity, hopefully resulting is general-purpose APIs for sensing. Finally, the hotspot model for traffic synthesis needs additional upgrades into a tool that would generate Big Data traces that would closely emulate realistic conditions in several real Big Data environments. As an immediate and currently pursued goal, this author is working on a hotspot model for traffic sources in a standard Hadoop cluster.

REFERENCES

1. M. Zhanikeev, Can we benefit from solid state drives in rich multimedia content processing, storage and streaming? ITE/IEICE Technical Report on Multimedia Storage (ITE-MMS), October 2013.
2. J. McDonald, *Fundamentals of Digital Switching. Applications of Communications Theory*, Springer, New York, USA, 1983.
3. M. Zhanikeev and Y. Tanaka, Popularity-based modeling of flash events in synthetic packet traces, *IEICE Technical Report on Communication Quality*, 112(288), pp. 1–6, November 2012.
4. Cut-Through and Store-and-Forward Ethernet Switching for Low-Latency Environments Cisco White Paper, 2014.
5. *Cut-Through Ethernet Switching: A Versatile Resource for Low Latency and High Performance*, NetOptics, 2014.
6. M. Zhanikeev and Y. Tanaka, Analytical models for L2 versus L3 QoS provisioning, *IEICE Technical Report on Photonic Networks*, 112(276), 13–18, November 2012.
7. B. Fortz and M. Thorup, Internet Traffic Engineering by Optimizing OSPF Weights, INFOCOM, pp. 519–528, March 2000.
8. K Supercomputer. [Online]. Available at: http://www.aics.riken.jp/en/ (Retrieved September 2014).
9. S. Gai, *Data Center Networks and Fibre Channels over Ethernet (FCoE)*. Lulu.com, 2008.
10. INCITS T11 Standardization Body. [Online]. Available at: http://www.t11.org/FCoE (Retrieved September 2014).
11. H.G. Perros, *Connection-Oriented Networks: SONET/SDH, ATM, MPLS, and Optical Networks*, Wiley and Sons, West Sussex, UK, 2005.
12. M. Zhanikeev, Experiences from measuring per-packet cost of software defined networking, *IEICE Technical Report on Service Computing (SC)*, 113(86), 31–34, June 2013.
13. M. Zhanikeev, Multi-Source stream aggregation in the cloud, Chapter 10 in *Book on Advanced Content Delivery and Streaming in the Cloud*, Wiley and Sons, West Sussex, UK, 2014.
14. M. Zhanikeev, Optimizing virtual machine migration for energy-efficient clouds, *IEICE Transactions on Communications*, E97-B(2), 450–458, February 2014.
15. Z. He and G. Liang, Research and Evaluation of Network Virtualization in Cloud Computing Environment, *3rd International Conference on Networking and Distributed Computing (ICNDC)*, pp. 40–44, October 2012.
16. H. Zang, J.P. Jue, L. Sahasrabuddhe, R. Ramamurthy, and B. Mukherjee, Dynamic lightpath establishment in wavelength-routed networks, *IEEE Communications Magazine*, 39(9), 100–108, 2001.
17. J. Jue, *Optical Networks*, Kluwer Academic Publishers, Norwell, MA, USA, 2001.
18. Congestion Notification, IEEE 802.1Qau Standard, IEEE, April 2010.
19. Enhanced Transmission Selection, IEEE 802.1Qaz Standard, June 2011.
20. Priority-Based Flow Control, IEEE 802.1Qbb Standard, June 2011.
21. Fibre Channel over Ethernet: A Pragmatic Approach to Data Center Network Convergence, Hewlett-Packard Whitepaper, 2010.
22. G. Lemasa and S. Gai, Fibre Channel over Ethernet in the Data Center: An Introduction, Cisco Whitepaper, 2007.
23. Assured Forwarding PHB Group, RFC2597, 1999.

24. An Expedited Forwarding PHB, RFC2598, 1999.
25. QoS: DSCP Classification Guidelines, RFC4594, 2006.
26. Greek Research Network (GRNET). [Online]. Available at: http://www.grnet.gr (Retrieved September 2014).
27. Greek Research Network (GRNET). [Online]. Available at: http://netmon.grnet.gr/network-map/gmindex.php (Retrieved September 2014).
28. GRNET Advanced Network Services (ANS) Provisioning Tool. [Online]. Available at: http://anstool2.grnet.gr (Retrieved September 2014).
29. OpenVSwitch project. [Online]. Available at: https://github.com/noxrepo/pox (Retrieved September 2014).
30. M. Tsugawa and J. Fortes, Characterizing User-level Network Virtualization: Performance, Overheads and Limits, 4th *IEEE International Conference on eScience*, Indianapolis, USA, pp. 204–206, 2008.
31. The Overhead of Software Tunneling. [Online]. Available at: http://networkheresy.com/category/open-vswitch/(Retrieved September 2014).
32. J.Y.L. Boudec and P. Thiran, *Network Calculus*, Springer-Verlag, New York, July 2001.
33. E. Kohler, R. Morris, B. Chen, J. Jannotti, and M. Kaashoek, The Click Modular Router, *ACM Transactions on Computer Systems (TOCS)*, 18(3), 263–297, August 2000.
34. J. Kim, S. Huh, K. Jang, K. Park, and S. Moon, The Power of Batching in the Click Modular Router, Asia-Pacific Workshop on Systems (APSYS), Seoul, Republic of Korea, Article 14, July 2012.
35. PICA8 Project for Low Latency Virtual Networking. [Online]. Available at: http://www.pica8.com/(Retrieved September 2014).
36. M. Zec, L. Rizzo, and M. Mikuc, DXR: Towards a Billion Routing Lookups per Second in Software, *ACM SIGCOMM Computer Communication Review*, 42(5), 30–36, 2012.
37. S. Han, S. Marshall, B. Chun, and S. Ratnasamy, MegaPipe: A new programming interface for scalable network I/O, *USENIX OSDI*, 1–14, 2012.
38. L. Rizzo, Netmap: A novel framework for fast packet I/O, *USENIX Annual Technical Conference*, pp. 1–12, June 2012.
39. T. Marian, K. Lee, and H. Weatherspoon, NetSlices: Scalable Multi-Core Packet Processing in User-Space, ANCS, October 2012.
40. J. Lockwood, N. McKeown, G. Watson, G. Gibb, P. Hartke, J. Naous, R. Raghuraman, and J. Luo, NetFPGA—An Open Platform for Gigabit-rate Network Switching and Routing, *IEEE International Conference on Microelectronic Systems Education (MSE)*, pp. 1–2, June 2007.
41. LAN Switching and Wireless, *CCNA Exploration Companion Guide*. Cisco, 2014.
42. Bouras, V. Kapoulas, V. Papapanagiotou, L. Poulopoulos, D. Primpas, and K. Stamos, *Extending QoS support from Layer 3 to Layer 2, 15th International Conference on Telecommunications (ICT)*, St. Petersburg, Russia, pp. 1–7, June 2008.
43. C.S. Chang, *Performance Guarantees in Communication Networks*, Springer-Verlag, New York, 2000.
44. Z. Wang, *Internet QoS: Architectures and Mechanisms for Quality of Service*, Morgan Kaufmann, 2001.
45. Definition of the Differentiated Services Field (DS Field) in the IPv4 and IPv6 Headers, RFC2474, 1999.
46. New Terminology and Clarifications for Diffserv, RFC3260, 2002.
47. M. Flannagan, *Cisco Catalyst QoS: Quality of Service in Campus Networks*, Cisco Press, June 2003.
48. A Lower Effort Per-Domain Behavior (PDB) for Differentiated Services, RFC3662, 2003.
49. R. Kachalia, *Borderless Campus 1.0: Design Guide*, Cisco Press, June 2011.
50. Varvitsiotis, V. Siris, D. Primpas, G. Fotiadis, A. Liakopoulos, and C. Bouras, Techniques for DiffServ-based QoS in Hierarchically Federated MAN Networks—the GRNET Case, 14th IEEE

Workshop on Local and Metropolitan Area Networks (LANMAN), Crete, Greece, pp. 1–6, September 2005.

51. Houidi, W. Louati, and D. Zeghlache, A Distributed Virtual Network Mapping Algorithm, *International Conference on Computers and Communications (ICC)*, 5634–5641, 2008.

52. G. Even, M. Medina, G. Schaffrath, and S. Schmid, Competitive and deterministic embeddings of virtual networks, *13th International Conference on Distributed Computing and Networking (ICDCN)*, 106–121, 2012.

53. P. Bodk, A. Fox, M. Franklin, M. Jordan, and D. Patterson, Characterizing, Modeling, and Generating Workload Spikes for Stateful Services, *1st ACM Symposium on Cloud Computing (SoCC)*, pp. 241–252, 2010.

54. R. Jankuniene and P. Tervydis, The Contention Resolution in OBS Network, *Elektronika ir Electrotechnika*, 20(6), 144–149, 2014.

55. M. Vuran and V. Gungor, On the interdependency of congestion and contention in wireless sensor networks, *ACM SENMETRICS*, 136–147, 2005.

Index